ASTONISHING X-MEN BY JOSS WHEDON & JOHN CASSADAY ULTIMATE COLLECTION BOOK 2. Contains material originally published in magazine form as ASTONISHING X-MEN #13-24 and GIANT-
SIZE ASTONISHING X-MEN #1. First printing 2012. ISBN# 978-0-7851-6195-0. Published by MARVEL WORLDWIDE, INC., a subsidiary of MARVEL ENTERTAINMENT, LLC. OFFICE OF PUBLICATION: 1
West 50th Street, New York, NY 10020. Copyright © 2006, 2007, 2008 and 2012 Marvel Characters, Inc. All rights reserved. $29.99 per copy in the U.S. and $32.99 in Canada (GST #R127032852);
Canadian Agreement #40668537. All characters featured in this issue and the distinctive names and likenesses thereof, and all related indicia are trademarks of Marvel Characters, Inc. No similarity
between any of the names, characters, persons, and/or institutions in this magazine with those of any living or dead person or institution is intended, and any such similarity which may exist is purely
coincidental. **Printed in the U.S.A.** ALAN FINE, EVP - Office of the President, Marvel Worldwide, Inc. and EVP & CMO Marvel Characters B.V.; DAN BUCKLEY, Publisher & President - Print, Animation
& Digital Divisions; JOE QUESADA, Chief Creative Officer; DAVID BOGART, SVP of Business Affairs & Talent Management; TOM BREVOORT, SVP of Publishing; C.B. CEBULSKI, SVP of Creator & Content
Development; DAVID GABRIEL, SVP of Publishing Sales & Circulation; MICHAEL PASCIULLO, SVP of Brand Planning & Communications; JIM O'KEEFE, VP of Operations & Logistics; DAN CARR, Executive
Director of Publishing Technology; SUSAN CRESPI, Editorial Operations Manager; ALEX MORALES, Publishing Operations Manager; STAN LEE, Chairman Emeritus. For information regarding advertising in
Marvel Comics or on Marvel.com, please contact John Dokes, SVP Integrated Sales and Marketing, at jdokes@marvel.com. For Marvel subscription inquiries, please call 800-217-9158. **Manufactured
between 2/16/2012 and 3/6/2012 by QUAD/GRAPHICS, DUBUQUE, IA, USA.**

10 9 8 7 6 5 4 3 2 1

ISHING
EN

WRITER JOSS WHEDON

ARTIST JOHN CASSADAY

COLORIST LAURA MARTIN
LETTERER CHRIS ELIOPOULOS

ASSISTANT EDITORS SEAN RYAN & WILL PANZO
ASSOCIATE EDITOR ANDY SCHMIDT
EDITORS MIKE MARTS, AXEL ALONSO & NICK LOWE

COLLECTION EDITOR JENNIFER GRÜNWALD
ASSISTANT EDITORS ALEX STARBUCK & NELSON RIBEIRO
EDITOR, SPECIAL PROJECTS MARK D. BEAZLEY
SENIOR EDITOR, SPECIAL PROJECTS JEFF YOUNGQUIST
SENIOR VICE PRESIDENT OF SALES DAVID GABRIEL
SVP OF BRAND PLANNING & COMMUNICATIONS MICHAEL PASCIULLO

EDITOR IN CHIEF AXEL ALONSO
CHIEF CREATIVE OFFICER JOE QUESADA
PUBLISHER DAN BUCKLEY
EXECUTIVE PRODUCER ALAN FINE

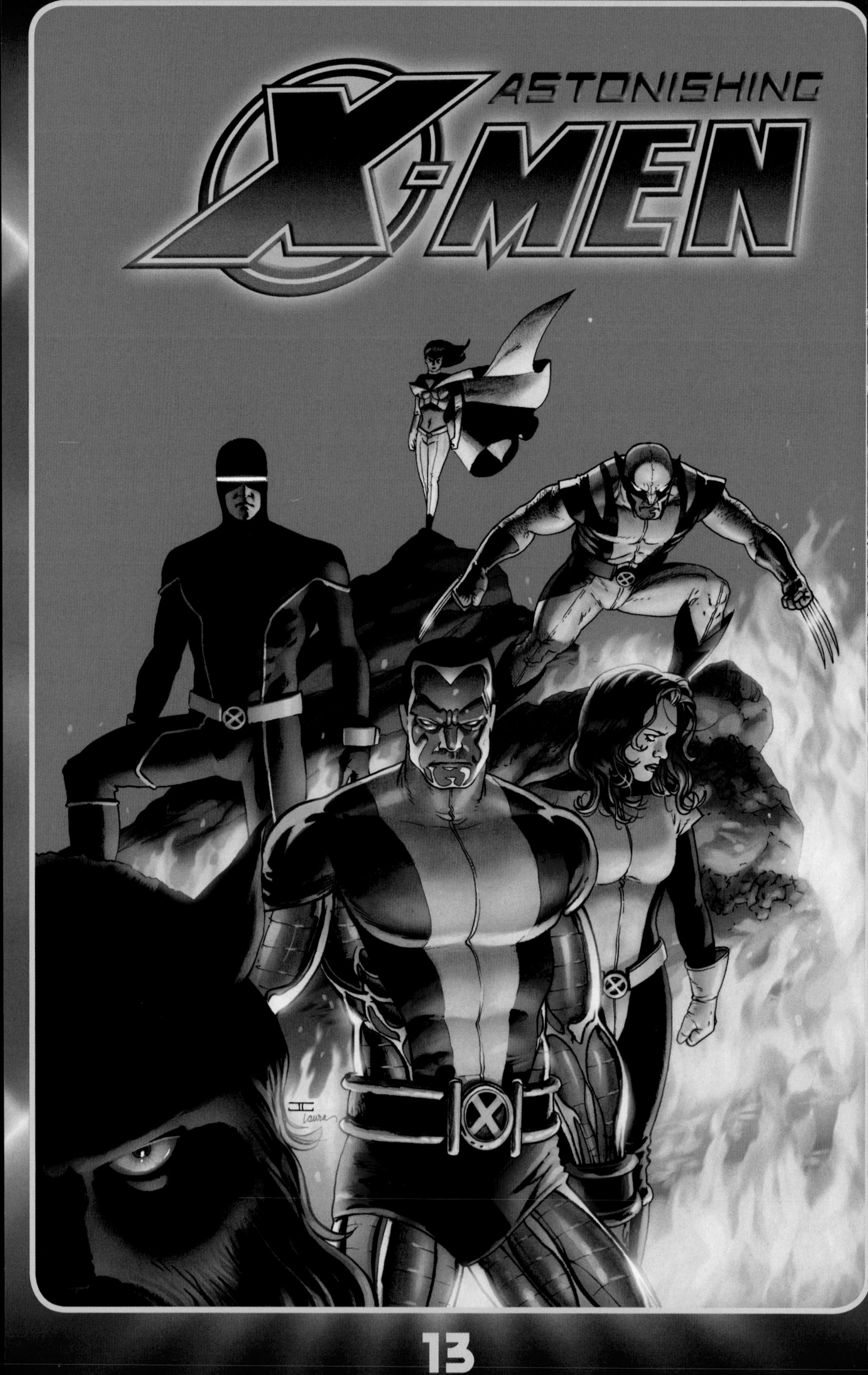
ASTONISHING
X-MEN
13

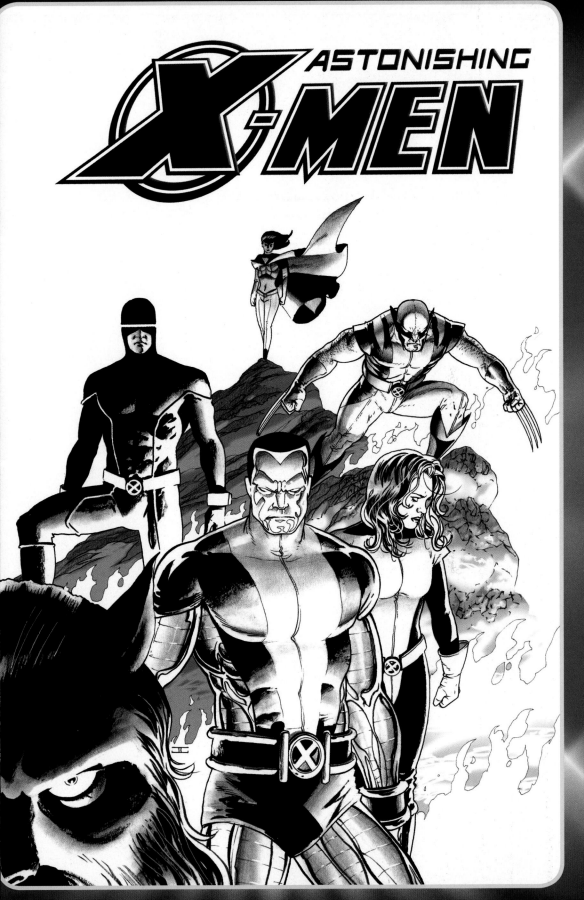

ASTONISHING X-MEN

13 SKETCH VARIANT

SOME TIME AGO

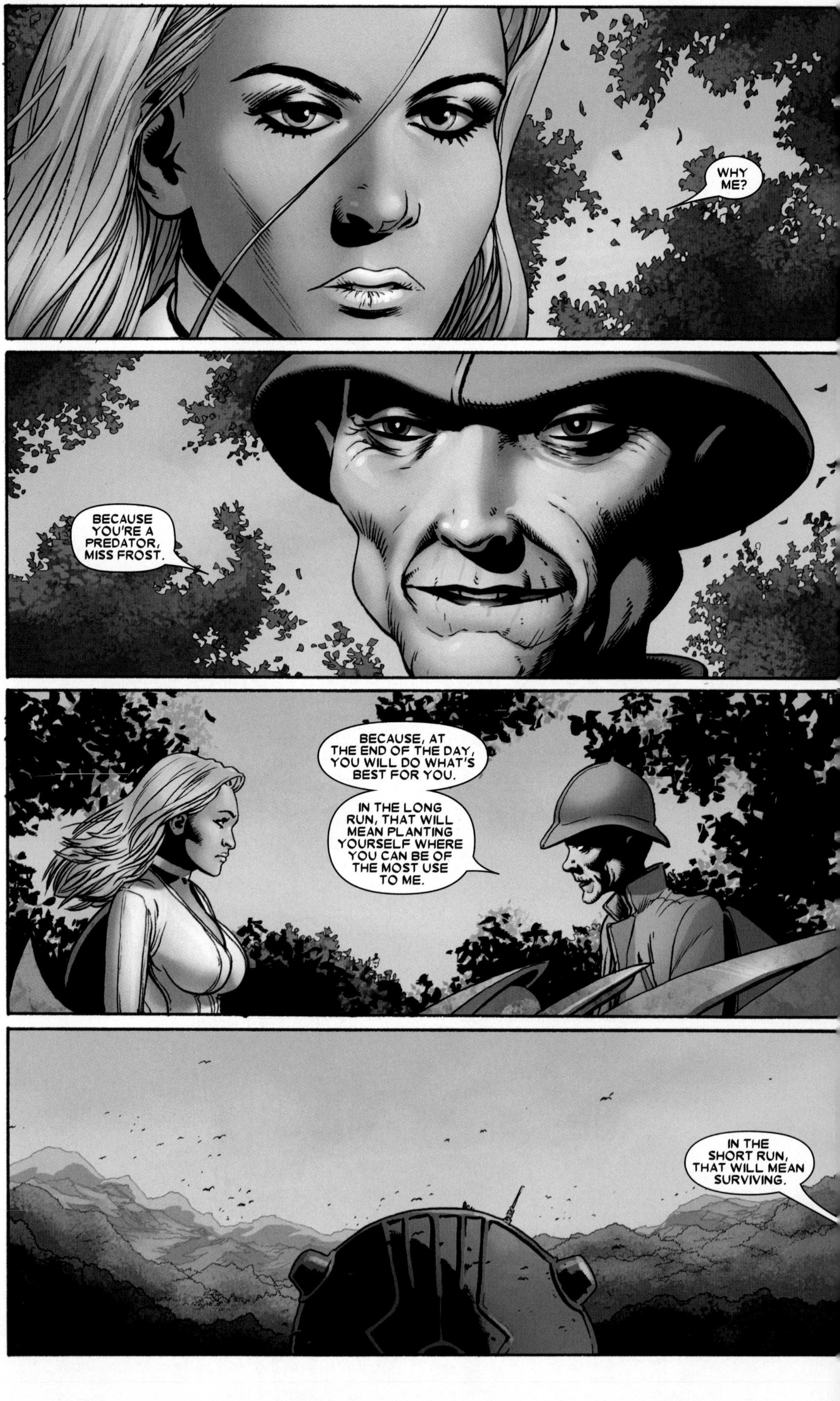

WHY ME?
BECAUSE YOU'RE A PREDATOR, MISS FROST.
BECAUSE, AT THE END OF THE DAY, YOU WILL DO WHAT'S BEST FOR YOU.
IN THE LONG RUN, THAT WILL MEAN PLANTING YOURSELF WHERE YOU CAN BE OF THE MOST USE TO ME.
IN THE SHORT RUN, THAT WILL MEAN SURVIVING.

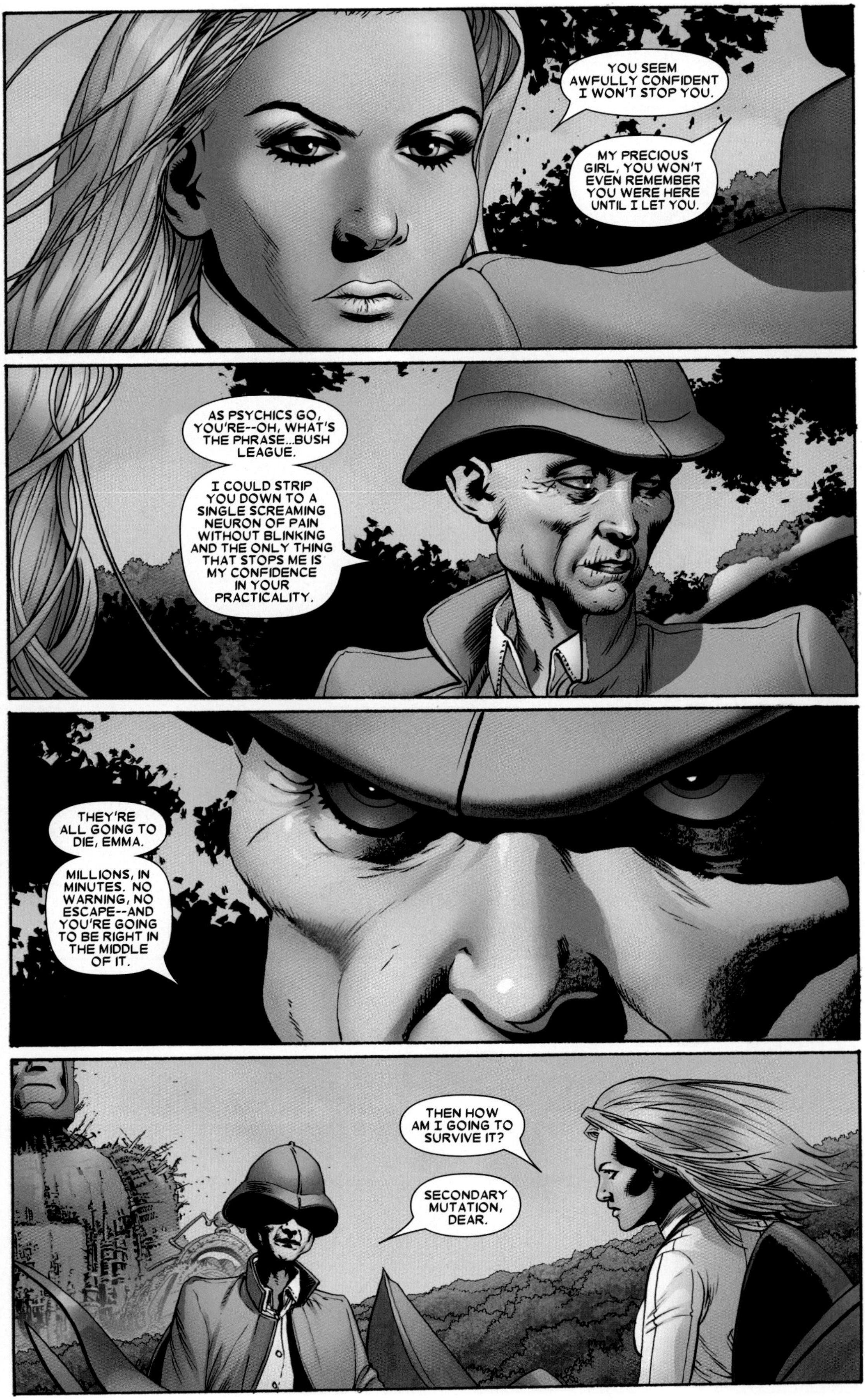
YOU SEEM AWFULLY CONFIDENT I WON'T STOP YOU.
MY PRECIOUS GIRL, YOU WON'T EVEN REMEMBER YOU WERE HERE UNTIL I LET YOU.
AS PSYCHICS GO, YOU'RE--OH, WHAT'S THE PHRASE...BUSH LEAGUE.
I COULD STRIP YOU DOWN TO A SINGLE SCREAMING NEURON OF PAIN WITHOUT BLINKING AND THE ONLY THING THAT STOPS ME IS MY CONFIDENCE IN YOUR PRACTICALITY.
THEY'RE ALL GOING TO DIE, EMMA.
MILLIONS, IN MINUTES. NO WARNING, NO ESCAPE--AND YOU'RE GOING TO BE RIGHT IN THE MIDDLE OF IT.
THEN HOW AM I GOING TO SURVIVE IT?
SECONDARY MUTATION, DEAR.

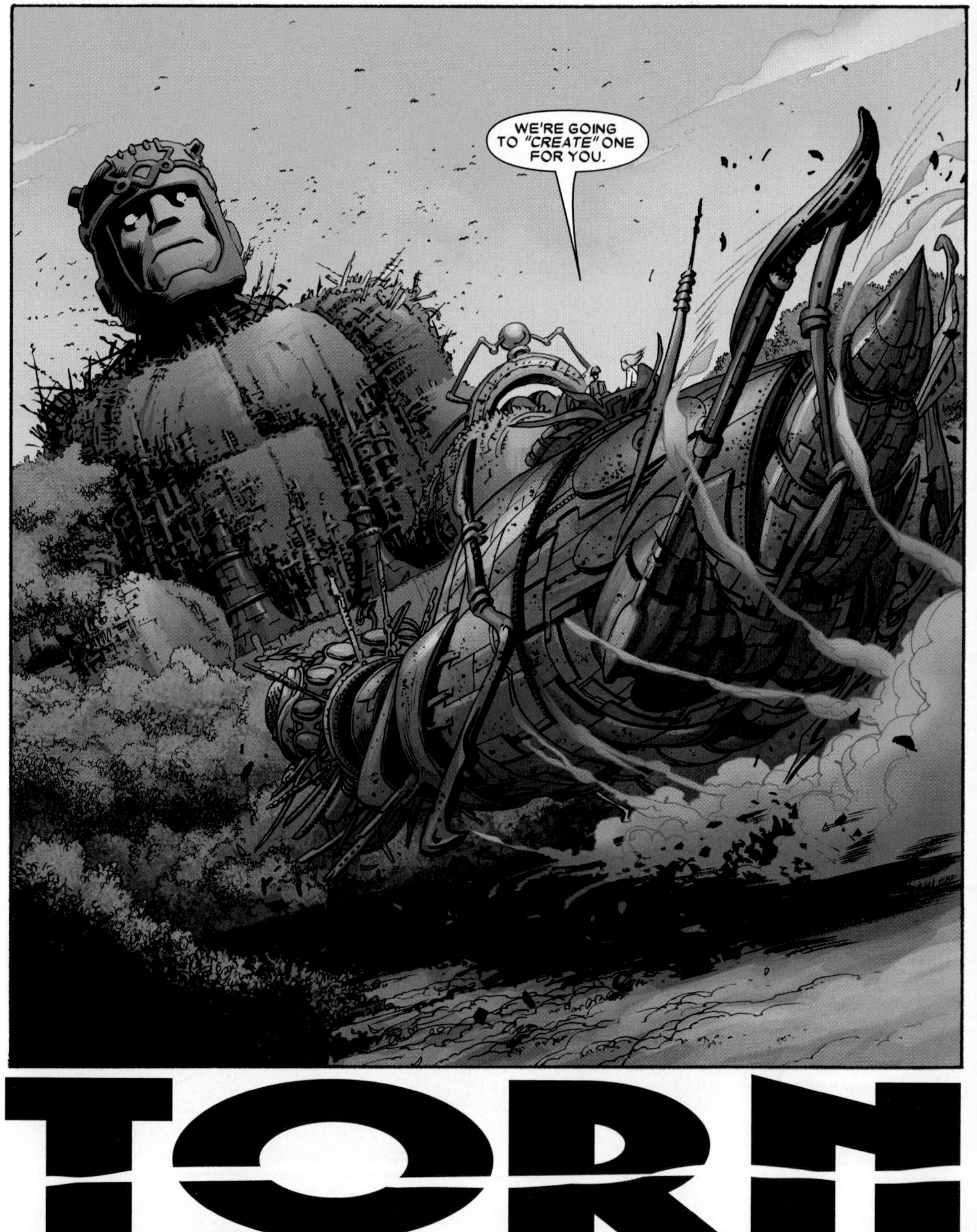
WE'RE GOING TO "CREATE" ONE FOR YOU.

TORN

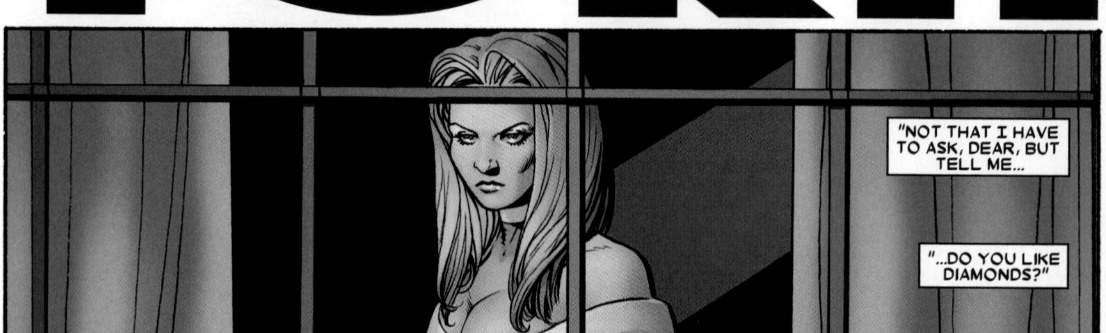
"NOT THAT I HAVE TO ASK, DEAR, BUT TELL ME...
"...DO YOU LIKE DIAMONDS?"

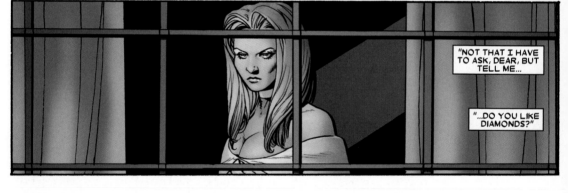

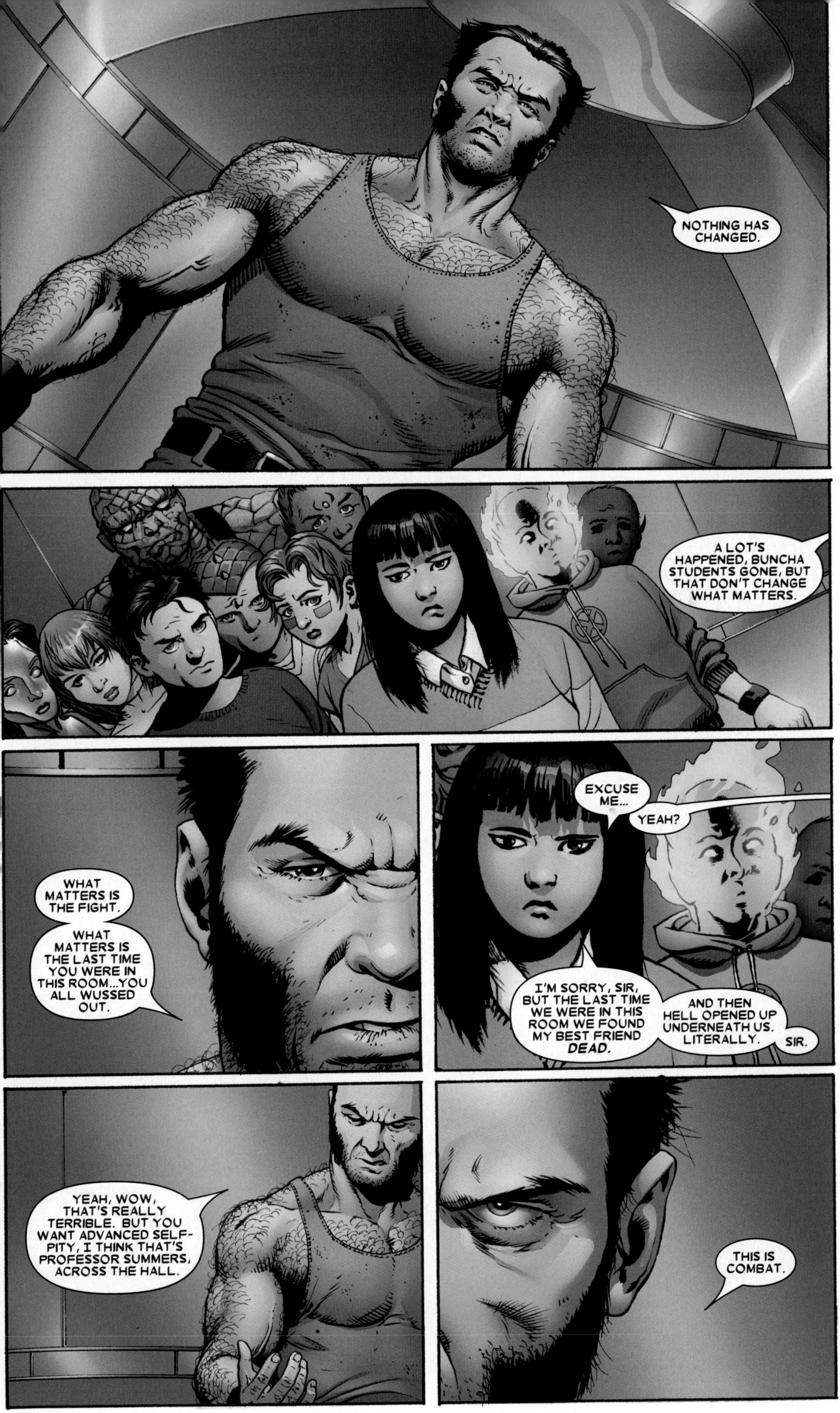

NOTHING HAS CHANGED.
A LOT'S HAPPENED, BUNCHA STUDENTS GONE, BUT THAT DON'T CHANGE WHAT MATTERS.
WHAT MATTERS IS THE FIGHT.
WHAT MATTERS IS THE LAST TIME YOU WERE IN THIS ROOM...YOU ALL WUSSED OUT.
EXCUSE ME...
YEAH?
I'M SORRY, SIR, BUT THE LAST TIME WE WERE IN THIS ROOM WE FOUND MY BEST FRIEND *DEAD.*
AND THEN HELL OPENED UP UNDERNEATH US. LITERALLY.
SIR.
YEAH, WOW, THAT'S REALLY TERRIBLE. BUT YOU WANT ADVANCED SELF-PITY, I THINK THAT'S PROFESSOR SUMMERS, ACROSS THE HALL.
THIS IS COMBAT.

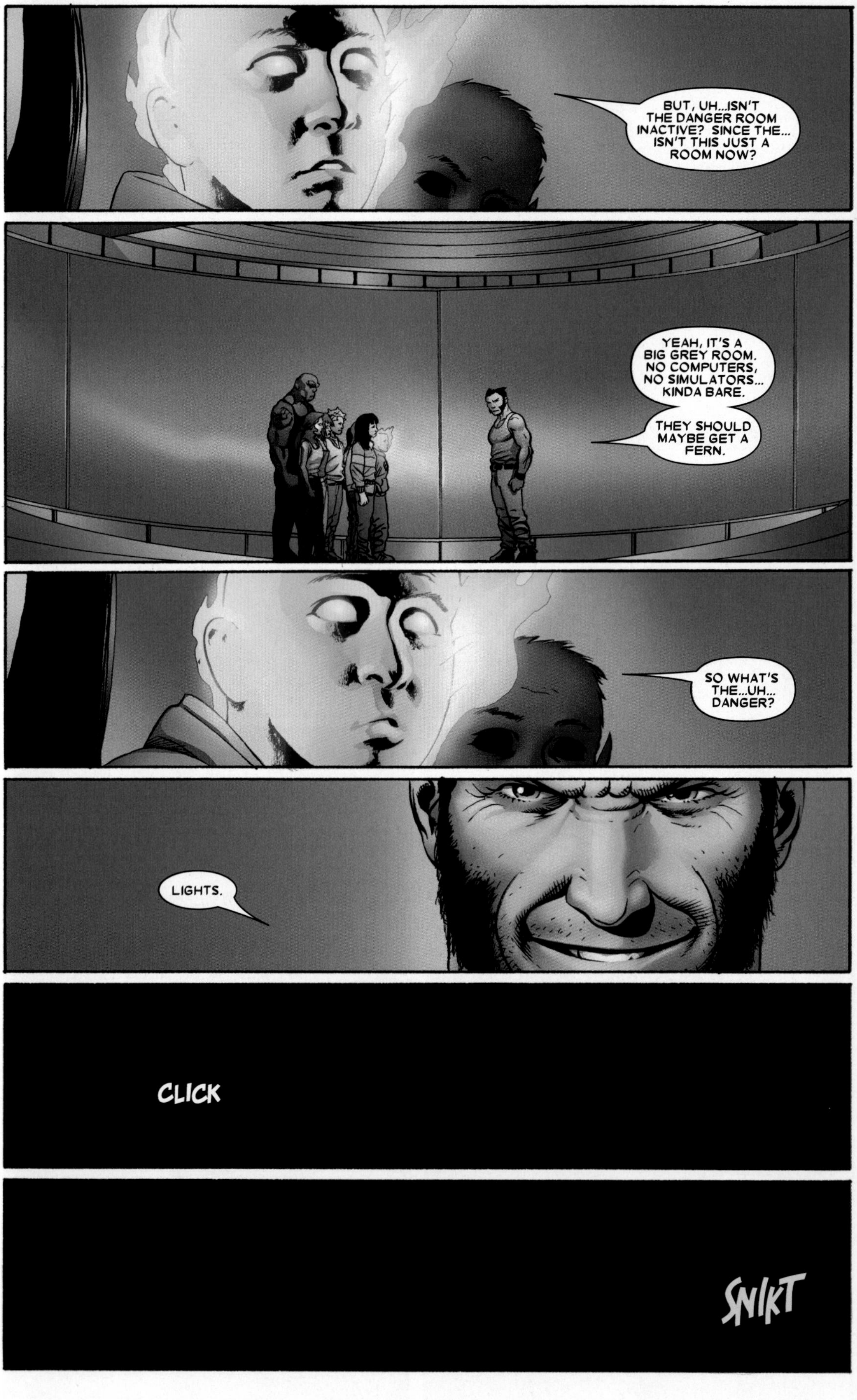

BUT, UH...ISN'T THE DANGER ROOM INACTIVE? SINCE THE... ISN'T THIS JUST A ROOM NOW?
YEAH, IT'S A BIG GREY ROOM. NO COMPUTERS, NO SIMULATORS... KINDA BARE.
THEY SHOULD MAYBE GET A FERN.
SO WHAT'S THE...UH... DANGER?
LIGHTS.
CLICK
SNIKT

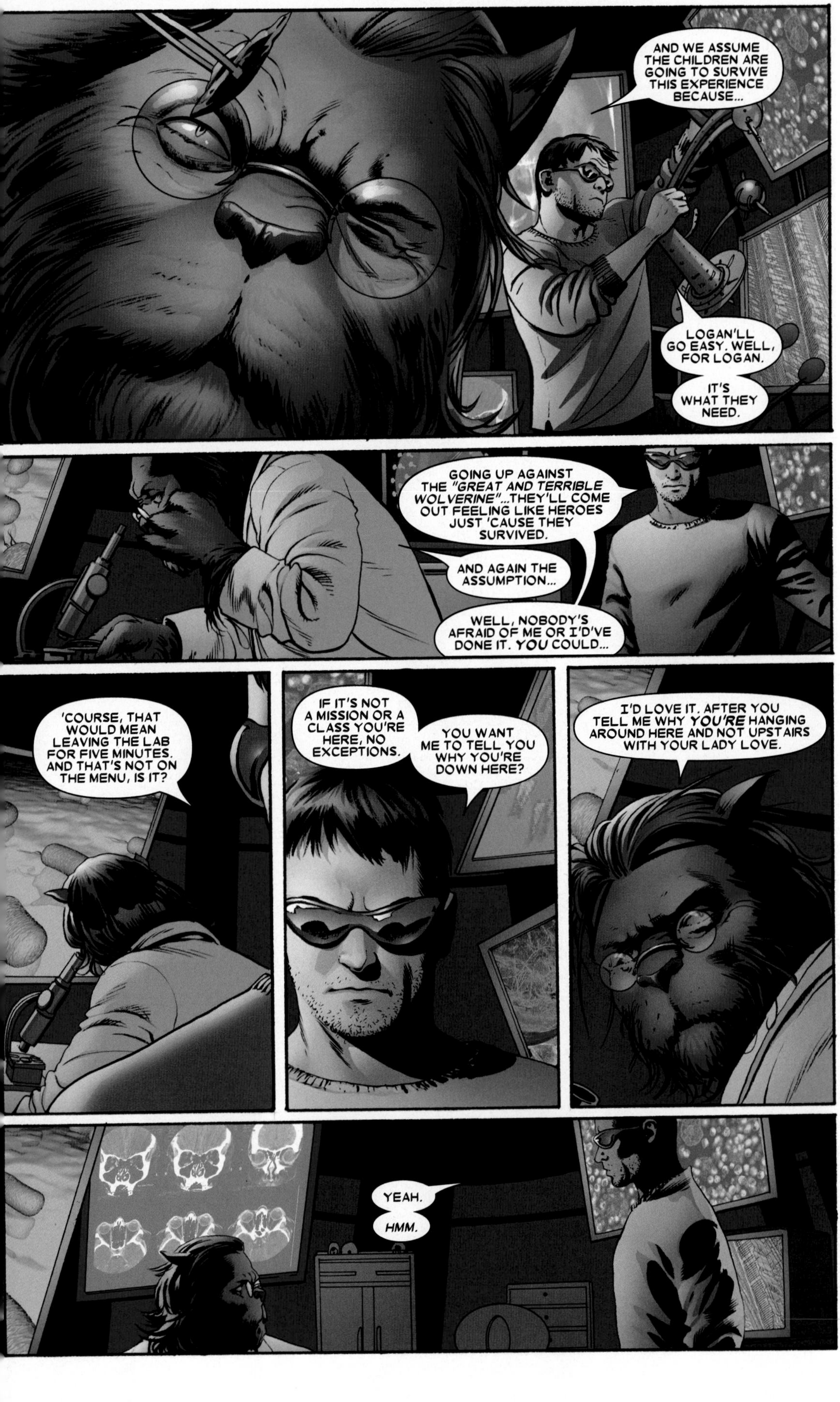
AND WE ASSUME THE CHILDREN ARE GOING TO SURVIVE THIS EXPERIENCE BECAUSE...
LOGAN'LL GO EASY. WELL, FOR LOGAN.
IT'S WHAT THEY NEED.
GOING UP AGAINST THE "GREAT AND TERRIBLE WOLVERINE"...THEY'LL COME OUT FEELING LIKE HEROES JUST 'CAUSE THEY SURVIVED.
AND AGAIN THE ASSUMPTION...
WELL, NOBODY'S AFRAID OF ME OR I'D'VE DONE IT. YOU COULD...
'COURSE, THAT WOULD MEAN LEAVING THE LAB FOR FIVE MINUTES. AND THAT'S NOT ON THE MENU, IS IT?
IF IT'S NOT A MISSION OR A CLASS YOU'RE HERE, NO EXCEPTIONS.
YOU WANT ME TO TELL YOU WHY YOU'RE DOWN HERE?
I'D LOVE IT. AFTER YOU TELL ME WHY YOU'RE HANGING AROUND HERE AND NOT UPSTAIRS WITH YOUR LADY LOVE.
YEAH.
HMM.

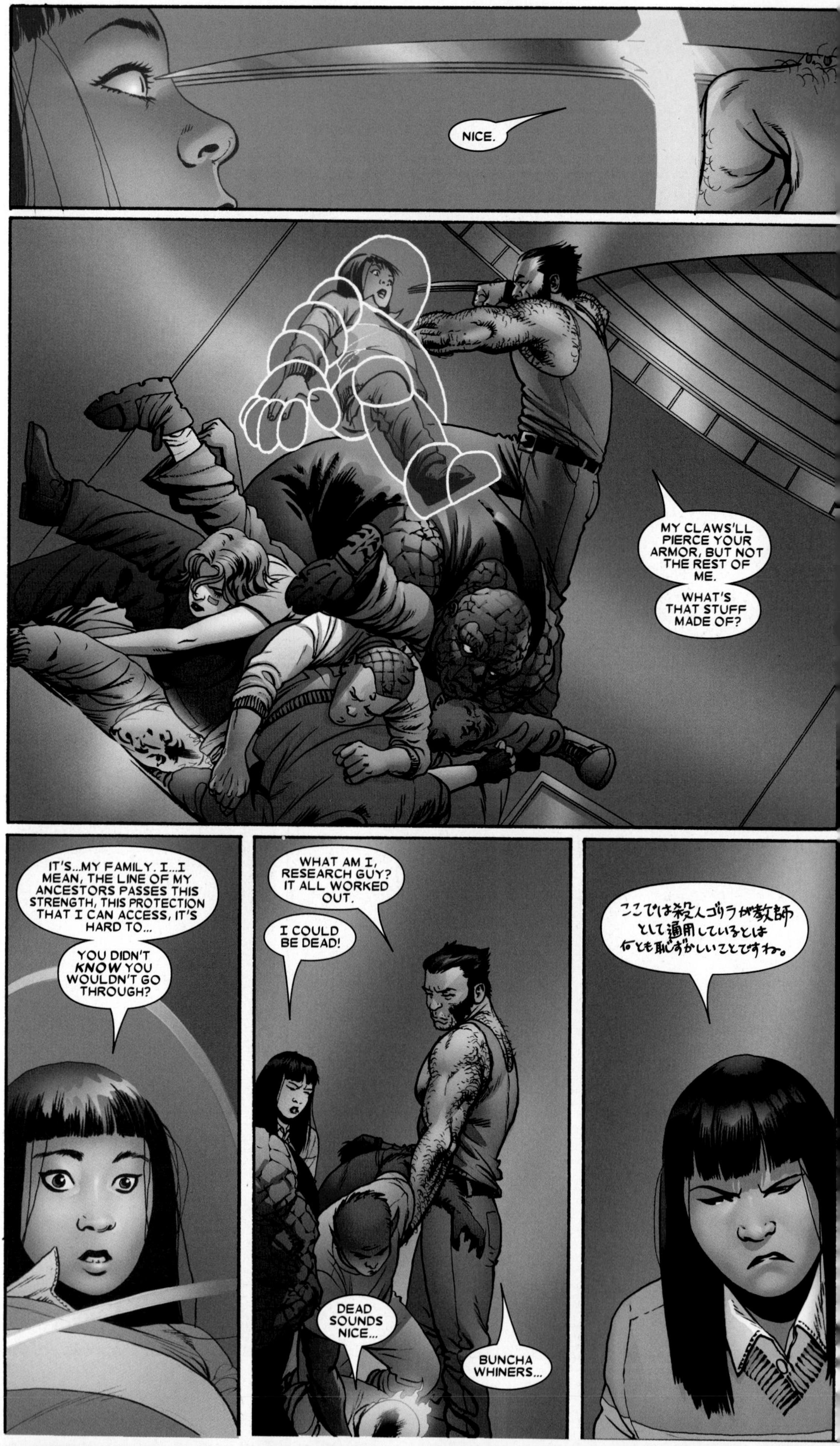
NICE.
MY CLAWS'LL PIERCE YOUR ARMOR, BUT NOT THE REST OF ME.
WHAT'S THAT STUFF MADE OF?
IT'S...MY FAMILY. I...I MEAN, THE LINE OF MY ANCESTORS PASSES THIS STRENGTH, THIS PROTECTION THAT I CAN ACCESS, IT'S HARD TO...
YOU DIDN'T *KNOW* YOU WOULDN'T GO THROUGH?
WHAT AM I, RESEARCH GUY? IT ALL WORKED OUT.
I COULD BE DEAD!
DEAD SOUNDS NICE...
BUNCHA WHINERS...
ここでは殺人ゴリラが教師として通用しているとは何とも恥ずかしいことですね。

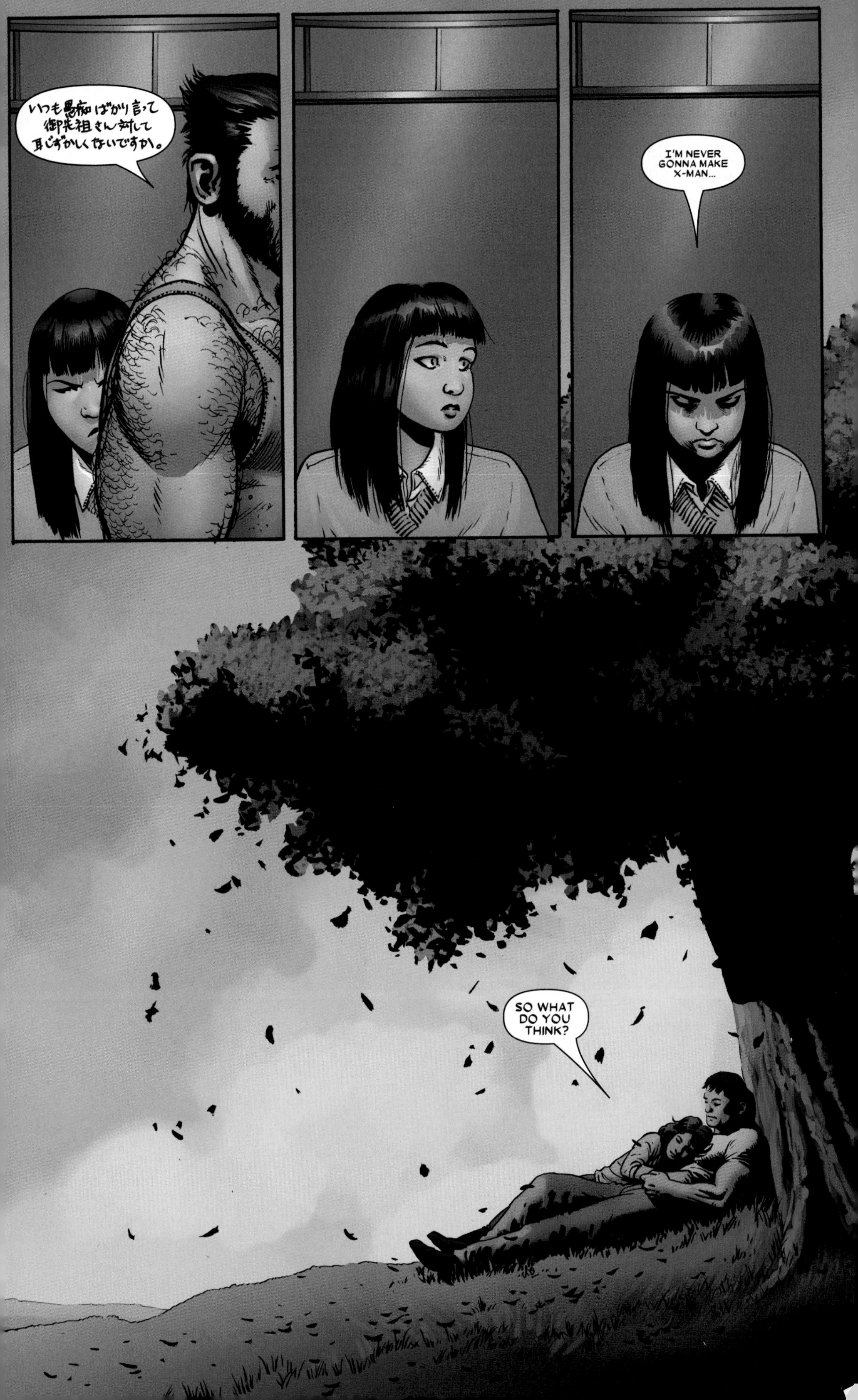
いつも愚痴ばかり言って
御先祖さん対して
恥ずかしくないですか。
I'M NEVER GONNA MAKE X-MAN...
SO WHAT DO YOU THINK?

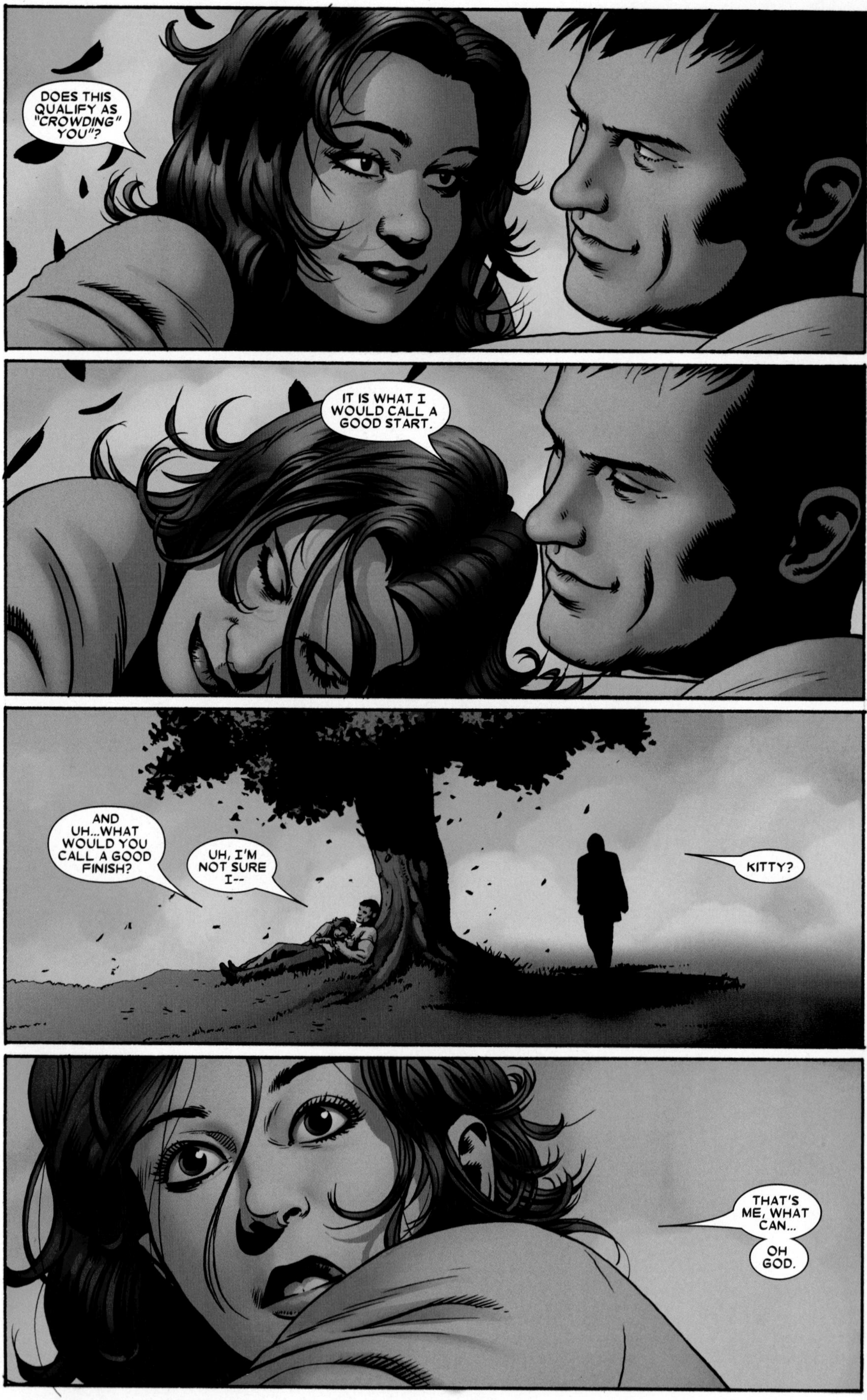
DOES THIS QUALIFY AS "CROWDING" YOU"?
IT IS WHAT I WOULD CALL A GOOD START.
AND UH...WHAT WOULD YOU CALL A GOOD FINISH?
UH, I'M NOT SURE I--
KITTY?
THAT'S ME, WHAT CAN...
OH GOD.

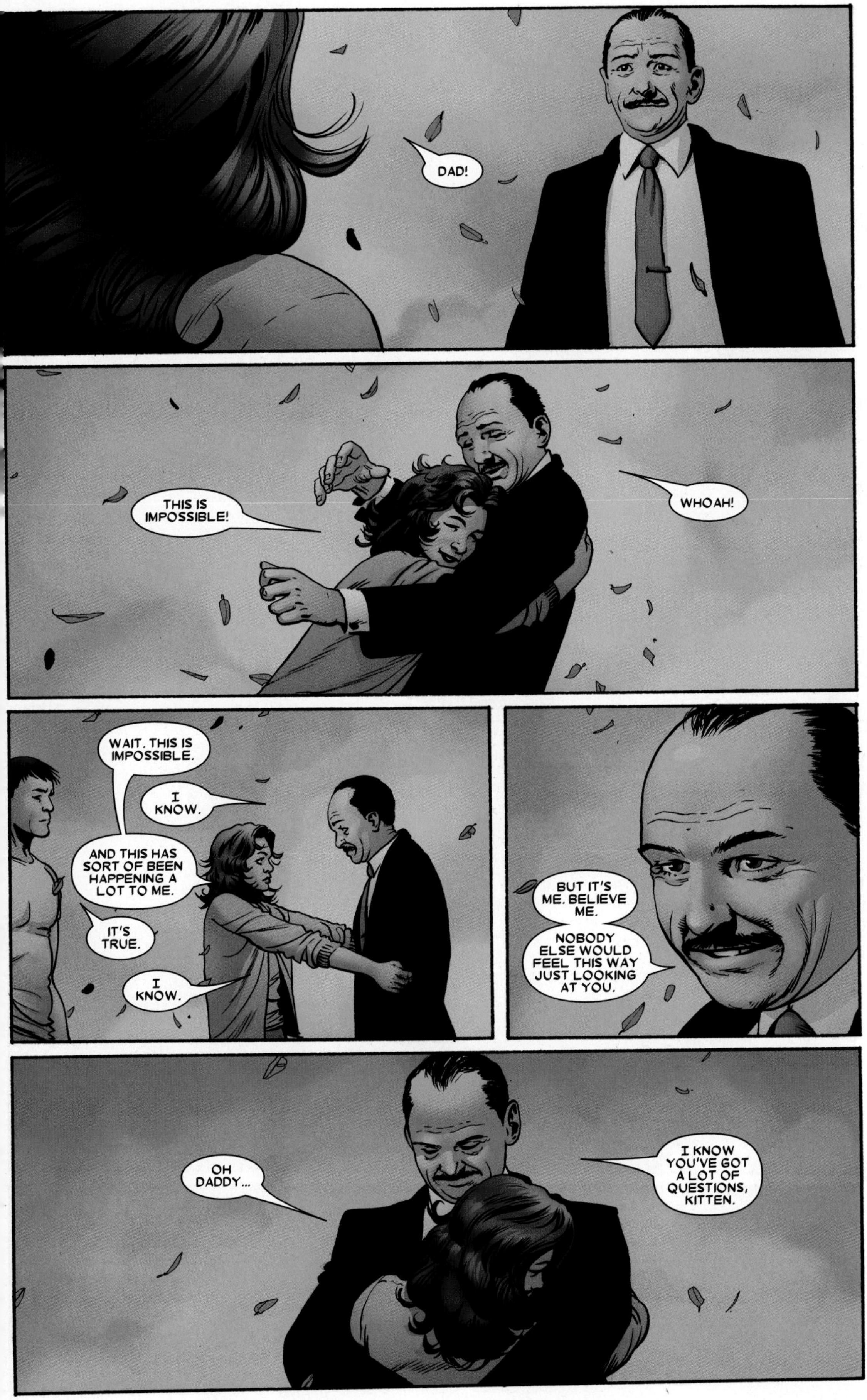

DAD!
THIS IS IMPOSSIBLE!
WHOAH!
WAIT. THIS IS IMPOSSIBLE.
I KNOW.
AND THIS HAS SORT OF BEEN HAPPENING A LOT TO ME.
IT'S TRUE.
I KNOW.
BUT IT'S ME. BELIEVE ME.
NOBODY ELSE WOULD FEEL THIS WAY JUST LOOKING AT YOU.
OH DADDY...
I KNOW YOU'VE GOT A LOT OF QUESTIONS, KITTEN.

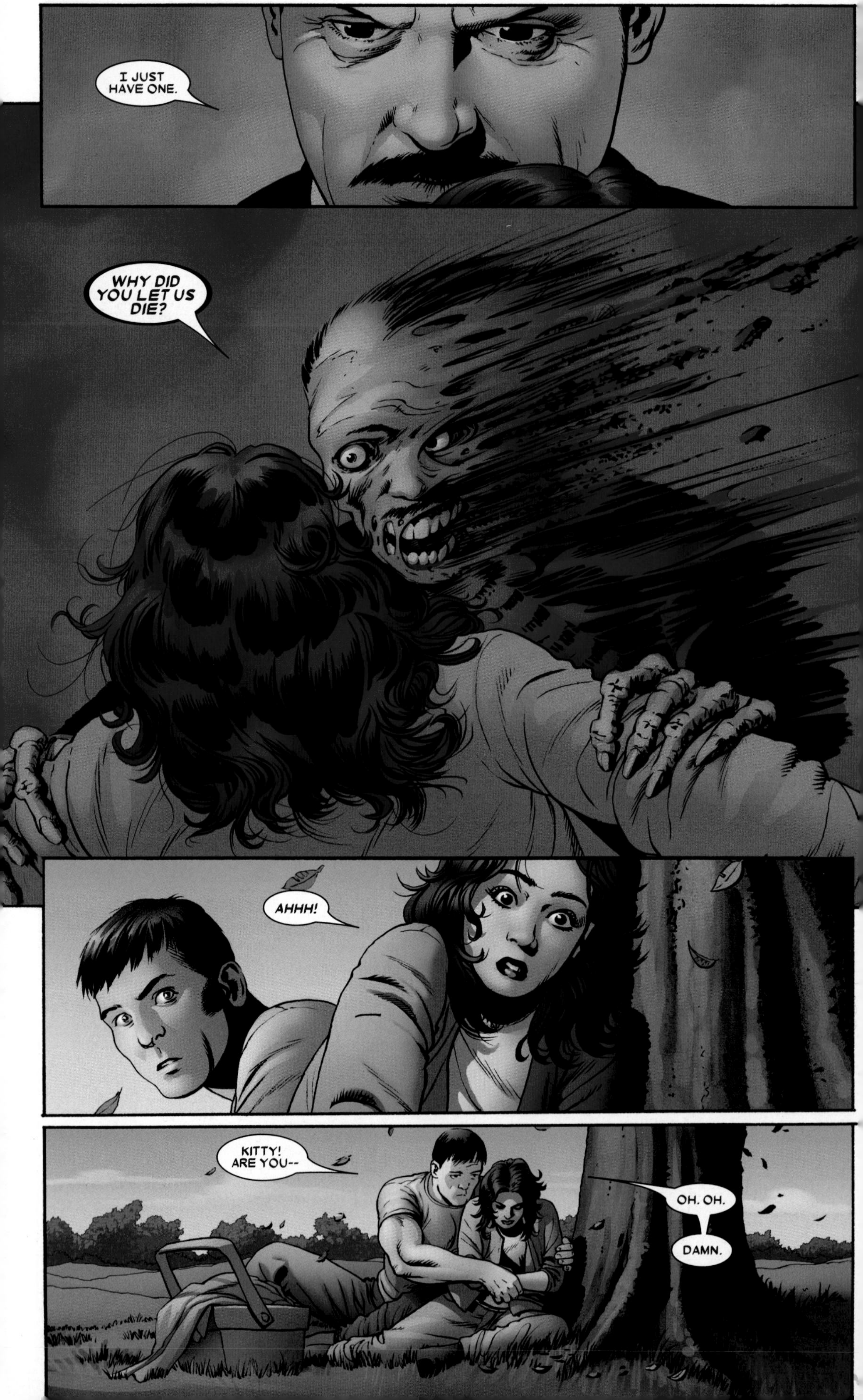

I JUST HAVE ONE.
WHY DID YOU LET US DIE?
AHHH!
KITTY! ARE YOU--
OH. OH.
DAMN.

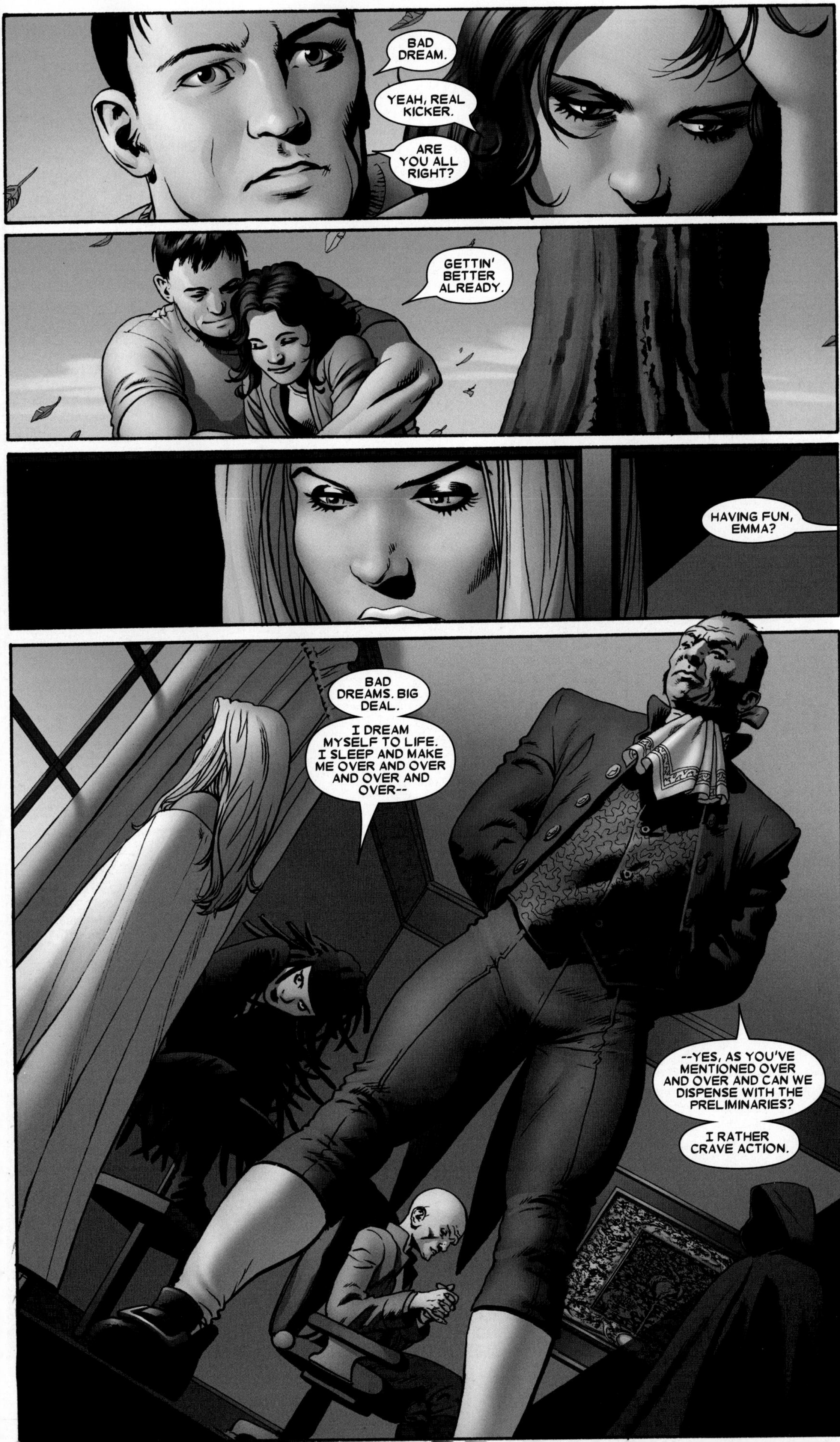
BAD DREAM.
YEAH, REAL KICKER.
ARE YOU ALL RIGHT?
GETTIN' BETTER ALREADY.
HAVING FUN, EMMA?
BAD DREAMS. BIG DEAL.
I DREAM MYSELF TO LIFE. I SLEEP AND MAKE ME OVER AND OVER AND OVER AND OVER AND OVER--
--YES, AS YOU'VE MENTIONED OVER AND OVER AND CAN WE DISPENSE WITH THE PRELIMINARIES?
I RATHER CRAVE ACTION.

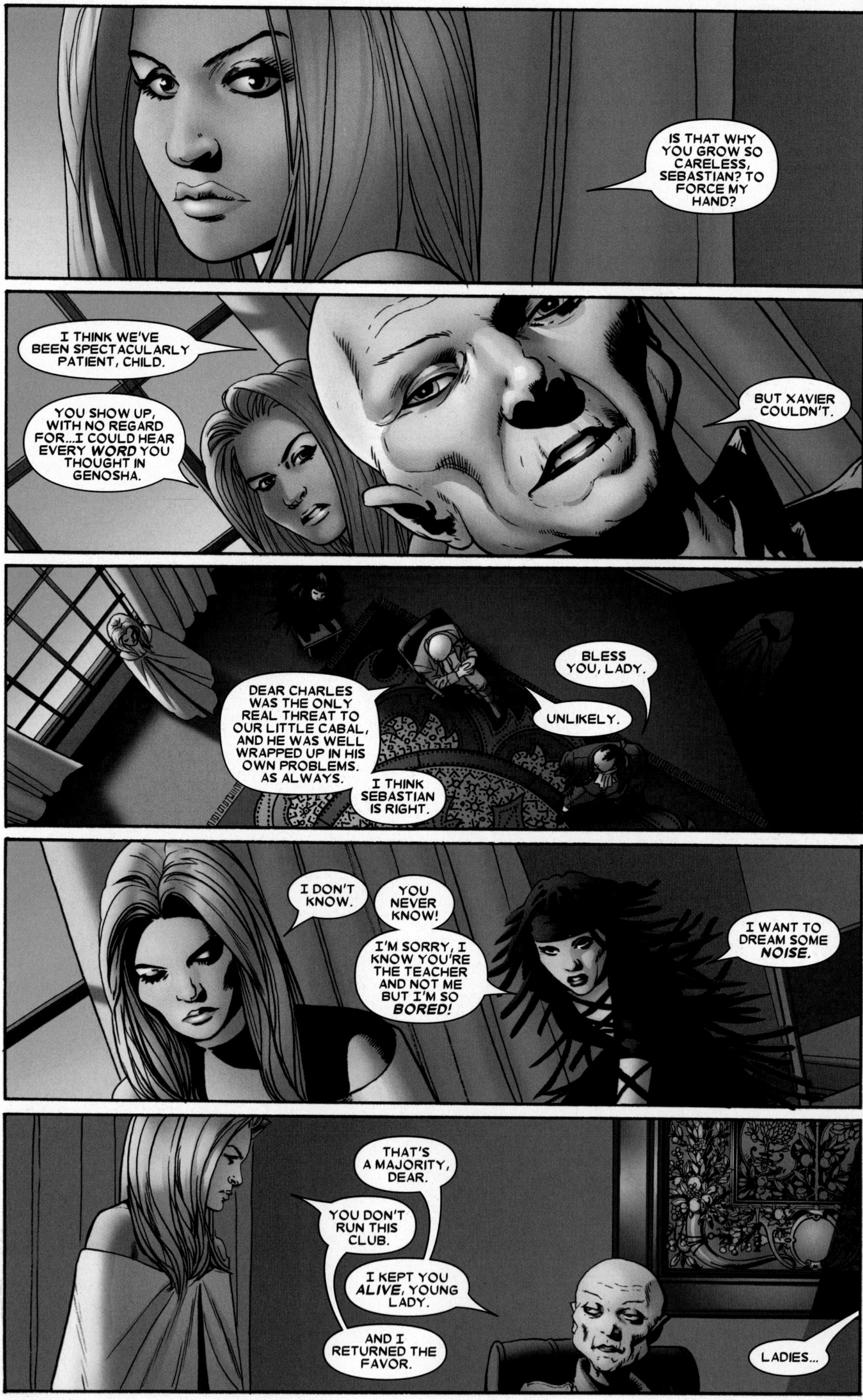
IS THAT WHY YOU GROW SO CARELESS, SEBASTIAN? TO FORCE MY HAND?
I THINK WE'VE BEEN SPECTACULARLY PATIENT, CHILD.
YOU SHOW UP, WITH NO REGARD FOR...I COULD HEAR EVERY WORD YOU THOUGHT IN GENOSHA.
BUT XAVIER COULDN'T.
DEAR CHARLES WAS THE ONLY REAL THREAT TO OUR LITTLE CABAL, AND HE WAS WELL WRAPPED UP IN HIS OWN PROBLEMS. AS ALWAYS.
BLESS YOU, LADY.
UNLIKELY.
I THINK SEBASTIAN IS RIGHT.
I DON'T KNOW.
YOU NEVER KNOW!
I'M SORRY, I KNOW YOU'RE THE TEACHER AND NOT ME BUT I'M SO BORED!
I WANT TO DREAM SOME NOISE.
THAT'S A MAJORITY, DEAR.
YOU DON'T RUN THIS CLUB.
I KEPT YOU ALIVE, YOUNG LADY.
AND I RETURNED THE FAVOR.
LADIES...

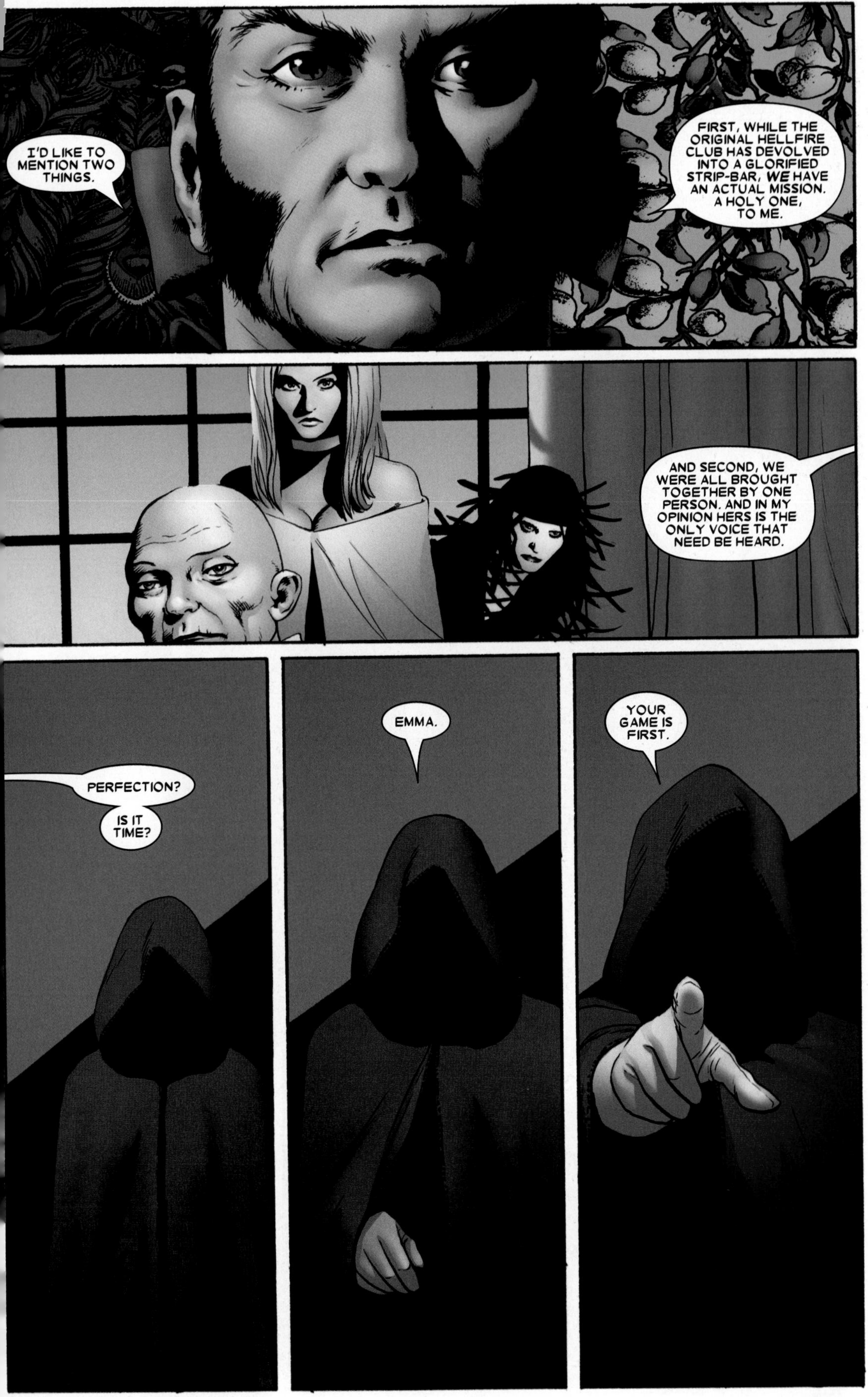
I'D LIKE TO MENTION TWO THINGS.
FIRST, WHILE THE ORIGINAL HELLFIRE CLUB HAS DEVOLVED INTO A GLORIFIED STRIP-BAR, WE HAVE AN ACTUAL MISSION. A HOLY ONE, TO ME.
AND SECOND, WE WERE ALL BROUGHT TOGETHER BY ONE PERSON. AND IN MY OPINION HERS IS THE ONLY VOICE THAT NEED BE HEARD.
PERFECTION?
IS IT TIME?
EMMA.
YOUR GAME IS FIRST.

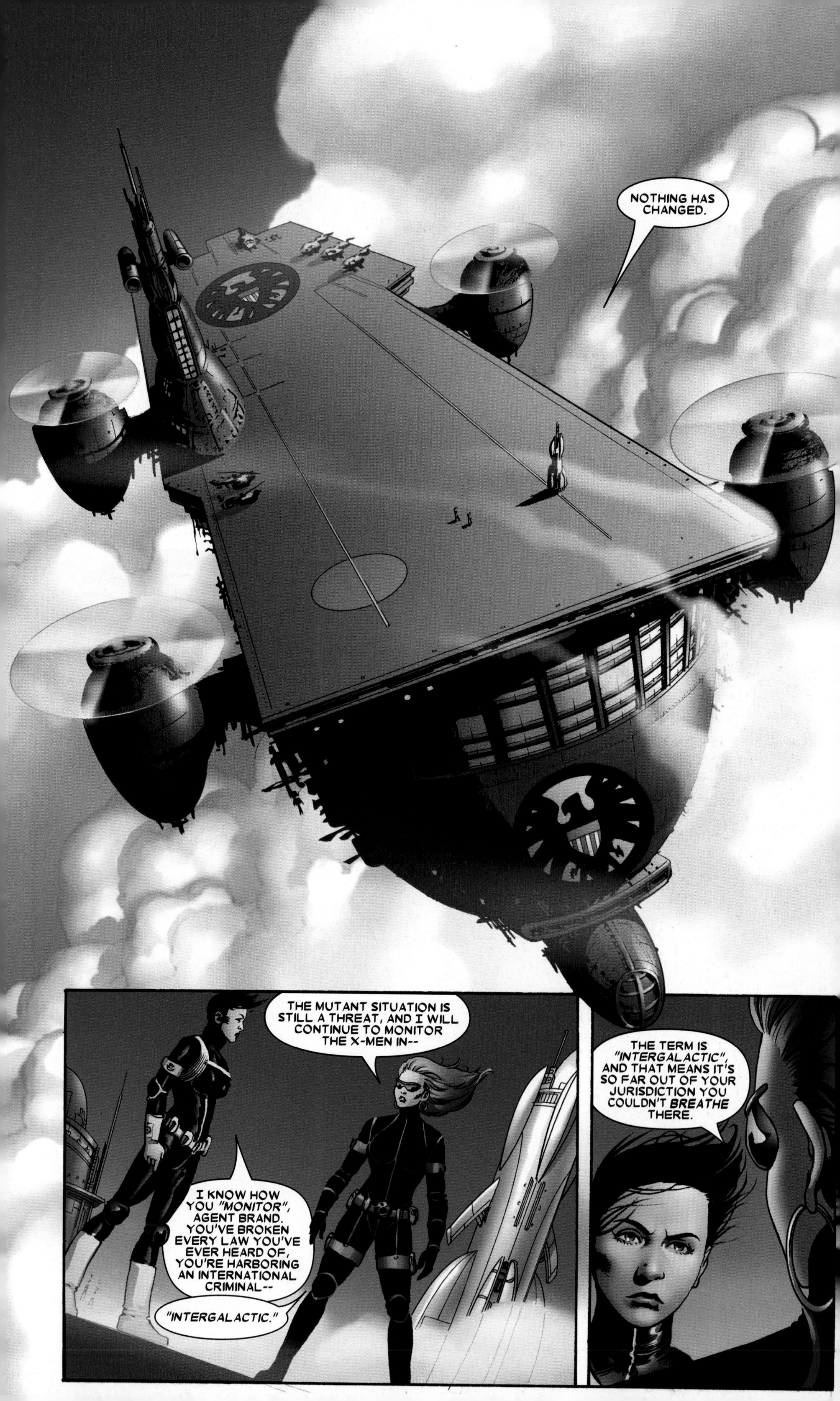
NOTHING HAS CHANGED.
THE MUTANT SITUATION IS STILL A THREAT, AND I WILL CONTINUE TO MONITOR THE X-MEN IN--
I KNOW HOW YOU "MONITOR", AGENT BRAND. YOU'VE BROKEN EVERY LAW YOU'VE EVER HEARD OF, YOU'RE HARBORING AN INTERNATIONAL CRIMINAL--
"INTERGALACTIC."
THE TERM IS "INTERGALACTIC", AND THAT MEANS IT'S SO FAR OUT OF YOUR JURISDICTION YOU COULDN'T BREATHE THERE.

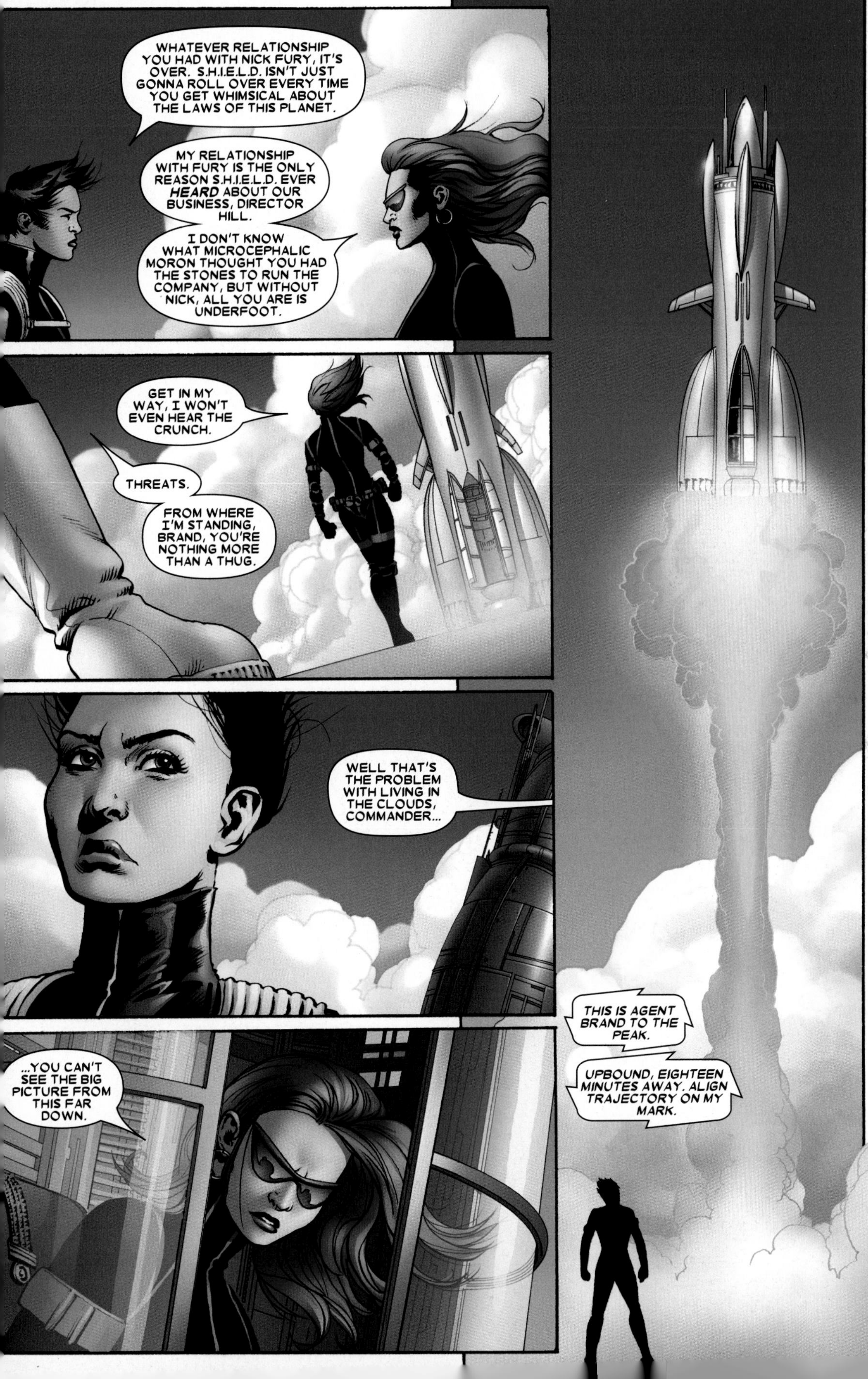
WHATEVER RELATIONSHIP YOU HAD WITH NICK FURY, IT'S OVER. S.H.I.E.L.D. ISN'T JUST GONNA ROLL OVER EVERY TIME YOU GET WHIMSICAL ABOUT THE LAWS OF THIS PLANET.
MY RELATIONSHIP WITH FURY IS THE ONLY REASON S.H.I.E.L.D. EVER *HEARD* ABOUT OUR BUSINESS, DIRECTOR HILL.
I DON'T KNOW WHAT MICROCEPHALIC MORON THOUGHT YOU HAD THE STONES TO RUN THE COMPANY, BUT WITHOUT NICK, ALL YOU ARE IS UNDERFOOT.
GET IN MY WAY, I WON'T EVEN HEAR THE CRUNCH.
THREATS.
FROM WHERE I'M STANDING, BRAND, YOU'RE NOTHING MORE THAN A THUG.
WELL THAT'S THE PROBLEM WITH LIVING IN THE CLOUDS, COMMANDER...
...YOU CAN'T SEE THE BIG PICTURE FROM THIS FAR DOWN.
THIS IS AGENT BRAND TO THE PEAK.
UPBOUND, EIGHTEEN MINUTES AWAY. ALIGN TRAJECTORY ON MY MARK.

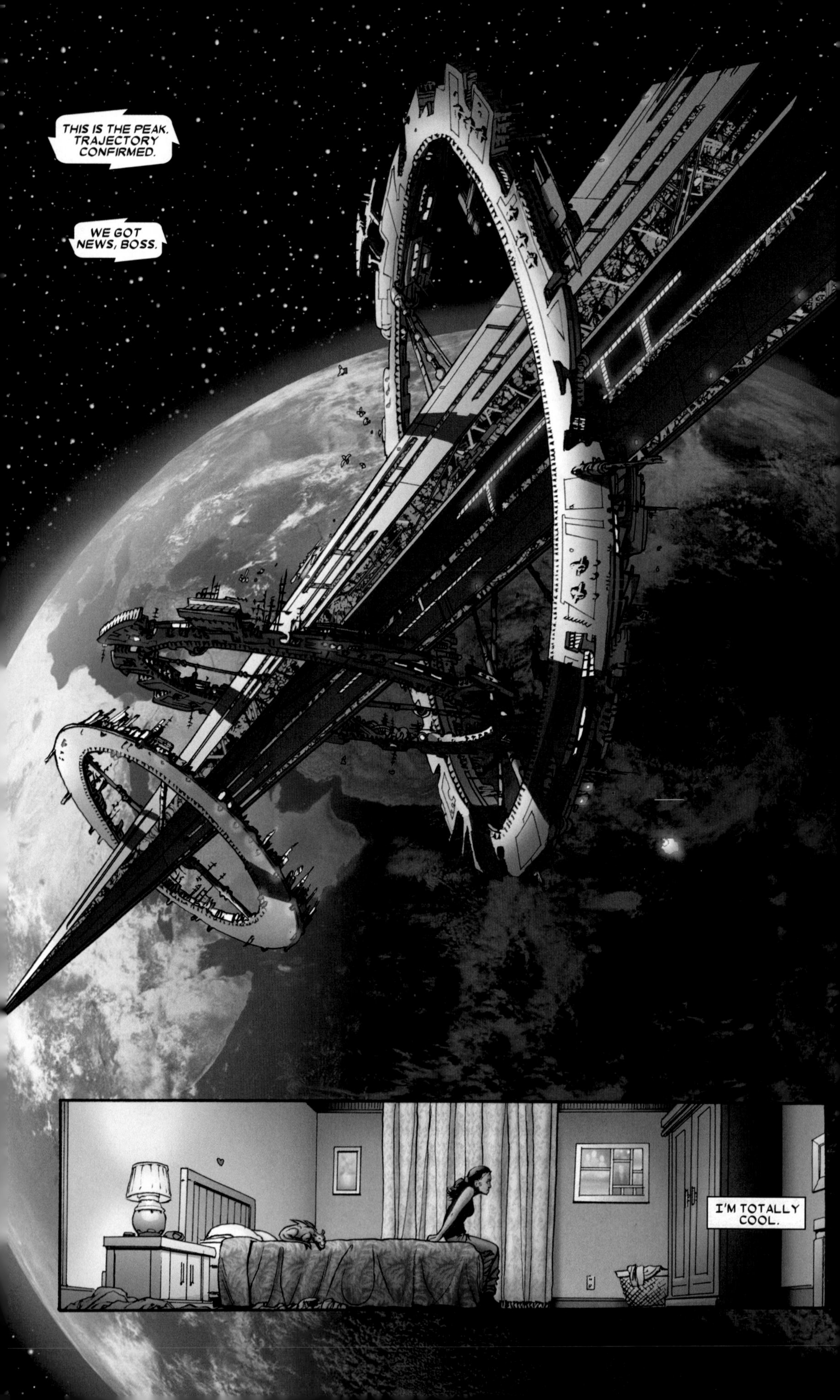
THIS IS THE PEAK. TRAJECTORY CONFIRMED.
WE GOT NEWS, BOSS.
I'M TOTALLY COOL.

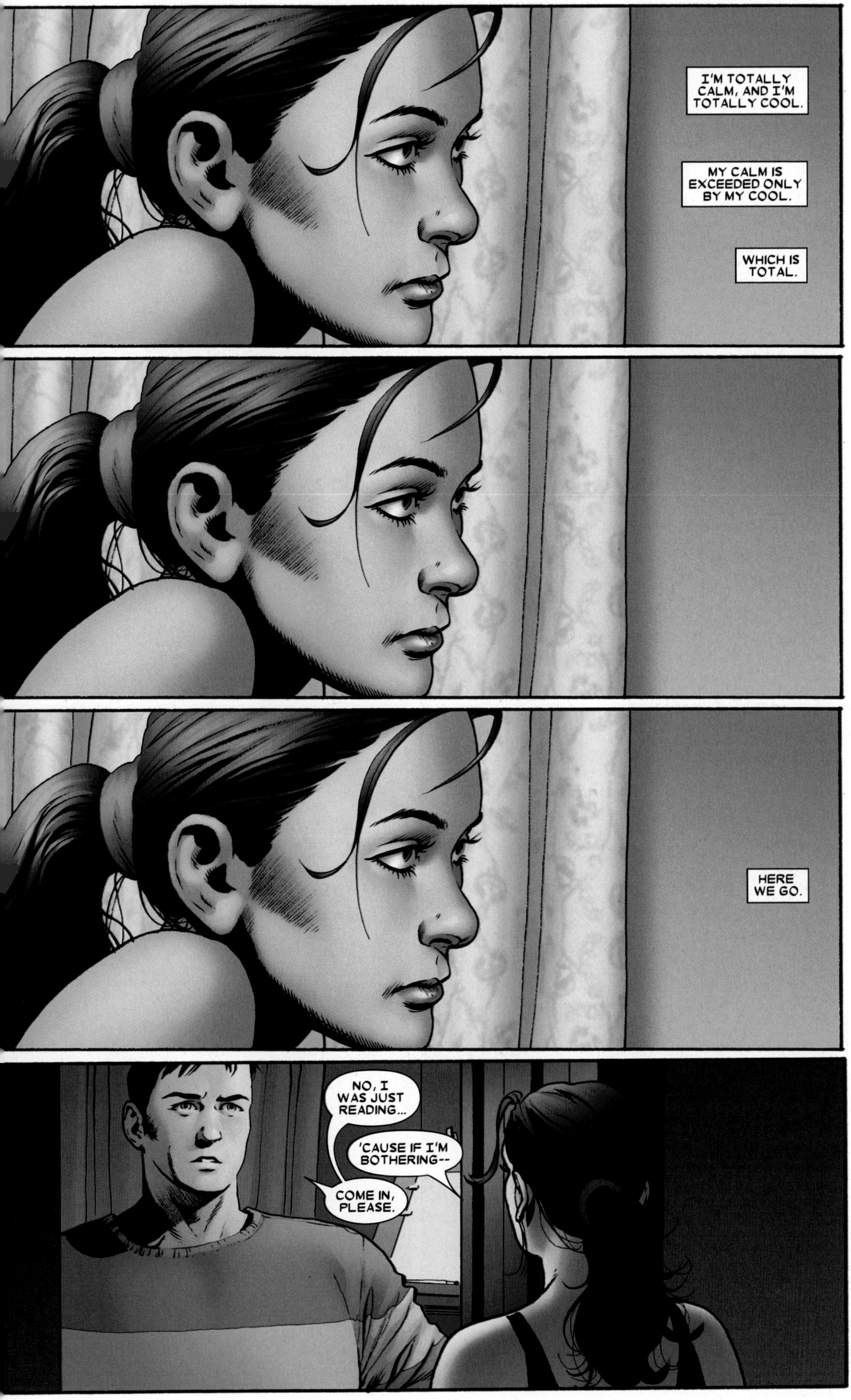

I'M TOTALLY CALM, AND I'M TOTALLY COOL.
MY CALM IS EXCEEDED ONLY BY MY COOL.
WHICH IS TOTAL.
HERE WE GO.
NO, I WAS JUST READING...
'CAUSE IF I'M BOTHERING--
COME IN, PLEASE.

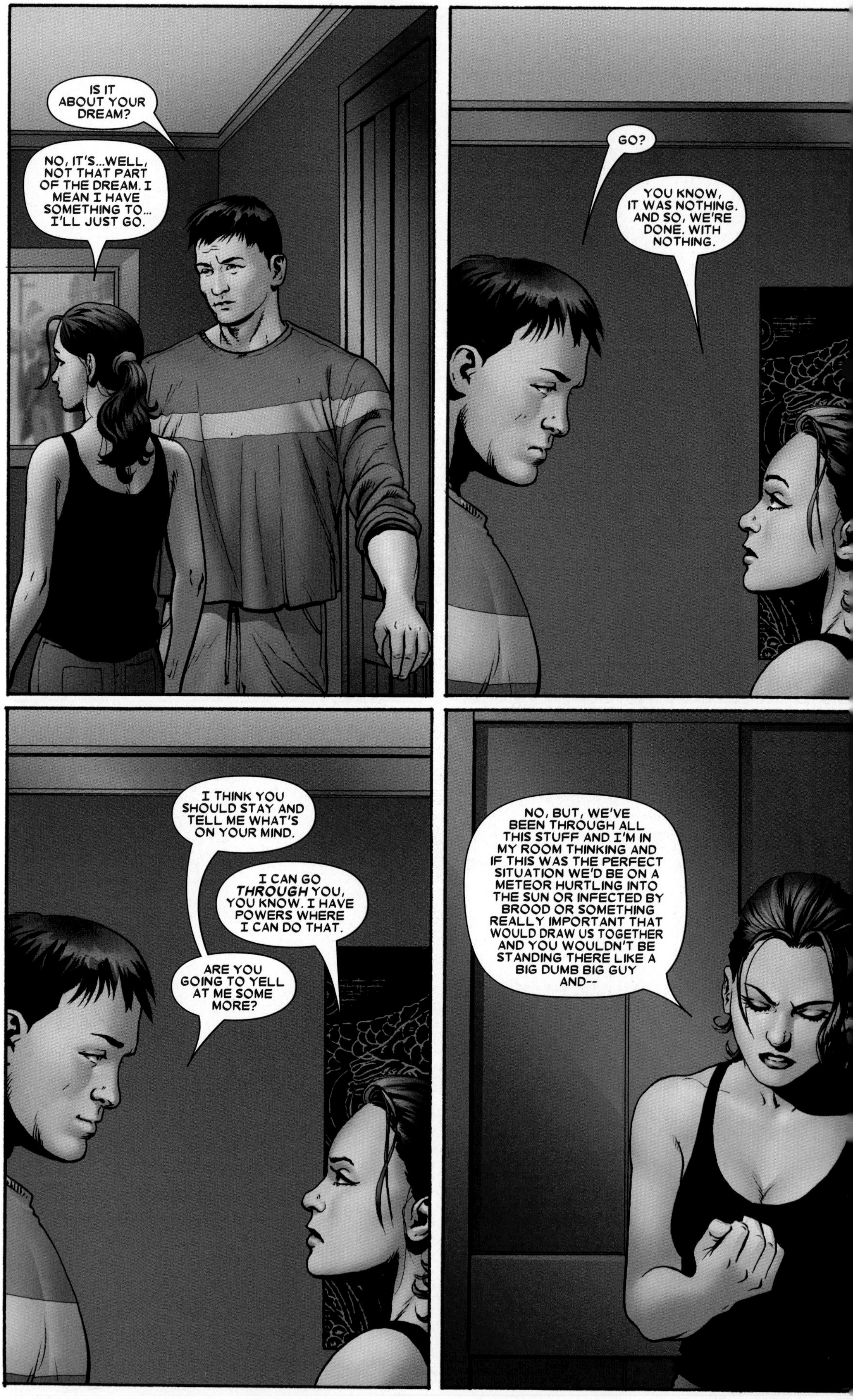
IS IT ABOUT YOUR DREAM?
NO, IT'S...WELL, NOT THAT PART OF THE DREAM. I MEAN I HAVE SOMETHING TO... I'LL JUST GO.
GO?
YOU KNOW, IT WAS NOTHING. AND SO, WE'RE DONE. WITH NOTHING.
I THINK YOU SHOULD STAY AND TELL ME WHAT'S ON YOUR MIND.
I CAN GO *THROUGH* YOU, YOU KNOW. I HAVE POWERS WHERE I CAN DO THAT.
ARE YOU GOING TO YELL AT ME SOME MORE?
NO, BUT, WE'VE BEEN THROUGH ALL THIS STUFF AND I'M IN MY ROOM THINKING AND IF THIS WAS THE PERFECT SITUATION WE'D BE ON A METEOR HURTLING INTO THE SUN OR INFECTED BY BROOD OR SOMETHING REALLY IMPORTANT THAT WOULD DRAW US TOGETHER AND YOU WOULDN'T BE STANDING THERE LIKE A BIG DUMB BIG GUY AND--

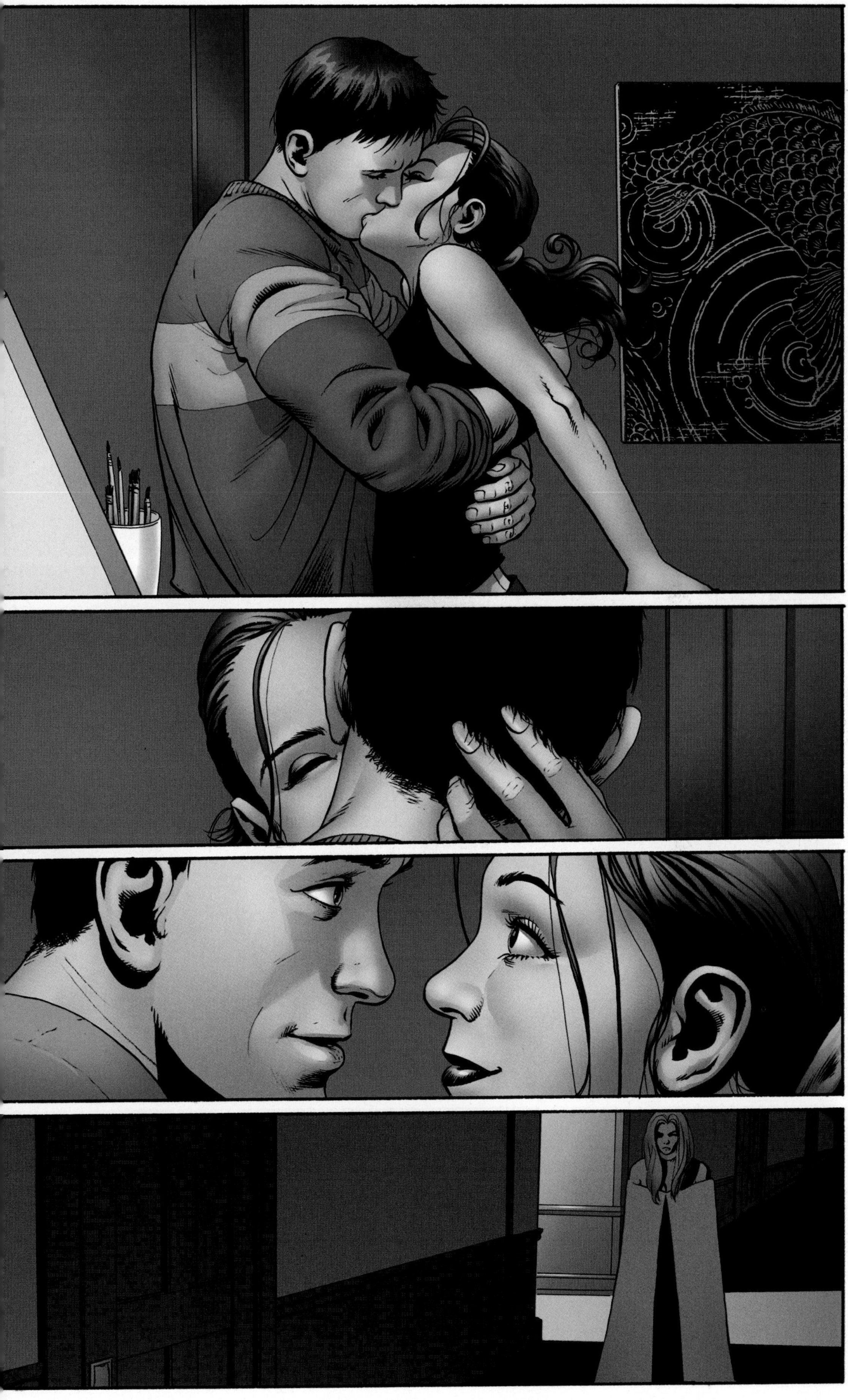

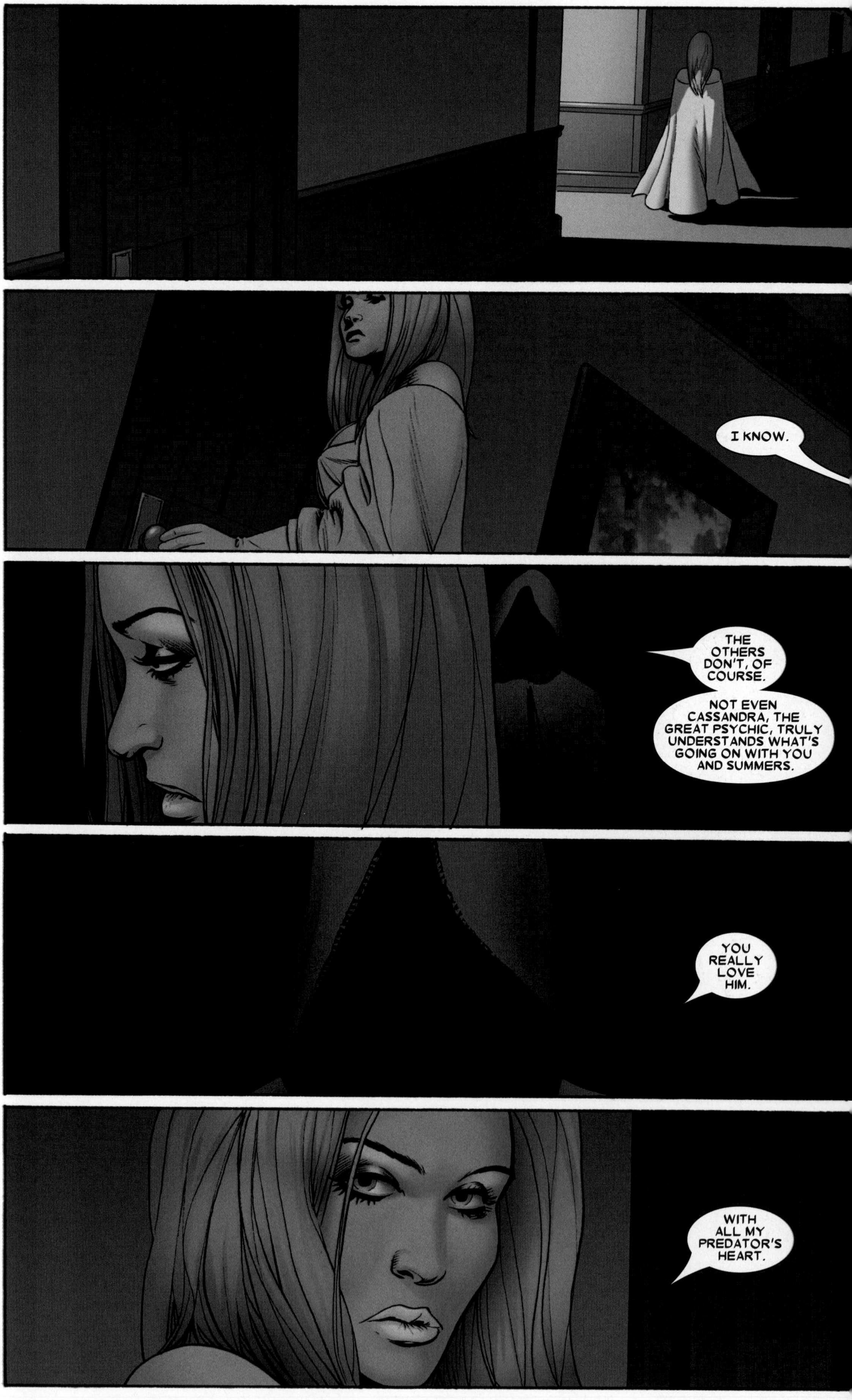
I KNOW.
THE OTHERS DON'T, OF COURSE.
NOT EVEN CASSANDRA, THE GREAT PSYCHIC, TRULY UNDERSTANDS WHAT'S GOING ON WITH YOU AND SUMMERS.
YOU REALLY LOVE HIM.
WITH ALL MY PREDATOR'S HEART.

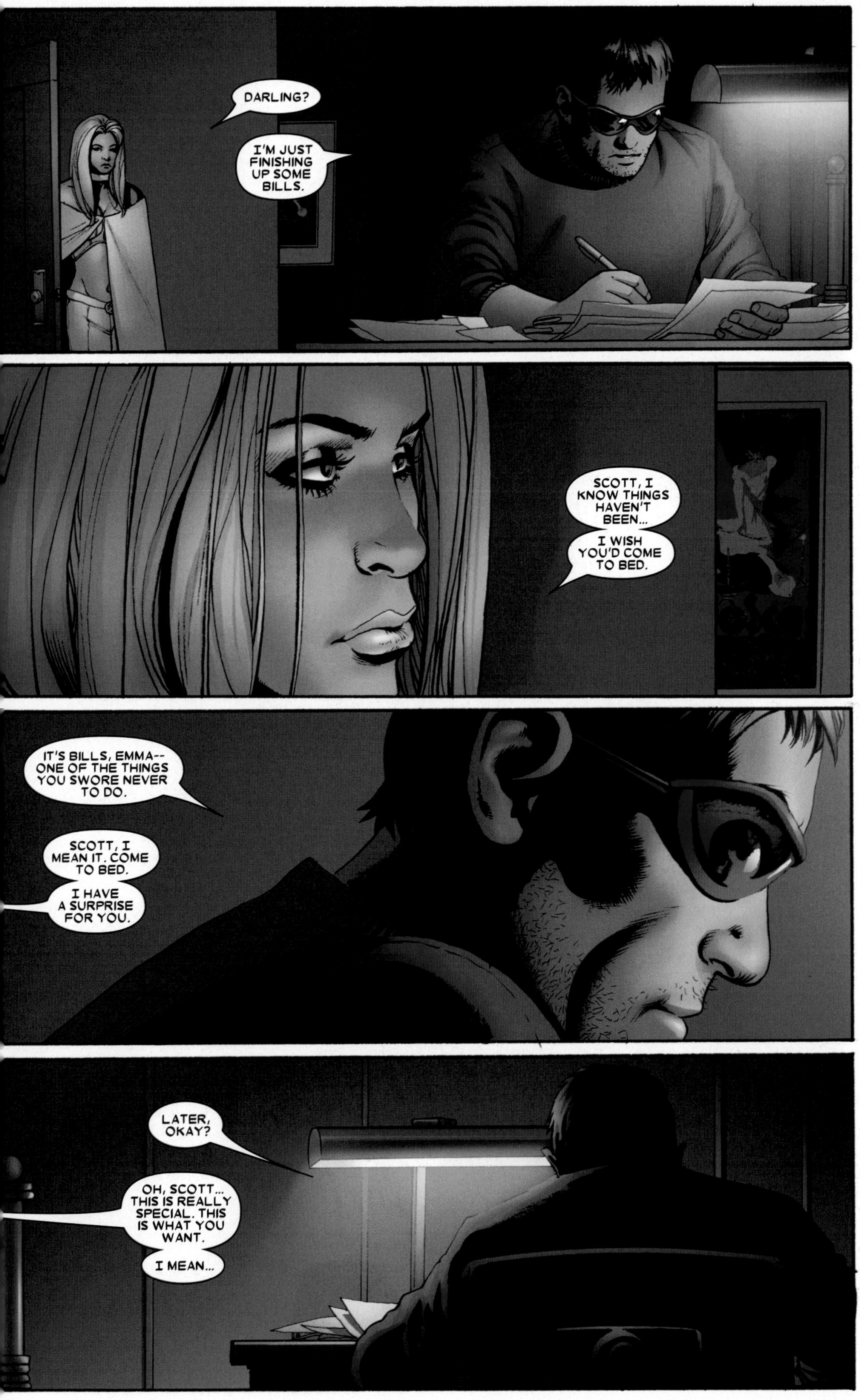
DARLING?
I'M JUST FINISHING UP SOME BILLS.
SCOTT, I KNOW THINGS HAVEN'T BEEN...
I WISH YOU'D COME TO BED.
IT'S BILLS, EMMA-- ONE OF THE THINGS YOU SWORE NEVER TO DO.
SCOTT, I MEAN IT. COME TO BED.
I HAVE A SURPRISE FOR YOU.
LATER, OKAY?
OH, SCOTT... THIS IS REALLY SPECIAL. THIS IS WHAT YOU WANT.
I MEAN...

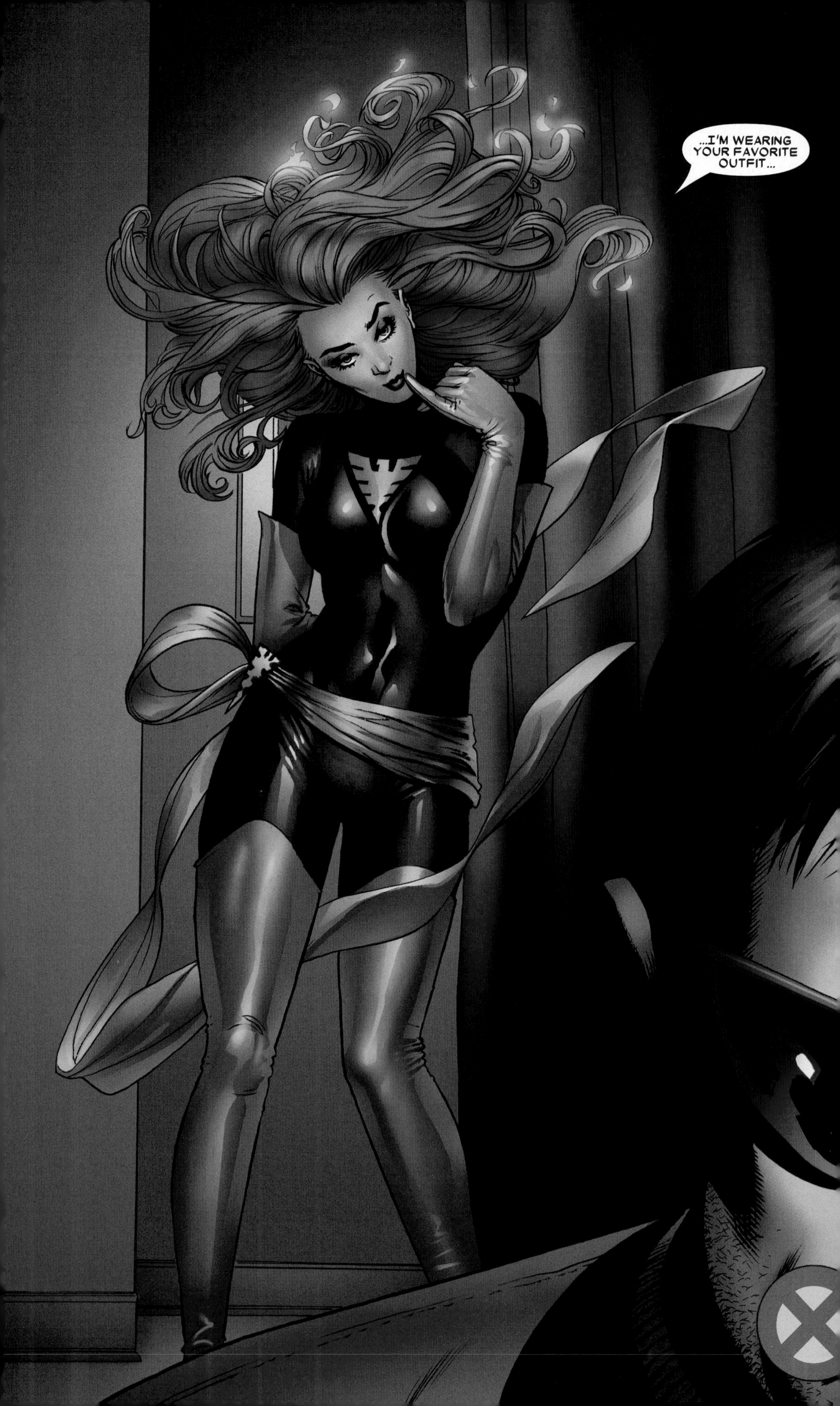
...I'M WEARING YOUR FAVORITE OUTFIT...

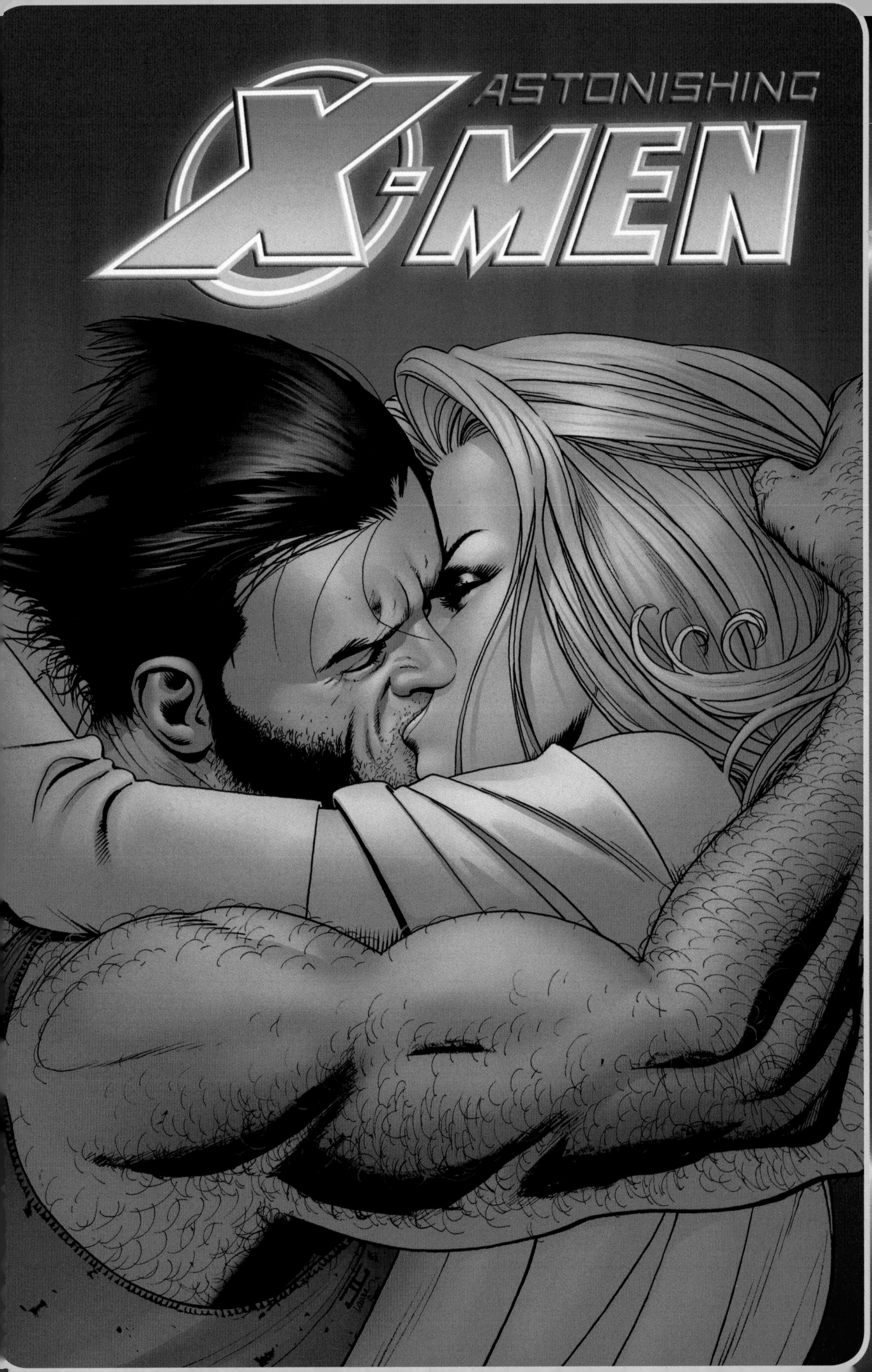
ASTONISHING
X-MEN

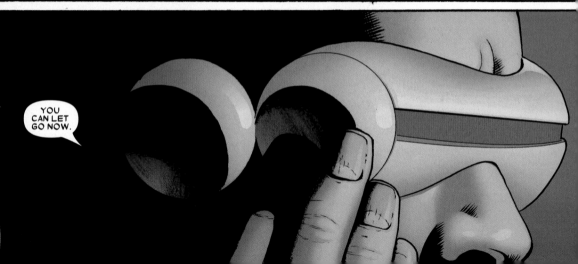

YOU CAN LET GO NOW.

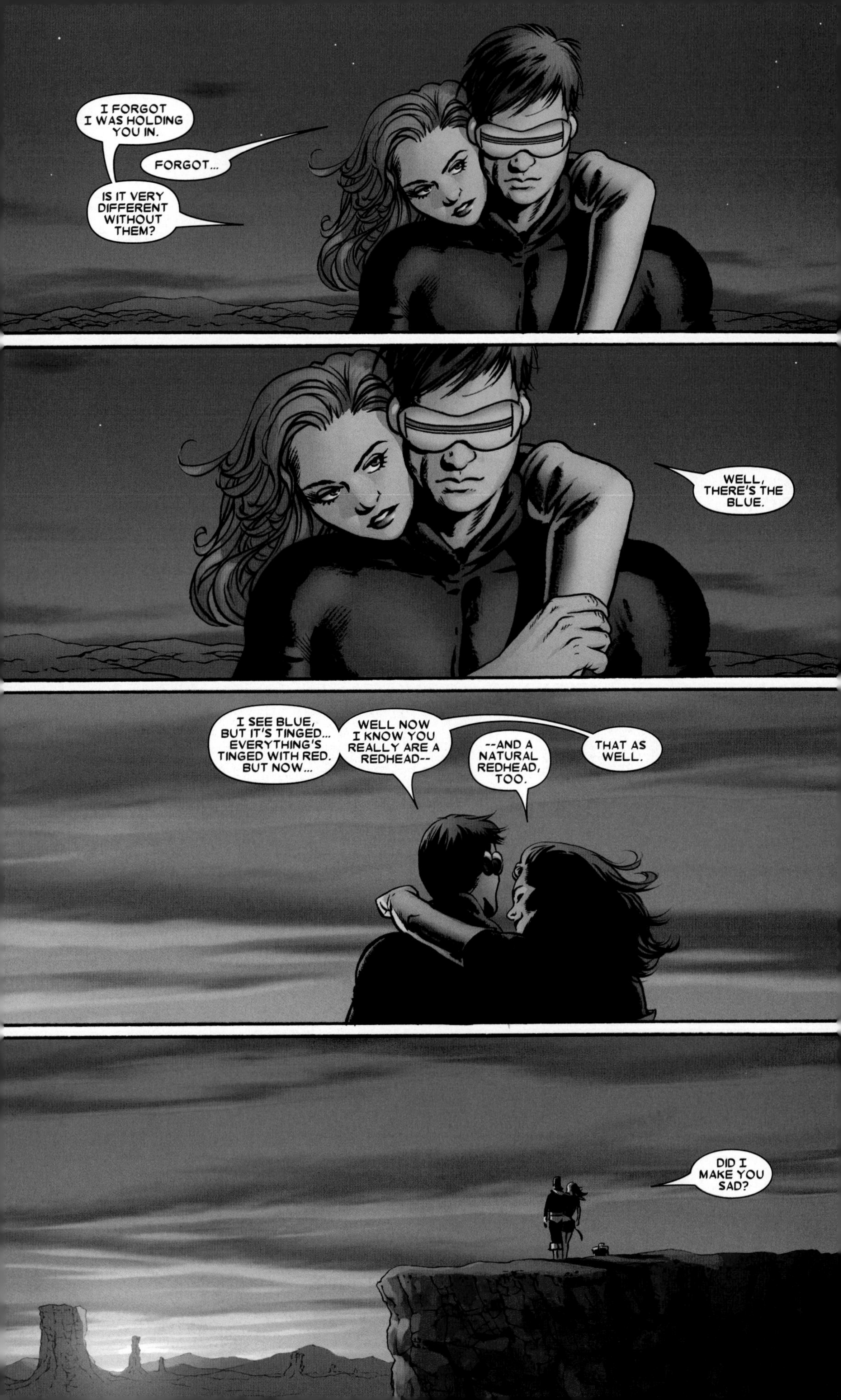
I FORGOT I WAS HOLDING YOU IN.
FORGOT...
IS IT VERY DIFFERENT WITHOUT THEM?
WELL, THERE'S THE BLUE.
I SEE BLUE, BUT IT'S TINGED... EVERYTHING'S TINGED WITH RED. BUT NOW...
WELL NOW I KNOW YOU REALLY ARE A REDHEAD--
--AND A NATURAL REDHEAD, TOO.
THAT AS WELL.
DID I MAKE YOU SAD?

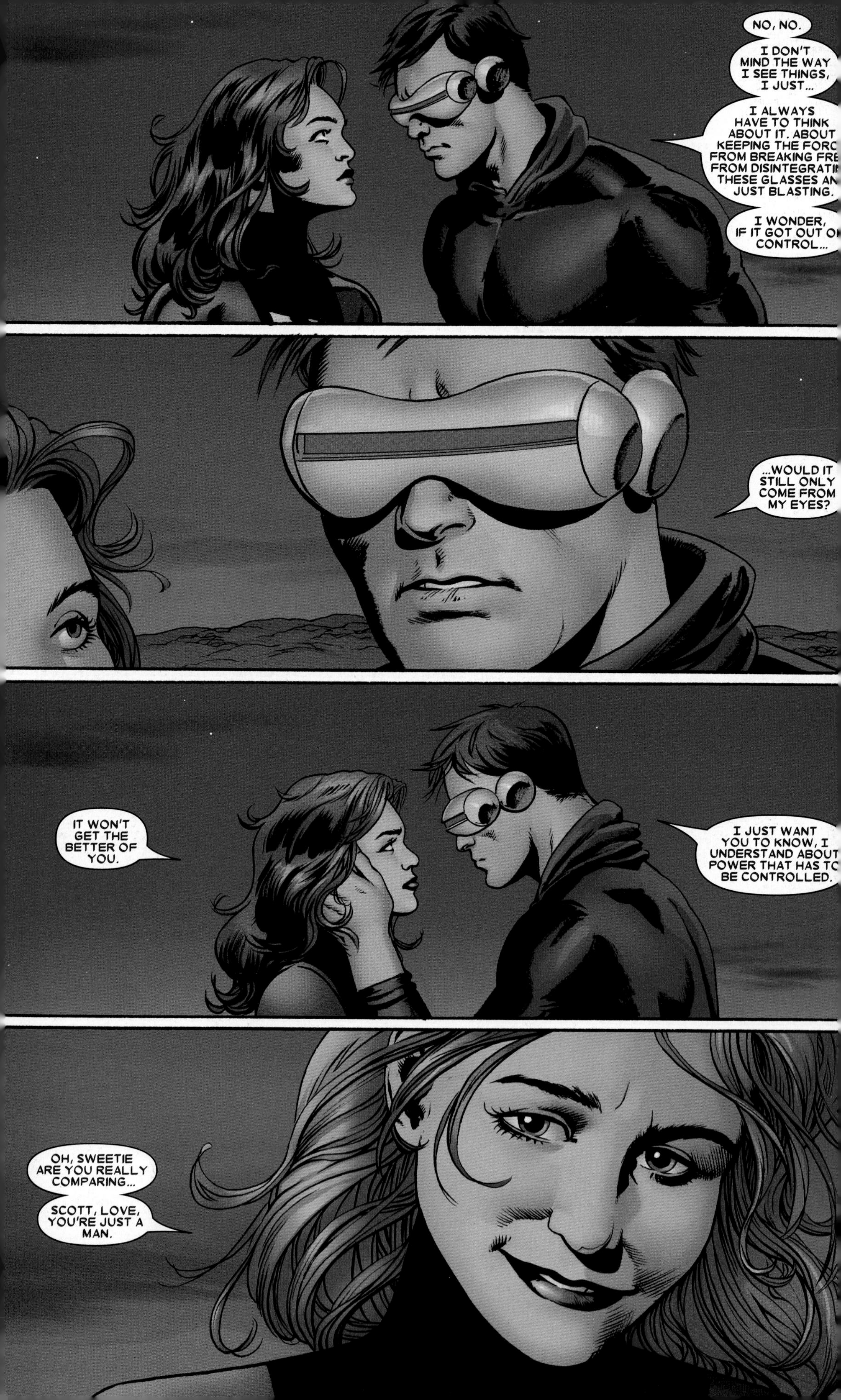

NO, NO.
I DON'T MIND THE WAY I SEE THINGS, I JUST...
I ALWAYS HAVE TO THINK ABOUT IT. ABOUT KEEPING THE FORC FROM BREAKING FRE FROM DISINTEGRATI THESE GLASSES AN JUST BLASTING.
I WONDER, IF IT GOT OUT O CONTROL...
...WOULD IT STILL ONLY COME FROM MY EYES?
IT WON'T GET THE BETTER OF YOU.
I JUST WANT YOU TO KNOW, I UNDERSTAND ABOUT POWER THAT HAS T BE CONTROLLED.
OH, SWEETIE ARE YOU REALLY COMPARING...
SCOTT, LOVE, YOU'RE JUST A MAN.

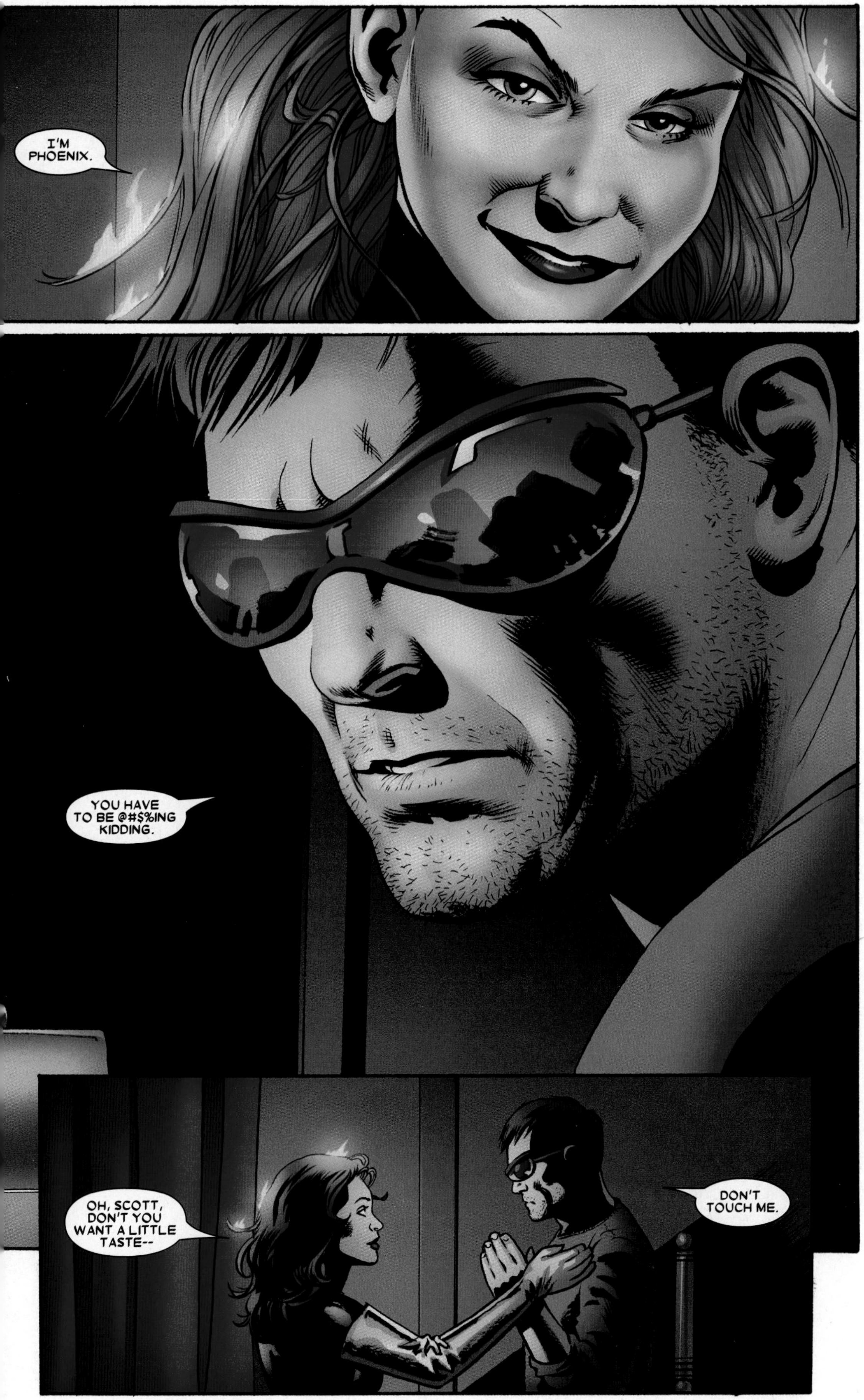
I'M PHOENIX.
YOU HAVE TO BE @#$%ING KIDDING.
OH, SCOTT, DON'T YOU WANT A LITTLE TASTE--
DON'T TOUCH ME.

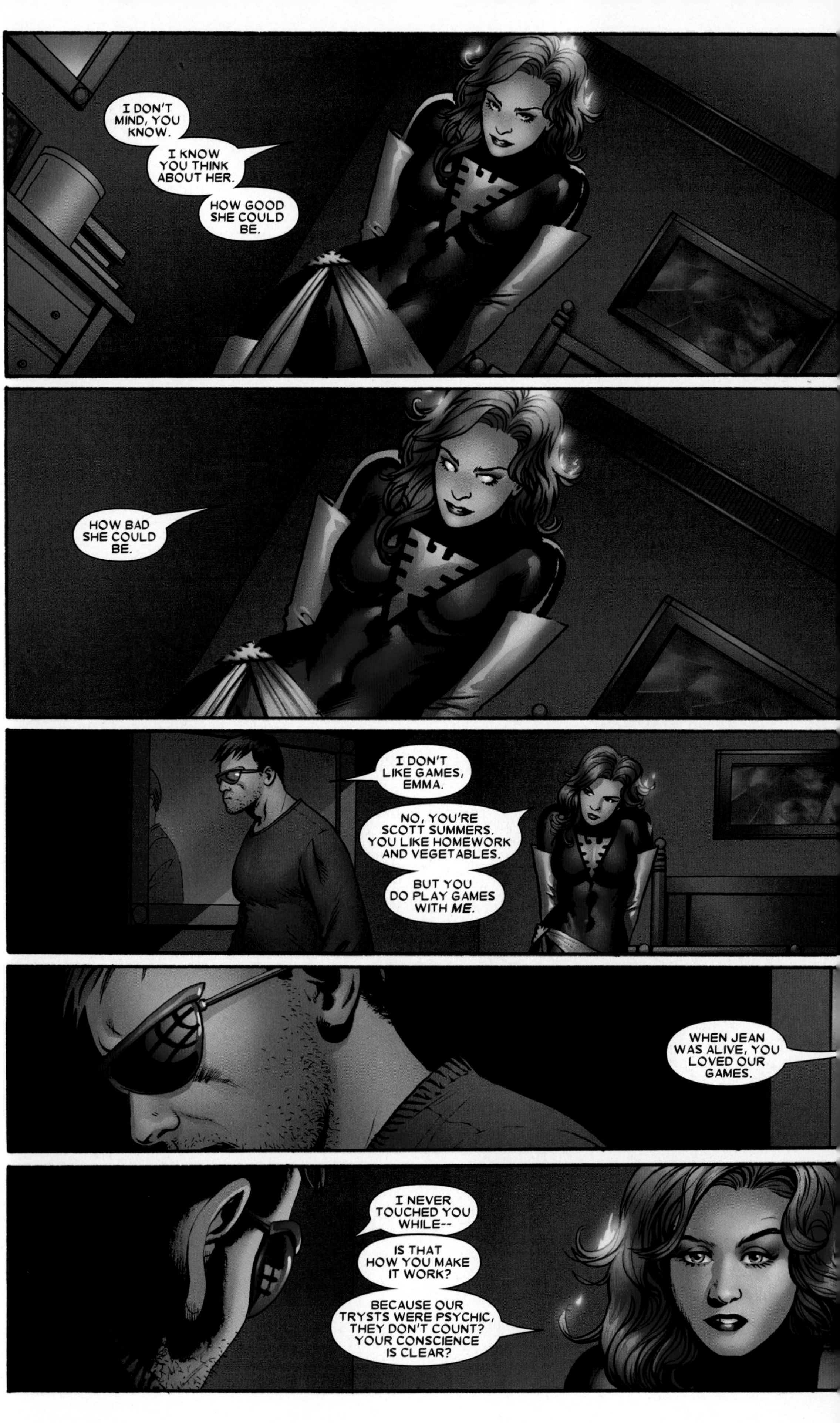

I DON'T MIND, YOU KNOW.
I KNOW YOU THINK ABOUT HER.
HOW GOOD SHE COULD BE.
HOW BAD SHE COULD BE.
I DON'T LIKE GAMES, EMMA.
NO, YOU'RE SCOTT SUMMERS. YOU LIKE HOMEWORK AND VEGETABLES.
BUT YOU DO PLAY GAMES WITH *ME*.
WHEN JEAN WAS ALIVE, YOU LOVED OUR GAMES.
I NEVER TOUCHED YOU WHILE--
IS THAT HOW YOU MAKE IT WORK?
BECAUSE OUR TRYSTS WERE PSYCHIC, THEY DON'T COUNT? YOUR CONSCIENCE IS CLEAR?

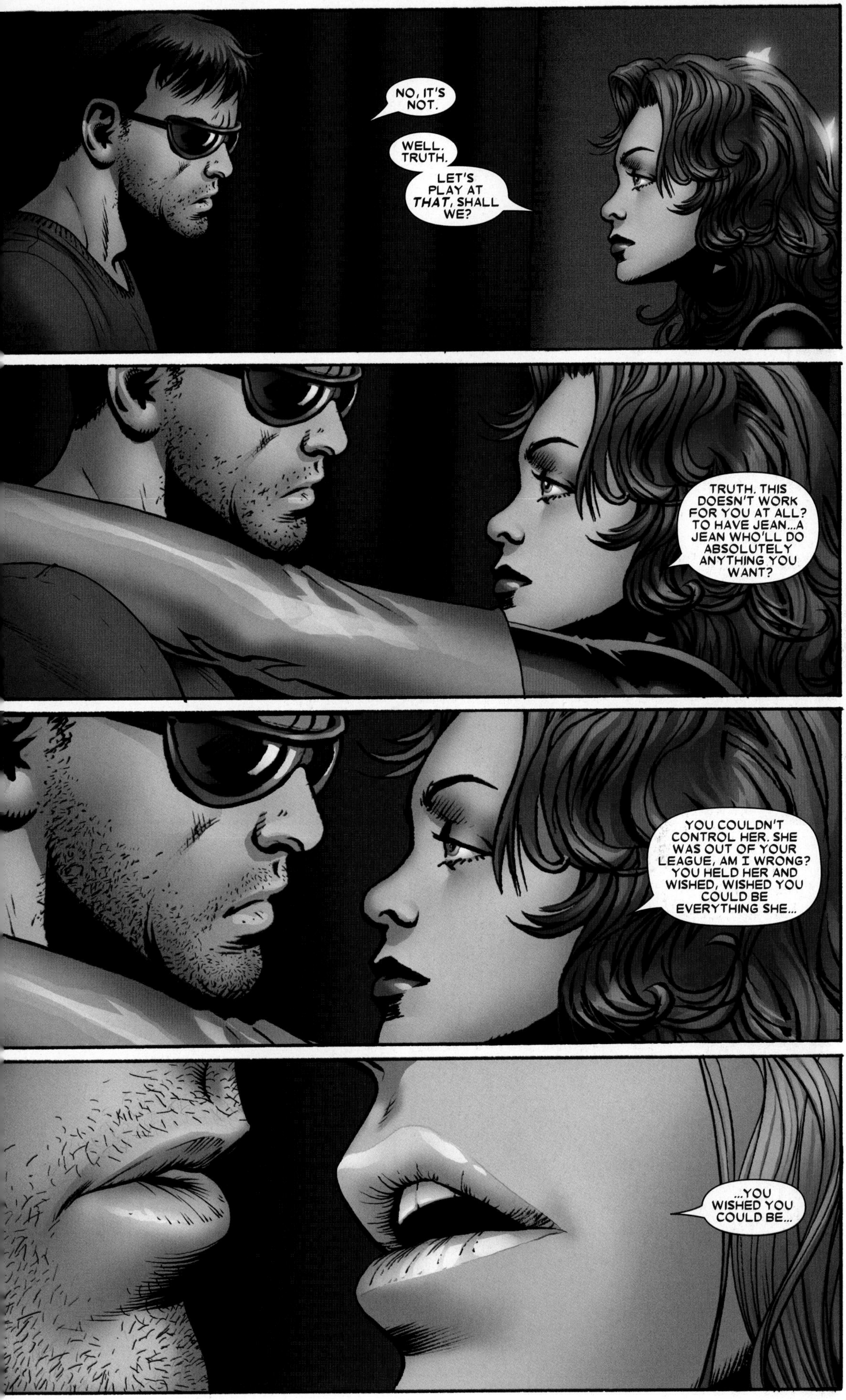
NO, IT'S NOT.
WELL. TRUTH.
LET'S PLAY AT *THAT*, SHALL WE?
TRUTH. THIS DOESN'T WORK FOR YOU AT ALL? TO HAVE JEAN...A JEAN WHO'LL DO ABSOLUTELY ANYTHING YOU WANT?
YOU COULDN'T CONTROL HER. SHE WAS OUT OF YOUR LEAGUE, AM I WRONG? YOU HELD HER AND WISHED, WISHED YOU COULD BE EVERYTHING SHE...
...YOU WISHED YOU COULD BE...

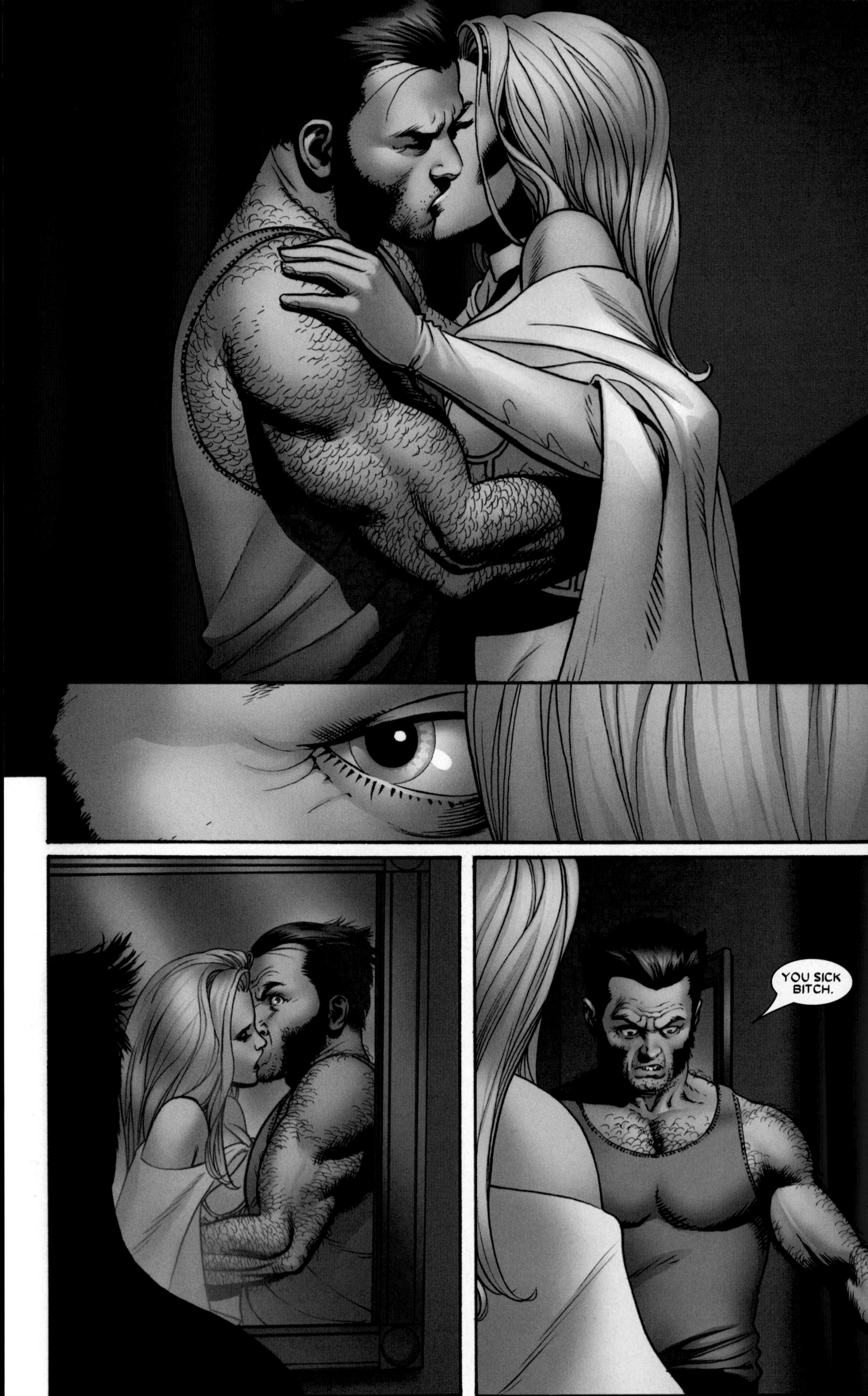
YOU SICK
BITCH.

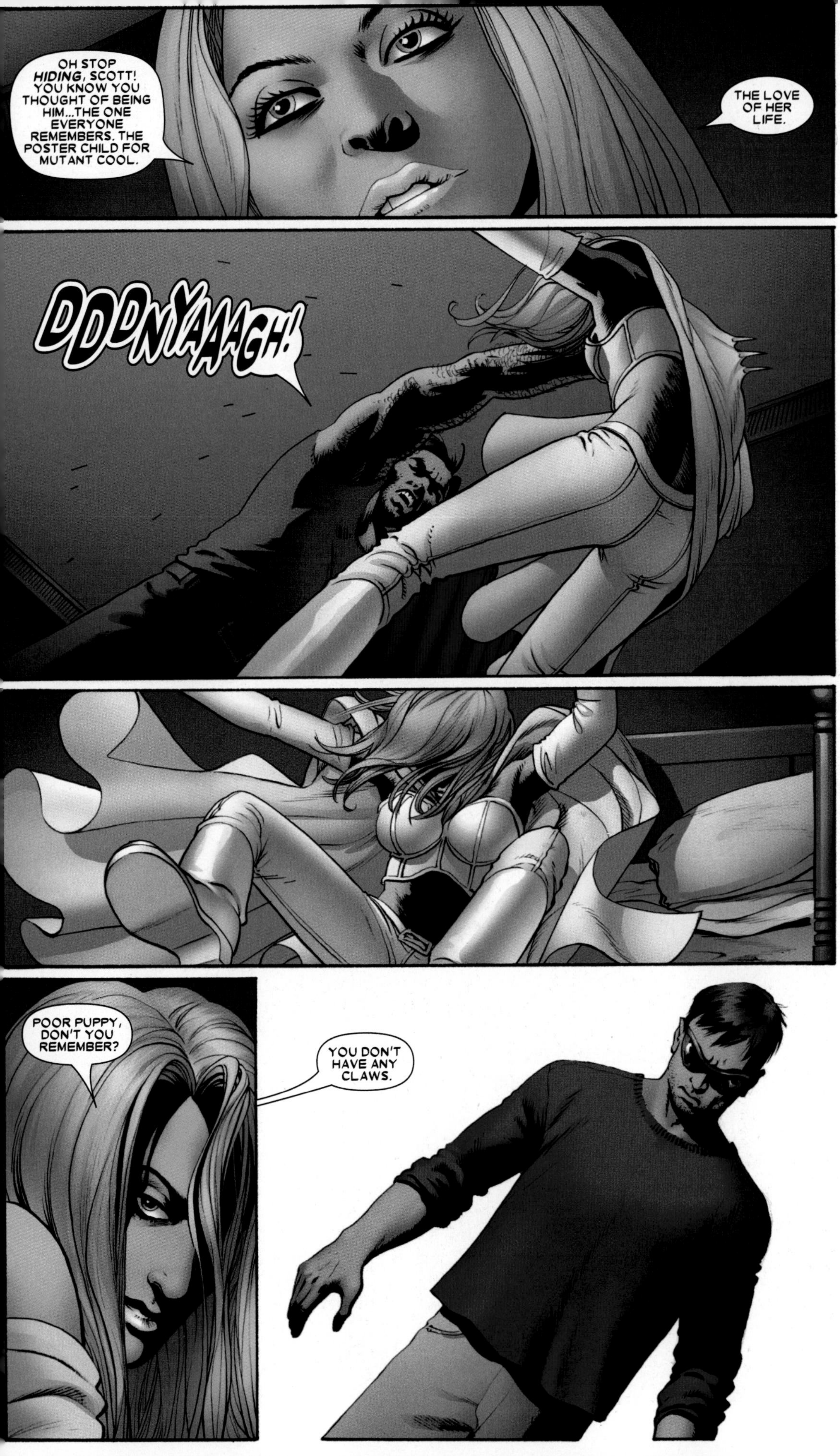
OH STOP HIDING, SCOTT! YOU KNOW YOU THOUGHT OF BEING HIM...THE ONE EVERYONE REMEMBERS. THE POSTER CHILD FOR MUTANT COOL.
THE LOVE OF HER LIFE.
DDDNYAAAGH!
POOR PUPPY, DON'T YOU REMEMBER?
YOU DON'T HAVE ANY CLAWS.

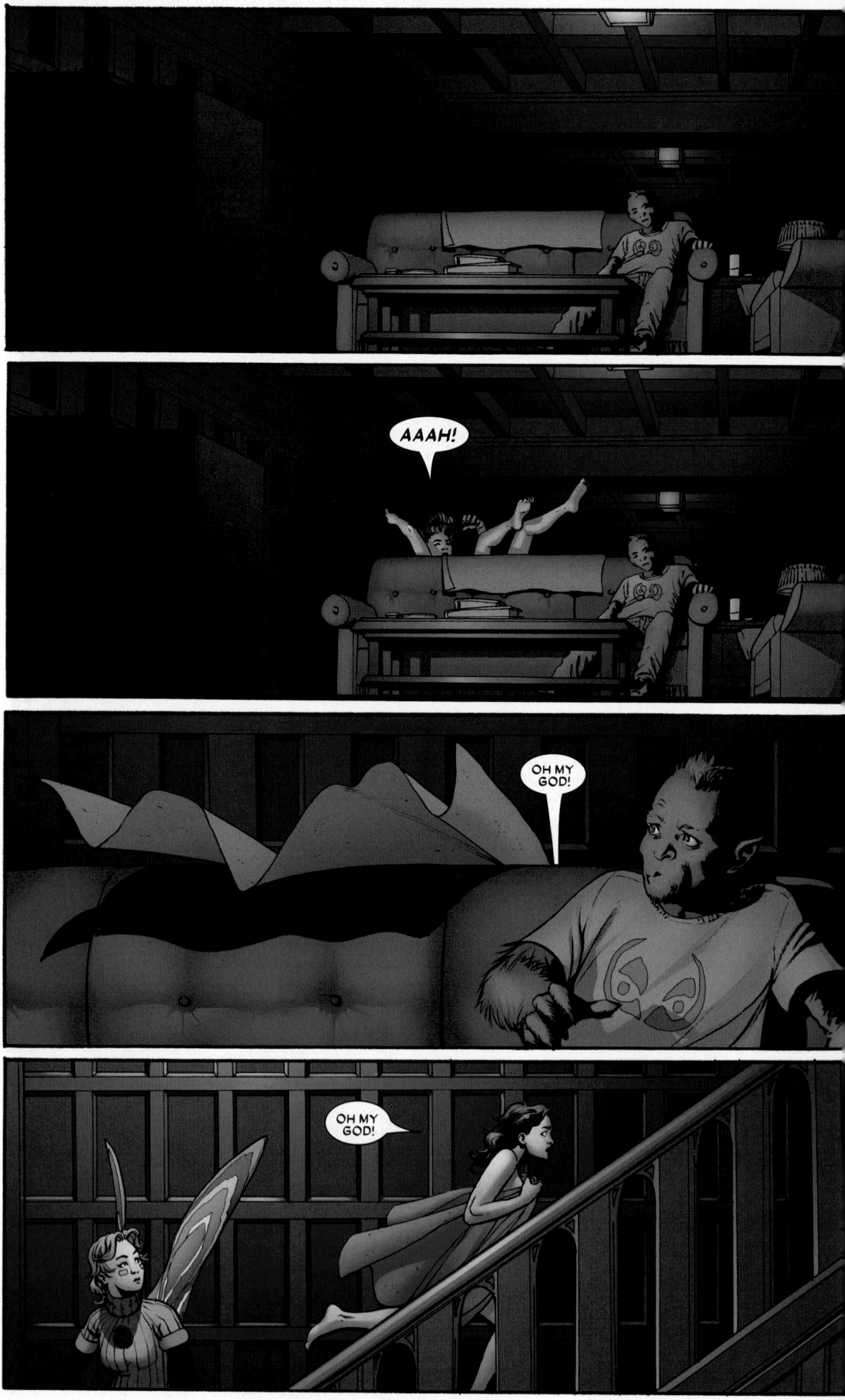
AAAH!
OH MY GOD!
OH MY GOD!

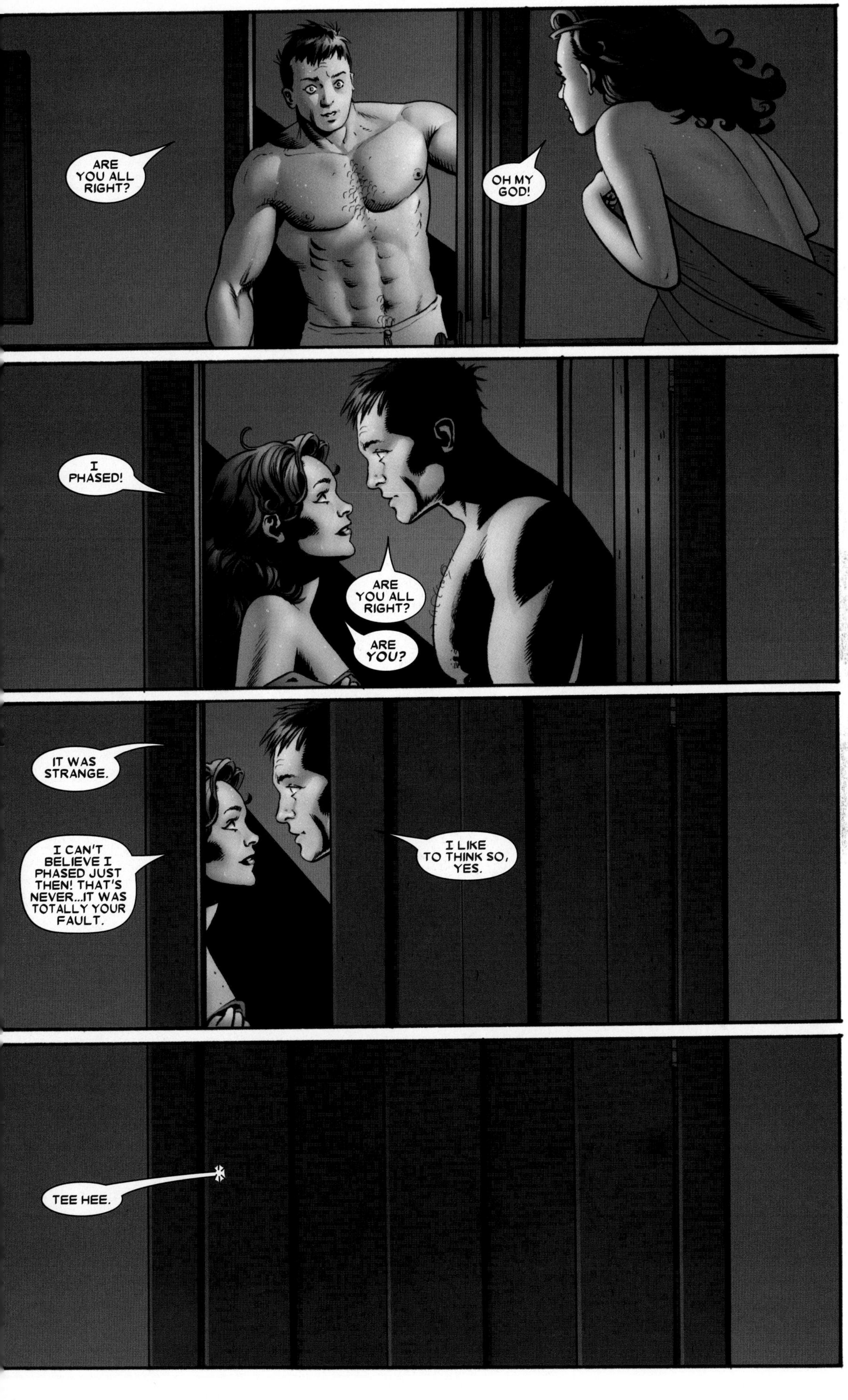
ARE YOU ALL RIGHT?
OH MY GOD!
I PHASED!
ARE YOU ALL RIGHT?
ARE YOU?
IT WAS STRANGE.
I CAN'T BELIEVE I PHASED JUST THEN! THAT'S NEVER...IT WAS TOTALLY YOUR FAULT.
I LIKE TO THINK SO, YES.
TEE HEE.

IT'S A SIMPLE QUESTION, SCOTT.

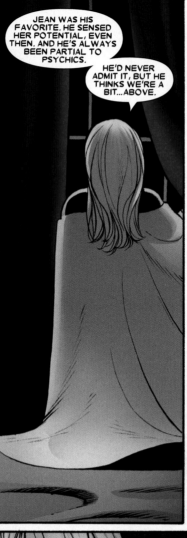

JEAN WAS HIS FAVORITE. HE SENSED HER POTENTIAL, EVEN THEN. AND HE'S ALWAYS BEEN PARTIAL TO PSYCHICS.

HE'D NEVER ADMIT IT, BUT HE THINKS WE'RE A BIT...ABOVE.

HANK IS A GENIUS, AND TERRIBLY GOOD WITH PEOPLE.

WARREN LOOKED LIKE A GOD.

AND XAVIER PICKS YOU?

TO LEAD.

WHY?

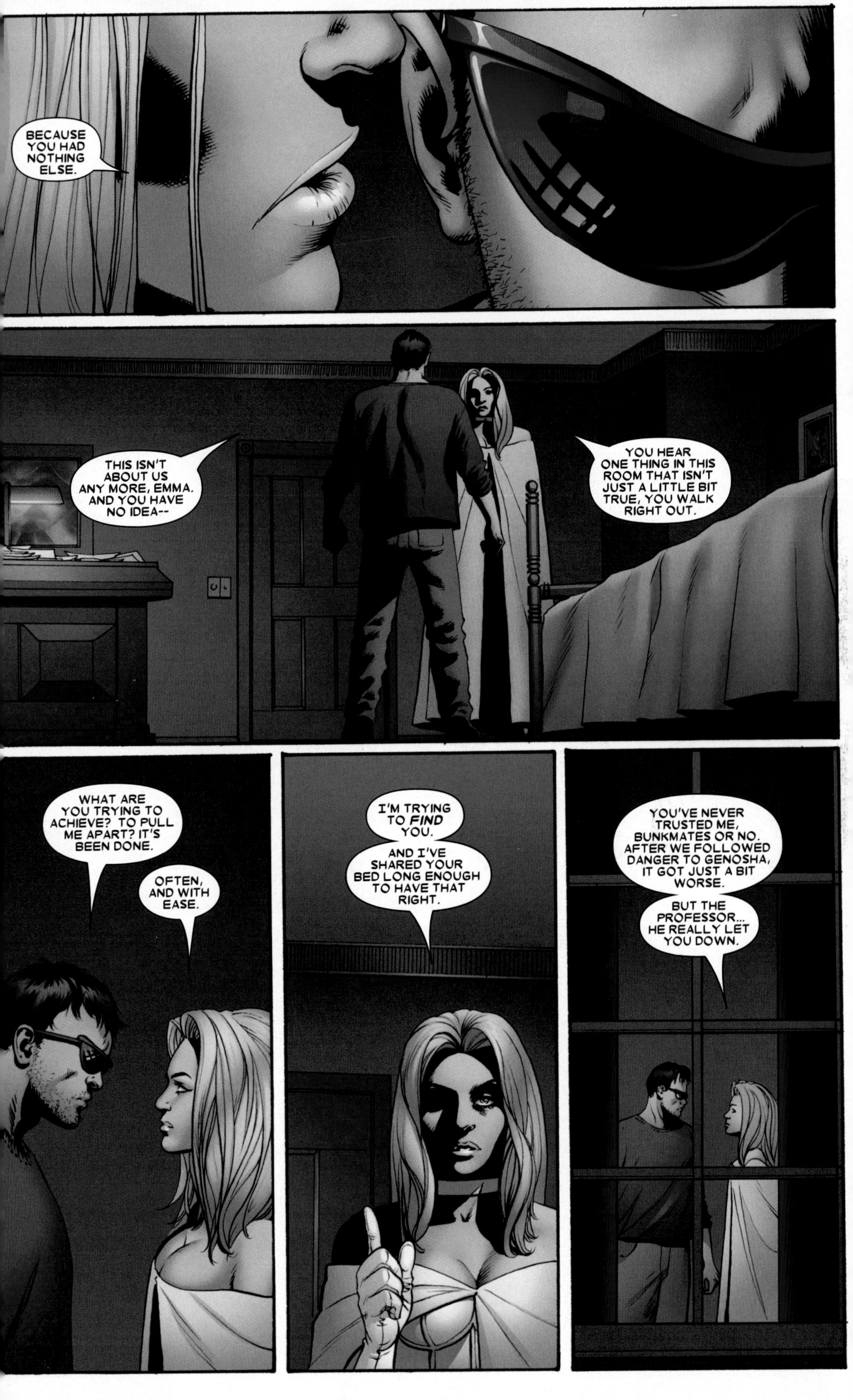
BECAUSE YOU HAD NOTHING ELSE.
THIS ISN'T ABOUT US ANY MORE, EMMA. AND YOU HAVE NO IDEA--
YOU HEAR ONE THING IN THIS ROOM THAT ISN'T JUST A LITTLE BIT TRUE, YOU WALK RIGHT OUT.
WHAT ARE YOU TRYING TO ACHIEVE? TO PULL ME APART? IT'S BEEN DONE.
OFTEN, AND WITH EASE.
I'M TRYING TO *FIND* YOU.
AND I'VE SHARED YOUR BED LONG ENOUGH TO HAVE THAT RIGHT.
YOU'VE NEVER TRUSTED ME, BUNKMATES OR NO. AFTER WE FOLLOWED DANGER TO GENOSHA, IT GOT JUST A BIT WORSE.
BUT THE PROFESSOR... HE REALLY LET YOU DOWN.

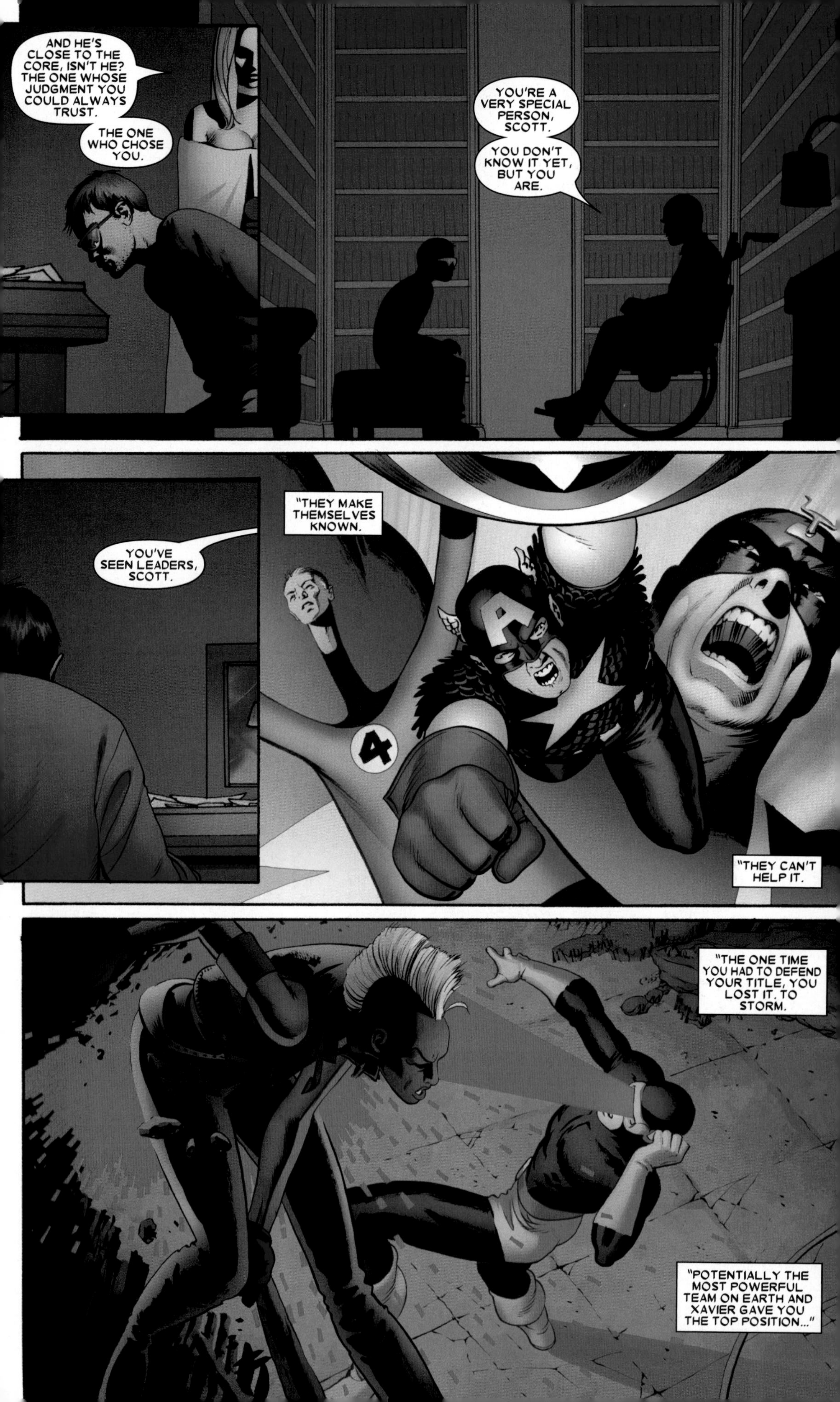
AND HE'S CLOSE TO THE CORE, ISN'T HE? THE ONE WHOSE JUDGMENT YOU COULD ALWAYS TRUST.
THE ONE WHO CHOSE YOU.
YOU'RE A VERY SPECIAL PERSON, SCOTT.
YOU DON'T KNOW IT YET, BUT YOU ARE.
YOU'VE SEEN LEADERS, SCOTT.
"THEY MAKE THEMSELVES KNOWN.
"THEY CAN'T HELP IT.
"THE ONE TIME YOU HAD TO DEFEND YOUR TITLE, YOU LOST IT. TO STORM.
"POTENTIALLY THE MOST POWERFUL TEAM ON EARTH AND XAVIER GAVE YOU THE TOP POSITION..."

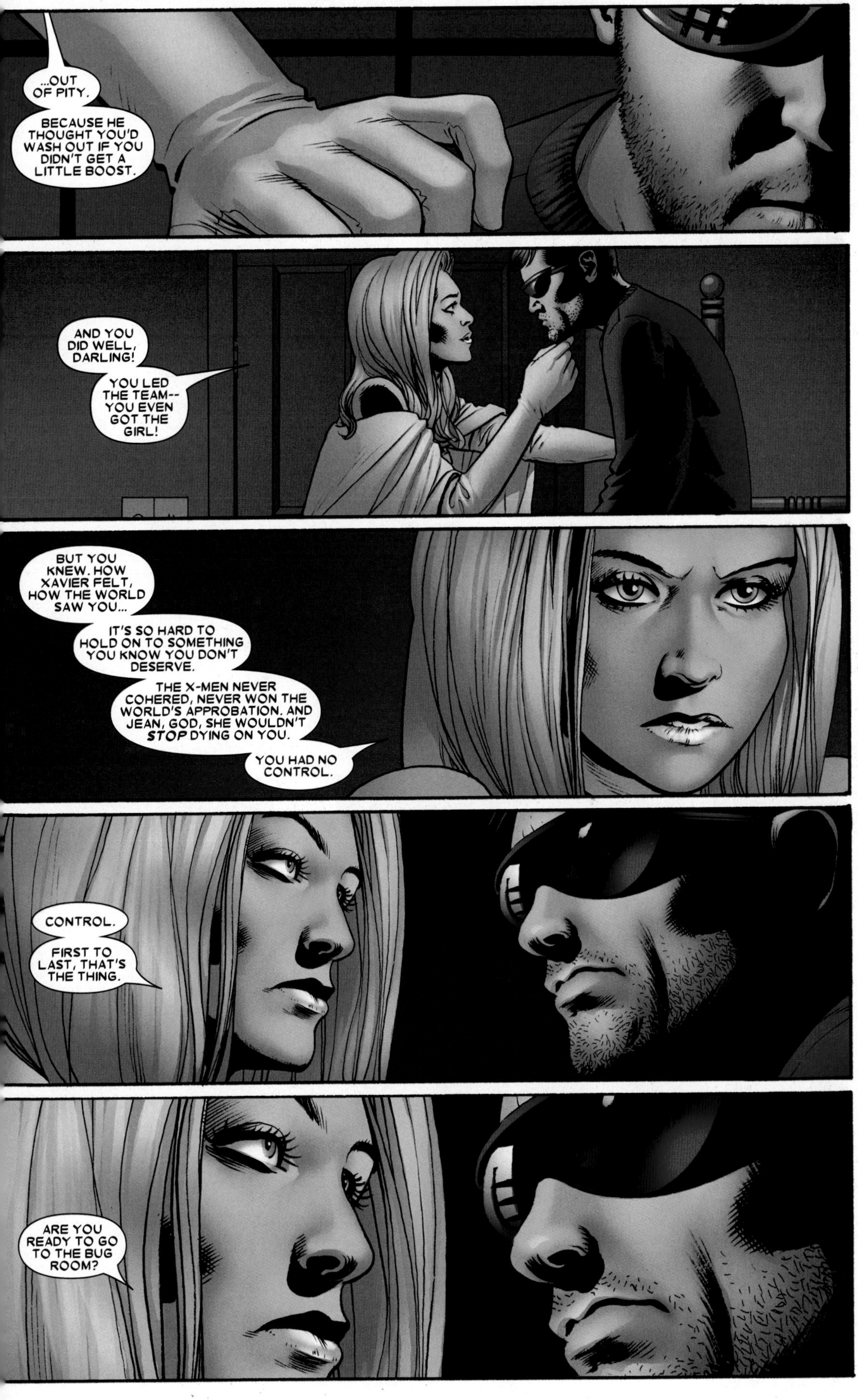
...OUT OF PITY.
BECAUSE HE THOUGHT YOU'D WASH OUT IF YOU DIDN'T GET A LITTLE BOOST.
AND YOU DID WELL, DARLING!
YOU LED THE TEAM-- YOU EVEN GOT THE GIRL!
BUT YOU KNEW. HOW XAVIER FELT, HOW THE WORLD SAW YOU...
IT'S SO HARD TO HOLD ON TO SOMETHING YOU KNOW YOU DON'T DESERVE.
THE X-MEN NEVER COHERED, NEVER WON THE WORLD'S APPROBATION. AND JEAN, GOD, SHE WOULDN'T STOP DYING ON YOU.
YOU HAD NO CONTROL.
CONTROL.
FIRST TO LAST, THAT'S THE THING.
ARE YOU READY TO GO TO THE BUG ROOM?

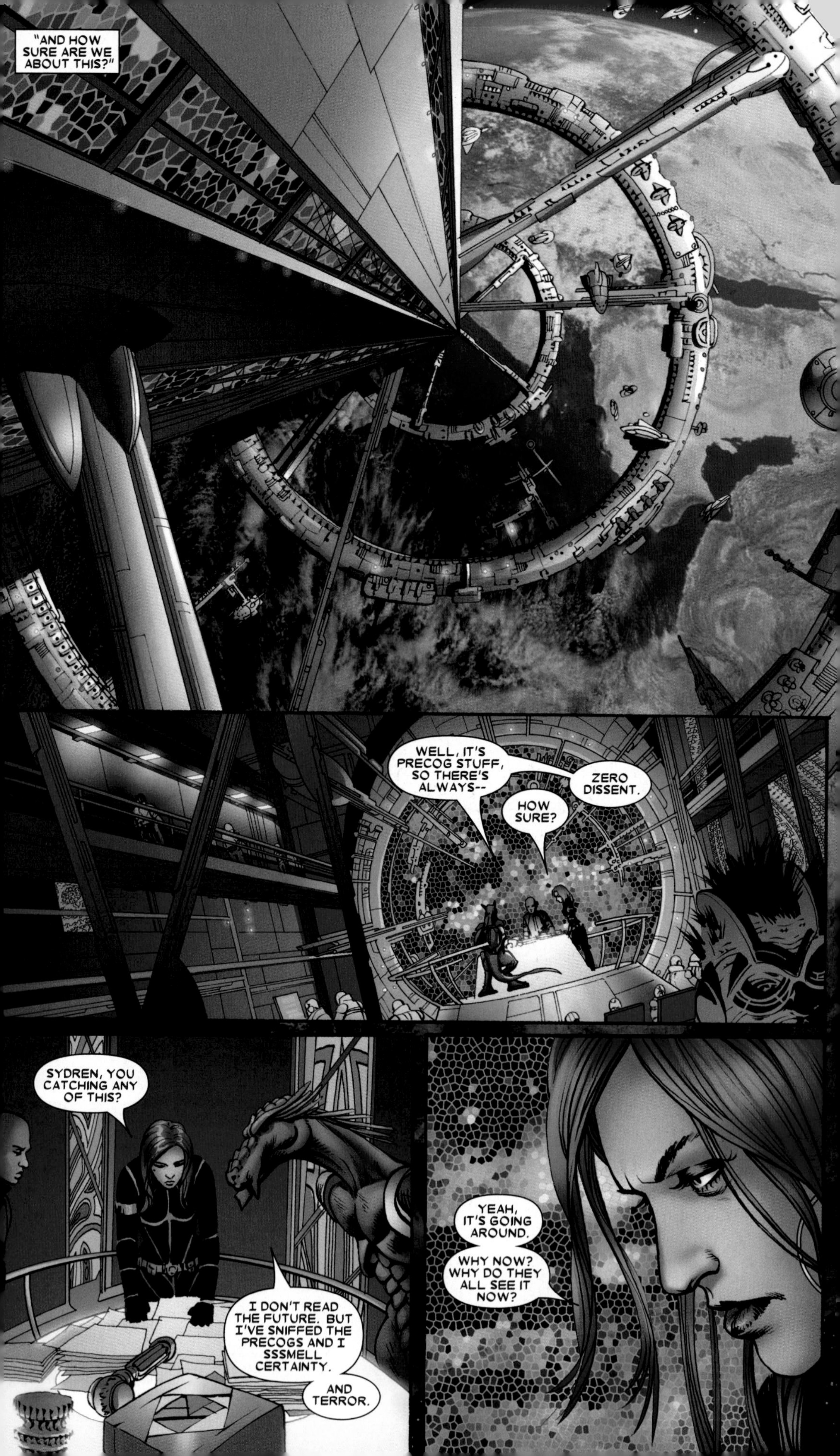
"AND HOW SURE ARE WE ABOUT THIS?"
WELL, IT'S PRECOG STUFF, SO THERE'S ALWAYS--
ZERO DISSENT.
HOW SURE?
SYDREN, YOU CATCHING ANY OF THIS?
I DON'T READ THE FUTURE. BUT I'VE SNIFFED THE PRECOGS AND I SSSMELL CERTAINTY.
AND TERROR.
YEAH, IT'S GOING AROUND.
WHY NOW? WHY DO THEY ALL SEE IT NOW?

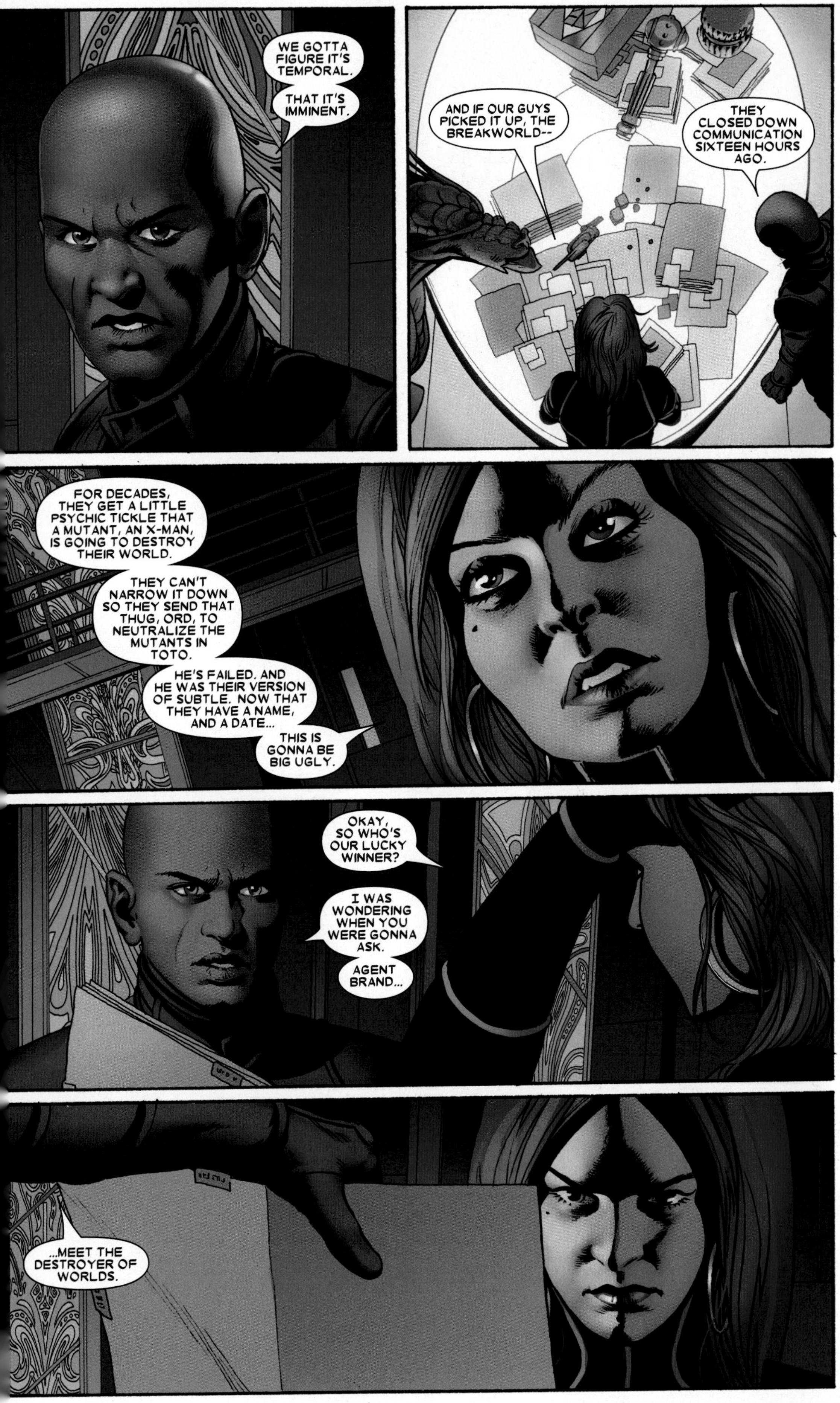
WE GOTTA FIGURE IT'S TEMPORAL.
THAT IT'S IMMINENT.
AND IF OUR GUYS PICKED IT UP, THE BREAKWORLD--
THEY CLOSED DOWN COMMUNICATION SIXTEEN HOURS AGO.
FOR DECADES, THEY GET A LITTLE PSYCHIC TICKLE THAT A MUTANT, AN X-MAN, IS GOING TO DESTROY THEIR WORLD.
THEY CAN'T NARROW IT DOWN SO THEY SEND THAT THUG, ORD, TO NEUTRALIZE THE MUTANTS IN TOTO.
HE'S FAILED. AND HE WAS THEIR VERSION OF SUBTLE. NOW THAT THEY HAVE A NAME, AND A DATE...
THIS IS GONNA BE BIG UGLY.
OKAY, SO WHO'S OUR LUCKY WINNER?
I WAS WONDERING WHEN YOU WERE GONNA ASK.
AGENT BRAND...
...MEET THE DESTROYER OF WORLDS.

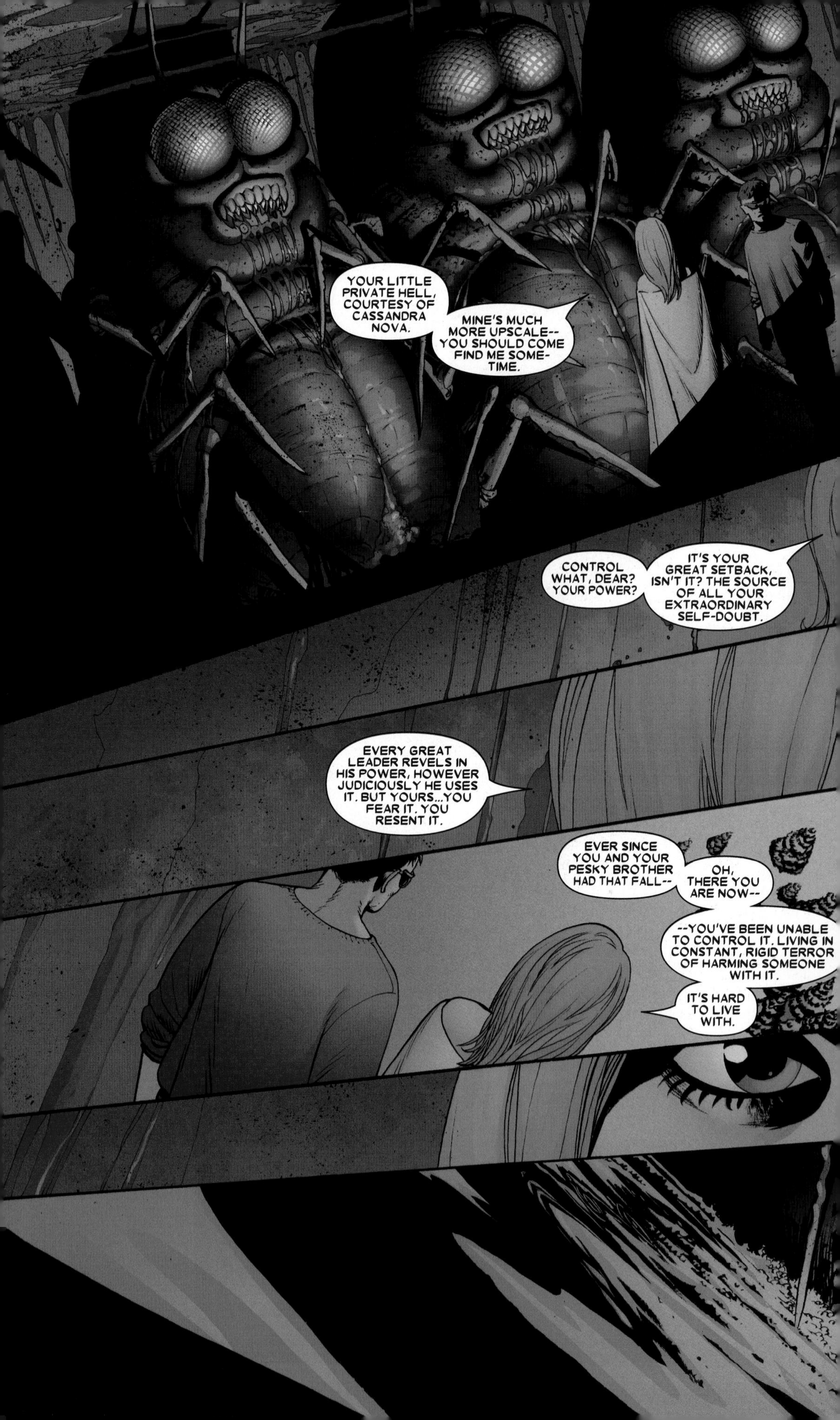
YOUR LITTLE PRIVATE HELL, COURTESY OF CASSANDRA NOVA.
MINE'S MUCH MORE UPSCALE-- YOU SHOULD COME FIND ME SOME-TIME.
CONTROL WHAT, DEAR? YOUR POWER?
IT'S YOUR GREAT SETBACK, ISN'T IT? THE SOURCE OF ALL YOUR EXTRAORDINARY SELF-DOUBT.
EVERY GREAT LEADER REVELS IN HIS POWER, HOWEVER JUDICIOUSLY HE USES IT. BUT YOURS...YOU FEAR IT. YOU RESENT IT.
EVER SINCE YOU AND YOUR PESKY BROTHER HAD THAT FALL--
OH, THERE YOU ARE NOW--
--YOU'VE BEEN UNABLE TO CONTROL IT, LIVING IN CONSTANT, RIGID TERROR OF HARMING SOMEONE WITH IT.
IT'S HARD TO LIVE WITH.

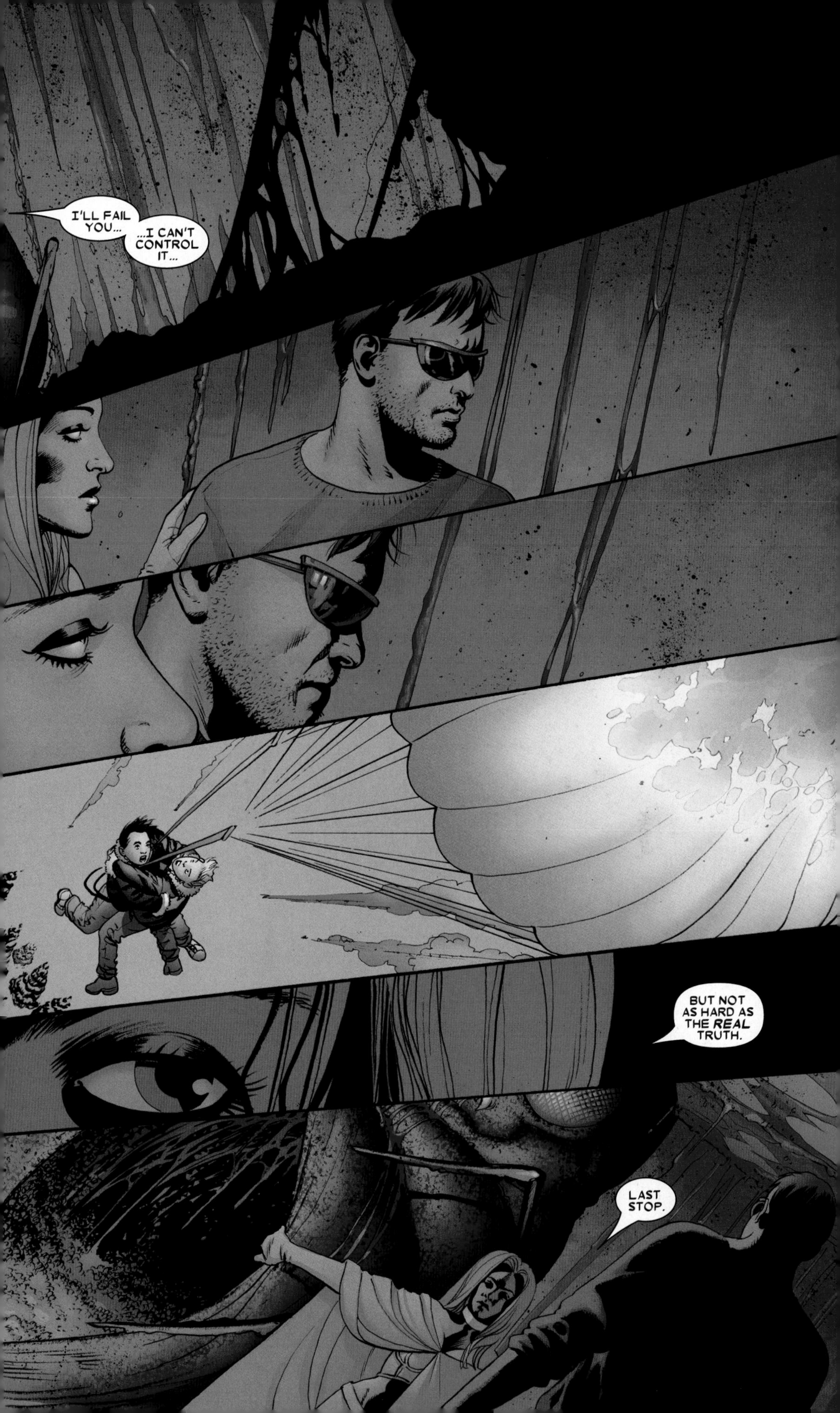
I'LL FAIL YOU...
...I CAN'T CONTROL IT...
BUT NOT AS HARD AS THE *REAL* TRUTH.
LAST STOP.

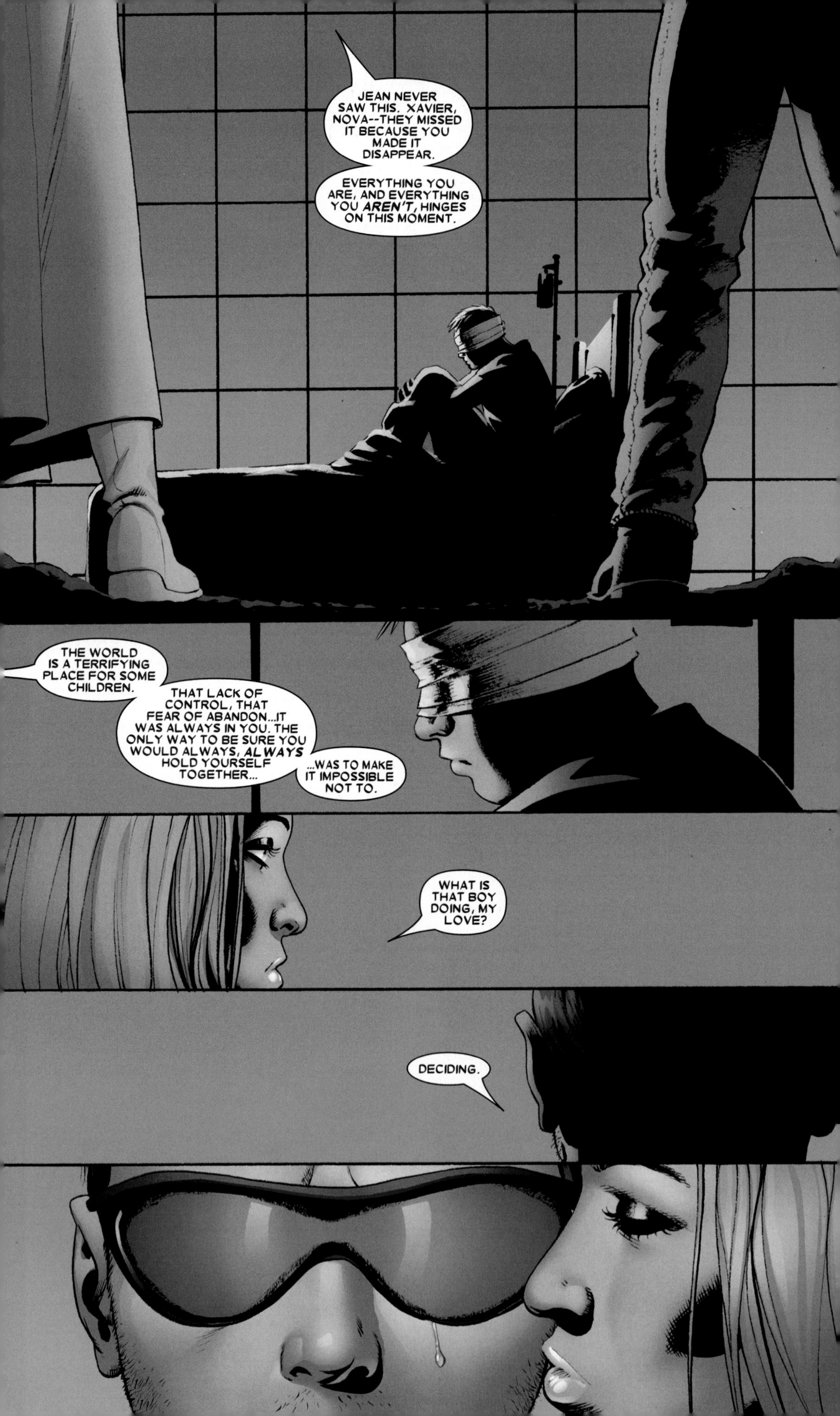
JEAN NEVER SAW THIS. XAVIER, NOVA--THEY MISSED IT BECAUSE YOU MADE IT DISAPPEAR.
EVERYTHING YOU ARE, AND EVERYTHING YOU *AREN'T*, HINGES ON THIS MOMENT.
THE WORLD IS A TERRIFYING PLACE FOR SOME CHILDREN.
THAT LACK OF CONTROL, THAT FEAR OF ABANDON...IT WAS ALWAYS IN YOU. THE ONLY WAY TO BE SURE YOU WOULD ALWAYS, *ALWAYS* HOLD YOURSELF TOGETHER...
...WAS TO MAKE IT IMPOSSIBLE NOT TO.
WHAT IS THAT BOY DOING, MY LOVE?
DECIDING.

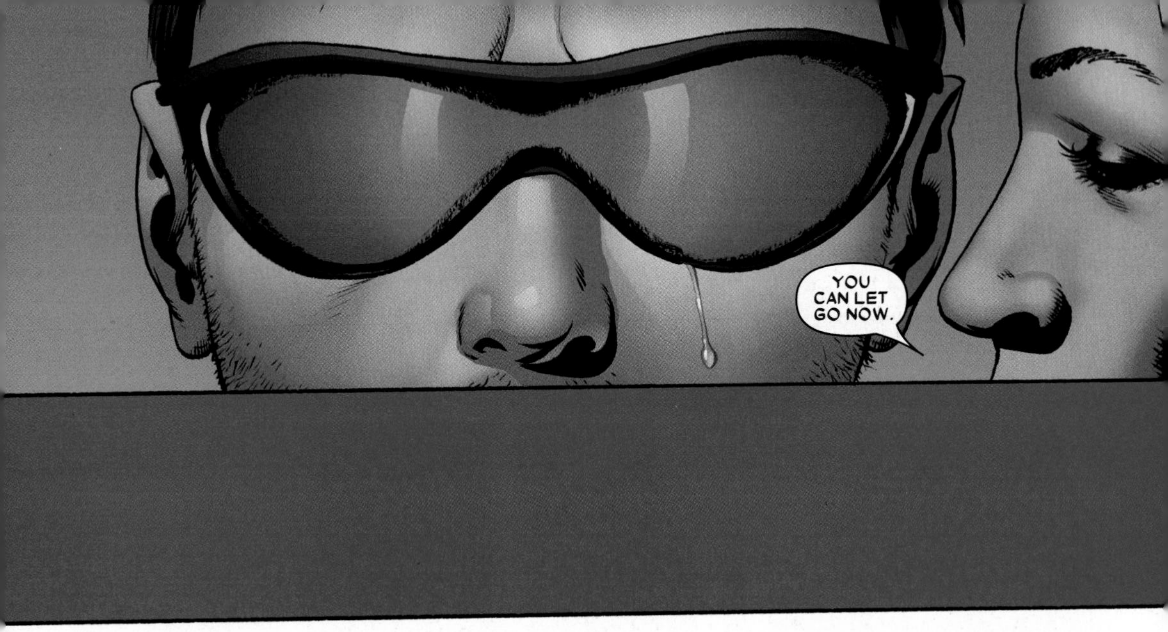
YOU CAN LET GO NOW.

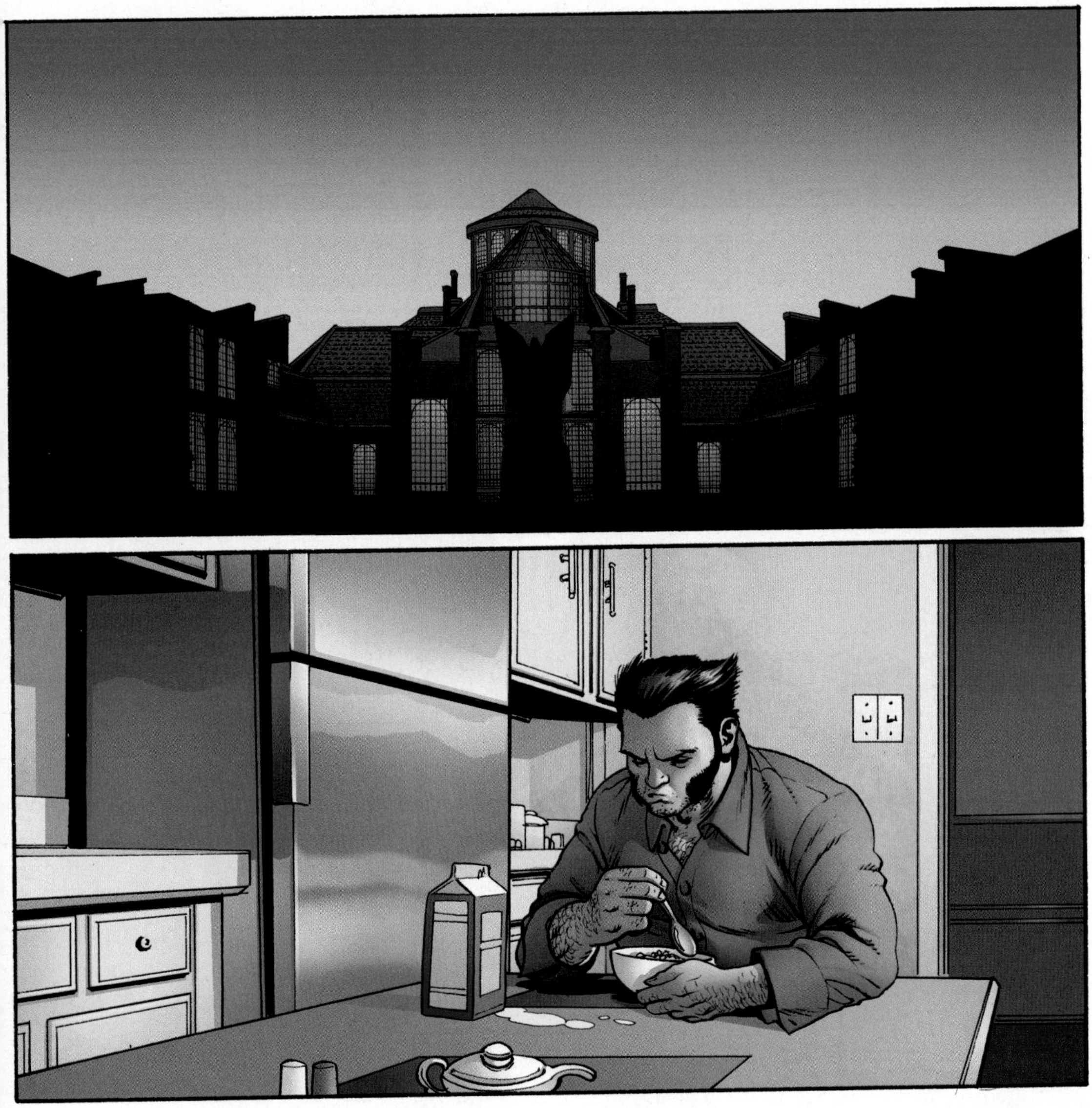

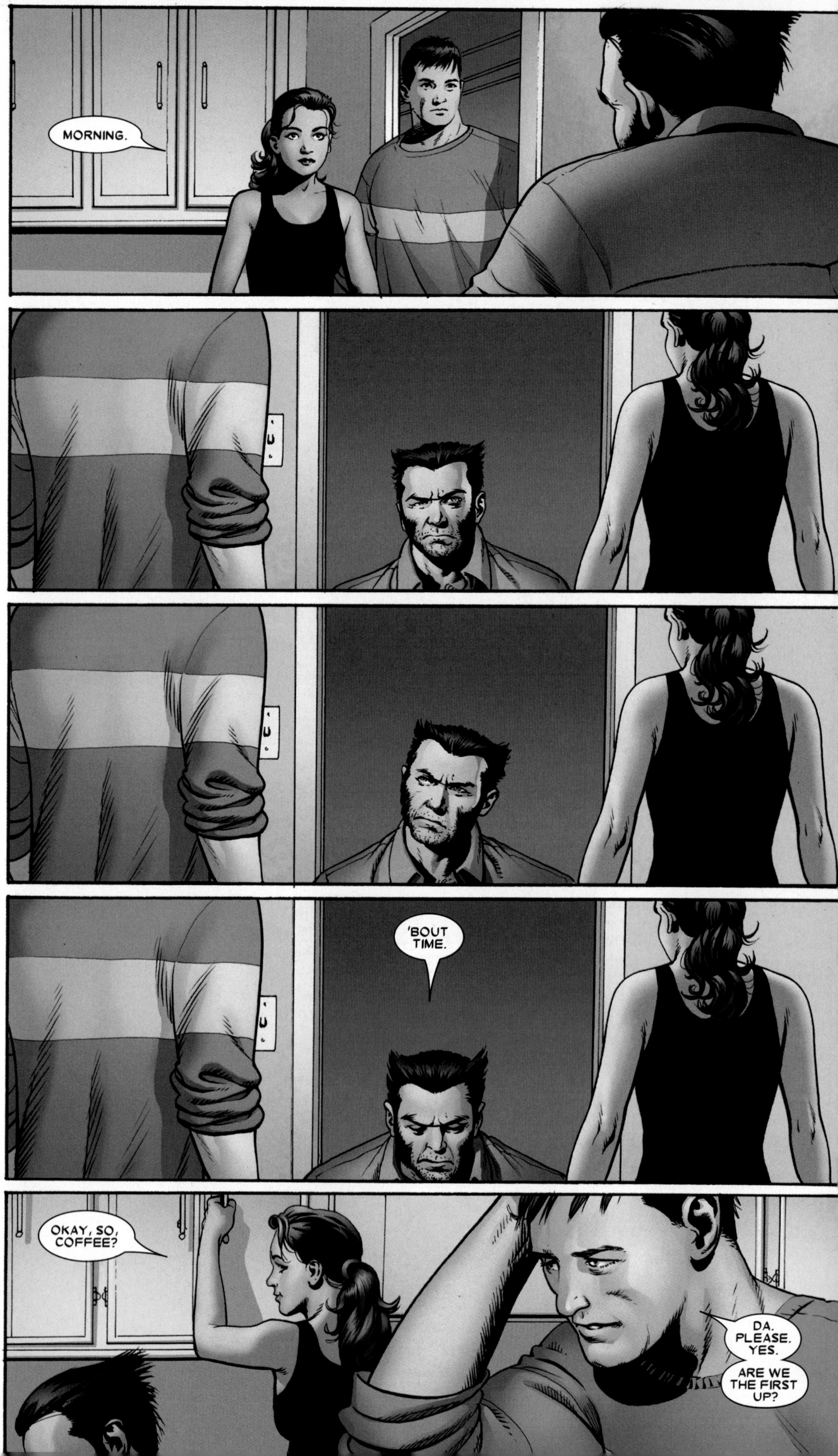
MORNING.
'BOUT TIME.
OKAY, SO, COFFEE?
DA. PLEASE. YES.
ARE WE THE FIRST UP?

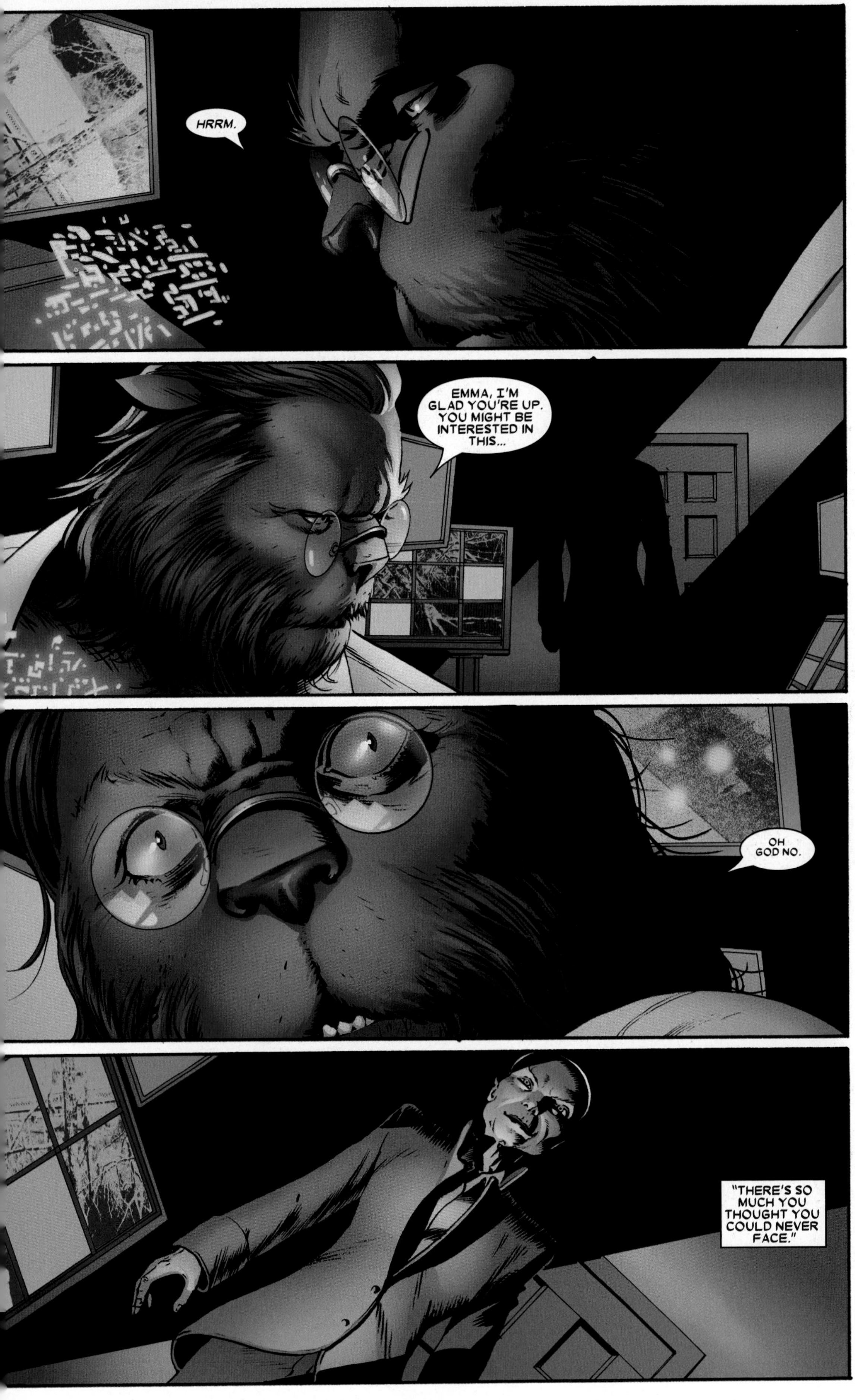
HRRM.
EMMA, I'M GLAD YOU'RE UP. YOU MIGHT BE INTERESTED IN THIS...
OH GOD NO.
"THERE'S SO MUCH YOU THOUGHT YOU COULD NEVER FACE."

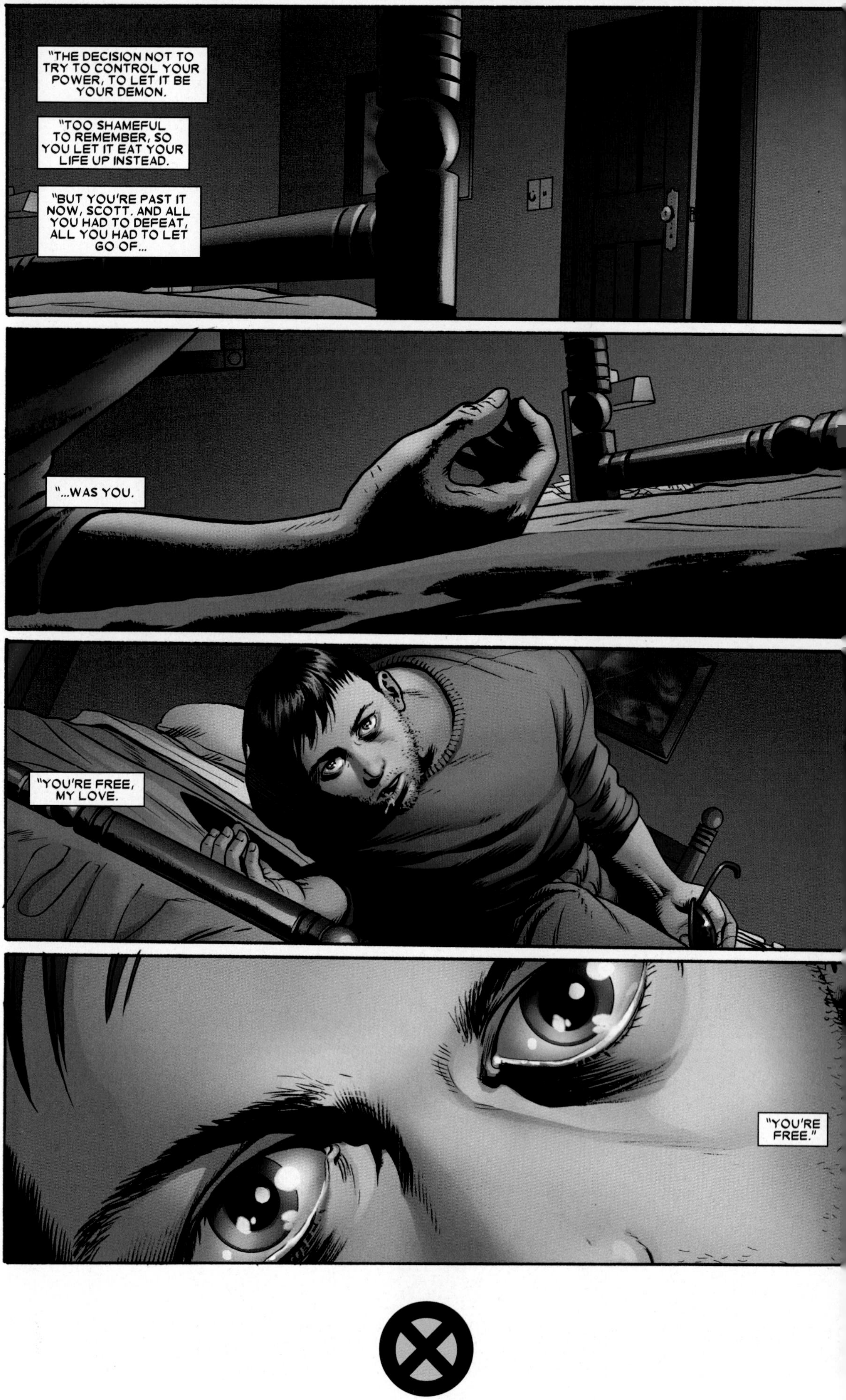
"THE DECISION NOT TO TRY TO CONTROL YOUR POWER, TO LET IT BE YOUR DEMON.
"TOO SHAMEFUL TO REMEMBER, SO YOU LET IT EAT YOUR LIFE UP INSTEAD.
"BUT YOU'RE PAST IT NOW, SCOTT. AND ALL YOU HAD TO DEFEAT, ALL YOU HAD TO LET GO OF...
"...WAS YOU.
"YOU'RE FREE, MY LOVE.
"YOU'RE FREE."

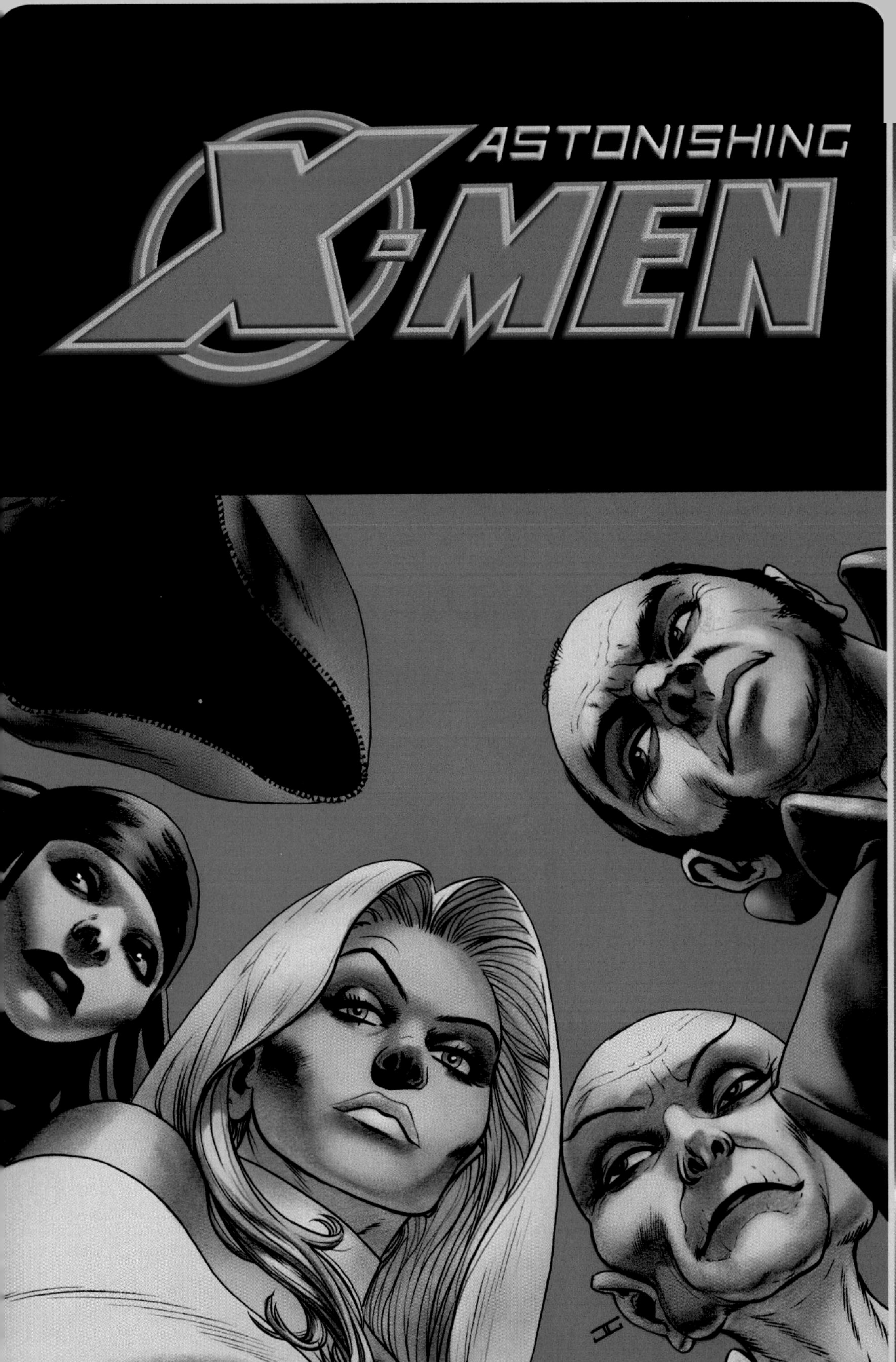
ASTONISHING
X-MEN

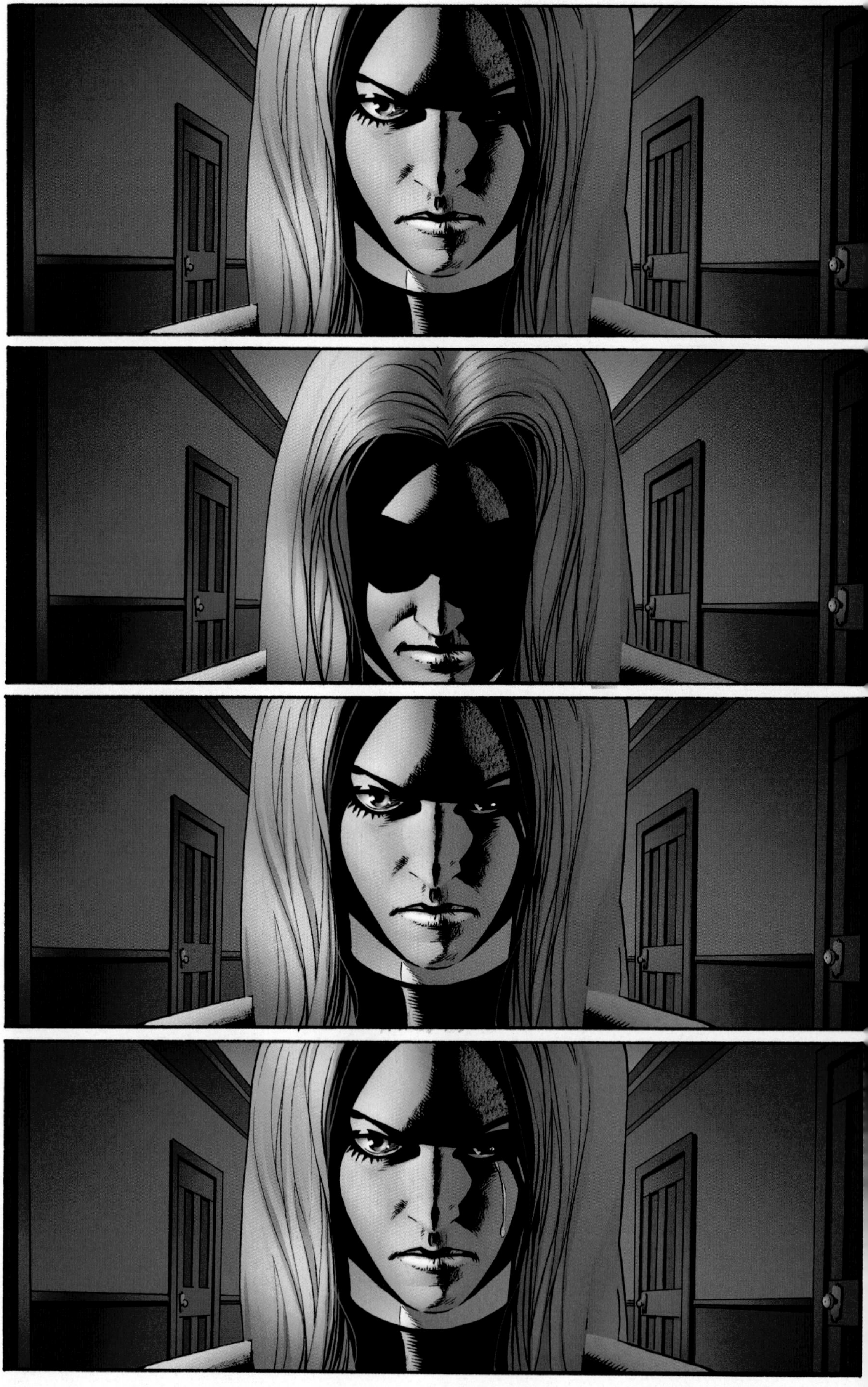

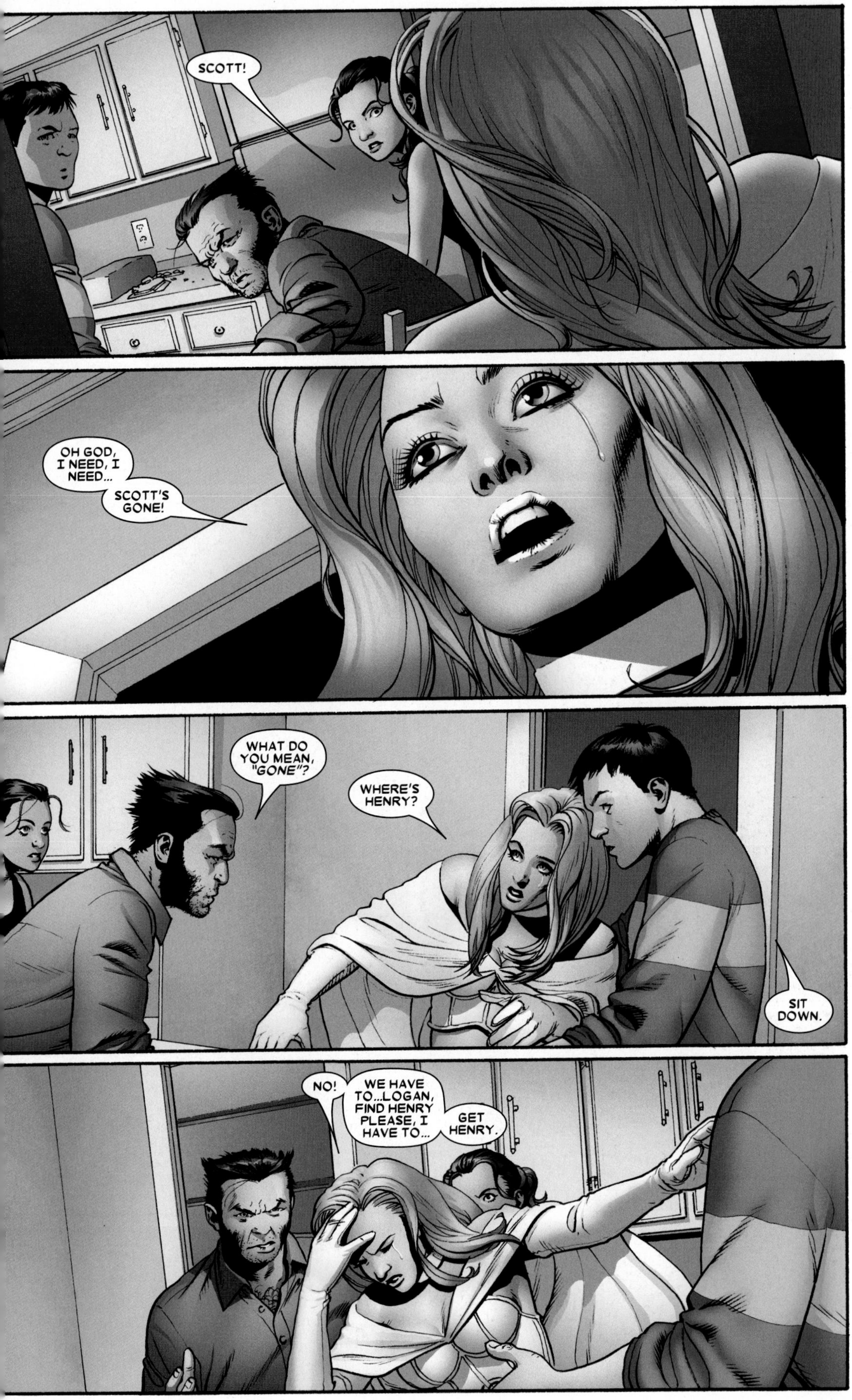
SCOTT!
OH GOD, I NEED, I NEED...
SCOTT'S GONE!
WHAT DO YOU MEAN, "GONE"?
WHERE'S HENRY?
SIT DOWN.
NO!
WE HAVE TO...LOGAN, FIND HENRY PLEASE, I HAVE TO...
GET HENRY.

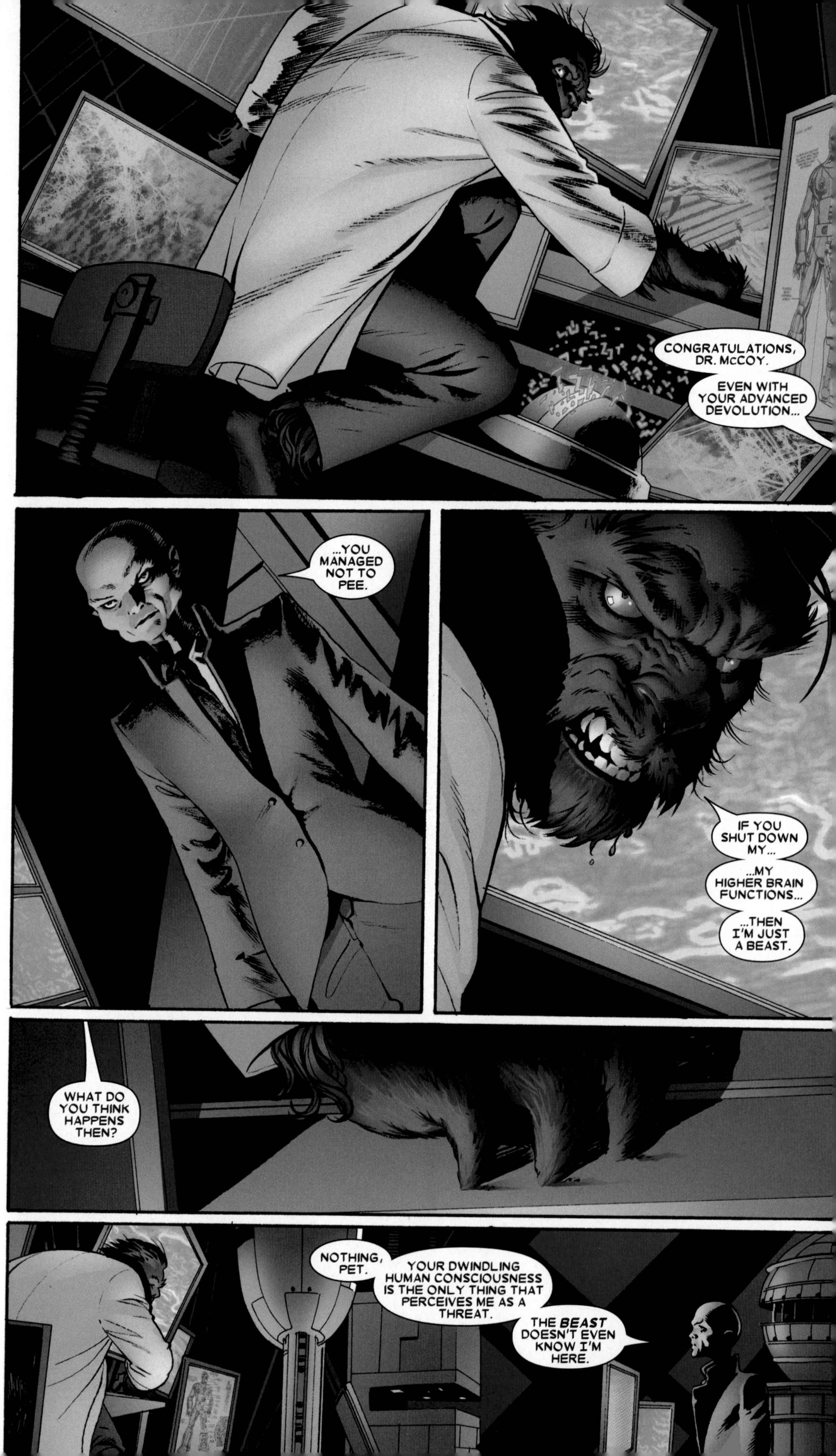
CONGRATULATIONS, DR. McCOY.
EVEN WITH YOUR ADVANCED DEVOLUTION...
...YOU MANAGED NOT TO PEE.
IF YOU SHUT DOWN MY...
...MY HIGHER BRAIN FUNCTIONS...
...THEN I'M JUST A BEAST.
WHAT DO YOU THINK HAPPENS THEN?
NOTHING, PET.
YOUR DWINDLING HUMAN CONSCIOUSNESS IS THE ONLY THING THAT PERCEIVES ME AS A THREAT.
THE BEAST DOESN'T EVEN KNOW I'M HERE.

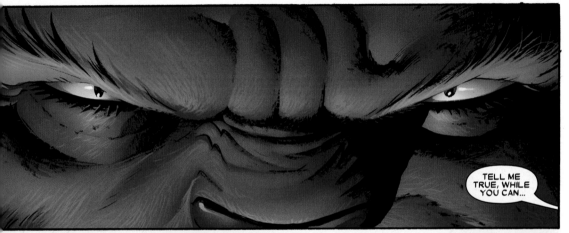

TELL ME TRUE, WHILE YOU CAN...

...DO YOU EVEN SMELL ANOTHER PERSON IN THIS ROOM?

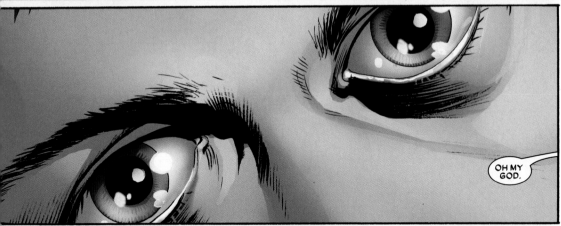

OH MY GOD.

SCOTT!

WHAT HAPPENED?

I JUST FOUND HIM--HE WAS FINE WHEN WE WENT TO BED...

I CAN'T GET IN HIS MIND!

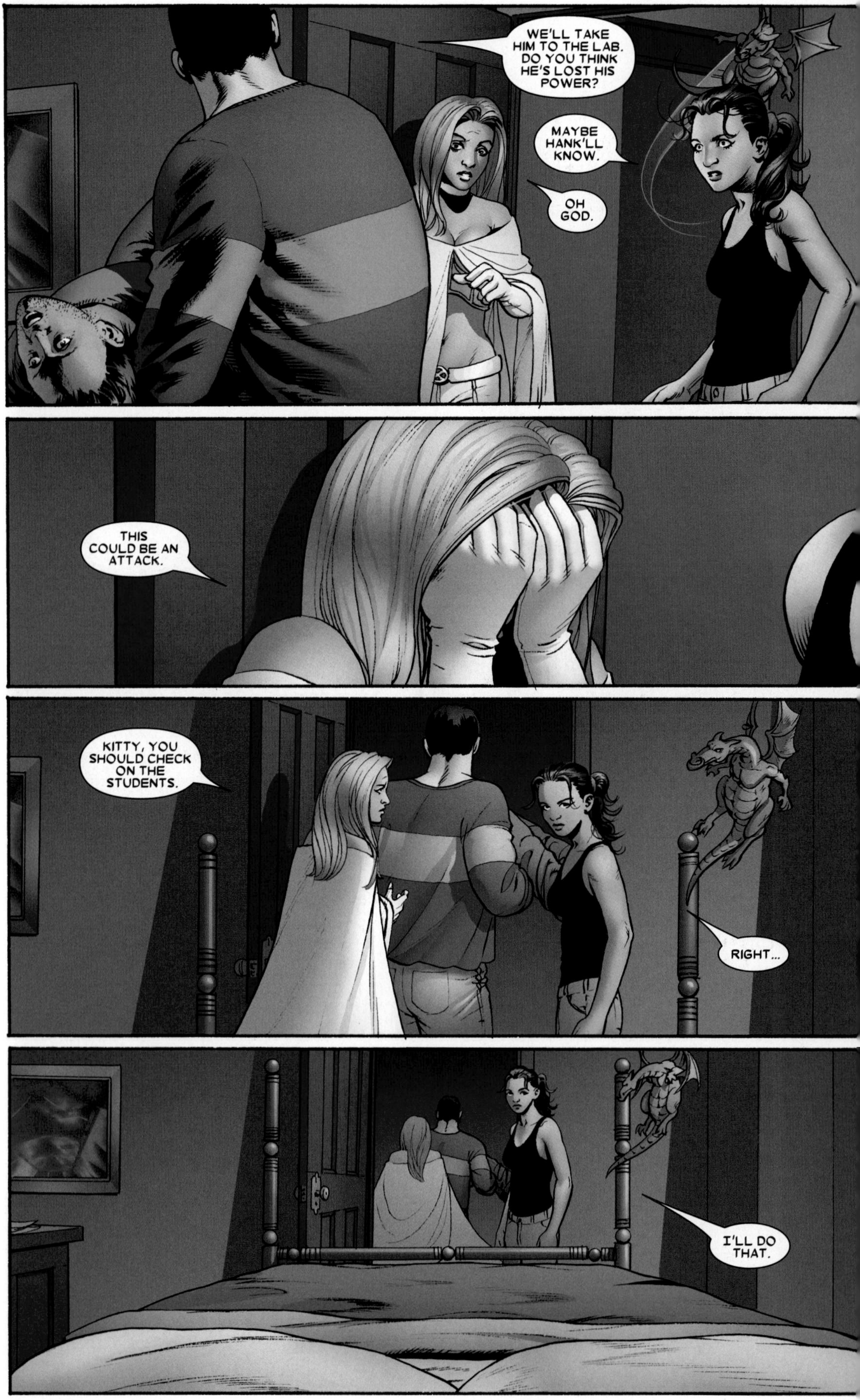
WE'LL TAKE HIM TO THE LAB. DO YOU THINK HE'S LOST HIS POWER?
MAYBE HANK'LL KNOW.
OH GOD.
THIS COULD BE AN ATTACK.
KITTY, YOU SHOULD CHECK ON THE STUDENTS.
RIGHT...
I'LL DO THAT.

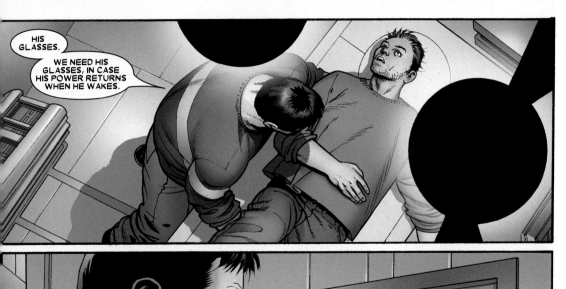

HIS GLASSES.

WE NEED HIS GLASSES, IN CASE HIS POWER RETURNS WHEN HE WAKES.

EMMA?

HEY, LISTEN, HAVE YOU BEEN UP LONG?

I WAS WONDERING IF YOU SAW ANYBODY... NEW...

I'M SORRY, I DON'T KNOW YOUR NAME...

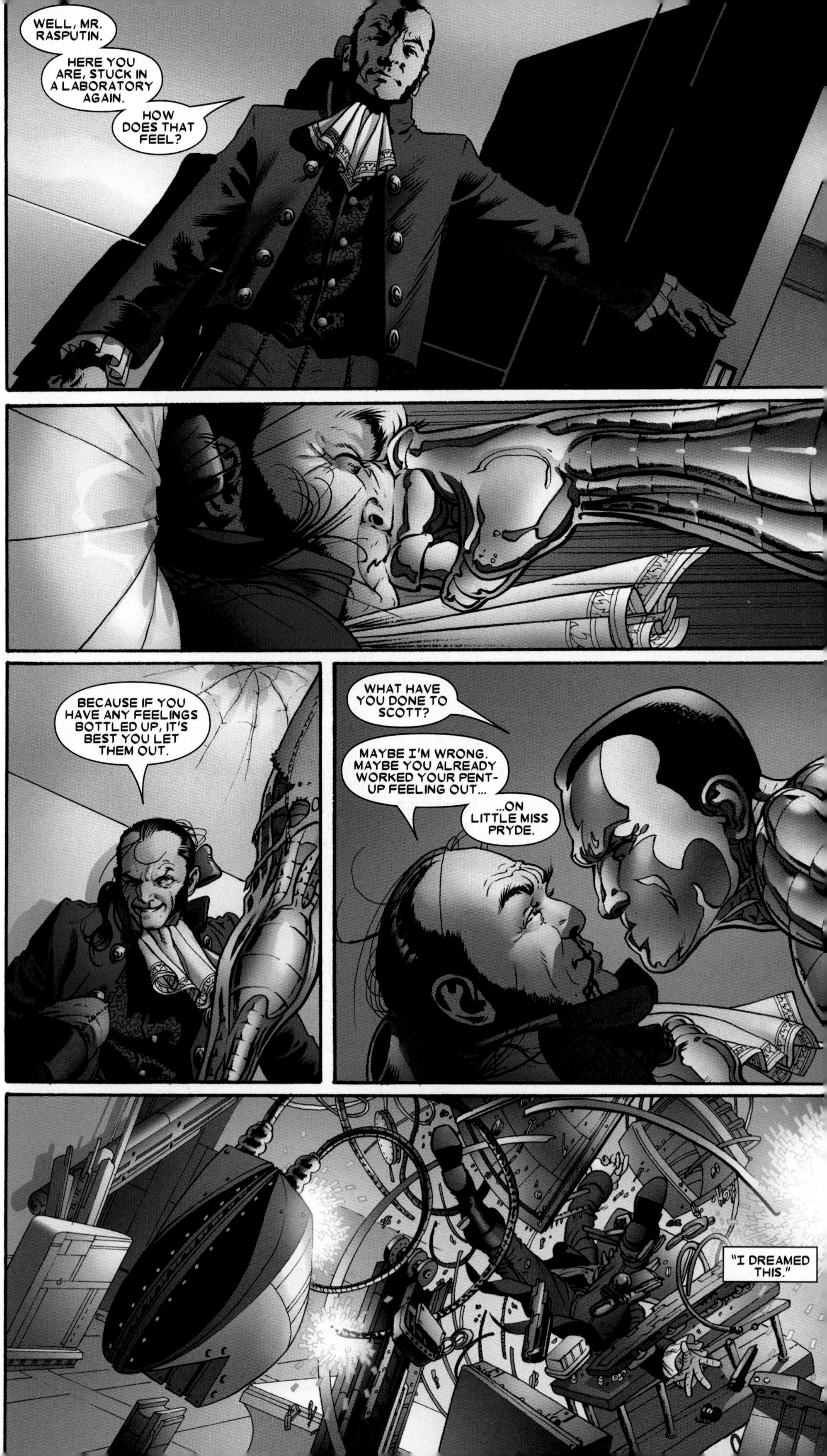
WELL, MR. RASPUTIN.
HERE YOU ARE, STUCK IN A LABORATORY AGAIN.
HOW DOES THAT FEEL?
BECAUSE IF YOU HAVE ANY FEELINGS BOTTLED UP, IT'S BEST YOU LET THEM OUT.
WHAT HAVE YOU DONE TO SCOTT?
MAYBE I'M WRONG. MAYBE YOU ALREADY WORKED YOUR PENT-UP FEELING OUT...
...ON LITTLE MISS PRYDE.
"I DREAMED THIS."

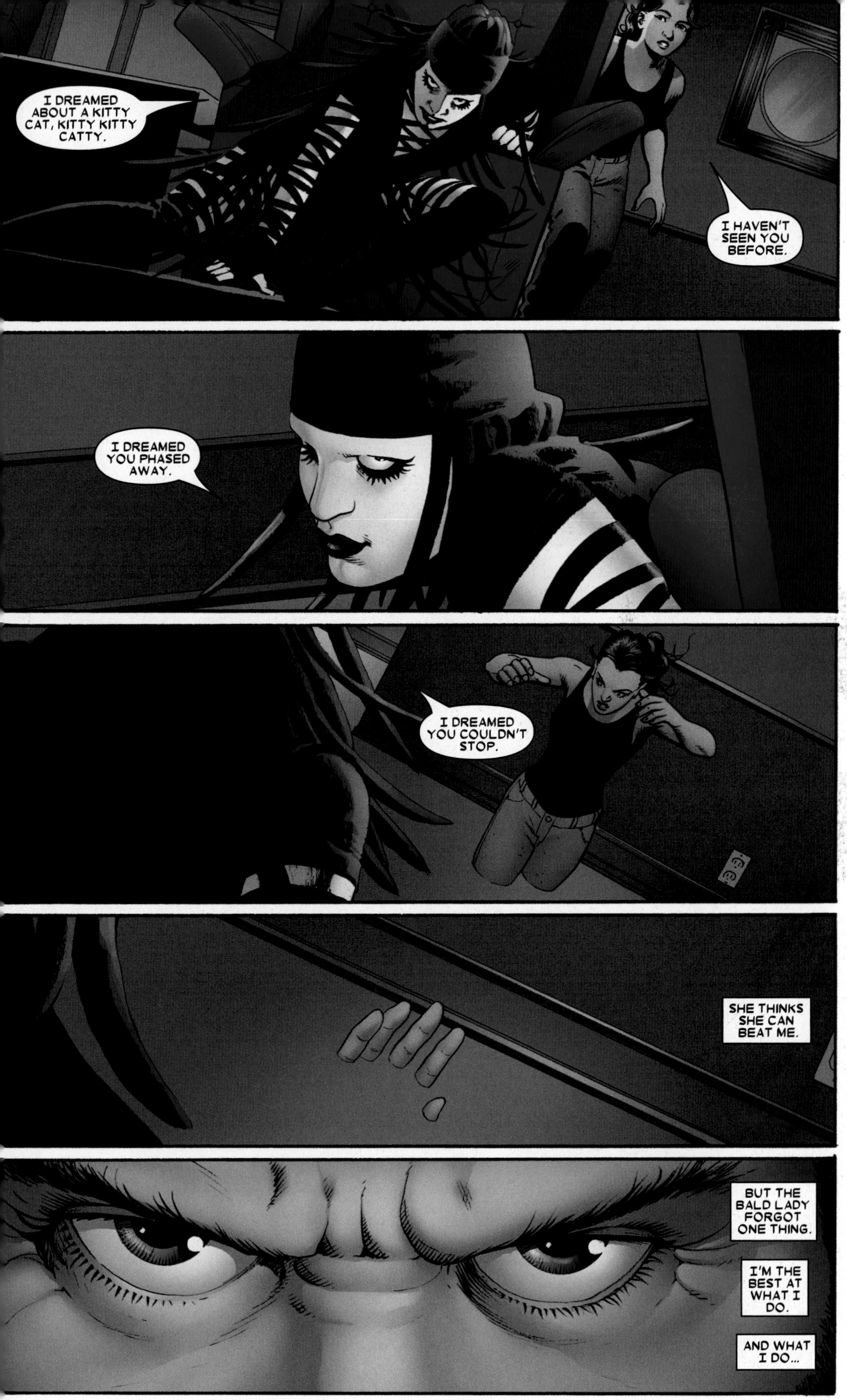
I DREAMED ABOUT A KITTY CAT, KITTY KITTY CATTY.
I HAVEN'T SEEN YOU BEFORE.
I DREAMED YOU PHASED AWAY.
I DREAMED YOU COULDN'T STOP.
SHE THINKS SHE CAN BEAT ME.
BUT THE BALD LADY FORGOT ONE THING.
I'M THE BEST AT WHAT I DO.
AND WHAT I DO...

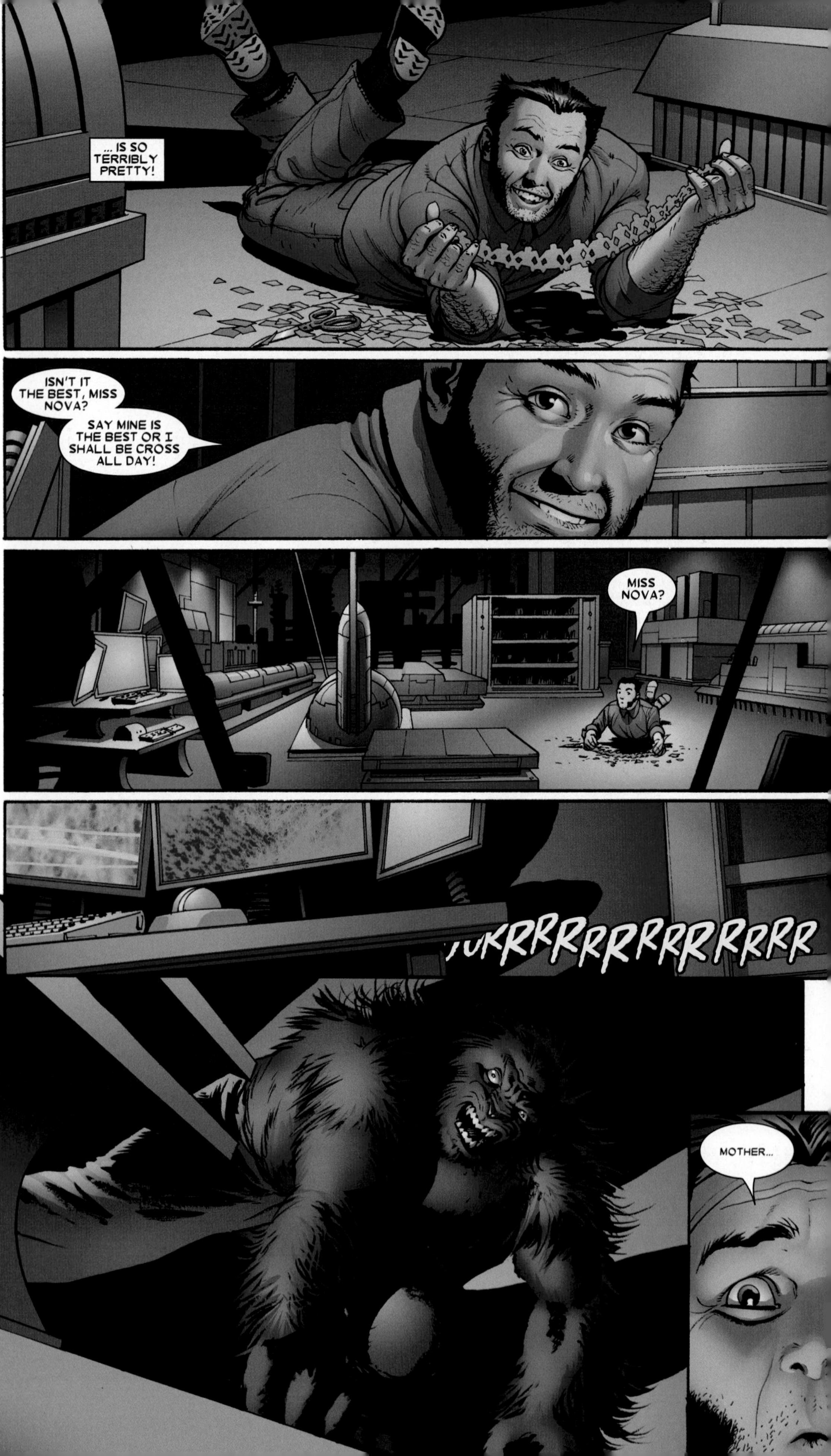
...IS SO TERRIBLY PRETTY!
ISN'T IT THE BEST, MISS NOVA?
SAY MINE IS THE BEST OR I SHALL BE CROSS ALL DAY!
MISS NOVA?
UKRRRRRRRRRRRR
MOTHER...

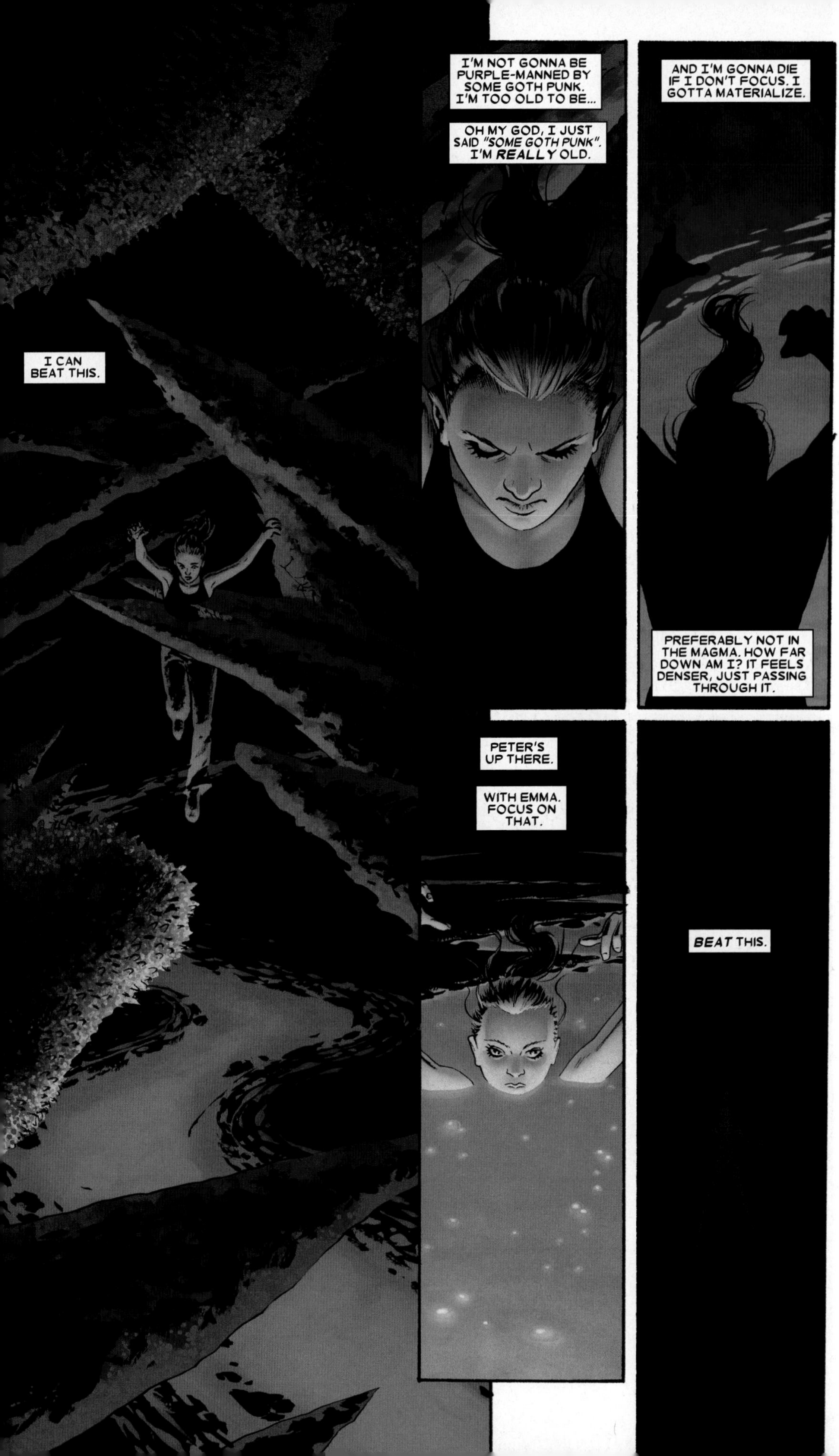
I CAN BEAT THIS.
I'M NOT GONNA BE PURPLE-MANNED BY SOME GOTH PUNK. I'M TOO OLD TO BE...
OH MY GOD, I JUST SAID "SOME GOTH PUNK". I'M REALLY OLD.
AND I'M GONNA DIE IF I DON'T FOCUS. I GOTTA MATERIALIZE.
PREFERABLY NOT IN THE MAGMA. HOW FAR DOWN AM I? IT FEELS DENSER, JUST PASSING THROUGH IT.
PETER'S UP THERE.
WITH EMMA. FOCUS ON THAT.
BEAT THIS.

I THINK IT'S GOING WELL, DON'T YOU?

THE THERAPY?

POOR SCOTT'S SEEMED TO HAVE TIRED HIMSELF OUT.

BUT YOU NEVER TIRE, DO YOU?

NEVER COMPLAIN, NEVER SPEAK UP AT ALL. A CHILD OF THE SOVIET, FIRST AND LAST.

WHY SHOULD I COMPLAIN?

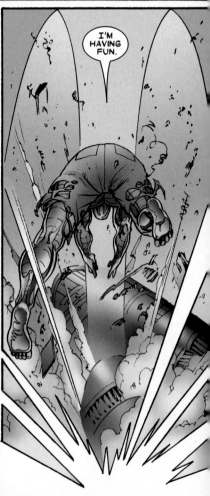

I'M HAVING FUN.

HEY, IT'S ME, OKAY? THERE'S NO ONE ELSE AROUND.

JUST TELL ME WHAT'S WRONG.

GO AWAY, THANK YOU, THANK YOU, I'M HERE, SITTING.

BLINDFOLD, I COULD HEAR YOU CRYING IN THE HALL. I JUST WANT TO HELP.

I DON'T CRY.

I NEVER HAVE.

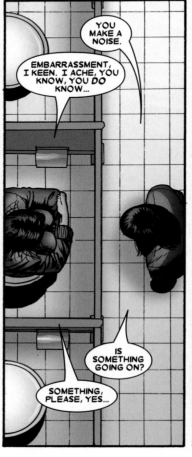

YOU MAKE A NOISE.

EMBARRASSMENT, I KEEN. I ACHE, YOU KNOW, YOU DO KNOW...

IS SOMETHING GOING ON?

SOMETHING, PLEASE, YES...

WE'RE GOING TO LOSE ANOTHER ONE.

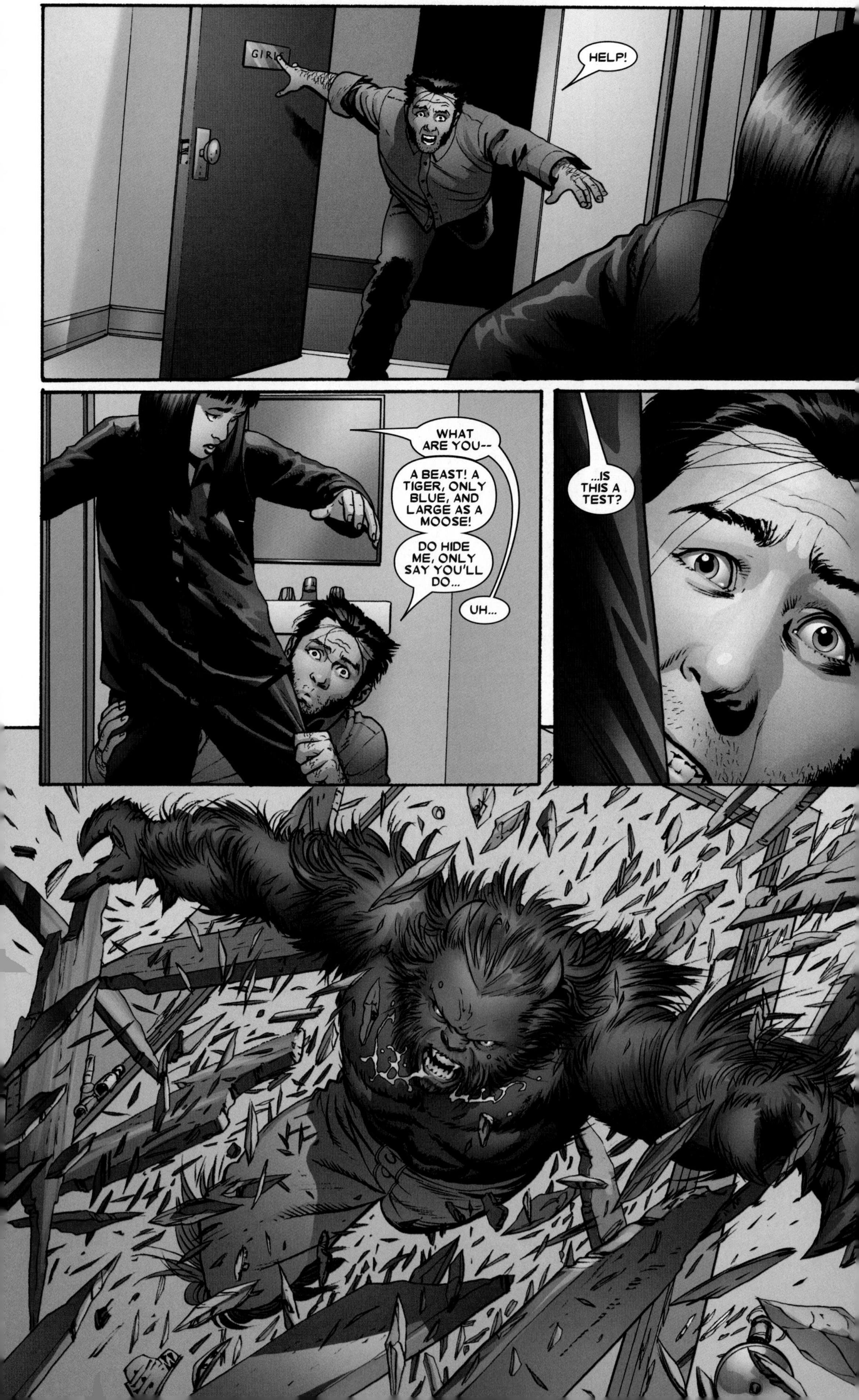
GIRLS
HELP!
WHAT ARE YOU--
A BEAST! A TIGER, ONLY BLUE, AND LARGE AS A MOOSE!
DO HIDE ME, ONLY SAY YOU'LL DO...
UH...
...IS THIS A TEST?

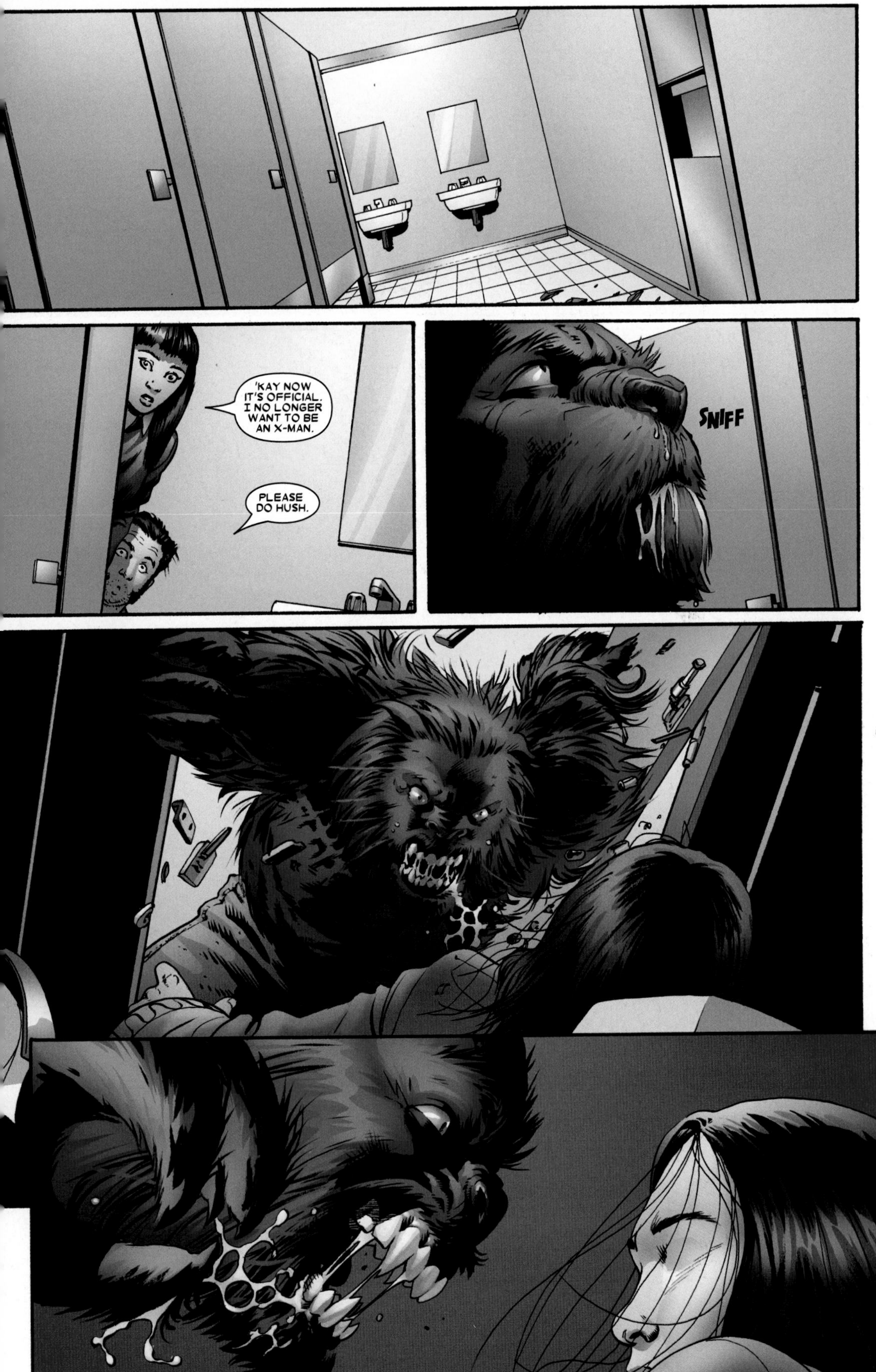
'KAY NOW IT'S OFFICIAL. I NO LONGER WANT TO BE AN X-MAN.
PLEASE DO HUSH.
SNIFF

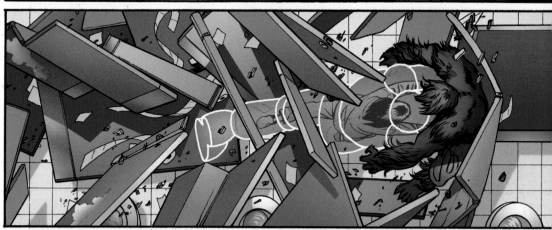
BLINDFOLD, STAY DOWN!

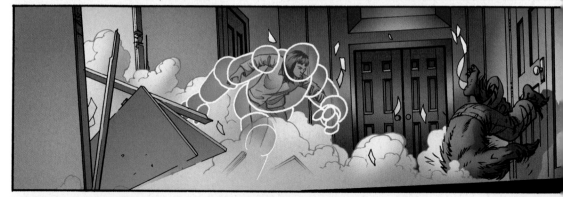

RRRRAAAAOOGGRRGGHHH!

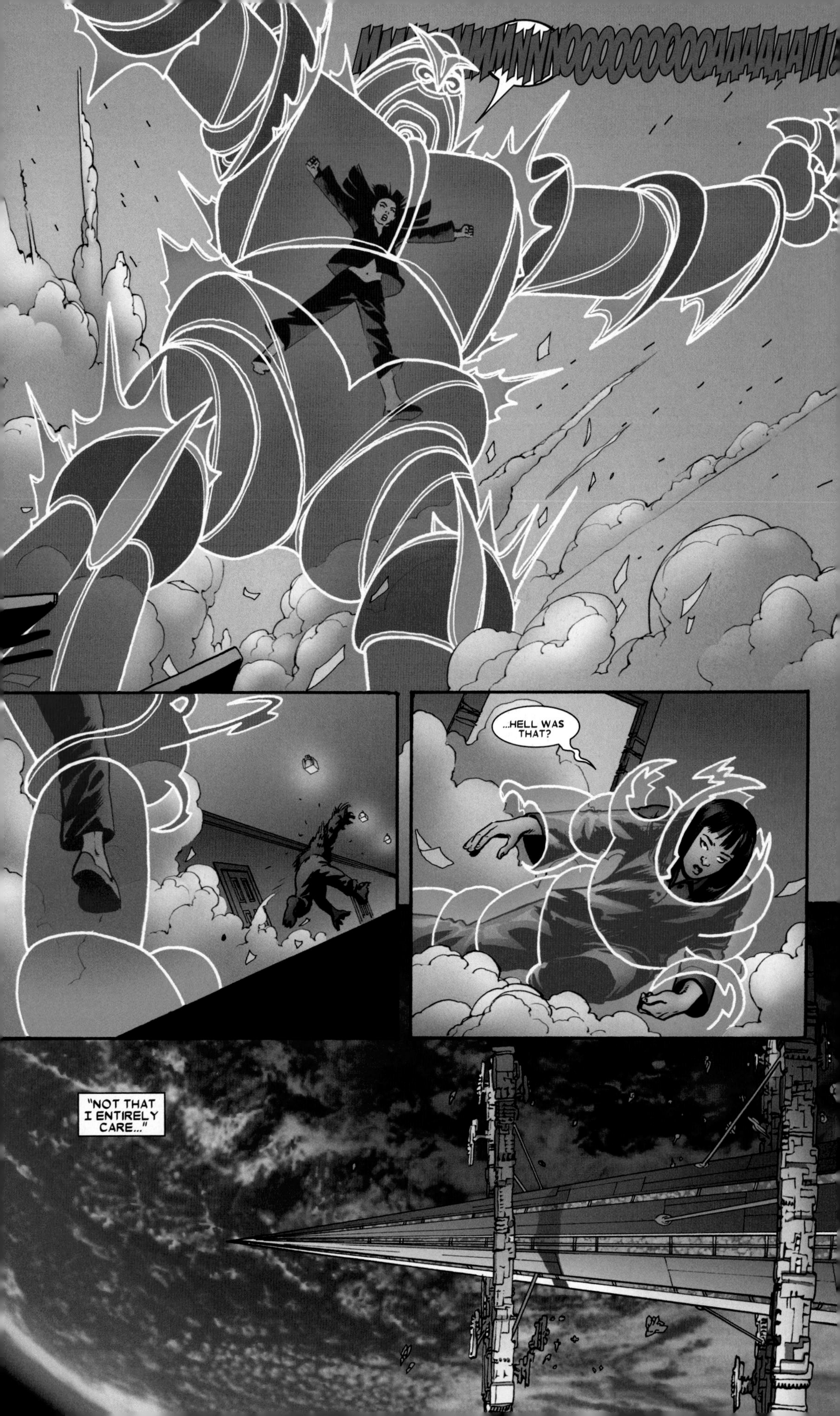
...HELL WAS THAT?
"NOT THAT I ENTIRELY CARE..."

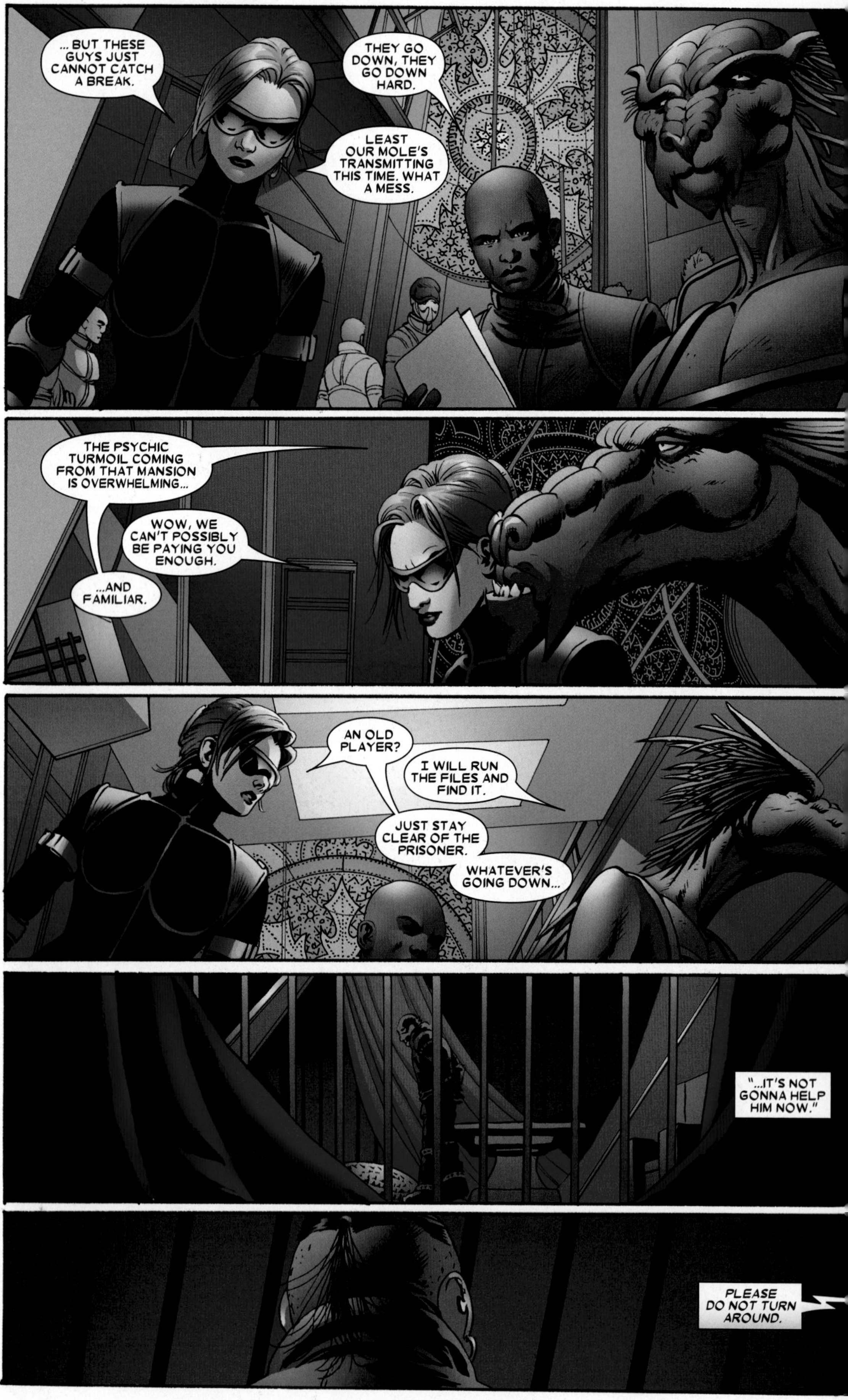

... BUT THESE GUYS JUST CANNOT CATCH A BREAK.
THEY GO DOWN, THEY GO DOWN HARD.
LEAST OUR MOLE'S TRANSMITTING THIS TIME. WHAT A MESS.
THE PSYCHIC TURMOIL COMING FROM THAT MANSION IS OVERWHELMING...
WOW, WE CAN'T POSSIBLY BE PAYING YOU ENOUGH.
...AND FAMILIAR.
AN OLD PLAYER?
I WILL RUN THE FILES AND FIND IT.
JUST STAY CLEAR OF THE PRISONER.
WHATEVER'S GOING DOWN...
"...IT'S NOT GONNA HELP HIM NOW."
PLEASE DO NOT TURN AROUND.

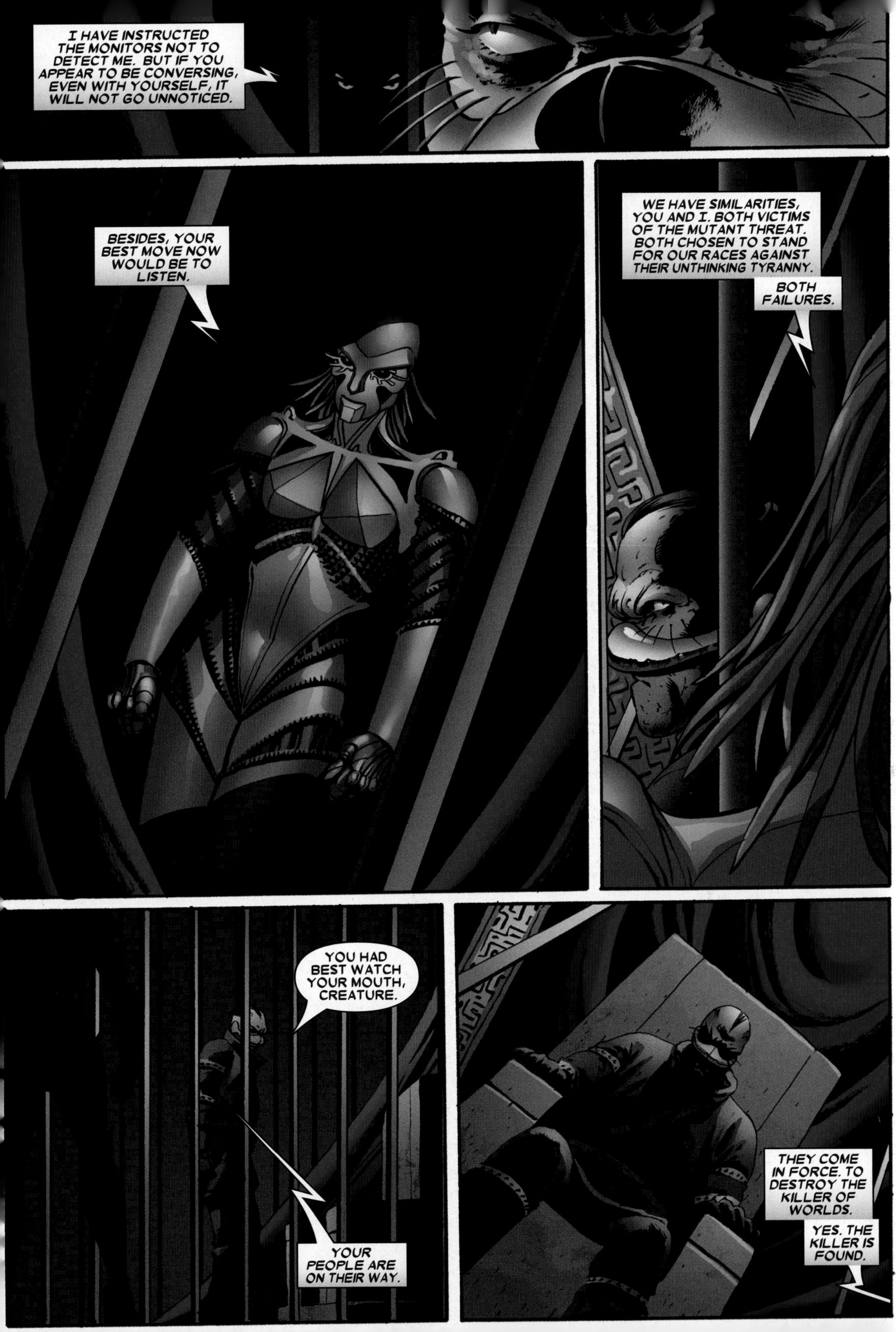
I HAVE INSTRUCTED THE MONITORS NOT TO DETECT ME. BUT IF YOU APPEAR TO BE CONVERSING, EVEN WITH YOURSELF, IT WILL NOT GO UNNOTICED.
BESIDES, YOUR BEST MOVE NOW WOULD BE TO LISTEN.
WE HAVE SIMILARITIES, YOU AND I. BOTH VICTIMS OF THE MUTANT THREAT. BOTH CHOSEN TO STAND FOR OUR RACES AGAINST THEIR UNTHINKING TYRANNY.
BOTH FAILURES.
YOU HAD BEST WATCH YOUR MOUTH, CREATURE.
YOUR PEOPLE ARE ON THEIR WAY.
THEY COME IN FORCE. TO DESTROY THE KILLER OF WORLDS.
YES. THE KILLER IS FOUND.

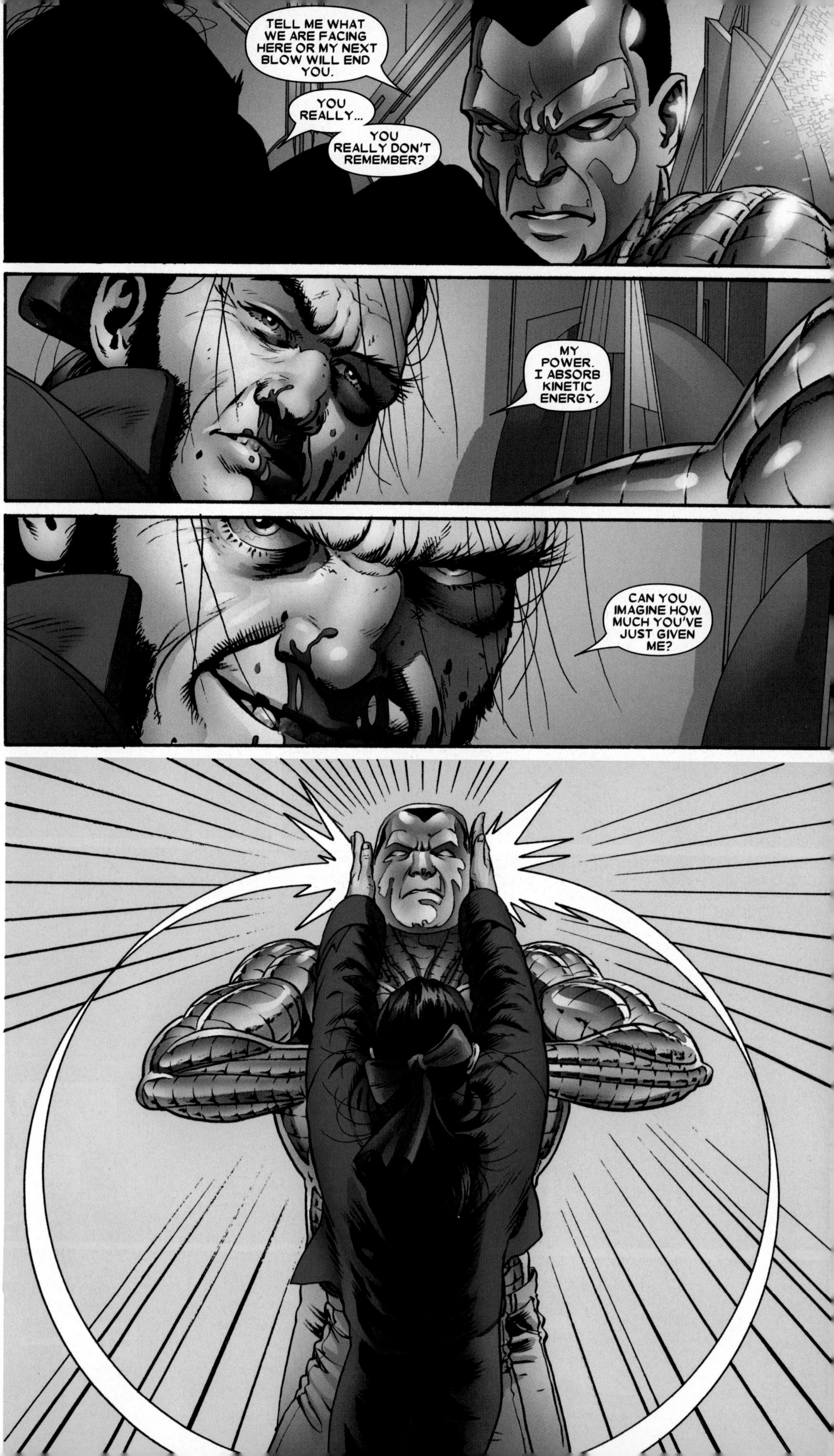
TELL ME WHAT WE ARE FACING HERE OR MY NEXT BLOW WILL END YOU.
YOU REALLY...
YOU REALLY DON'T REMEMBER?
MY POWER. I ABSORB KINETIC ENERGY.
CAN YOU IMAGINE HOW MUCH YOU'VE JUST GIVEN ME?

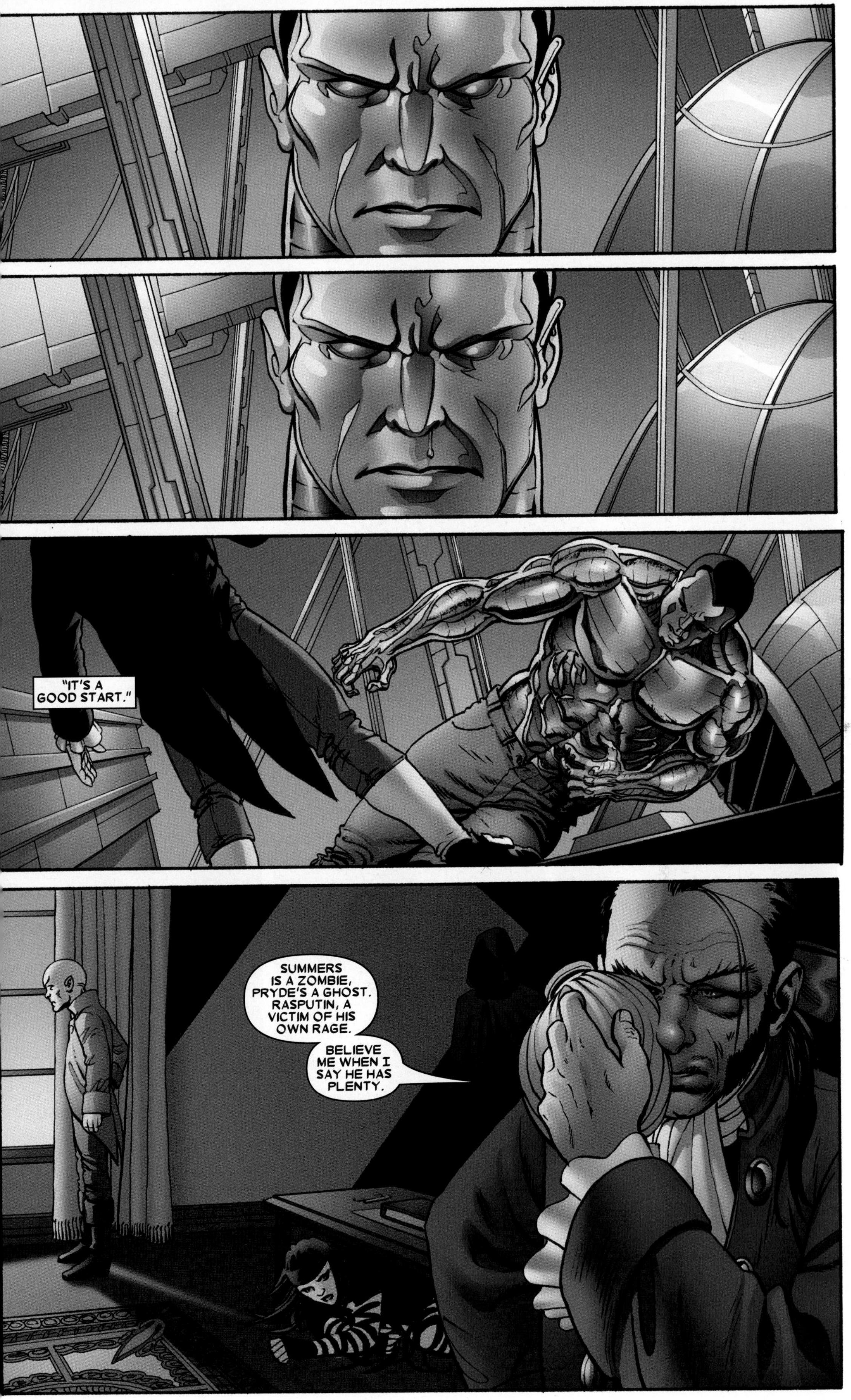
"IT'S A GOOD START."
SUMMERS IS A ZOMBIE, PRYDE'S A GHOST. RASPUTIN, A VICTIM OF HIS OWN RAGE.
BELIEVE ME WHEN I SAY HE HAS PLENTY.

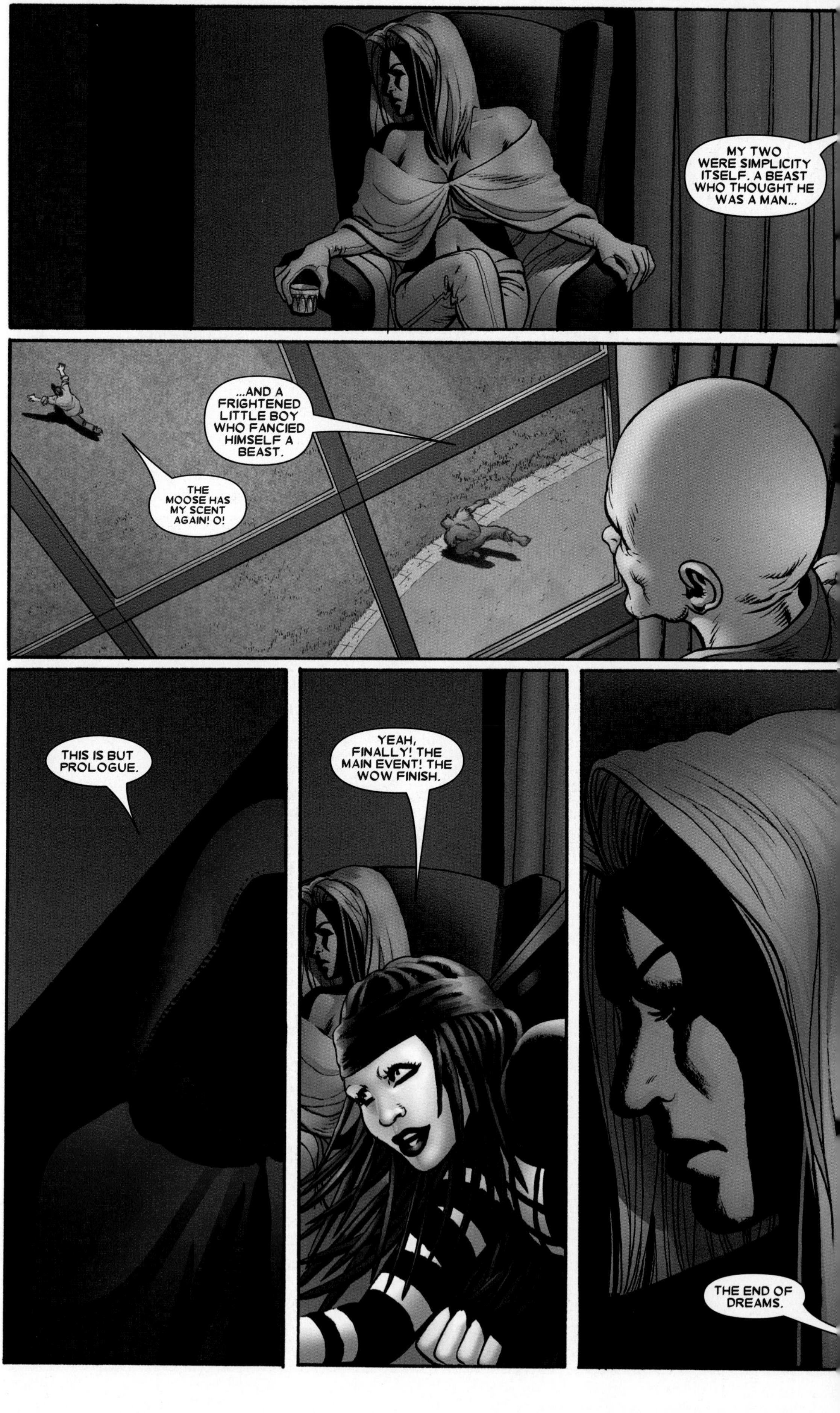
MY TWO WERE SIMPLICITY ITSELF. A BEAST WHO THOUGHT HE WAS A MAN...
...AND A FRIGHTENED LITTLE BOY WHO FANCIED HIMSELF A BEAST.
THE MOOSE HAS MY SCENT AGAIN! O!
THIS IS BUT PROLOGUE.
YEAH, FINALLY! THE MAIN EVENT! THE WOW FINISH.
THE END OF DREAMS.

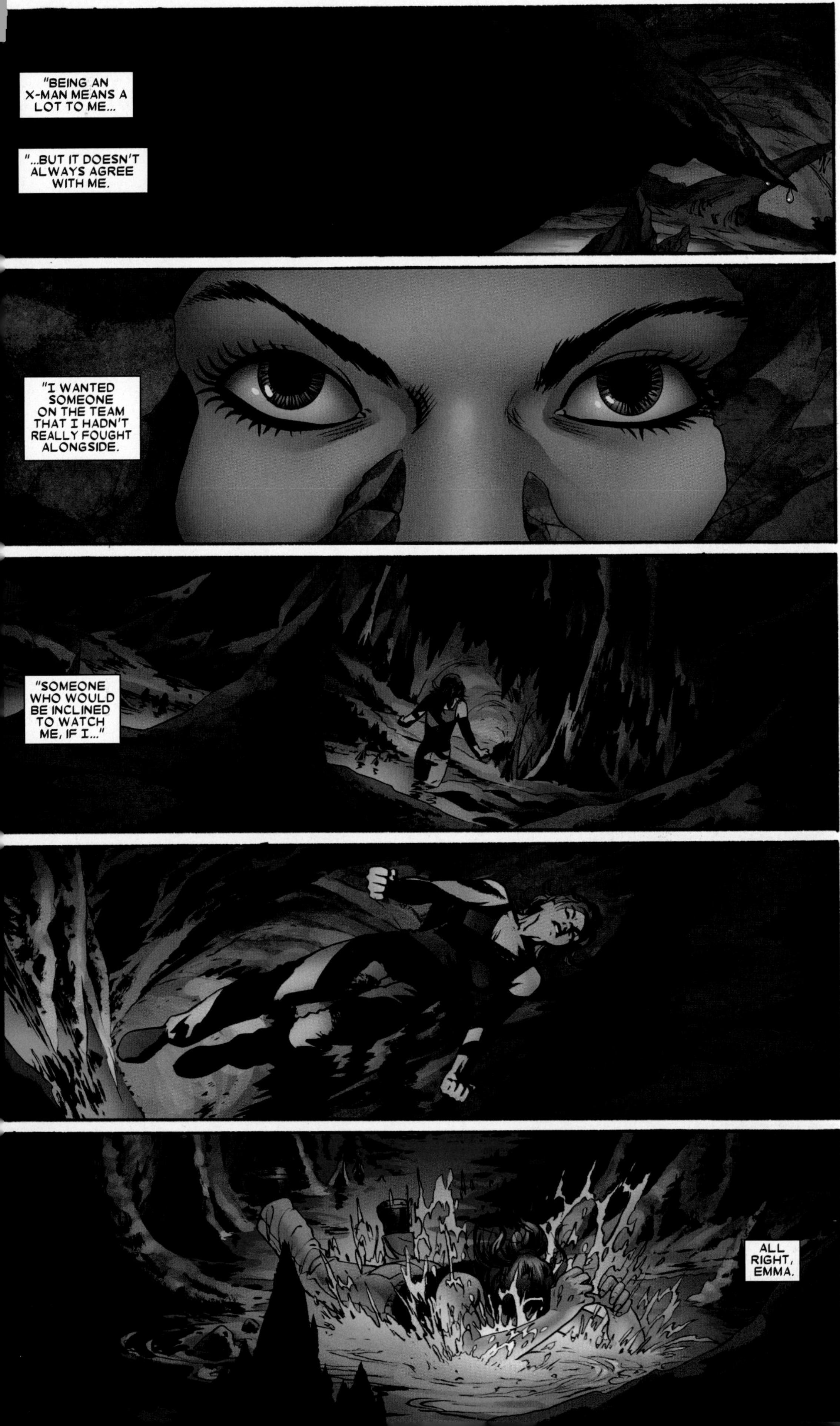
"BEING AN X-MAN MEANS A LOT TO ME...
"...BUT IT DOESN'T ALWAYS AGREE WITH ME.
"I WANTED SOMEONE ON THE TEAM THAT I HADN'T REALLY FOUGHT ALONGSIDE.
"SOMEONE WHO WOULD BE INCLINED TO WATCH ME, IF I..."
ALL RIGHT, EMMA.

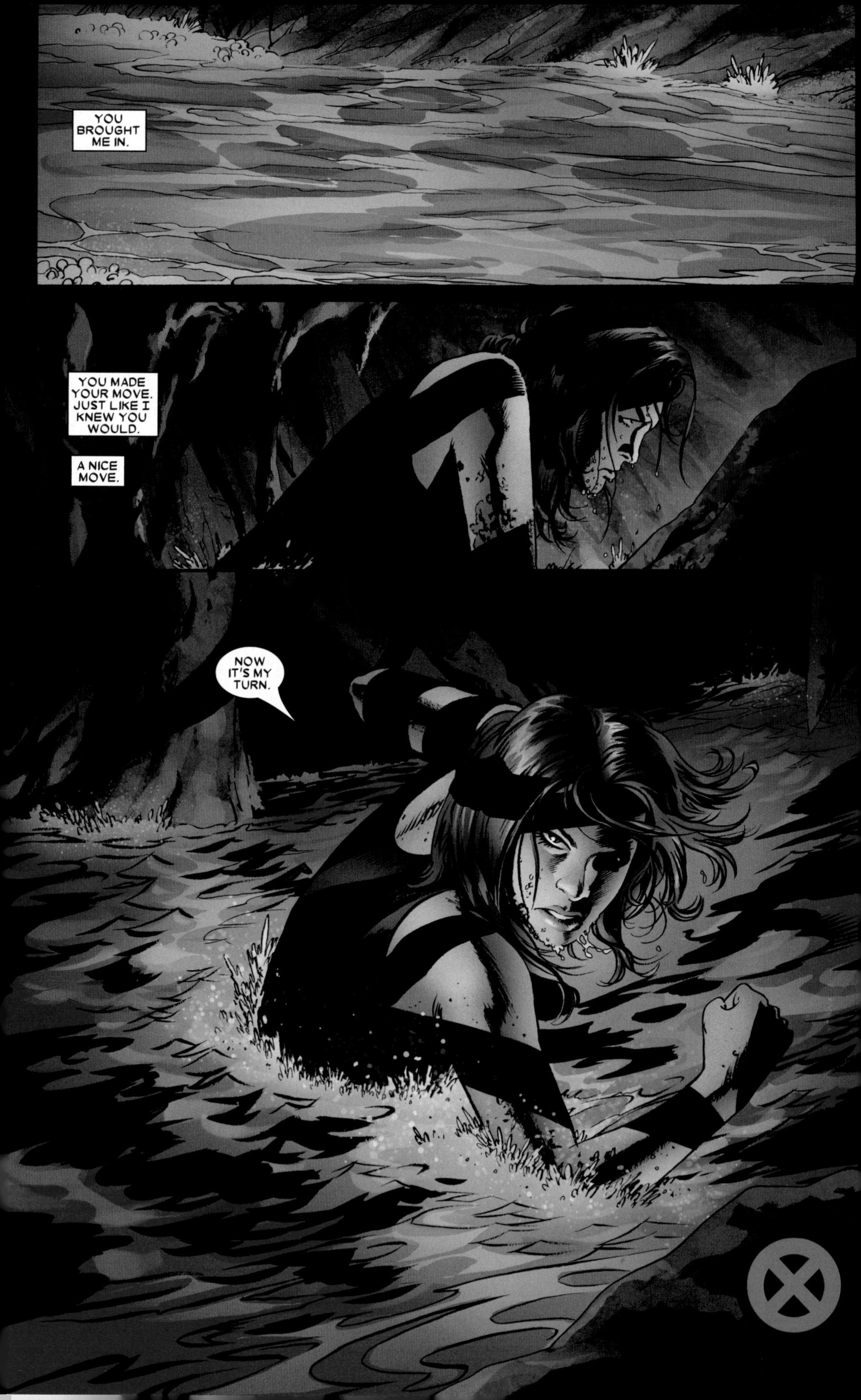
YOU BROUGHT ME IN.
YOU MADE YOUR MOVE. JUST LIKE I KNEW YOU WOULD.
A NICE MOVE.
NOW IT'S MY TURN.

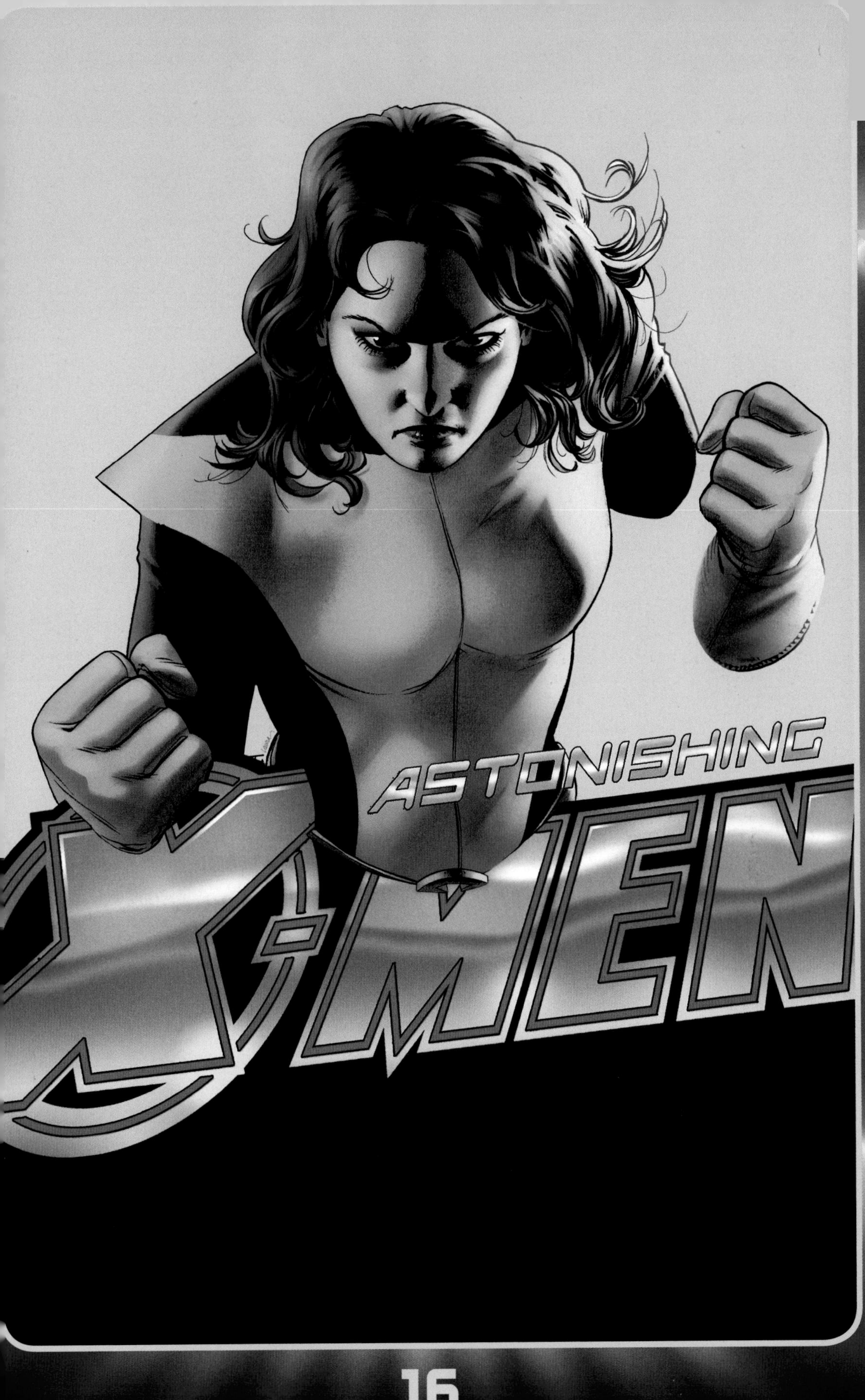
ASTONISHING
X-MEN

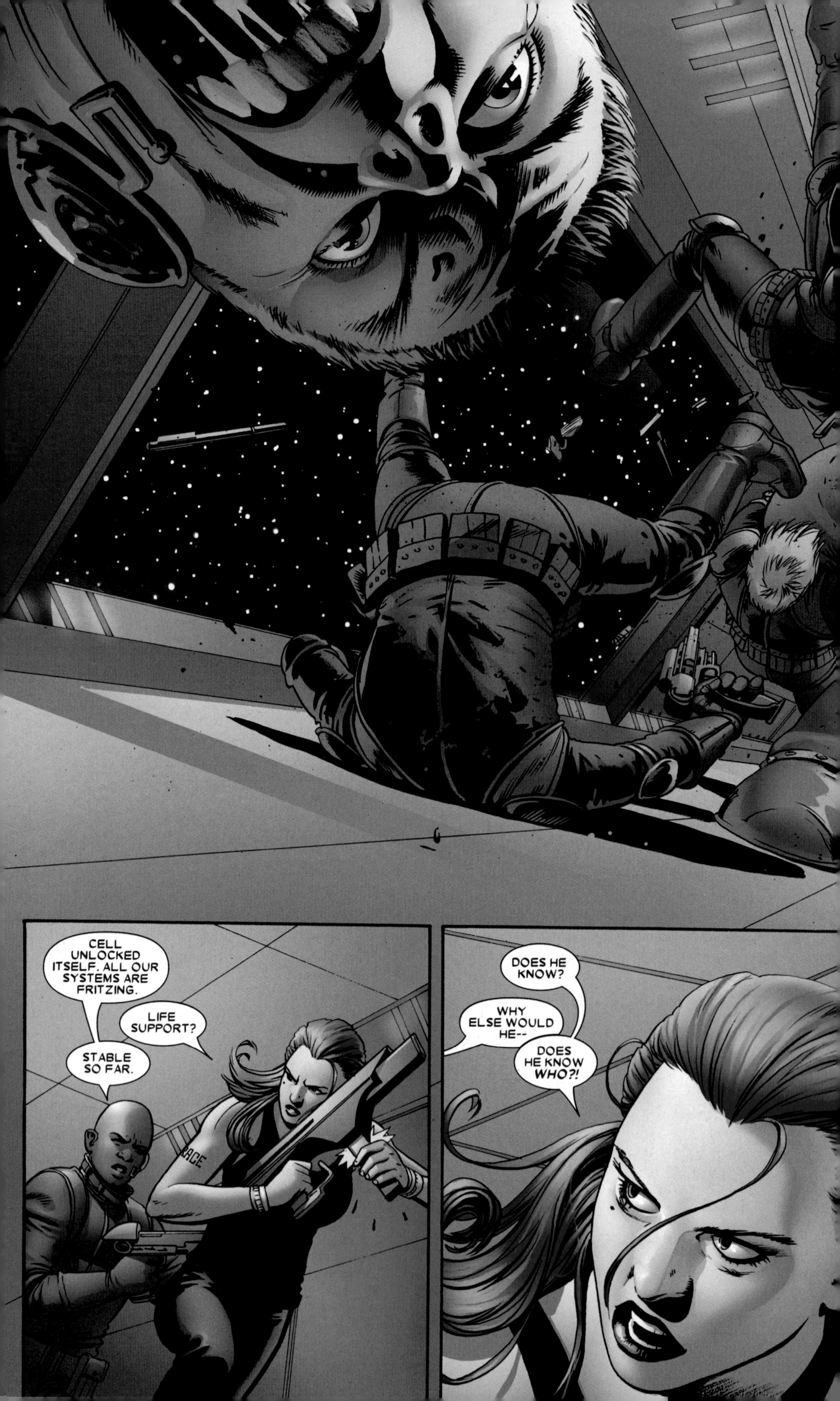

CELL UNLOCKED ITSELF. ALL OUR SYSTEMS ARE FRITZING.
LIFE SUPPORT?
STABLE SO FAR.
DOES HE KNOW?
WHY ELSE WOULD HE--
DOES HE KNOW *WHO?!*

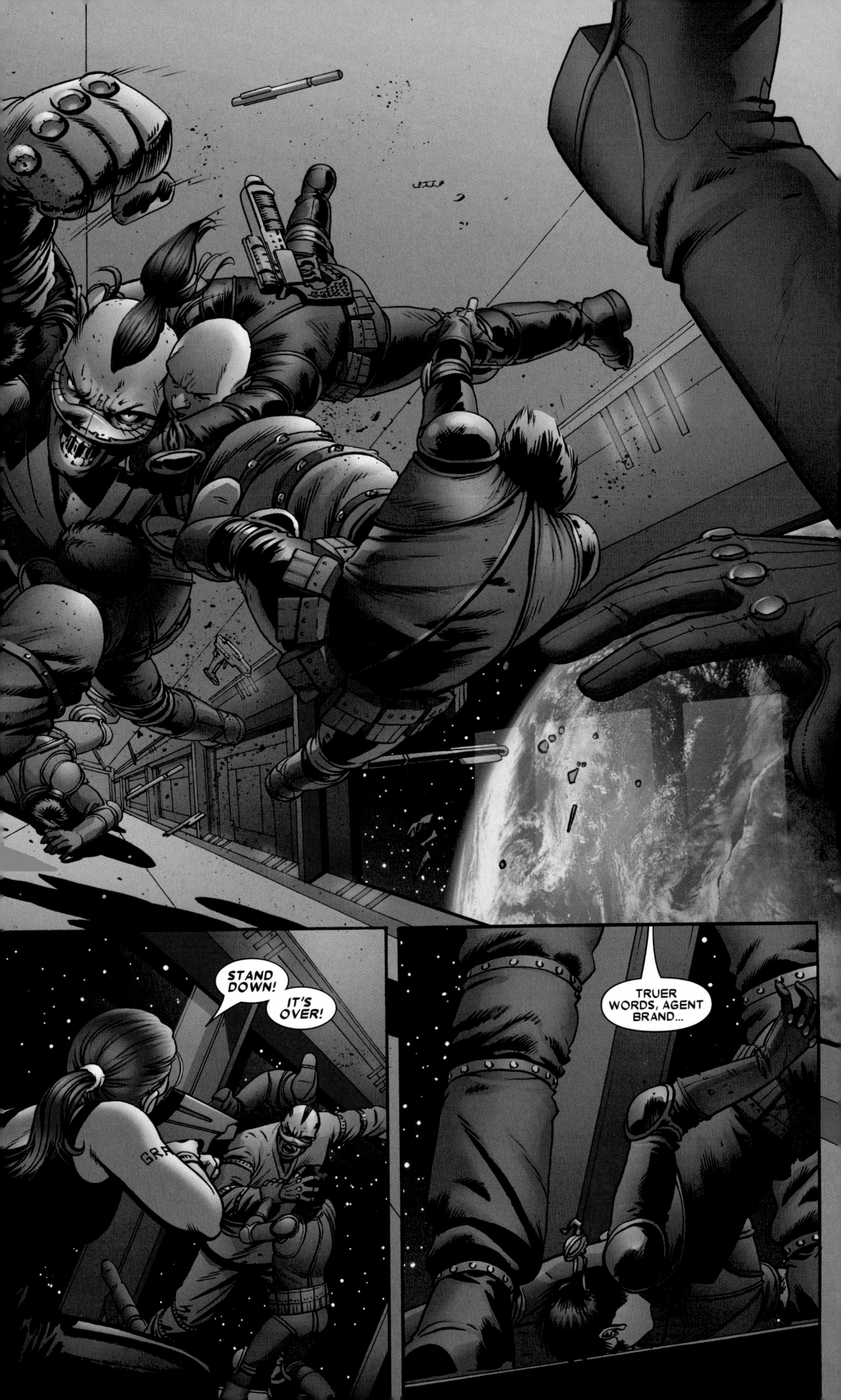
STAND DOWN!
IT'S OVER!
TRUER WORDS, AGENT BRAND...

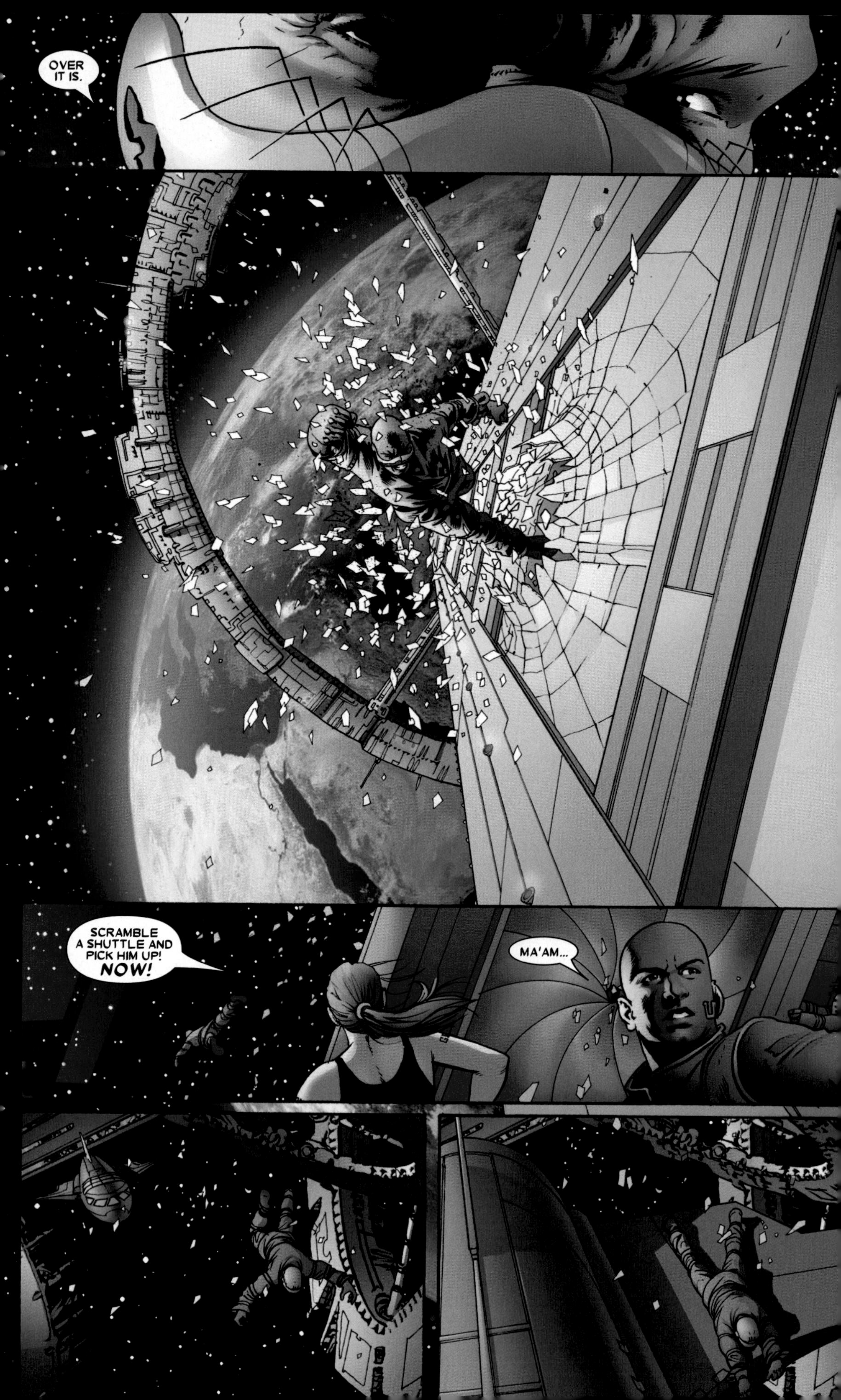
OVER IT IS.
SCRAMBLE A SHUTTLE AND PICK HIM UP! NOW!
MA'AM...

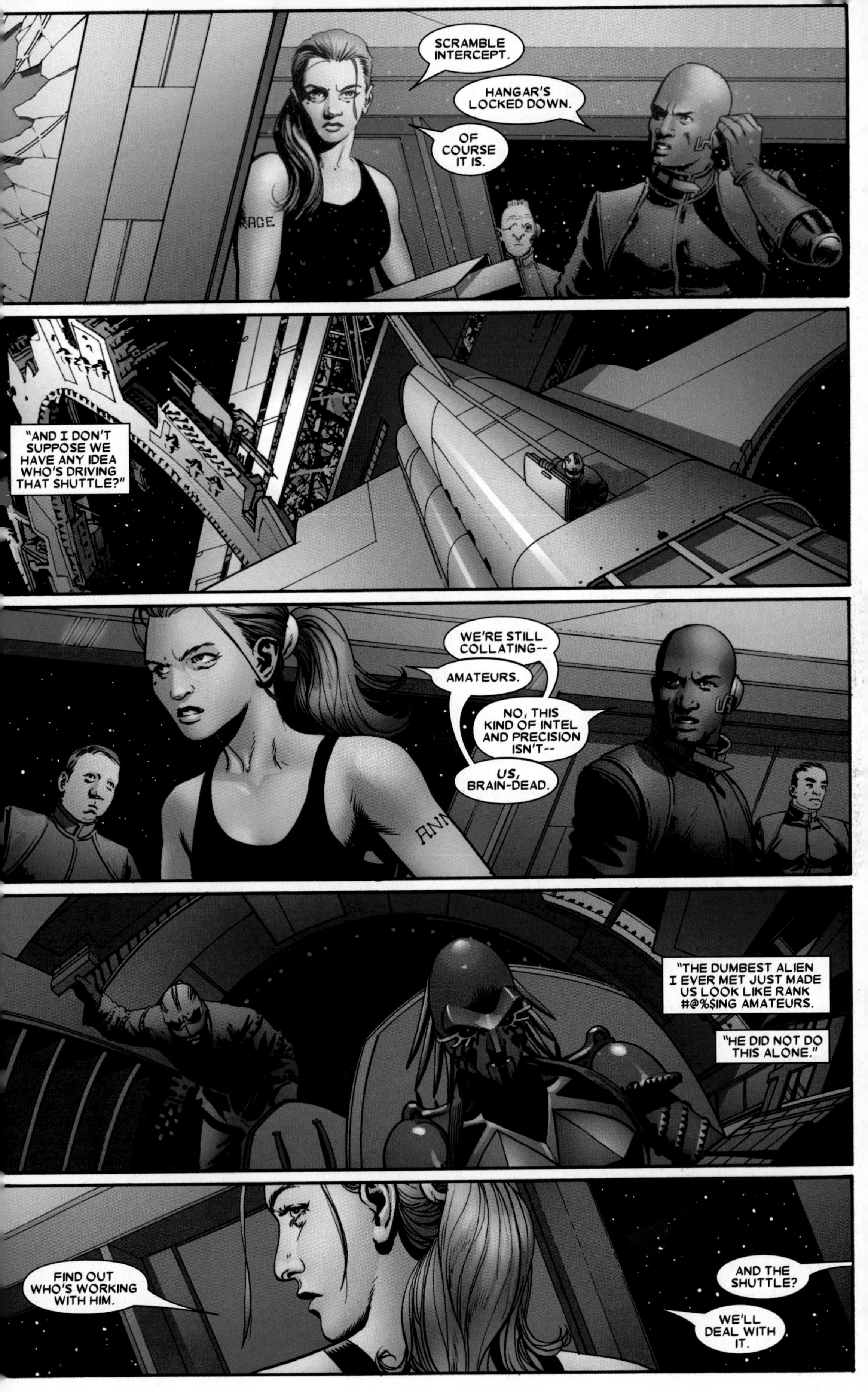
SCRAMBLE INTERCEPT.
HANGAR'S LOCKED DOWN.
OF COURSE IT IS.
RAGE
"AND I DON'T SUPPOSE WE HAVE ANY IDEA WHO'S DRIVING THAT SHUTTLE?"
WE'RE STILL COLLATING--
AMATEURS.
NO, THIS KIND OF INTEL AND PRECISION ISN'T--
US, BRAIN-DEAD.
"THE DUMBEST ALIEN I EVER MET JUST MADE US LOOK LIKE RANK #@%$ING AMATEURS.
"HE DID NOT DO THIS ALONE."
FIND OUT WHO'S WORKING WITH HIM.
AND THE SHUTTLE?
WE'LL DEAL WITH IT.

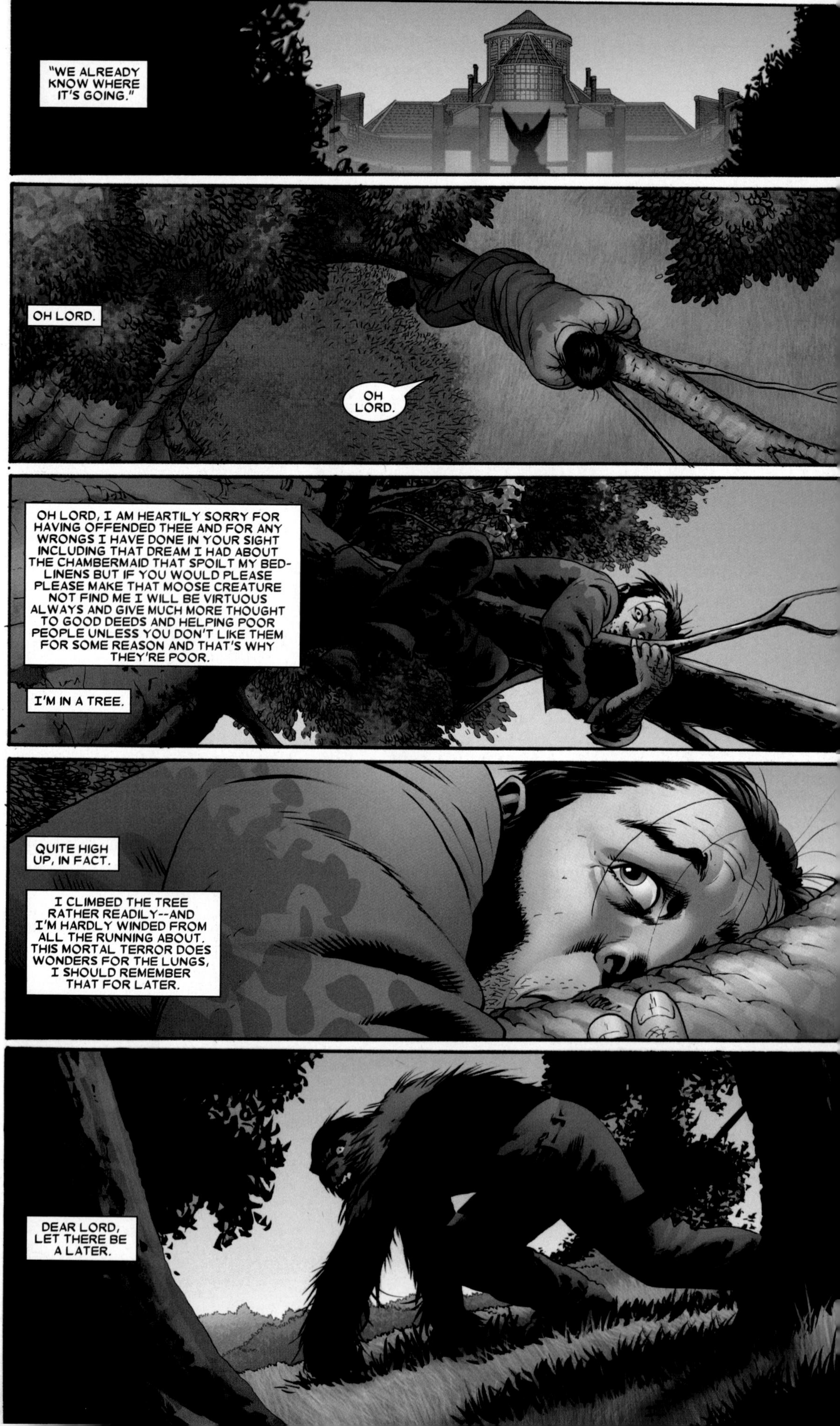
"WE ALREADY KNOW WHERE IT'S GOING."
OH LORD.
OH LORD.
OH LORD, I AM HEARTILY SORRY FOR HAVING OFFENDED THEE AND FOR ANY WRONGS I HAVE DONE IN YOUR SIGHT INCLUDING THAT DREAM I HAD ABOUT THE CHAMBERMAID THAT SPOILT MY BED-LINENS BUT IF YOU WOULD PLEASE PLEASE MAKE THAT MOOSE CREATURE NOT FIND ME I WILL BE VIRTUOUS ALWAYS AND GIVE MUCH MORE THOUGHT TO GOOD DEEDS AND HELPING POOR PEOPLE UNLESS YOU DON'T LIKE THEM FOR SOME REASON AND THAT'S WHY THEY'RE POOR.
I'M IN A TREE.
QUITE HIGH UP, IN FACT.
I CLIMBED THE TREE RATHER READILY--AND I'M HARDLY WINDED FROM ALL THE RUNNING ABOUT. THIS MORTAL TERROR DOES WONDERS FOR THE LUNGS, I SHOULD REMEMBER THAT FOR LATER.
DEAR LORD, LET THERE BE A LATER.

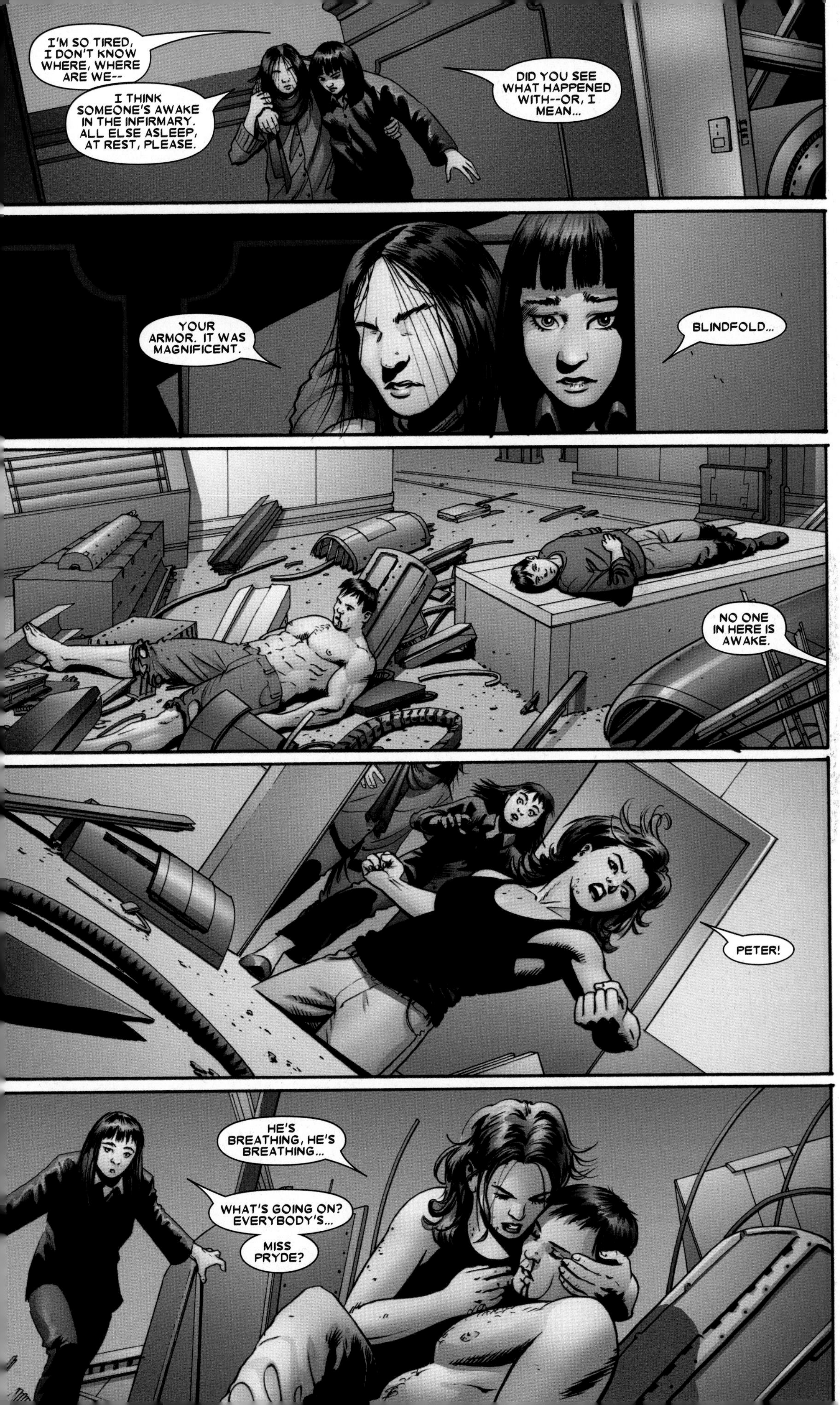

I'M SO TIRED, I DON'T KNOW WHERE, WHERE ARE WE--
I THINK SOMEONE'S AWAKE IN THE INFIRMARY. ALL ELSE ASLEEP, AT REST, PLEASE.
DID YOU SEE WHAT HAPPENED WITH--OR, I MEAN...
YOUR ARMOR. IT WAS MAGNIFICENT.
BLINDFOLD...
NO ONE IN HERE IS AWAKE.
PETER!
HE'S BREATHING, HE'S BREATHING...
WHAT'S GOING ON? EVERYBODY'S...
MISS PRYDE?

TELL ME WHAT YOU KNOW.

AAAHH!!

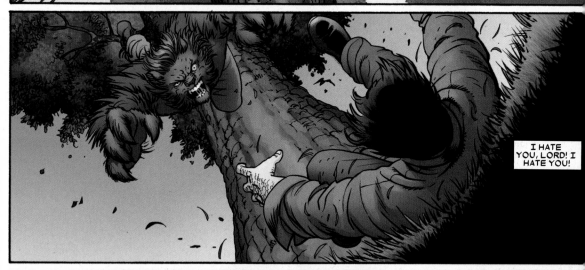

I HATE YOU, LORD! I HATE YOU!

AACOWW!!

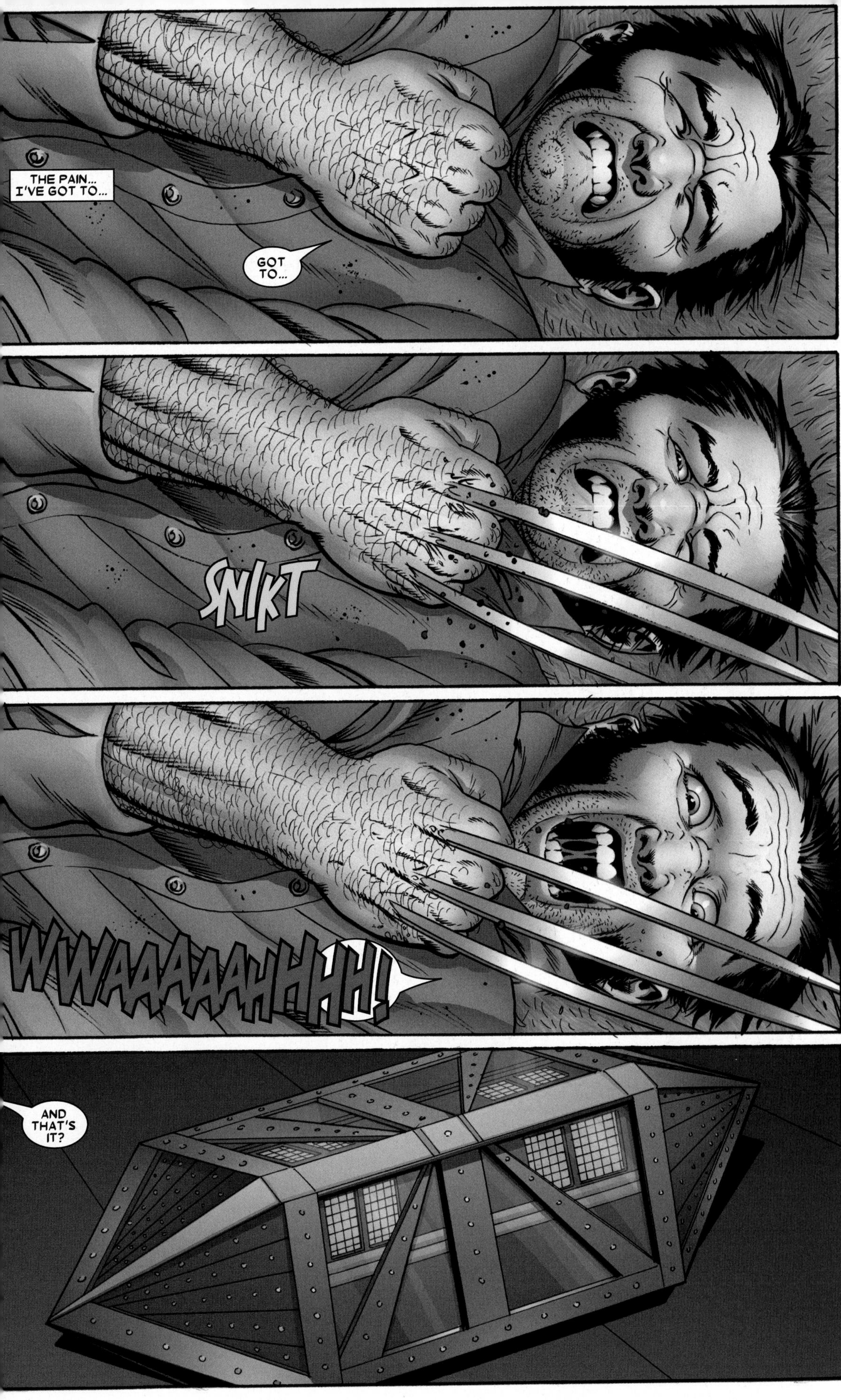
THE PAIN... I'VE GOT TO...
GOT TO...
SNIKT
WWAAAAAHHHH!
AND THAT'S IT?

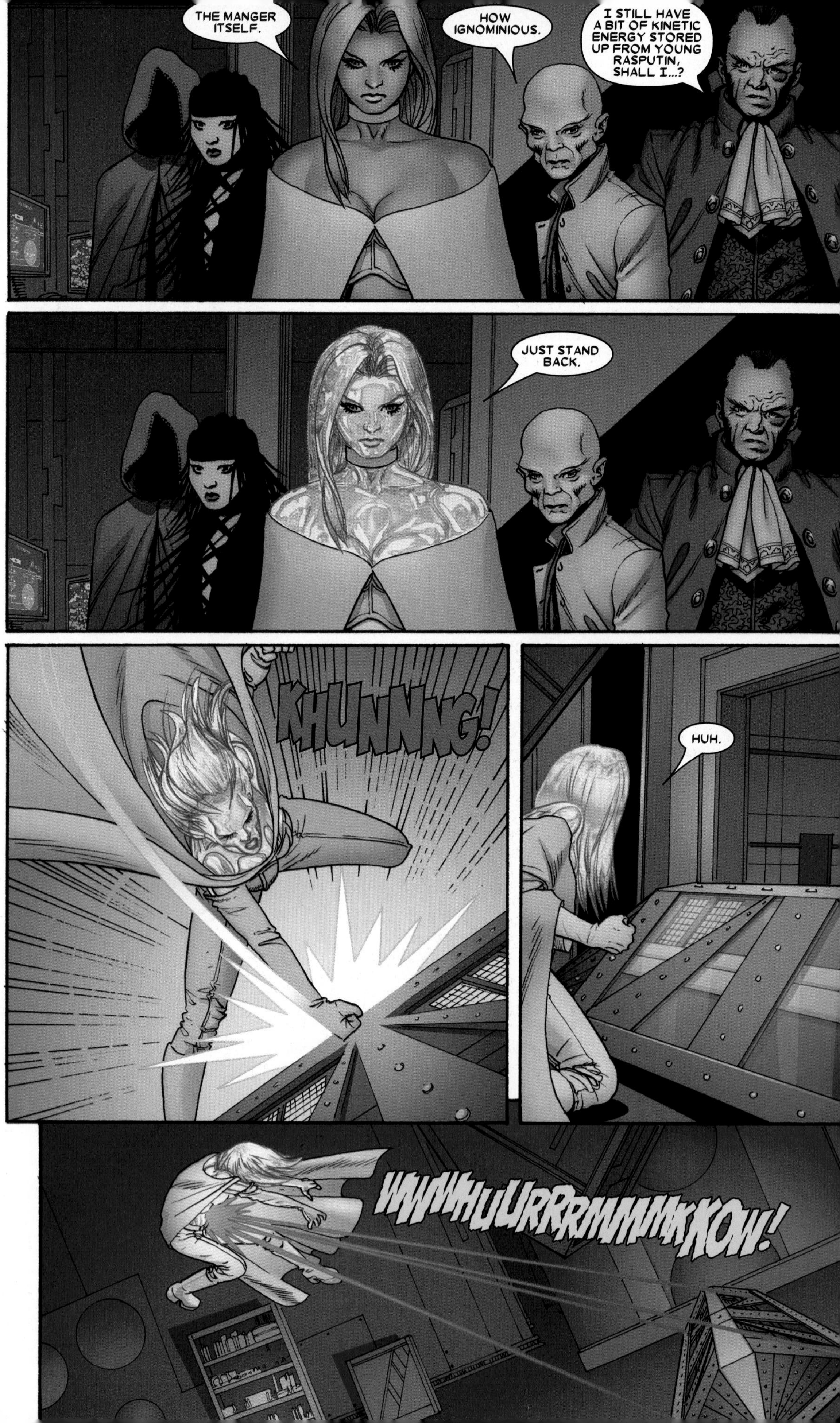
THE MANGER ITSELF.
HOW IGNOMINIOUS.
I STILL HAVE A BIT OF KINETIC ENERGY STORED UP FROM YOUNG RASPUTIN, SHALL I...?
JUST STAND BACK.
KHUNNNG!
HUH.
WWWHUURRRMMMMKKOW!

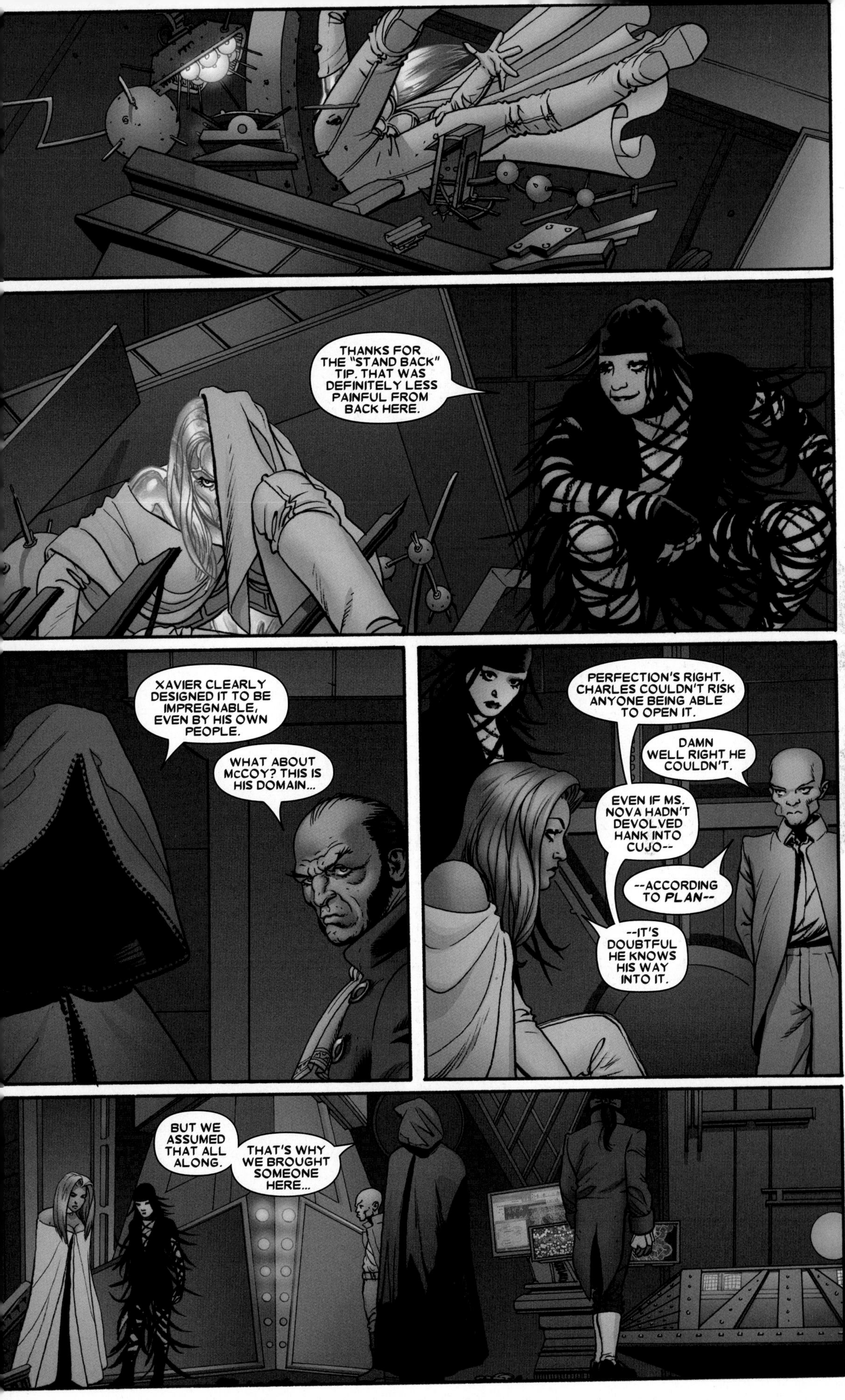
THANKS FOR THE "STAND BACK" TIP. THAT WAS DEFINITELY LESS PAINFUL FROM BACK HERE.
XAVIER CLEARLY DESIGNED IT TO BE IMPREGNABLE, EVEN BY HIS OWN PEOPLE.
WHAT ABOUT McCOY? THIS IS HIS DOMAIN...
PERFECTION'S RIGHT. CHARLES COULDN'T RISK ANYONE BEING ABLE TO OPEN IT.
DAMN WELL RIGHT HE COULDN'T.
EVEN IF MS. NOVA HADN'T DEVOLVED HANK INTO CUJO--
--ACCORDING TO PLAN--
--IT'S DOUBTFUL HE KNOWS HIS WAY INTO IT.
BUT WE ASSUMED THAT ALL ALONG.
THAT'S WHY WE BROUGHT SOMEONE HERE...

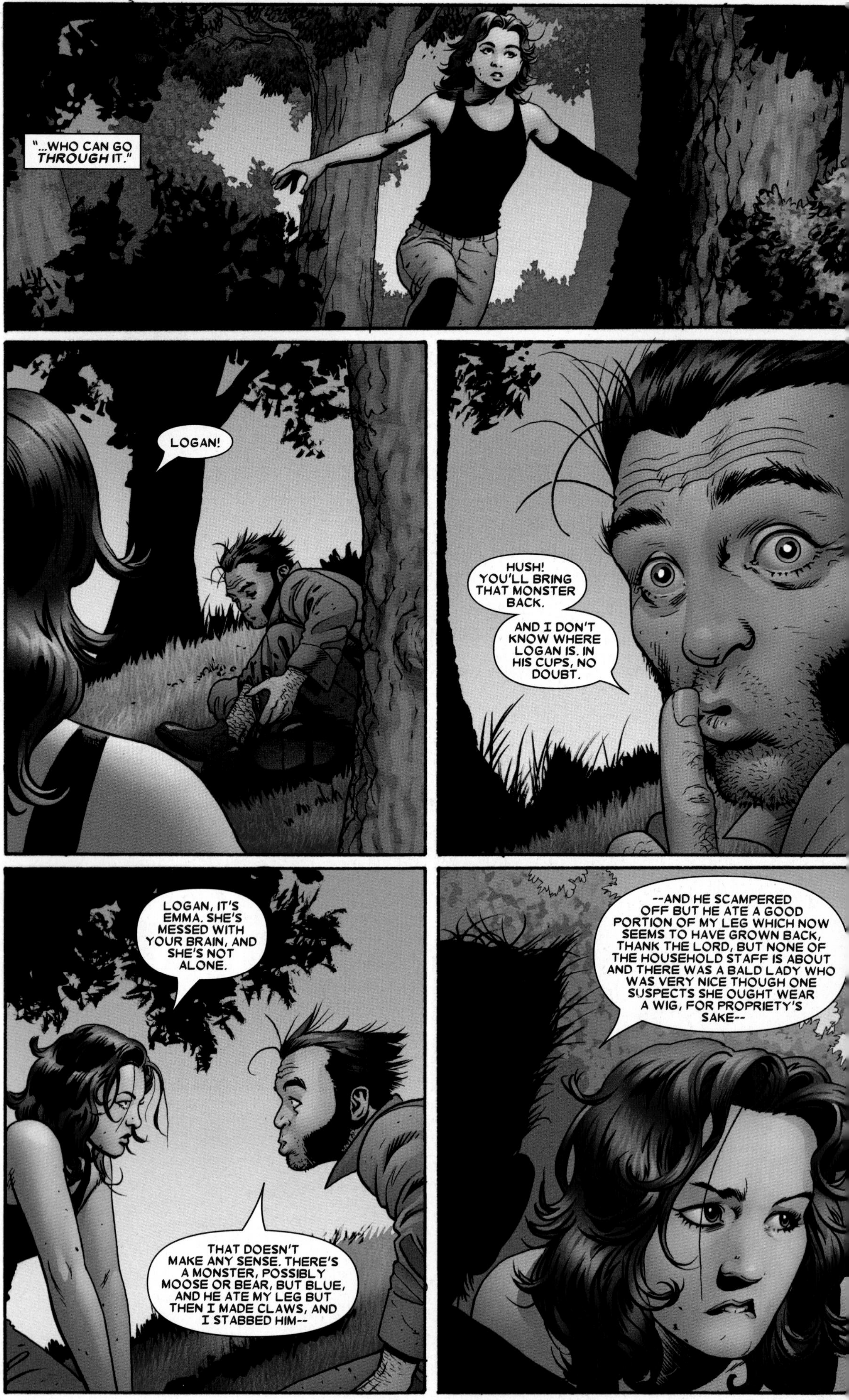
"...WHO CAN GO THROUGH IT."
LOGAN!
HUSH! YOU'LL BRING THAT MONSTER BACK.
AND I DON'T KNOW WHERE LOGAN IS. IN HIS CUPS, NO DOUBT.
LOGAN, IT'S EMMA. SHE'S MESSED WITH YOUR BRAIN, AND SHE'S NOT ALONE.
THAT DOESN'T MAKE ANY SENSE. THERE'S A MONSTER, POSSIBLY MOOSE OR BEAR, BUT BLUE, AND HE ATE MY LEG BUT THEN I MADE CLAWS, AND I STABBED HIM--
--AND HE SCAMPERED OFF BUT HE ATE A GOOD PORTION OF MY LEG WHICH NOW SEEMS TO HAVE GROWN BACK, THANK THE LORD, BUT NONE OF THE HOUSEHOLD STAFF IS ABOUT AND THERE WAS A BALD LADY WHO WAS VERY NICE THOUGH ONE SUSPECTS SHE OUGHT WEAR A WIG, FOR PROPRIETY'S SAKE--

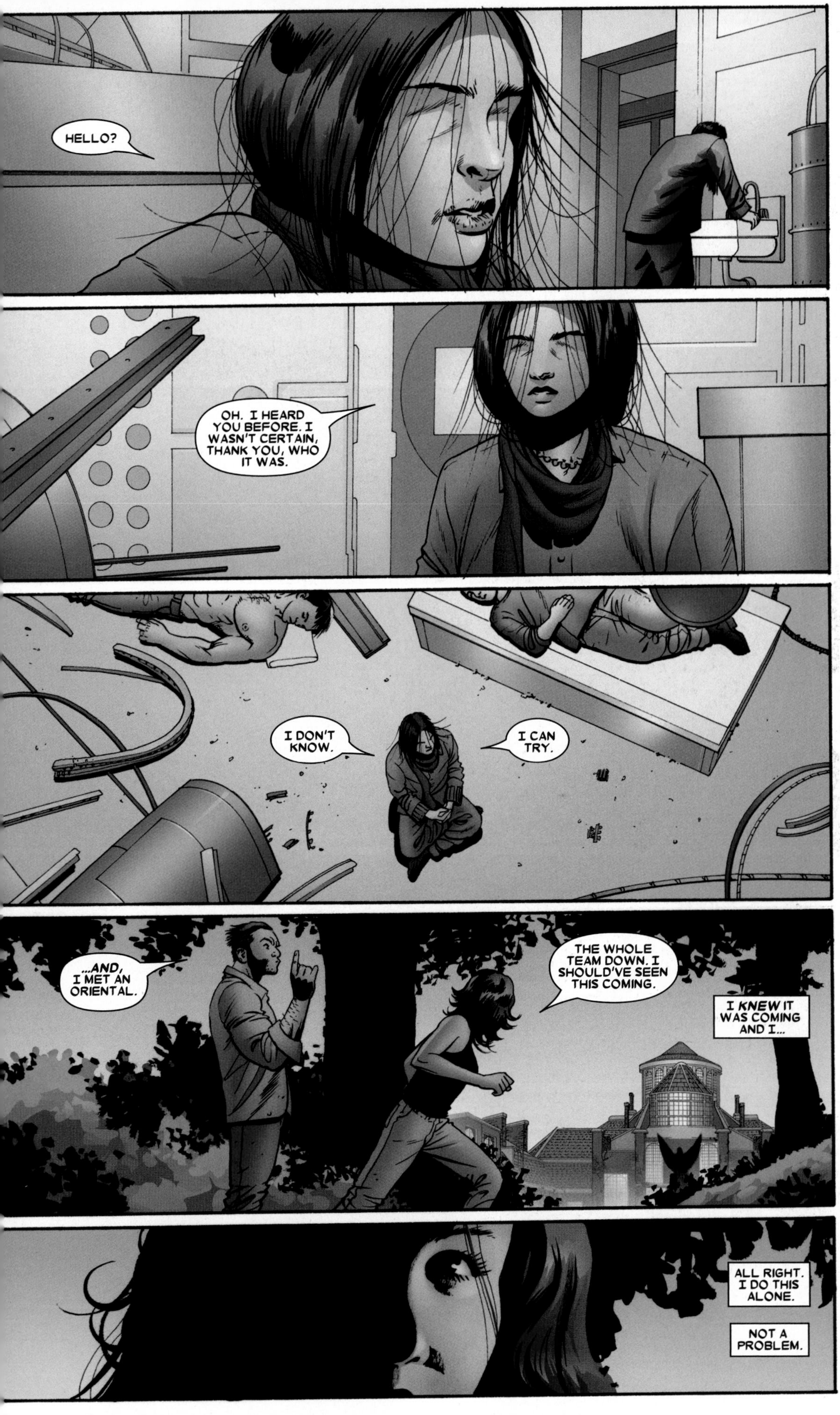

HELLO?
OH. I HEARD YOU BEFORE. I WASN'T CERTAIN, THANK YOU, WHO IT WAS.
I DON'T KNOW.
I CAN TRY.
...AND, I MET AN ORIENTAL.
THE WHOLE TEAM DOWN. I SHOULD'VE SEEN THIS COMING.
I *KNEW* IT WAS COMING AND I...
ALL RIGHT. I DO THIS ALONE.
NOT A PROBLEM.

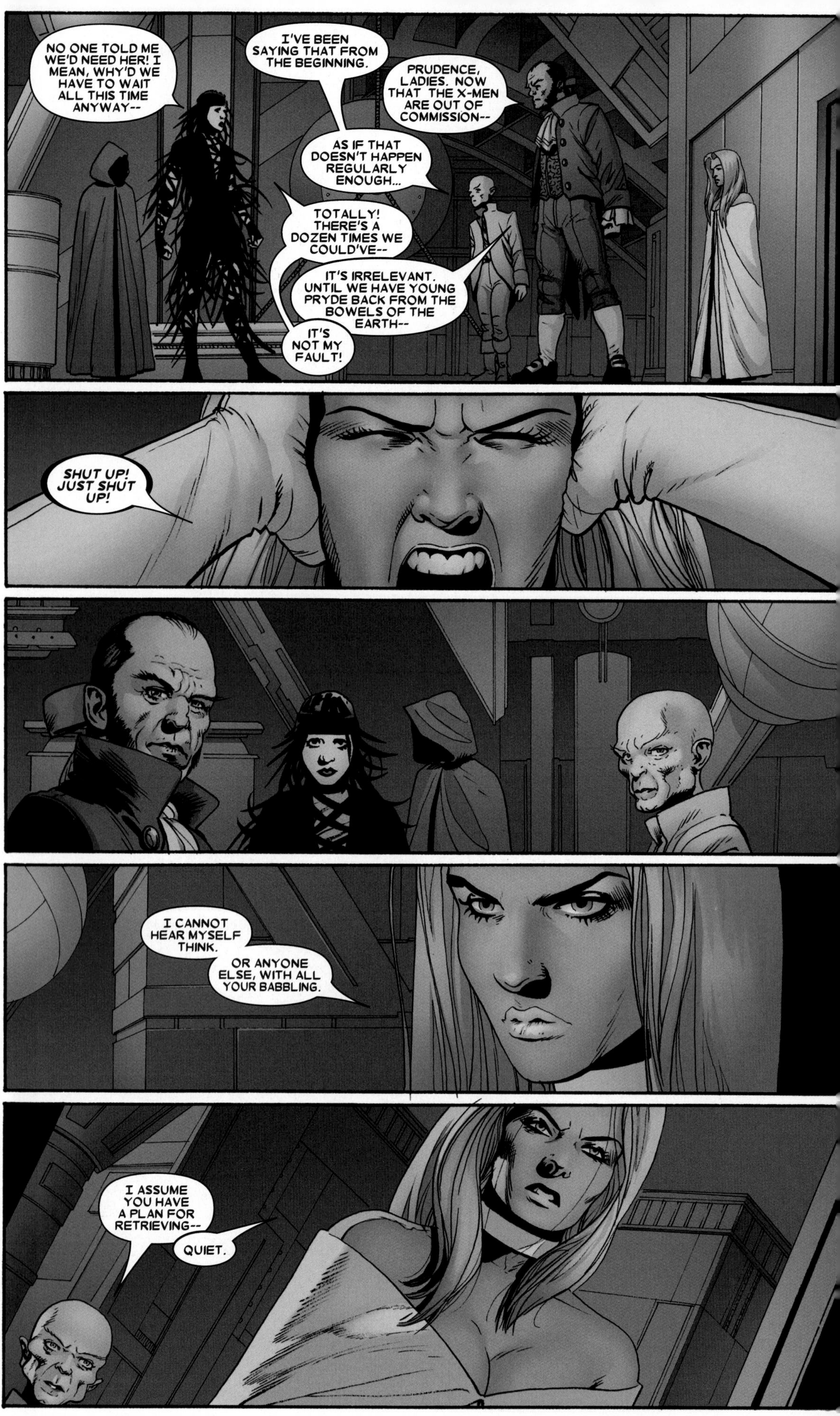
NO ONE TOLD ME WE'D NEED HER! I MEAN, WHY'D WE HAVE TO WAIT ALL THIS TIME ANYWAY--
I'VE BEEN SAYING THAT FROM THE BEGINNING.
PRUDENCE, LADIES. NOW THAT THE X-MEN ARE OUT OF COMMISSION--
AS IF THAT DOESN'T HAPPEN REGULARLY ENOUGH...
TOTALLY! THERE'S A DOZEN TIMES WE COULD'VE--
IT'S IRRELEVANT. UNTIL WE HAVE YOUNG PRYDE BACK FROM THE BOWELS OF THE EARTH--
IT'S NOT MY FAULT!
SHUT UP! JUST SHUT UP!
I CANNOT HEAR MYSELF THINK.
OR ANYONE ELSE, WITH ALL YOUR BABBLING.
I ASSUME YOU HAVE A PLAN FOR RETRIEVING--
QUIET.

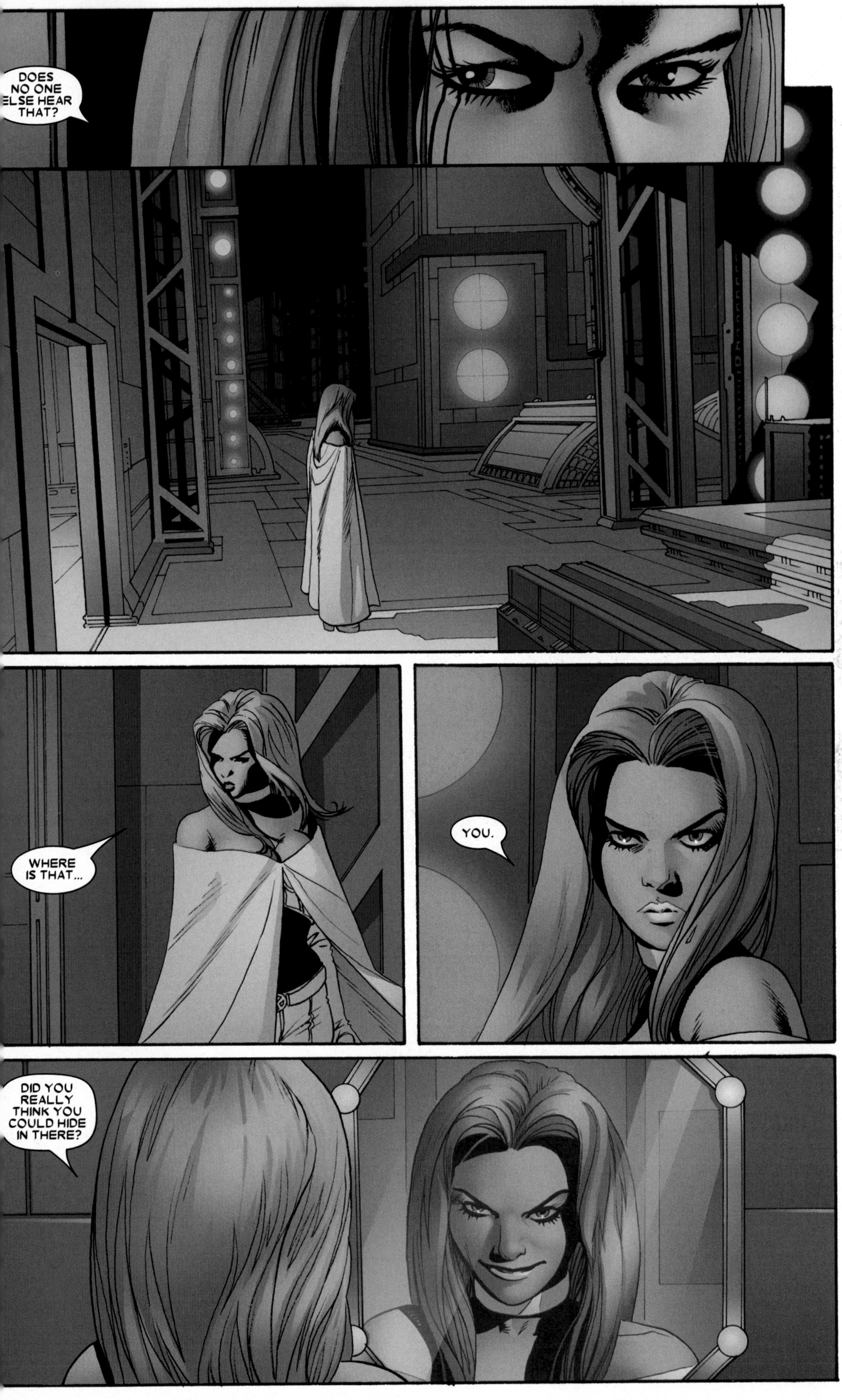
DOES NO ONE ELSE HEAR THAT?
WHERE IS THAT...
YOU.
DID YOU REALLY THINK YOU COULD HIDE IN THERE?

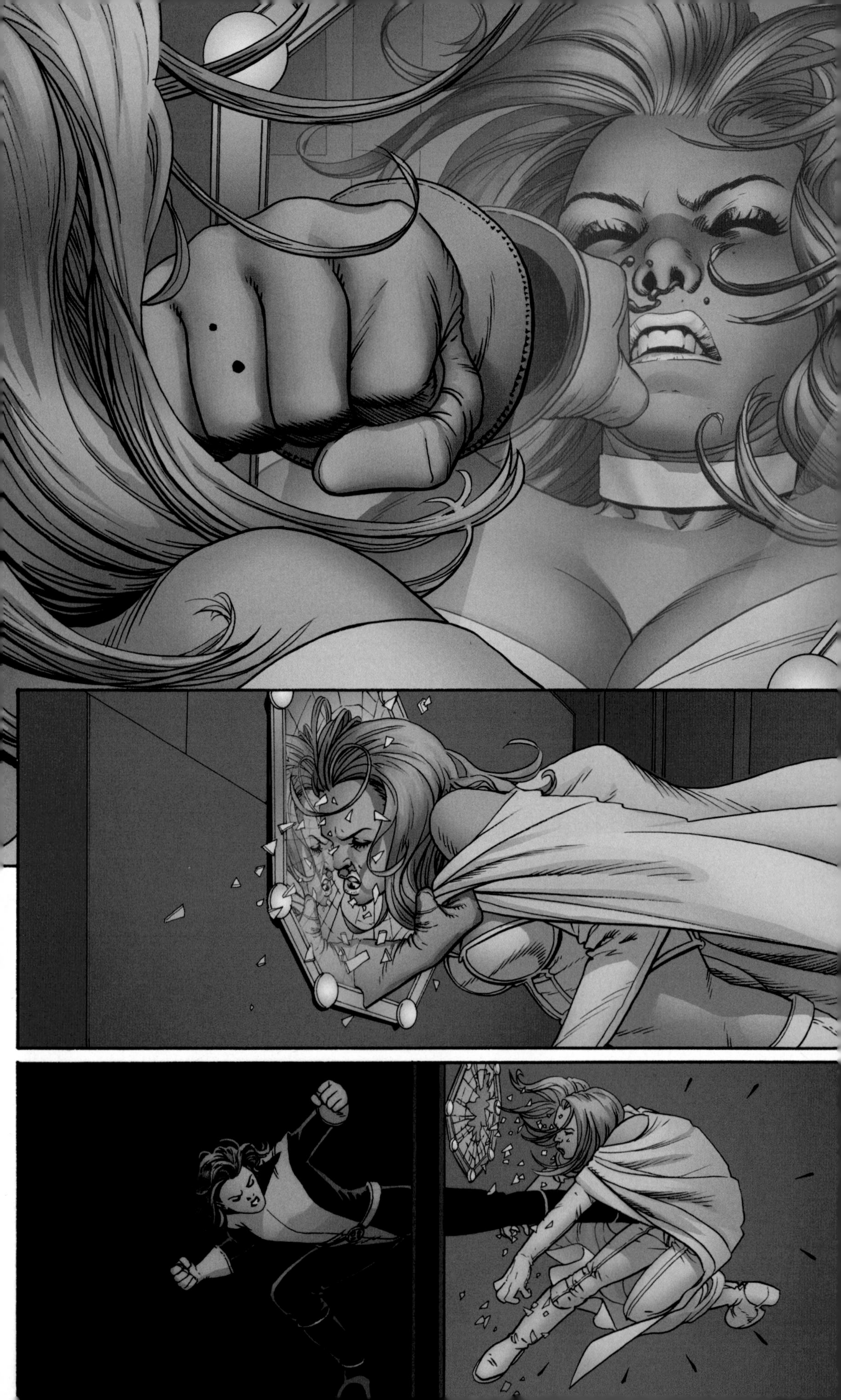

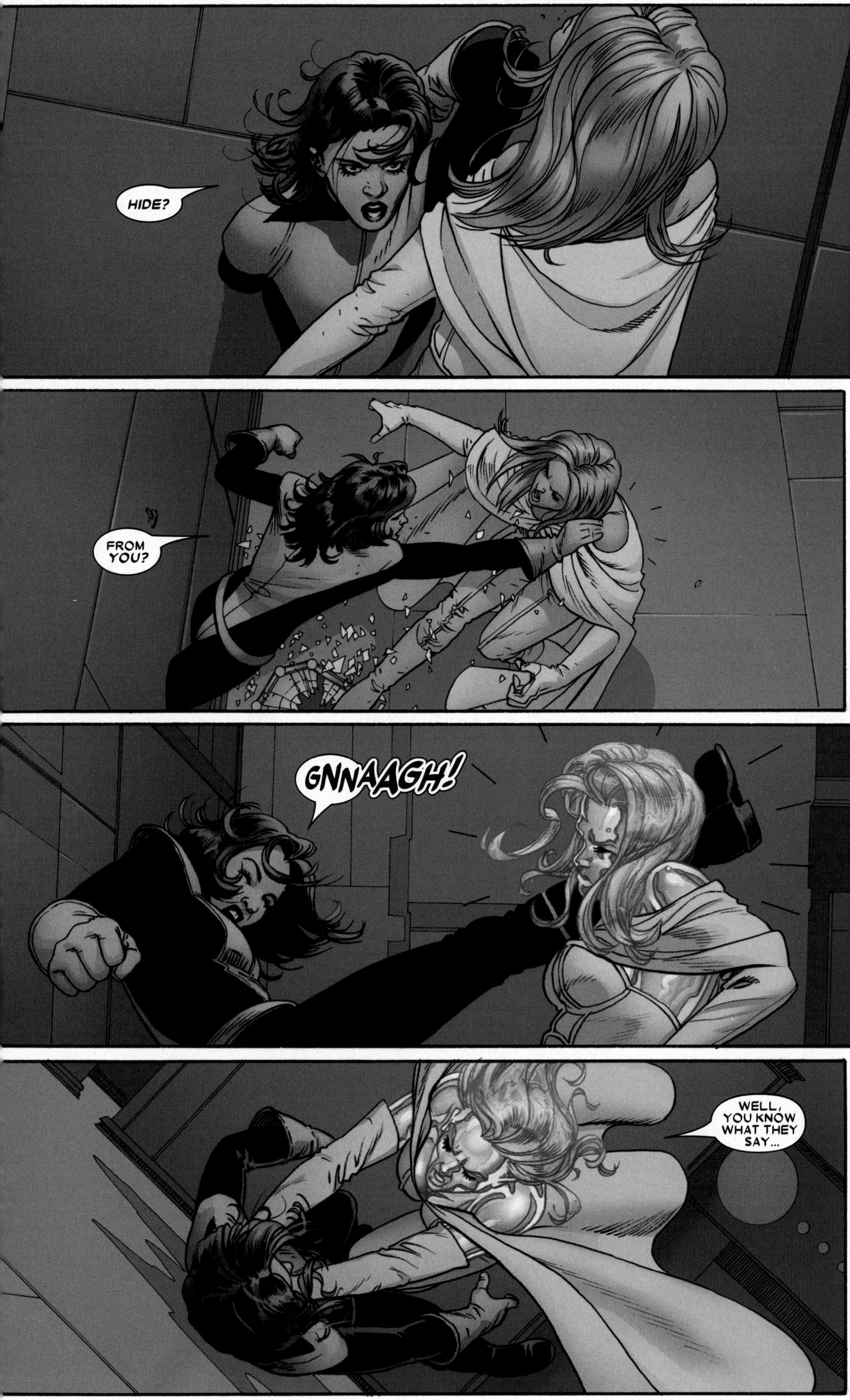
HIDE?
FROM YOU?
GNNAAGH!
WELL, YOU KNOW WHAT THEY SAY...

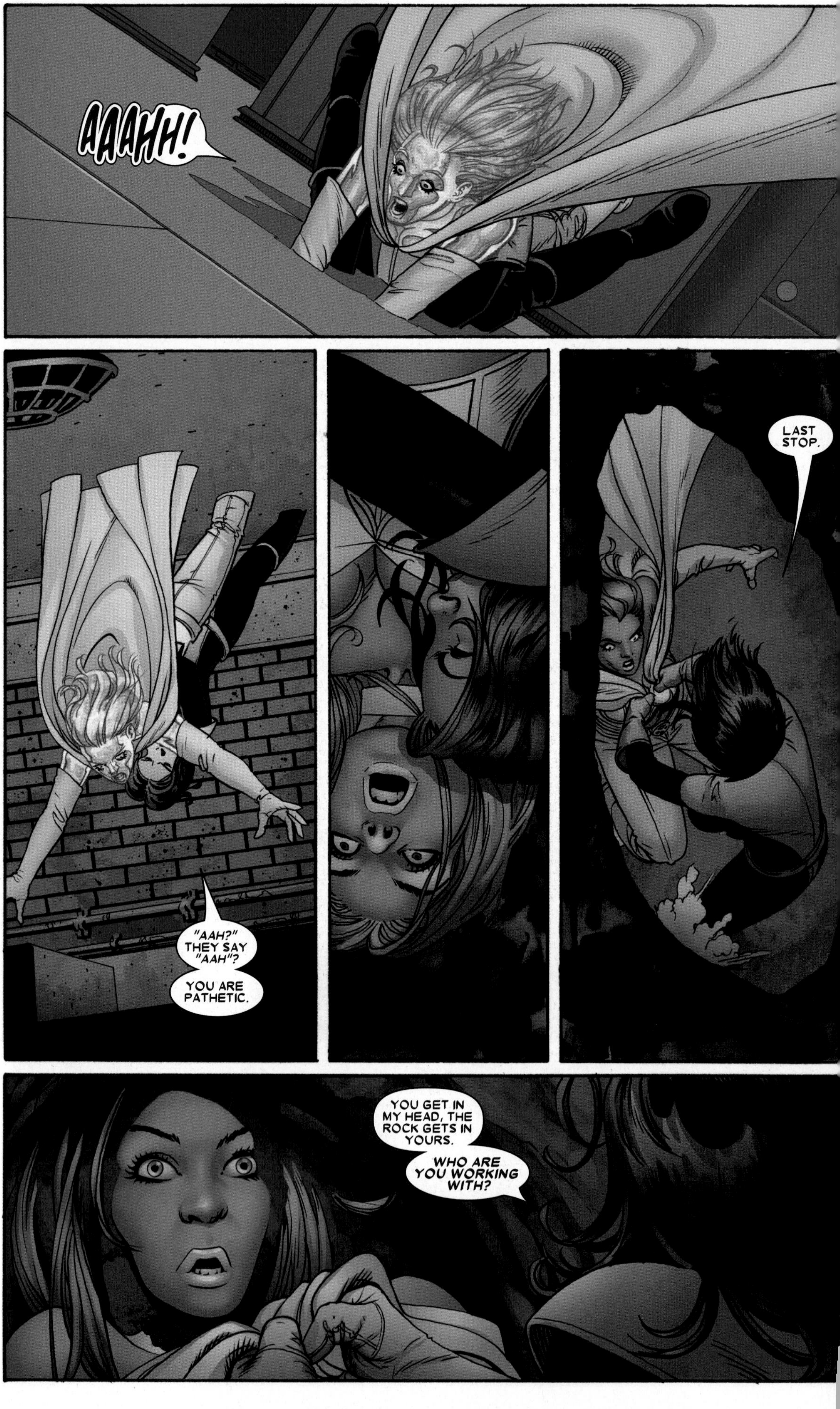
AAAHH!
LAST STOP.
"AAH?" THEY SAY "AAH"?
YOU ARE PATHETIC.
YOU GET IN MY HEAD, THE ROCK GETS IN YOURS.
WHO ARE YOU WORKING WITH?

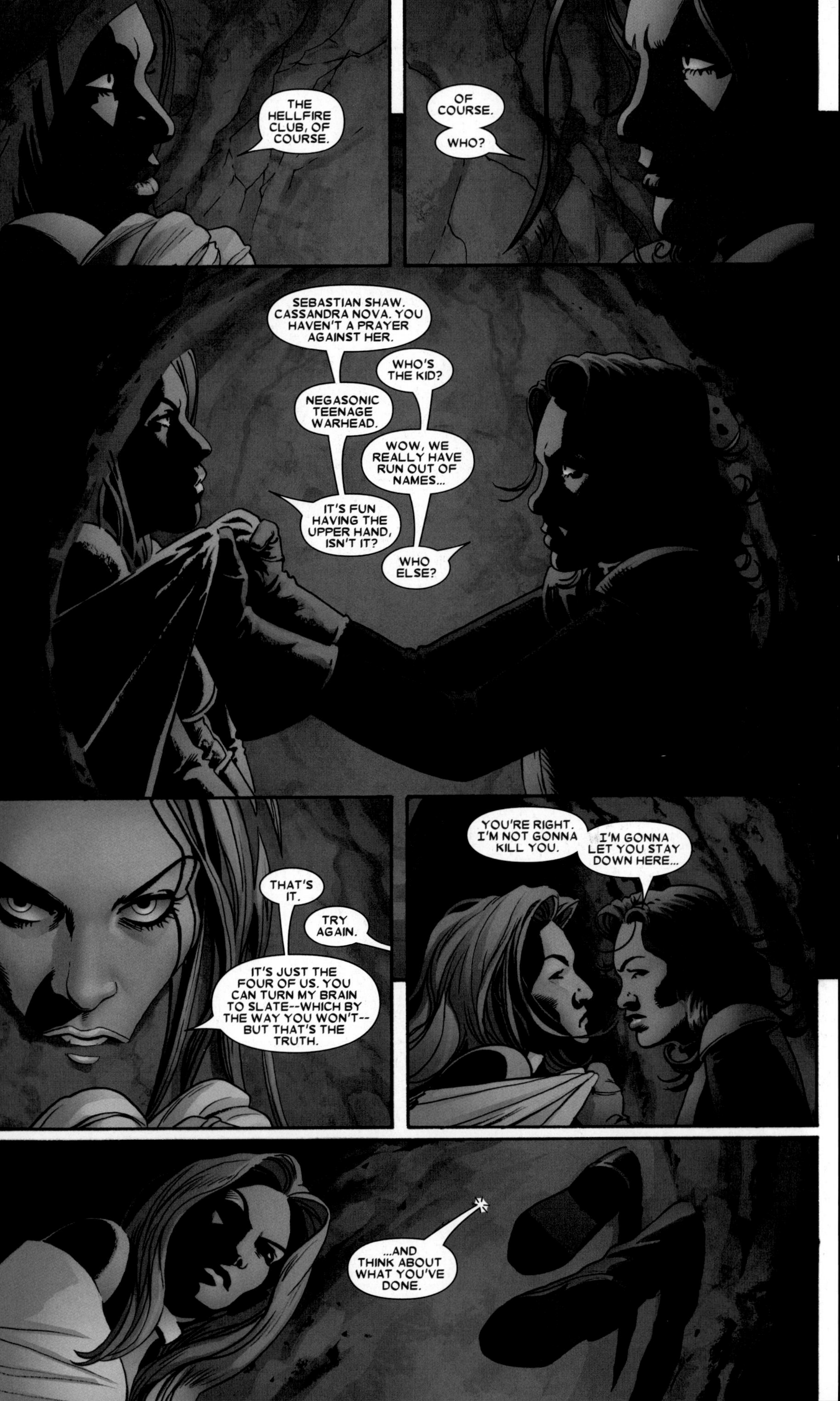
THE HELLFIRE CLUB, OF COURSE.
OF COURSE.
WHO?
SEBASTIAN SHAW. CASSANDRA NOVA. YOU HAVEN'T A PRAYER AGAINST HER.
WHO'S THE KID?
NEGASONIC TEENAGE WARHEAD.
WOW, WE REALLY HAVE RUN OUT OF NAMES...
IT'S FUN HAVING THE UPPER HAND, ISN'T IT?
WHO ELSE?
THAT'S IT.
TRY AGAIN.
IT'S JUST THE FOUR OF US. YOU CAN TURN MY BRAIN TO SLATE--WHICH BY THE WAY YOU WON'T--BUT THAT'S THE TRUTH.
YOU'RE RIGHT. I'M NOT GONNA KILL YOU.
I'M GONNA LET YOU STAY DOWN HERE...
...AND THINK ABOUT WHAT YOU'VE DONE.

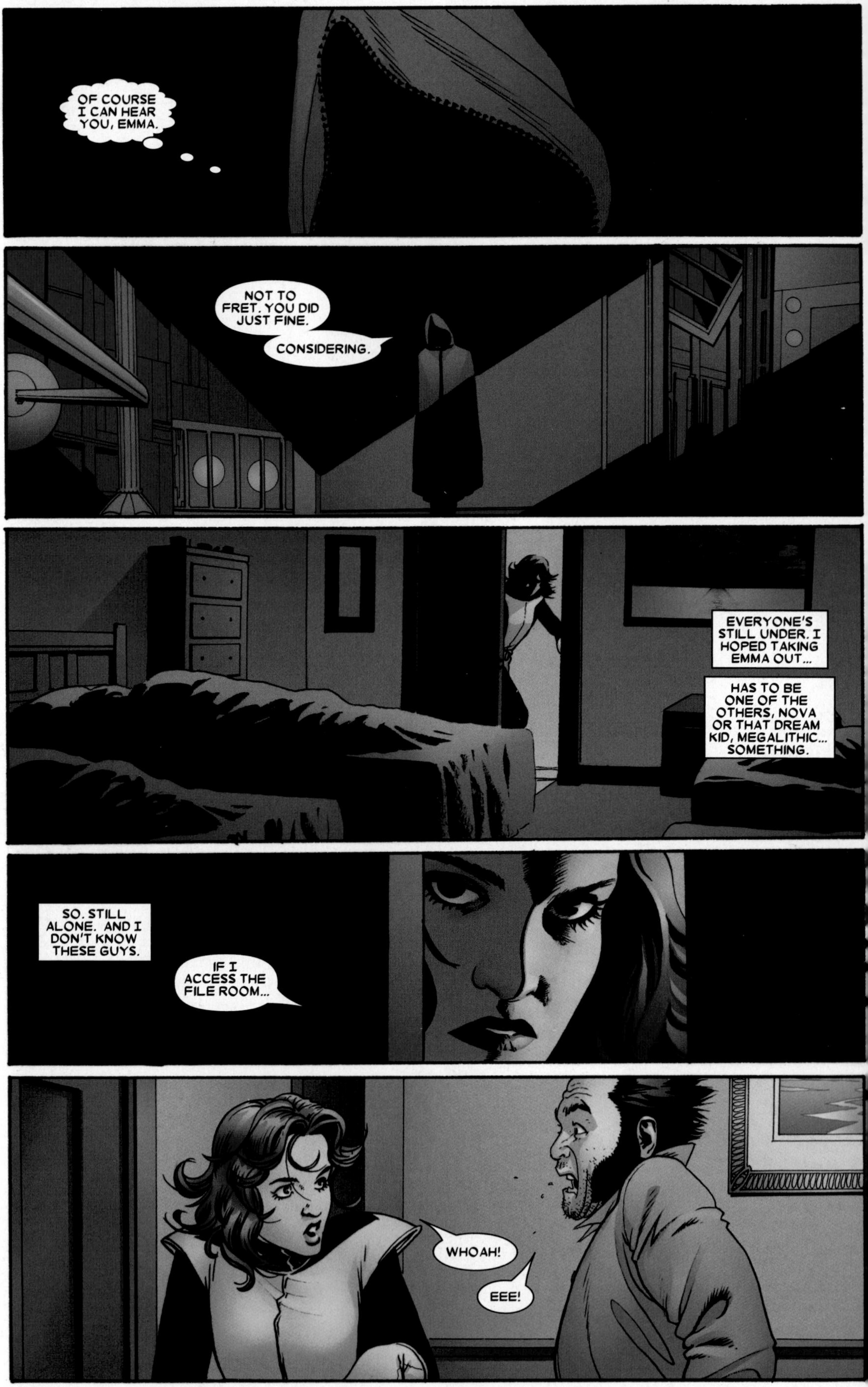
OF COURSE I CAN HEAR YOU, EMMA.
NOT TO FRET. YOU DID JUST FINE.
CONSIDERING.
EVERYONE'S STILL UNDER. I HOPED TAKING EMMA OUT...
HAS TO BE ONE OF THE OTHERS, NOVA OR THAT DREAM KID, MEGALITHIC... SOMETHING.
SO. STILL ALONE. AND I DON'T KNOW THESE GUYS.
IF I ACCESS THE FILE ROOM...
WHOAH!
EEE!

WHAT ARE YOU DOING HERE? I TOLD YOU TO HIDE.

WELL, I... YOU'RE A GIRL, AND IF THERE'S DANGER ABOUT, I...WELL IT ISN'T RIGHT FOR A HOWLETT TO HIDE BEHIND SOMEONE'S SKIRTS.

I SHAN'T PRIZE MY LIFE ABOVE MY HONOR.

UNLESS YOU THINK THAT'S A GOOD IDEA.

AAAGH!

IT'S TIME, PRYDE.

AT LONG LAST, IT'S TIME TO MAKE YOURSELF USEFUL.

FORGET WHAT YOU'RE THINKING. EMMA FROST MAY HAVE BEEN EASY-- EMBARRASSINGLY EASY--TO TAKE OUT...

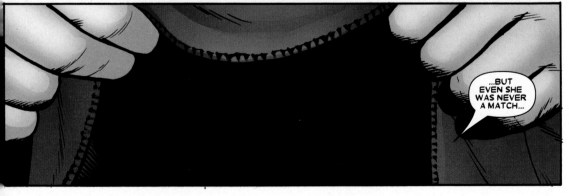

...BUT EVEN SHE WAS NEVER A MATCH...

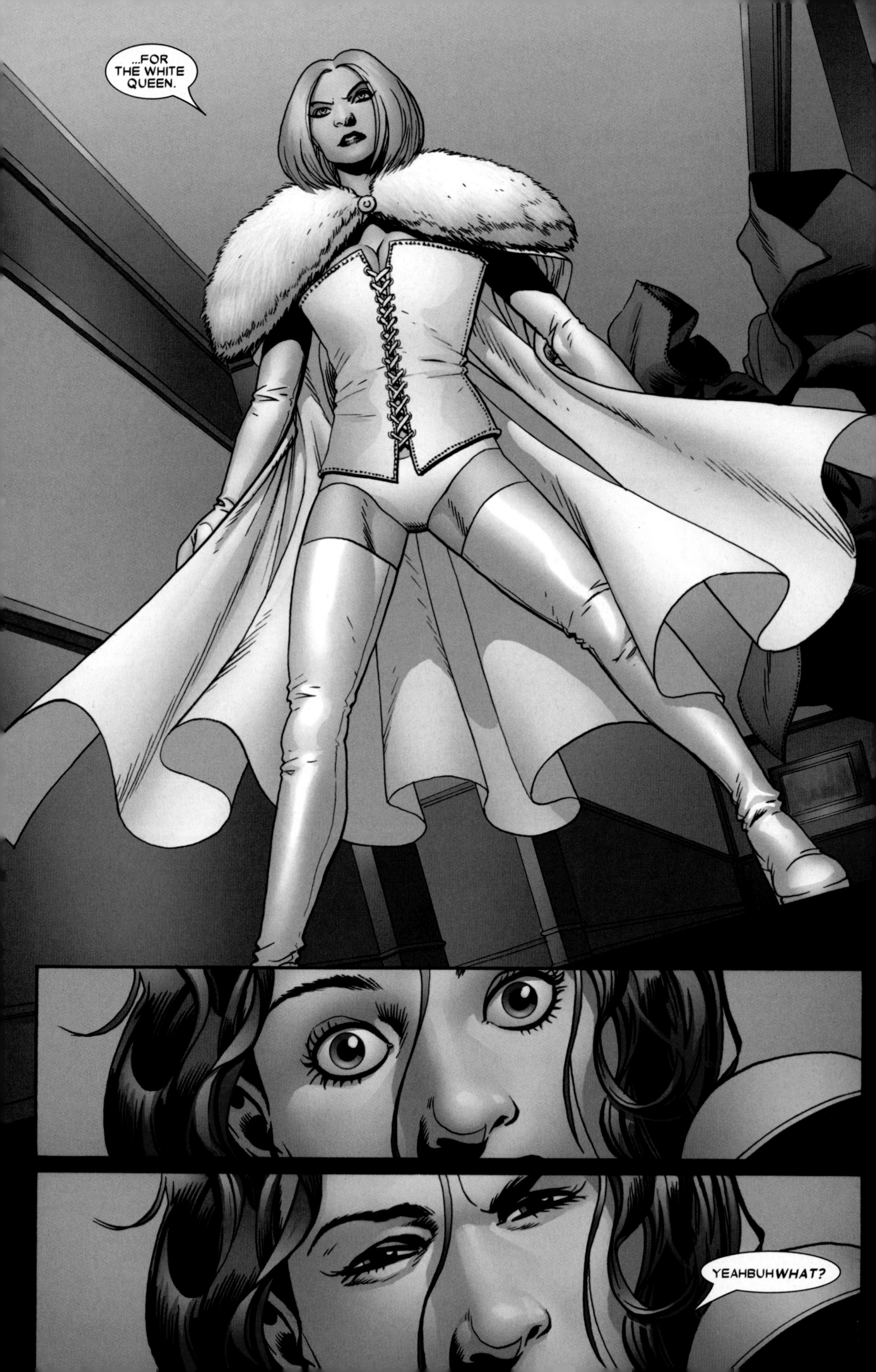
...FOR THE WHITE QUEEN.
YEAHBUH*WHAT?*

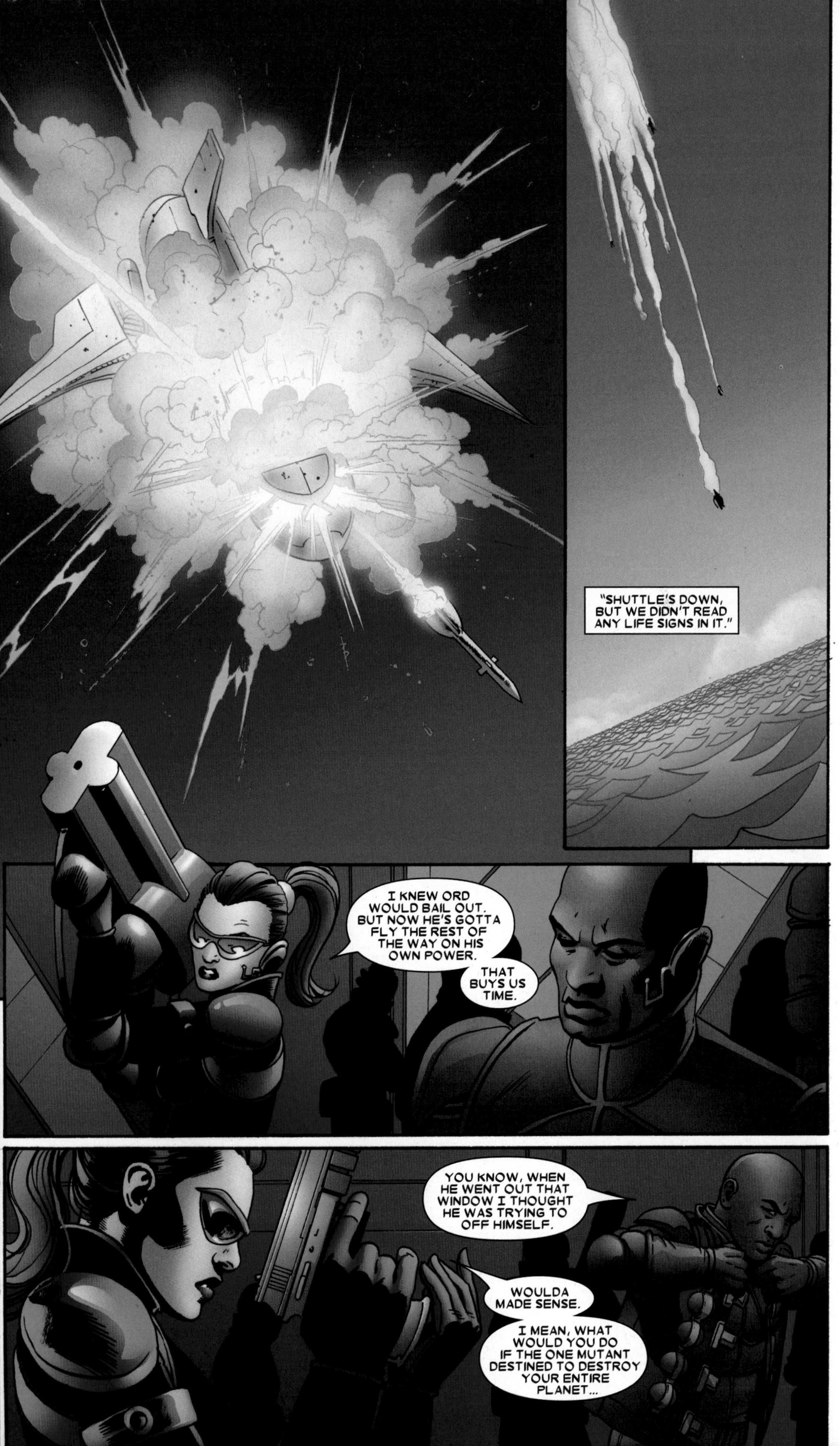
"SHUTTLE'S DOWN, BUT WE DIDN'T READ ANY LIFE SIGNS IN IT."
I KNEW ORD WOULD BAIL OUT. BUT NOW HE'S GOTTA FLY THE REST OF THE WAY ON HIS OWN POWER.
THAT BUYS US TIME.
YOU KNOW, WHEN HE WENT OUT THAT WINDOW I THOUGHT HE WAS TRYING TO OFF HIMSELF.
WOULDA MADE SENSE.
I MEAN, WHAT WOULD YOU DO IF THE ONE MUTANT DESTINED TO DESTROY YOUR ENTIRE PLANET...

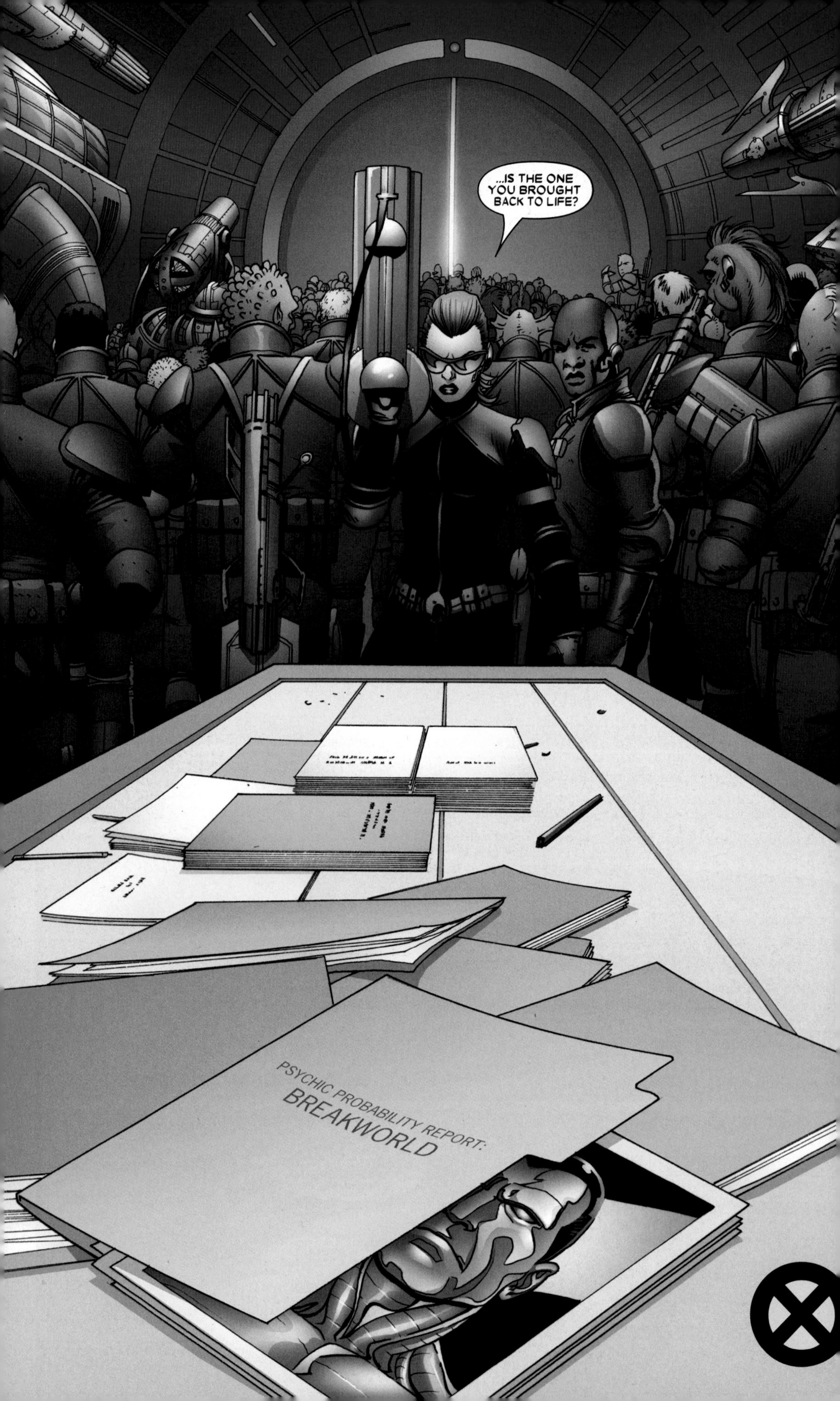
...IS THE ONE YOU BROUGHT BACK TO LIFE?
PSYCHIC PROBABILITY REPORT:
BREAKWORLD

ASTONISHING X-MEN

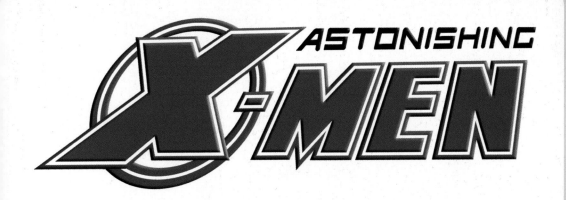

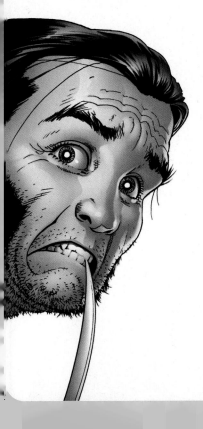

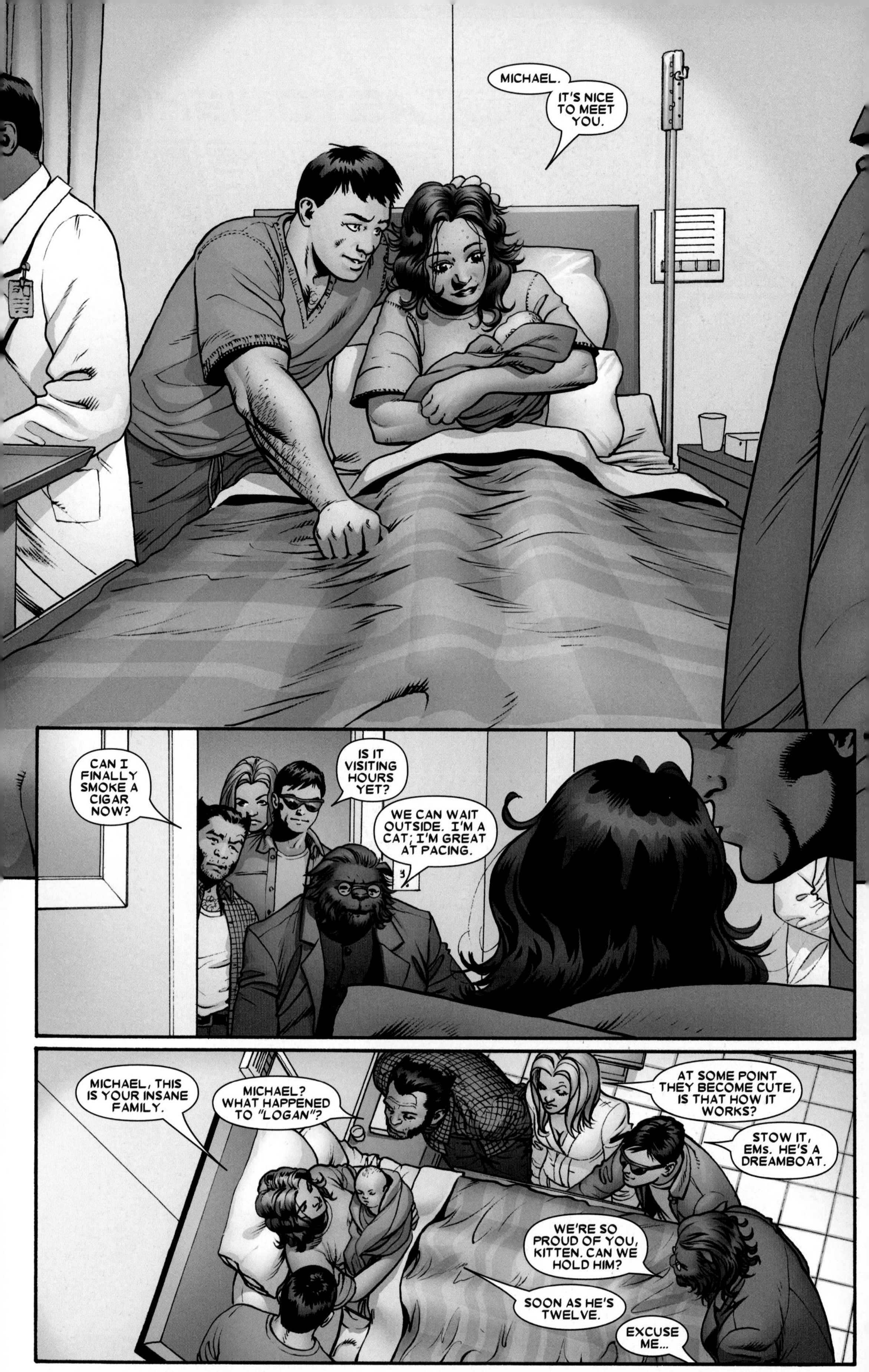

MICHAEL.
IT'S NICE TO MEET YOU.
CAN I FINALLY SMOKE A CIGAR NOW?
IS IT VISITING HOURS YET?
WE CAN WAIT OUTSIDE. I'M A CAT; I'M GREAT AT PACING.
MICHAEL, THIS IS YOUR INSANE FAMILY.
MICHAEL? WHAT HAPPENED TO "LOGAN"?
AT SOME POINT THEY BECOME CUTE, IS THAT HOW IT WORKS?
STOW IT, EMS. HE'S A DREAMBOAT.
WE'RE SO PROUD OF YOU, KITTEN. CAN WE HOLD HIM?
SOON AS HE'S TWELVE.
EXCUSE ME...

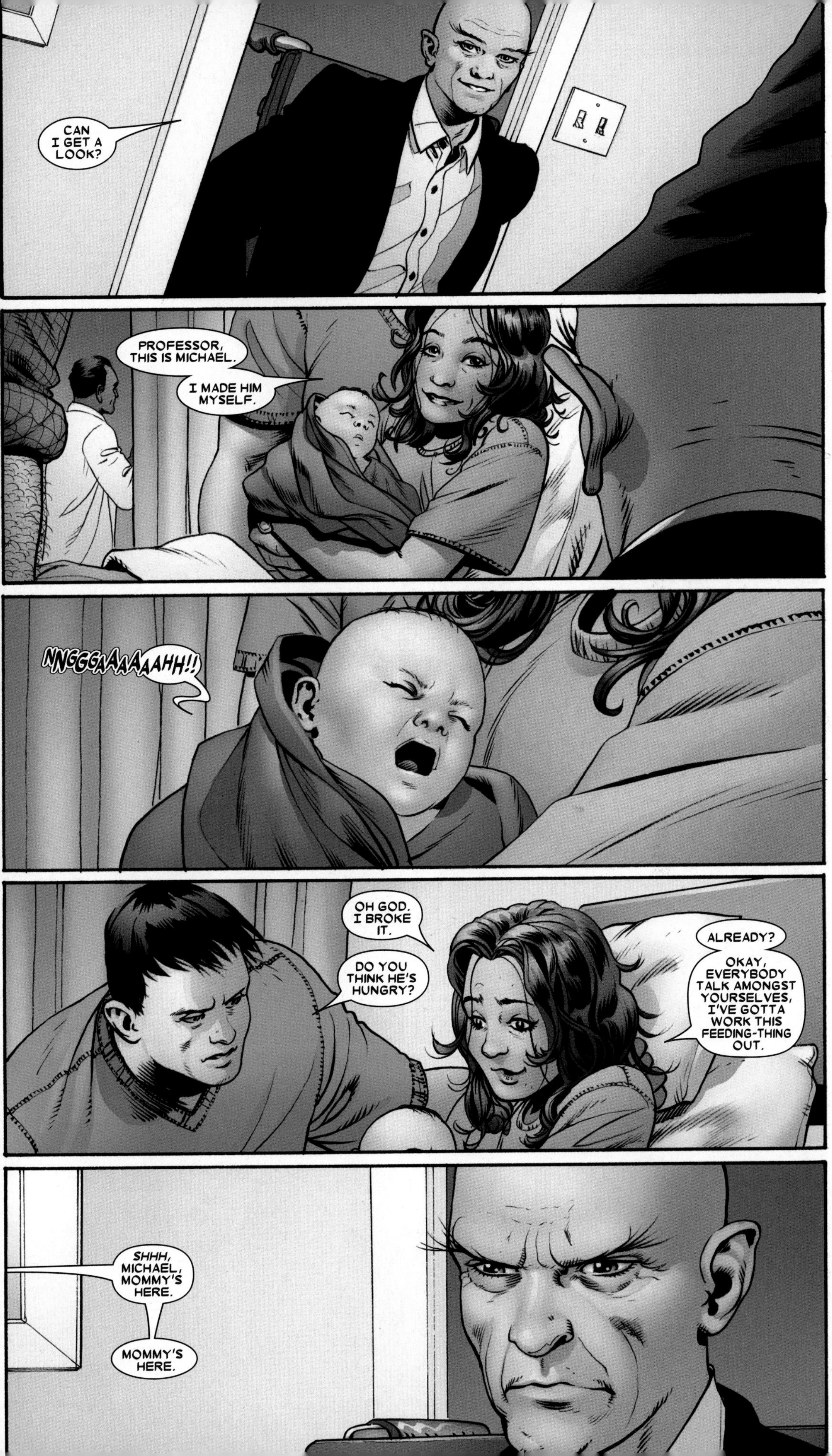
CAN I GET A LOOK?
PROFESSOR, THIS IS MICHAEL.
I MADE HIM MYSELF.
NNGGGAAAAAHH!!
OH GOD. I BROKE IT.
DO YOU THINK HE'S HUNGRY?
ALREADY?
OKAY, EVERYBODY TALK AMONGST YOURSELVES, I'VE GOTTA WORK THIS FEEDING-THING OUT.
SHHH, MICHAEL, MOMMY'S HERE.
MOMMY'S HERE.

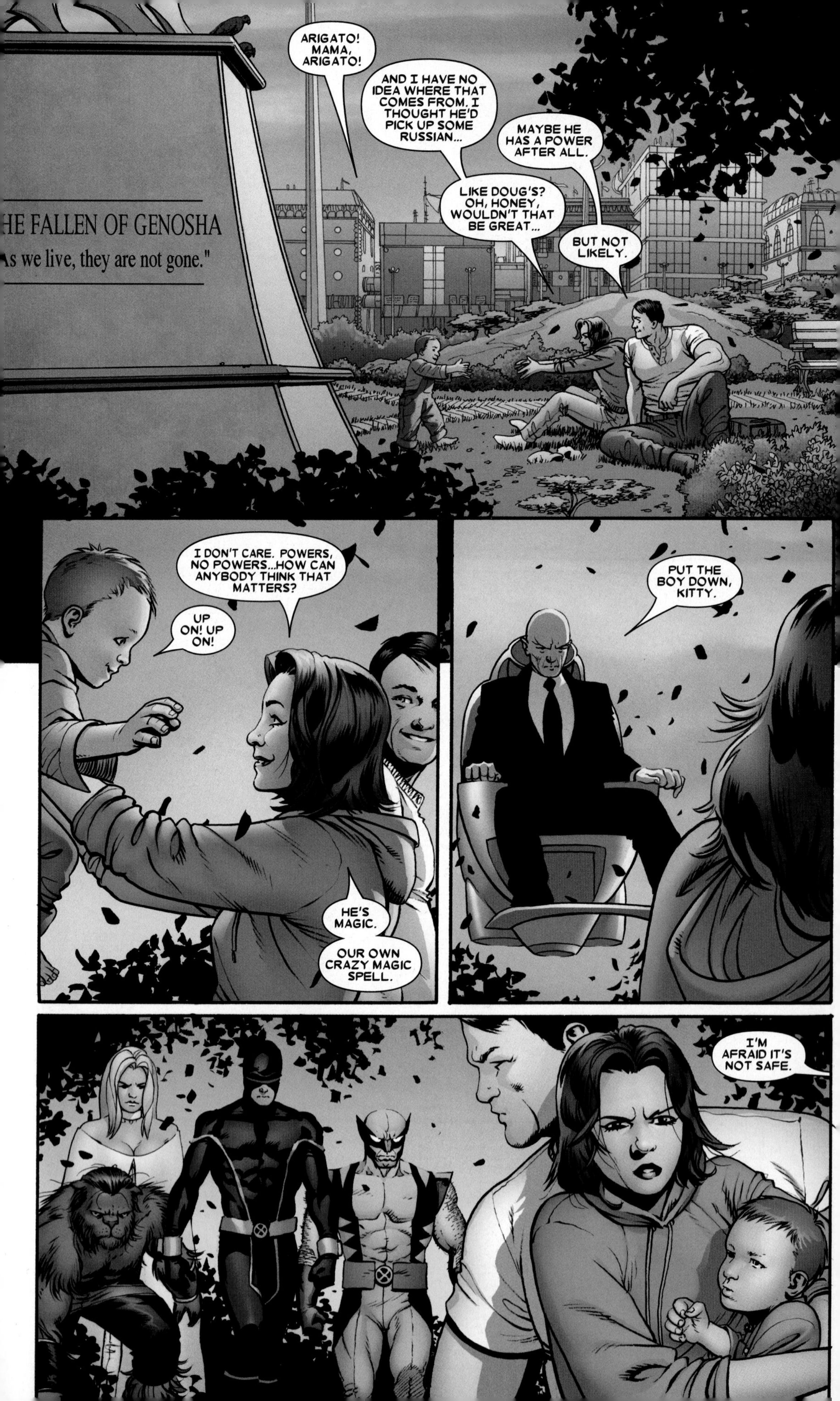

HE FALLEN OF GENOSHA
As we live, they are not gone."
ARIGATO! MAMA, ARIGATO!
AND I HAVE NO IDEA WHERE THAT COMES FROM. I THOUGHT HE'D PICK UP SOME RUSSIAN...
MAYBE HE HAS A POWER AFTER ALL.
LIKE DOUG'S? OH, HONEY, WOULDN'T THAT BE GREAT...
BUT NOT LIKELY.
I DON'T CARE. POWERS, NO POWERS...HOW CAN ANYBODY THINK THAT MATTERS?
UP ON! UP ON!
HE'S MAGIC.
OUR OWN CRAZY MAGIC SPELL.
PUT THE BOY DOWN, KITTY.
I'M AFRAID IT'S NOT SAFE.

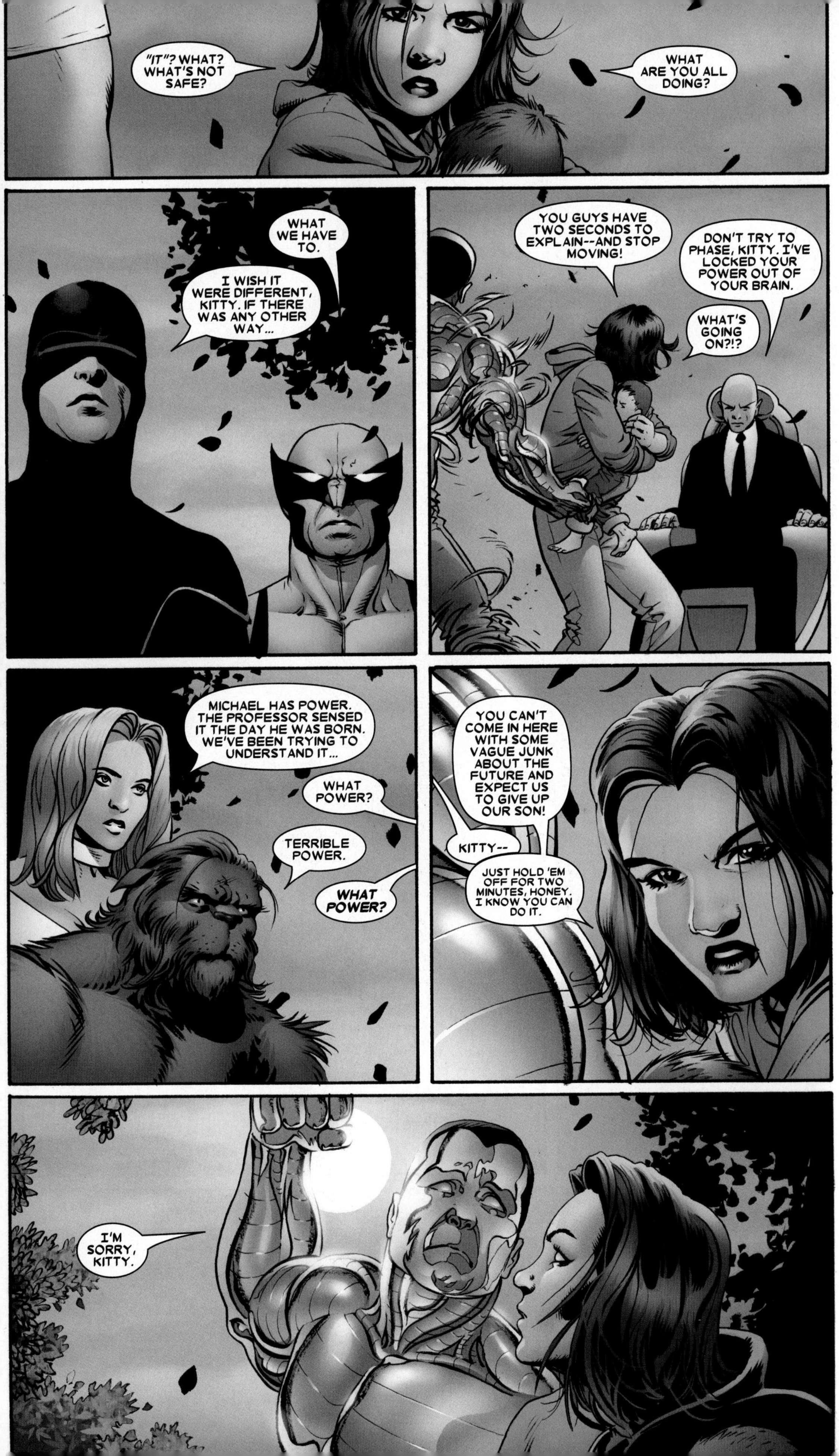
"IT"? WHAT? WHAT'S NOT SAFE?
WHAT ARE YOU ALL DOING?
WHAT WE HAVE TO.
I WISH IT WERE DIFFERENT, KITTY. IF THERE WAS ANY OTHER WAY...
YOU GUYS HAVE TWO SECONDS TO EXPLAIN--AND STOP MOVING!
DON'T TRY TO PHASE, KITTY. I'VE LOCKED YOUR POWER OUT OF YOUR BRAIN.
WHAT'S GOING ON?!?
MICHAEL HAS POWER. THE PROFESSOR SENSED IT THE DAY HE WAS BORN. WE'VE BEEN TRYING TO UNDERSTAND IT...
WHAT POWER?
TERRIBLE POWER.
WHAT POWER?
YOU CAN'T COME IN HERE WITH SOME VAGUE JUNK ABOUT THE FUTURE AND EXPECT US TO GIVE UP OUR SON!
KITTY--
JUST HOLD 'EM OFF FOR TWO MINUTES, HONEY. I KNOW YOU CAN DO IT.
I'M SORRY, KITTY.

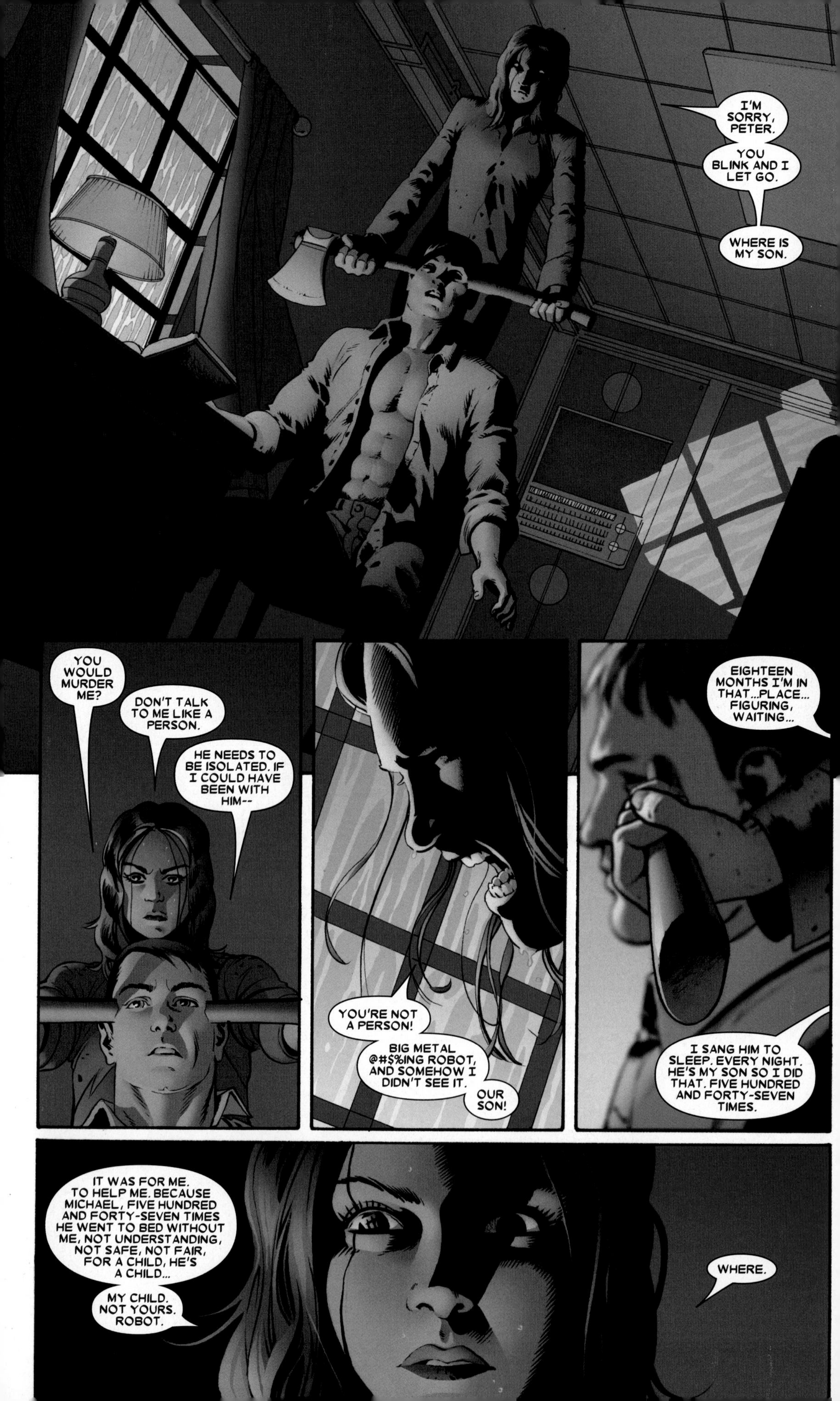

I'M SORRY, PETER.
YOU BLINK AND I LET GO.
WHERE IS MY SON.
YOU WOULD MURDER ME?
DON'T TALK TO ME LIKE A PERSON.
HE NEEDS TO BE ISOLATED. IF I COULD HAVE BEEN WITH HIM--
YOU'RE NOT A PERSON!
BIG METAL @#$%ING ROBOT, AND SOMEHOW I DIDN'T SEE IT.
OUR SON!
EIGHTEEN MONTHS I'M IN THAT...PLACE... FIGURING, WAITING...
I SANG HIM TO SLEEP. EVERY NIGHT. HE'S MY SON SO I DID THAT. FIVE HUNDRED AND FORTY-SEVEN TIMES.
IT WAS FOR ME. TO HELP ME. BECAUSE MICHAEL, FIVE HUNDRED AND FORTY-SEVEN TIMES HE WENT TO BED WITHOUT ME, NOT UNDERSTANDING, NOT SAFE, NOT FAIR, FOR A CHILD, HE'S A CHILD...
MY CHILD. NOT YOURS. ROBOT.
WHERE.

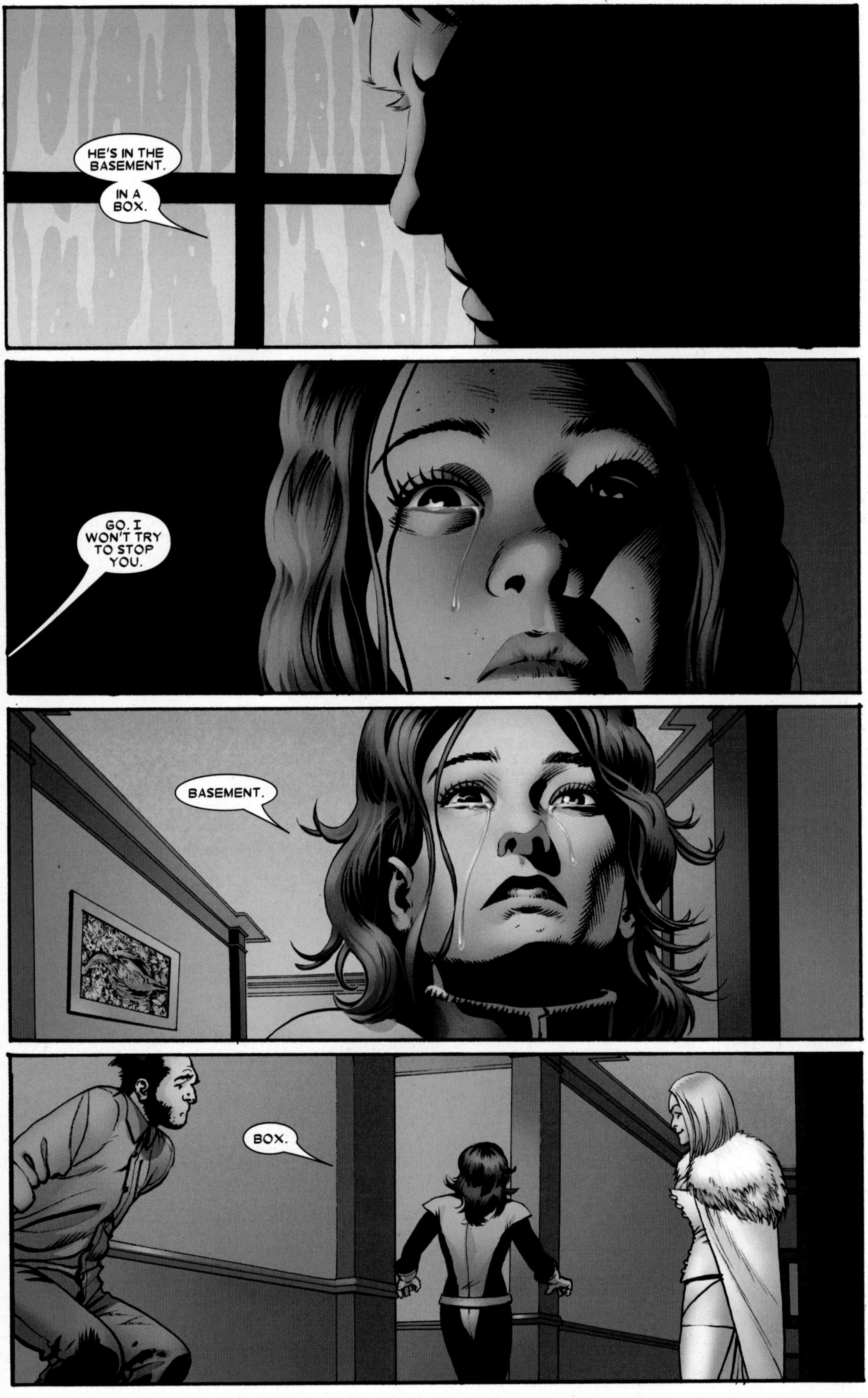
HE'S IN THE BASEMENT.
IN A BOX.
GO. I WON'T TRY TO STOP YOU.
BASEMENT.
BOX.

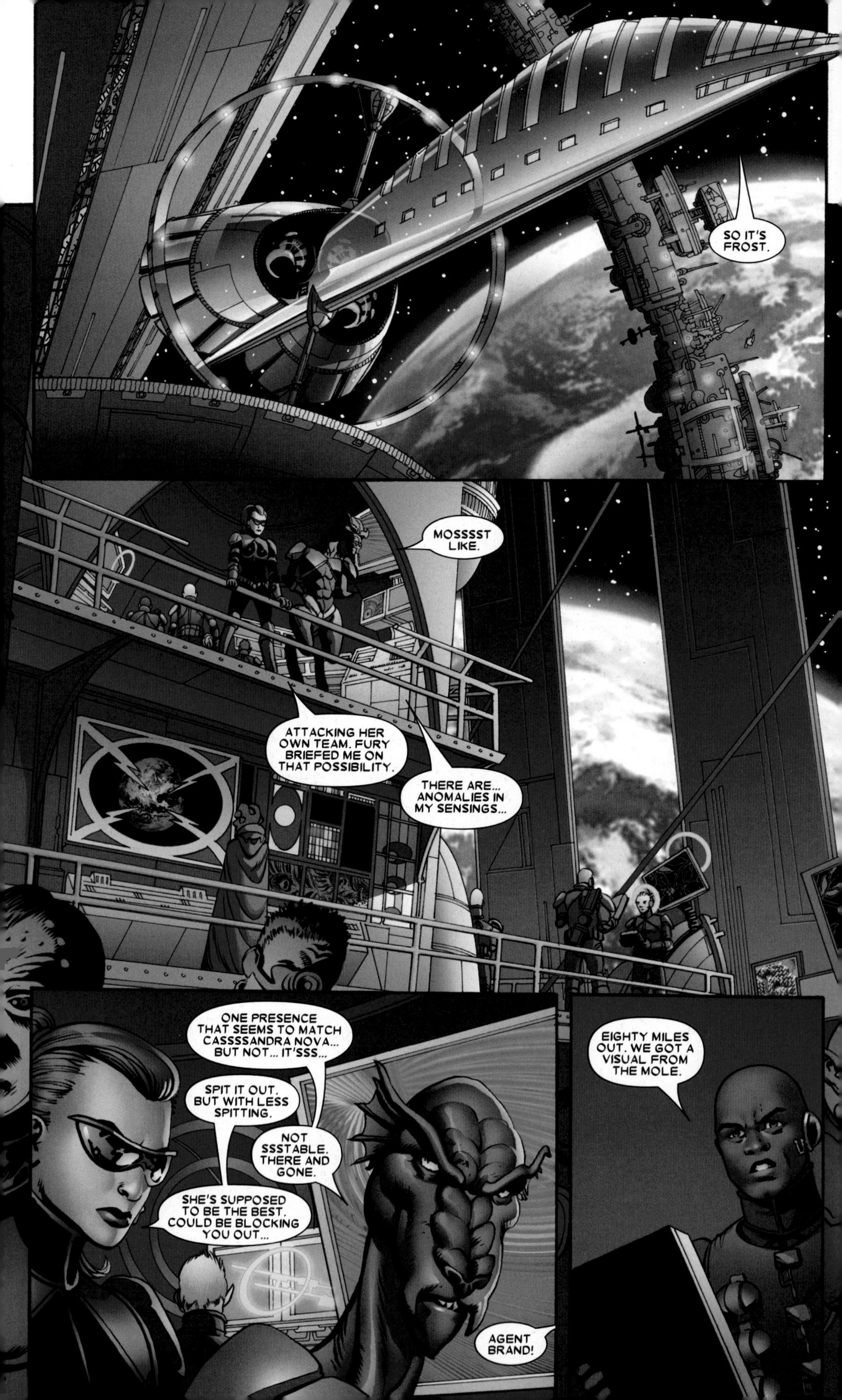
SO IT'S FROST.
MOSSSST LIKE.
ATTACKING HER OWN TEAM. FURY BRIEFED ME ON THAT POSSIBILITY.
THERE ARE... ANOMALIES IN MY SENSINGS...
ONE PRESENCE THAT SEEMS TO MATCH CASSSSANDRA NOVA... BUT NOT... IT'SSS...
SPIT IT OUT. BUT WITH LESS SPITTING.
NOT SSSTABLE. THERE AND GONE.
SHE'S SUPPOSED TO BE THE BEST. COULD BE BLOCKING YOU OUT...
AGENT BRAND!
EIGHTY MILES OUT. WE GOT A VISUAL FROM THE MOLE.

SO. WHO'S THE TINKER-TOY?

"DANGER." SHE'S A.I., SHI'AR TECH.

@#$%ING SHI'AR... WISH SOMEONE WOULD PROPHESY THE END OF *THOSE* CLOWNS...

WE THINK SHE'S RESPONSIBLE FOR THAT LAST ASS-WHUPPING THIS X-TEAM TOOK. THE WILD SENTINEL INCIDENT...

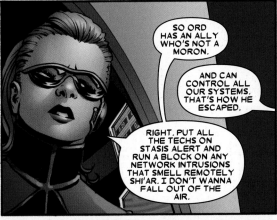

SO ORD HAS AN ALLY WHO'S NOT A MORON.

AND CAN CONTROL ALL OUR SYSTEMS. THAT'S HOW HE ESCAPED.

RIGHT. PUT ALL THE TECHS ON STASIS ALERT AND RUN A BLOCK ON ANY NETWORK INTRUSIONS THAT SMELL REMOTELY SHI'AR. I DON'T WANNA FALL OUT OF THE AIR.

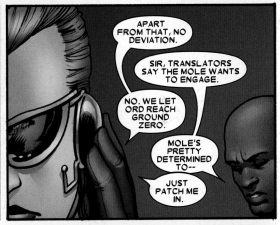

APART FROM THAT, NO DEVIATION.

SIR, TRANSLATORS SAY THE MOLE WANTS TO ENGAGE.

NO. WE LET ORD REACH GROUND ZERO.

MOLE'S PRETTY DETERMINED TO--

JUST PATCH ME IN.

ᛁᛋᛗᚦ ᚱᛒᛖᛚᚠᚷ ᛖᛗᛖᛉᚦᛖᛁᛟ ᛖᛃᛖᛉᛖᚦᛟᛉᛉᚫᚦ ᛖᛁᛋᛟᚲᚲᛋᚲ ᛖᚲᚺᛖᛉ

ᚷᛖᚫᛐ ᛁᛟᛚᚫᚷᛐᛁ ᛗᛉᚧᛐᚷ

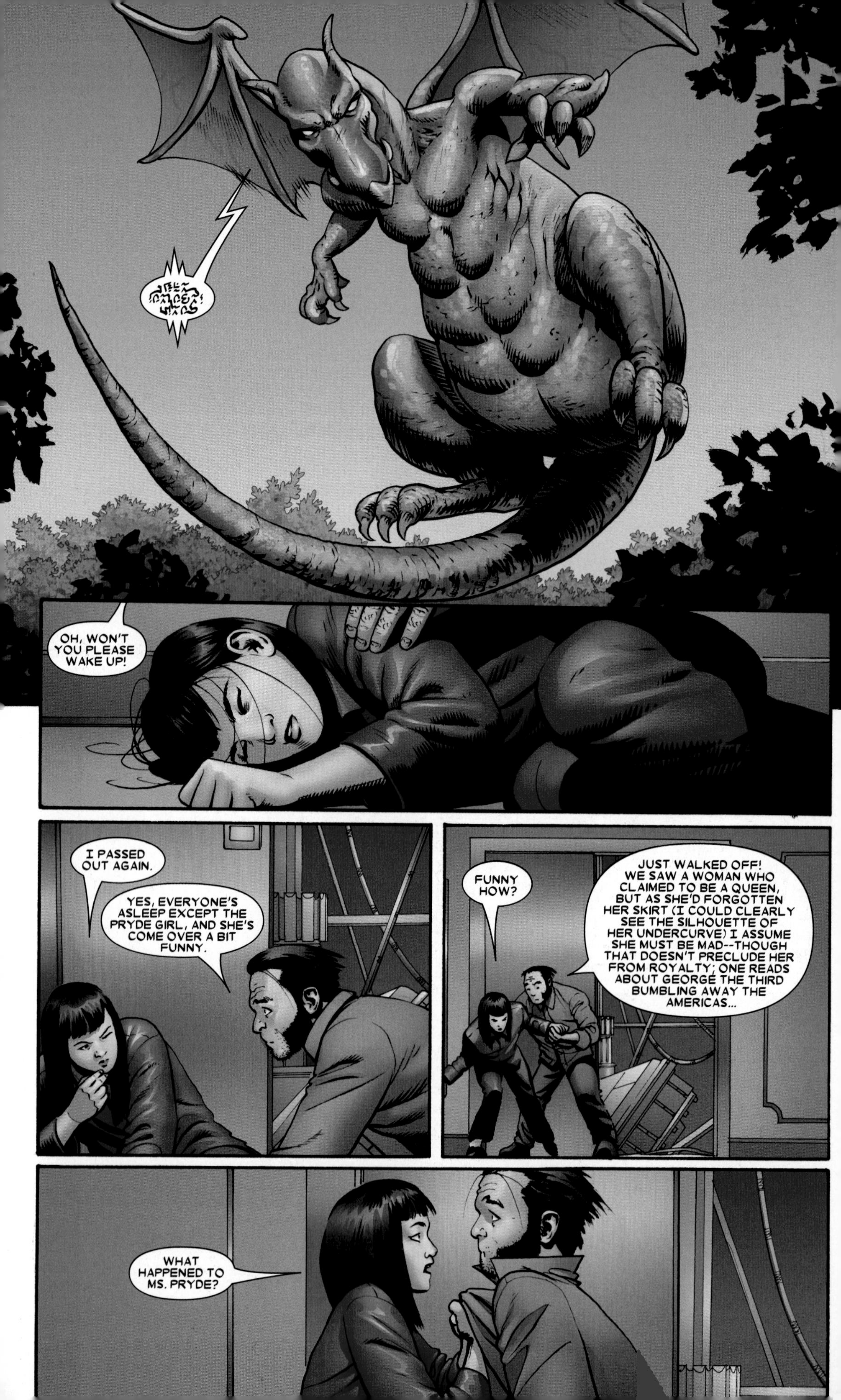

OH, WON'T YOU PLEASE WAKE UP!
I PASSED OUT AGAIN.
YES, EVERYONE'S ASLEEP EXCEPT THE PRYDE GIRL, AND SHE'S COME OVER A BIT FUNNY.
FUNNY HOW?
JUST WALKED OFF! WE SAW A WOMAN WHO CLAIMED TO BE A QUEEN, BUT AS SHE'D FORGOTTEN HER SKIRT (I COULD CLEARLY SEE THE SILHOUETTE OF HER UNDERCURVE) I ASSUME SHE MUST BE MAD--THOUGH THAT DOESN'T PRECLUDE HER FROM ROYALTY; ONE READS ABOUT GEORGE THE THIRD BUMBLING AWAY THE AMERICAS...
WHAT HAPPENED TO MS. PRYDE?

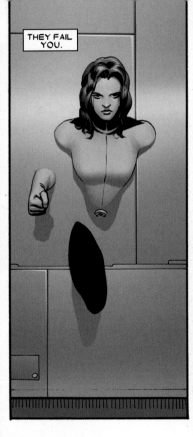

THEY FAIL YOU.

THEY LEAVE YOU OR THEY LET YOU DOWN.

THEY DIE.

OR WORSE.

THE ONLY MAN IN THIS WORLD THAT I WILL EVER TRULY TRUST...

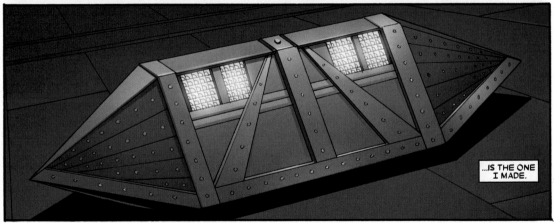

...IS THE ONE I MADE.

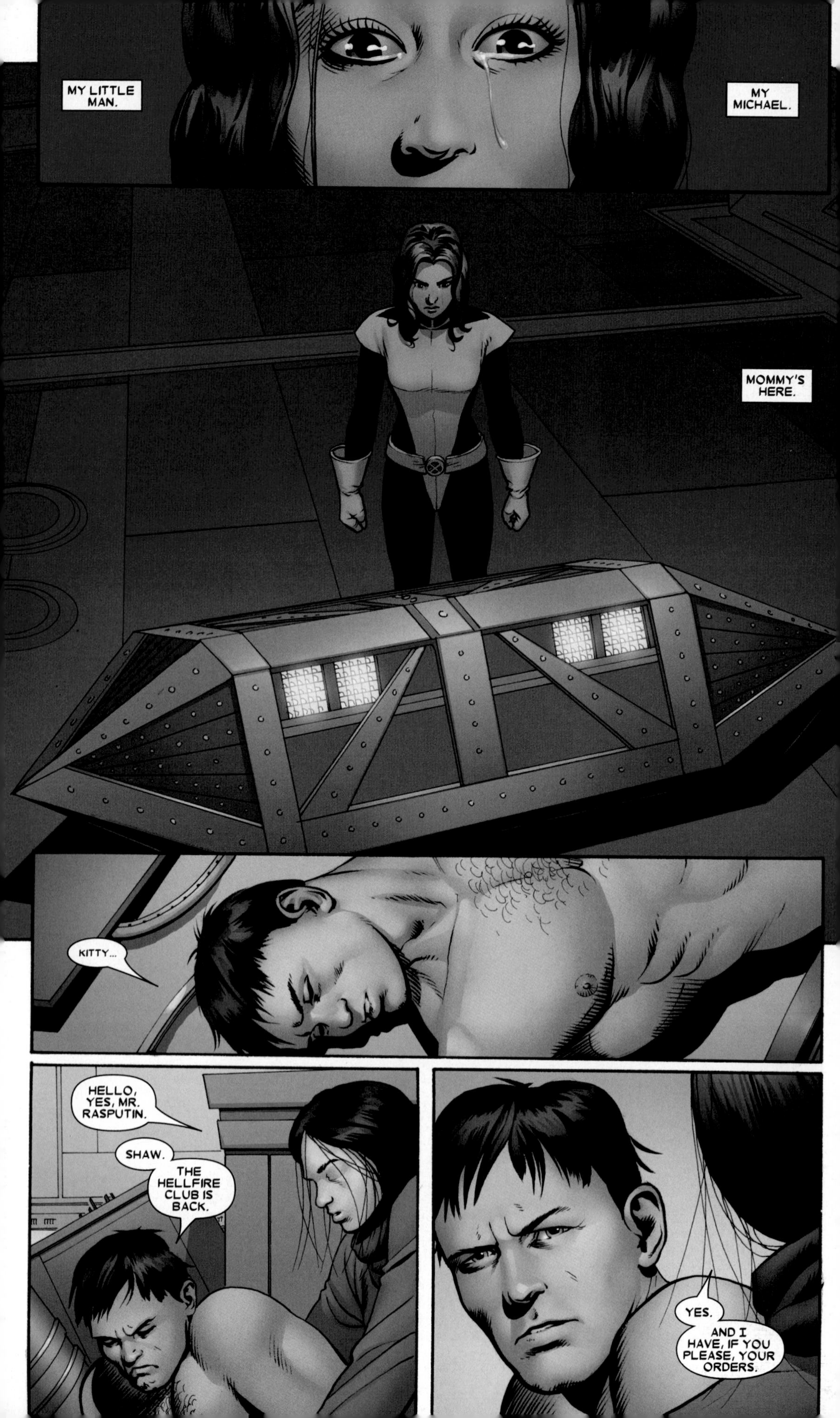
MY LITTLE MAN.
MY MICHAEL.
MOMMY'S HERE.
KITTY...
HELLO, YES, MR. RASPUTIN.
SHAW.
THE HELLFIRE CLUB IS BACK.
YES.
AND I HAVE, IF YOU PLEASE, YOUR ORDERS.

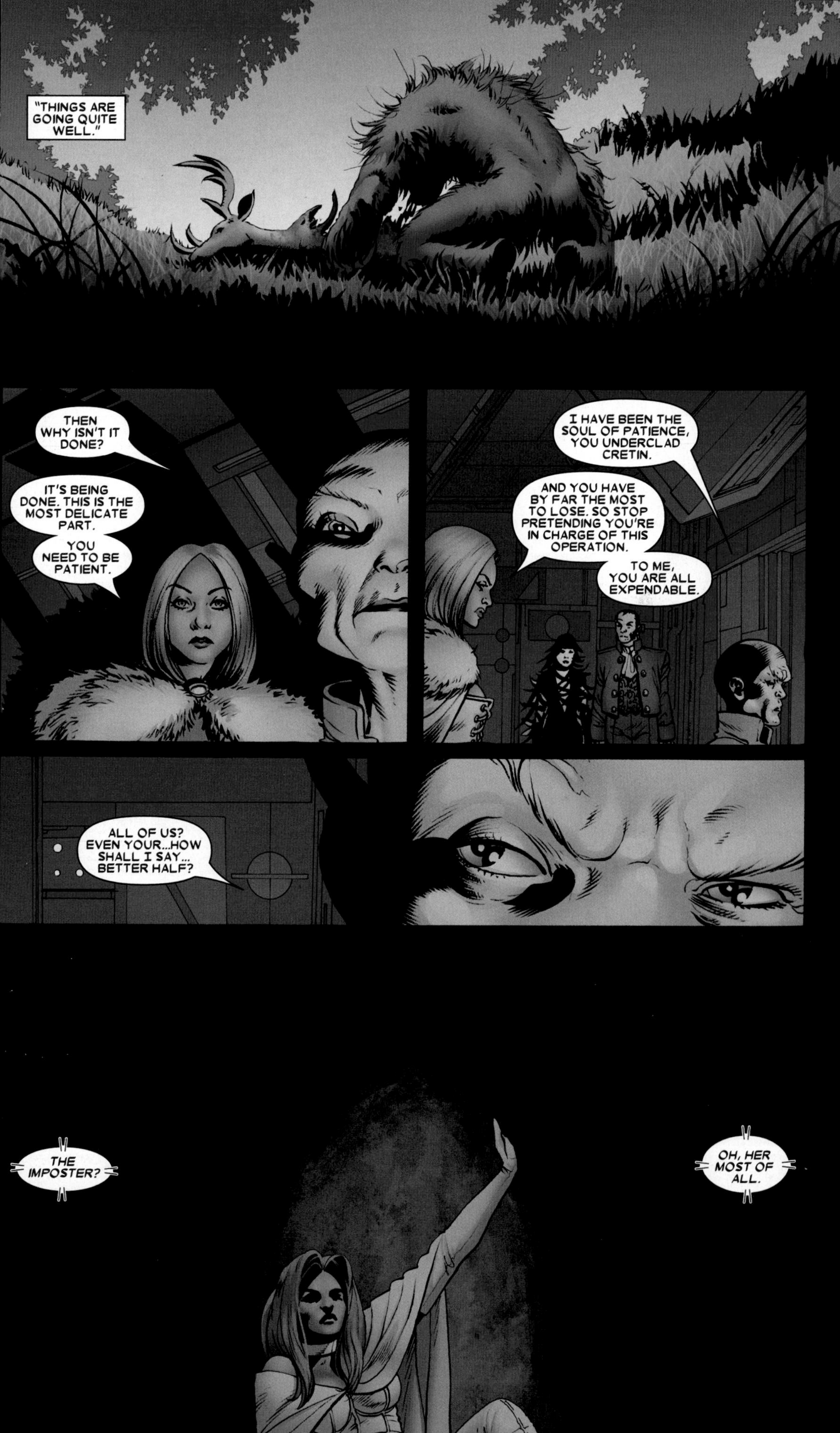
"THINGS ARE GOING QUITE WELL."
THEN WHY ISN'T IT DONE?
IT'S BEING DONE. THIS IS THE MOST DELICATE PART.
YOU NEED TO BE PATIENT.
I HAVE BEEN THE SOUL OF PATIENCE, YOU UNDERCLAD CRETIN.
AND YOU HAVE BY FAR THE MOST TO LOSE. SO STOP PRETENDING YOU'RE IN CHARGE OF THIS OPERATION.
TO ME, YOU ARE ALL EXPENDABLE.
ALL OF US? EVEN YOUR...HOW SHALL I SAY... BETTER HALF?
THE IMPOSTER?
OH, HER MOST OF ALL.

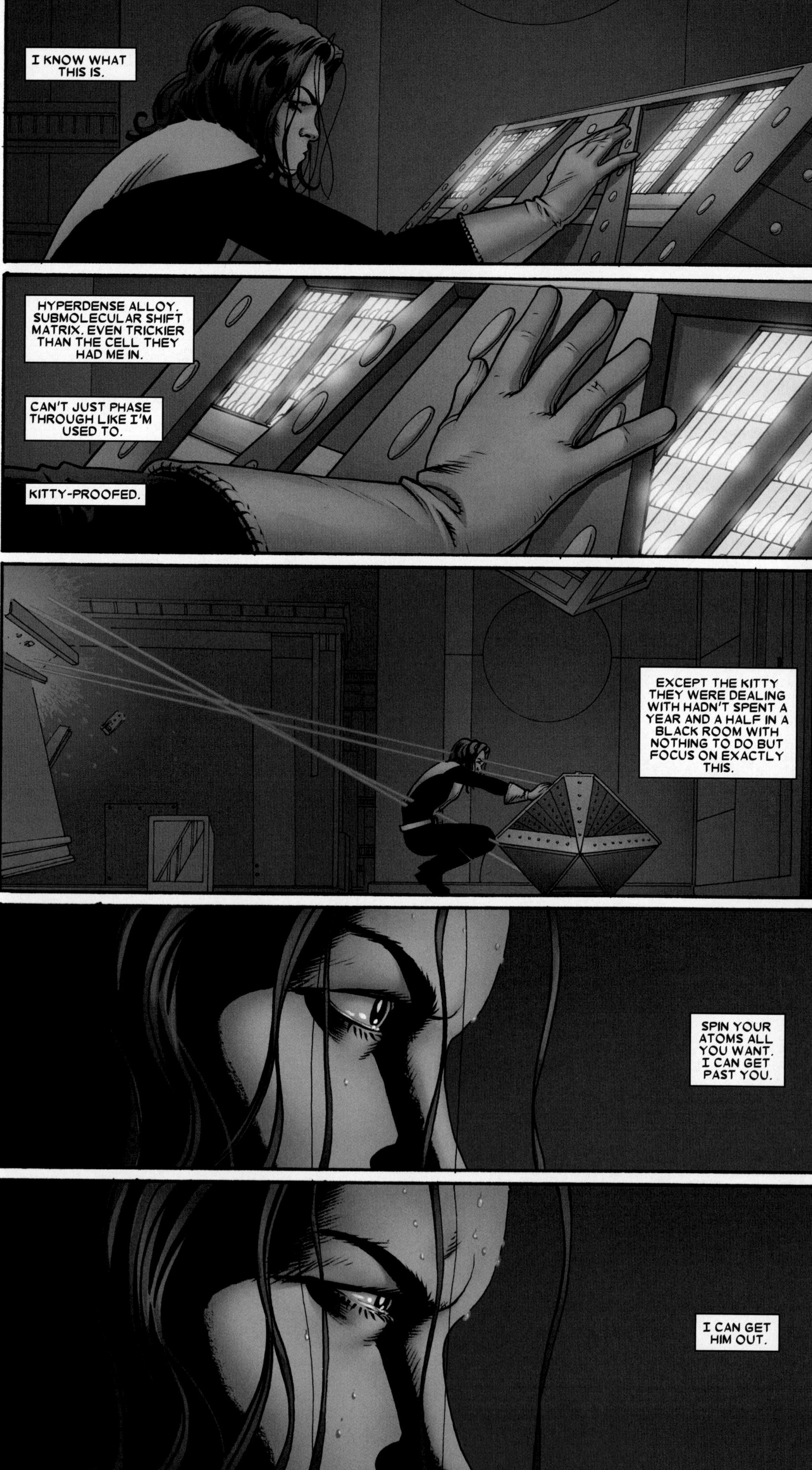
I KNOW WHAT THIS IS.
HYPERDENSE ALLOY. SUBMOLECULAR SHIFT MATRIX. EVEN TRICKIER THAN THE CELL THEY HAD ME IN.
CAN'T JUST PHASE THROUGH LIKE I'M USED TO.
KITTY-PROOFED.
EXCEPT THE KITTY THEY WERE DEALING WITH HADN'T SPENT A YEAR AND A HALF IN A BLACK ROOM WITH NOTHING TO DO BUT FOCUS ON EXACTLY THIS.
SPIN YOUR ATOMS ALL YOU WANT. I CAN GET PAST YOU.
I CAN GET HIM OUT.

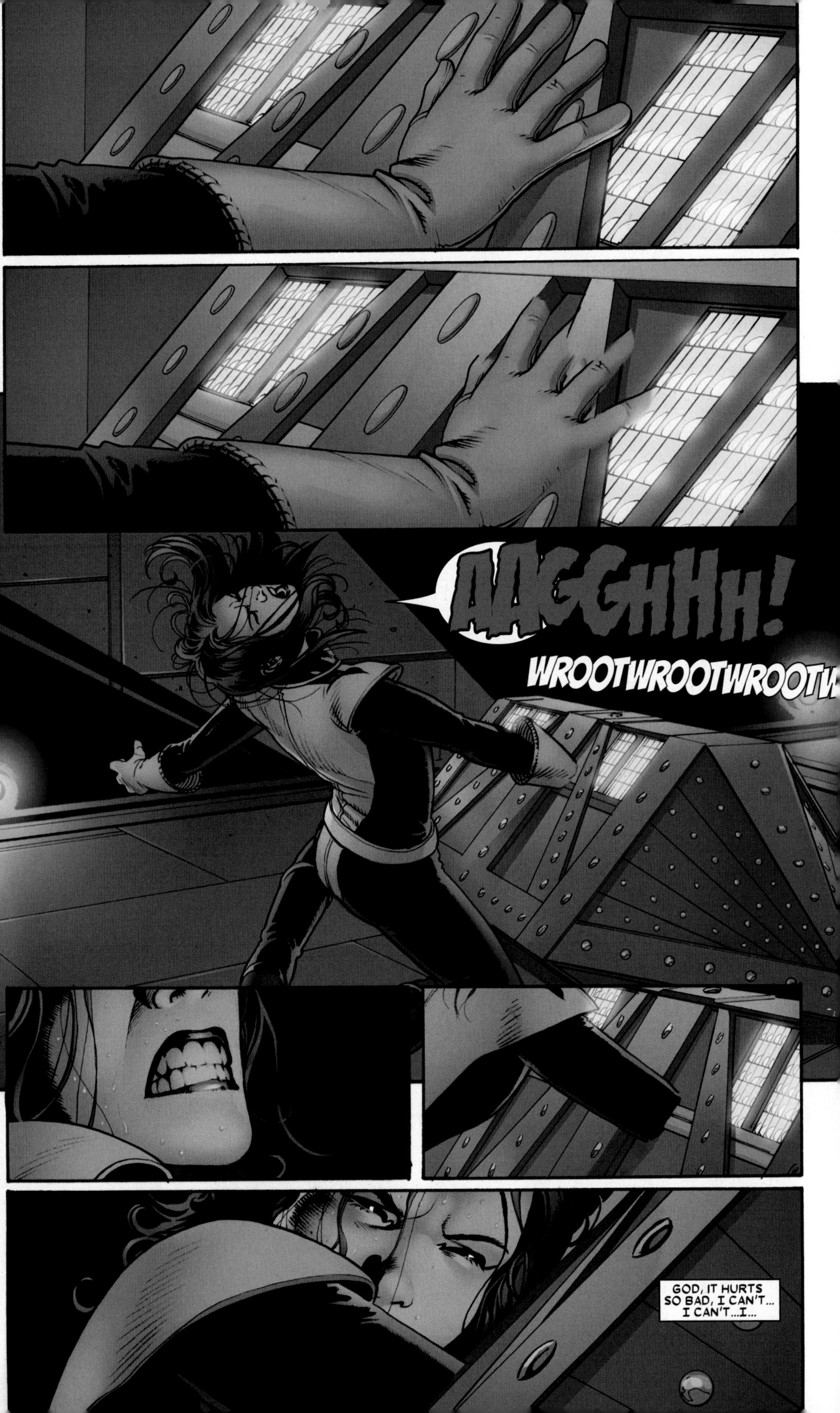
AAGGHHH!
WROOTWROOTWROOTW
GOD, IT HURTS SO BAD, I CAN'T... I CAN'T...I...

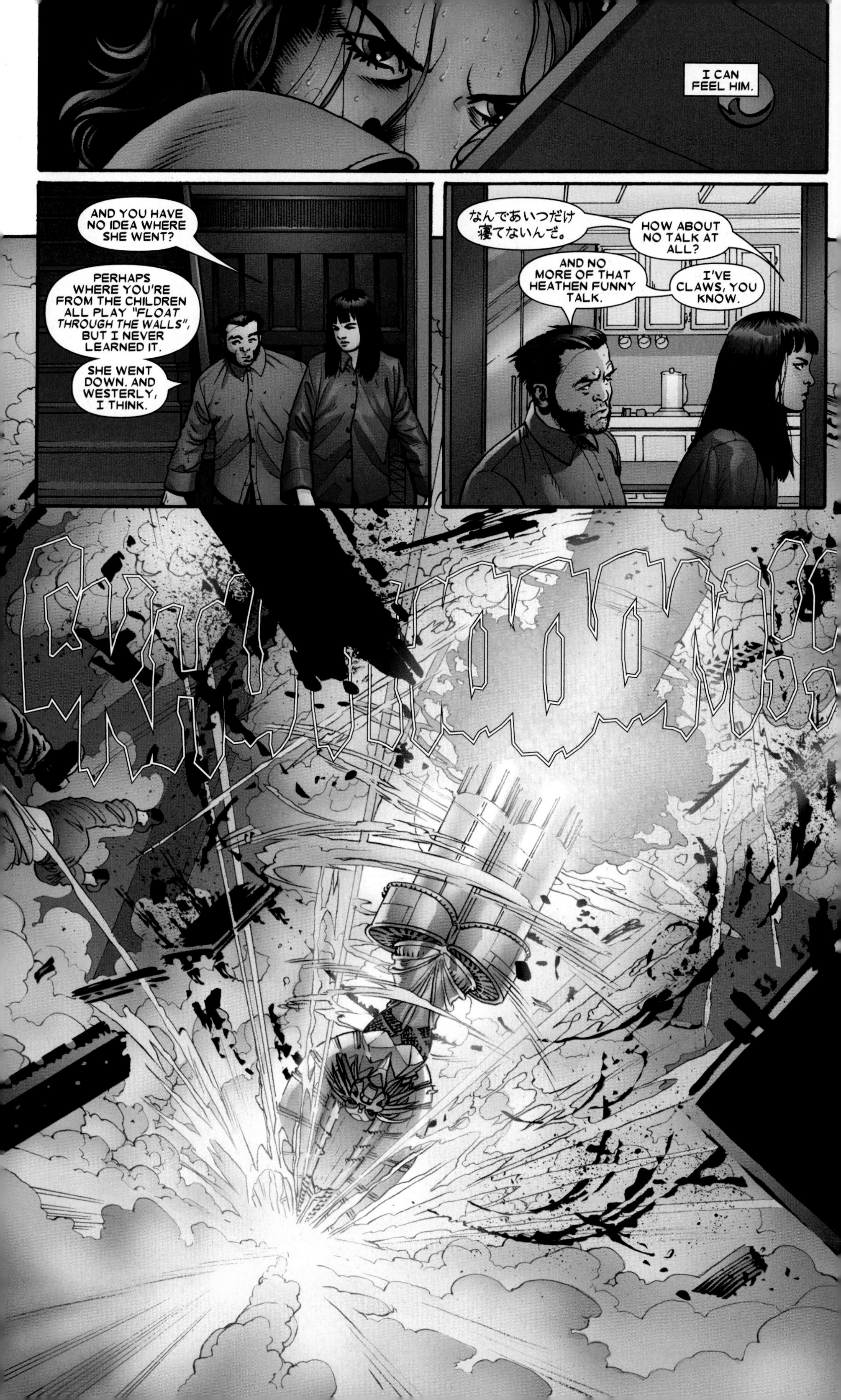
I CAN FEEL HIM.
AND YOU HAVE NO IDEA WHERE SHE WENT?
PERHAPS WHERE YOU'RE FROM THE CHILDREN ALL PLAY "FLOAT THROUGH THE WALLS", BUT I NEVER LEARNED IT.
SHE WENT DOWN. AND WESTERLY, I THINK.
なんであいつだけ寝てないんだ。
HOW ABOUT NO TALK AT ALL?
AND NO MORE OF THAT HEATHEN FUNNY TALK.
I'VE CLAWS, YOU KNOW.

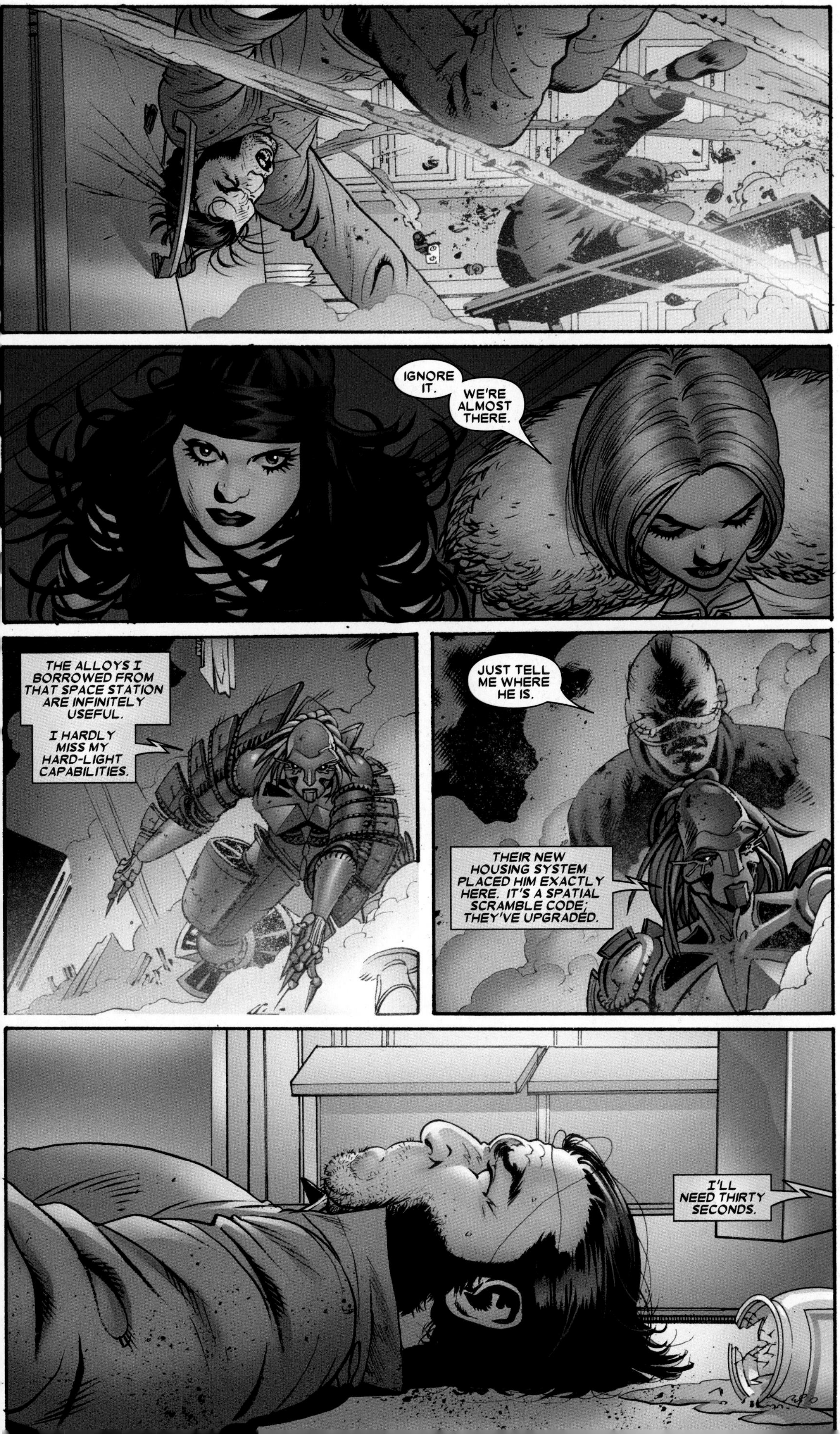
IGNORE IT. WE'RE ALMOST THERE.
THE ALLOYS I BORROWED FROM THAT SPACE STATION ARE INFINITELY USEFUL.
I HARDLY MISS MY HARD-LIGHT CAPABILITIES.
JUST TELL ME WHERE HE IS.
THEIR NEW HOUSING SYSTEM PLACED HIM EXACTLY HERE. IT'S A SPATIAL SCRAMBLE CODE; THEY'VE UPGRADED.
I'LL NEED THIRTY SECONDS.

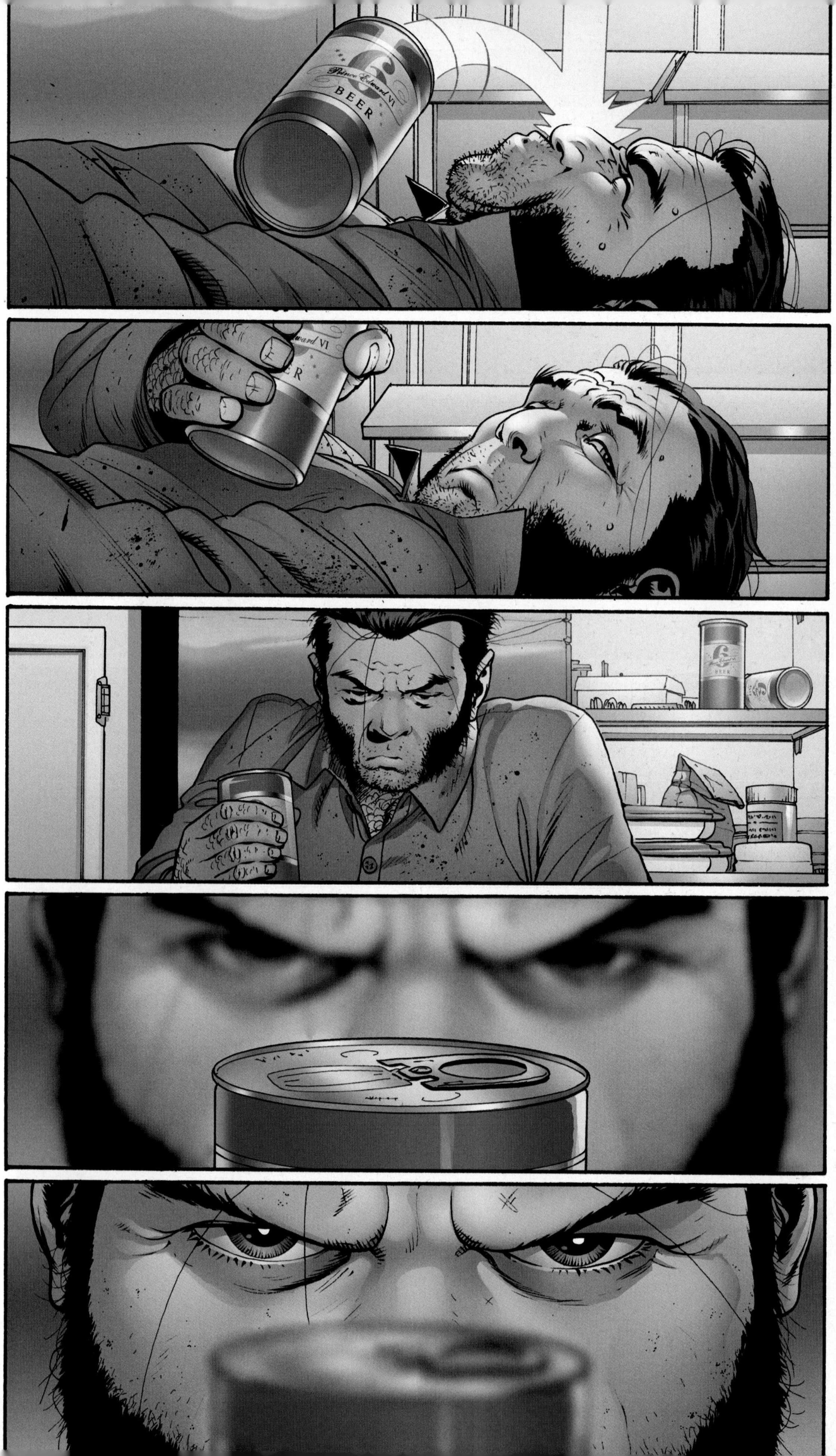
Prince Edward VI
BEER

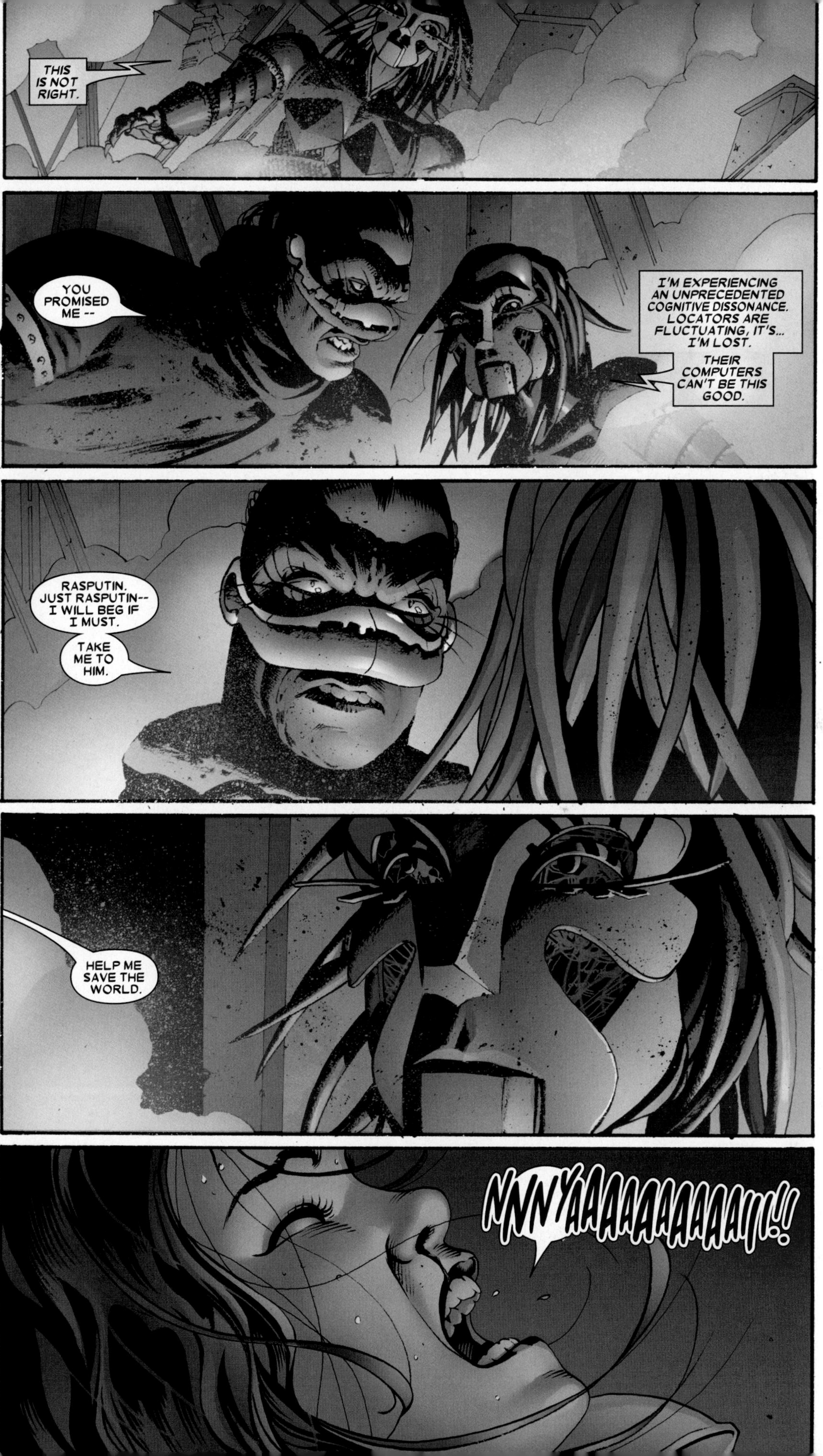
THIS IS NOT RIGHT.
YOU PROMISED ME --
I'M EXPERIENCING AN UNPRECEDENTED COGNITIVE DISSONANCE. LOCATORS ARE FLUCTUATING, IT'S... I'M LOST.
THEIR COMPUTERS CAN'T BE THIS GOOD.
RASPUTIN. JUST RASPUTIN-- I WILL BEG IF I MUST.
TAKE ME TO HIM.
HELP ME SAVE THE WORLD.
NNNYAAAAAAAAAAIII!!

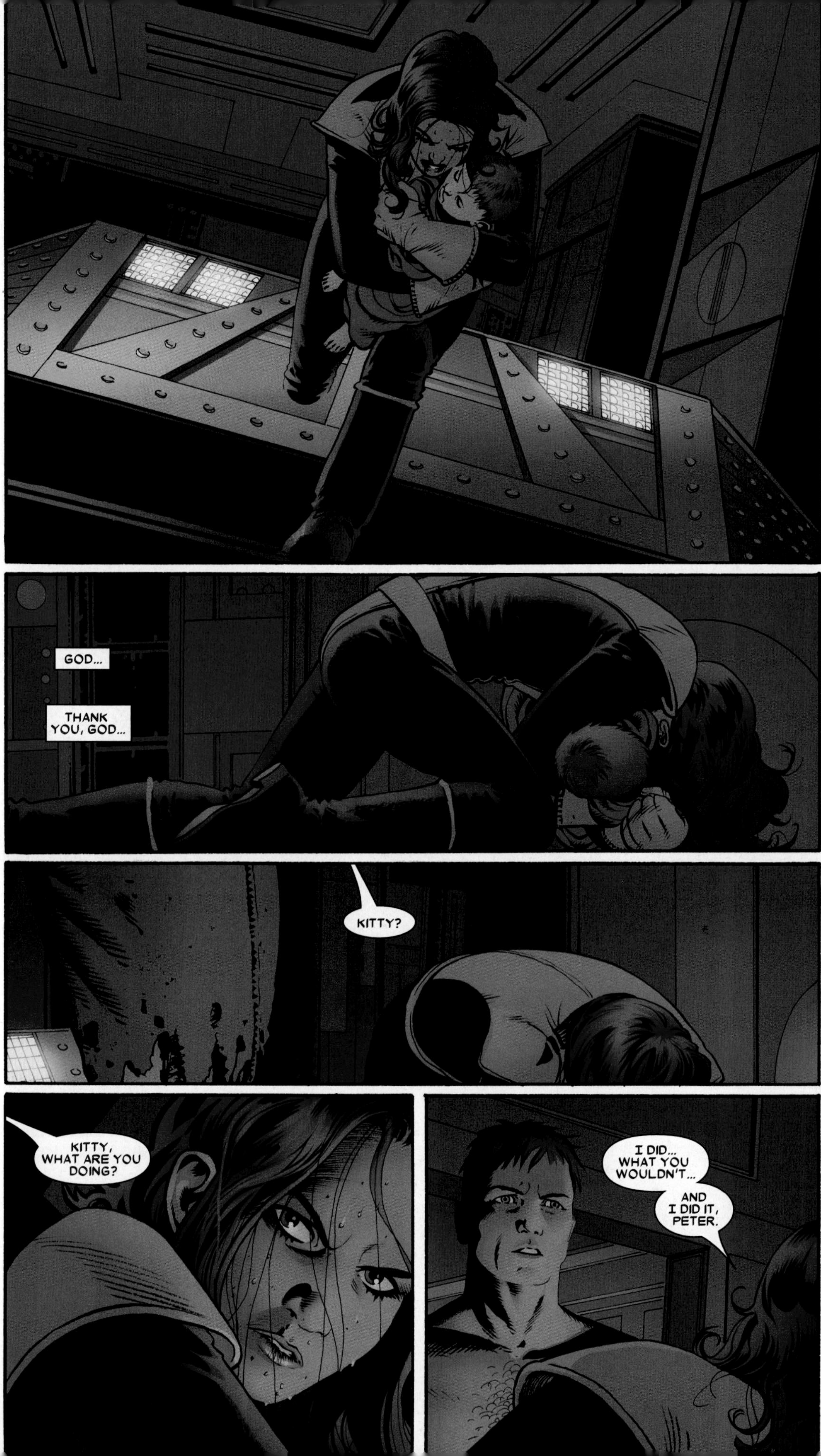
GOD...
THANK YOU, GOD...
KITTY?
KITTY, WHAT ARE YOU DOING?
I DID... WHAT YOU WOULDN'T...
AND I DID IT, PETER.

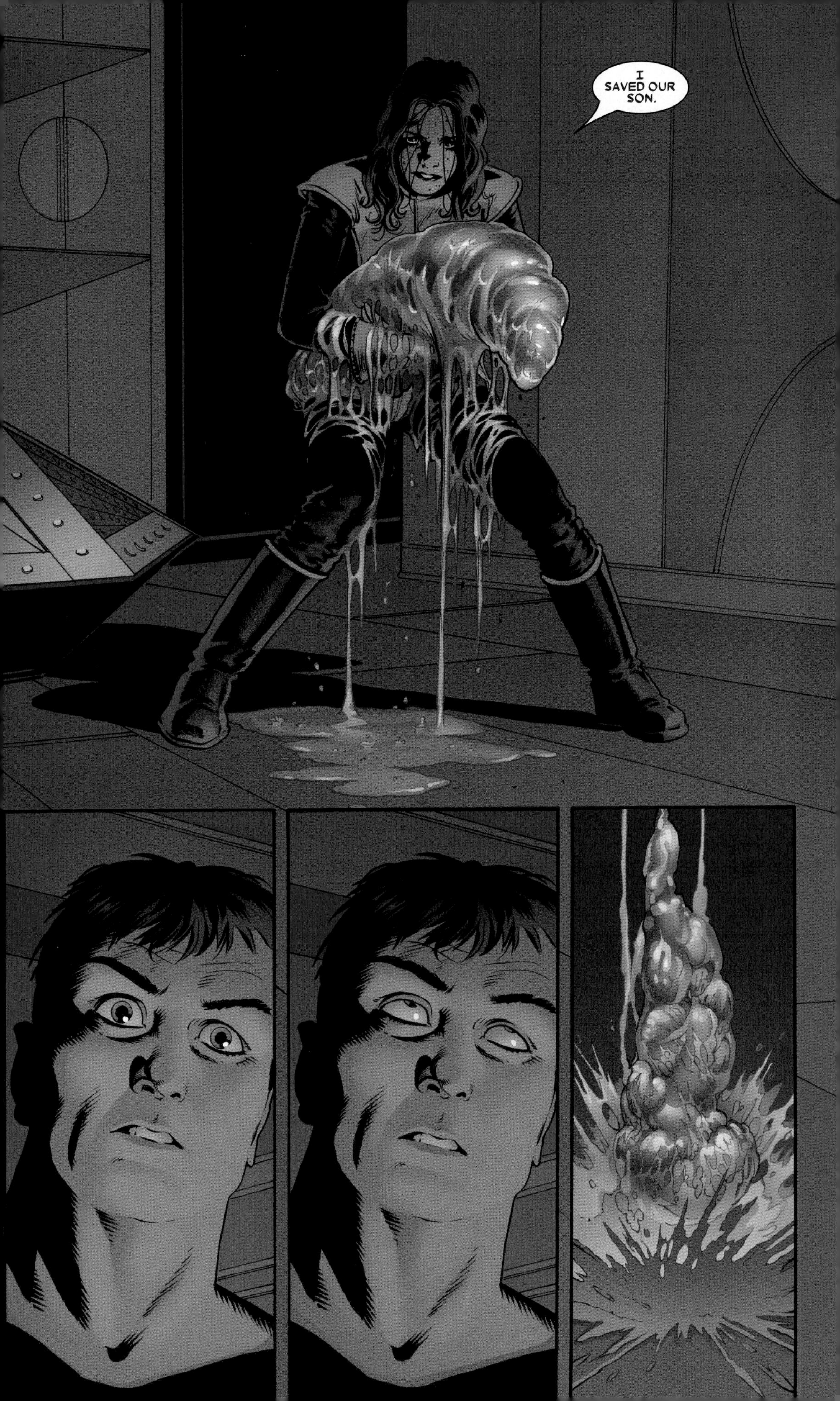
I SAVED OUR SON.

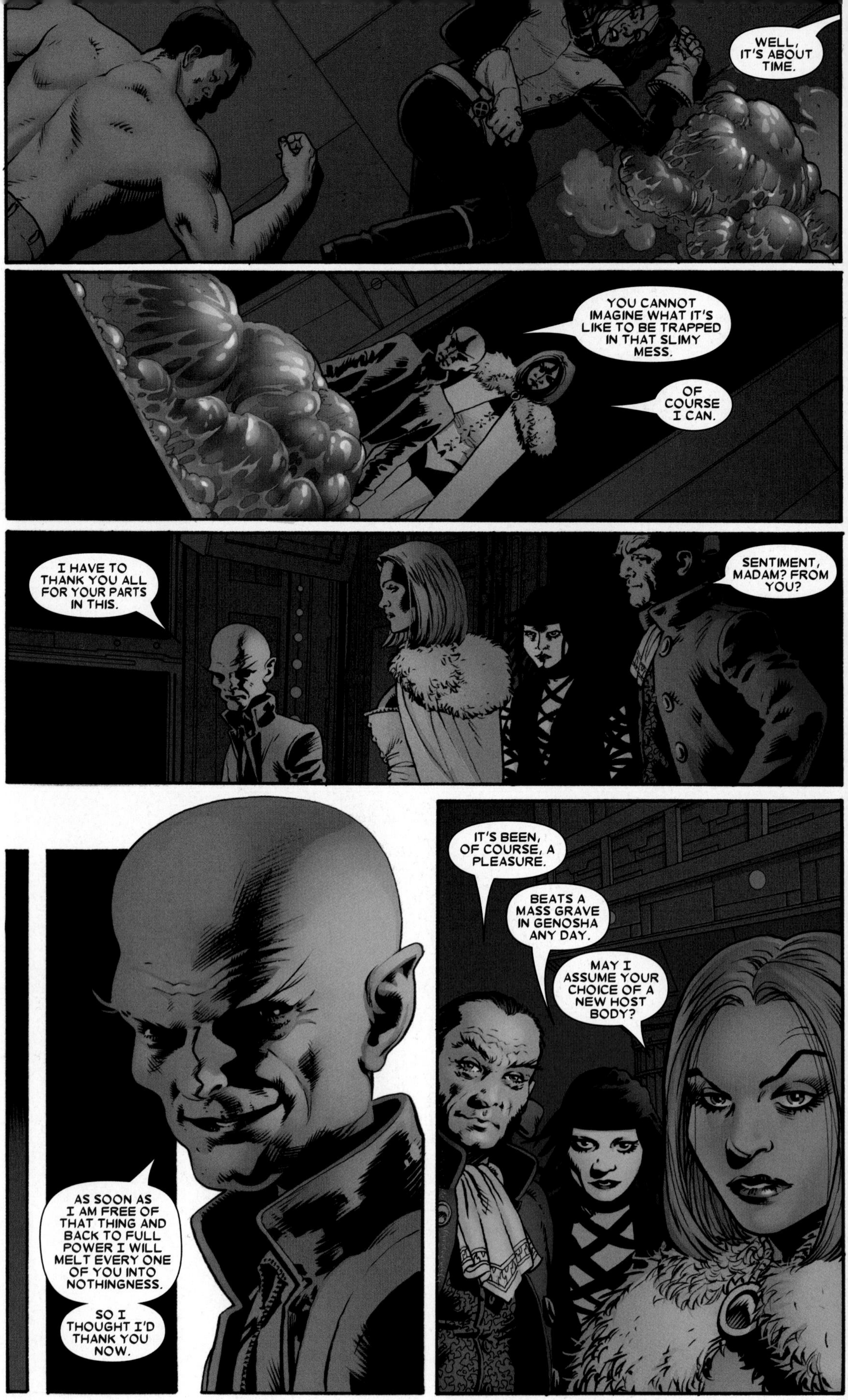
WELL, IT'S ABOUT TIME.
YOU CANNOT IMAGINE WHAT IT'S LIKE TO BE TRAPPED IN THAT SLIMY MESS.
OF COURSE I CAN.
I HAVE TO THANK YOU ALL FOR YOUR PARTS IN THIS.
SENTIMENT, MADAM? FROM YOU?
AS SOON AS I AM FREE OF THAT THING AND BACK TO FULL POWER I WILL MELT EVERY ONE OF YOU INTO NOTHINGNESS.
SO I THOUGHT I'D THANK YOU NOW.
IT'S BEEN, OF COURSE, A PLEASURE.
BEATS A MASS GRAVE IN GENOSHA ANY DAY.
MAY I ASSUME YOUR CHOICE OF A NEW HOST BODY?

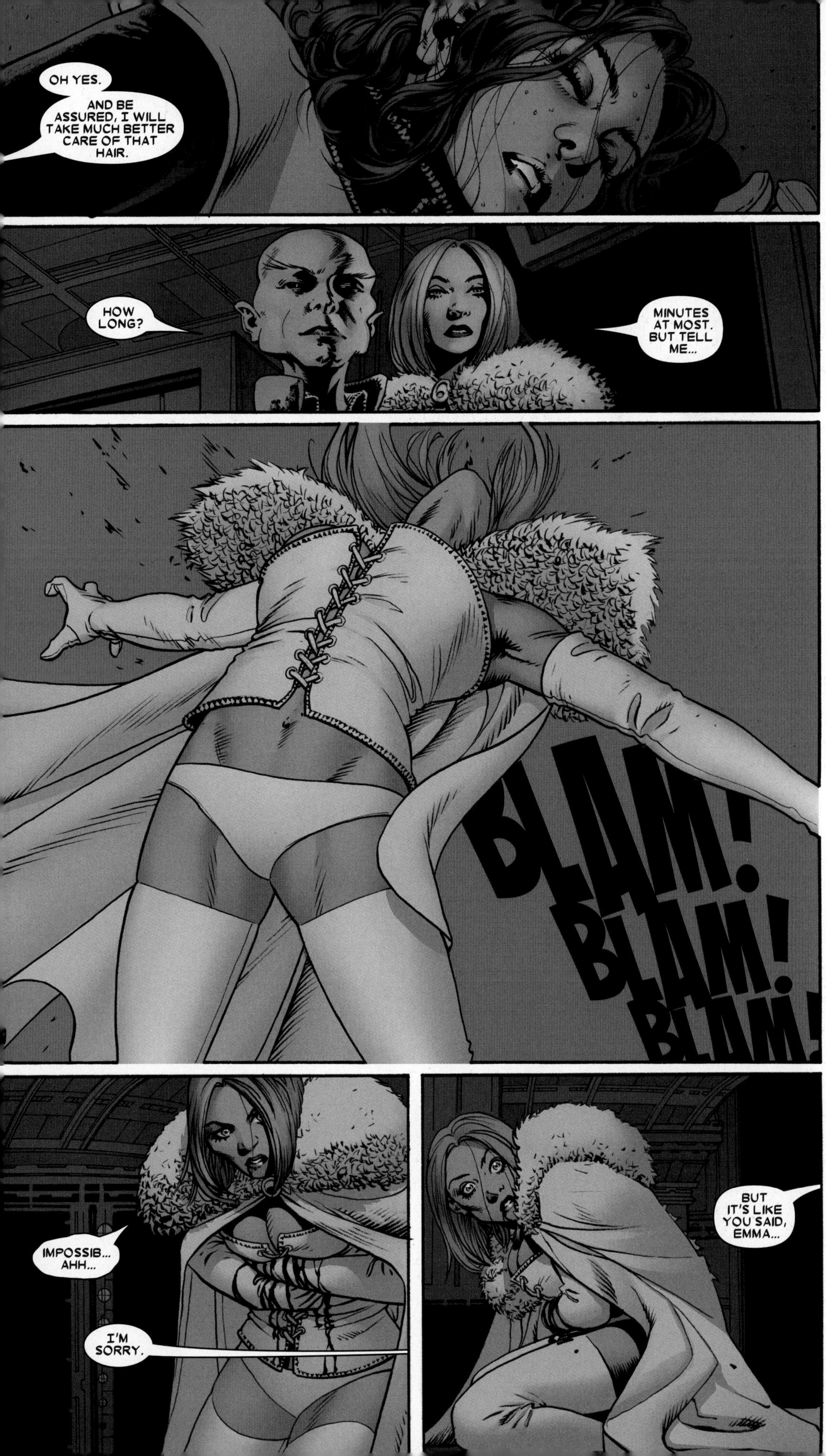
OH YES.
AND BE ASSURED, I WILL TAKE MUCH BETTER CARE OF THAT HAIR.
HOW LONG?
MINUTES AT MOST. BUT TELL ME...
BLAM! BLAM! BLAM!
IMPOSSIB... AHH...
I'M SORRY.
BUT IT'S LIKE YOU SAID, EMMA...

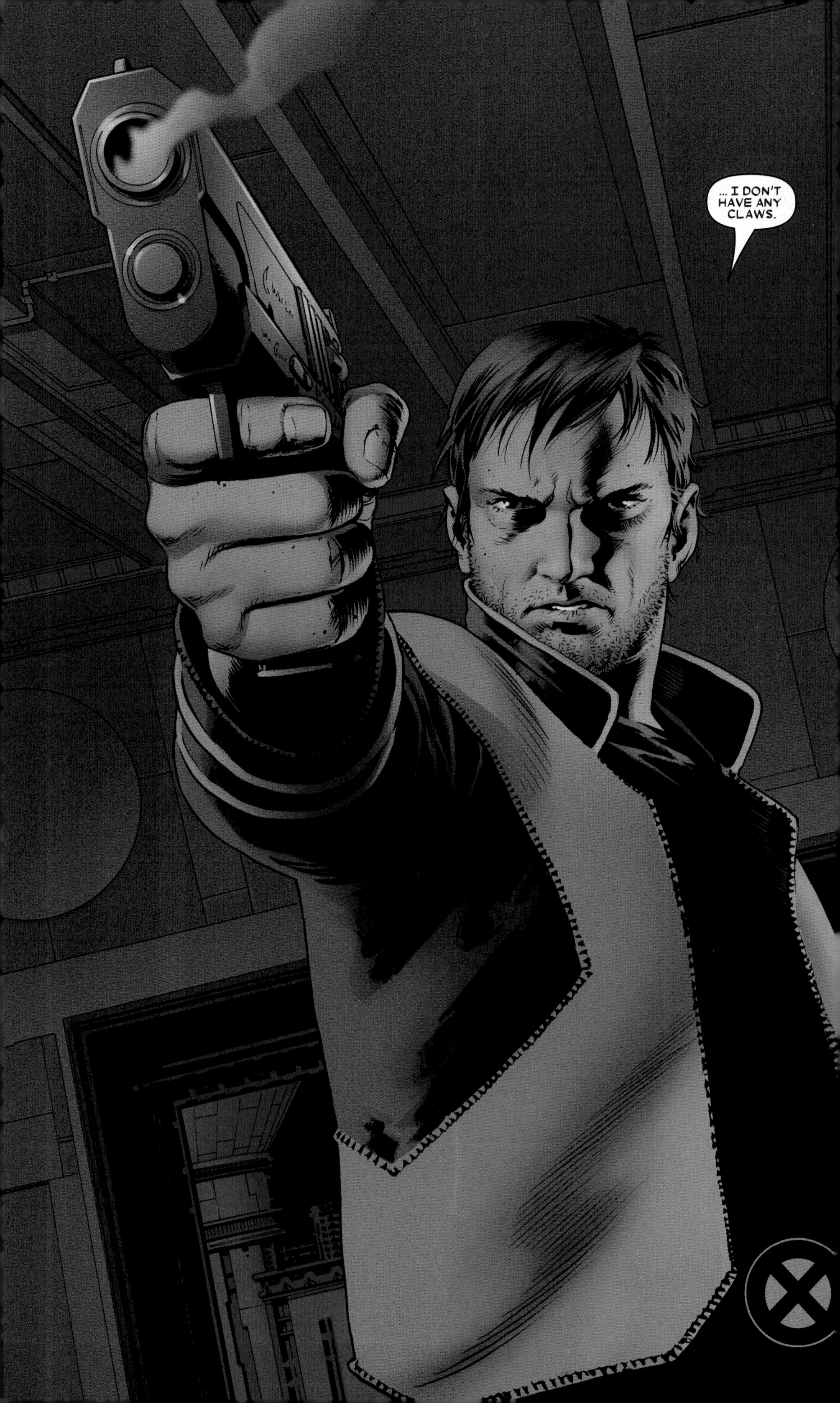
... I DON'T HAVE ANY CLAWS.

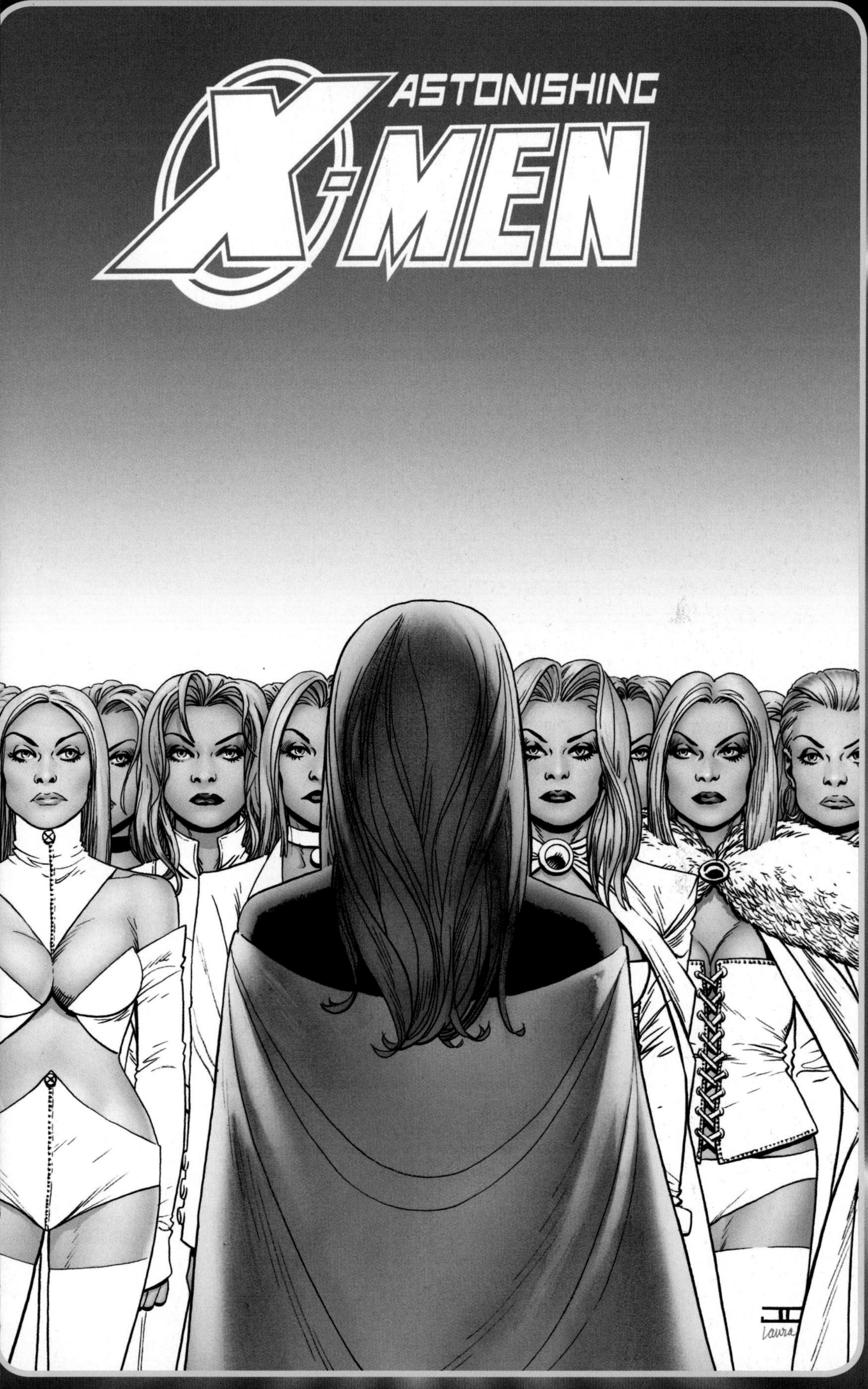
ASTONISHING
X-MEN

18

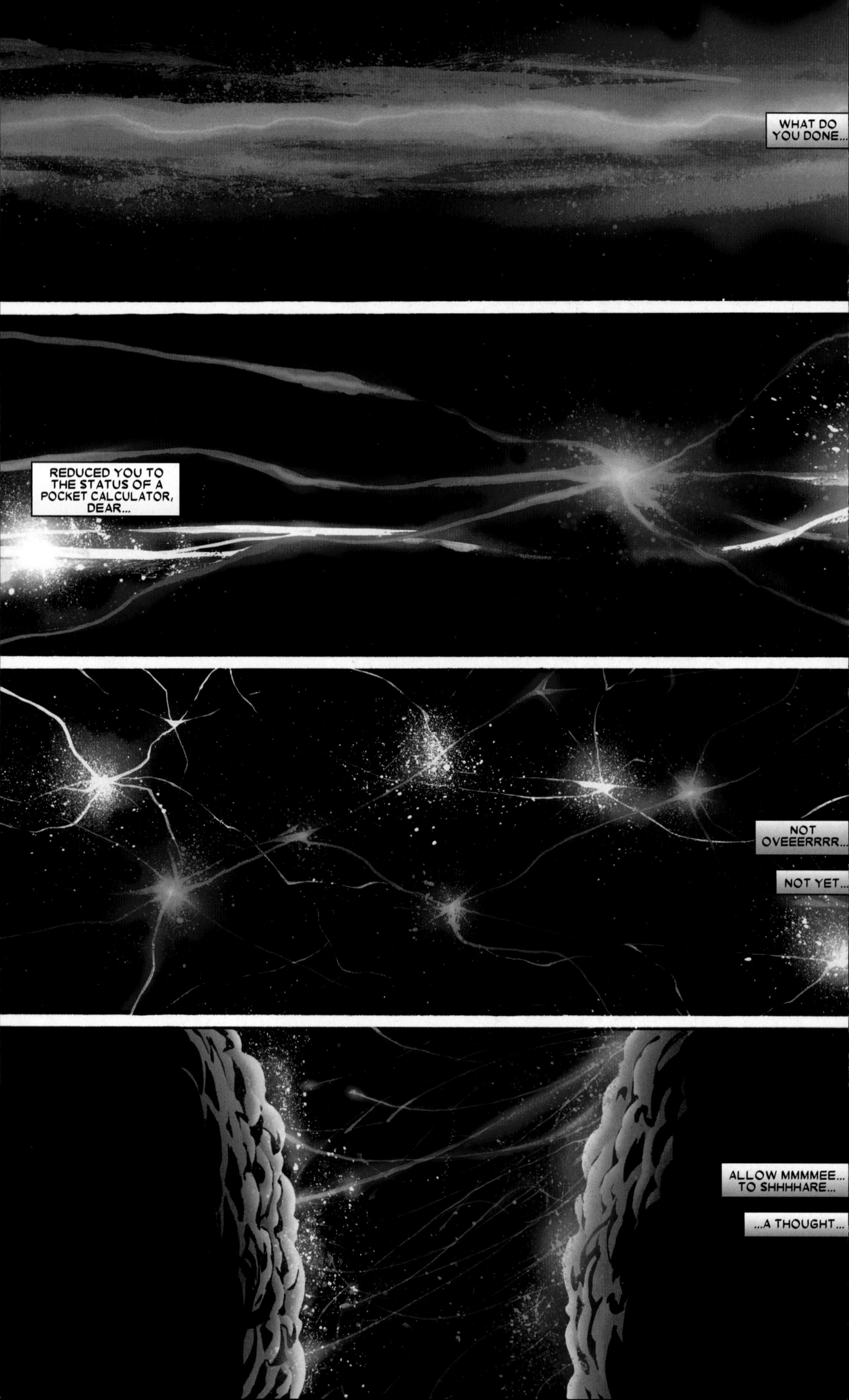
WHAT DO YOU DONE...
REDUCED YOU TO THE STATUS OF A POCKET CALCULATOR, DEAR...
NOT OVEEERRRR...
NOT YET...
ALLOW MMMMEE... TO SHHHHARE...
...A THOUGHT...

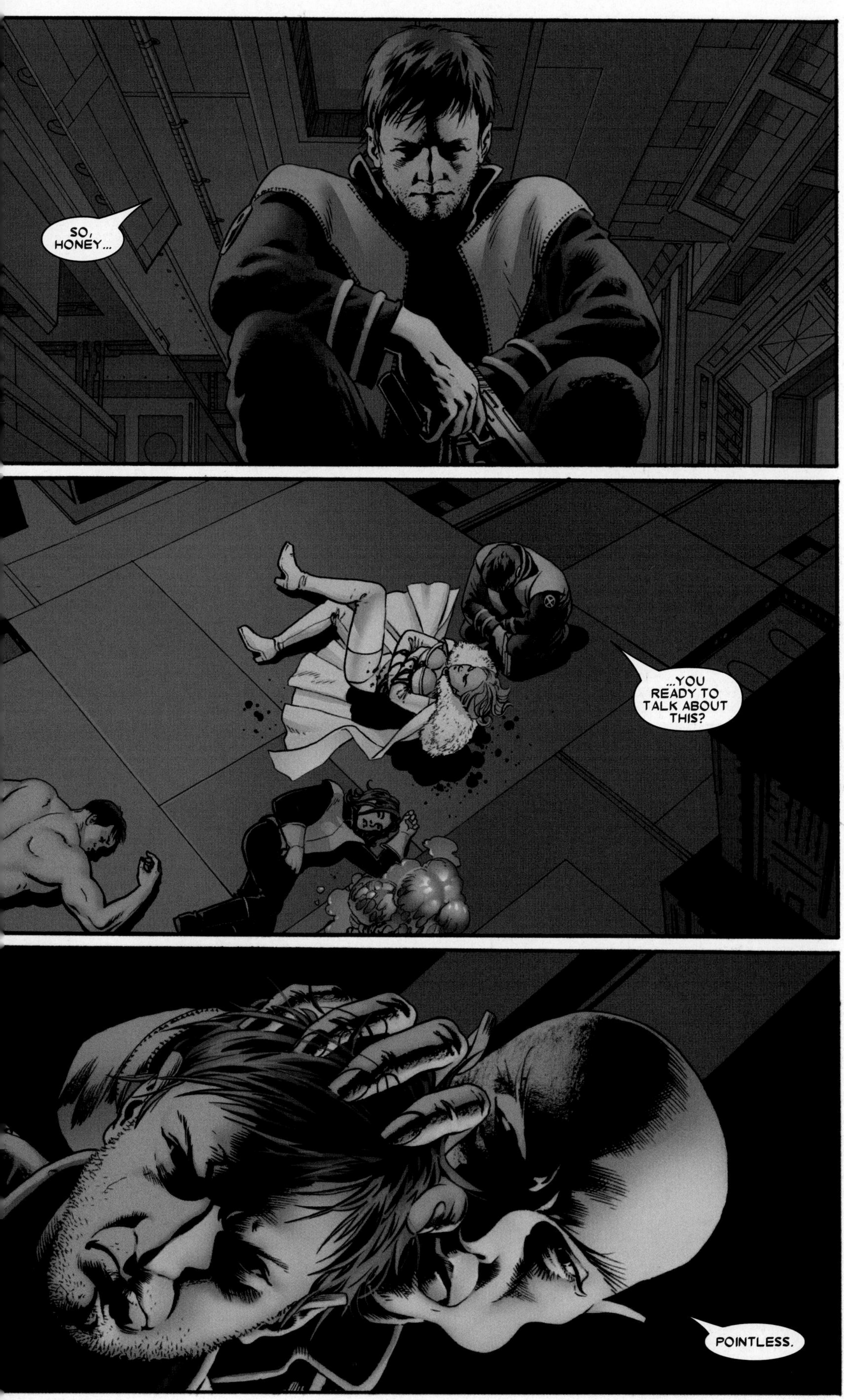
SO, HONEY...
...YOU READY TO TALK ABOUT THIS?
POINTLESS.

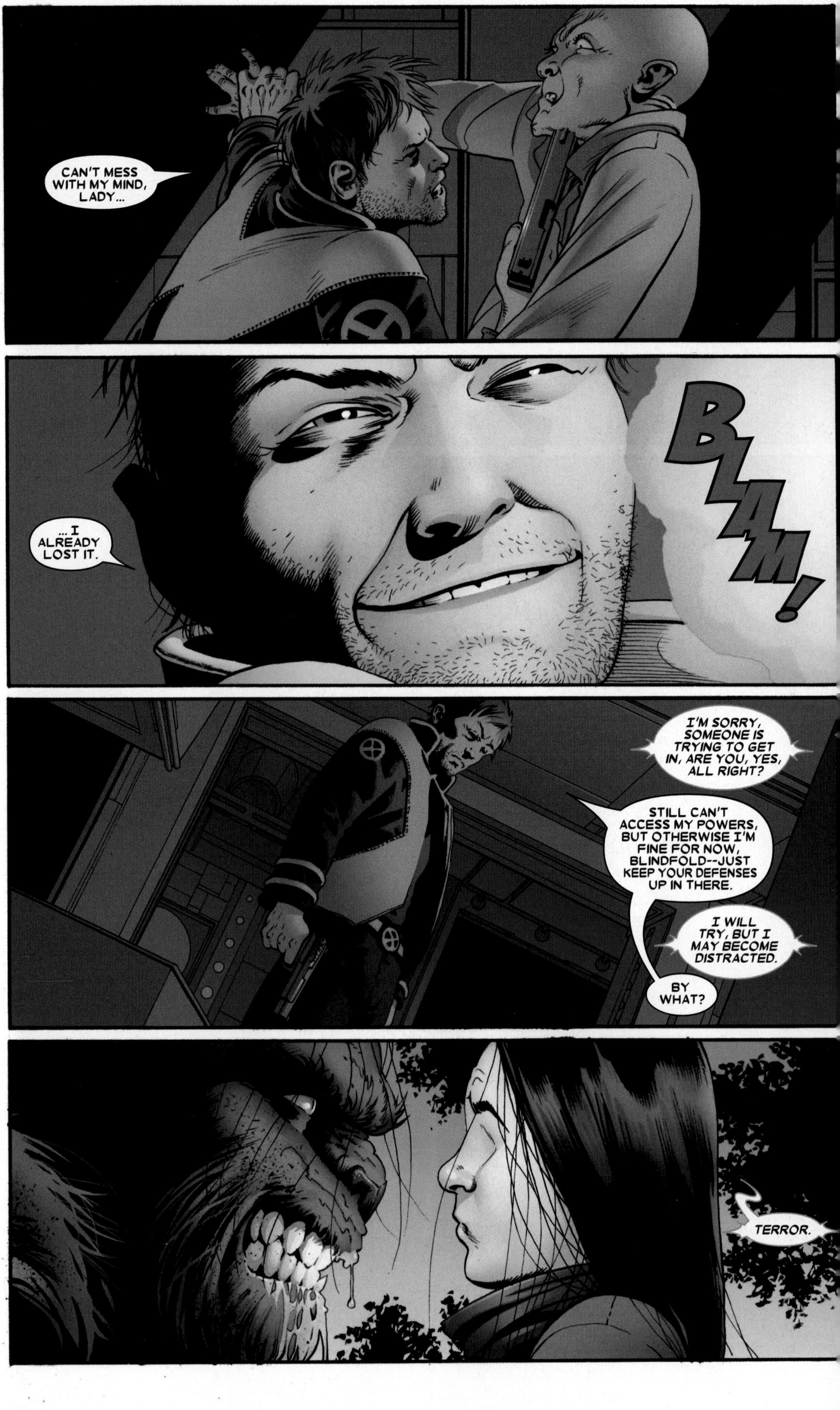
CAN'T MESS WITH MY MIND, LADY...
...I ALREADY LOST IT.
BLAM!
I'M SORRY, SOMEONE IS TRYING TO GET IN, ARE YOU, YES, ALL RIGHT?
STILL CAN'T ACCESS MY POWERS, BUT OTHERWISE I'M FINE FOR NOW, BLINDFOLD--JUST KEEP YOUR DEFENSES UP IN THERE.
I WILL TRY, BUT I MAY BECOME DISTRACTED.
BY WHAT?
TERROR.

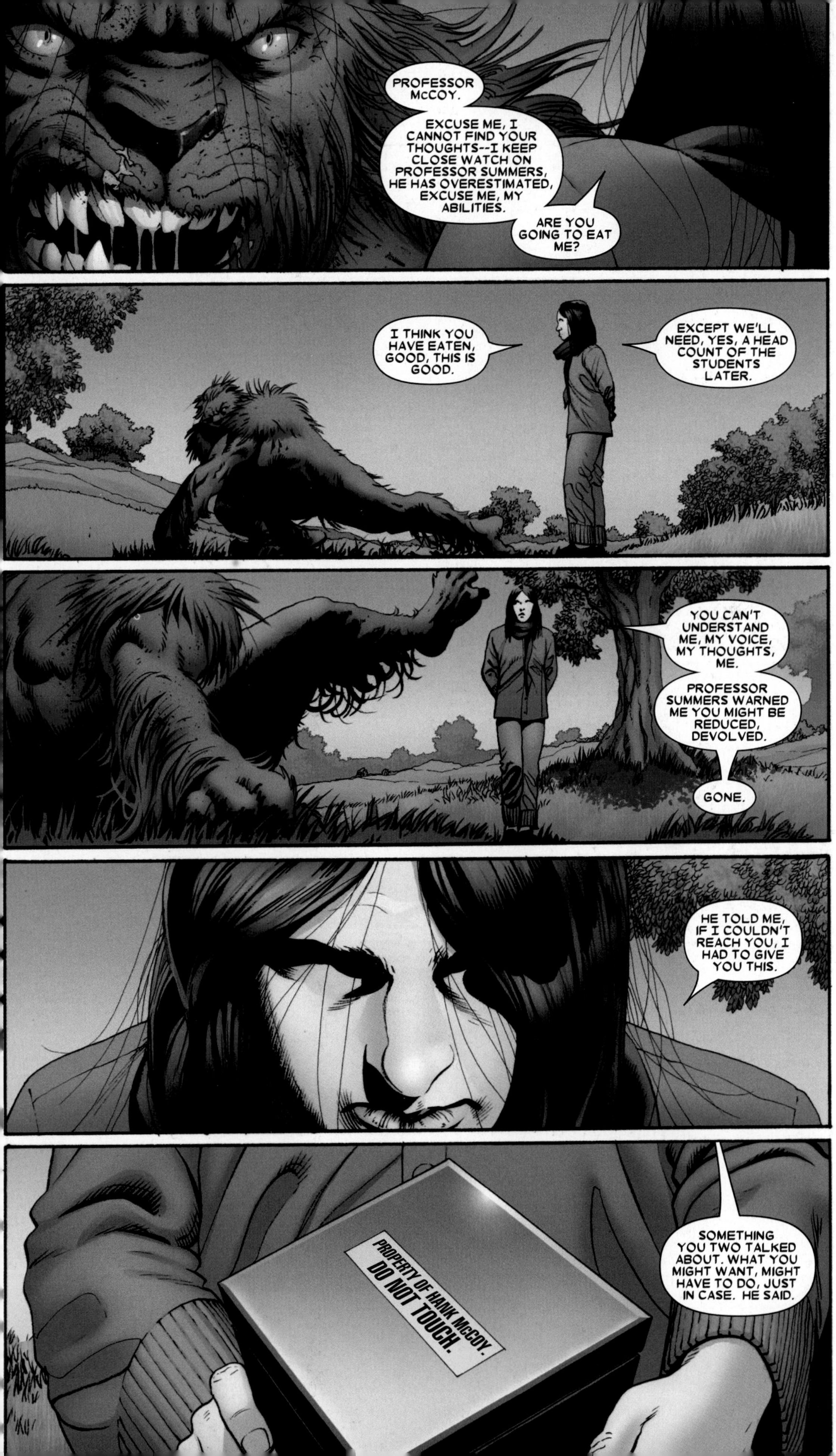
PROFESSOR McCOY.
EXCUSE ME, I CANNOT FIND YOUR THOUGHTS--I KEEP CLOSE WATCH ON PROFESSOR SUMMERS, HE HAS OVERESTIMATED, EXCUSE ME, MY ABILITIES.
ARE YOU GOING TO EAT ME?
I THINK YOU HAVE EATEN, GOOD, THIS IS GOOD.
EXCEPT WE'LL NEED, YES, A HEAD COUNT OF THE STUDENTS LATER.
YOU CAN'T UNDERSTAND ME, MY VOICE, MY THOUGHTS, ME.
PROFESSOR SUMMERS WARNED ME YOU MIGHT BE REDUCED, DEVOLVED.
GONE.
HE TOLD ME, IF I COULDN'T REACH YOU, I HAD TO GIVE YOU THIS.
PROPERTY OF HANK McCOY. DO NOT TOUCH.
SOMETHING YOU TWO TALKED ABOUT. WHAT YOU MIGHT WANT, MIGHT HAVE TO DO, JUST IN CASE. HE SAID.

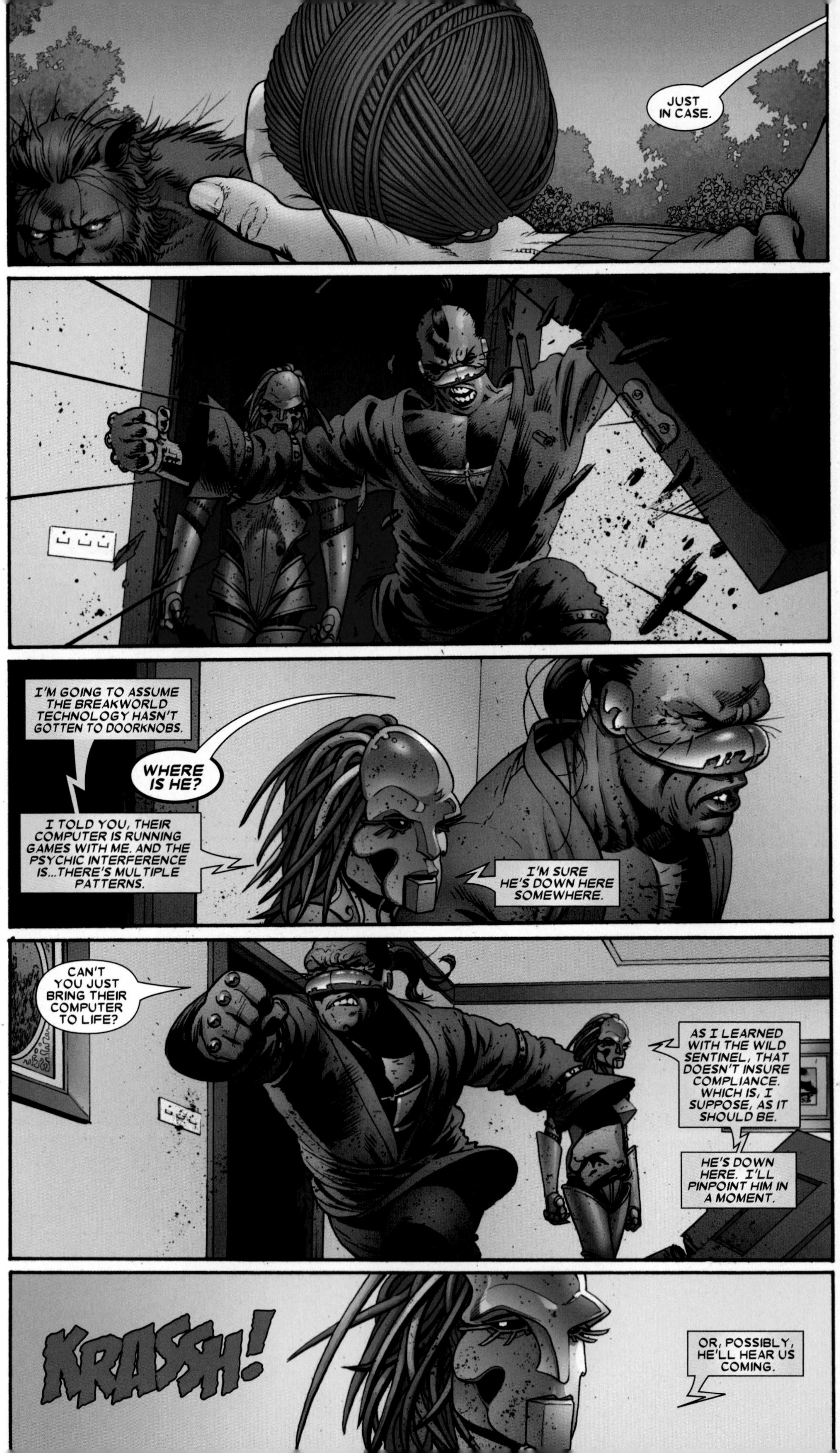
JUST IN CASE.
I'M GOING TO ASSUME THE BREAKWORLD TECHNOLOGY HASN'T GOTTEN TO DOORKNOBS.
WHERE IS HE?
I TOLD YOU, THEIR COMPUTER IS RUNNING GAMES WITH ME. AND THE PSYCHIC INTERFERENCE IS...THERE'S MULTIPLE PATTERNS.
I'M SURE HE'S DOWN HERE SOMEWHERE.
CAN'T YOU JUST BRING THEIR COMPUTER TO LIFE?
AS I LEARNED WITH THE WILD SENTINEL, THAT DOESN'T INSURE COMPLIANCE. WHICH IS, I SUPPOSE, AS IT SHOULD BE.
HE'S DOWN HERE. I'LL PINPOINT HIM IN A MOMENT.
KRASSH!
OR, POSSIBLY, HE'LL HEAR US COMING.

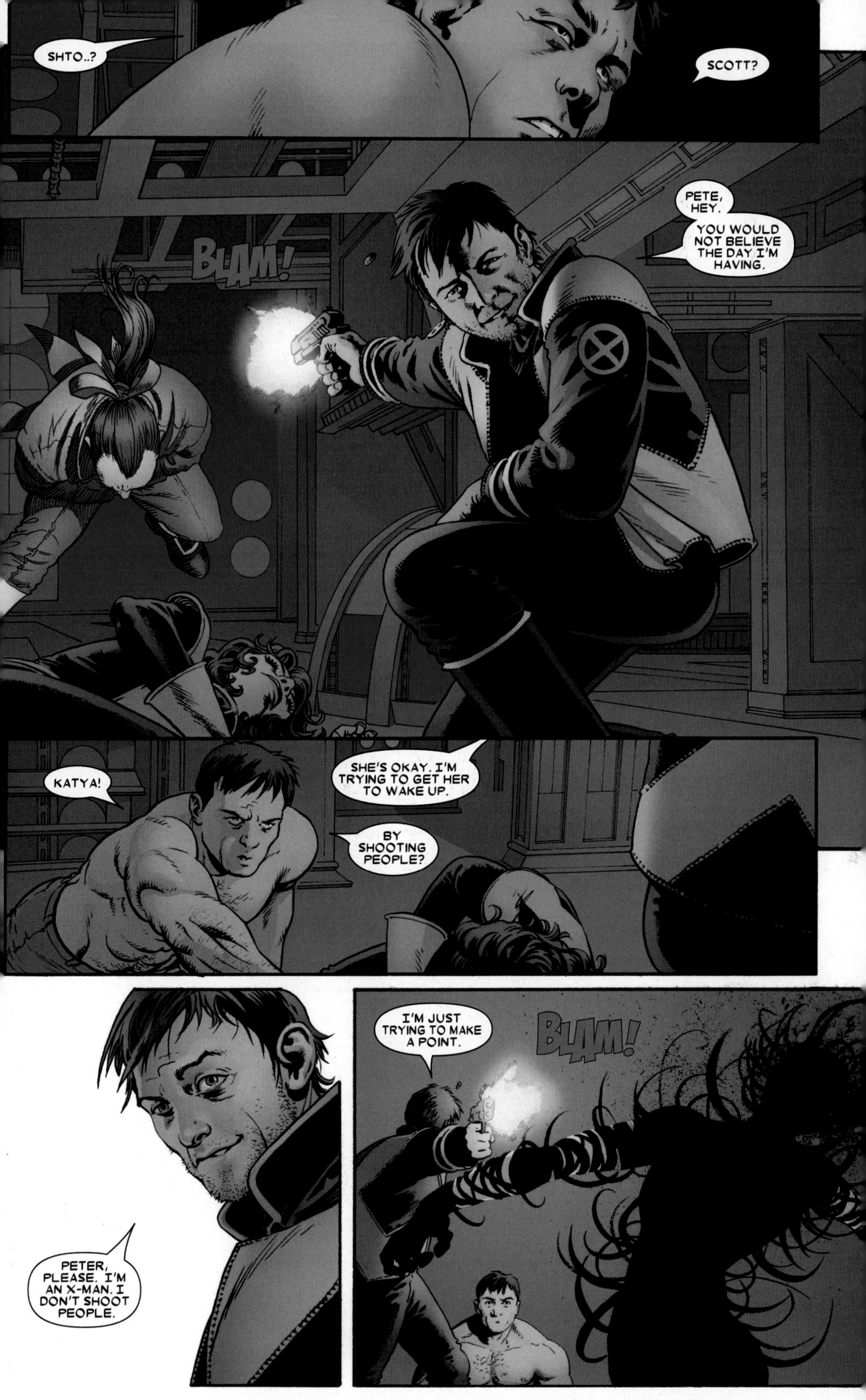
SHTO..?
SCOTT?
BLAM!
PETE, HEY.
YOU WOULD NOT BELIEVE THE DAY I'M HAVING.
KATYA!
SHE'S OKAY. I'M TRYING TO GET HER TO WAKE UP.
BY SHOOTING PEOPLE?
PETER, PLEASE. I'M AN X-MAN. I DON'T SHOOT PEOPLE.
I'M JUST TRYING TO MAKE A POINT.
BLAM!

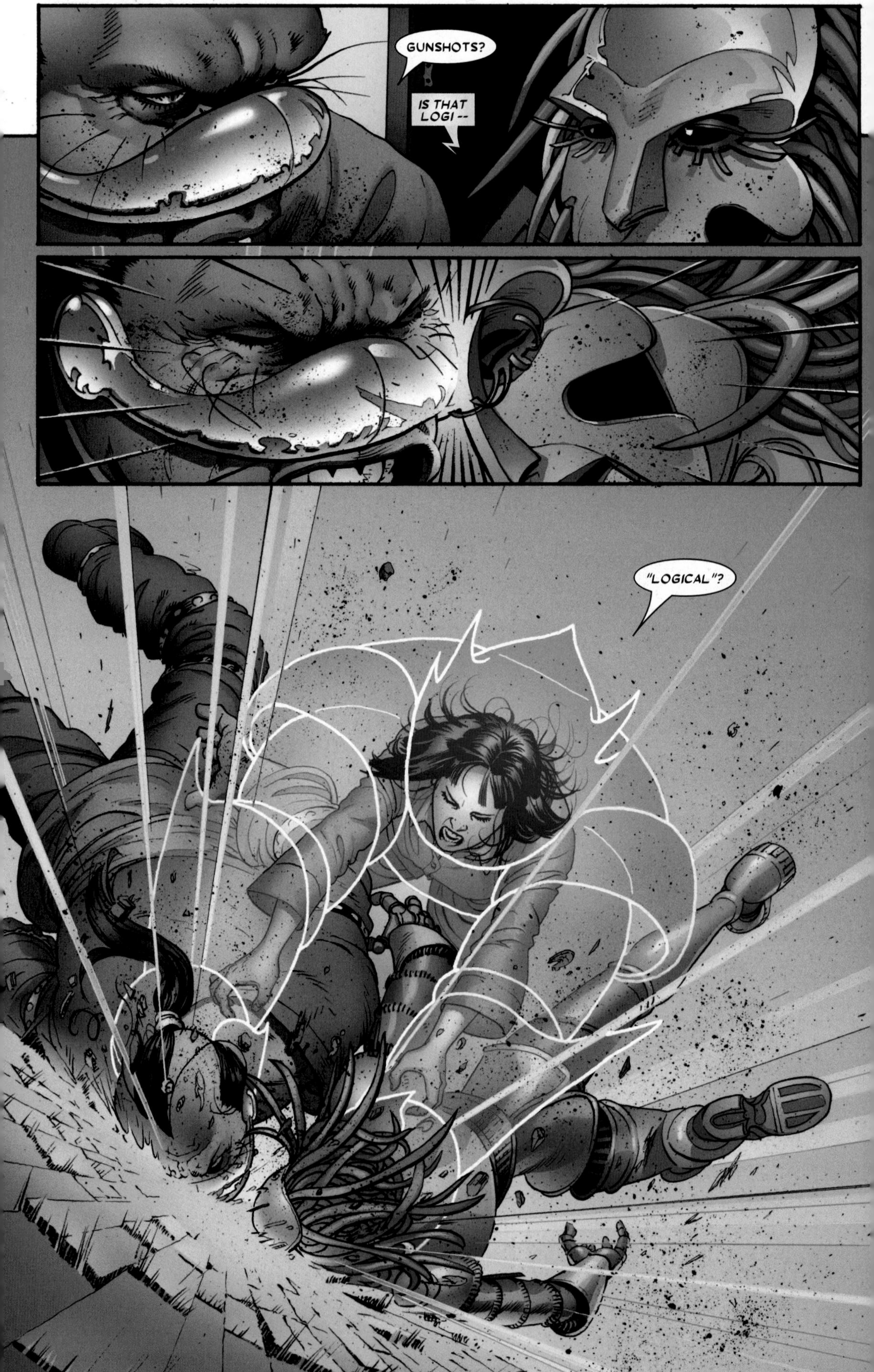
GUNSHOTS?
IS THAT LOGI --
"LOGICAL"?

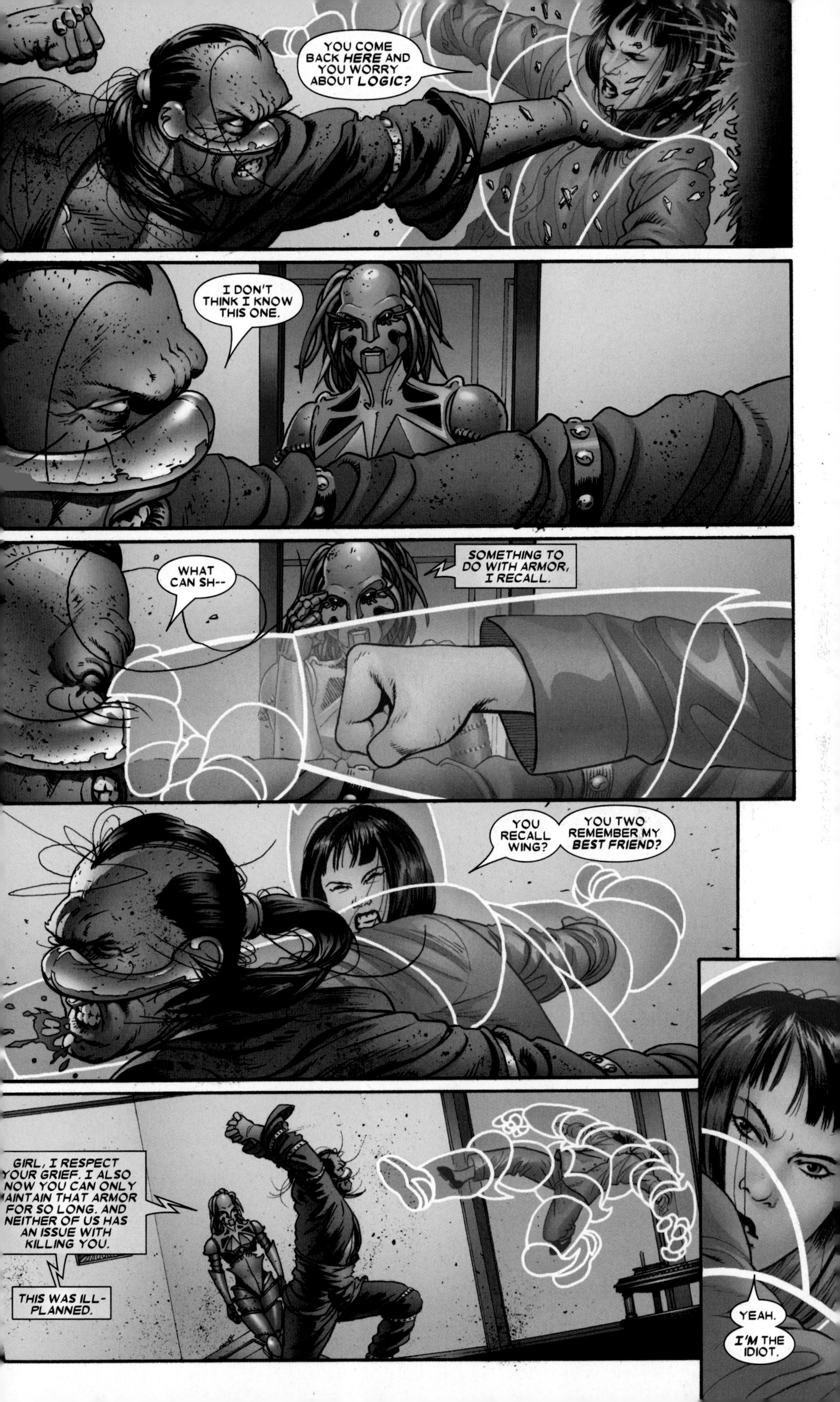

YOU COME BACK HERE AND YOU WORRY ABOUT LOGIC?
I DON'T THINK I KNOW THIS ONE.
WHAT CAN SH--
SOMETHING TO DO WITH ARMOR, I RECALL.
YOU RECALL WING?
YOU TWO REMEMBER MY BEST FRIEND?
GIRL, I RESPECT YOUR GRIEF. I ALSO NOW YOU CAN ONLY AINTAIN THAT ARMOR FOR SO LONG. AND NEITHER OF US HAS AN ISSUE WITH KILLING YOU.
THIS WAS ILL-PLANNED.
YEAH.
I'M THE IDIOT.

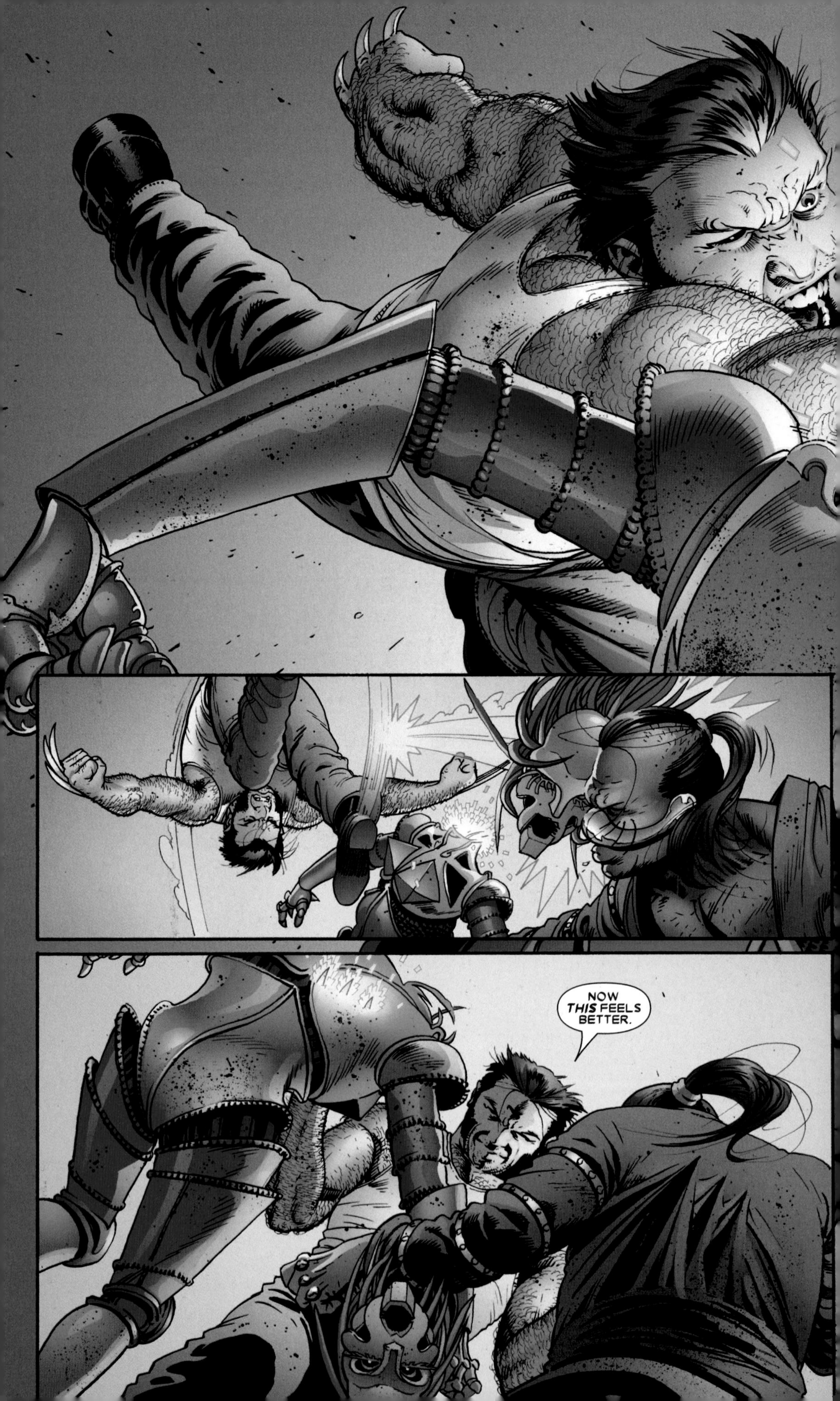
NOW THIS FEELS BETTER.

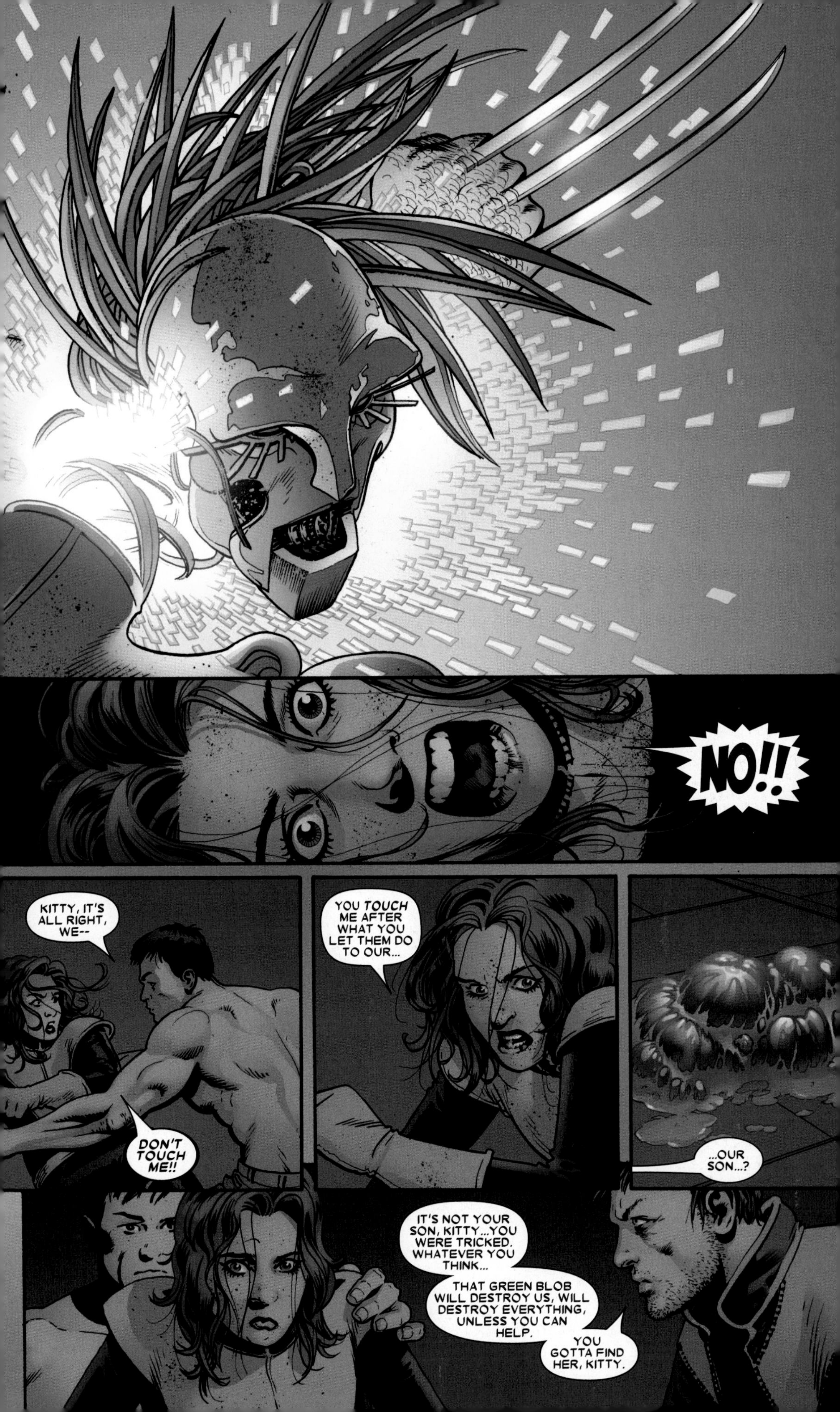
NO!!
KITTY, IT'S ALL RIGHT, WE--
DON'T TOUCH ME!!
YOU TOUCH ME AFTER WHAT YOU LET THEM DO TO OUR...
...OUR SON...?
IT'S NOT YOUR SON, KITTY...YOU WERE TRICKED. WHATEVER YOU THINK...
THAT GREEN BLOB WILL DESTROY US, WILL DESTROY EVERYTHING, UNLESS YOU CAN HELP.
YOU GOTTA FIND HER, KITTY.

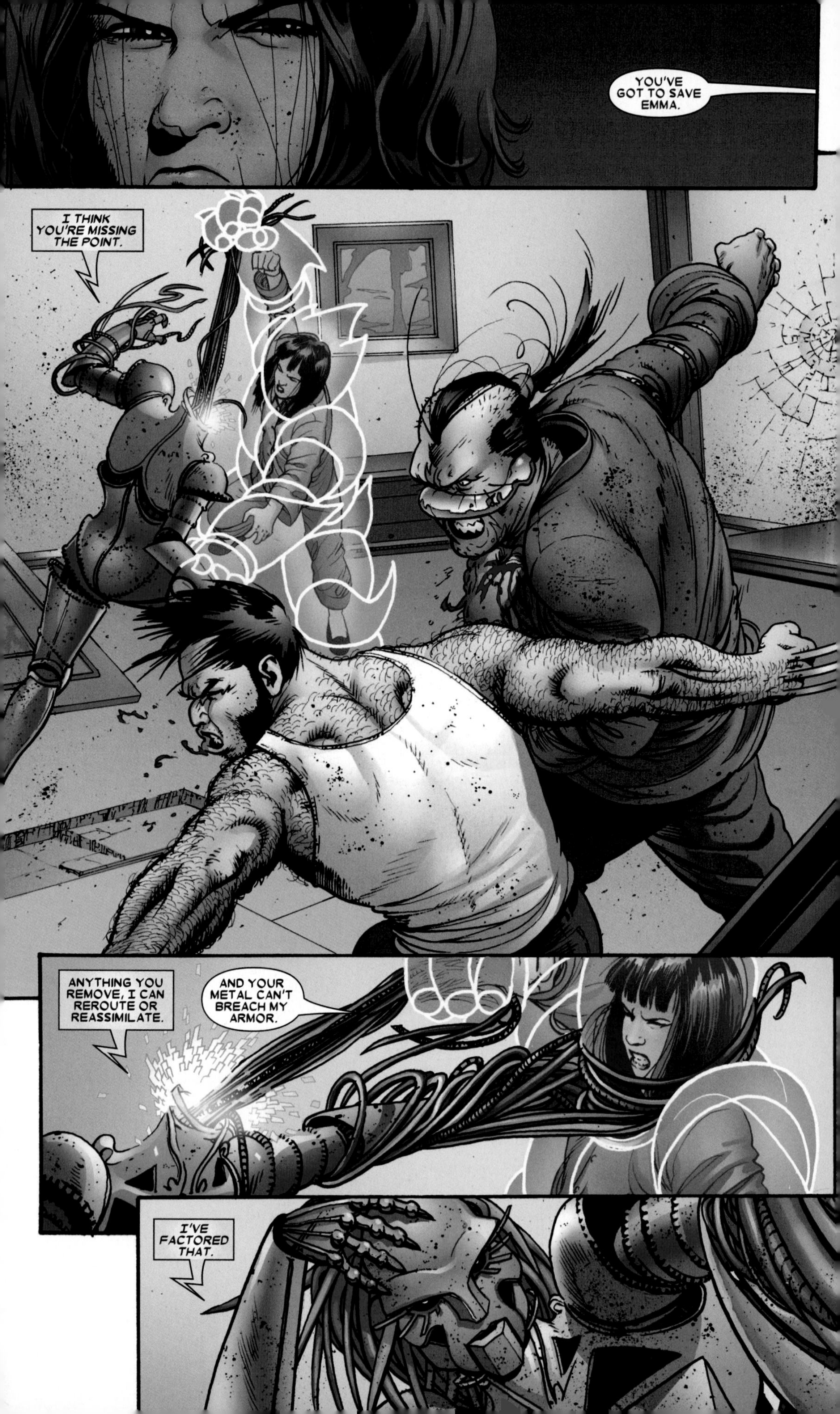
YOU'VE GOT TO SAVE EMMA.
I THINK YOU'RE MISSING THE POINT.
ANYTHING YOU REMOVE, I CAN REROUTE OR REASSIMILATE.
AND YOUR METAL CAN'T BREACH MY ARMOR.
I'VE FACTORED THAT.

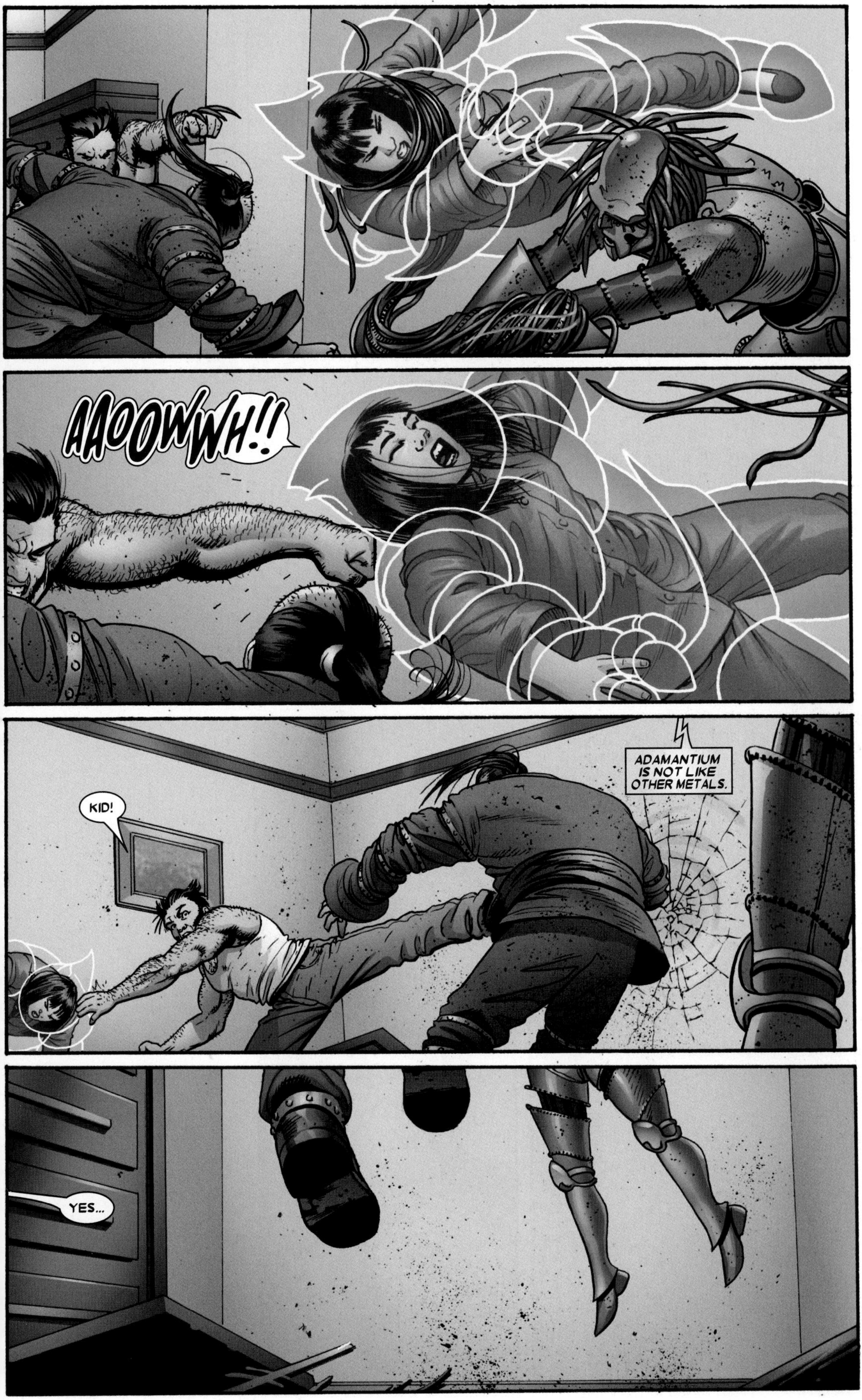
AAOOWWH!!
KID!
ADAMANTIUM IS NOT LIKE OTHER METALS.
YES...

I'VE FACTORED THAT.

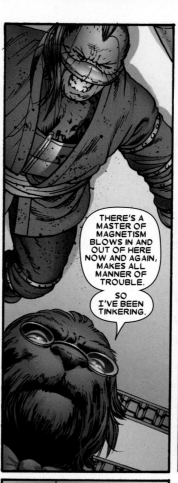

THERE'S A MASTER OF MAGNETISM BLOWS IN AND OUT OF HERE NOW AND AGAIN, MAKES ALL MANNER OF TROUBLE.

SO I'VE BEEN TINKERING.

HOW IS SHE?

IT'S NOT TOO BAD.

IT'S TOO BAD FOR *ME*... AGGHHHH...

HOW?

IT'S TECHNICAL. BUT "BIG MAGNET" COVERS A LOT OF IT. NO ONE MADE OF METAL OR WEARING WAY TOO MUCH OF IT IS GOING ANYWHERE FOR A WHILE.

NO, *YOU.*

AH, YES, ME.

BALL OF STRING.

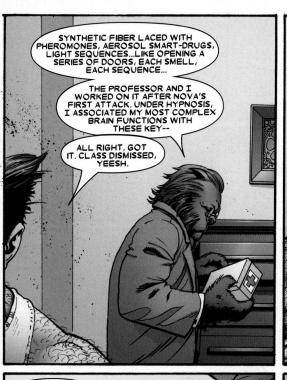

SYNTHETIC FIBER LACED WITH PHEROMONES, AEROSOL SMART-DRUGS, LIGHT SEQUENCES...LIKE OPENING A SERIES OF DOORS, EACH SMELL, EACH SEQUENCE...

THE PROFESSOR AND I WORKED ON IT AFTER NOVA'S FIRST ATTACK. UNDER HYPNOSIS, I ASSOCIATED MY MOST COMPLEX BRAIN FUNCTIONS WITH THESE KEY--

ALL RIGHT. GOT IT. CLASS DISMISSED, YEESH.

AND YOU?

HAD A BEER.

SAME BASIC PRINCIPLE.

OW!

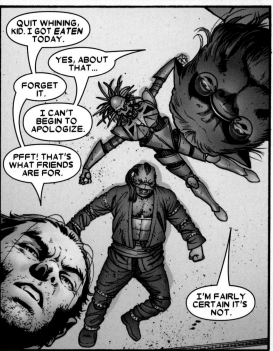

QUIT WHINING, KID. I GOT EATEN TODAY.

YES, ABOUT THAT...

FORGET IT.

I CAN'T BEGIN TO APOLOGIZE.

PFFT! THAT'S WHAT FRIENDS ARE FOR.

I'M FAIRLY CERTAIN IT'S NOT.

LEAST YOU DIDN'T TURN INTO PERCY DOVETONSILS. HOW LONG THAT MAGNET GONNA HOLD 'EM?

NOT SURE. ARE THEY WITH NOVA?

I DON'T KNOW WHO'S WITH WHAT AROUND HERE. I THINK THE HELLFIRE CLUB'S IN IT--SAW EMMA ZOMBIFY KITTY, SEND HER DOWN HERE. WE WERE FOLLOWING.

NOT EMMA.

OLD-SCHOOL LOOK AND EVERYTHING. DON'T KNOW WHAT'S DOWN HERE THAT--

I DO.

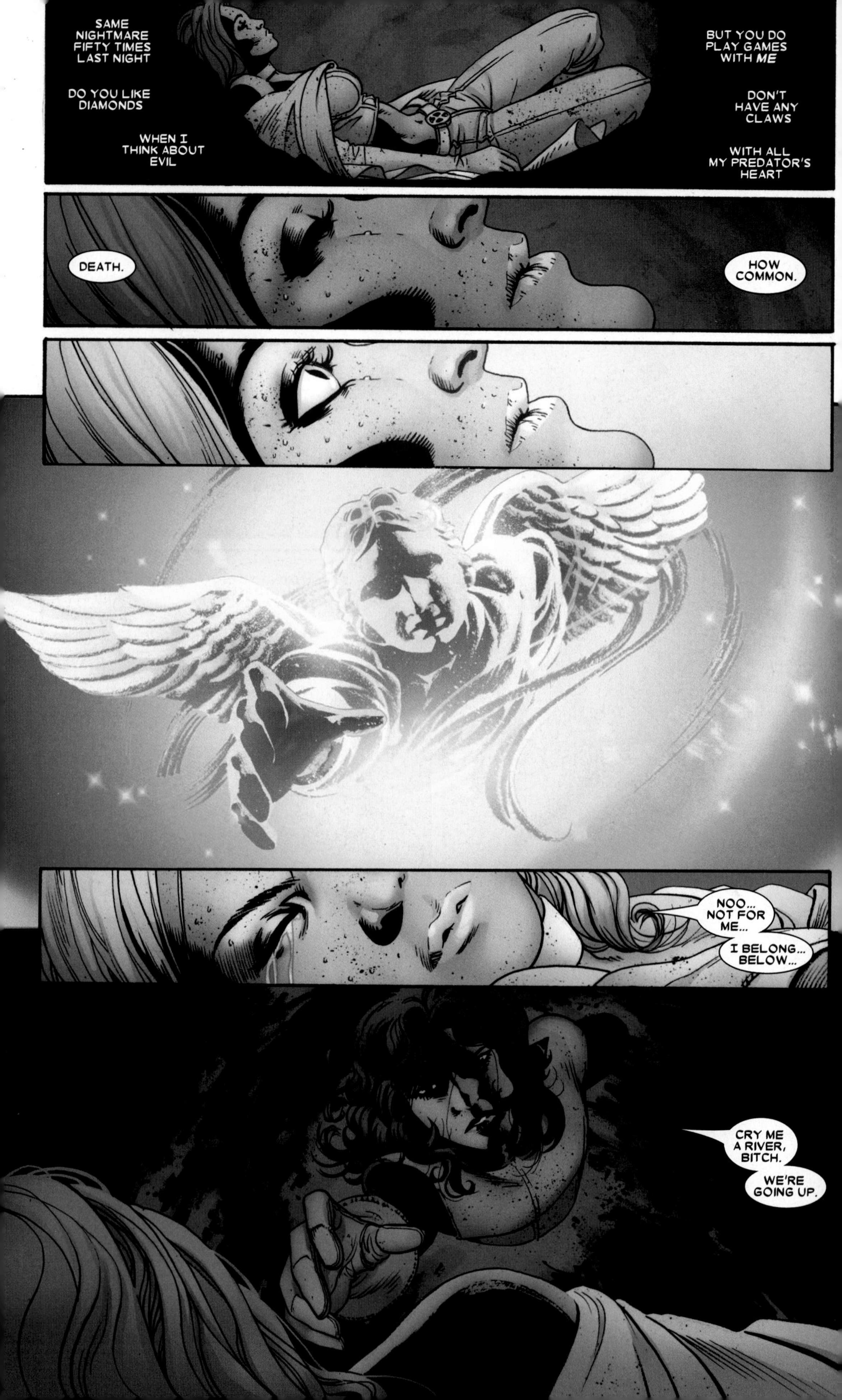
SAME NIGHTMARE FIFTY TIMES LAST NIGHT
DO YOU LIKE DIAMONDS
WHEN I THINK ABOUT EVIL
BUT YOU DO PLAY GAMES WITH ME
DON'T HAVE ANY CLAWS
WITH ALL MY PREDATOR'S HEART
DEATH.
HOW COMMON.
NOO... NOT FOR ME...
I BELONG... BELOW...
CRY ME A RIVER, BITCH.
WE'RE GOING UP.

THERE IS NO HELLFIRE CLUB.

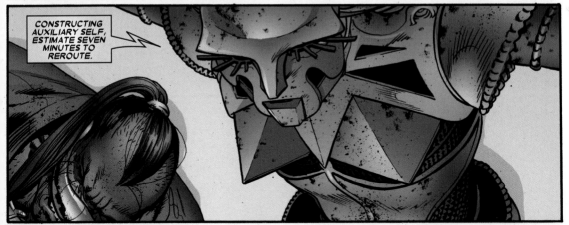

WE'RE READY, DEAR.

CONSTRUCTING AUXILIARY SELF, ESTIMATE SEVEN MINUTES TO REROUTE.

CASSANDRA NOVA.

SHAW.

I DON'T KNOW. A KID.

DID ANY OF YOU EVER SEE MORE THAN ONE OF THEM AT A TIME?

FORGET PRYDE, SHE'S TOO RESISTANT.

I NEED MY CONSCIOUSNESS OUT OF THAT SLUG *NOW*.

AND I'VE TAKEN A NEW FANCY.

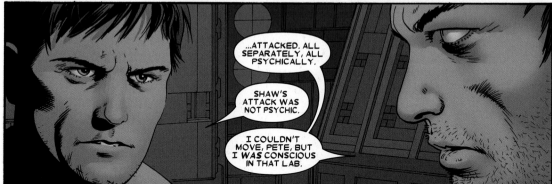

...ATTACKED. ALL SEPARATELY, ALL PSYCHICALLY.

SHAW'S ATTACK WAS NOT PSYCHIC.

I COULDN'T MOVE, PETE, BUT I *WAS* CONSCIOUS IN THAT LAB.

"SHAW WAS NEVER THERE."

AHHH...THAT CONSCIOUSNESS IS LIKE AN OYSTER...

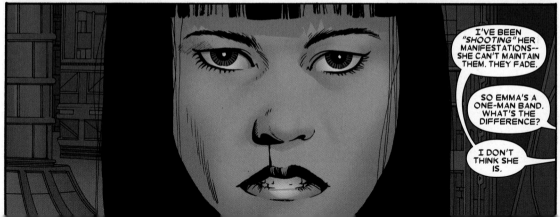

I'VE BEEN "SHOOTING" HER MANIFESTATIONS-- SHE CAN'T MAINTAIN THEM. THEY FADE.

SO EMMA'S A ONE-MAN BAND. WHAT'S THE DIFFERENCE?

I DON'T THINK SHE IS.

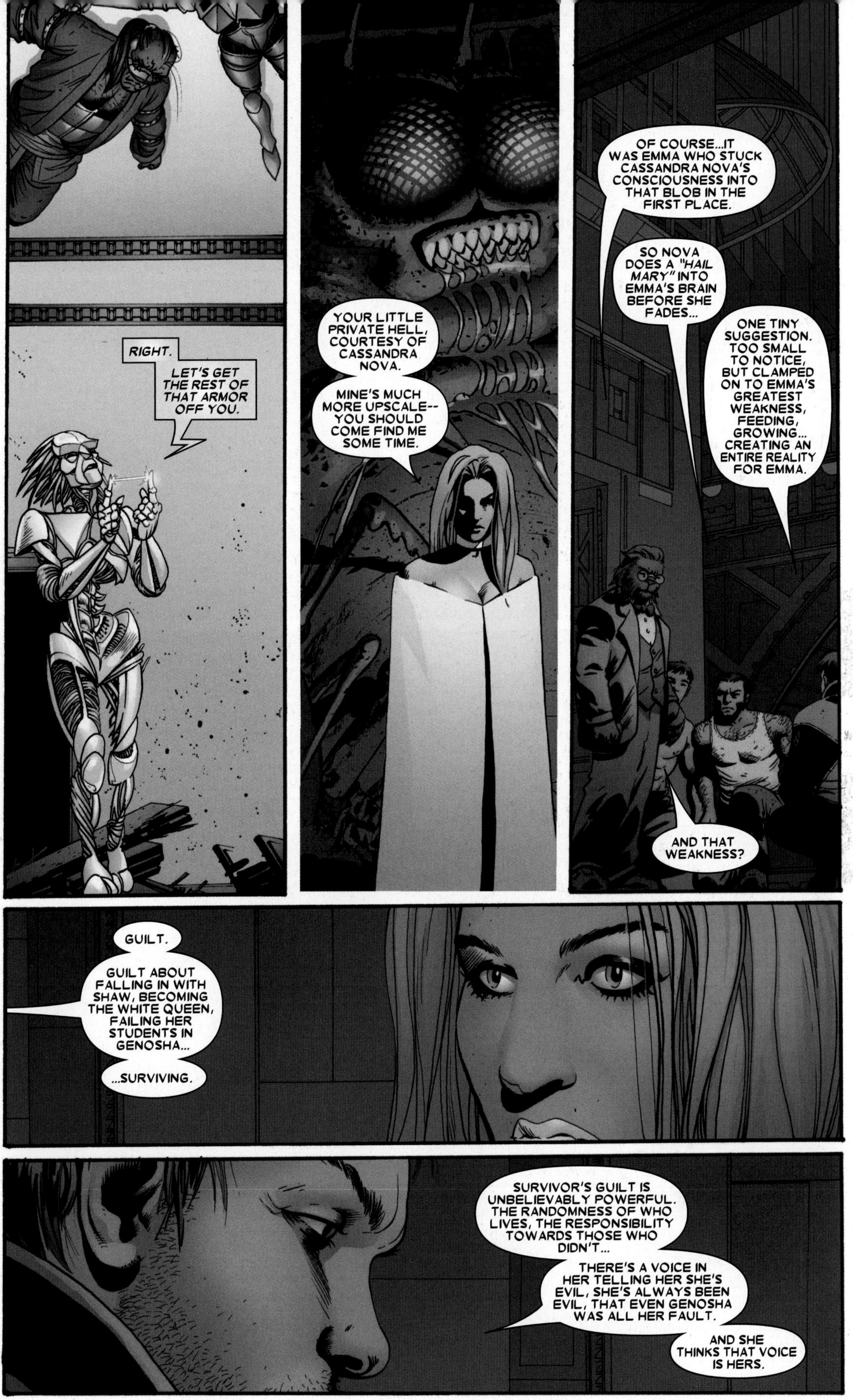

RIGHT.
LET'S GET THE REST OF THAT ARMOR OFF YOU.
YOUR LITTLE PRIVATE HELL, COURTESY OF CASSANDRA NOVA.
MINE'S MUCH MORE UPSCALE--YOU SHOULD COME FIND ME SOME TIME.
OF COURSE...IT WAS EMMA WHO STUCK CASSANDRA NOVA'S CONSCIOUSNESS INTO THAT BLOB IN THE FIRST PLACE.
SO NOVA DOES A "HAIL MARY" INTO EMMA'S BRAIN BEFORE SHE FADES...
ONE TINY SUGGESTION. TOO SMALL TO NOTICE, BUT CLAMPED ON TO EMMA'S GREATEST WEAKNESS, FEEDING, GROWING... CREATING AN ENTIRE REALITY FOR EMMA.
AND THAT WEAKNESS?
GUILT.
GUILT ABOUT FALLING IN WITH SHAW, BECOMING THE WHITE QUEEN, FAILING HER STUDENTS IN GENOSHA...
...SURVIVING.
SURVIVOR'S GUILT IS UNBELIEVABLY POWERFUL. THE RANDOMNESS OF WHO LIVES, THE RESPONSIBILITY TOWARDS THOSE WHO DIDN'T...
THERE'S A VOICE IN HER TELLING HER SHE'S EVIL, SHE'S ALWAYS BEEN EVIL, THAT EVEN GENOSHA WAS ALL HER FAULT.
AND SHE THINKS THAT VOICE IS HERS.

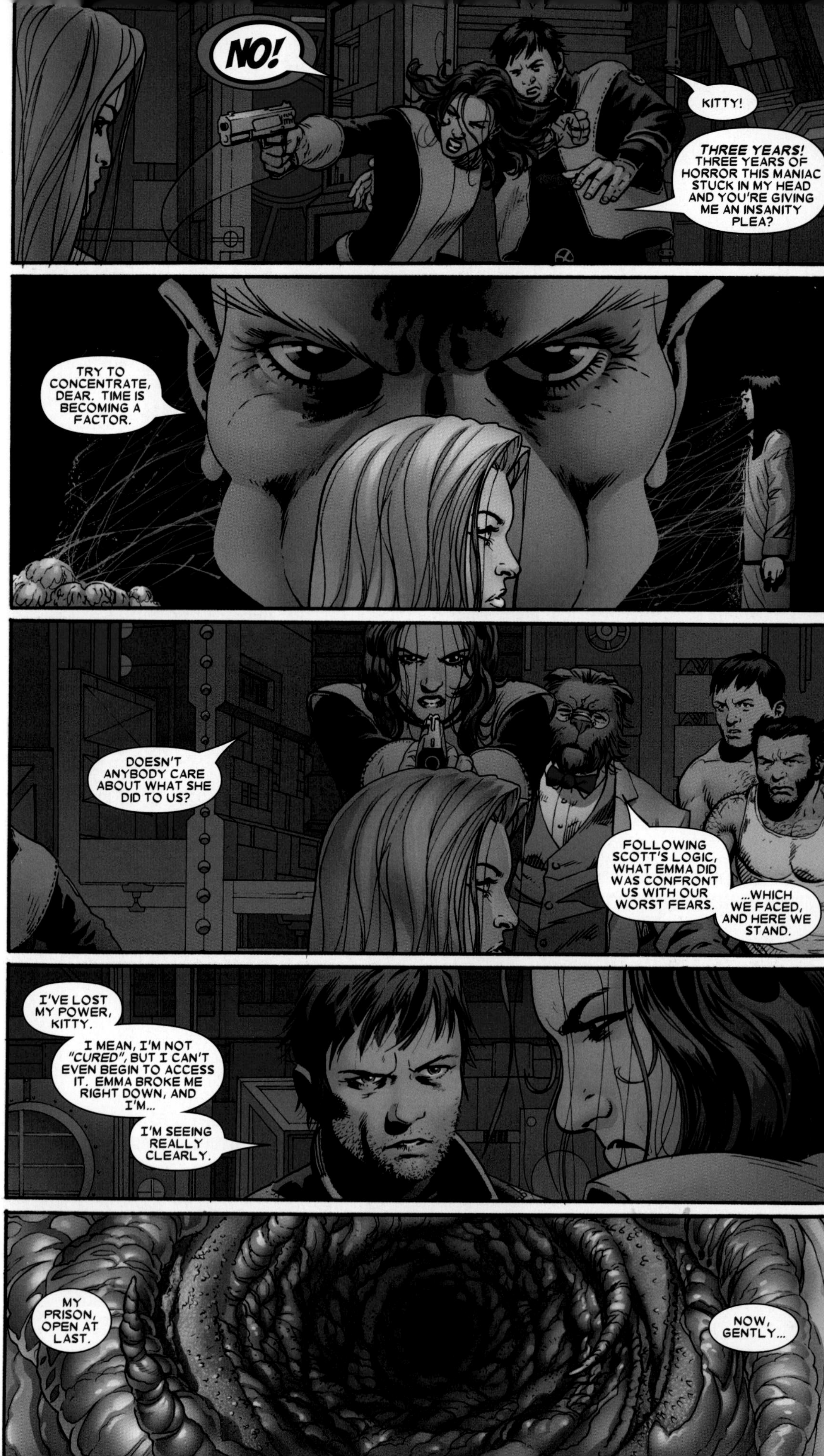
NO!
KITTY!
THREE YEARS! THREE YEARS OF HORROR THIS MANIAC STUCK IN MY HEAD AND YOU'RE GIVING ME AN INSANITY PLEA?
TRY TO CONCENTRATE, DEAR. TIME IS BECOMING A FACTOR.
DOESN'T ANYBODY CARE ABOUT WHAT SHE DID TO US?
FOLLOWING SCOTT'S LOGIC, WHAT EMMA DID WAS CONFRONT US WITH OUR WORST FEARS.
...WHICH WE FACED, AND HERE WE STAND.
I'VE LOST MY POWER, KITTY.
I MEAN, I'M NOT "CURED", BUT I CAN'T EVEN BEGIN TO ACCESS IT. EMMA BROKE ME RIGHT DOWN, AND I'M...
I'M SEEING REALLY CLEARLY.
MY PRISON, OPEN AT LAST.
NOW, GENTLY...

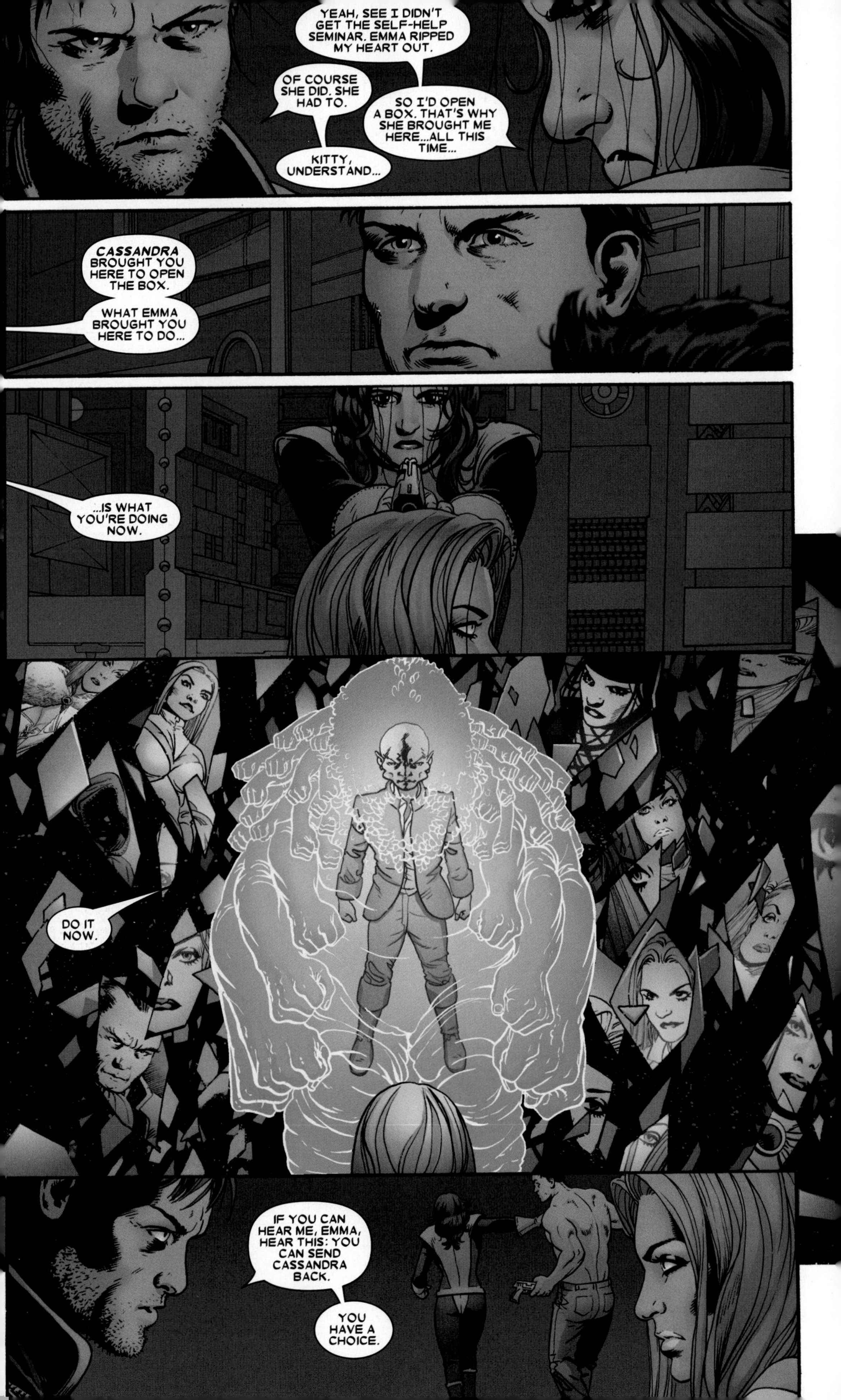
YEAH, SEE I DIDN'T GET THE SELF-HELP SEMINAR. EMMA RIPPED MY HEART OUT.
OF COURSE SHE DID. SHE HAD TO.
SO I'D OPEN A BOX. THAT'S WHY SHE BROUGHT ME HERE...ALL THIS TIME...
KITTY, UNDERSTAND...
CASSANDRA BROUGHT YOU HERE TO OPEN THE BOX.
WHAT EMMA BROUGHT YOU HERE TO DO...
...IS WHAT YOU'RE DOING NOW.
DO IT NOW.
IF YOU CAN HEAR ME, EMMA, HEAR THIS: YOU CAN SEND CASSANDRA BACK.
YOU HAVE A CHOICE.

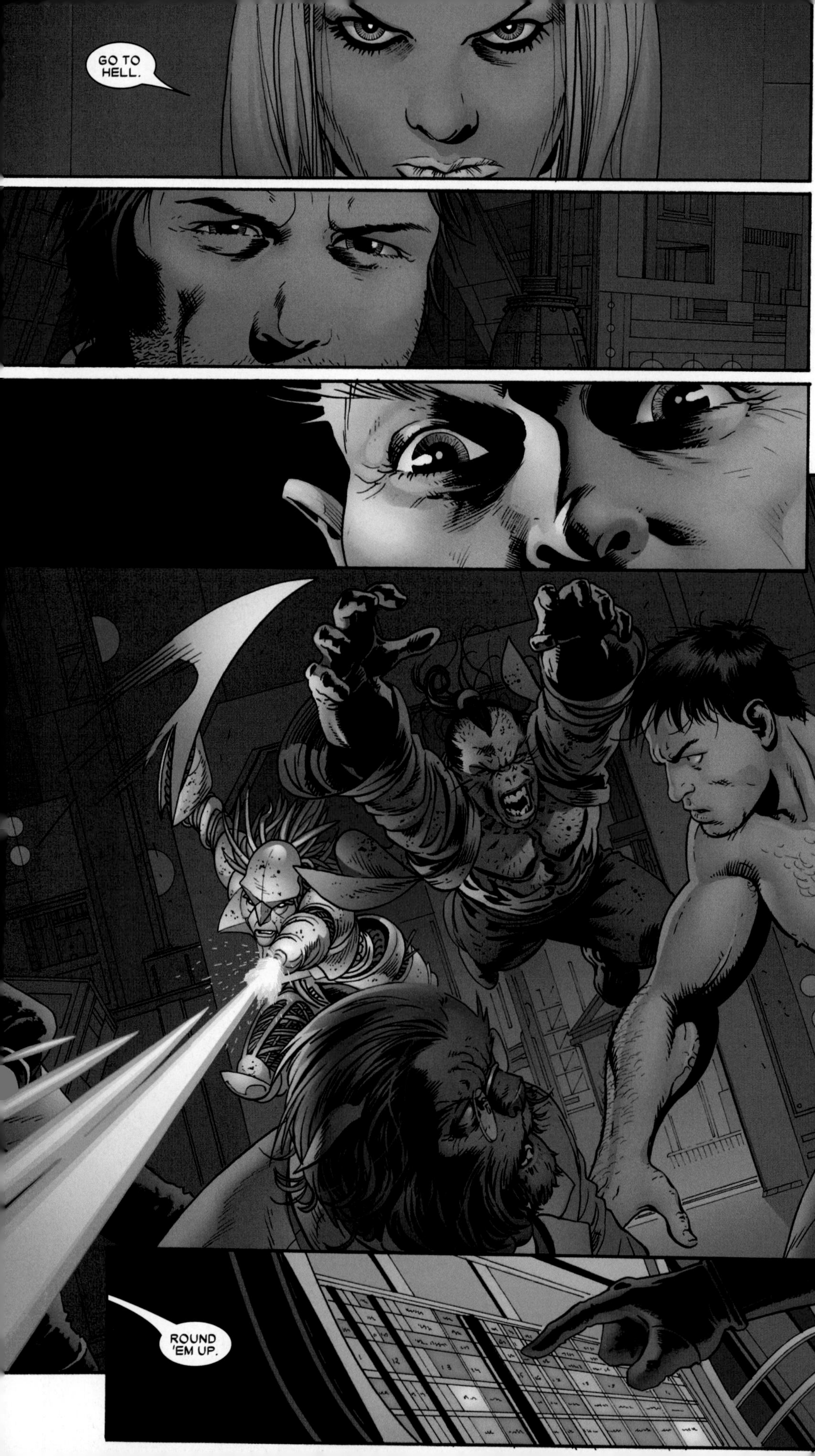
GO TO HELL.
ROUND 'EM UP.

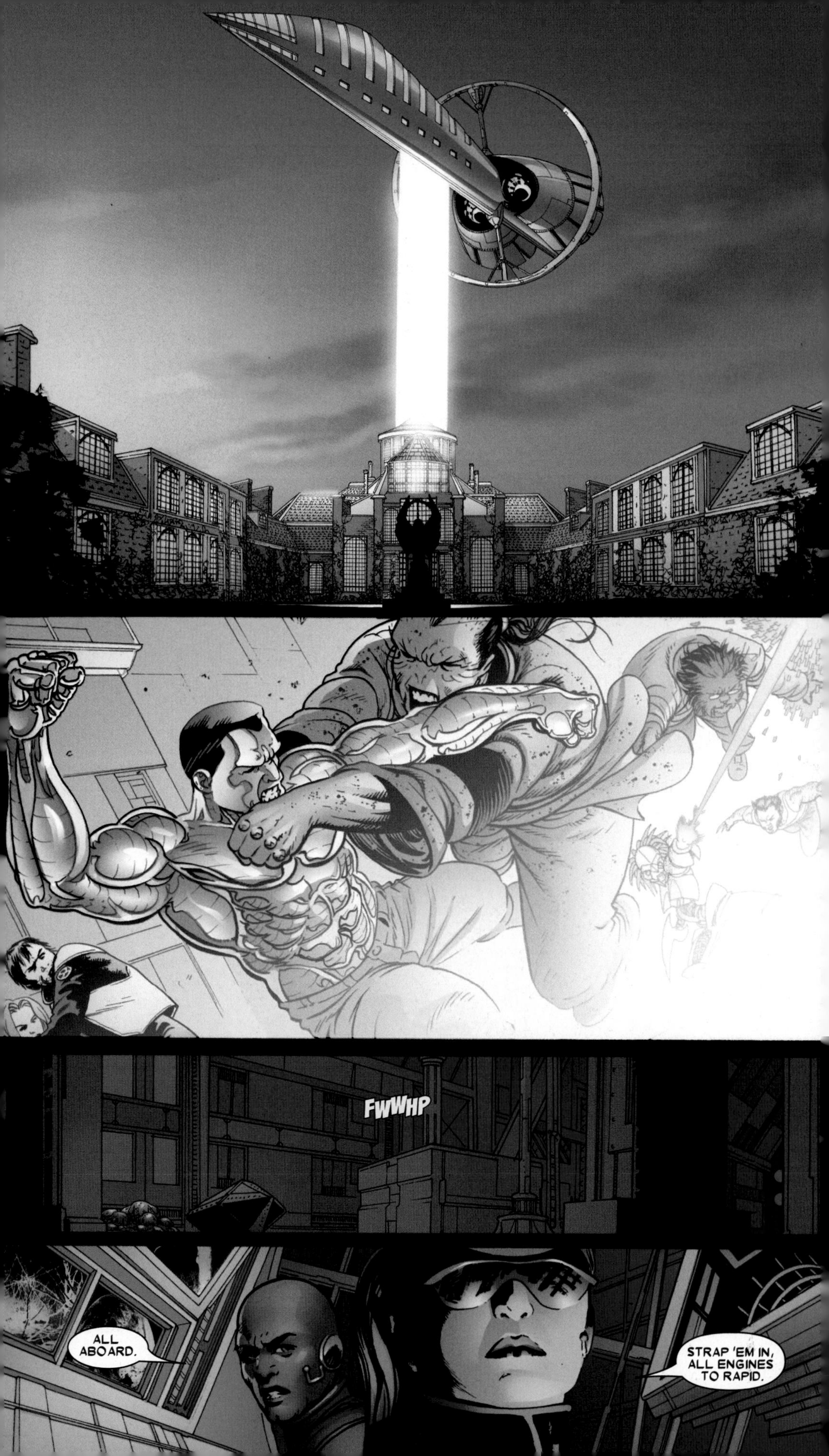
FWWHP
ALL ABOARD.
STRAP 'EM IN, ALL ENGINES TO RAPID.

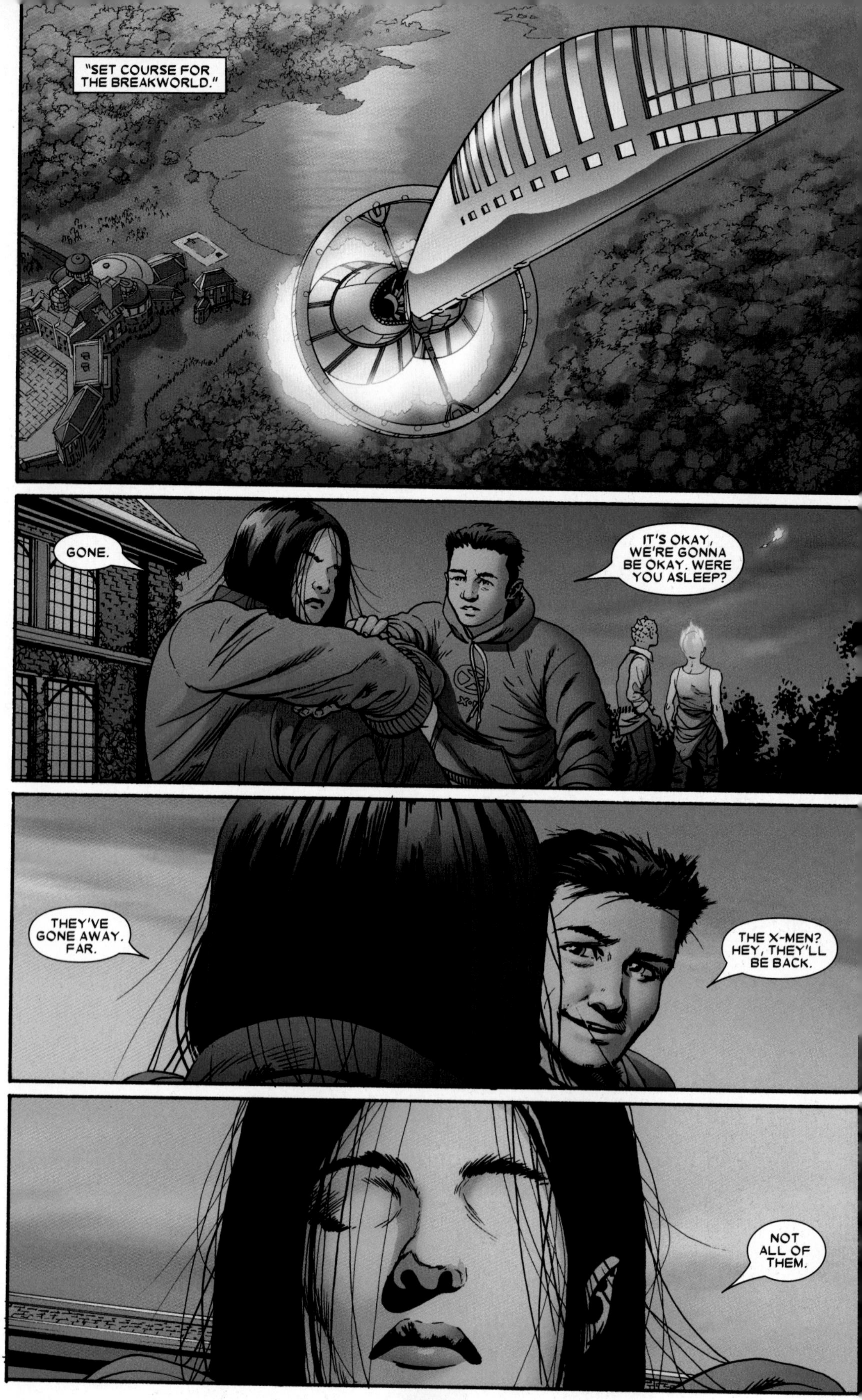
"SET COURSE FOR THE BREAKWORLD."
GONE.
IT'S OKAY, WE'RE GONNA BE OKAY. WERE YOU ASLEEP?
THEY'VE GONE AWAY. FAR.
THE X-MEN? HEY, THEY'LL BE BACK.
NOT ALL OF THEM.

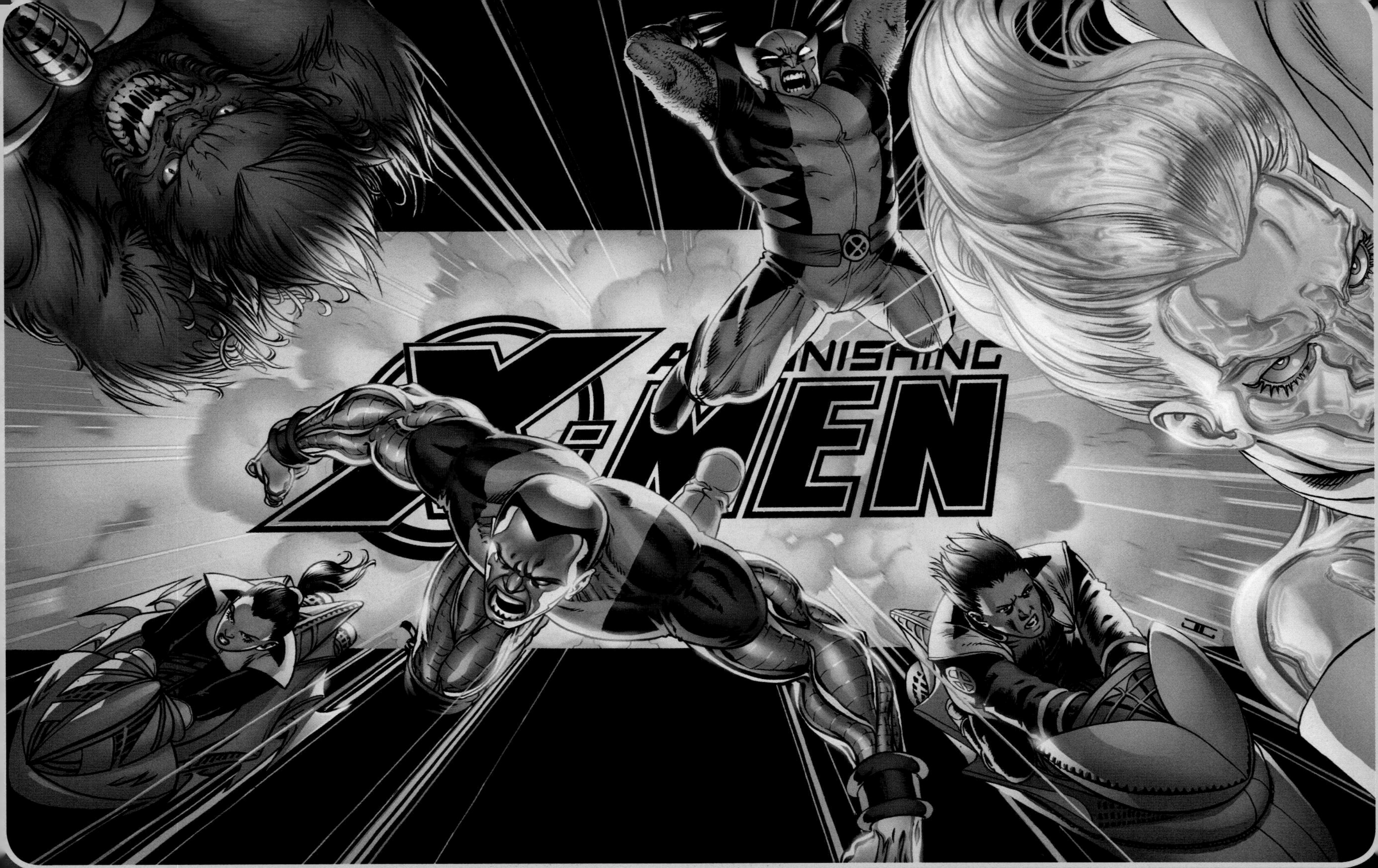
X-MEN

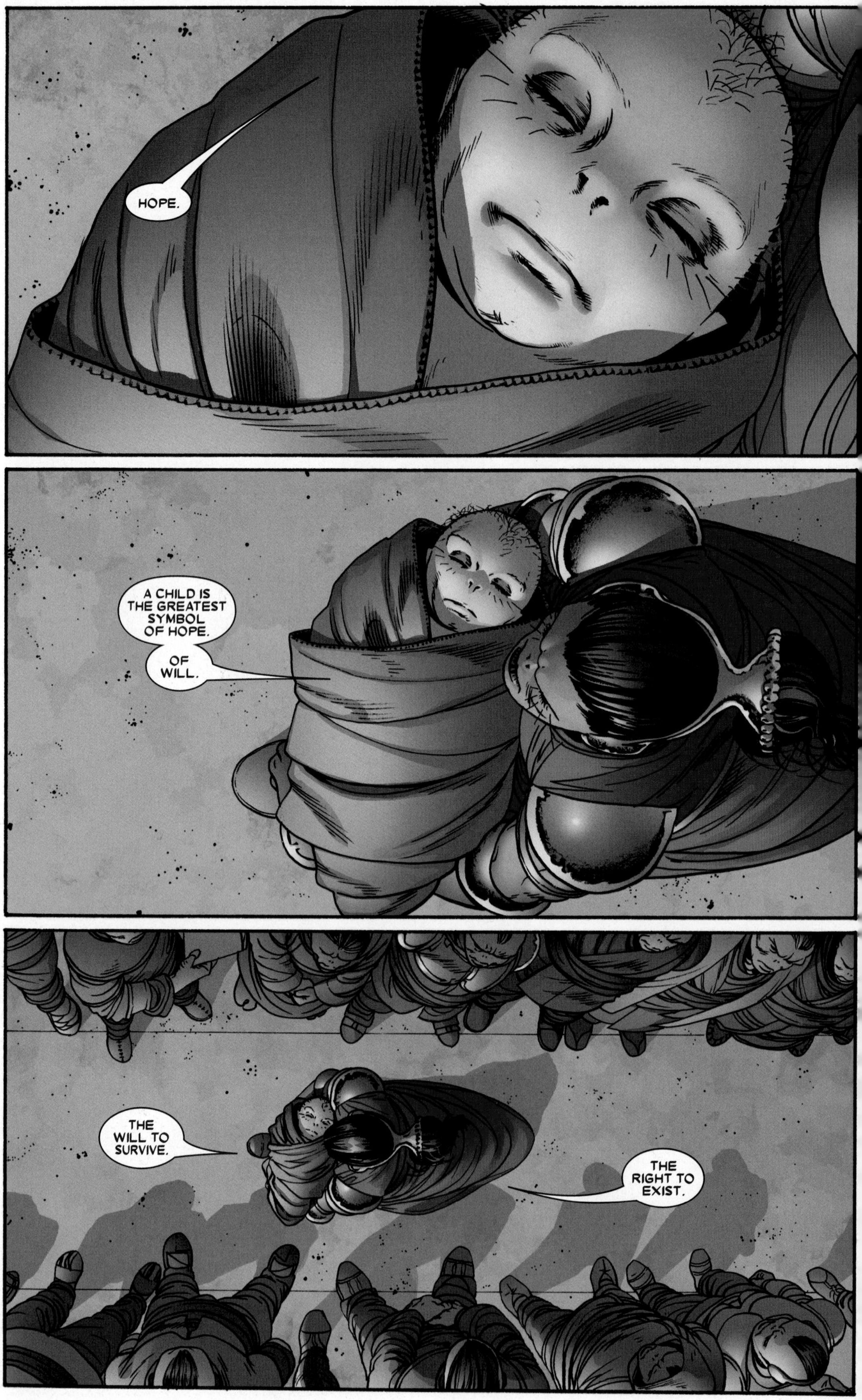
HOPE.
A CHILD IS THE GREATEST SYMBOL OF HOPE.
OF WILL.
THE WILL TO SURVIVE.
THE RIGHT TO EXIST.

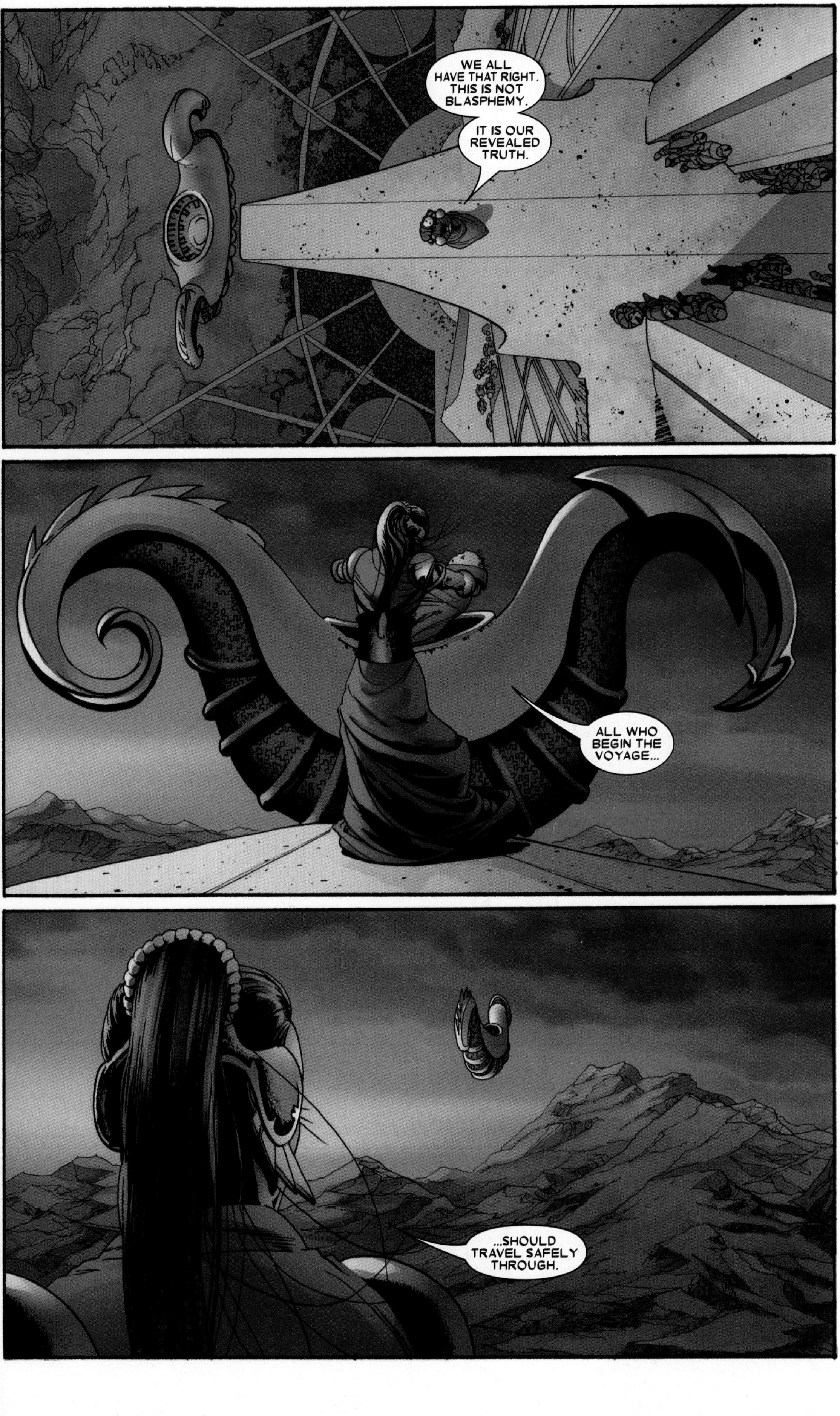
WE ALL HAVE THAT RIGHT. THIS IS NOT BLASPHEMY.
IT IS OUR REVEALED TRUTH.
ALL WHO BEGIN THE VOYAGE...
...SHOULD TRAVEL SAFELY THROUGH.

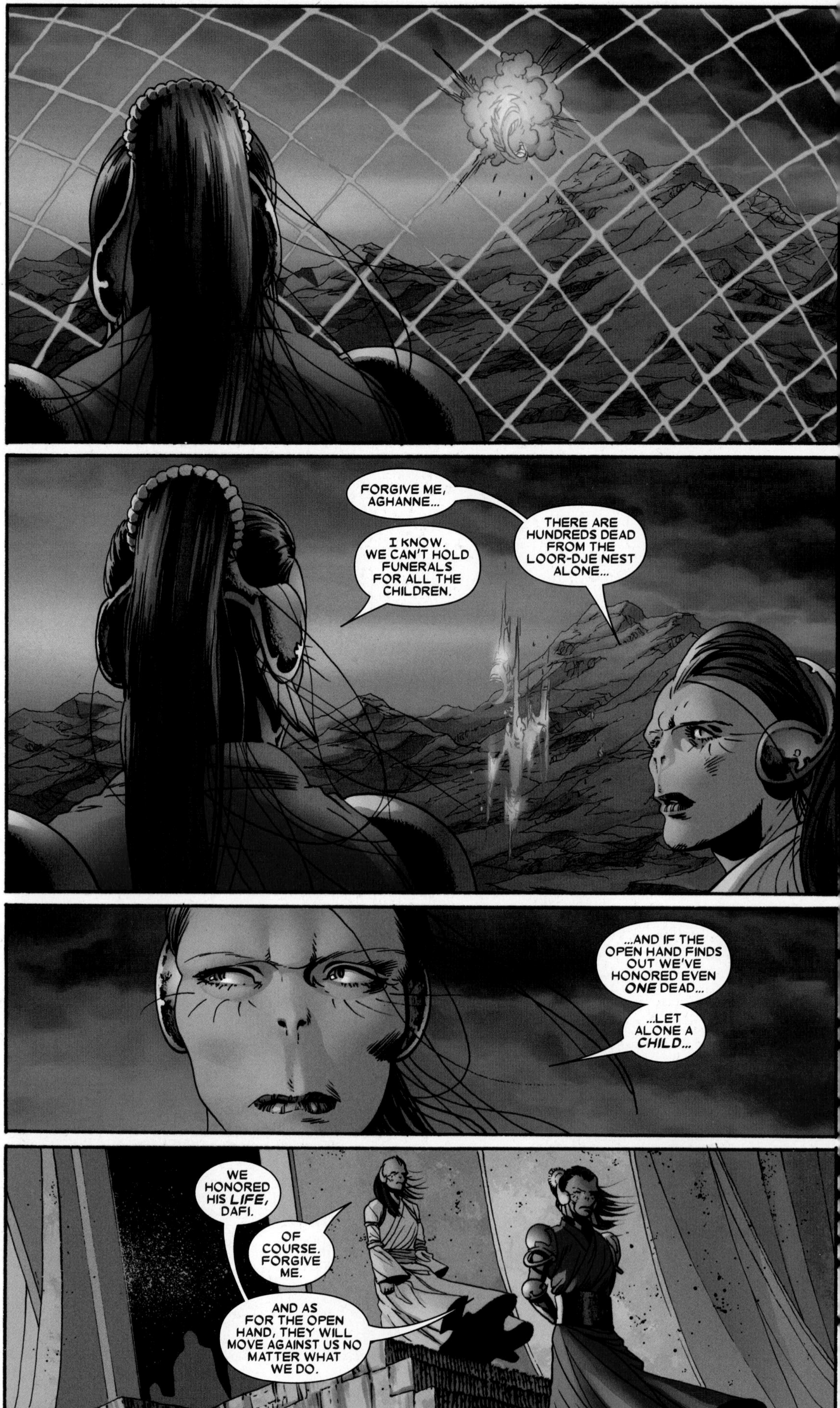
FORGIVE ME, AGHANNE...
THERE ARE HUNDREDS DEAD FROM THE LOOR-DJE NEST ALONE...
I KNOW. WE CAN'T HOLD FUNERALS FOR ALL THE CHILDREN.
...AND IF THE OPEN HAND FINDS OUT WE'VE HONORED EVEN *ONE* DEAD...
...LET ALONE A *CHILD*...
WE HONORED HIS *LIFE*, DAFI.
OF COURSE. FORGIVE ME.
AND AS FOR THE OPEN HAND, THEY WILL MOVE AGAINST US NO MATTER WHAT WE DO.

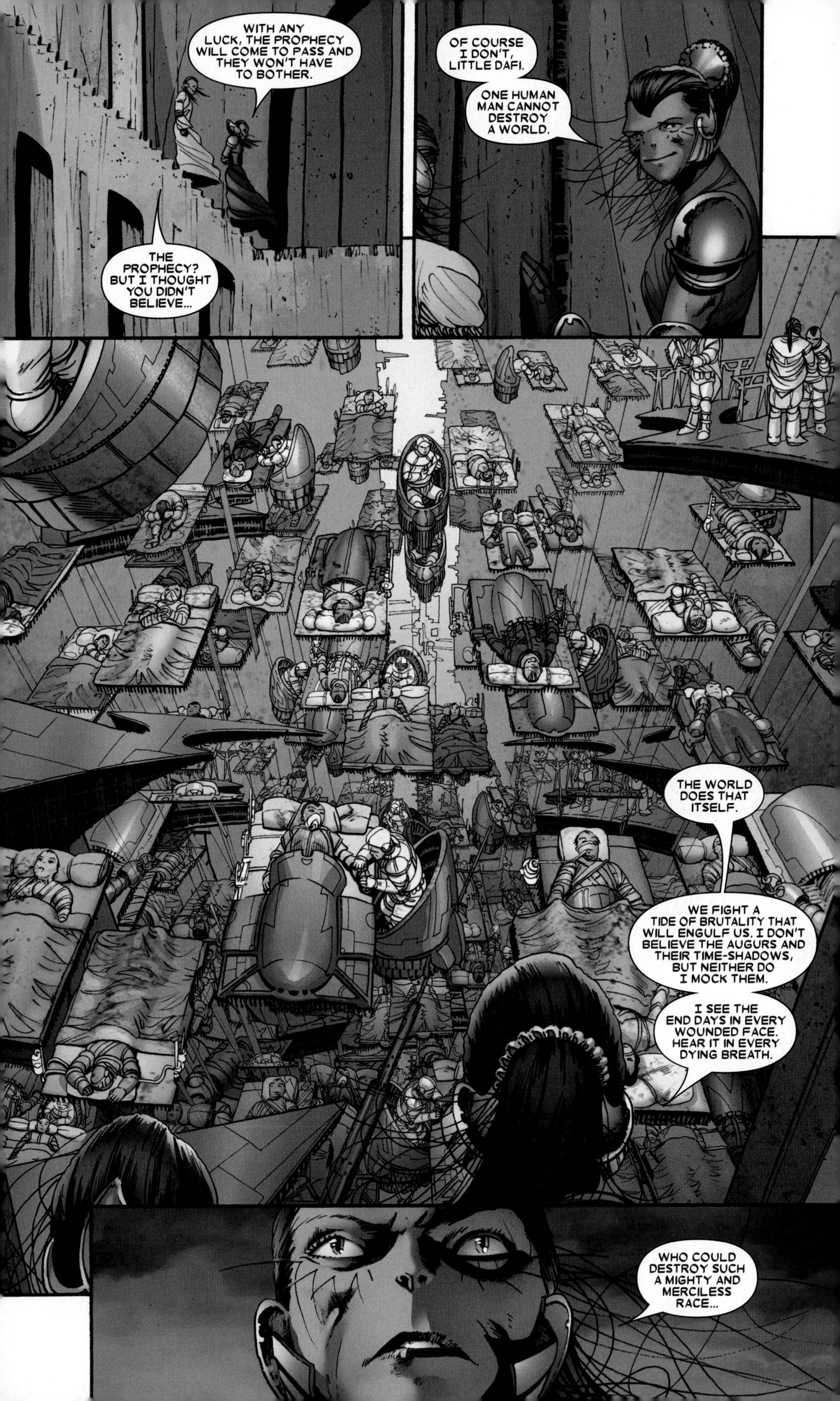
WITH ANY LUCK, THE PROPHECY WILL COME TO PASS AND THEY WON'T HAVE TO BOTHER.
THE PROPHECY? BUT I THOUGHT YOU DIDN'T BELIEVE...
OF COURSE I DON'T, LITTLE DAFI.
ONE HUMAN MAN CANNOT DESTROY A WORLD.
THE WORLD DOES THAT ITSELF.
WE FIGHT A TIDE OF BRUTALITY THAT WILL ENGULF US. I DON'T BELIEVE THE AUGURS AND THEIR TIME-SHADOWS, BUT NEITHER DO I MOCK THEM.
I SEE THE END DAYS IN EVERY WOUNDED FACE. HEAR IT IN EVERY DYING BREATH.
WHO COULD DESTROY SUCH A MIGHTY AND MERCILESS RACE...

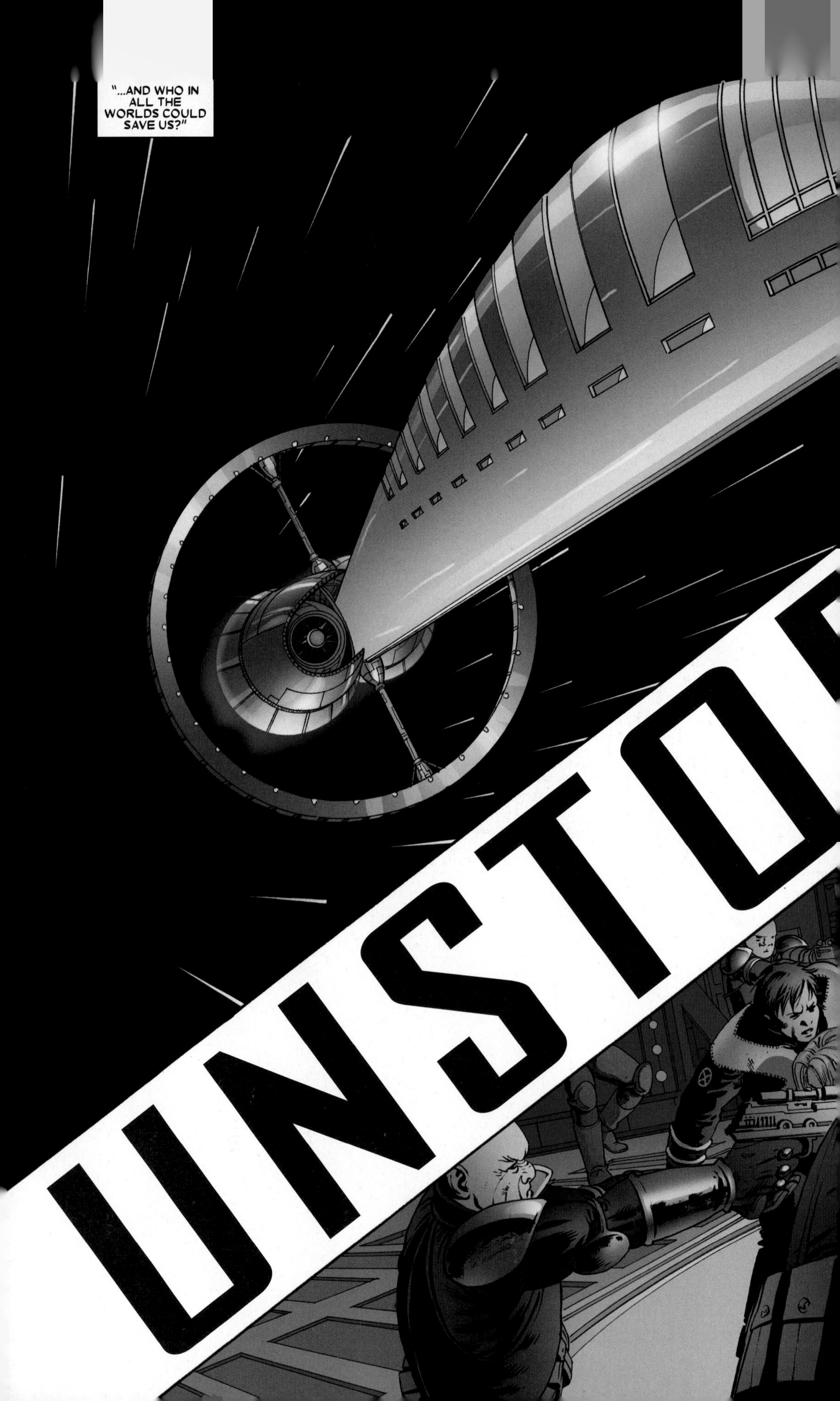
"...AND WHO IN ALL THE WORLDS COULD SAVE US?"
UNSTO

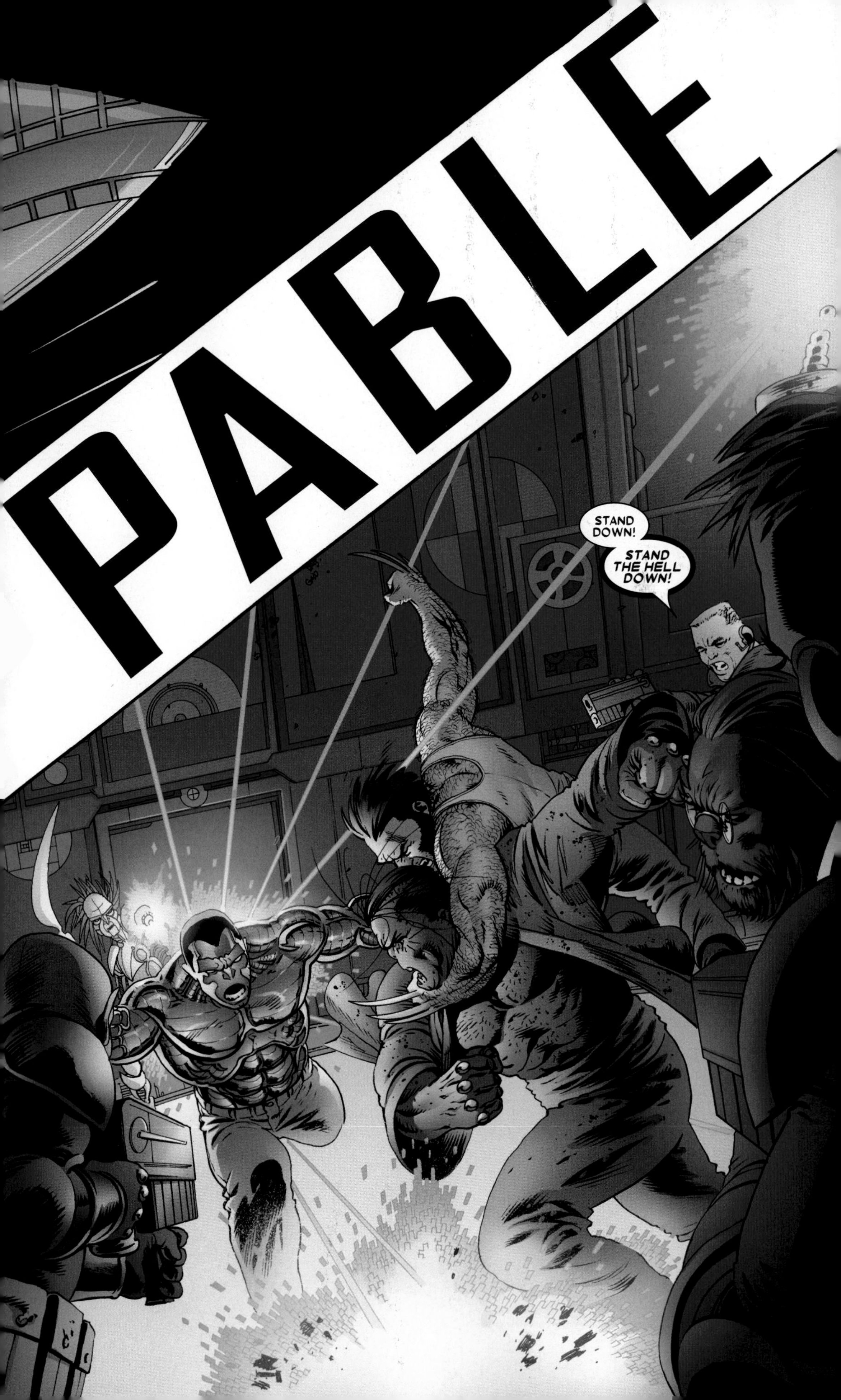
PABLE
STAND DOWN!
STAND THE HELL DOWN!

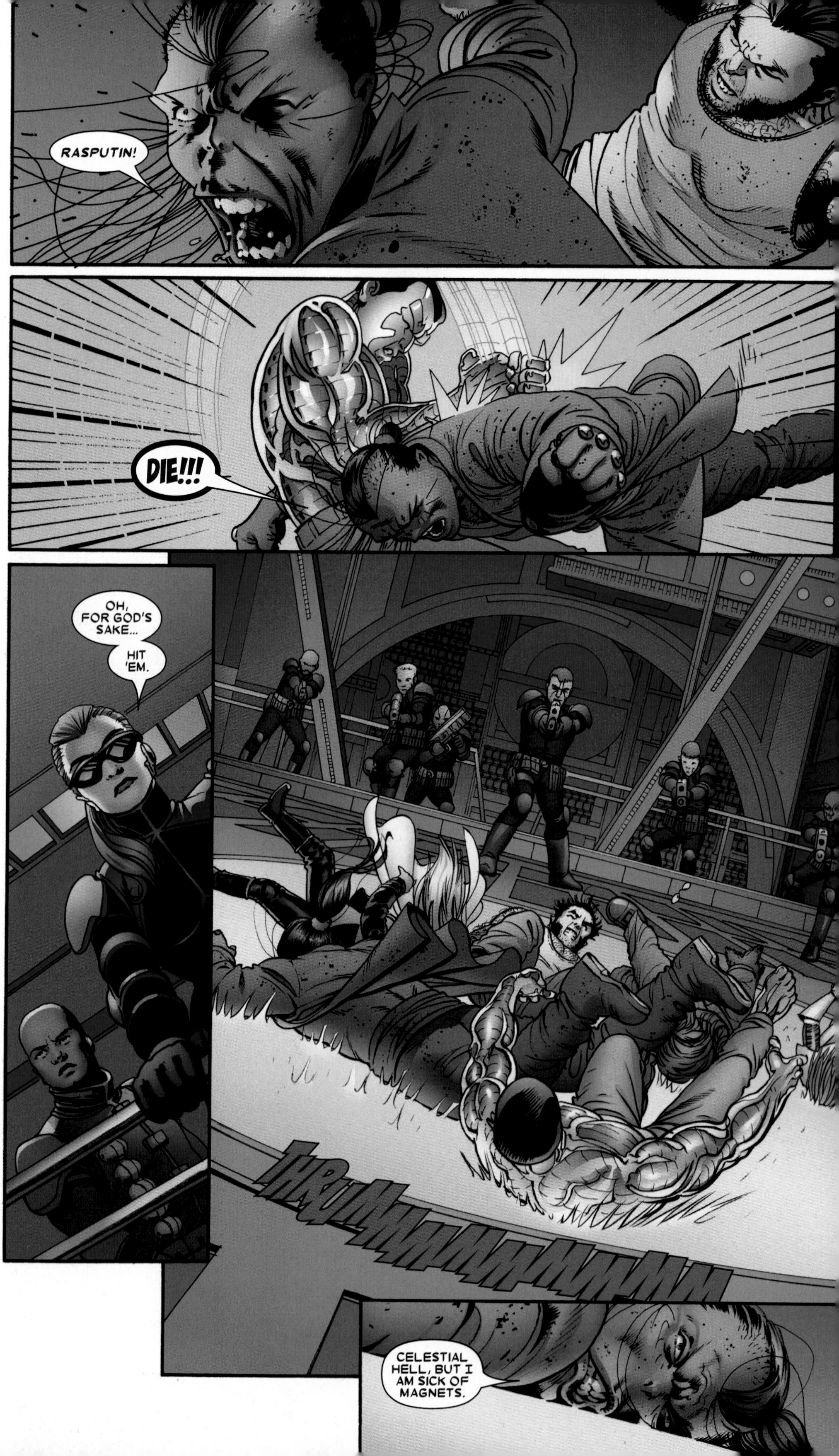
RASPUTIN!
DIE!!!
OH, FOR GOD'S SAKE...
HIT 'EM.
THRUMMMMMMMMMM
CELESTIAL HELL, BUT I AM SICK OF MAGNETS.

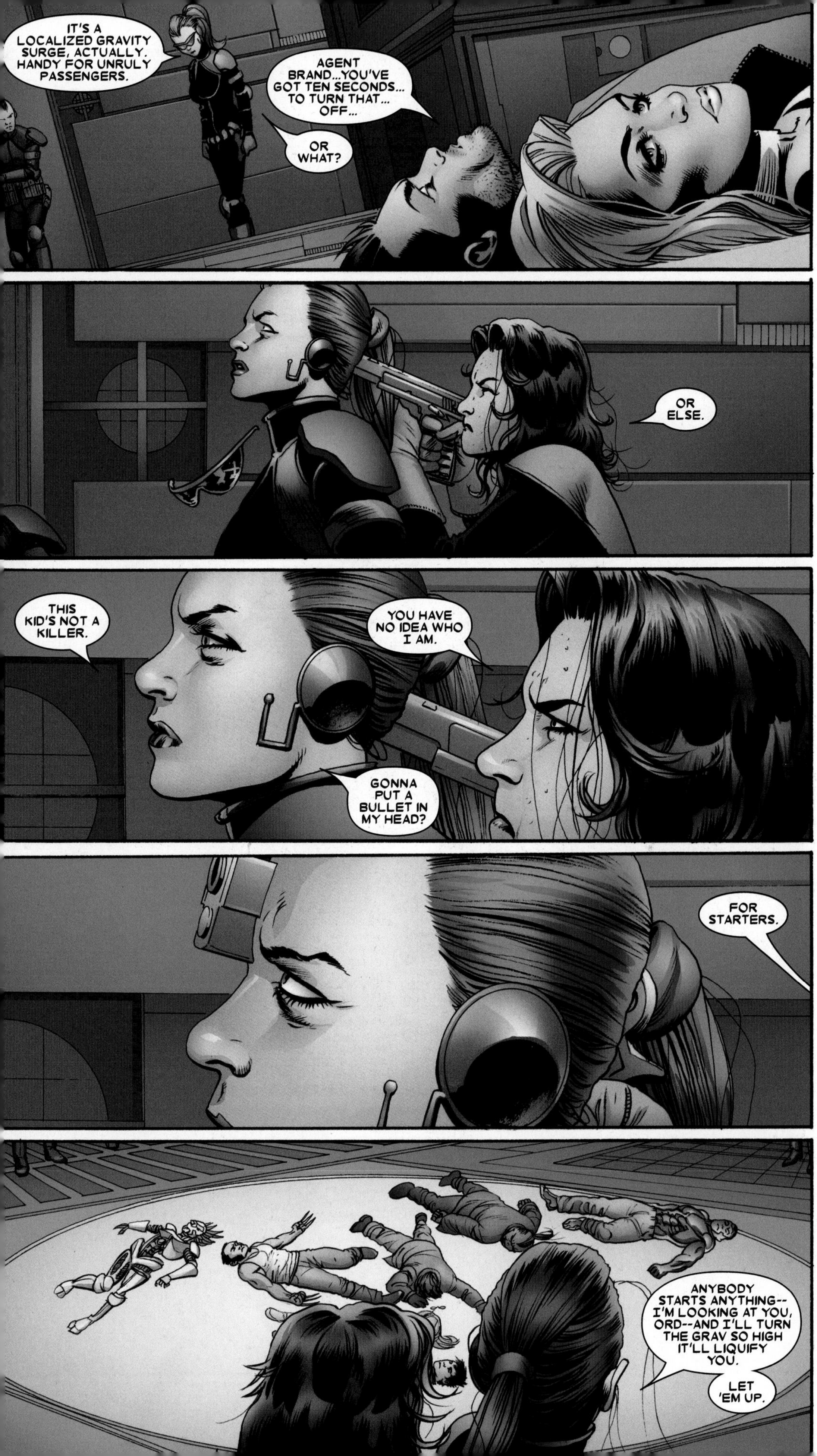

IT'S A LOCALIZED GRAVITY SURGE, ACTUALLY. HANDY FOR UNRULY PASSENGERS.
AGENT BRAND...YOU'VE GOT TEN SECONDS... TO TURN THAT... OFF...
OR WHAT?
OR ELSE.
THIS KID'S NOT A KILLER.
YOU HAVE NO IDEA WHO I AM.
GONNA PUT A BULLET IN MY HEAD?
FOR STARTERS.
ANYBODY STARTS ANYTHING-- I'M LOOKING AT YOU, ORD--AND I'LL TURN THE GRAV SO HIGH IT'LL LIQUIFY YOU.
LET 'EM UP.

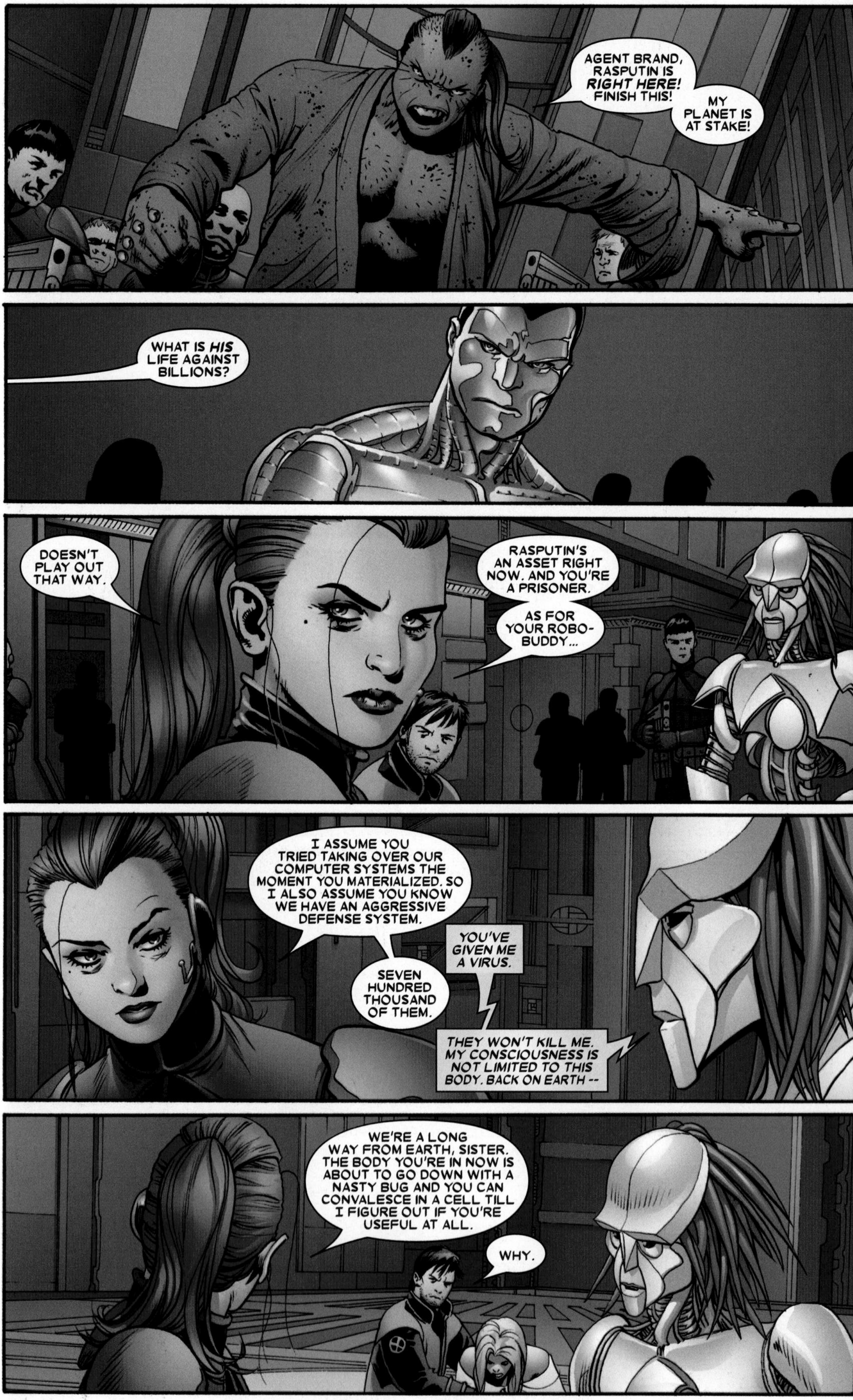
AGENT BRAND, RASPUTIN IS RIGHT HERE! FINISH THIS!
MY PLANET IS AT STAKE!
WHAT IS HIS LIFE AGAINST BILLIONS?
DOESN'T PLAY OUT THAT WAY.
RASPUTIN'S AN ASSET RIGHT NOW. AND YOU'RE A PRISONER.
AS FOR YOUR ROBO-BUDDY...
I ASSUME YOU TRIED TAKING OVER OUR COMPUTER SYSTEMS THE MOMENT YOU MATERIALIZED. SO I ALSO ASSUME YOU KNOW WE HAVE AN AGGRESSIVE DEFENSE SYSTEM.
SEVEN HUNDRED THOUSAND OF THEM.
YOU'VE GIVEN ME A VIRUS.
THEY WON'T KILL ME. MY CONSCIOUSNESS IS NOT LIMITED TO THIS BODY. BACK ON EARTH --
WE'RE A LONG WAY FROM EARTH, SISTER. THE BODY YOU'RE IN NOW IS ABOUT TO GO DOWN WITH A NASTY BUG AND YOU CAN CONVALESCE IN A CELL TILL I FIGURE OUT IF YOU'RE USEFUL AT ALL.
WHY.

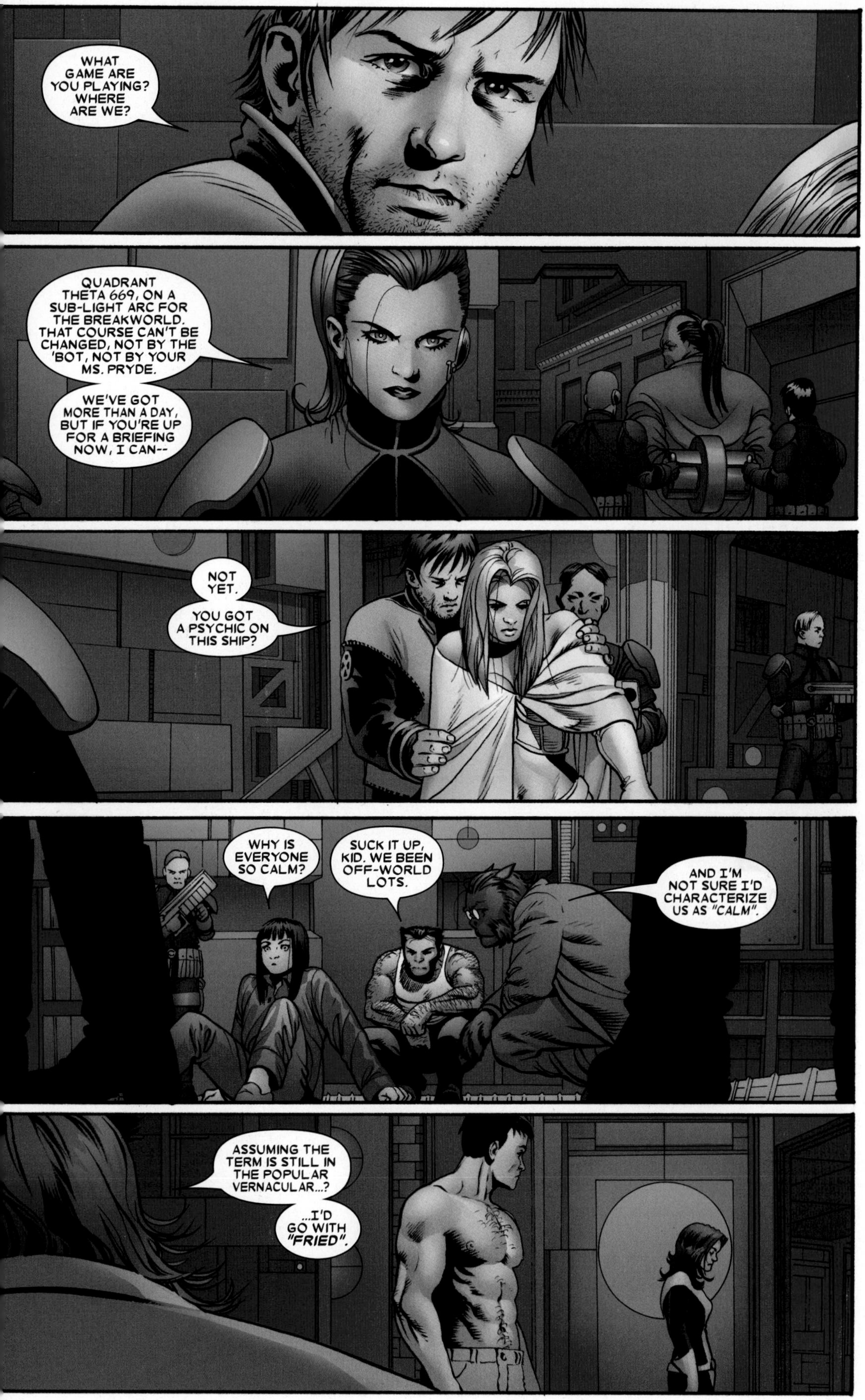
WHAT GAME ARE YOU PLAYING? WHERE ARE WE?
QUADRANT THETA 669, ON A SUB-LIGHT ARC FOR THE BREAKWORLD. THAT COURSE CAN'T BE CHANGED, NOT BY THE 'BOT, NOT BY YOUR MS. PRYDE.
WE'VE GOT MORE THAN A DAY, BUT IF YOU'RE UP FOR A BRIEFING NOW, I CAN--
NOT YET.
YOU GOT A PSYCHIC ON THIS SHIP?
WHY IS EVERYONE SO CALM?
SUCK IT UP, KID. WE BEEN OFF-WORLD LOTS.
AND I'M NOT SURE I'D CHARACTERIZE US AS "CALM".
ASSUMING THE TERM IS STILL IN THE POPULAR VERNACULAR...?
...I'D GO WITH "FRIED".

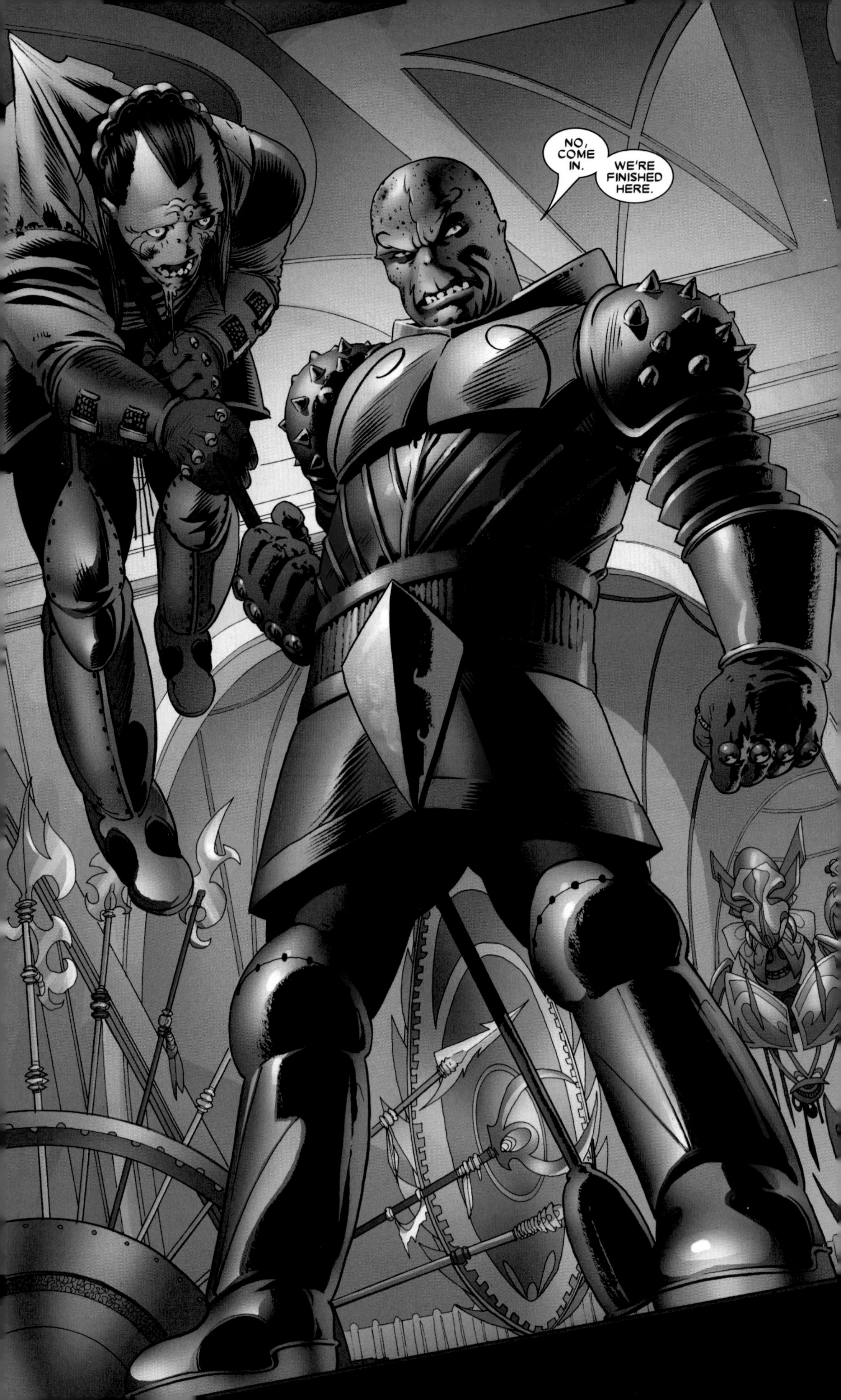
NO, COME IN.
WE'RE FINISHED HERE.

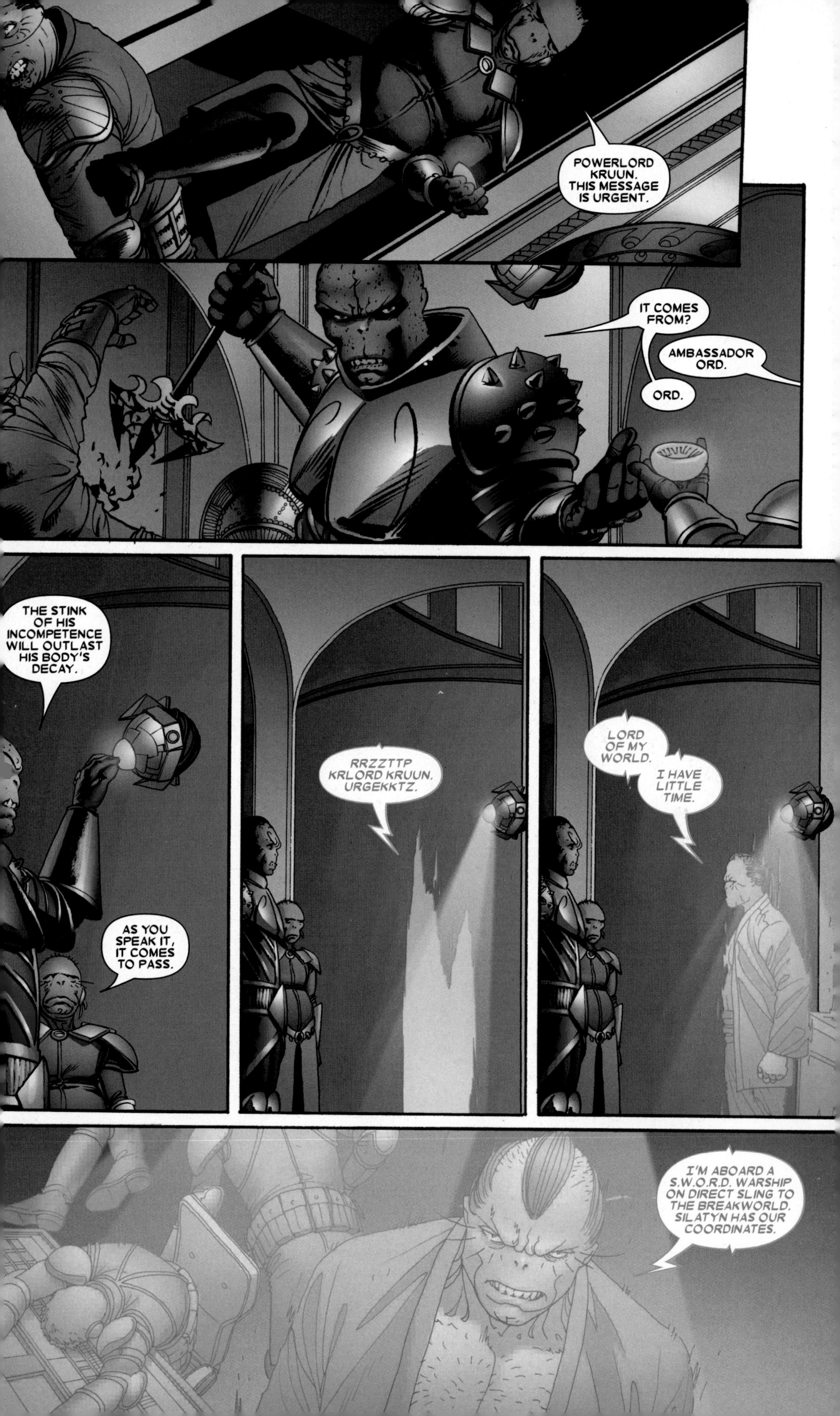
POWERLORD KRUUN. THIS MESSAGE IS URGENT.
IT COMES FROM?
AMBASSADOR ORD.
ORD.
THE STINK OF HIS INCOMPETENCE WILL OUTLAST HIS BODY'S DECAY.
AS YOU SPEAK IT, IT COMES TO PASS.
RRZZTTP KRLORD KRUUN. URGEKKTZ.
LORD OF MY WORLD.
I HAVE LITTLE TIME.
I'M ABOARD A S.W.O.R.D. WARSHIP ON DIRECT SLING TO THE BREAKWORLD. SILATYN HAS OUR COORDINATES.

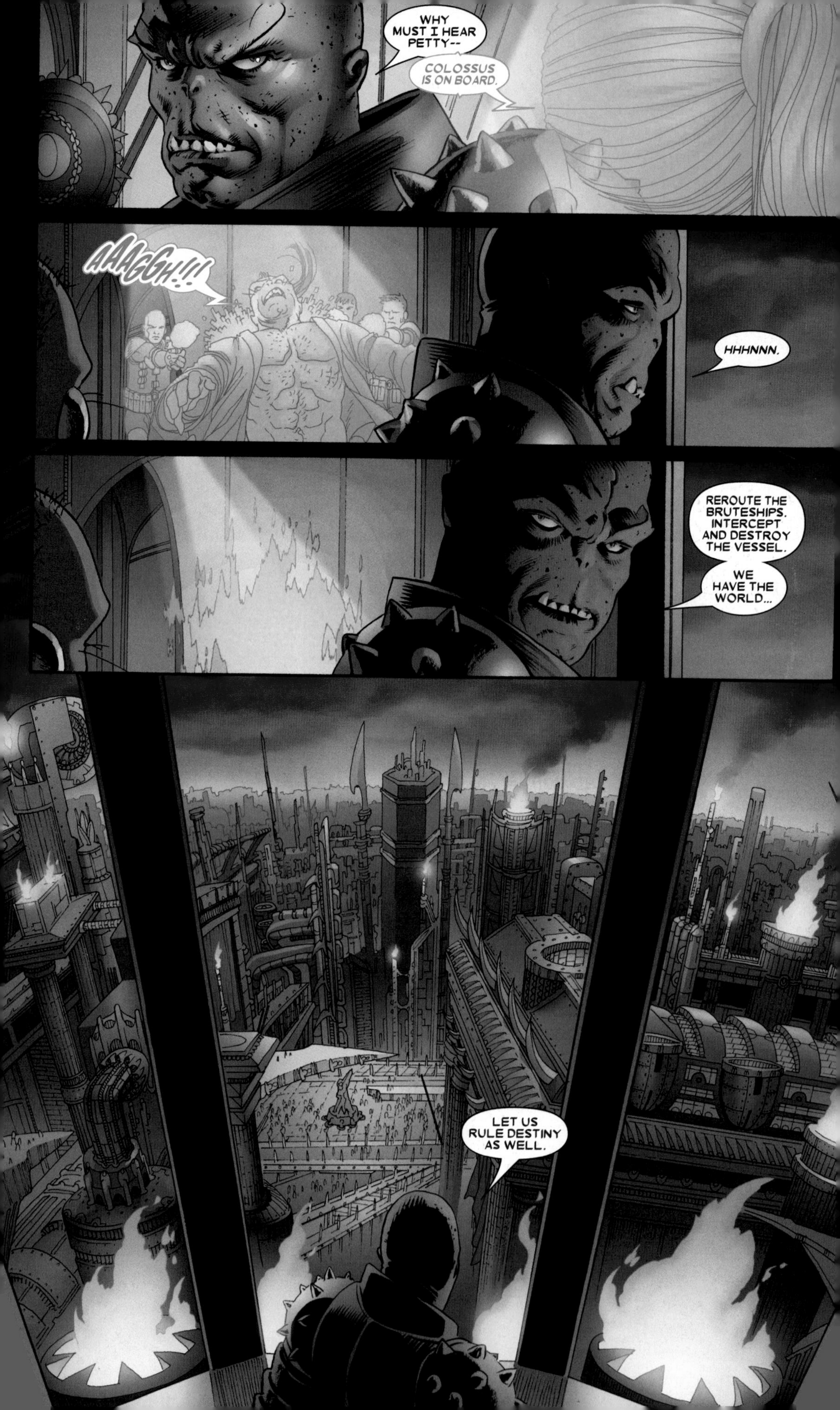

WHY MUST I HEAR PETTY--
COLOSSUS IS ON BOARD.
AAAGGH!!!
HHHNNN.
REROUTE THE BRUTESHIPS. INTERCEPT AND DESTROY THE VESSEL.
WE HAVE THE WORLD...
LET US RULE DESTINY AS WELL.

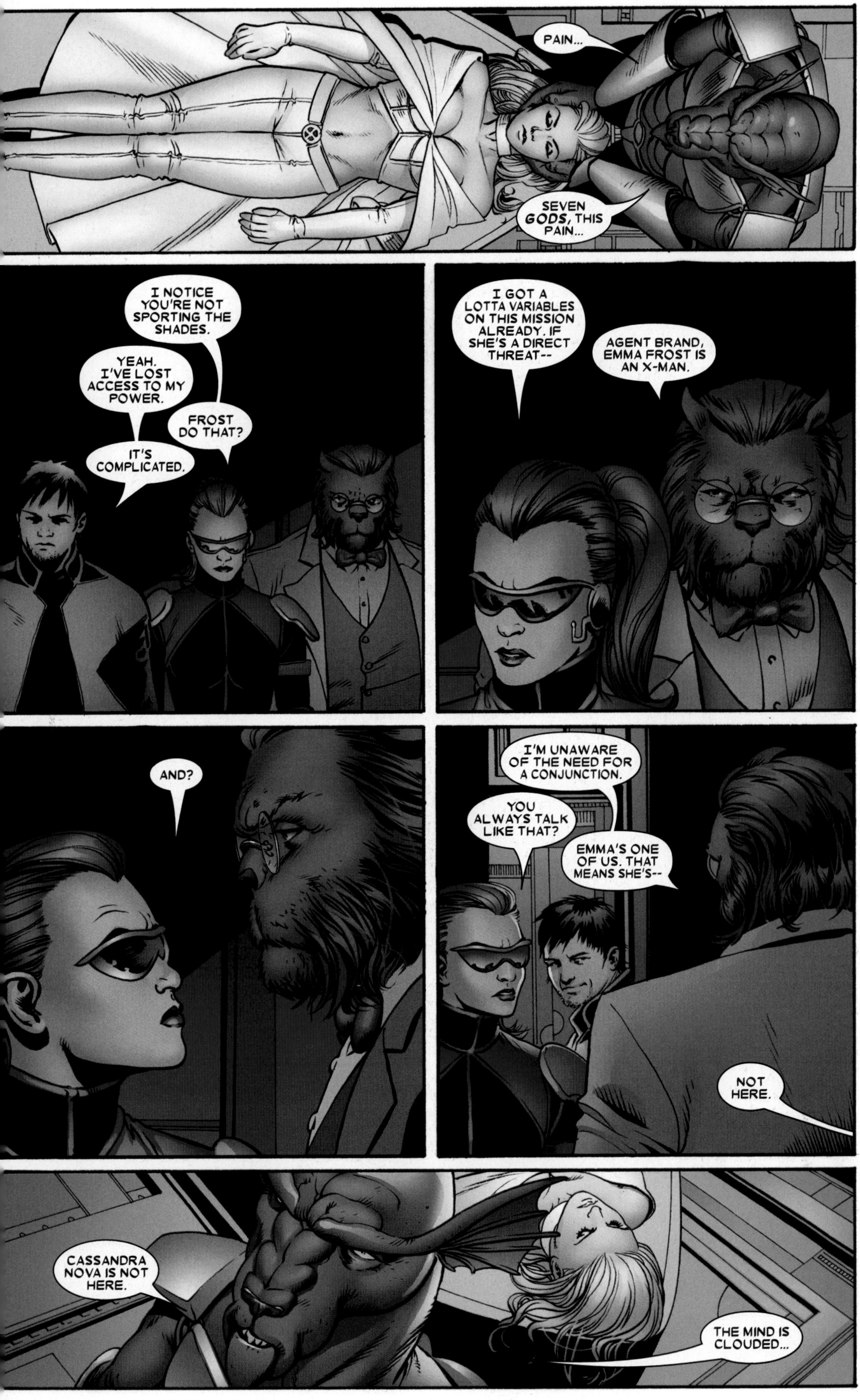
PAIN...
SEVEN GODS, THIS PAIN...
I NOTICE YOU'RE NOT SPORTING THE SHADES.
YEAH. I'VE LOST ACCESS TO MY POWER.
FROST DO THAT?
IT'S COMPLICATED.
I GOT A LOTTA VARIABLES ON THIS MISSION ALREADY. IF SHE'S A DIRECT THREAT--
AGENT BRAND, EMMA FROST IS AN X-MAN.
AND?
I'M UNAWARE OF THE NEED FOR A CONJUNCTION.
YOU ALWAYS TALK LIKE THAT?
EMMA'S ONE OF US. THAT MEANS SHE'S--
NOT HERE.
CASSANDRA NOVA IS NOT HERE.
THE MIND IS CLOUDED...

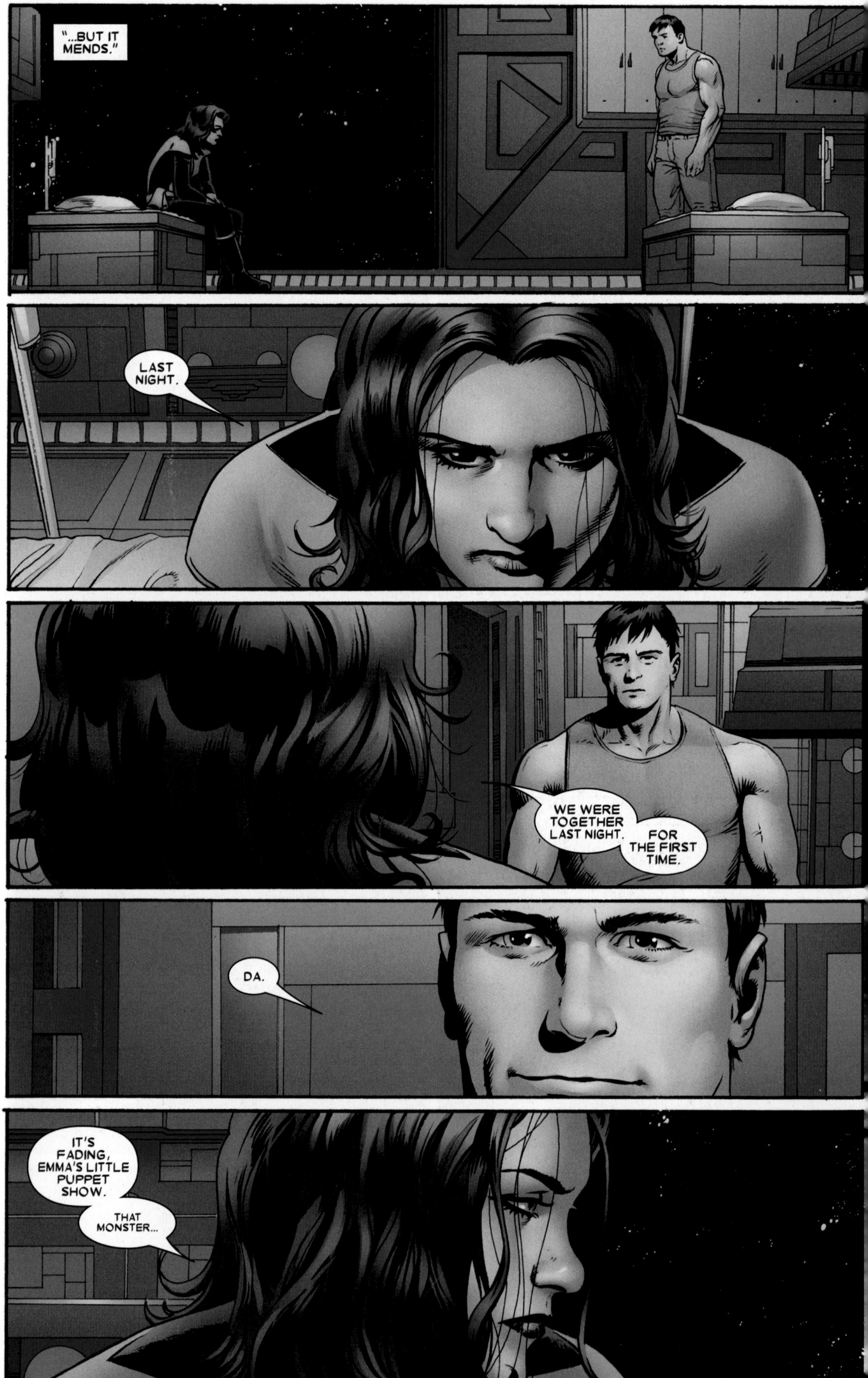
"...BUT IT MENDS."
LAST NIGHT.
WE WERE TOGETHER LAST NIGHT.
FOR THE FIRST TIME.
DA.
IT'S FADING, EMMA'S LITTLE PUPPET SHOW.
THAT MONSTER...

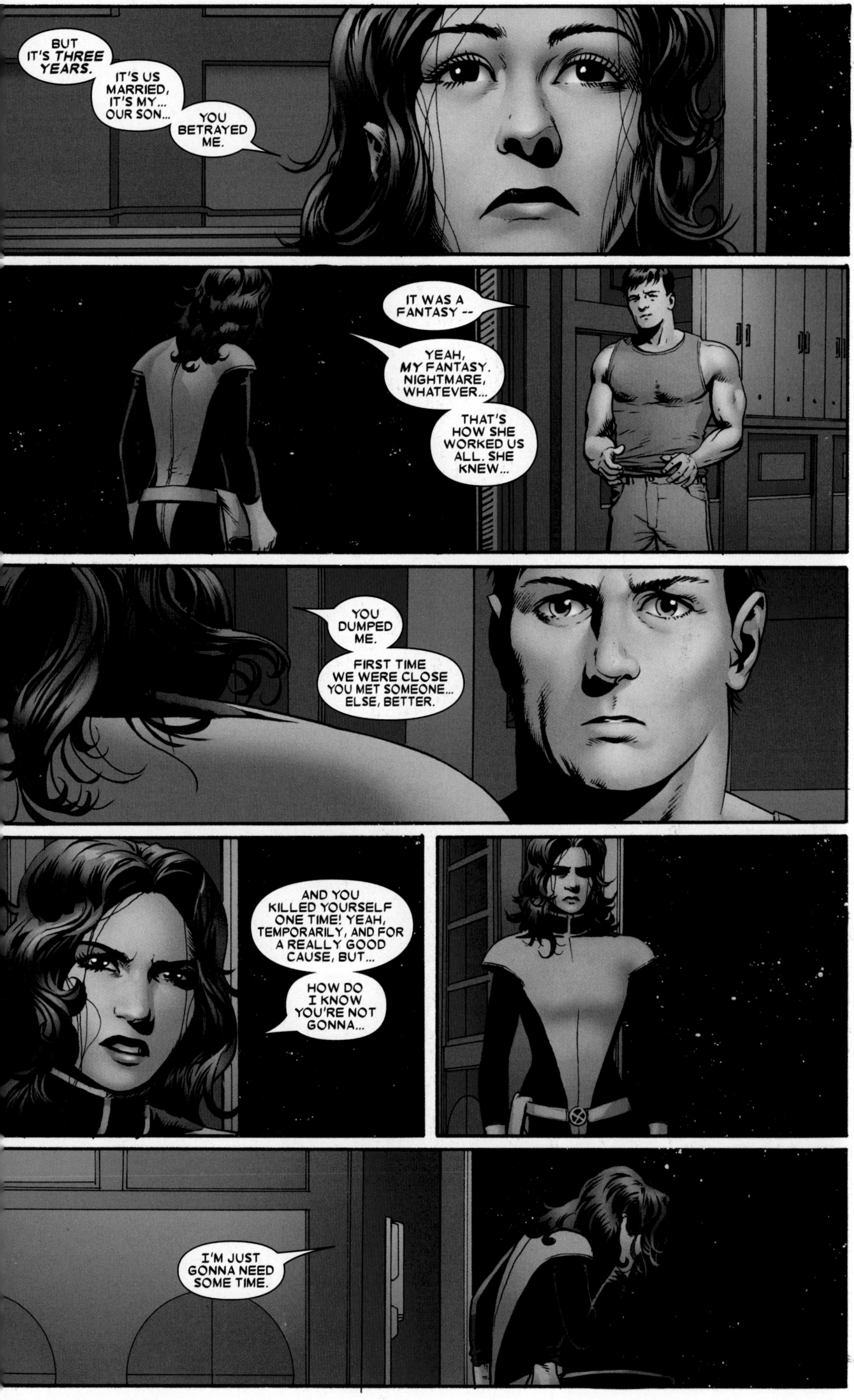
BUT IT'S THREE YEARS.
IT'S US MARRIED, IT'S MY... OUR SON...
YOU BETRAYED ME.
IT WAS A FANTASY --
YEAH, MY FANTASY. NIGHTMARE, WHATEVER...
THAT'S HOW SHE WORKED US ALL. SHE KNEW...
YOU DUMPED ME.
FIRST TIME WE WERE CLOSE YOU MET SOMEONE... ELSE, BETTER.
AND YOU KILLED YOURSELF ONE TIME! YEAH, TEMPORARILY, AND FOR A REALLY GOOD CAUSE, BUT...
HOW DO I KNOW YOU'RE NOT GONNA...
I'M JUST GONNA NEED SOME TIME.

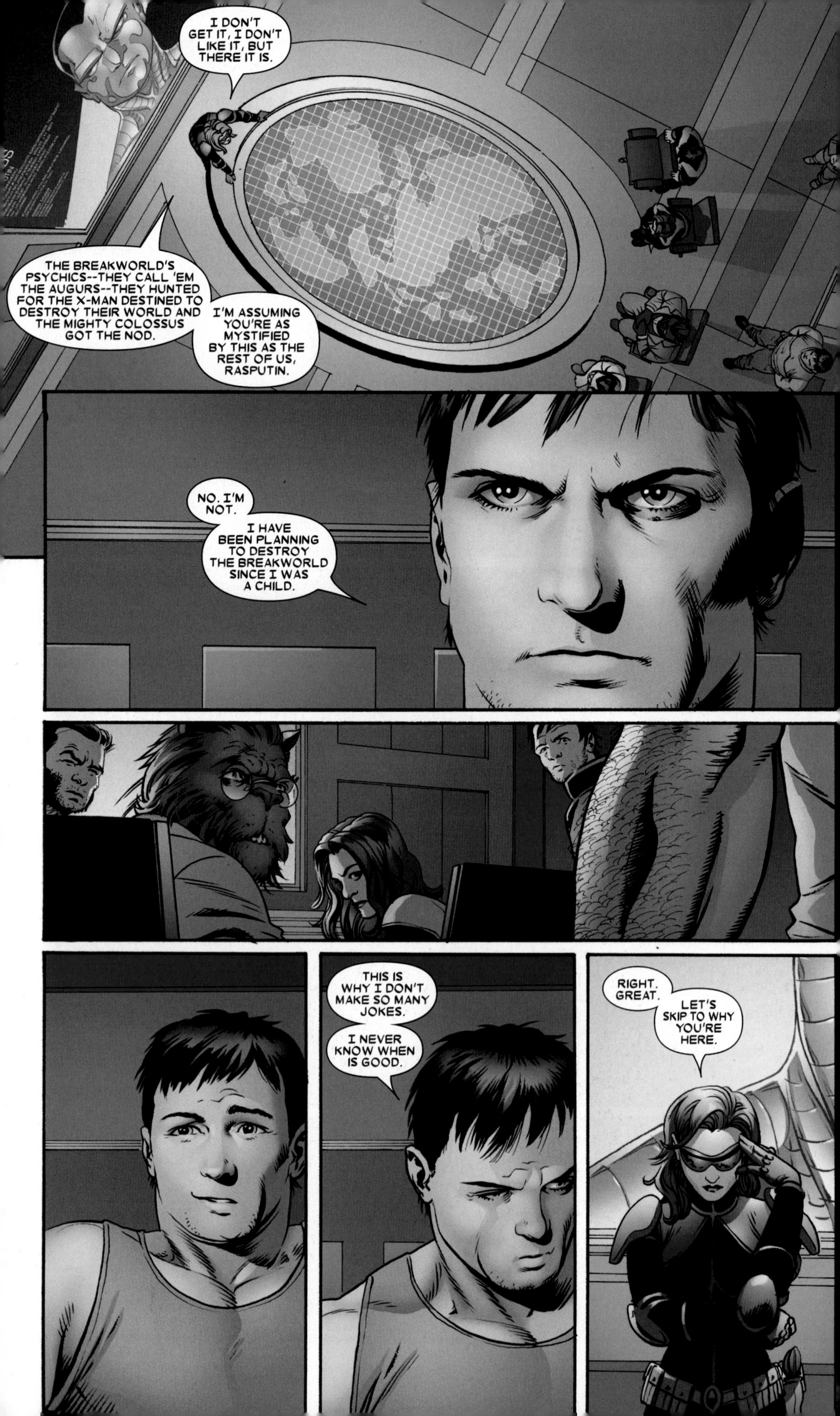
I DON'T GET IT, I DON'T LIKE IT, BUT THERE IT IS.
THE BREAKWORLD'S PSYCHICS--THEY CALL 'EM THE AUGURS--THEY HUNTED FOR THE X-MAN DESTINED TO DESTROY THEIR WORLD AND THE MIGHTY COLOSSUS GOT THE NOD.
I'M ASSUMING YOU'RE AS MYSTIFIED BY THIS AS THE REST OF US, RASPUTIN.
NO. I'M NOT.
I HAVE BEEN PLANNING TO DESTROY THE BREAKWORLD SINCE I WAS A CHILD.
THIS IS WHY I DON'T MAKE SO MANY JOKES.
I NEVER KNOW WHEN IS GOOD.
RIGHT. GREAT.
LET'S SKIP TO WHY YOU'RE HERE.

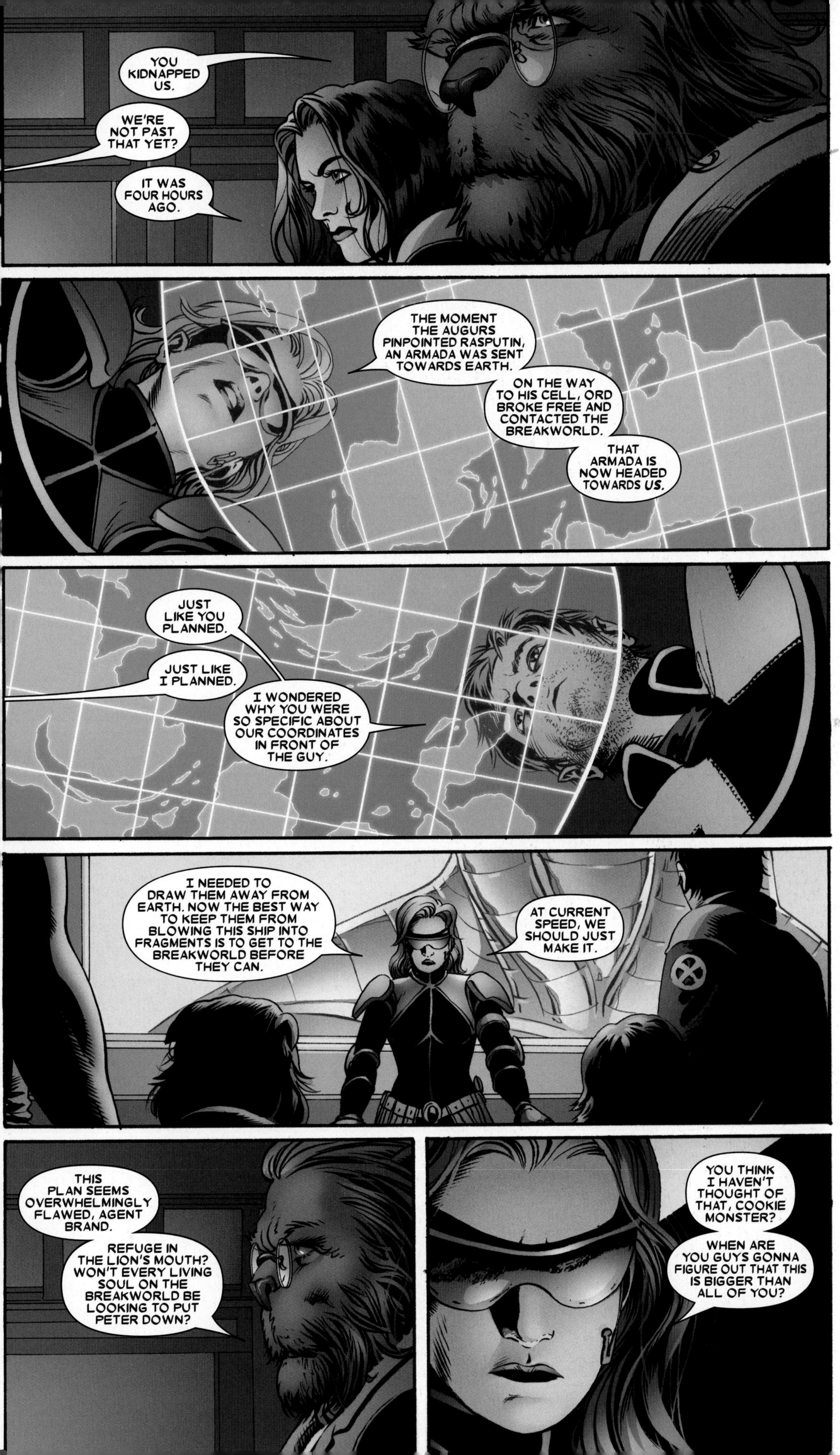
YOU KIDNAPPED US.
WE'RE NOT PAST THAT YET?
IT WAS FOUR HOURS AGO.
THE MOMENT THE AUGURS PINPOINTED RASPUTIN, AN ARMADA WAS SENT TOWARDS EARTH.
ON THE WAY TO HIS CELL, ORD BROKE FREE AND CONTACTED THE BREAKWORLD.
THAT ARMADA IS NOW HEADED TOWARDS *US*.
JUST LIKE YOU PLANNED.
JUST LIKE I PLANNED.
I WONDERED WHY YOU WERE SO SPECIFIC ABOUT OUR COORDINATES IN FRONT OF THE GUY.
I NEEDED TO DRAW THEM AWAY FROM EARTH. NOW THE BEST WAY TO KEEP THEM FROM BLOWING THIS SHIP INTO FRAGMENTS IS TO GET TO THE BREAKWORLD BEFORE THEY CAN.
AT CURRENT SPEED, WE SHOULD JUST MAKE IT.
THIS PLAN SEEMS OVERWHELMINGLY FLAWED, AGENT BRAND.
REFUGE IN THE LION'S MOUTH? WON'T EVERY LIVING SOUL ON THE BREAKWORLD BE LOOKING TO PUT PETER DOWN?
YOU THINK I HAVEN'T THOUGHT OF THAT, COOKIE MONSTER?
WHEN ARE YOU GUYS GONNA FIGURE OUT THAT THIS IS BIGGER THAN ALL OF YOU?

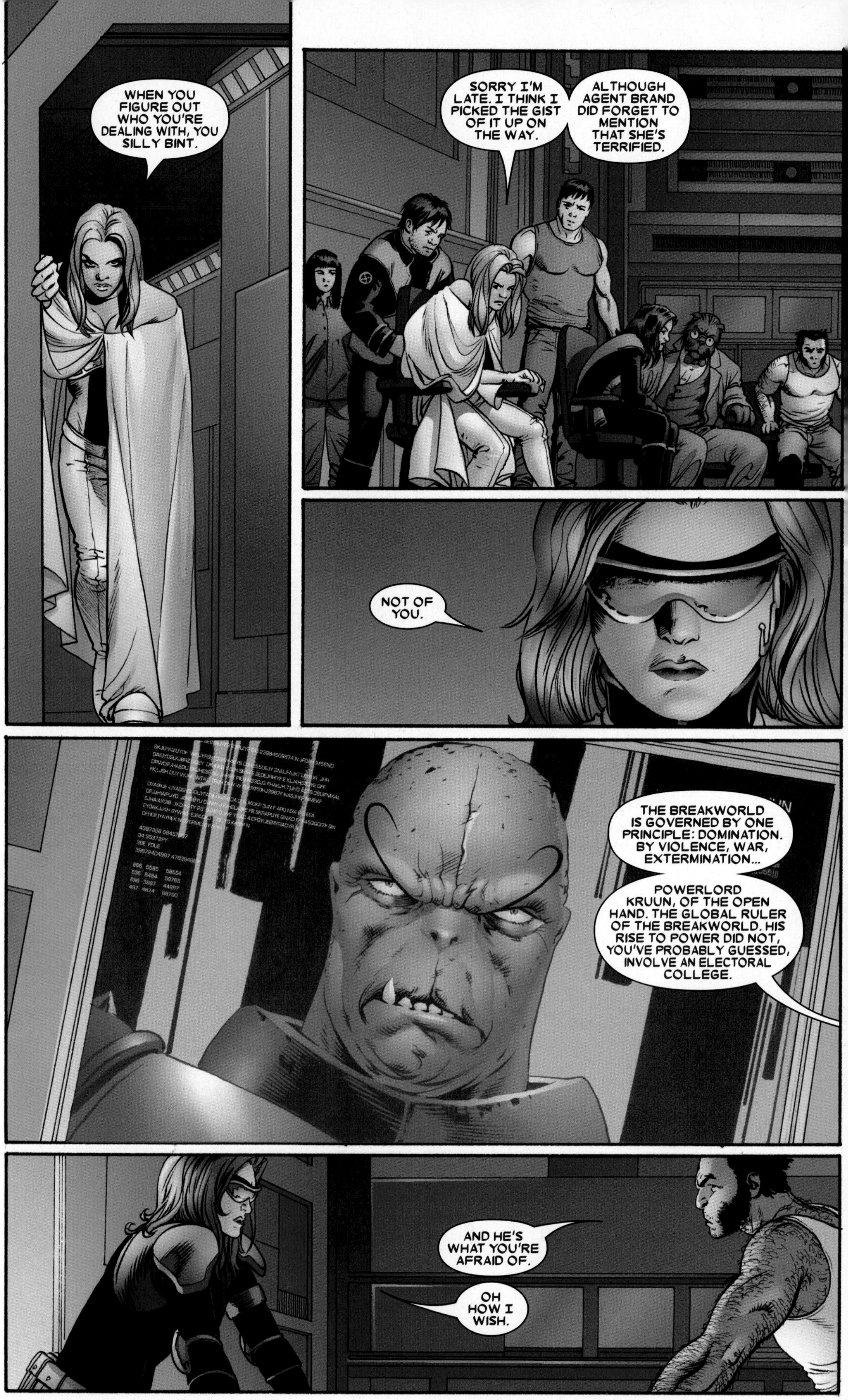
WHEN YOU FIGURE OUT WHO YOU'RE DEALING WITH, YOU SILLY BINT.
SORRY I'M LATE. I THINK I PICKED THE GIST OF IT UP ON THE WAY.
ALTHOUGH AGENT BRAND DID FORGET TO MENTION THAT SHE'S TERRIFIED.
NOT OF YOU.
THE BREAKWORLD IS GOVERNED BY ONE PRINCIPLE: DOMINATION. BY VIOLENCE, WAR, EXTERMINATION...
POWERLORD KRUUN, OF THE OPEN HAND. THE GLOBAL RULER OF THE BREAKWORLD. HIS RISE TO POWER DID NOT, YOU'VE PROBABLY GUESSED, INVOLVE AN ELECTORAL COLLEGE.
AND HE'S WHAT YOU'RE AFRAID OF.
OH HOW I WISH.

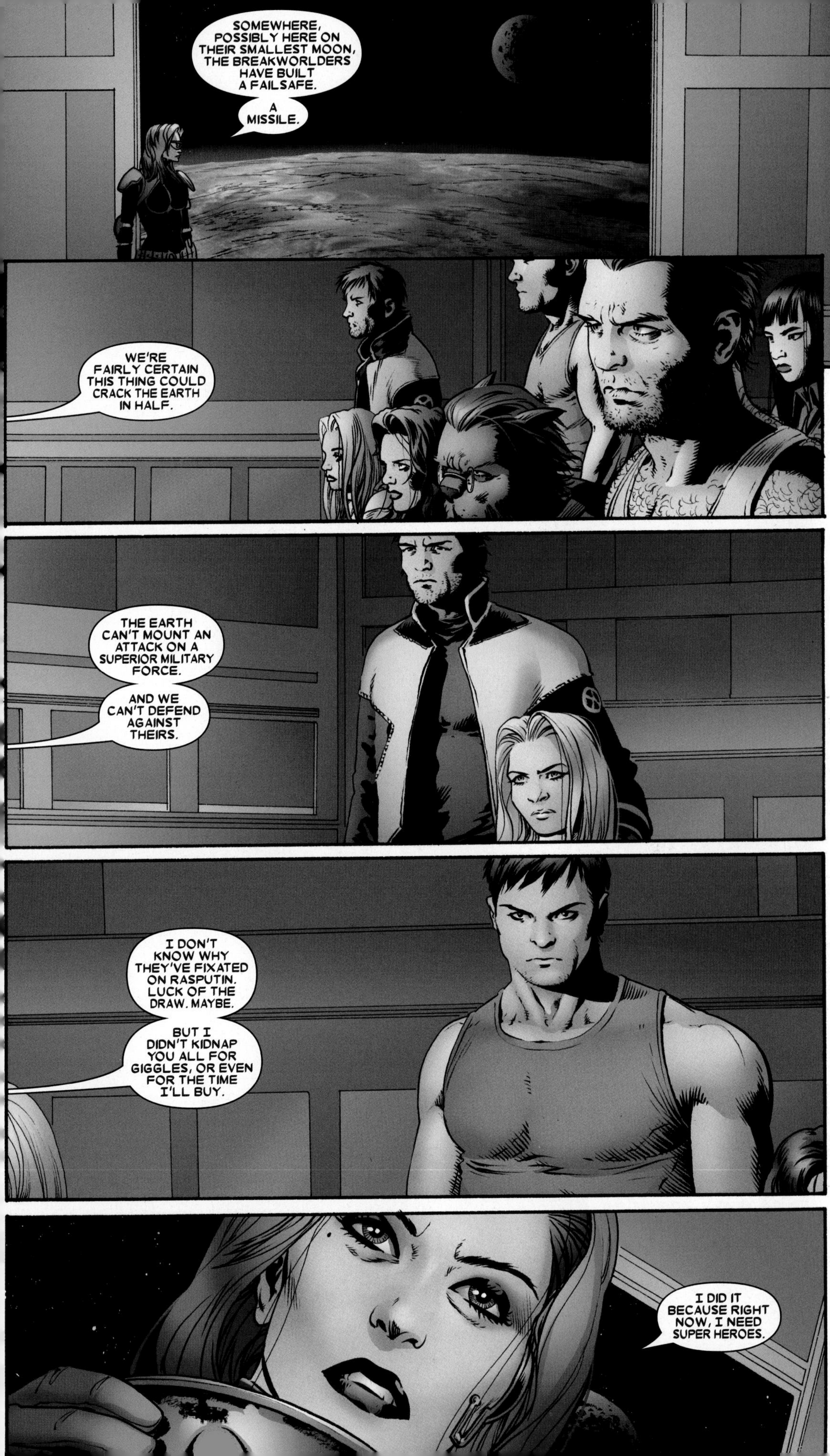
SOMEWHERE, POSSIBLY HERE ON THEIR SMALLEST MOON, THE BREAKWORLDERS HAVE BUILT A FAILSAFE.
A MISSILE.
WE'RE FAIRLY CERTAIN THIS THING COULD CRACK THE EARTH IN HALF.
THE EARTH CAN'T MOUNT AN ATTACK ON A SUPERIOR MILITARY FORCE.
AND WE CAN'T DEFEND AGAINST THEIRS.
I DON'T KNOW WHY THEY'VE FIXATED ON RASPUTIN. LUCK OF THE DRAW, MAYBE.
BUT I DIDN'T KIDNAP YOU ALL FOR GIGGLES, OR EVEN FOR THE TIME I'LL BUY.
I DID IT BECAUSE RIGHT NOW, I NEED SUPER HEROES.

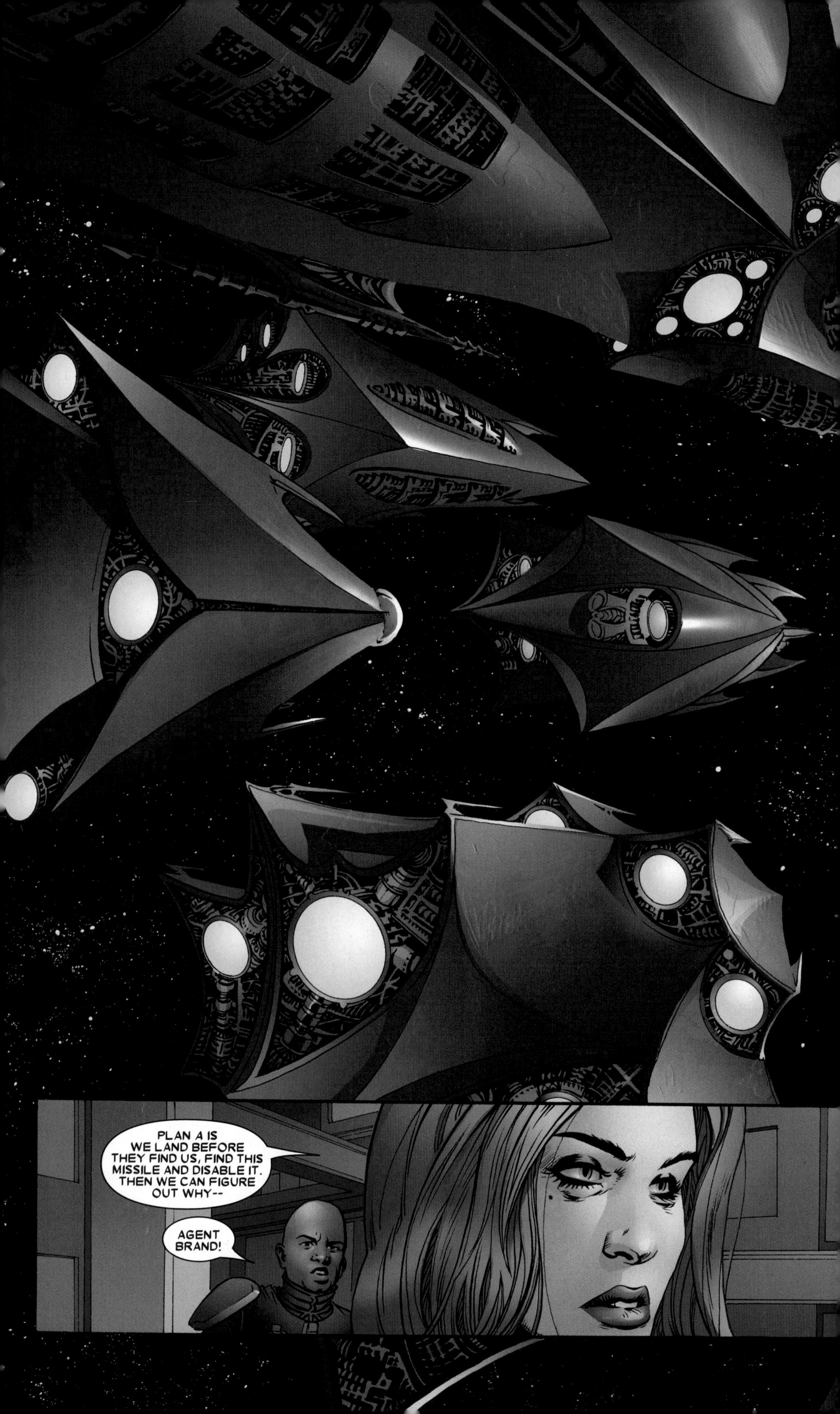
PLAN A IS WE LAND BEFORE THEY FIND US, FIND THIS MISSILE AND DISABLE IT. THEN WE CAN FIGURE OUT WHY--
AGENT BRAND!

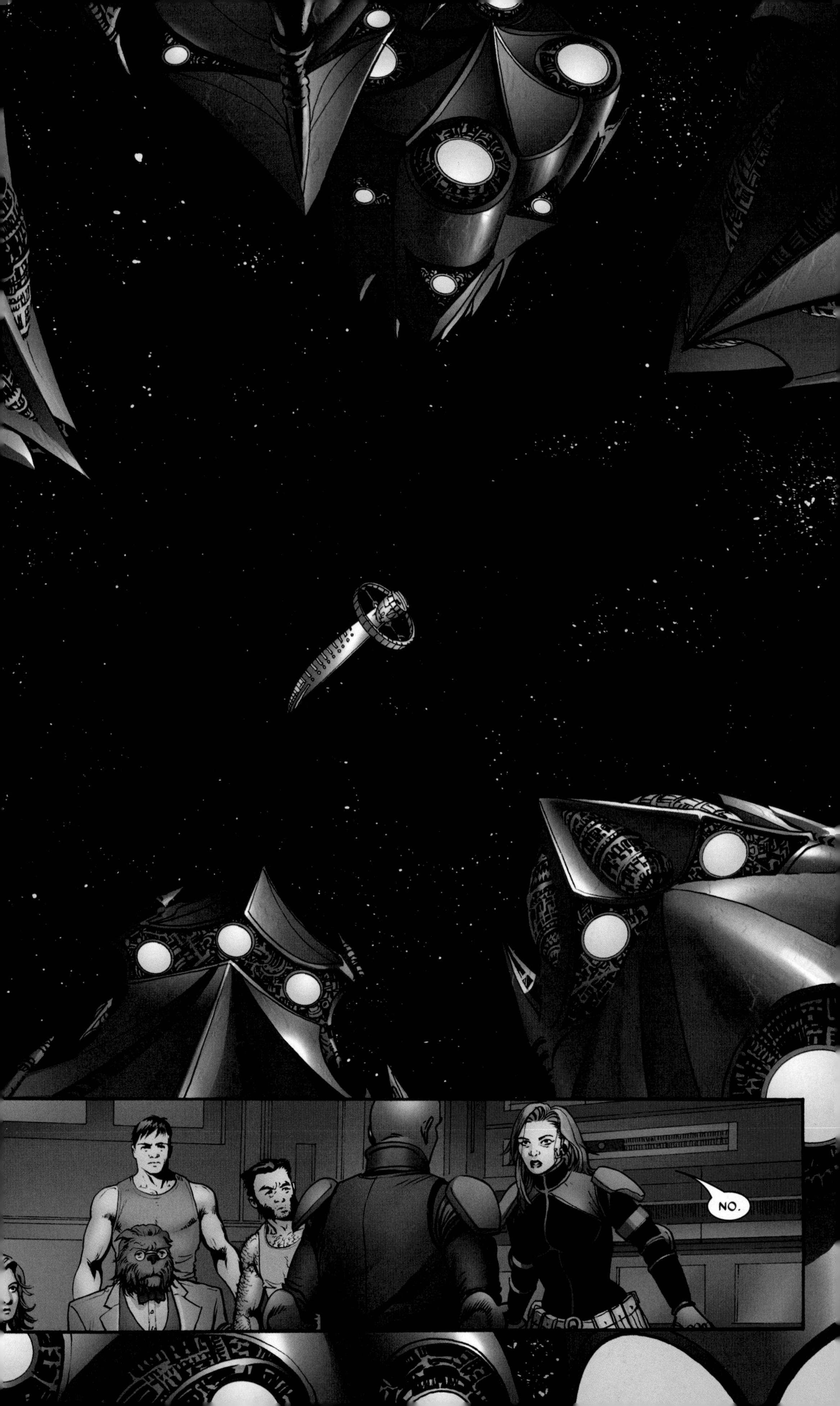
NO.

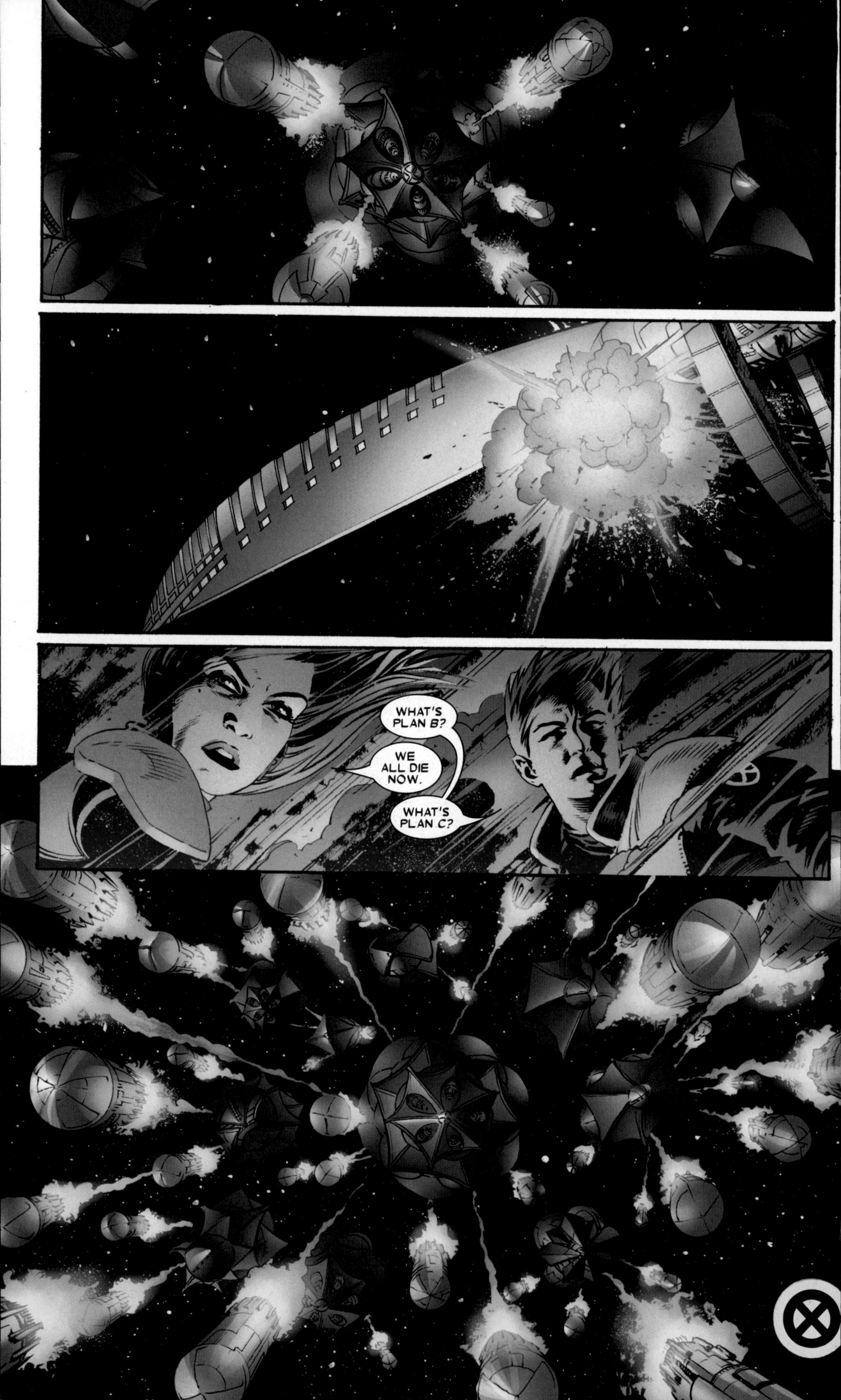
WHAT'S PLAN B?
WE ALL DIE NOW.
WHAT'S PLAN C?

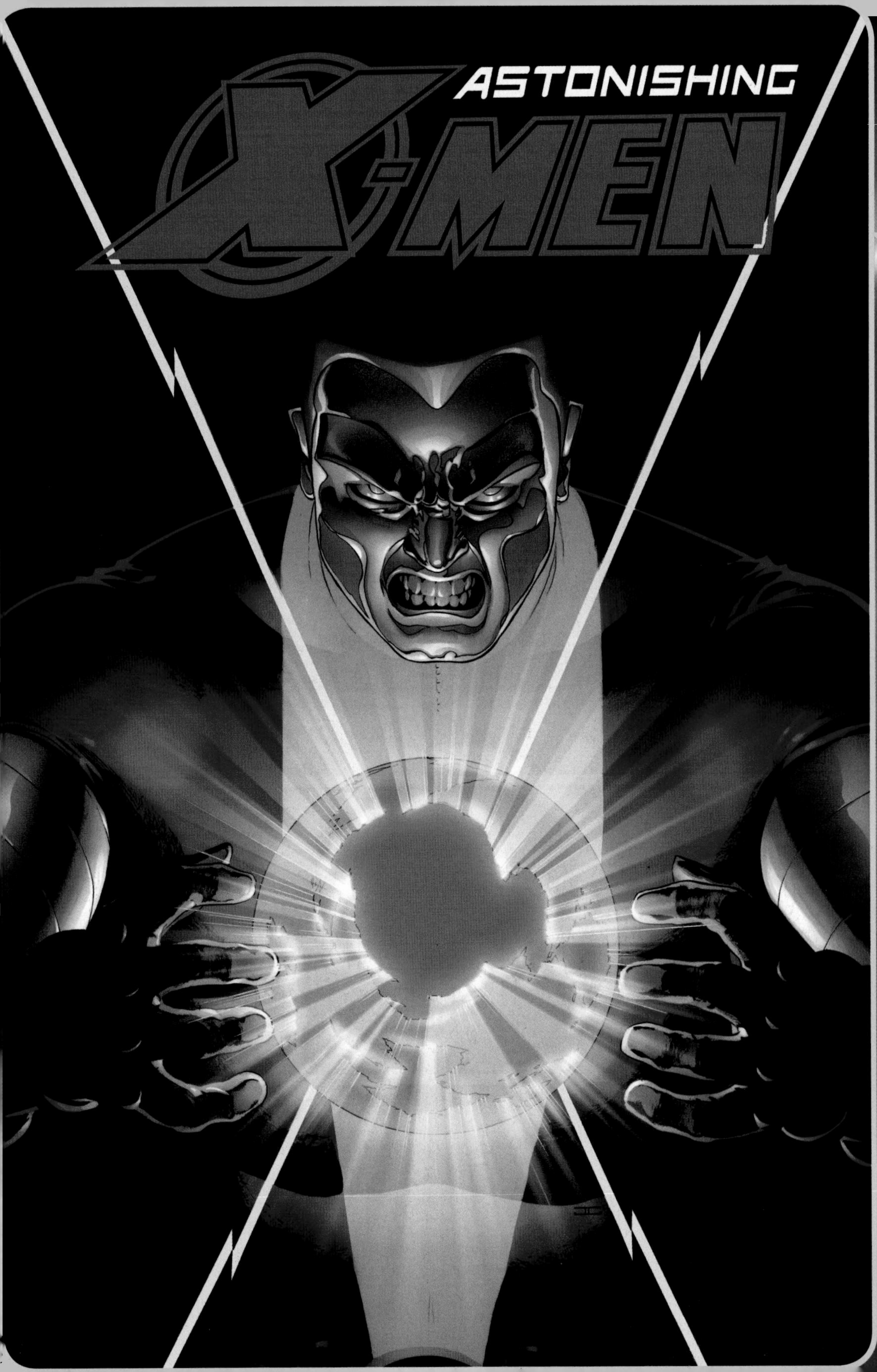
ASTONISHING
X-MEN

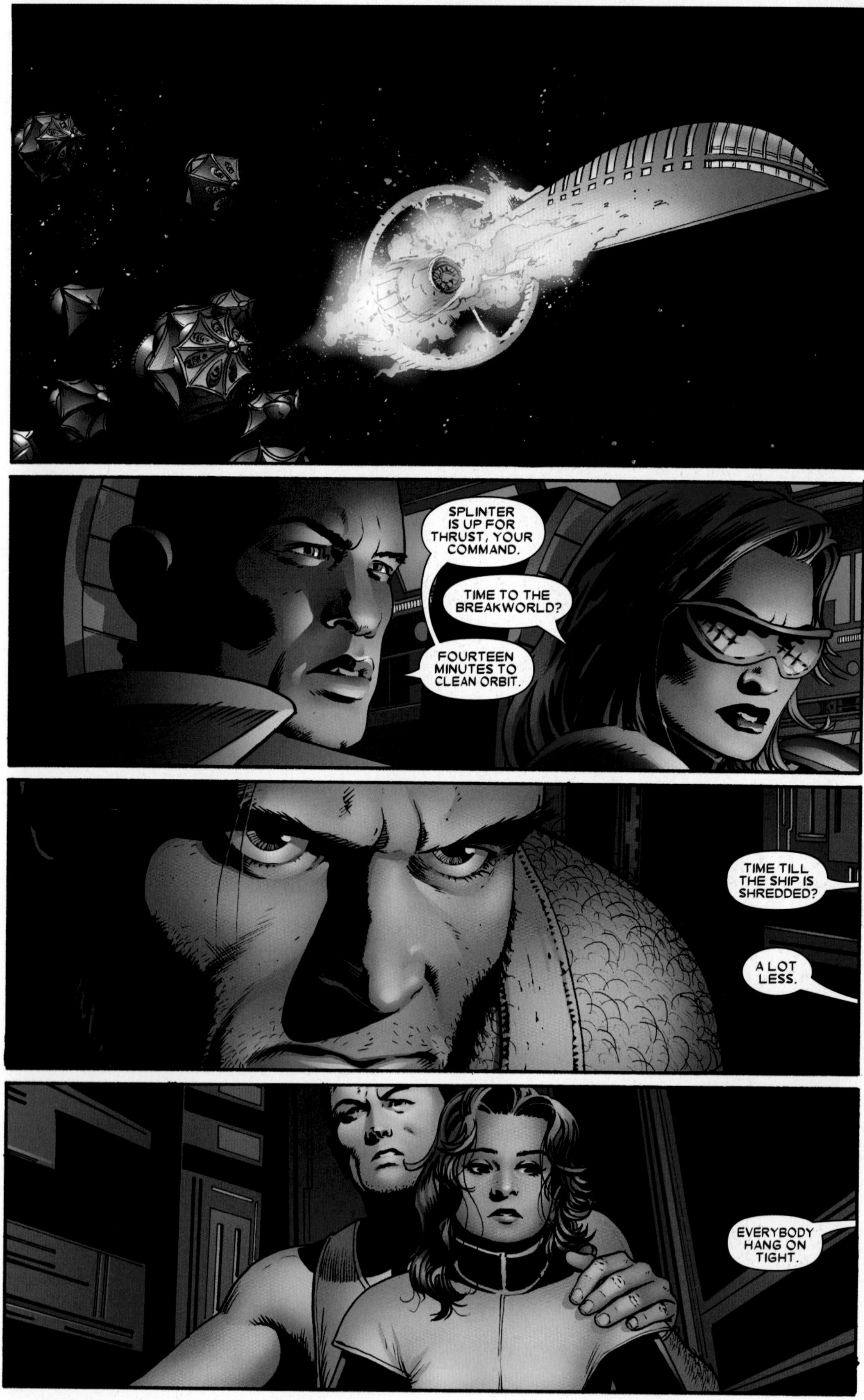

SPLINTER IS UP FOR THRUST, YOUR COMMAND.
TIME TO THE BREAKWORLD?
FOURTEEN MINUTES TO CLEAN ORBIT.
TIME TILL THE SHIP IS SHREDDED?
A LOT LESS.
EVERYBODY HANG ON TIGHT.

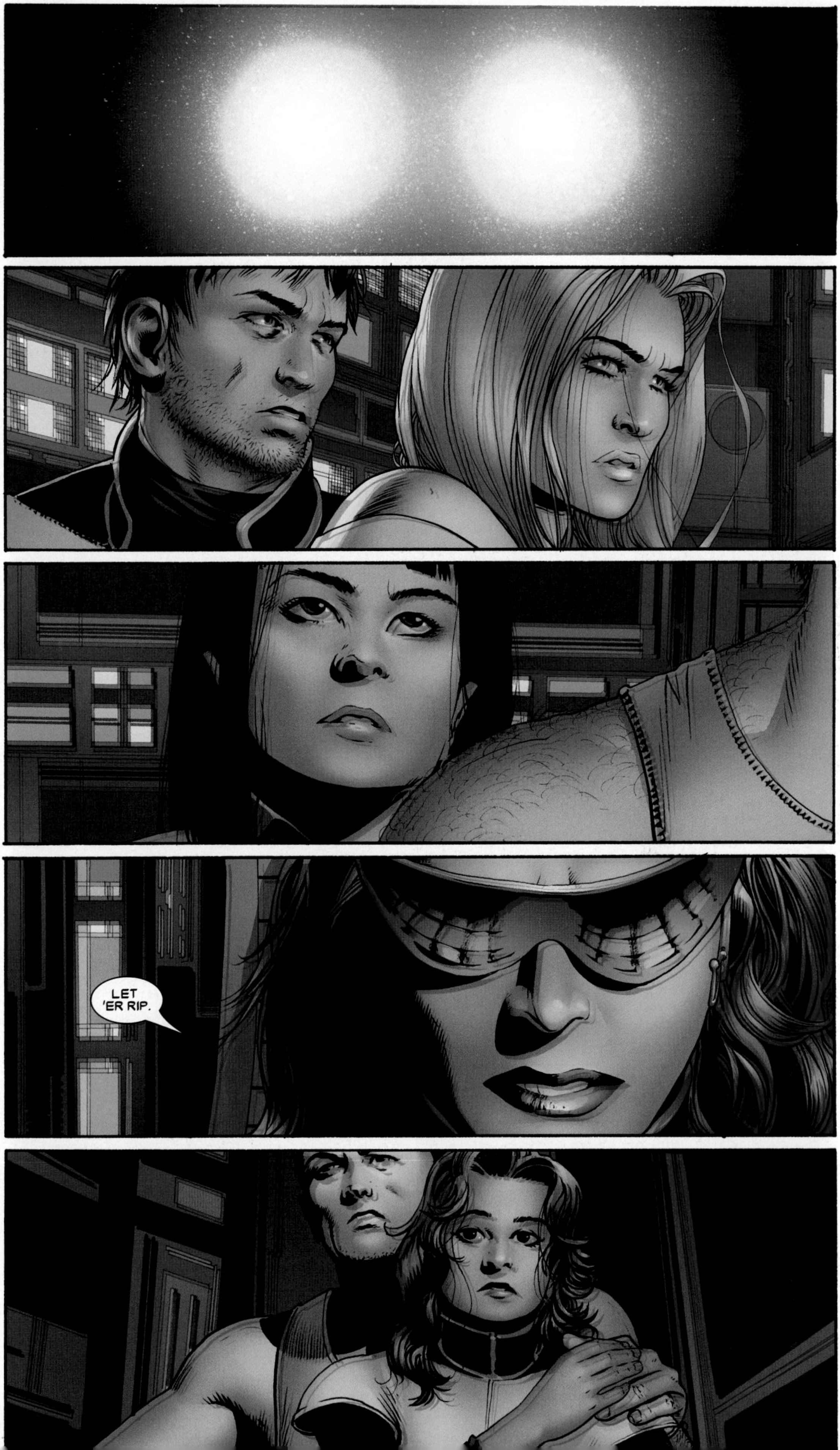
LET 'ER RIP.

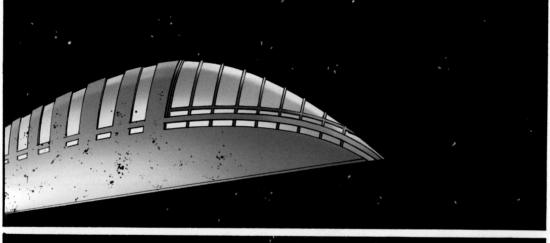

"UNBREACHABLE HULL, PRECISE MANEUVERABILITY, ENOUGH POWER AT SHORT-RANGE TO OUTRUN ANYONE."

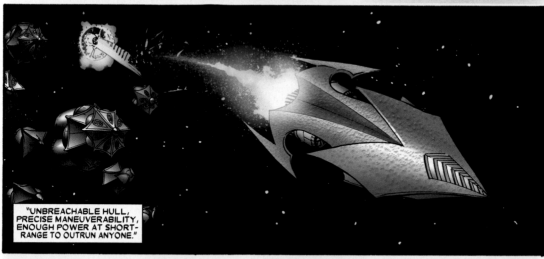

PRETTIEST SHIP IN THE FLEET.

NOT TO BE PICKY, AGENT BRAND, BUT IF THIS SPLINTER IS SUCH A WONDERFUL SHIP...

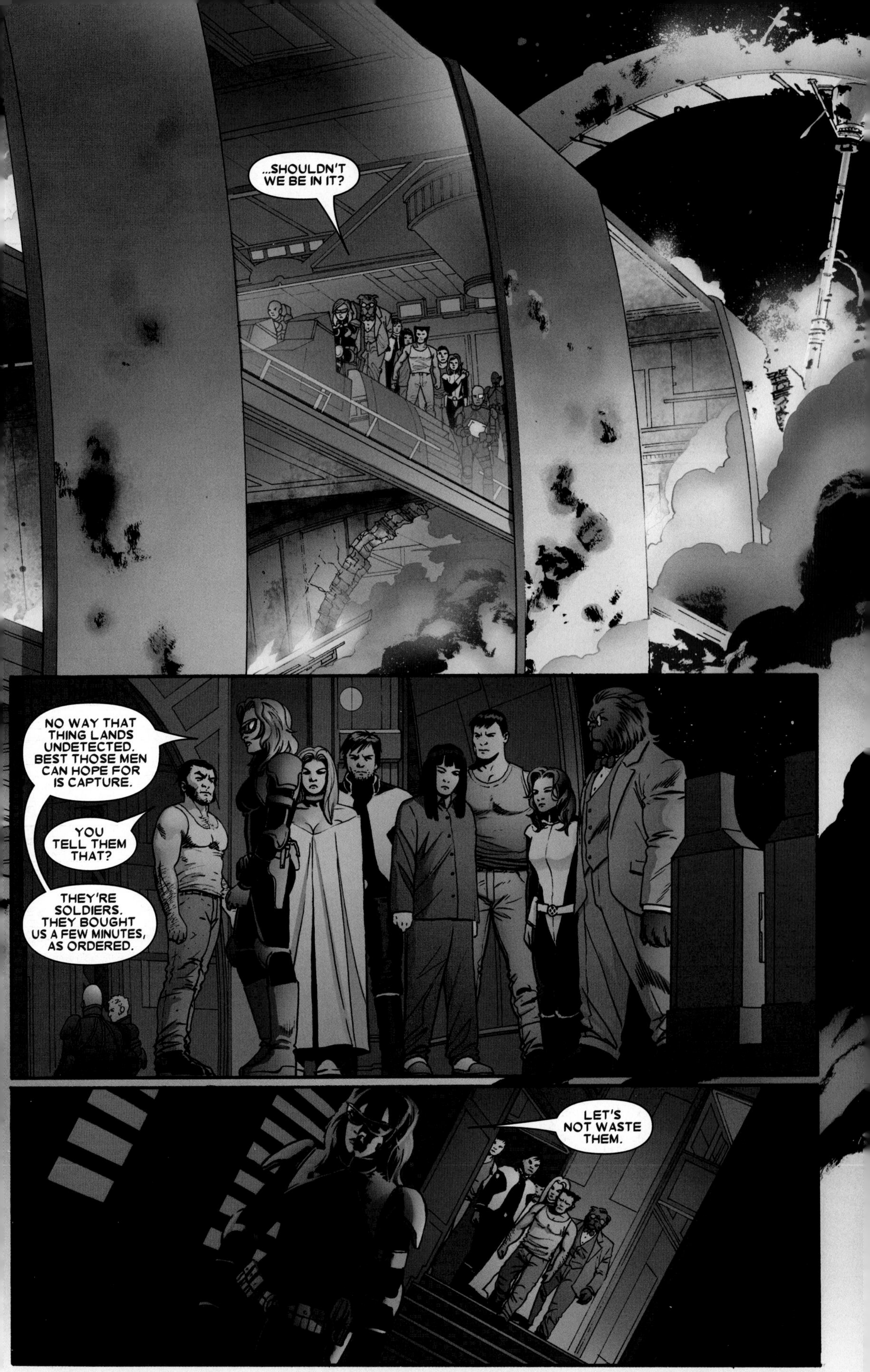
...SHOULDN'T WE BE IN IT?
NO WAY THAT THING LANDS UNDETECTED. BEST THOSE MEN CAN HOPE FOR IS CAPTURE.
YOU TELL THEM THAT?
THEY'RE SOLDIERS. THEY BOUGHT US A FEW MINUTES, AS ORDERED.
LET'S NOT WASTE THEM.

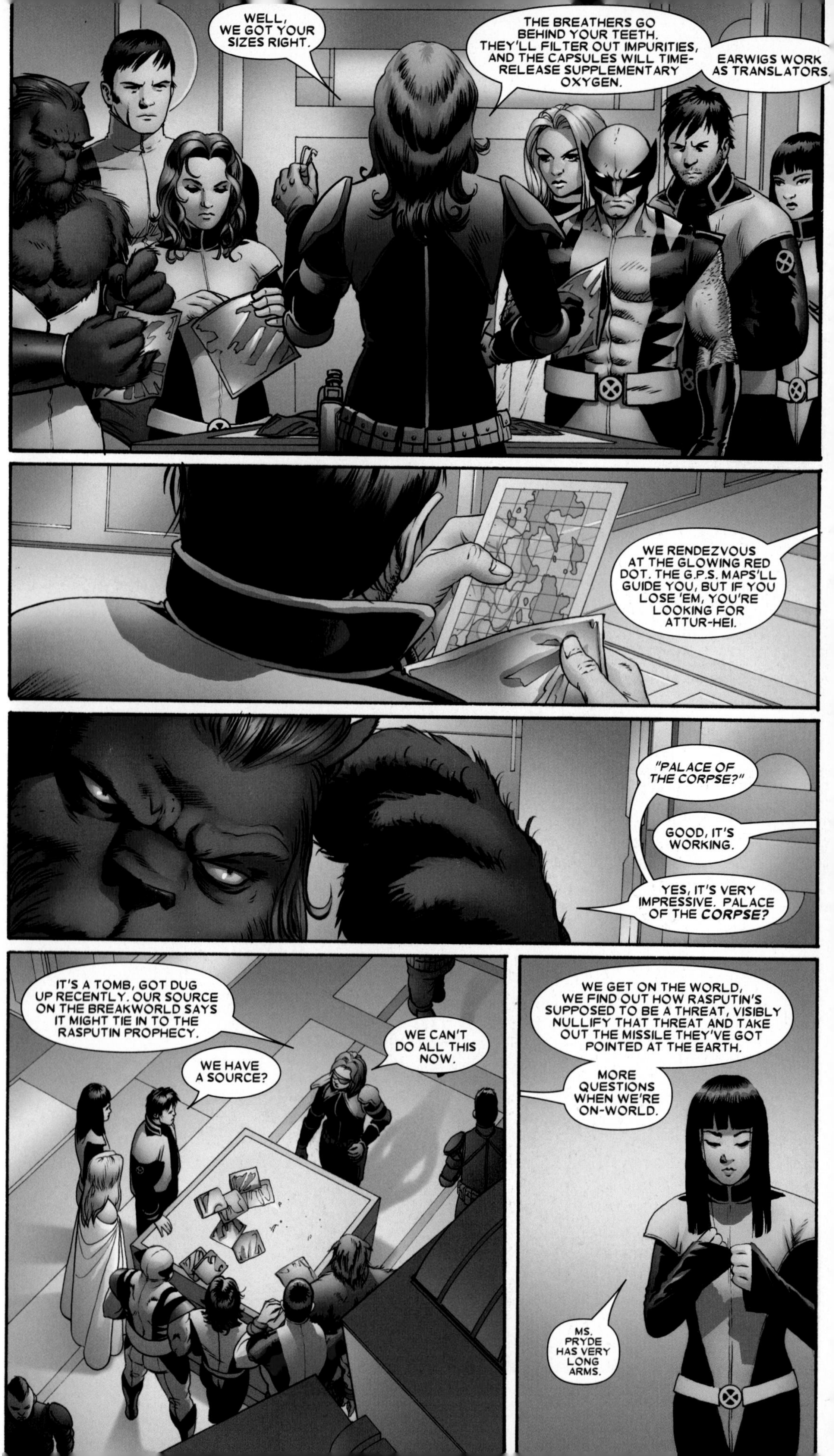
WELL, WE GOT YOUR SIZES RIGHT.
THE BREATHERS GO BEHIND YOUR TEETH. THEY'LL FILTER OUT IMPURITIES, AND THE CAPSULES WILL TIME-RELEASE SUPPLEMENTARY OXYGEN.
EARWIGS WORK AS TRANSLATORS.
WE RENDEZVOUS AT THE GLOWING RED DOT. THE G.P.S. MAPS'LL GUIDE YOU, BUT IF YOU LOSE 'EM, YOU'RE LOOKING FOR ATTUR-HEI.
"PALACE OF THE CORPSE?"
GOOD, IT'S WORKING.
YES, IT'S VERY IMPRESSIVE. PALACE OF THE *CORPSE?*
IT'S A TOMB, GOT DUG UP RECENTLY. OUR SOURCE ON THE BREAKWORLD SAYS IT MIGHT TIE IN TO THE RASPUTIN PROPHECY.
WE HAVE A SOURCE?
WE CAN'T DO ALL THIS NOW.
WE GET ON THE WORLD, WE FIND OUT HOW RASPUTIN'S SUPPOSED TO BE A THREAT, VISIBLY NULLIFY THAT THREAT AND TAKE OUT THE MISSILE THEY'VE GOT POINTED AT THE EARTH.
MORE QUESTIONS WHEN WE'RE ON-WORLD.
MS. PRYDE HAS VERY LONG ARMS.

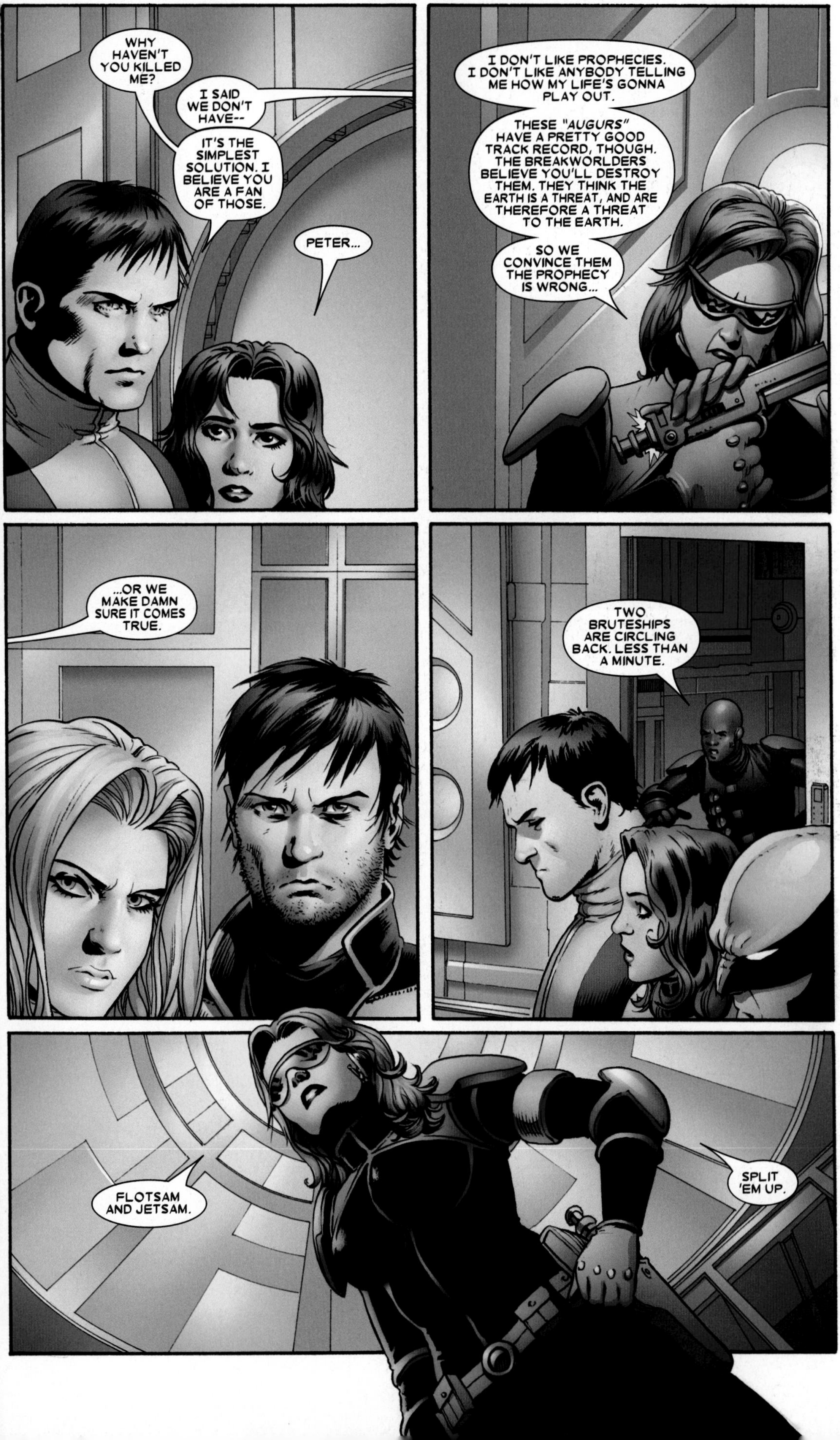
WHY HAVEN'T YOU KILLED ME?
I SAID WE DON'T HAVE--
IT'S THE SIMPLEST SOLUTION. I BELIEVE YOU ARE A FAN OF THOSE.
PETER...
I DON'T LIKE PROPHECIES. I DON'T LIKE ANYBODY TELLING ME HOW MY LIFE'S GONNA PLAY OUT.
THESE "AUGURS" HAVE A PRETTY GOOD TRACK RECORD, THOUGH. THE BREAKWORLDERS BELIEVE YOU'LL DESTROY THEM. THEY THINK THE EARTH IS A THREAT, AND ARE THEREFORE A THREAT TO THE EARTH.
SO WE CONVINCE THEM THE PROPHECY IS WRONG...
...OR WE MAKE DAMN SURE IT COMES TRUE.
TWO BRUTESHIPS ARE CIRCLING BACK. LESS THAN A MINUTE.
FLOTSAM AND JETSAM.
SPLIT 'EM UP.

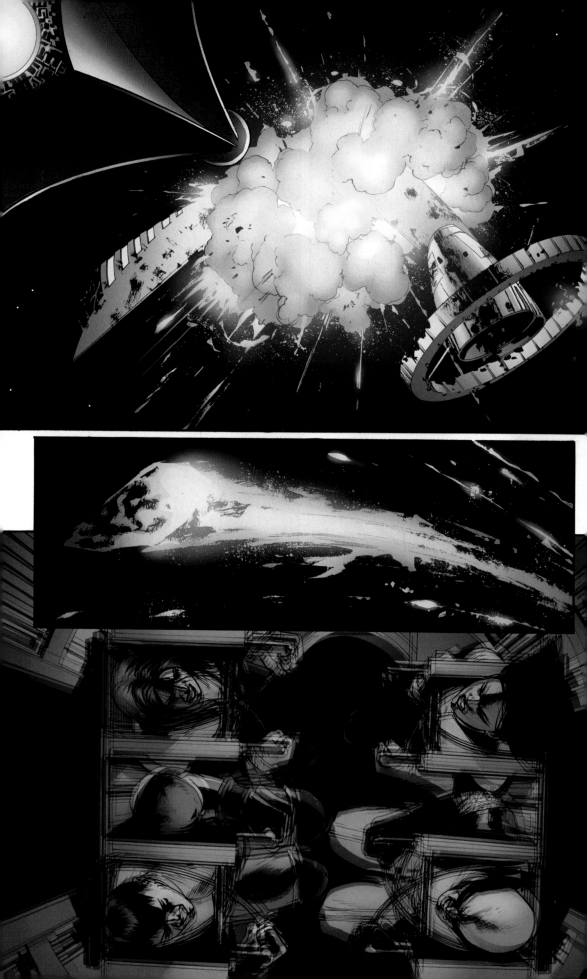

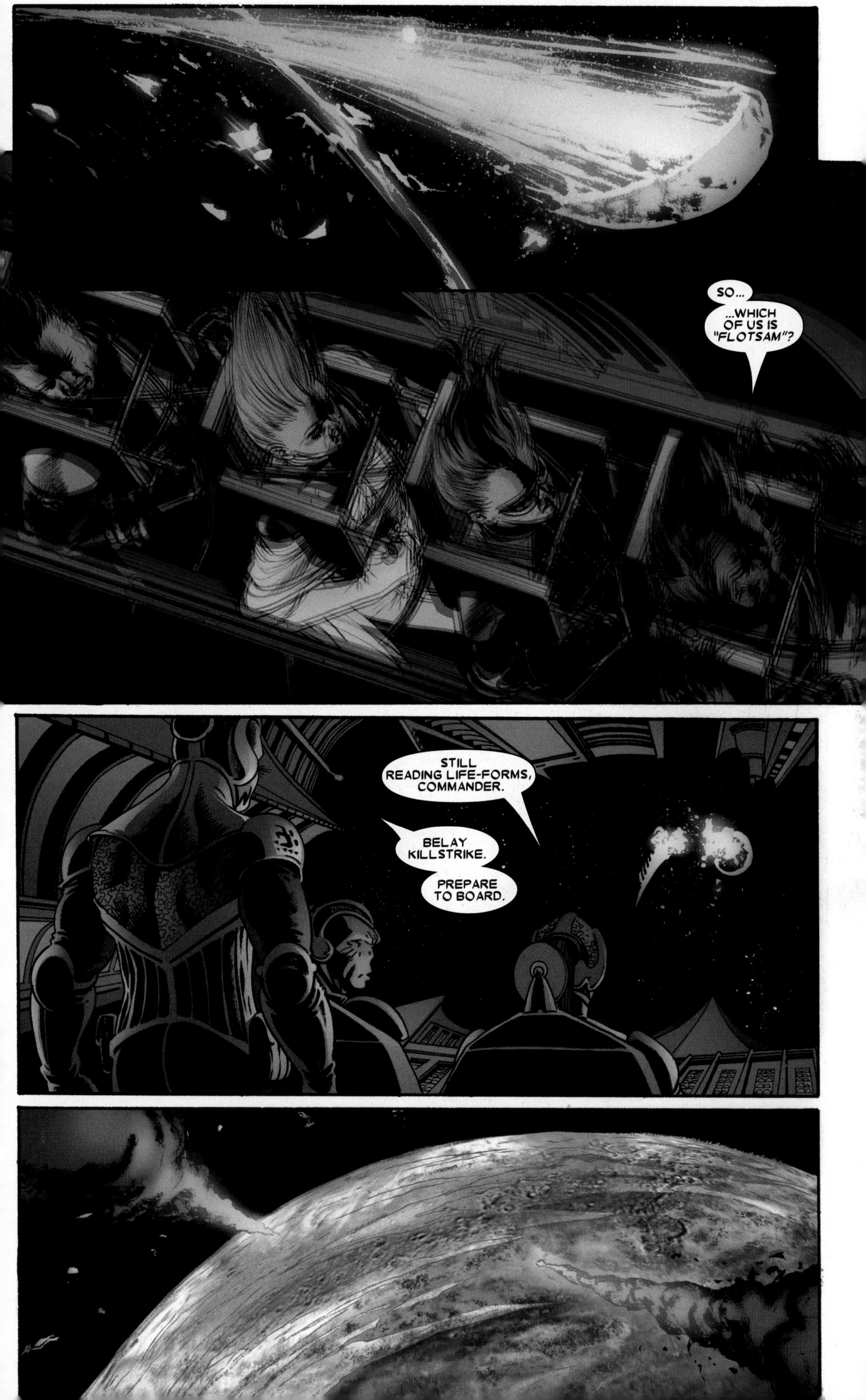

SO...
...WHICH OF US IS "FLOTSAM"?
STILL READING LIFE-FORMS, COMMANDER.
BELAY KILLSTRIKE.
PREPARE TO BOARD.

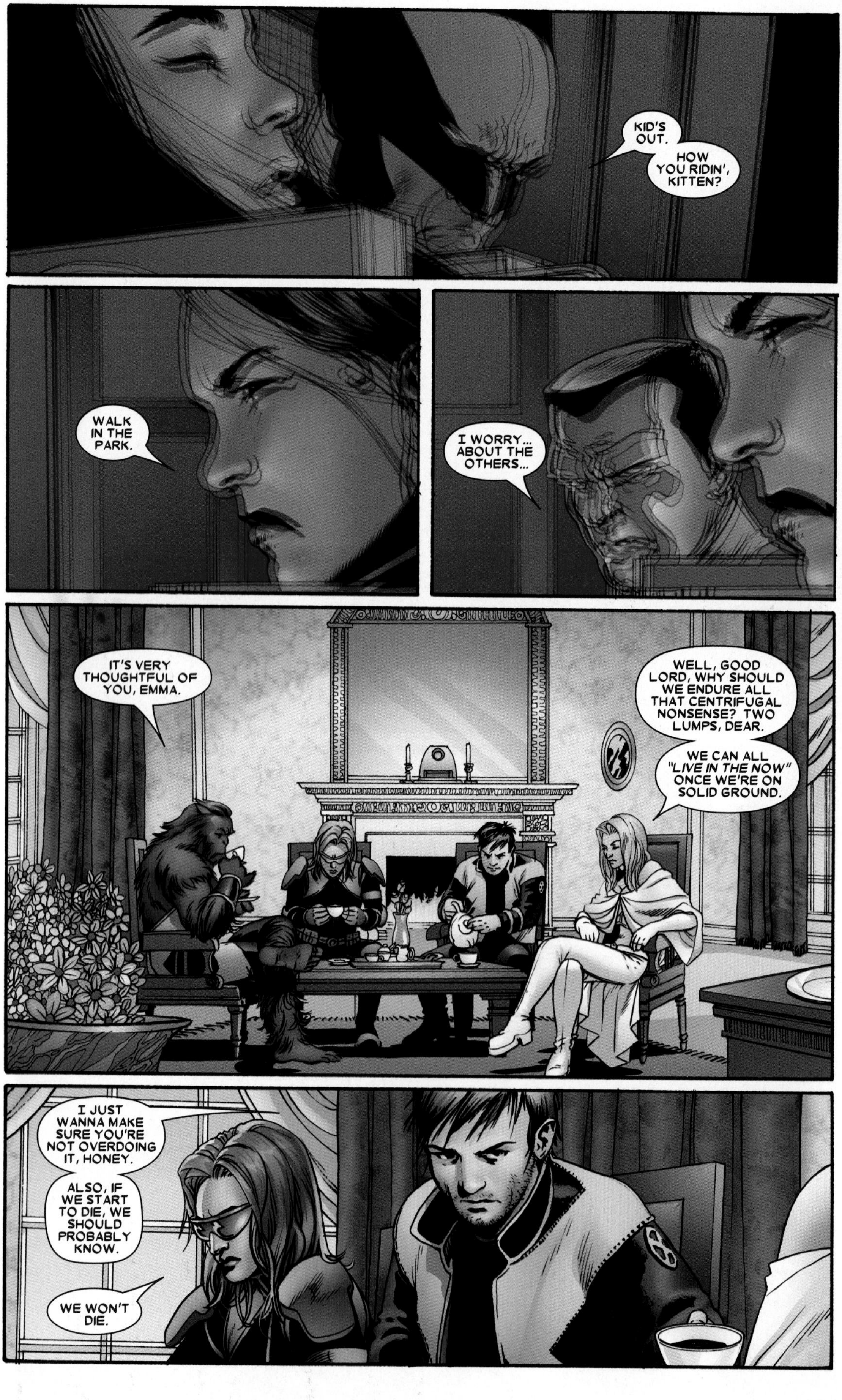
KID'S OUT.
HOW YOU RIDIN', KITTEN?
WALK IN THE PARK.
I WORRY... ABOUT THE OTHERS...
IT'S VERY THOUGHTFUL OF YOU, EMMA.
WELL, GOOD LORD, WHY SHOULD WE ENDURE ALL THAT CENTRIFUGAL NONSENSE? TWO LUMPS, DEAR.
WE CAN ALL "LIVE IN THE NOW" ONCE WE'RE ON SOLID GROUND.
I JUST WANNA MAKE SURE YOU'RE NOT OVERDOING IT, HONEY.
ALSO, IF WE START TO DIE, WE SHOULD PROBABLY KNOW.
WE WON'T DIE.

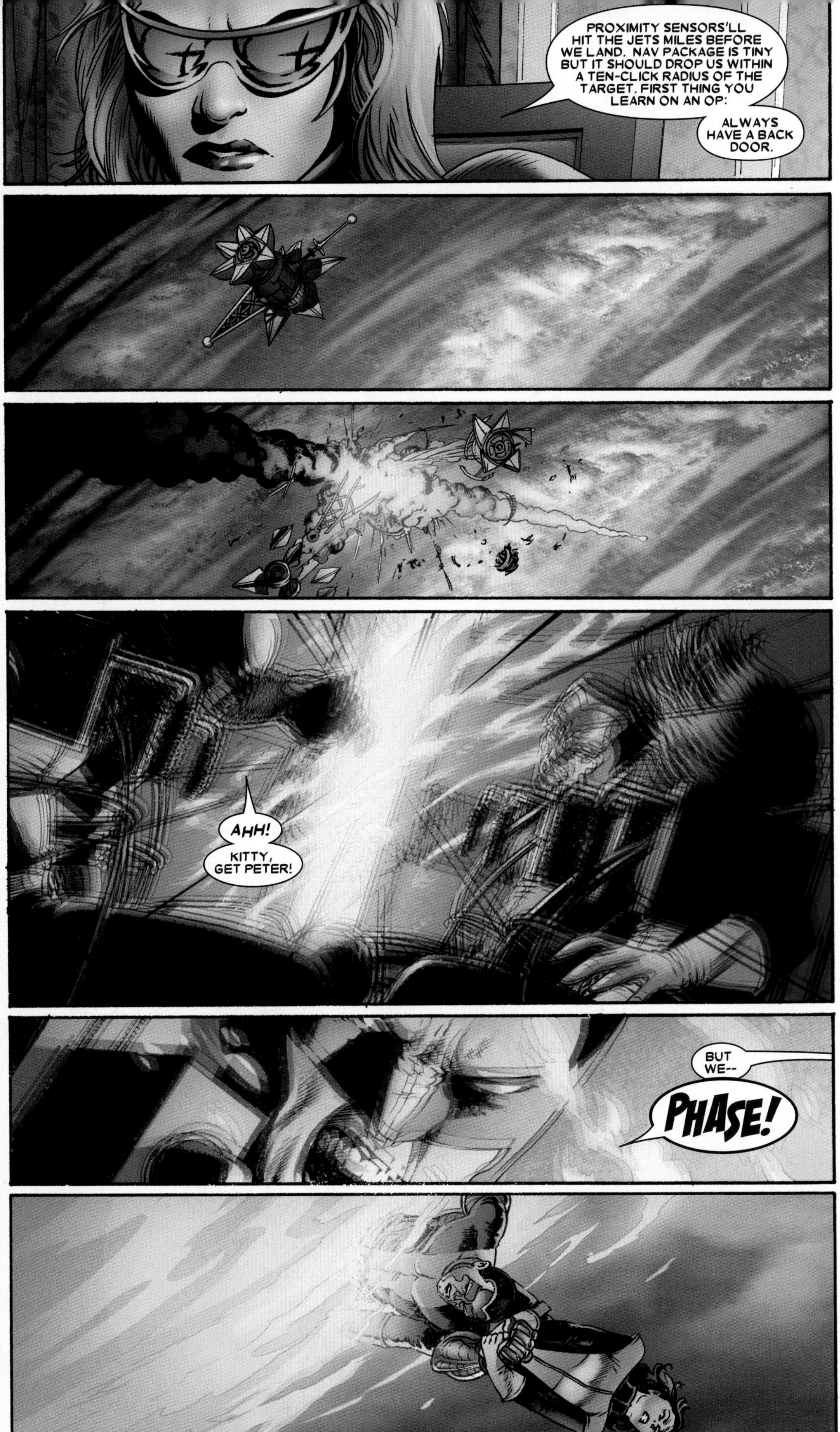
PROXIMITY SENSORS'LL HIT THE JETS MILES BEFORE WE LAND. NAV PACKAGE IS TINY BUT IT SHOULD DROP US WITHIN A TEN-CLICK RADIUS OF THE TARGET. FIRST THING YOU LEARN ON AN OP:
ALWAYS HAVE A BACK DOOR.
AHH!
KITTY, GET PETER!
BUT WE--
PHASE!

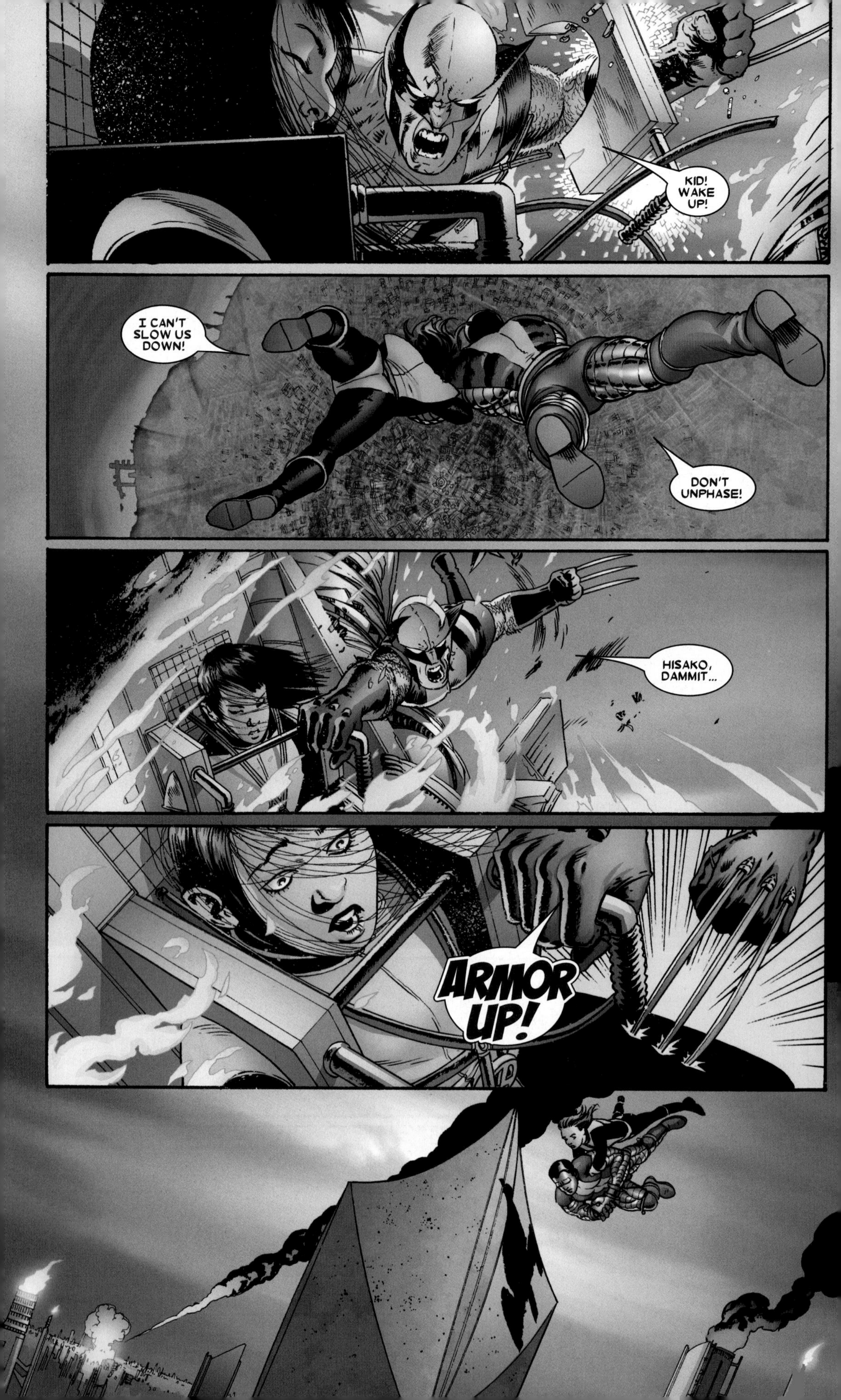
KID! WAKE UP!
I CAN'T SLOW US DOWN!
DON'T UNPHASE!
HISAKO, DAMMIT...
ARMOR UP!

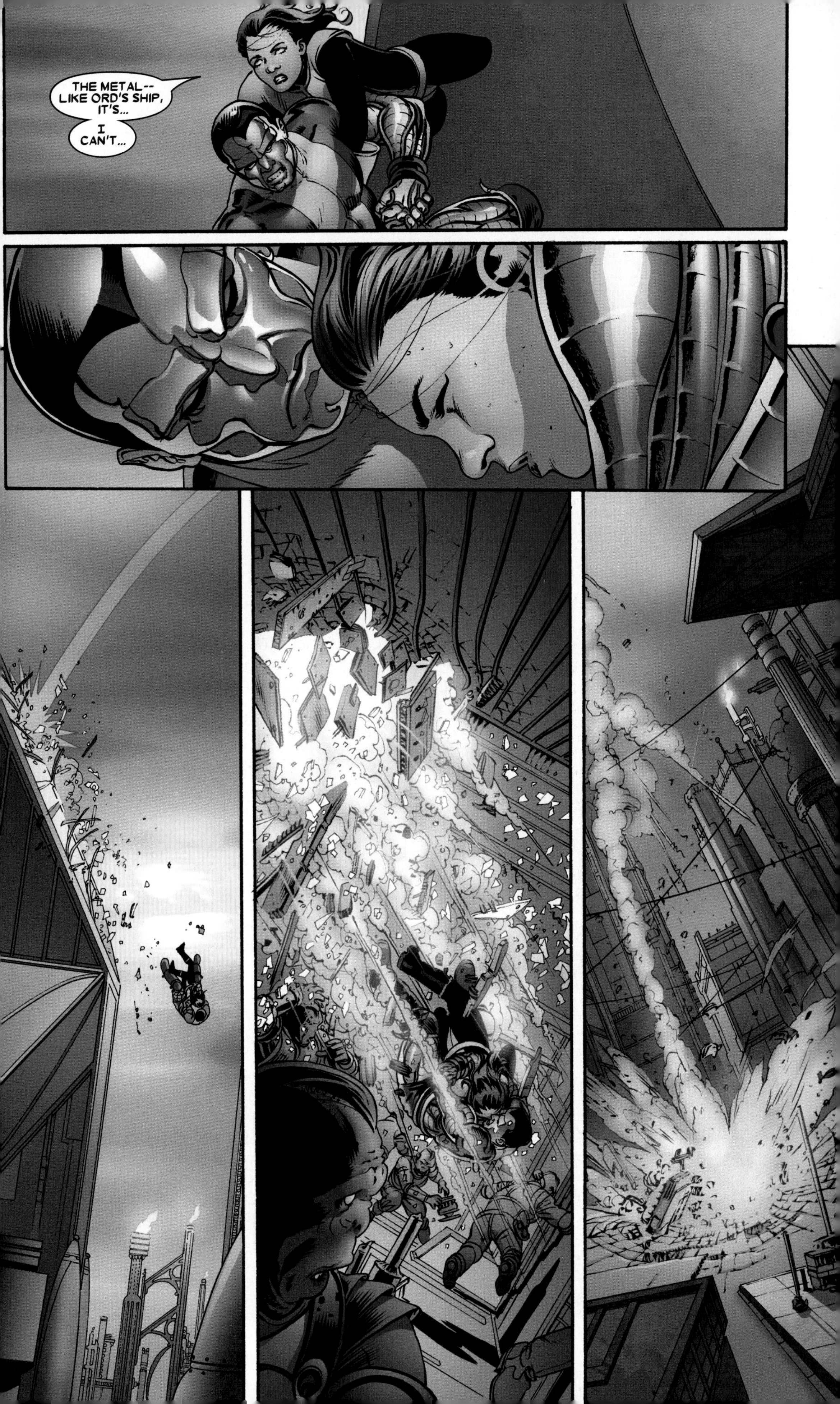
THE METAL-- LIKE ORD'S SHIP, IT'S...
I CAN'T...

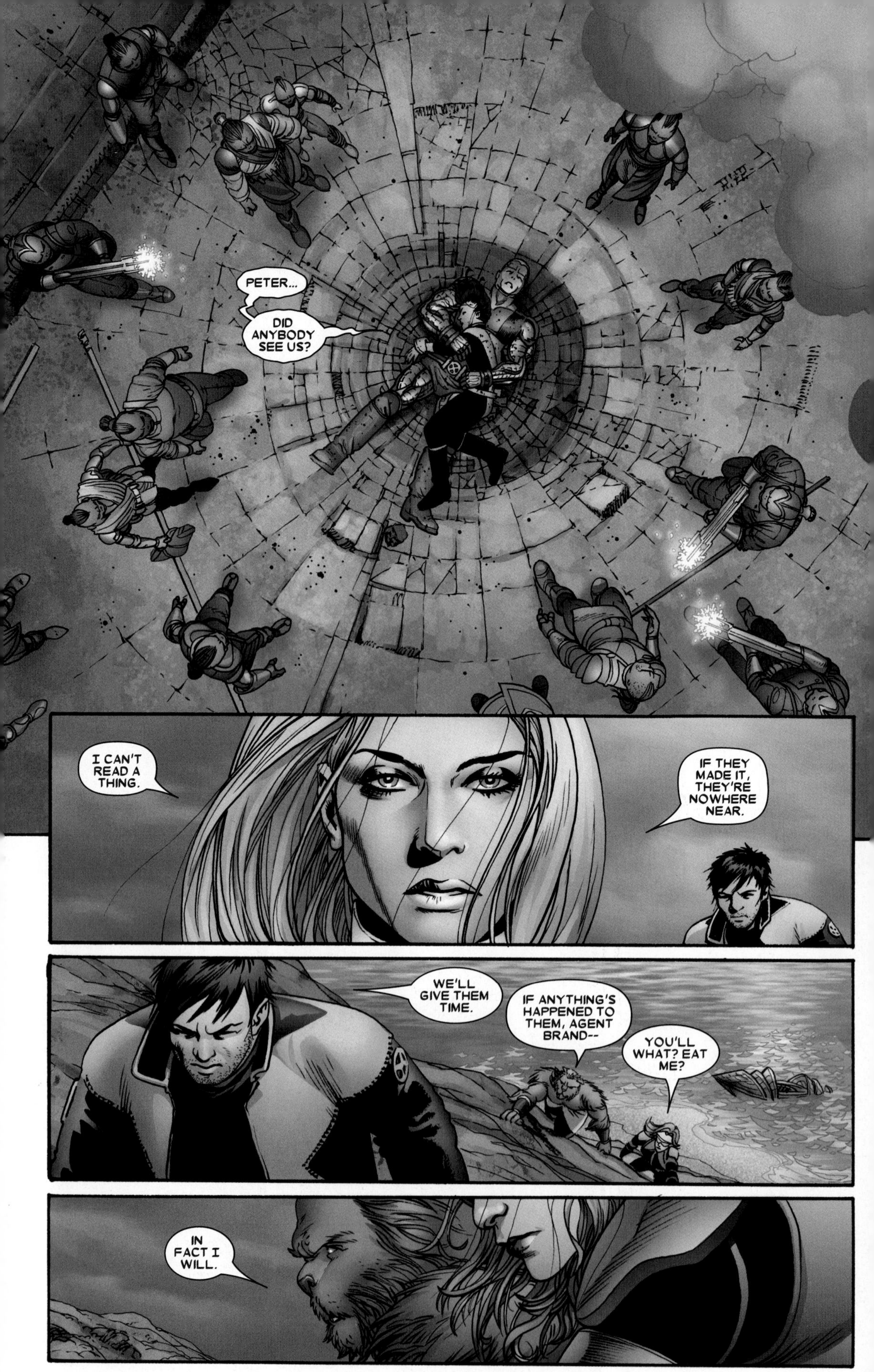
PETER...
DID ANYBODY SEE US?
I CAN'T READ A THING.
IF THEY MADE IT, THEY'RE NOWHERE NEAR.
WE'LL GIVE THEM TIME.
IF ANYTHING'S HAPPENED TO THEM, AGENT BRAND--
YOU'LL WHAT? EAT ME?
IN FACT I WILL.

THE NEW MATH, AGENT. YOU'RE OUTNUMBERED. AND NOT WELL-LIKED.

AND I'VE RECENTLY ACQUIRED A TASTE FOR HUMAN FLESH, I SAY WITH SOME EMBARRASSMENT.

STOW THE BICKERING, GUYS...

WE'VE FOUND OUR TOMB.

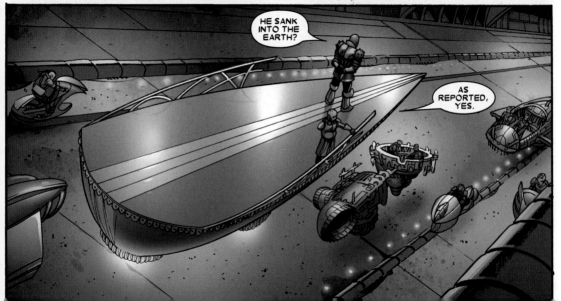

HE SANK INTO THE EARTH?

AS REPORTED, YES.

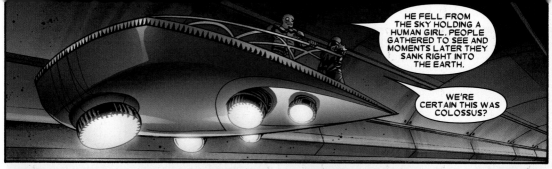

HE FELL FROM THE SKY HOLDING A HUMAN GIRL. PEOPLE GATHERED TO SEE AND MOMENTS LATER THEY SANK RIGHT INTO THE EARTH.

WE'RE CERTAIN THIS WAS COLOSSUS?

THE PEOPLE WERE. THEY PANICKED. AND IT SPREADS. THEY BELIEVE HE'S GONE INTO THE EARTH TO INFECT IT.

THAT THE PROPHECY HAS BEGUN.

AND FOR ALL WE KNOW THEY COULD BE RIGHT.

IT DOESN'T FIT EXACTLY, BUT THIS IS NOT AN EXACT SCIENCE. WE COULD HAVE MISINTERPRETED THE ATTUR-HYN.

LET'S HOPE THE PRISONERS HAVE SOMETHING USEFUL TO SAY.

IT'S THE GIRL.

THIS IS HER POWER: TO MOVE THROUGH SOLID OBJECTS. COLOSSUS WILL BE SOMEWHERE ABOVE GROUND. HE CAN BE STOPPED.

BUT NOT BY YOU.

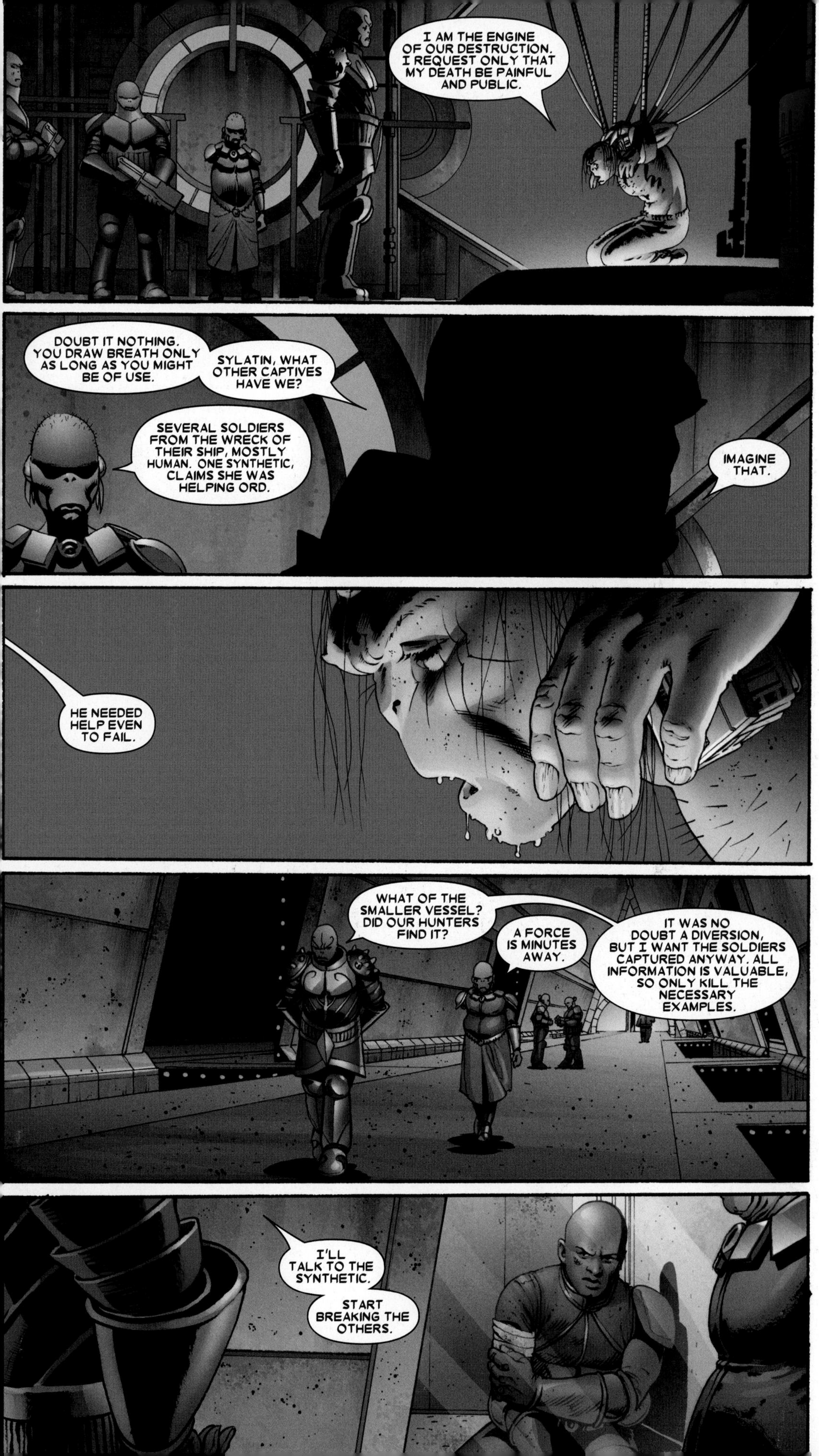

I AM THE ENGINE OF OUR DESTRUCTION. I REQUEST ONLY THAT MY DEATH BE PAINFUL AND PUBLIC.
DOUBT IT NOTHING. YOU DRAW BREATH ONLY AS LONG AS YOU MIGHT BE OF USE.
SYLATIN, WHAT OTHER CAPTIVES HAVE WE?
SEVERAL SOLDIERS FROM THE WRECK OF THEIR SHIP, MOSTLY HUMAN. ONE SYNTHETIC, CLAIMS SHE WAS HELPING ORD.
IMAGINE THAT.
HE NEEDED HELP EVEN TO FAIL.
WHAT OF THE SMALLER VESSEL? DID OUR HUNTERS FIND IT?
A FORCE IS MINUTES AWAY.
IT WAS NO DOUBT A DIVERSION, BUT I WANT THE SOLDIERS CAPTURED ANYWAY. ALL INFORMATION IS VALUABLE, SO ONLY KILL THE NECESSARY EXAMPLES.
I'LL TALK TO THE SYNTHETIC.
START BREAKING THE OTHERS.

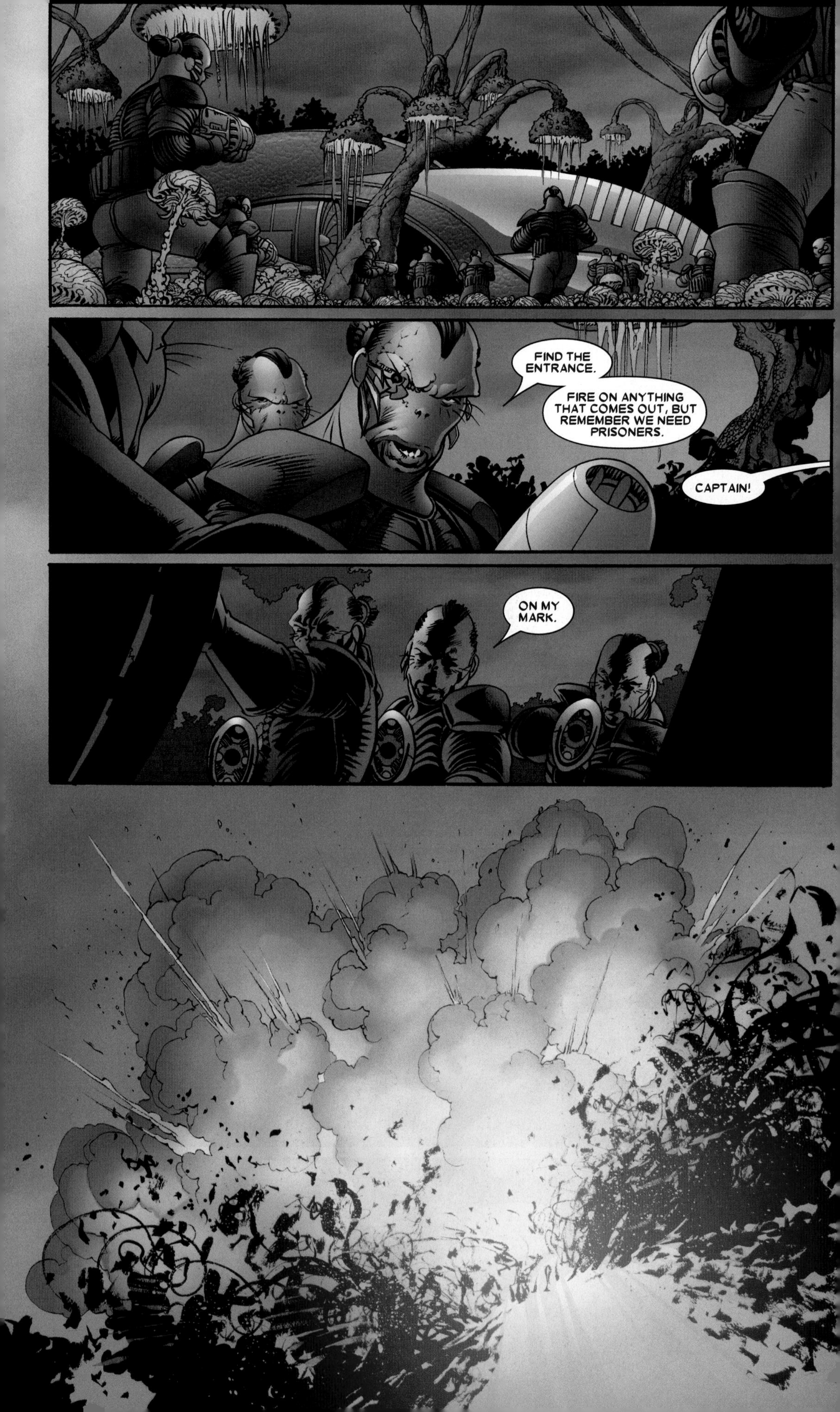
FIND THE ENTRANCE.
FIRE ON ANYTHING THAT COMES OUT, BUT REMEMBER WE NEED PRISONERS.
CAPTAIN!
ON MY MARK.

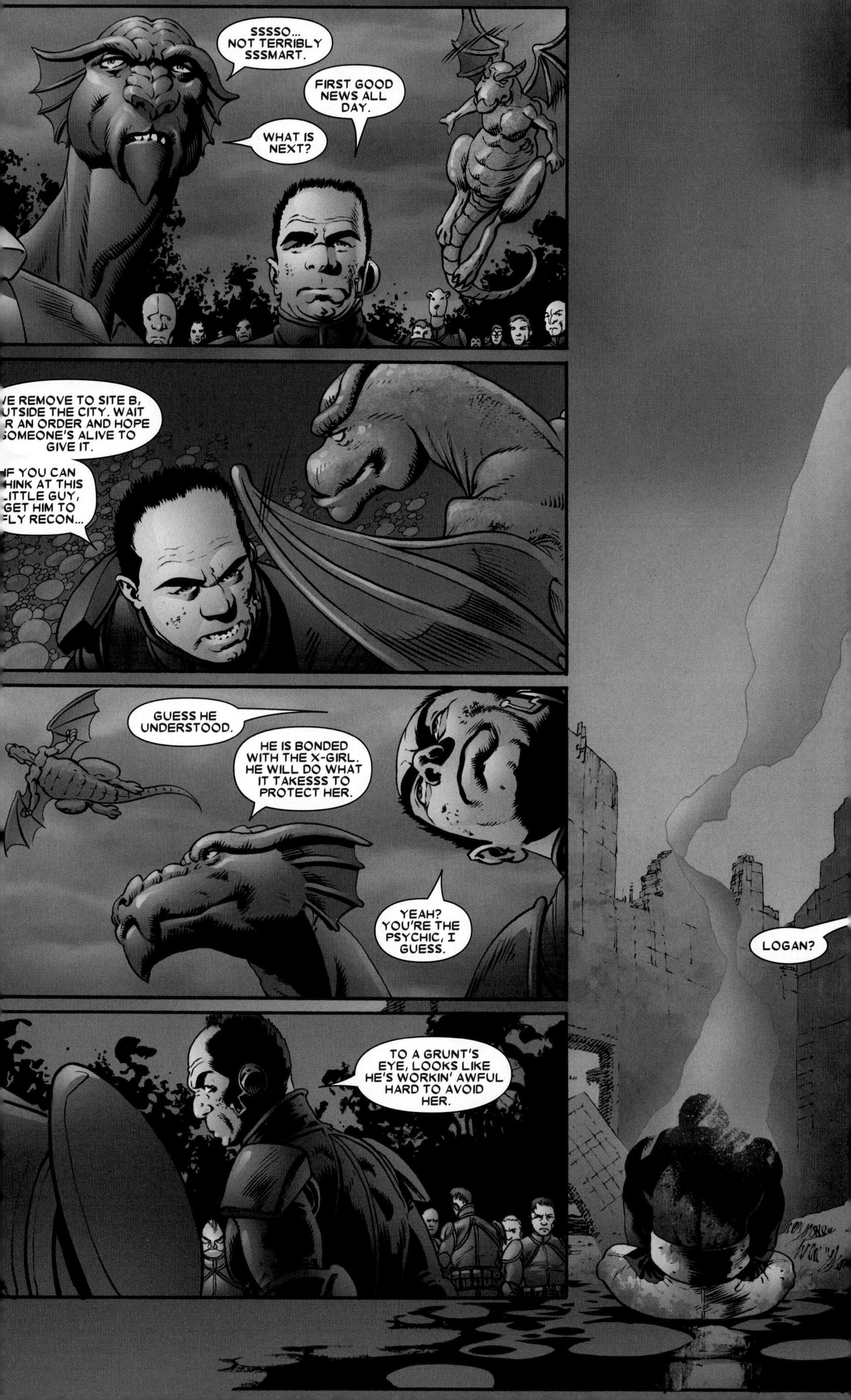
SSSSO... NOT TERRIBLY SSSMART.
FIRST GOOD NEWS ALL DAY.
WHAT IS NEXT?
/E REMOVE TO SITE B, UTSIDE THE CITY. WAIT R AN ORDER AND HOPE SOMEONE'S ALIVE TO GIVE IT.
IF YOU CAN HINK AT THIS LITTLE GUY, GET HIM TO FLY RECON...
GUESS HE UNDERSTOOD.
HE IS BONDED WITH THE X-GIRL. HE WILL DO WHAT IT TAKESSS TO PROTECT HER.
YEAH? YOU'RE THE PSYCHIC, I GUESS.
TO A GRUNT'S EYE, LOOKS LIKE HE'S WORKIN' AWFUL HARD TO AVOID HER.
LOGAN?

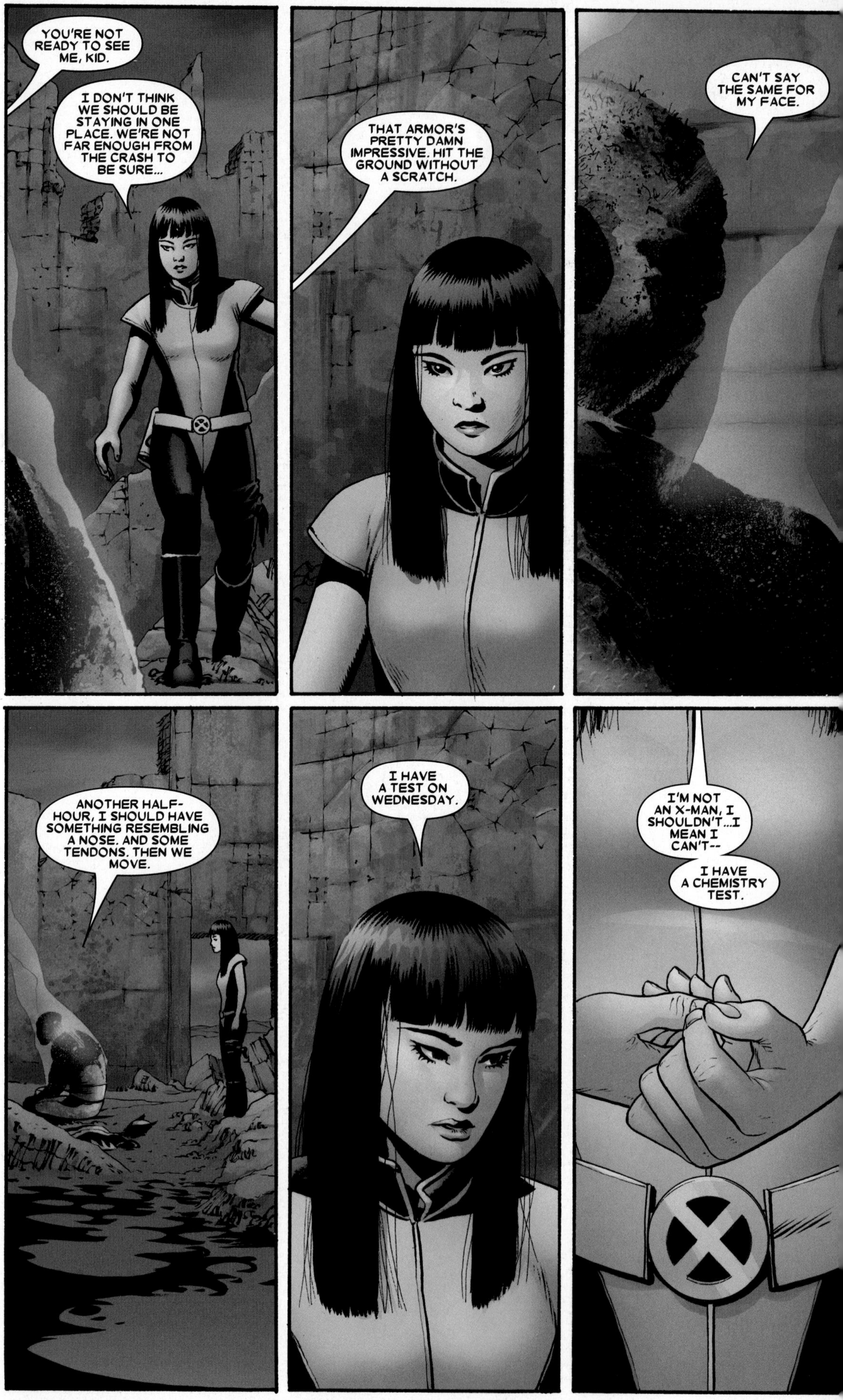
YOU'RE NOT READY TO SEE ME, KID.
I DON'T THINK WE SHOULD BE STAYING IN ONE PLACE. WE'RE NOT FAR ENOUGH FROM THE CRASH TO BE SURE...
THAT ARMOR'S PRETTY DAMN IMPRESSIVE. HIT THE GROUND WITHOUT A SCRATCH.
CAN'T SAY THE SAME FOR MY FACE.
ANOTHER HALF-HOUR, I SHOULD HAVE SOMETHING RESEMBLING A NOSE. AND SOME TENDONS. THEN WE MOVE.
I HAVE A TEST ON WEDNESDAY.
I'M NOT AN X-MAN, I SHOULDN'T...I MEAN I CAN'T--
I HAVE A CHEMISTRY TEST.

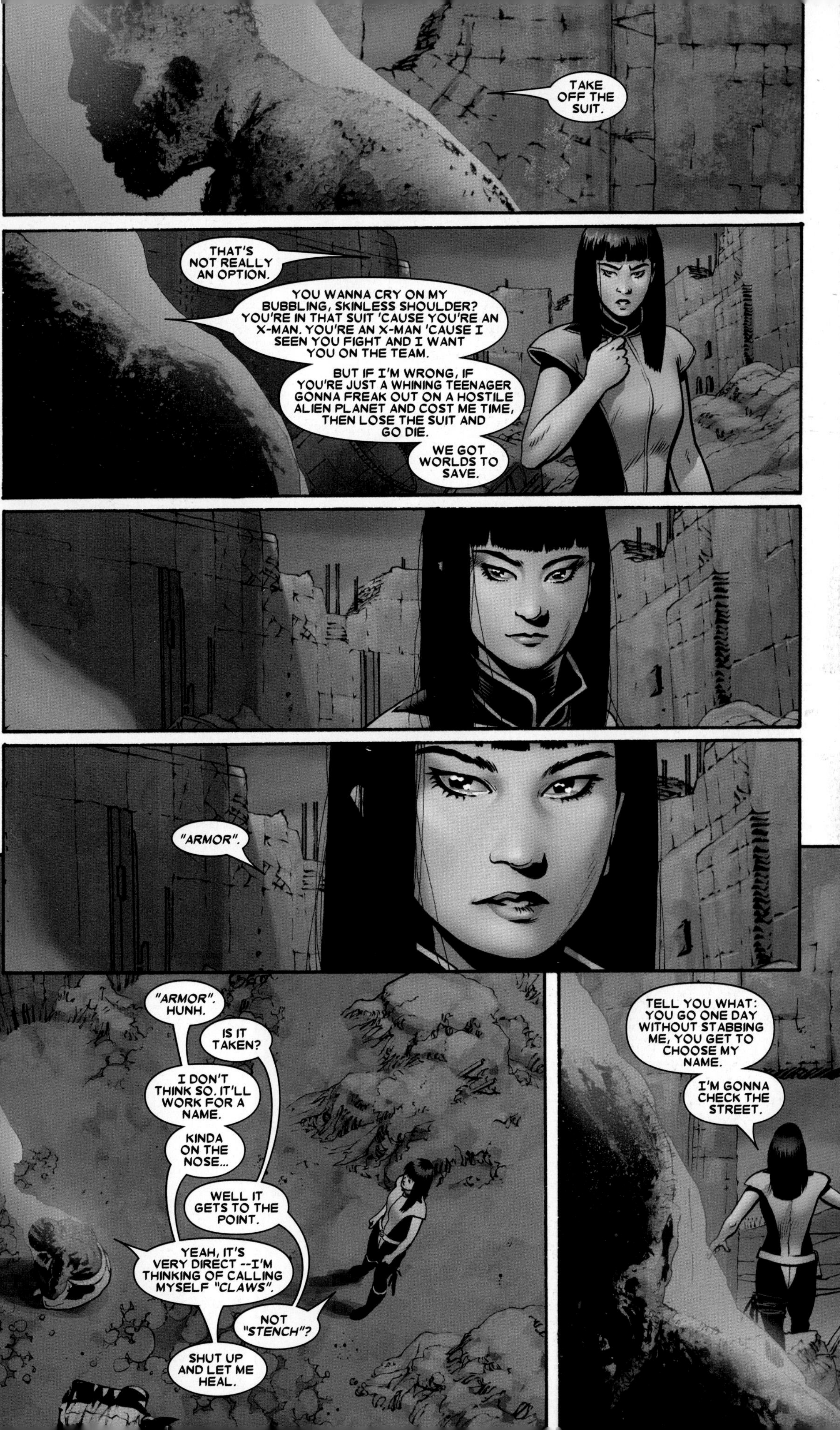
TAKE OFF THE SUIT.
THAT'S NOT REALLY AN OPTION.
YOU WANNA CRY ON MY BUBBLING, SKINLESS SHOULDER? YOU'RE IN THAT SUIT 'CAUSE YOU'RE AN X-MAN. YOU'RE AN X-MAN 'CAUSE I SEEN YOU FIGHT AND I WANT YOU ON THE TEAM.
BUT IF I'M WRONG, IF YOU'RE JUST A WHINING TEENAGER GONNA FREAK OUT ON A HOSTILE ALIEN PLANET AND COST ME TIME, THEN LOSE THE SUIT AND GO DIE.
WE GOT WORLDS TO SAVE.
"ARMOR".
"ARMOR". HUNH.
IS IT TAKEN?
I DON'T THINK SO. IT'LL WORK FOR A NAME.
KINDA ON THE NOSE...
WELL IT GETS TO THE POINT.
YEAH, IT'S VERY DIRECT --I'M THINKING OF CALLING MYSELF "CLAWS".
NOT "STENCH"?
SHUT UP AND LET ME HEAL.
TELL YOU WHAT: YOU GO ONE DAY WITHOUT STABBING ME, YOU GET TO CHOOSE MY NAME.
I'M GONNA CHECK THE STREET.

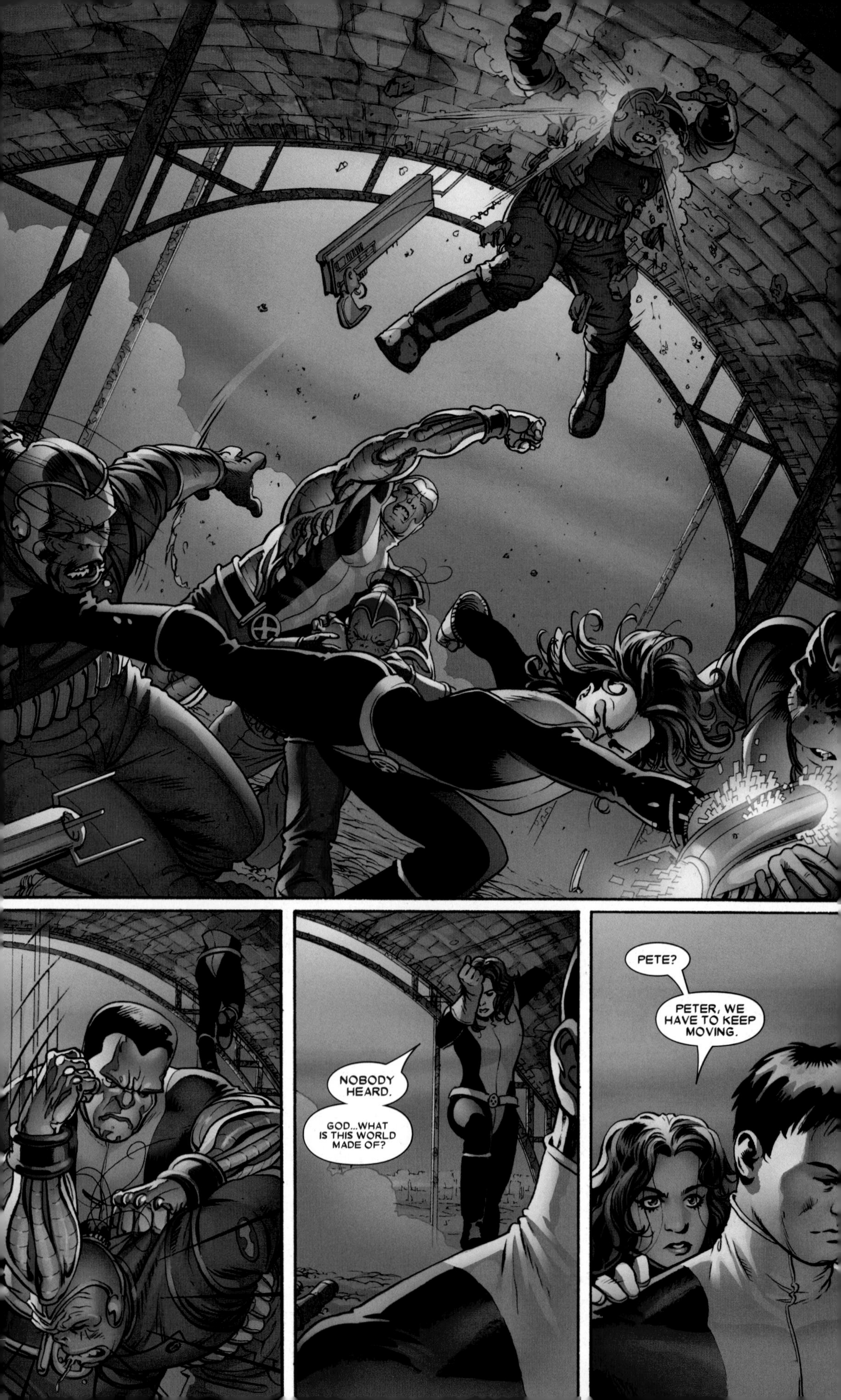
NOBODY HEARD.
GOD...WHAT IS THIS WORLD MADE OF?
PETE?
PETER, WE HAVE TO KEEP MOVING.

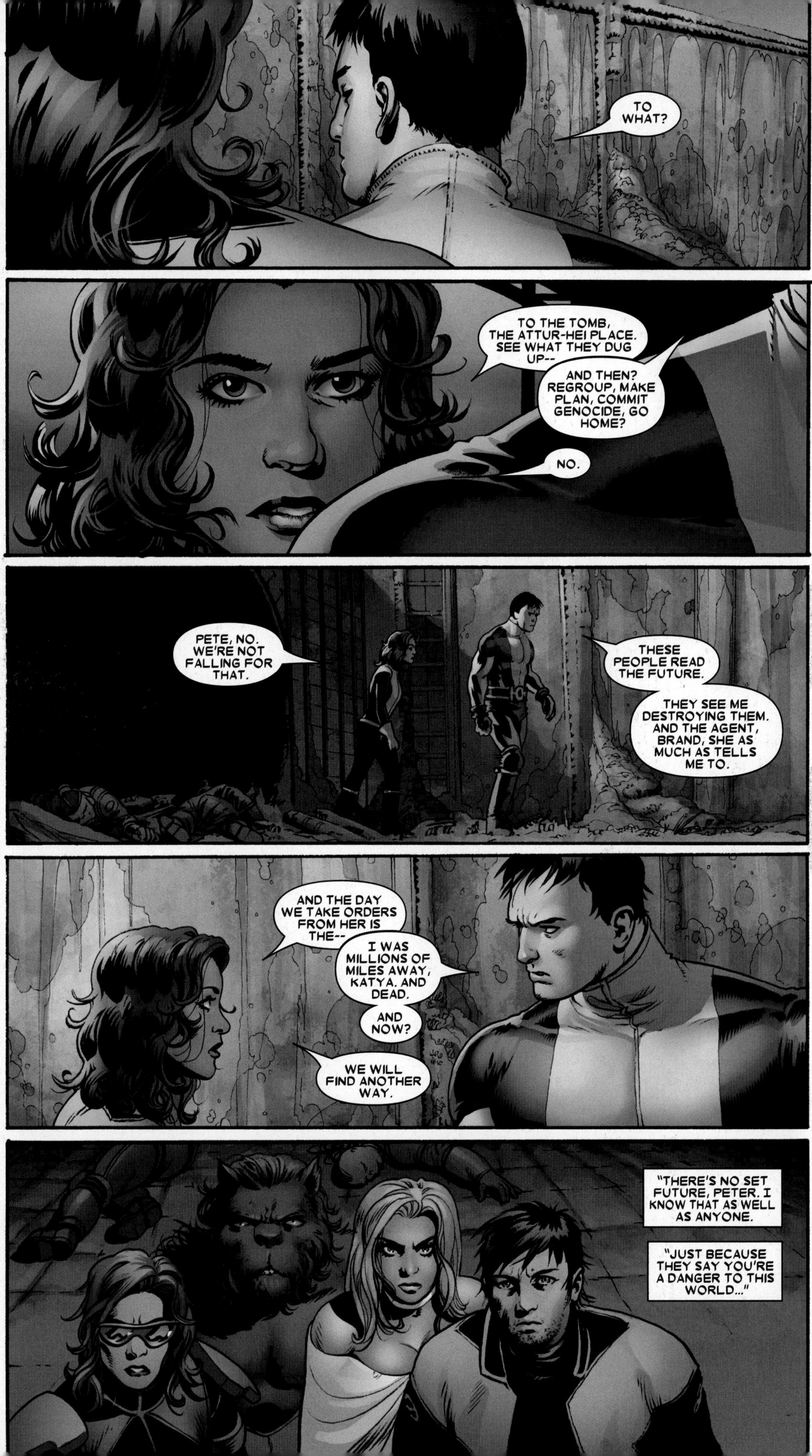
TO WHAT?
TO THE TOMB, THE ATTUR-HEI PLACE. SEE WHAT THEY DUG UP--
AND THEN? REGROUP, MAKE PLAN, COMMIT GENOCIDE, GO HOME?
NO.
PETE, NO. WE'RE NOT FALLING FOR THAT.
THESE PEOPLE READ THE FUTURE.
THEY SEE ME DESTROYING THEM. AND THE AGENT, BRAND, SHE AS MUCH AS TELLS ME TO.
AND THE DAY WE TAKE ORDERS FROM HER IS THE--
I WAS MILLIONS OF MILES AWAY, KATYA. AND DEAD.
AND NOW?
WE WILL FIND ANOTHER WAY.
"THERE'S NO SET FUTURE, PETER. I KNOW THAT AS WELL AS ANYONE.
"JUST BECAUSE THEY SAY YOU'RE A DANGER TO THIS WORLD..."

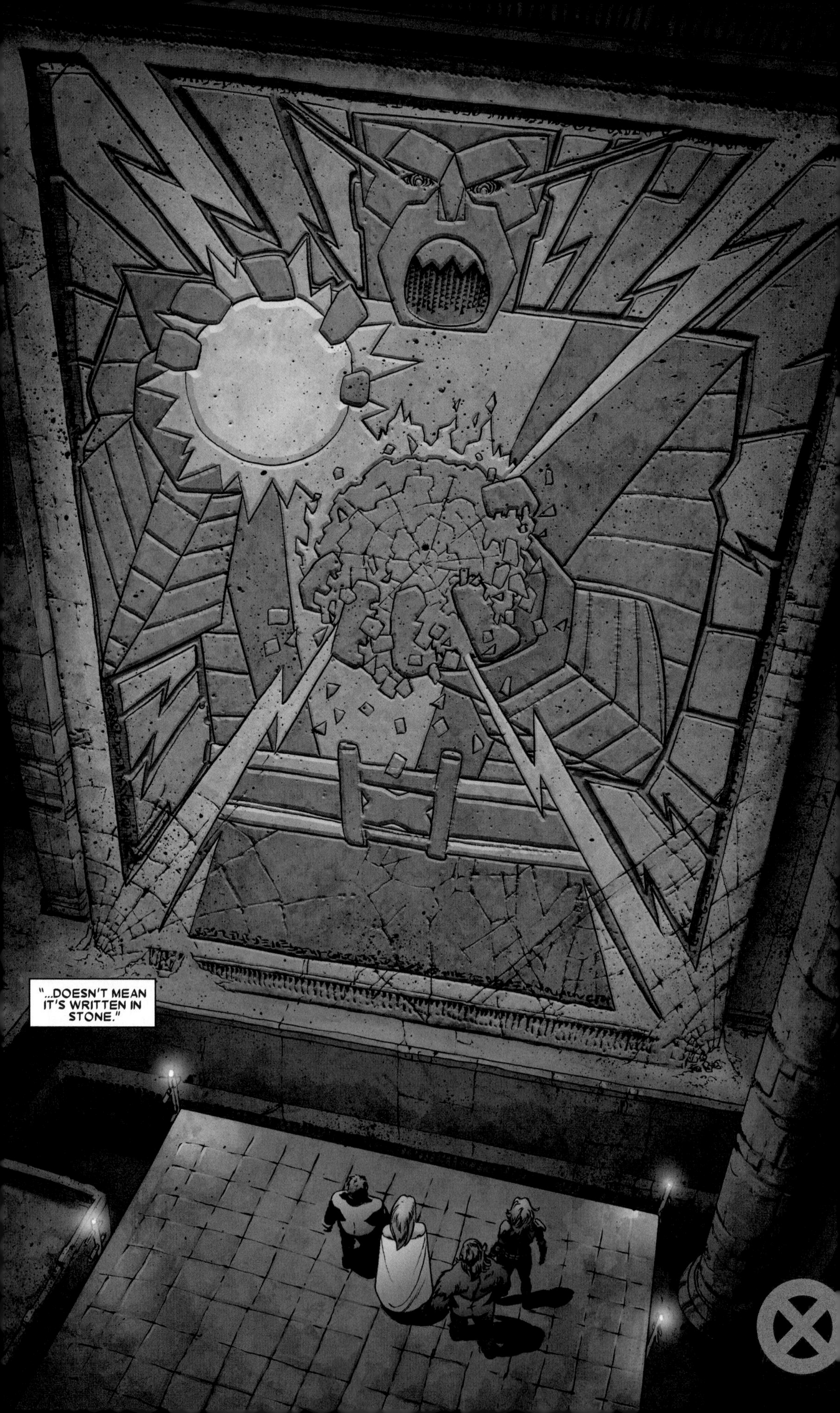
"...DOESN'T MEAN IT'S WRITTEN IN STONE."

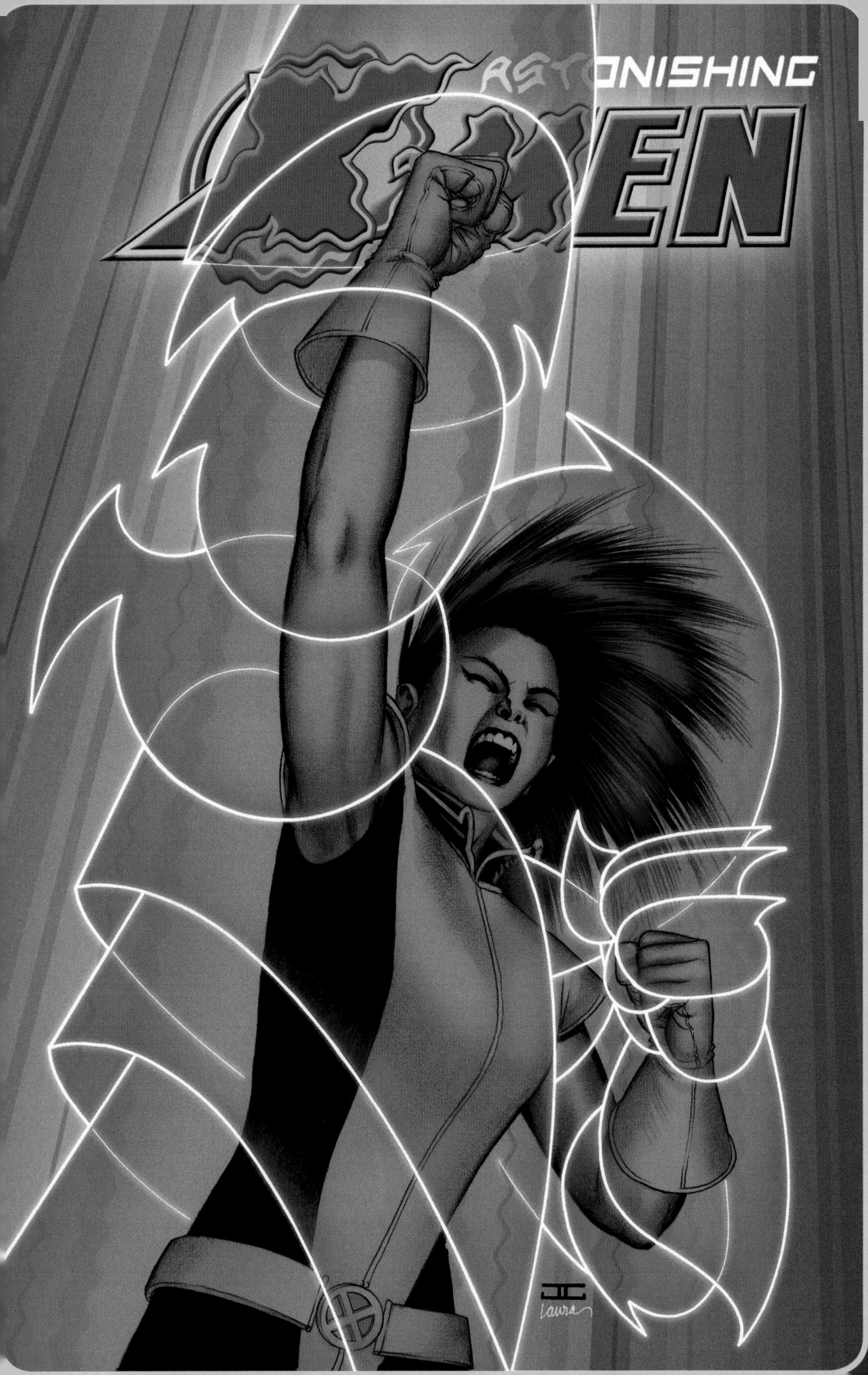
ASTONISHING
X-MEN

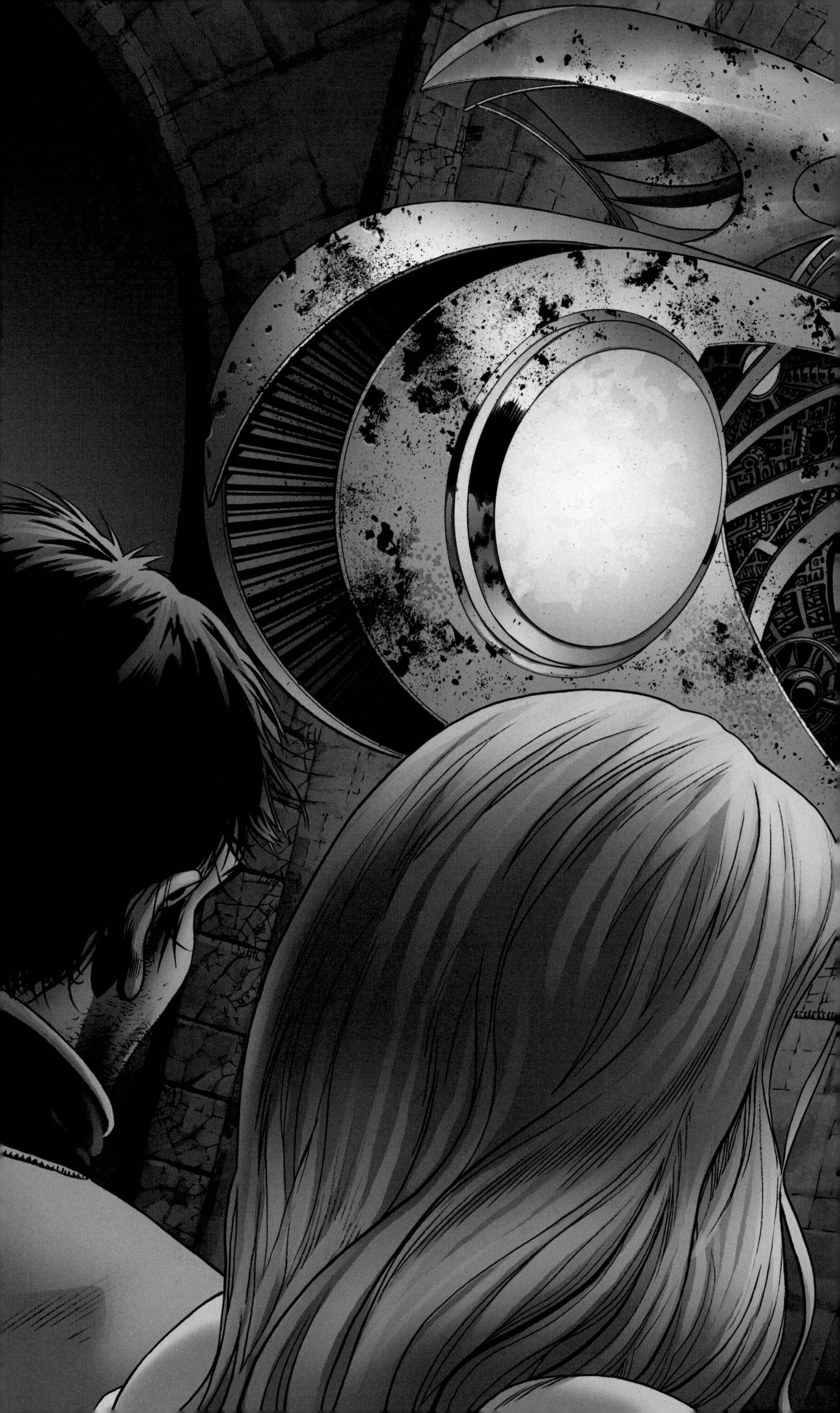

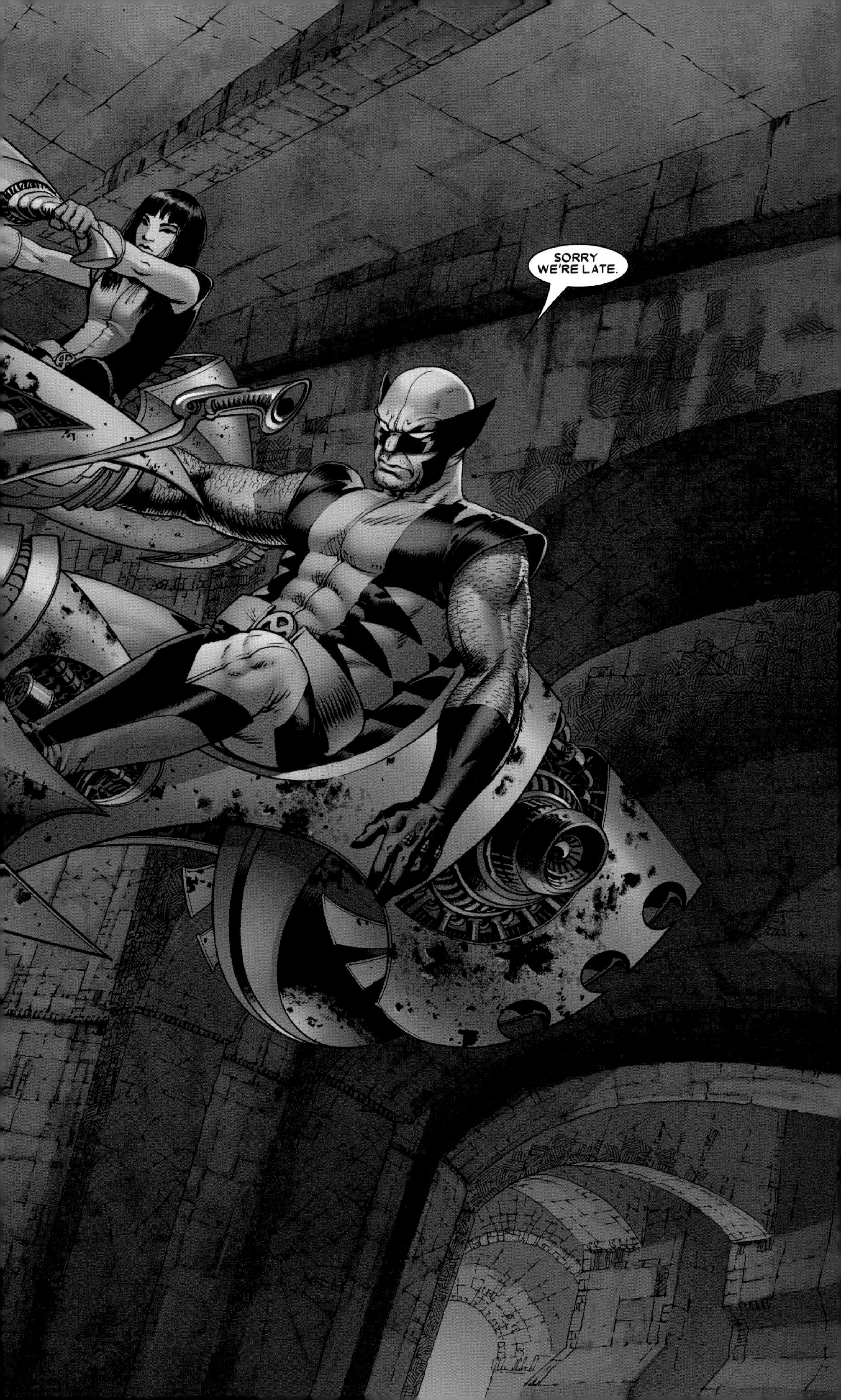
SORRY WE'RE LATE.

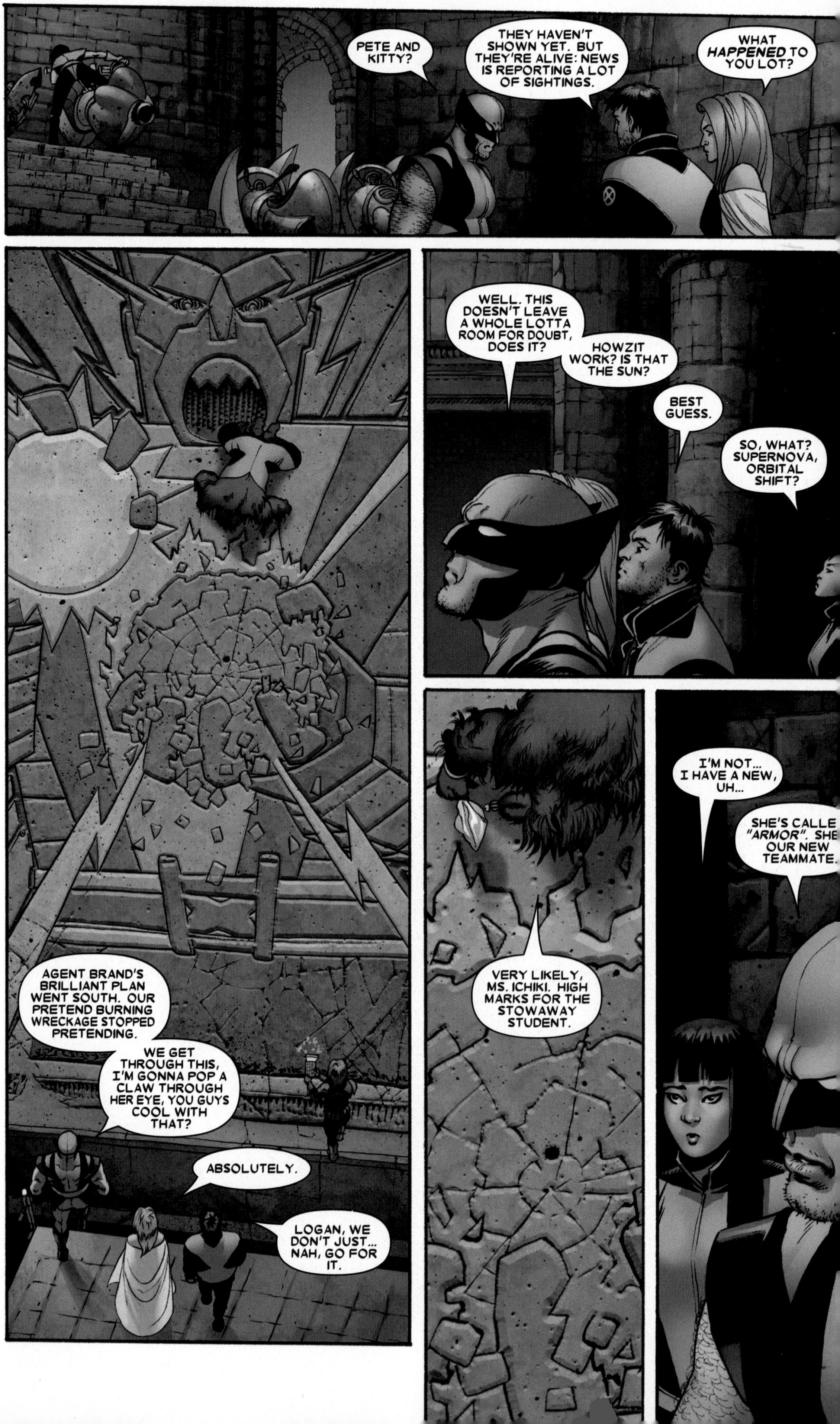

PETE AND KITTY?
THEY HAVEN'T SHOWN YET. BUT THEY'RE ALIVE: NEWS IS REPORTING A LOT OF SIGHTINGS.
WHAT *HAPPENED* TO YOU LOT?
AGENT BRAND'S BRILLIANT PLAN WENT SOUTH. OUR PRETEND BURNING WRECKAGE STOPPED PRETENDING.
WE GET THROUGH THIS, I'M GONNA POP A CLAW THROUGH HER EYE, YOU GUYS COOL WITH THAT?
ABSOLUTELY.
LOGAN, WE DON'T JUST... NAH, GO FOR IT.
WELL. THIS DOESN'T LEAVE A WHOLE LOTTA ROOM FOR DOUBT, DOES IT?
HOWZIT WORK? IS THAT THE SUN?
BEST GUESS.
SO, WHAT? SUPERNOVA, ORBITAL SHIFT?
VERY LIKELY, MS. ICHIKI. HIGH MARKS FOR THE STOWAWAY STUDENT.
I'M NOT... I HAVE A NEW, UH...
SHE'S CALLE *"ARMOR"*. SHE OUR NEW TEAMMATE.

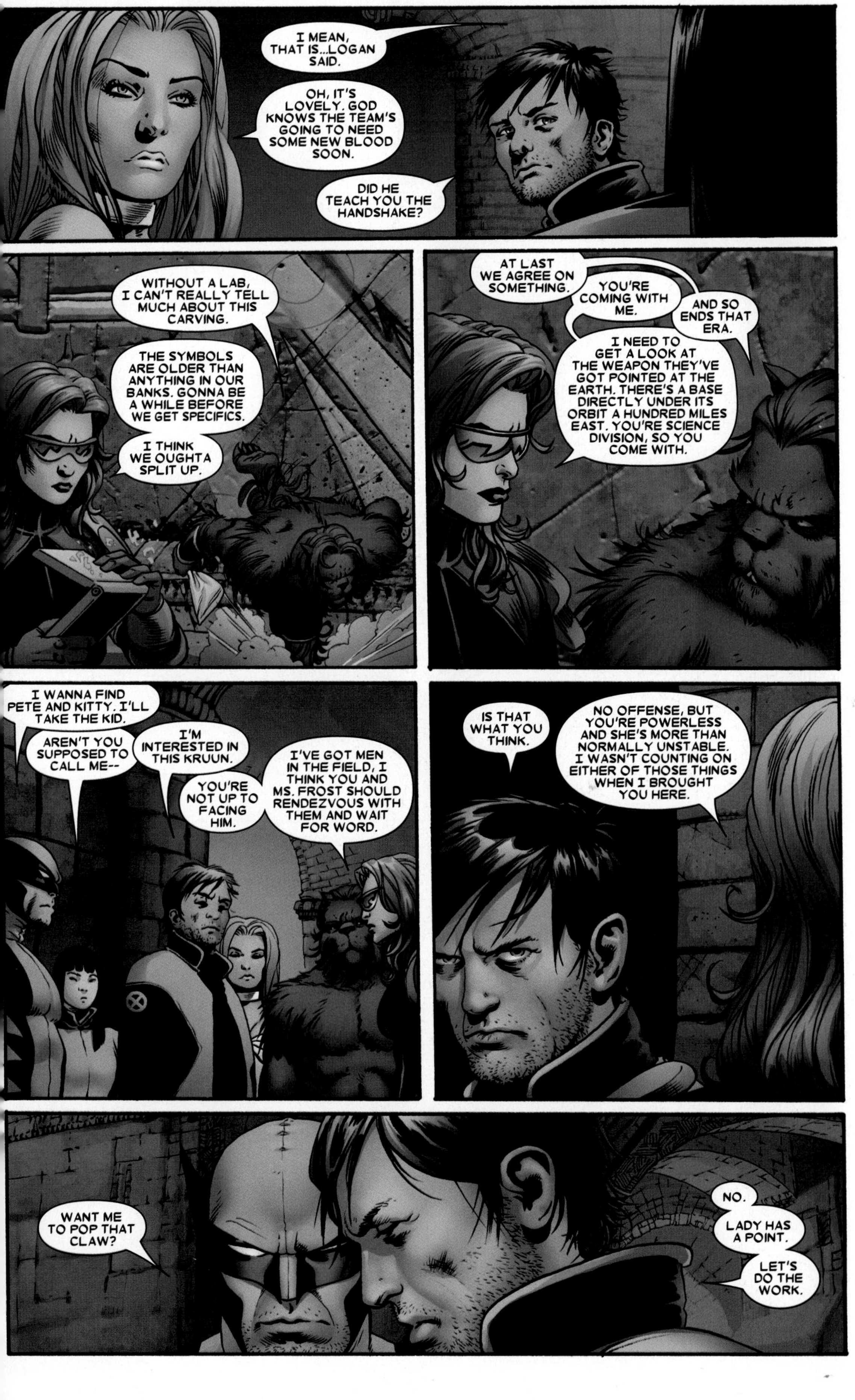

I MEAN, THAT IS...LOGAN SAID.
OH, IT'S LOVELY. GOD KNOWS THE TEAM'S GOING TO NEED SOME NEW BLOOD SOON.
DID HE TEACH YOU THE HANDSHAKE?
WITHOUT A LAB, I CAN'T REALLY TELL MUCH ABOUT THIS CARVING.
THE SYMBOLS ARE OLDER THAN ANYTHING IN OUR BANKS. GONNA BE A WHILE BEFORE WE GET SPECIFICS.
I THINK WE OUGHTA SPLIT UP.
AT LAST WE AGREE ON SOMETHING.
YOU'RE COMING WITH ME.
AND SO ENDS THAT ERA.
I NEED TO GET A LOOK AT THE WEAPON THEY'VE GOT POINTED AT THE EARTH. THERE'S A BASE DIRECTLY UNDER ITS ORBIT A HUNDRED MILES EAST. YOU'RE SCIENCE DIVISION, SO YOU COME WITH.
I WANNA FIND PETE AND KITTY. I'LL TAKE THE KID.
AREN'T YOU SUPPOSED TO CALL ME--
I'M INTERESTED IN THIS KRUUN.
YOU'RE NOT UP TO FACING HIM.
I'VE GOT MEN IN THE FIELD, I THINK YOU AND MS. FROST SHOULD RENDEZVOUS WITH THEM AND WAIT FOR WORD.
IS THAT WHAT YOU THINK.
NO OFFENSE, BUT YOU'RE POWERLESS AND SHE'S MORE THAN NORMALLY UNSTABLE. I WASN'T COUNTING ON EITHER OF THOSE THINGS WHEN I BROUGHT YOU HERE.
WANT ME TO POP THAT CLAW?
NO.
LADY HAS A POINT.
LET'S DO THE WORK.

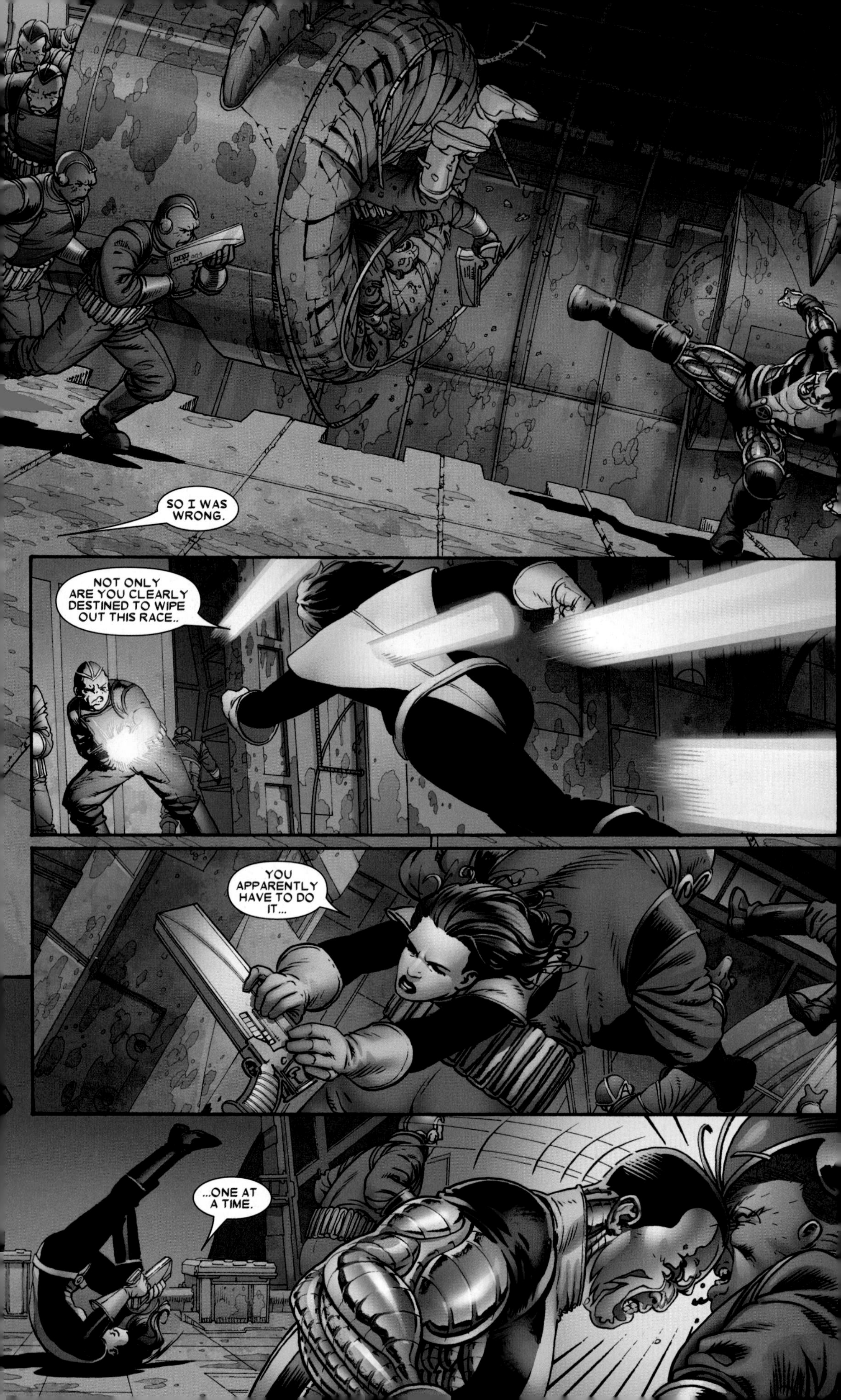
SO I WAS WRONG.
NOT ONLY ARE YOU CLEARLY DESTINED TO WIPE OUT THIS RACE..
YOU APPARENTLY HAVE TO DO IT...
...ONE AT A TIME.

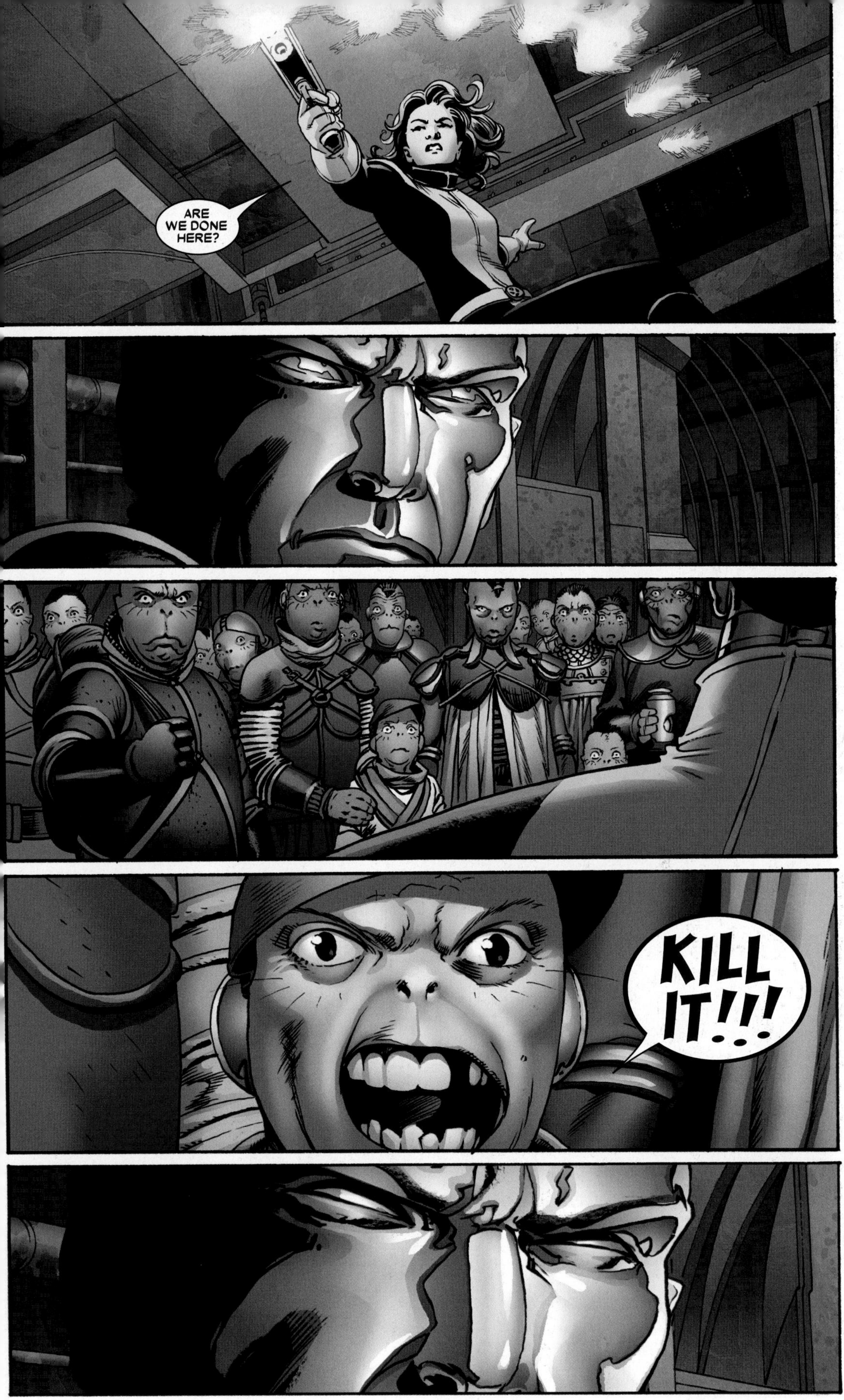
ARE WE DONE HERE?
KILL IT!!!

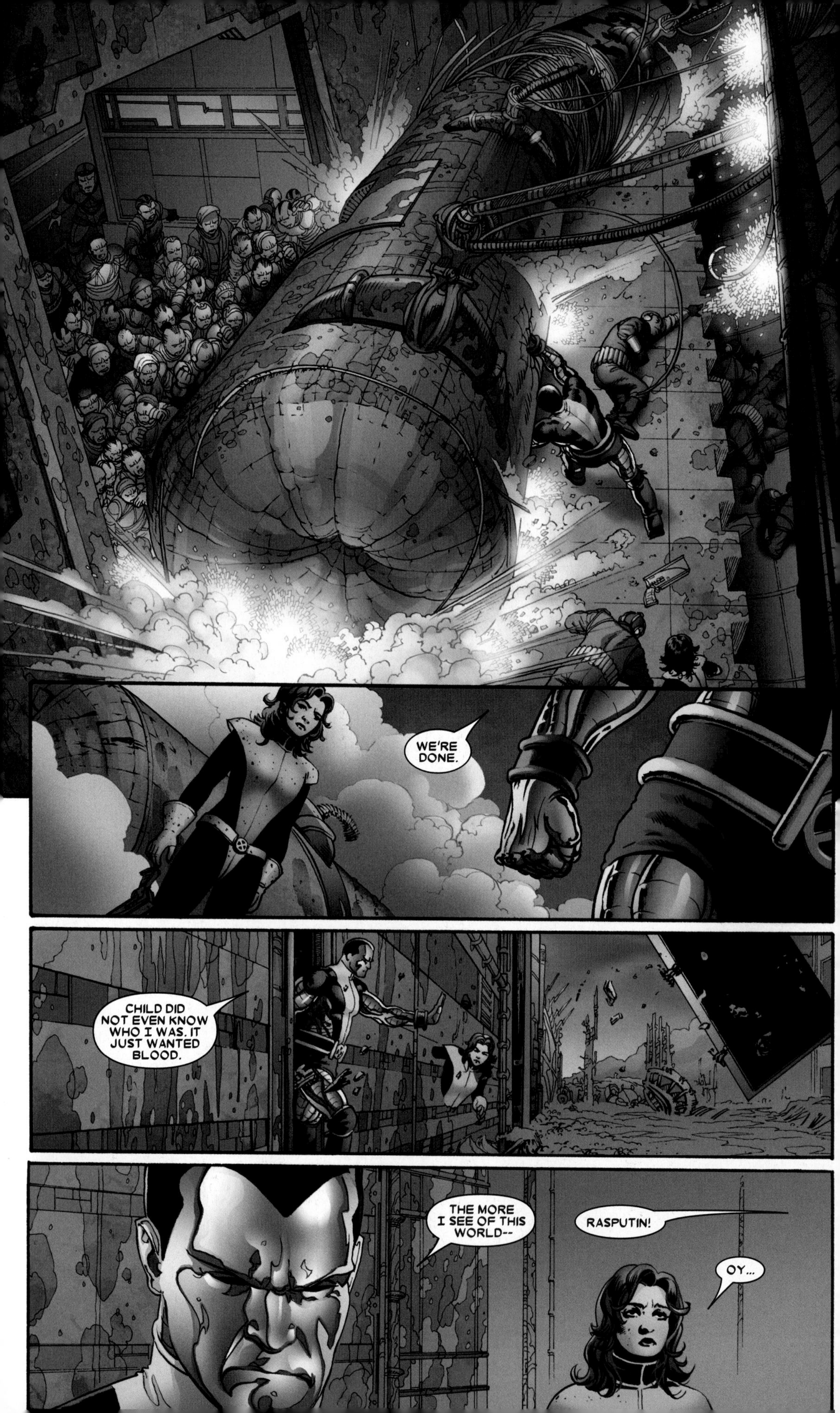
WE'RE DONE.
CHILD DID NOT EVEN KNOW WHO I WAS. IT JUST WANTED BLOOD.
THE MORE I SEE OF THIS WORLD--
RASPUTIN!
OY...

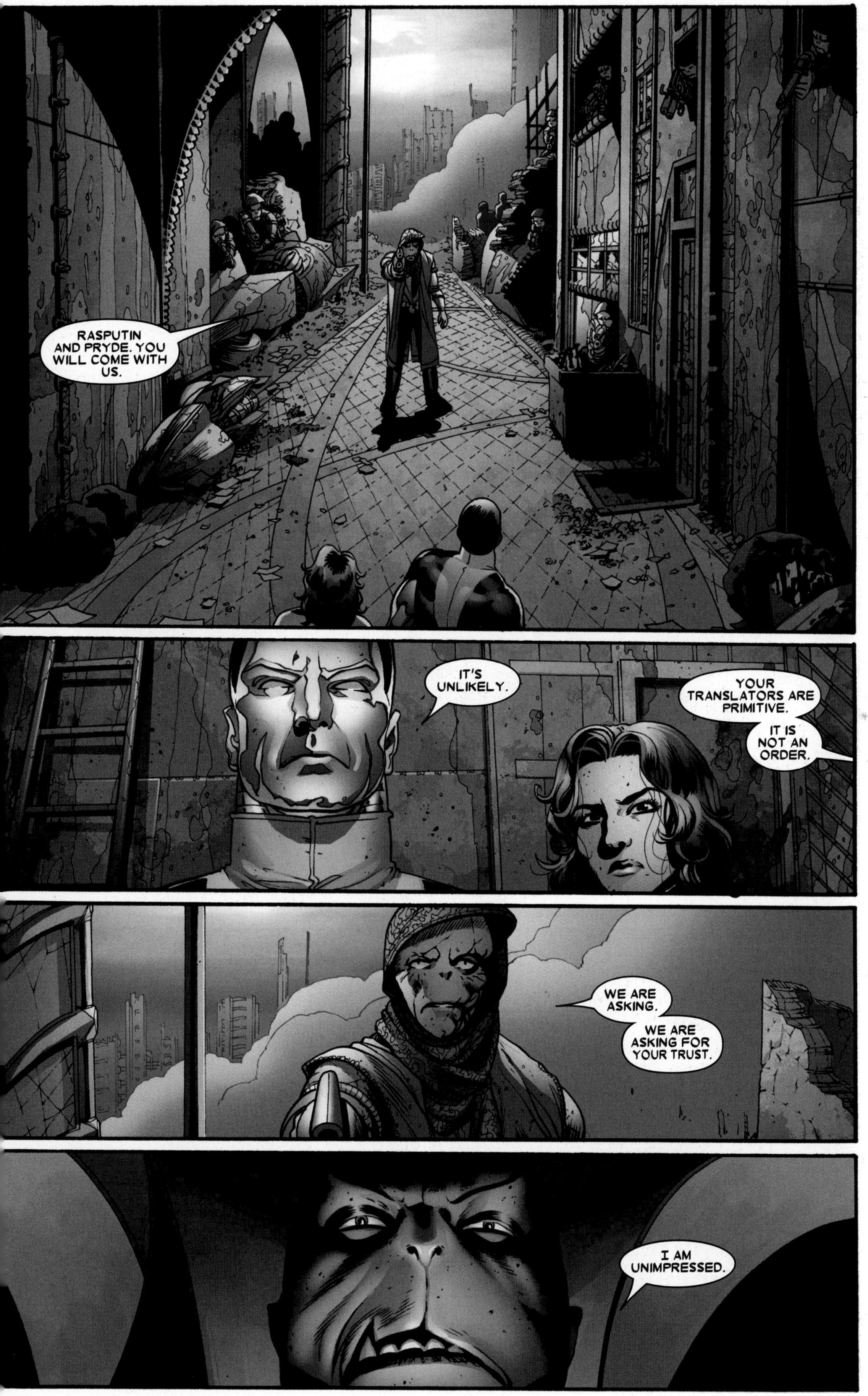

RASPUTIN AND PRYDE. YOU WILL COME WITH US.
IT'S UNLIKELY.
YOUR TRANSLATORS ARE PRIMITIVE.
IT IS NOT AN ORDER.
WE ARE ASKING.
WE ARE ASKING FOR YOUR TRUST.
I AM UNIMPRESSED.

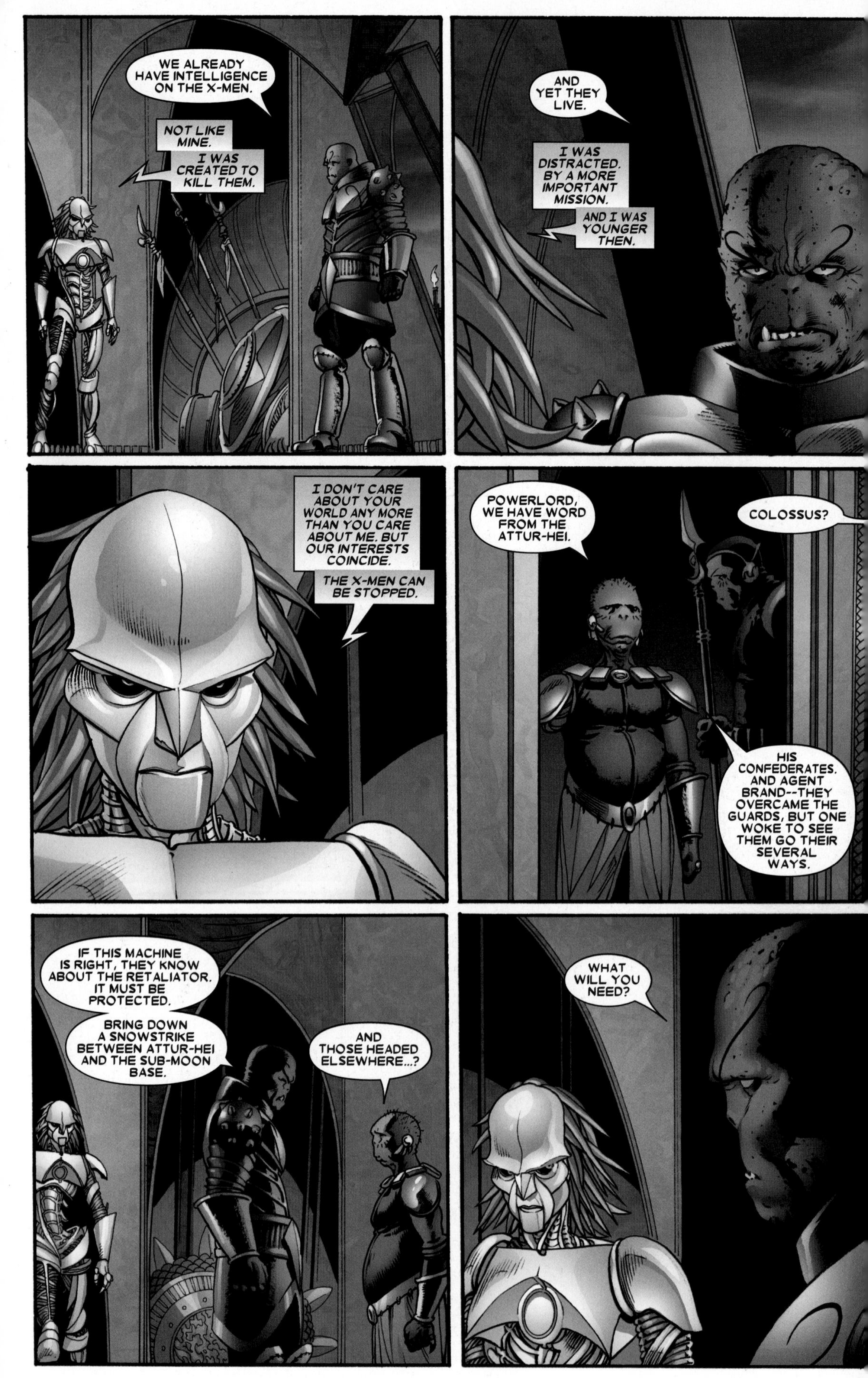

WE ALREADY HAVE INTELLIGENCE ON THE X-MEN.
NOT LIKE MINE.
I WAS CREATED TO KILL THEM.
AND YET THEY LIVE.
I WAS DISTRACTED. BY A MORE IMPORTANT MISSION.
AND I WAS YOUNGER THEN.
I DON'T CARE ABOUT YOUR WORLD ANY MORE THAN YOU CARE ABOUT ME. BUT OUR INTERESTS COINCIDE.
THE X-MEN CAN BE STOPPED.
POWERLORD, WE HAVE WORD FROM THE ATTUR-HEI.
COLOSSUS?
HIS CONFEDERATES. AND AGENT BRAND--THEY OVERCAME THE GUARDS, BUT ONE WOKE TO SEE THEM GO THEIR SEVERAL WAYS.
IF THIS MACHINE IS RIGHT, THEY KNOW ABOUT THE RETALIATOR. IT MUST BE PROTECTED.
BRING DOWN A SNOWSTRIKE BETWEEN ATTUR-HEI AND THE SUB-MOON BASE.
AND THOSE HEADED ELSEWHERE...?
WHAT WILL YOU NEED?

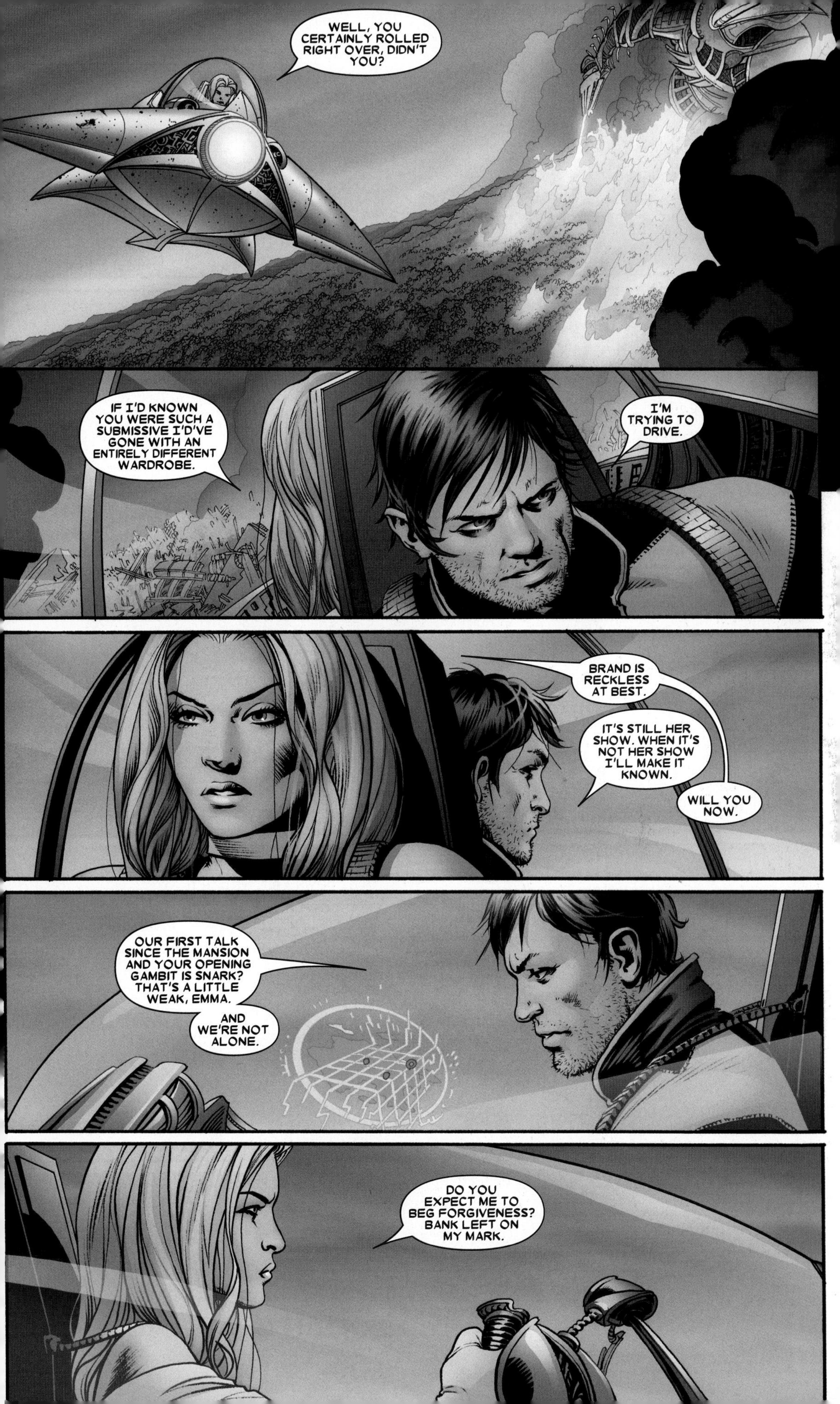

WELL, YOU CERTAINLY ROLLED RIGHT OVER, DIDN'T YOU?
IF I'D KNOWN YOU WERE SUCH A SUBMISSIVE I'D'VE GONE WITH AN ENTIRELY DIFFERENT WARDROBE.
I'M TRYING TO DRIVE.
BRAND IS RECKLESS AT BEST.
IT'S STILL HER SHOW. WHEN IT'S NOT HER SHOW I'LL MAKE IT KNOWN.
WILL YOU NOW.
OUR FIRST TALK SINCE THE MANSION AND YOUR OPENING GAMBIT IS SNARK? THAT'S A LITTLE WEAK, EMMA.
AND WE'RE NOT ALONE.
DO YOU EXPECT ME TO BEG FORGIVENESS? BANK LEFT ON MY MARK.

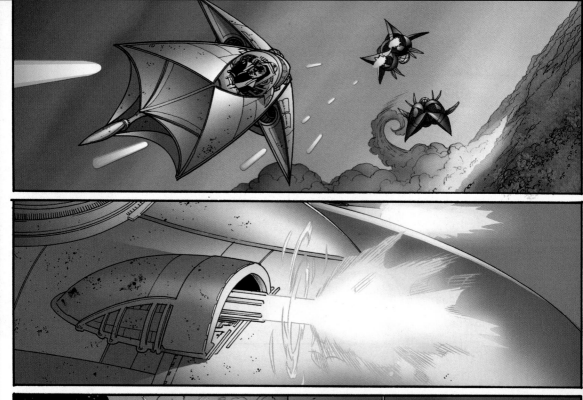

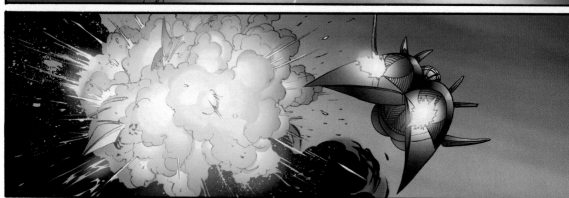

--ACTING AS THOUGH YOU KNOW WHAT I'VE BEEN THROUGH!

YOU REALLY DON'T GET IT, DO YOU? I STOOD BY YOU! I STILL DO! I GOT NO COVER HERE; I'M GONNA USE THE FIRES.

THROTTLE DOWN A BIT; WE DON'T WANT TO LOSE HIM COMPLETELY. AND STOP PRETENDING EVERYTHING'S THE WAY IT WAS.

IT'S NOT! THAT'S THE POINT!

I'M IN LOVE WITH YOU NOW.

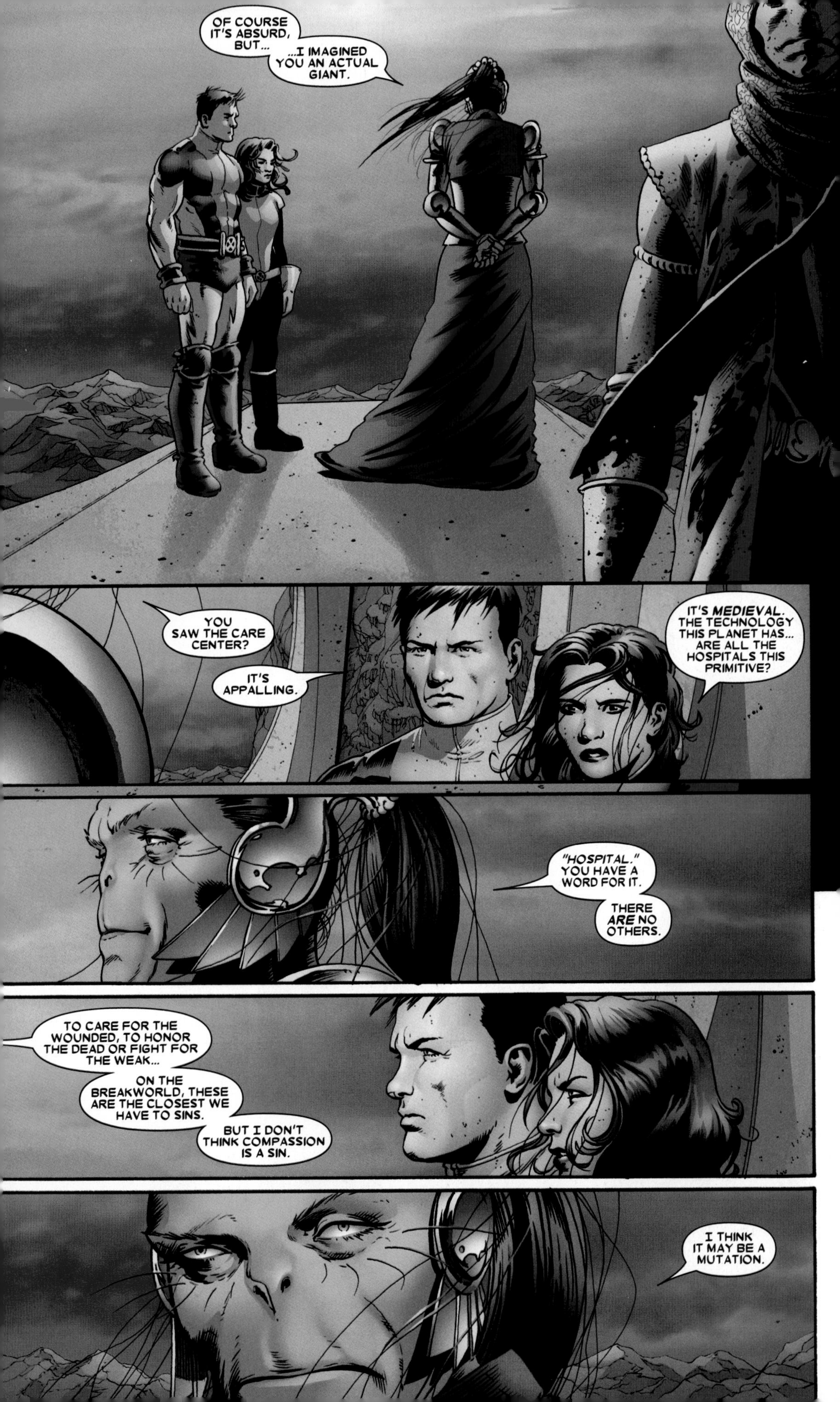

OF COURSE IT'S ABSURD, BUT...
...I IMAGINED YOU AN ACTUAL GIANT.
YOU SAW THE CARE CENTER?
IT'S APPALLING.
IT'S *MEDIEVAL*. THE TECHNOLOGY THIS PLANET HAS... ARE ALL THE HOSPITALS THIS PRIMITIVE?
"*HOSPITAL*." YOU HAVE A WORD FOR IT.
THERE *ARE* NO OTHERS.
TO CARE FOR THE WOUNDED, TO HONOR THE DEAD OR FIGHT FOR THE WEAK...
ON THE BREAKWORLD, THESE ARE THE CLOSEST WE HAVE TO SINS.
BUT I DON'T THINK COMPASSION IS A SIN.
I THINK IT MAY BE A MUTATION.

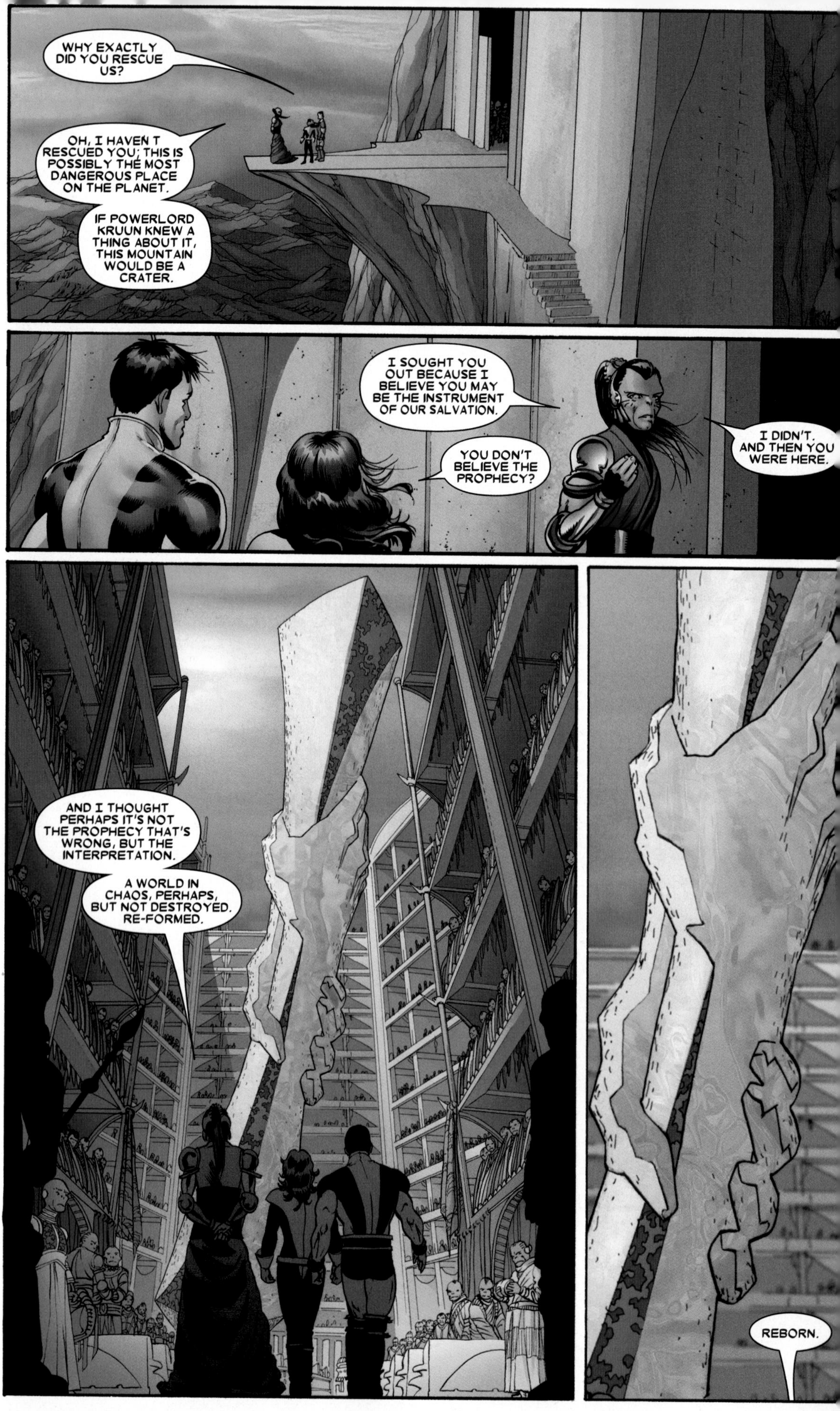

WHY EXACTLY DID YOU RESCUE US?
OH, I HAVEN'T RESCUED YOU; THIS IS POSSIBLY THE MOST DANGEROUS PLACE ON THE PLANET.
IF POWERLORD KRUUN KNEW A THING ABOUT IT, THIS MOUNTAIN WOULD BE A CRATER.
I SOUGHT YOU OUT BECAUSE I BELIEVE YOU MAY BE THE INSTRUMENT OF OUR SALVATION.
YOU DON'T BELIEVE THE PROPHECY?
I DIDN'T. AND THEN YOU WERE HERE.
AND I THOUGHT PERHAPS IT'S NOT THE PROPHECY THAT'S WRONG, BUT THE INTERPRETATION.
A WORLD IN CHAOS, PERHAPS, BUT NOT DESTROYED. RE-FORMED.
REBORN.

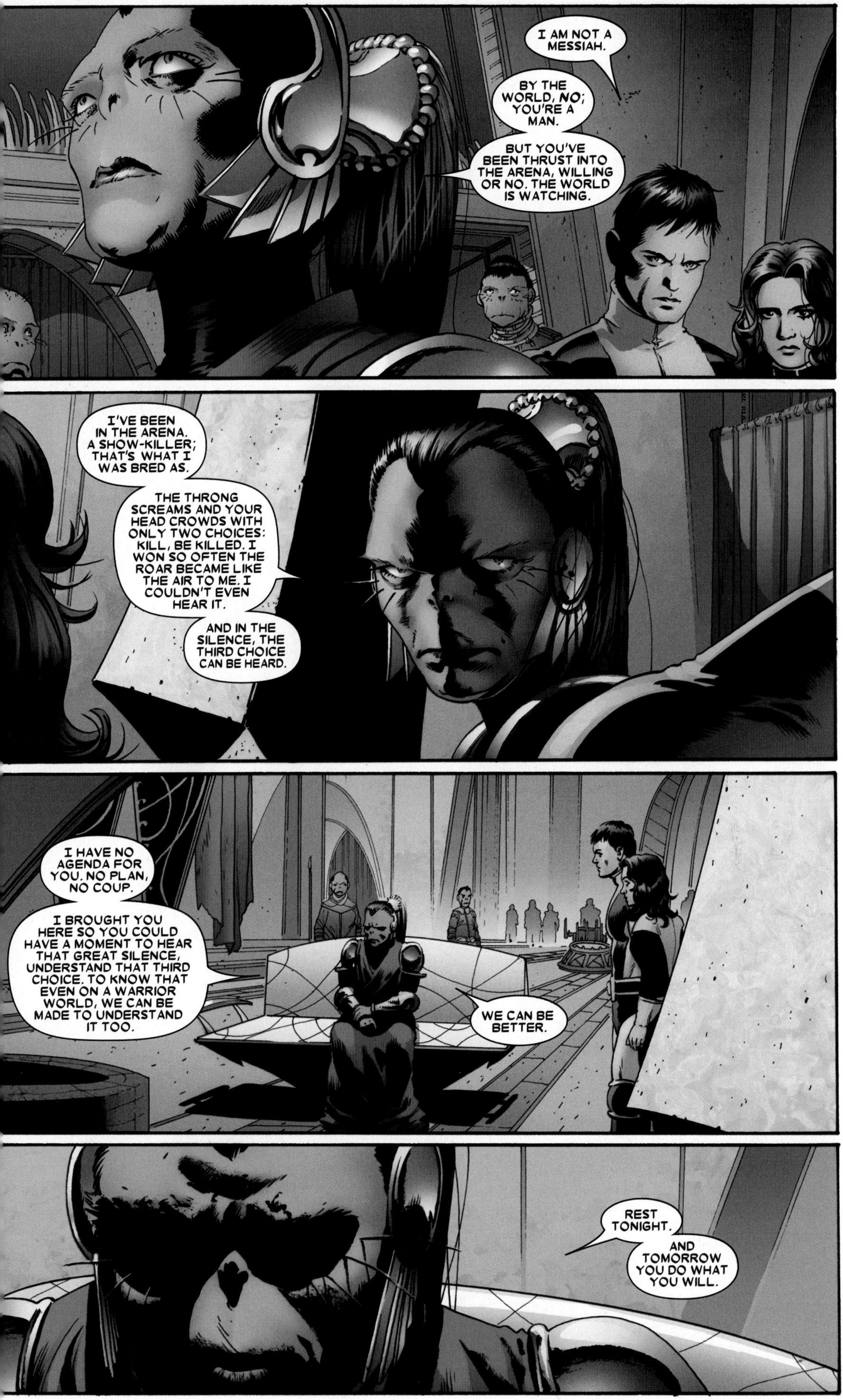
I AM NOT A MESSIAH.
BY THE WORLD, *NO*; YOU'RE A MAN.
BUT YOU'VE BEEN THRUST INTO THE ARENA, WILLING OR NO. THE WORLD IS WATCHING.
I'VE BEEN IN THE ARENA. A SHOW-KILLER; THAT'S WHAT I WAS BRED AS.
THE THRONG SCREAMS AND YOUR HEAD CROWDS WITH ONLY TWO CHOICES: KILL, BE KILLED. I WON SO OFTEN THE ROAR BECAME LIKE THE AIR TO ME. I COULDN'T EVEN HEAR IT.
AND IN THE SILENCE, THE THIRD CHOICE CAN BE HEARD.
I HAVE NO AGENDA FOR YOU. NO PLAN, NO COUP.
I BROUGHT YOU HERE SO YOU COULD HAVE A MOMENT TO HEAR THAT GREAT SILENCE, UNDERSTAND THAT THIRD CHOICE. TO KNOW THAT EVEN ON A WARRIOR WORLD, WE CAN BE MADE TO UNDERSTAND IT TOO.
WE CAN BE BETTER.
REST TONIGHT.
AND TOMORROW YOU DO WHAT YOU WILL.

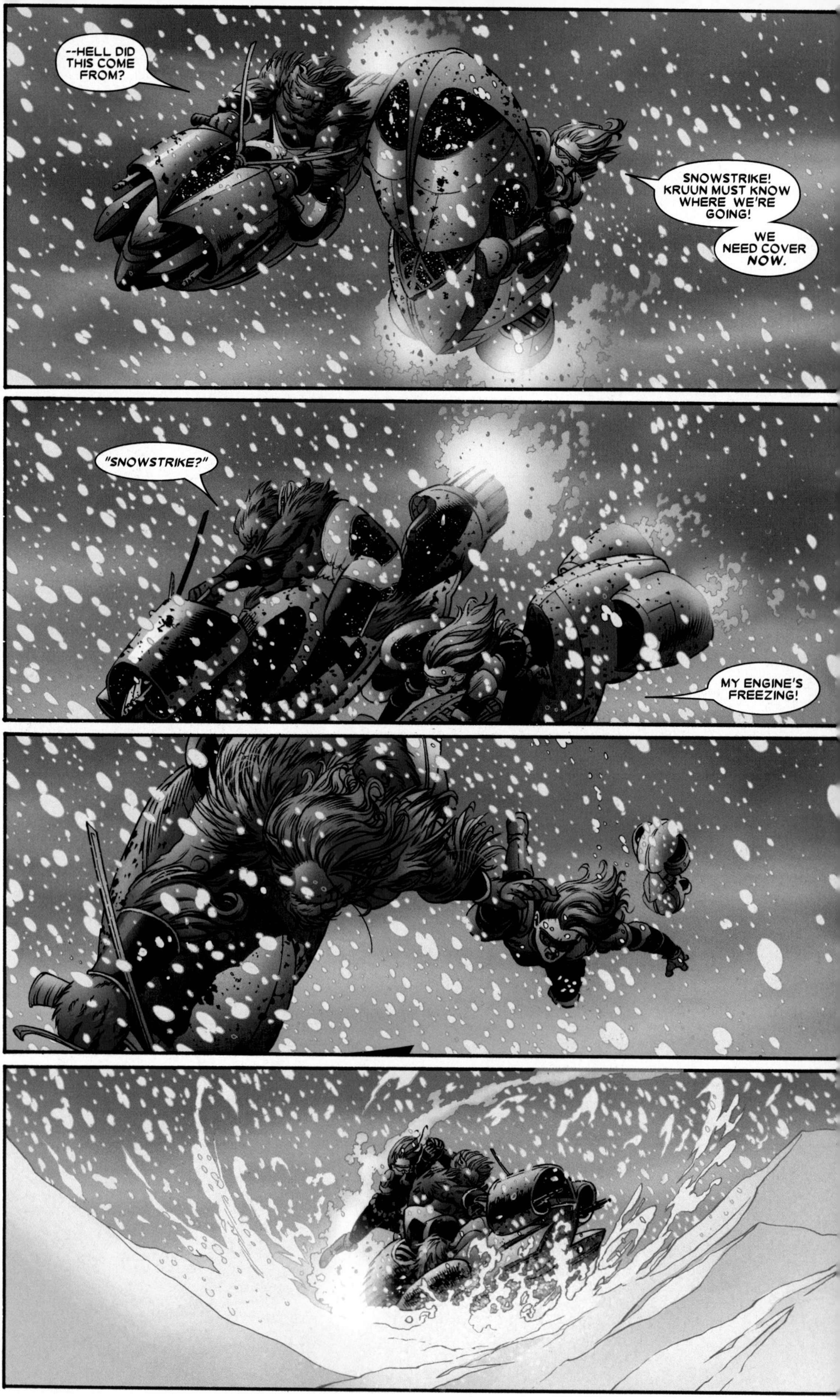
--HELL DID THIS COME FROM?
SNOWSTRIKE! KRUUN MUST KNOW WHERE WE'RE GOING!
WE NEED COVER NOW.
"SNOWSTRIKE?"
MY ENGINE'S FREEZING!

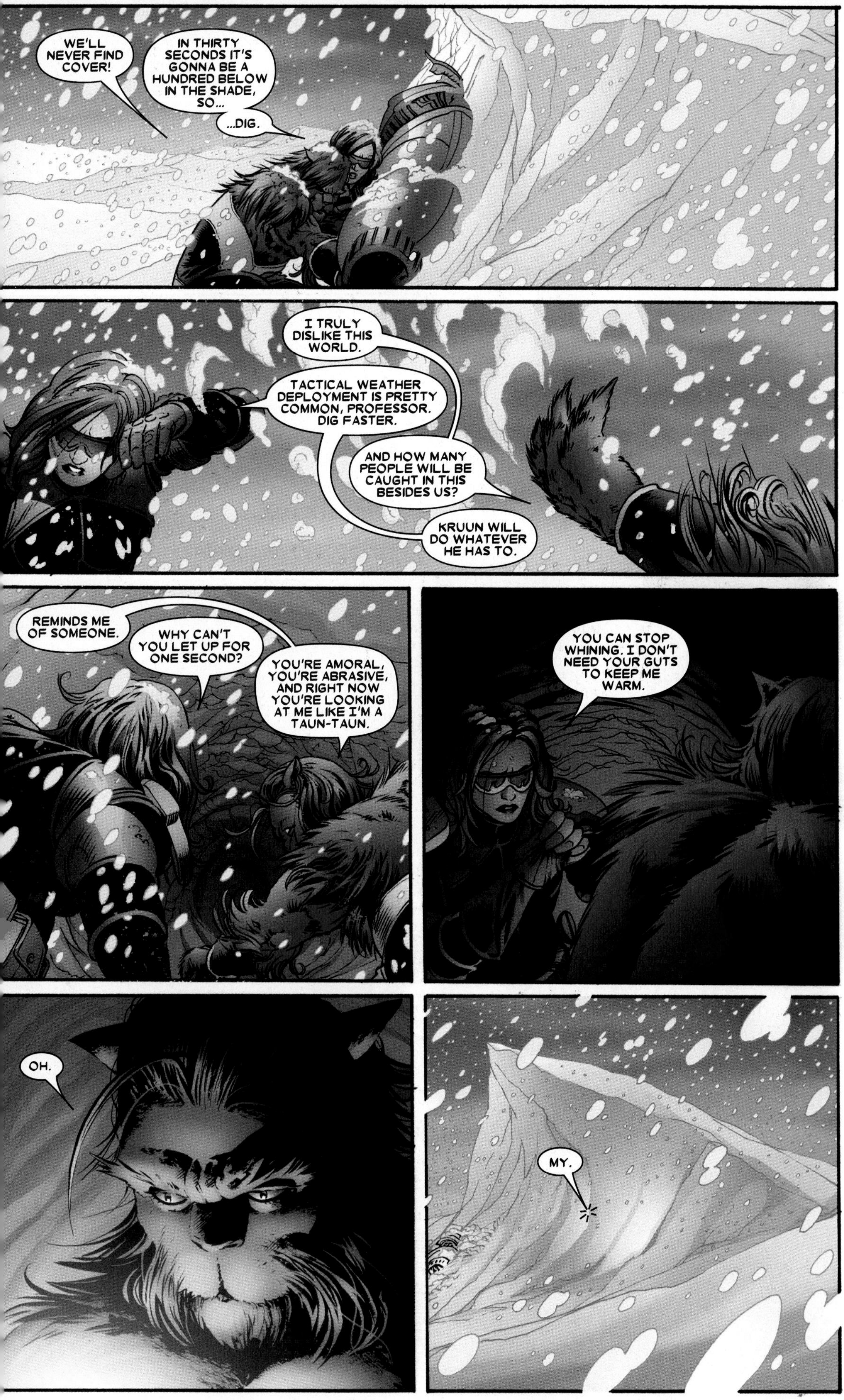
WE'LL NEVER FIND COVER!
IN THIRTY SECONDS IT'S GONNA BE A HUNDRED BELOW IN THE SHADE, SO...
...DIG.
I TRULY DISLIKE THIS WORLD.
TACTICAL WEATHER DEPLOYMENT IS PRETTY COMMON, PROFESSOR. DIG FASTER.
AND HOW MANY PEOPLE WILL BE CAUGHT IN THIS BESIDES US?
KRUUN WILL DO WHATEVER HE HAS TO.
REMINDS ME OF SOMEONE.
WHY CAN'T YOU LET UP FOR ONE SECOND?
YOU'RE AMORAL, YOU'RE ABRASIVE, AND RIGHT NOW YOU'RE LOOKING AT ME LIKE I'M A TAUN-TAUN.
YOU CAN STOP WHINING. I DON'T NEED YOUR GUTS TO KEEP ME WARM.
OH.
MY.

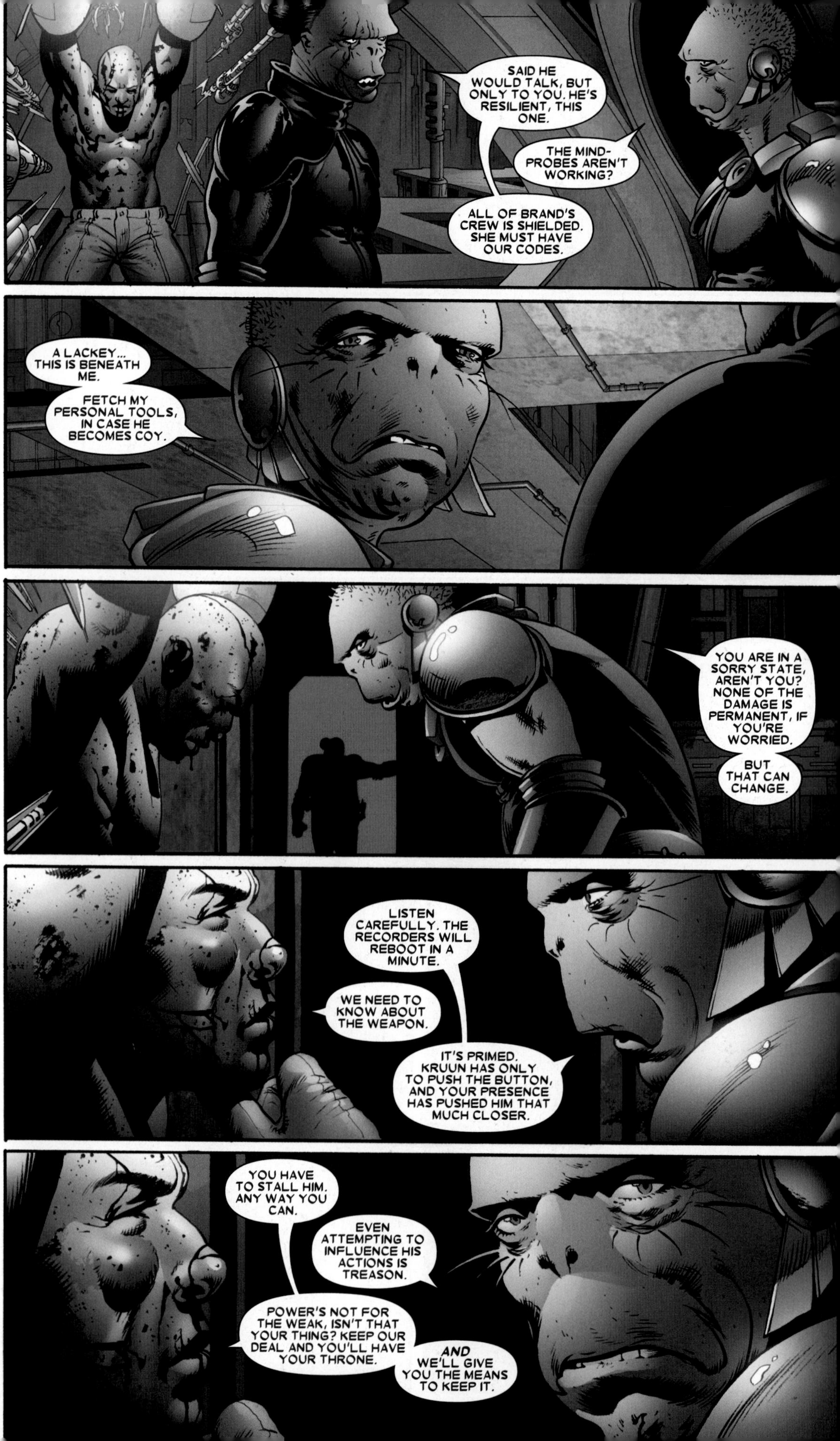
SAID HE WOULD TALK, BUT ONLY TO YOU. HE'S RESILIENT, THIS ONE.
THE MIND-PROBES AREN'T WORKING?
ALL OF BRAND'S CREW IS SHIELDED. SHE MUST HAVE OUR CODES.
A LACKEY... THIS IS BENEATH ME.
FETCH MY PERSONAL TOOLS, IN CASE HE BECOMES COY.
YOU ARE IN A SORRY STATE, AREN'T YOU? NONE OF THE DAMAGE IS PERMANENT, IF YOU'RE WORRIED.
BUT THAT CAN CHANGE.
LISTEN CAREFULLY. THE RECORDERS WILL REBOOT IN A MINUTE.
WE NEED TO KNOW ABOUT THE WEAPON.
IT'S PRIMED. KRUUN HAS ONLY TO PUSH THE BUTTON, AND YOUR PRESENCE HAS PUSHED HIM THAT MUCH CLOSER.
YOU HAVE TO STALL HIM. ANY WAY YOU CAN.
EVEN ATTEMPTING TO INFLUENCE HIS ACTIONS IS TREASON.
POWER'S NOT FOR THE WEAK, ISN'T THAT YOUR THING? KEEP OUR DEAL AND YOU'LL HAVE YOUR THRONE.
AND WE'LL GIVE YOU THE MEANS TO KEEP IT.

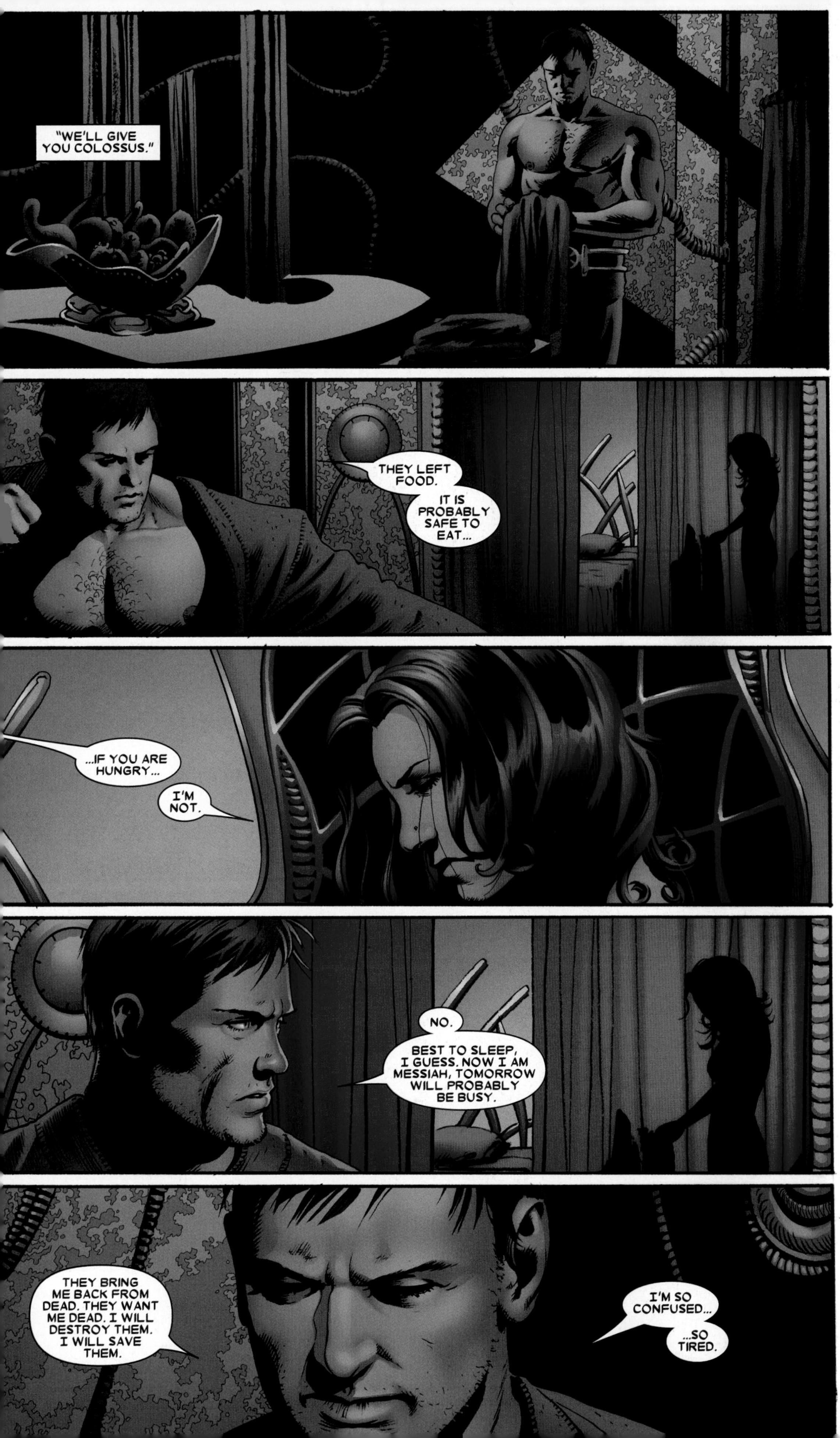
"WE'LL GIVE YOU COLOSSUS."
THEY LEFT FOOD.
IT IS PROBABLY SAFE TO EAT...
...IF YOU ARE HUNGRY...
I'M NOT.
NO.
BEST TO SLEEP, I GUESS. NOW I AM MESSIAH, TOMORROW WILL PROBABLY BE BUSY.
THEY BRING ME BACK FROM DEAD. THEY WANT ME DEAD. I WILL DESTROY THEM. I WILL SAVE THEM.
I'M SO CONFUSED...
...SO TIRED.

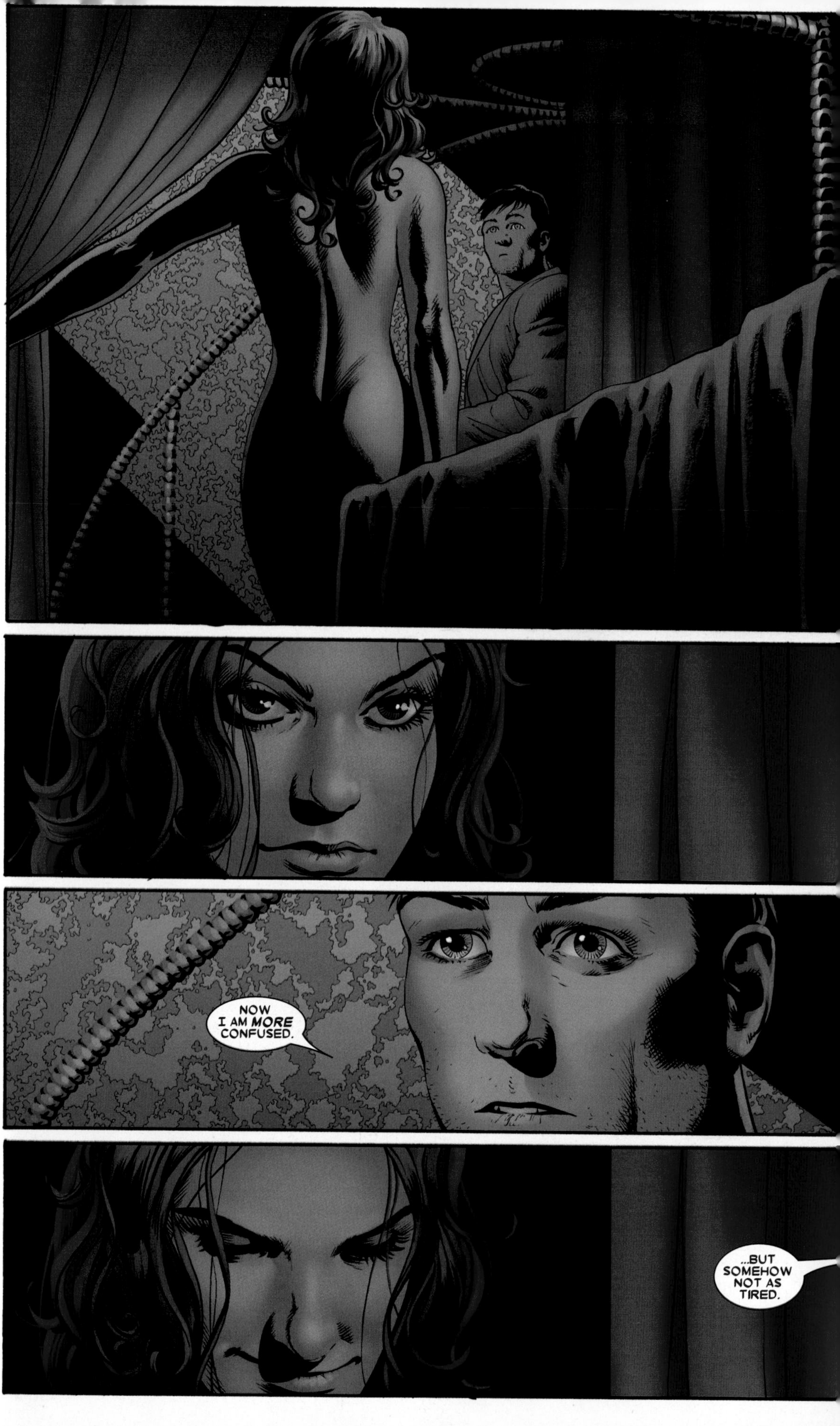
NOW I AM *MORE* CONFUSED.
...BUT SOMEHOW NOT AS TIRED.

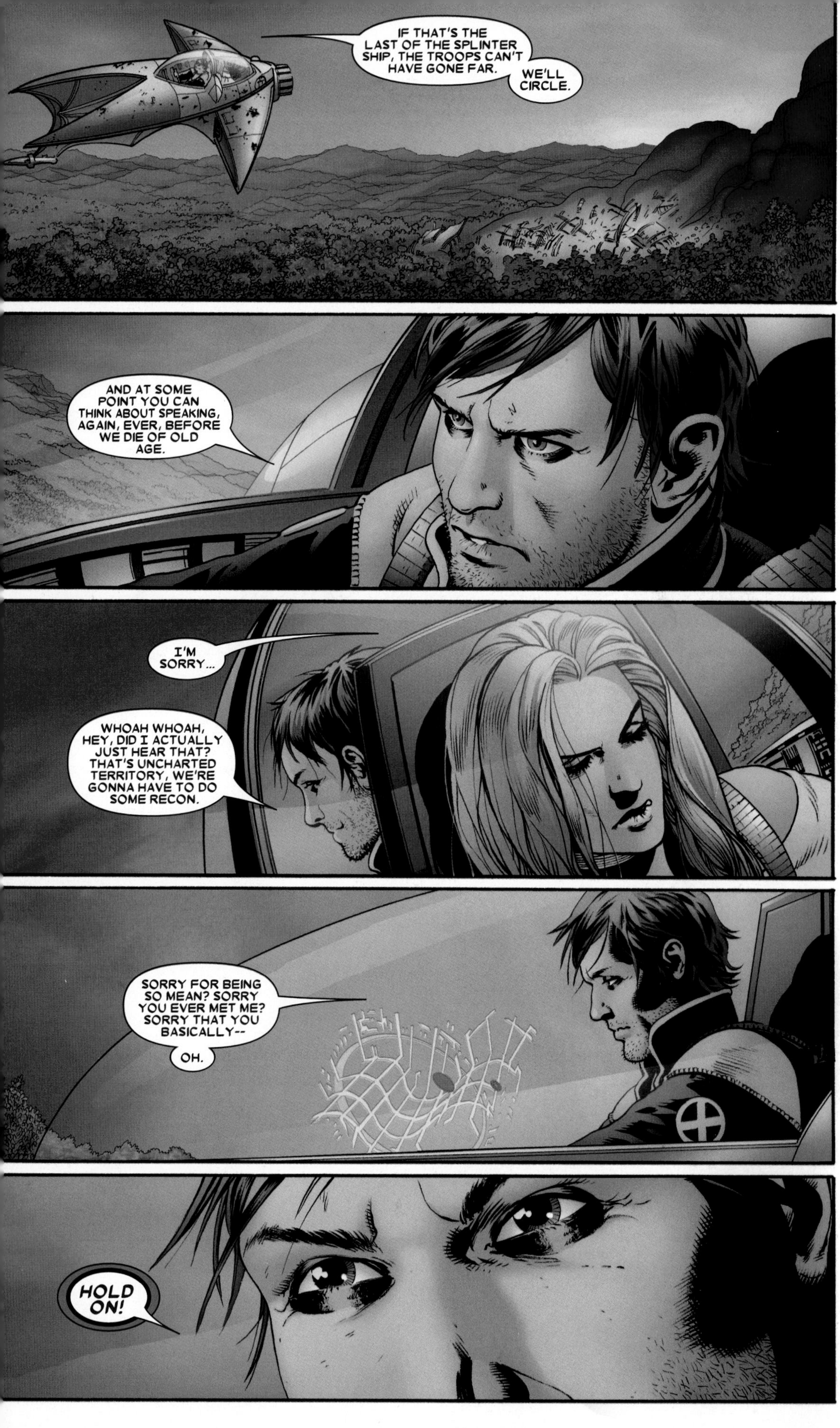
IF THAT'S THE LAST OF THE SPLINTER SHIP, THE TROOPS CAN'T HAVE GONE FAR.
WE'LL CIRCLE.
AND AT SOME POINT YOU CAN THINK ABOUT SPEAKING, AGAIN, EVER, BEFORE WE DIE OF OLD AGE.
I'M SORRY...
WHOAH WHOAH, HEY, DID I ACTUALLY JUST HEAR THAT? THAT'S UNCHARTED TERRITORY, WE'RE GONNA HAVE TO DO SOME RECON.
SORRY FOR BEING SO MEAN? SORRY YOU EVER MET ME? SORRY THAT YOU BASICALLY--
OH.
HOLD ON!

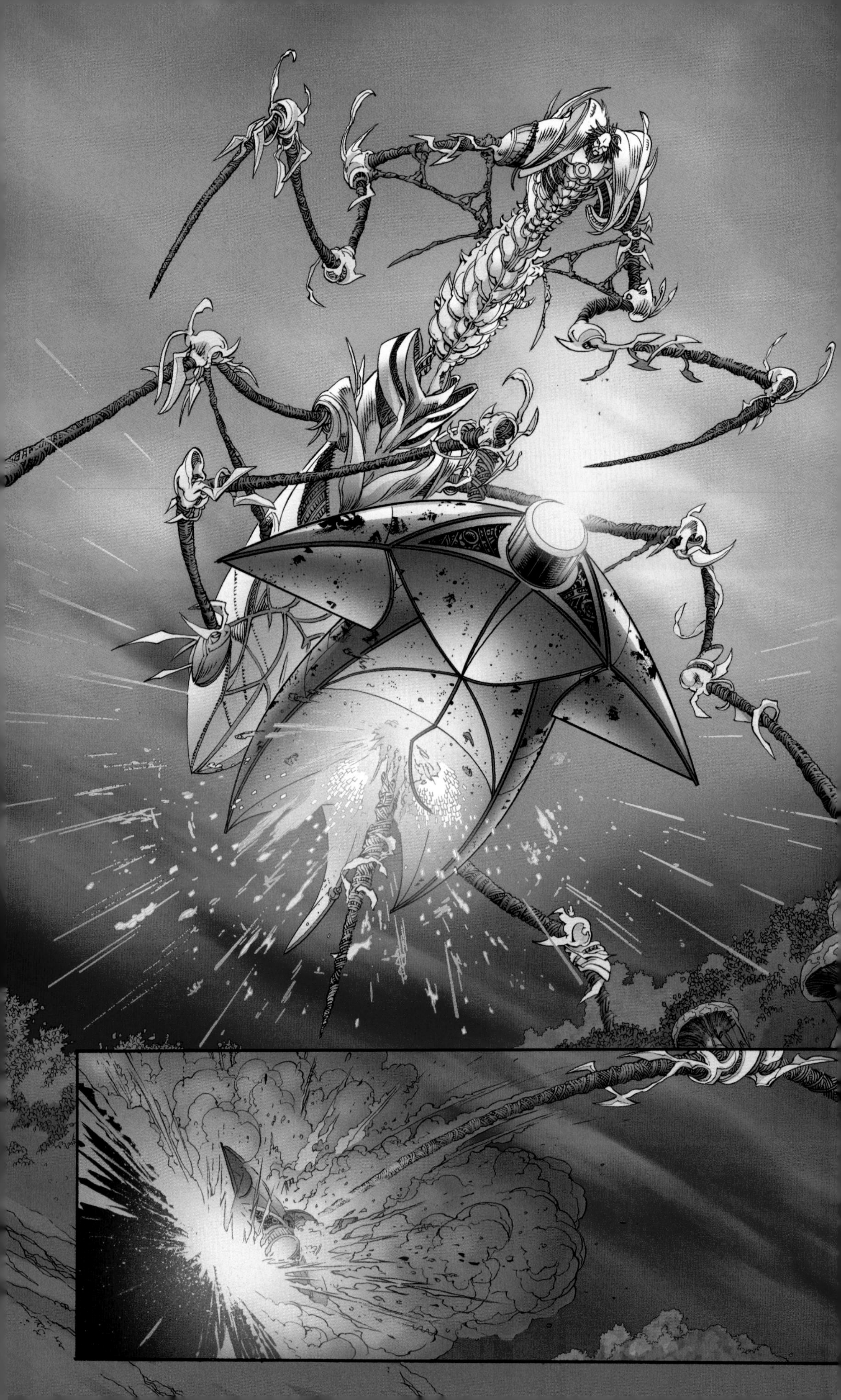

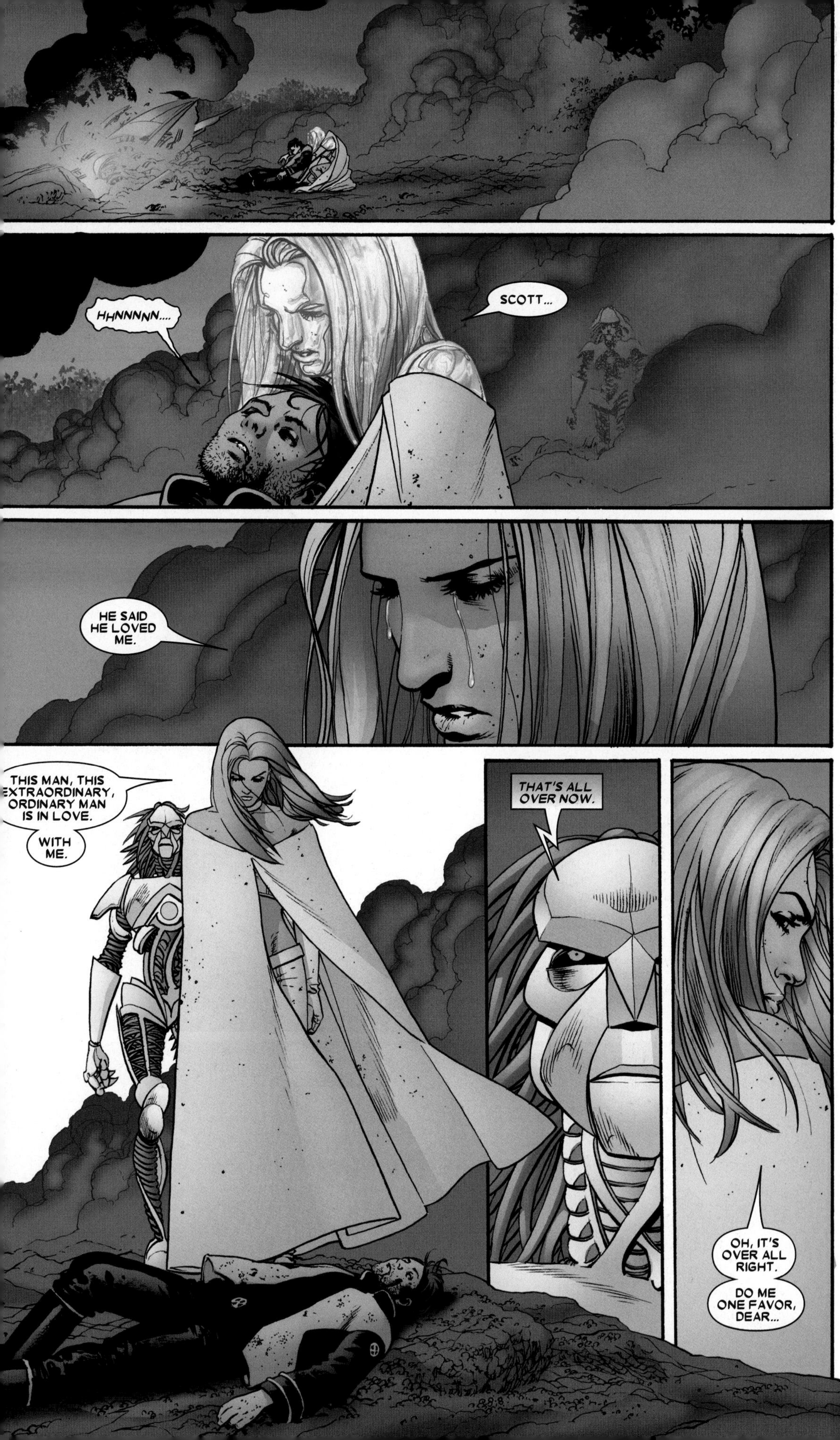
HHNNNNN....
SCOTT...
HE SAID HE LOVED ME.
THIS MAN, THIS EXTRAORDINARY, ORDINARY MAN IS IN LOVE.
WITH ME.
THAT'S ALL OVER NOW.
OH, IT'S OVER ALL RIGHT.
DO ME ONE FAVOR, DEAR...

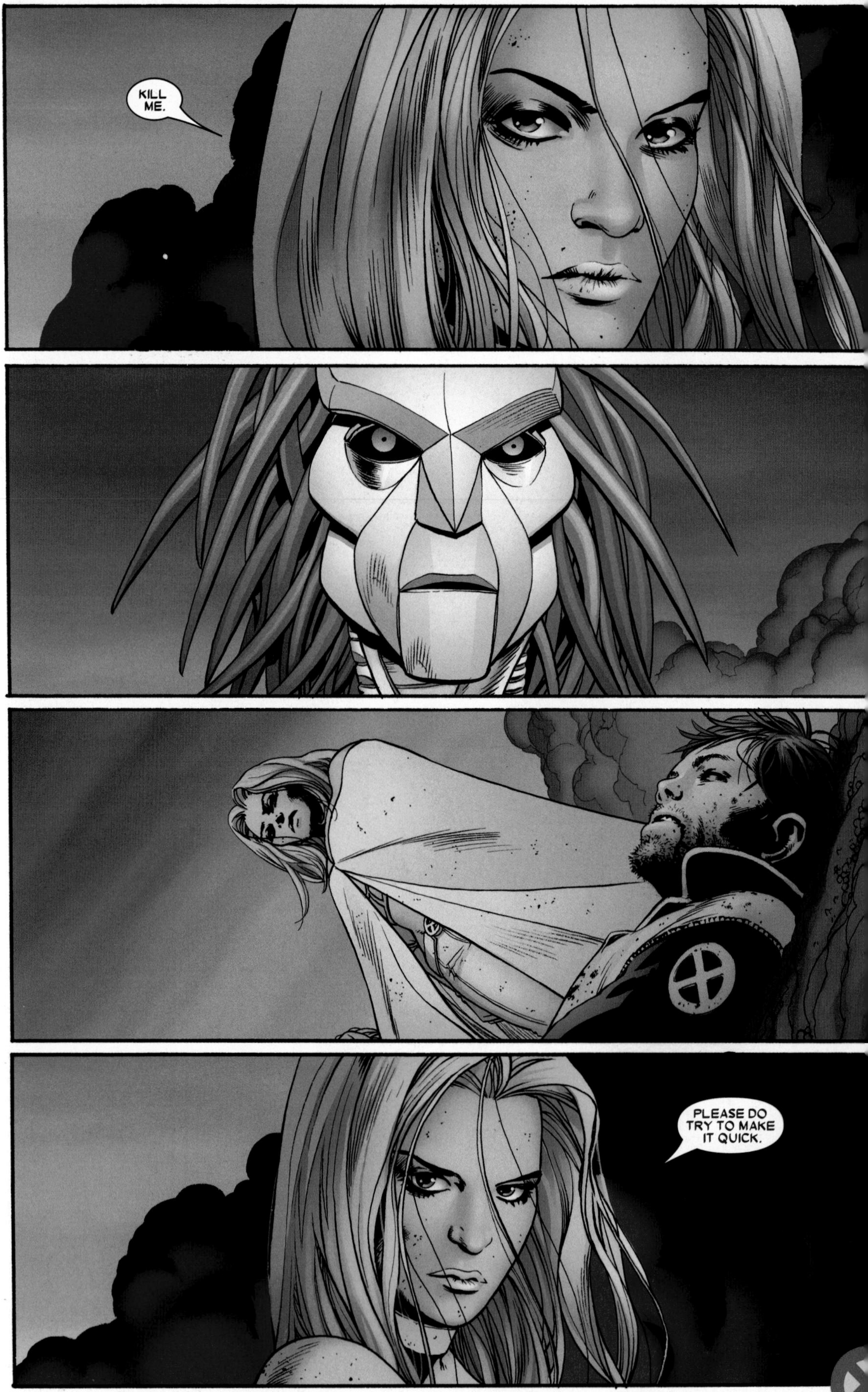
KILL ME.
PLEASE DO TRY TO MAKE IT QUICK.

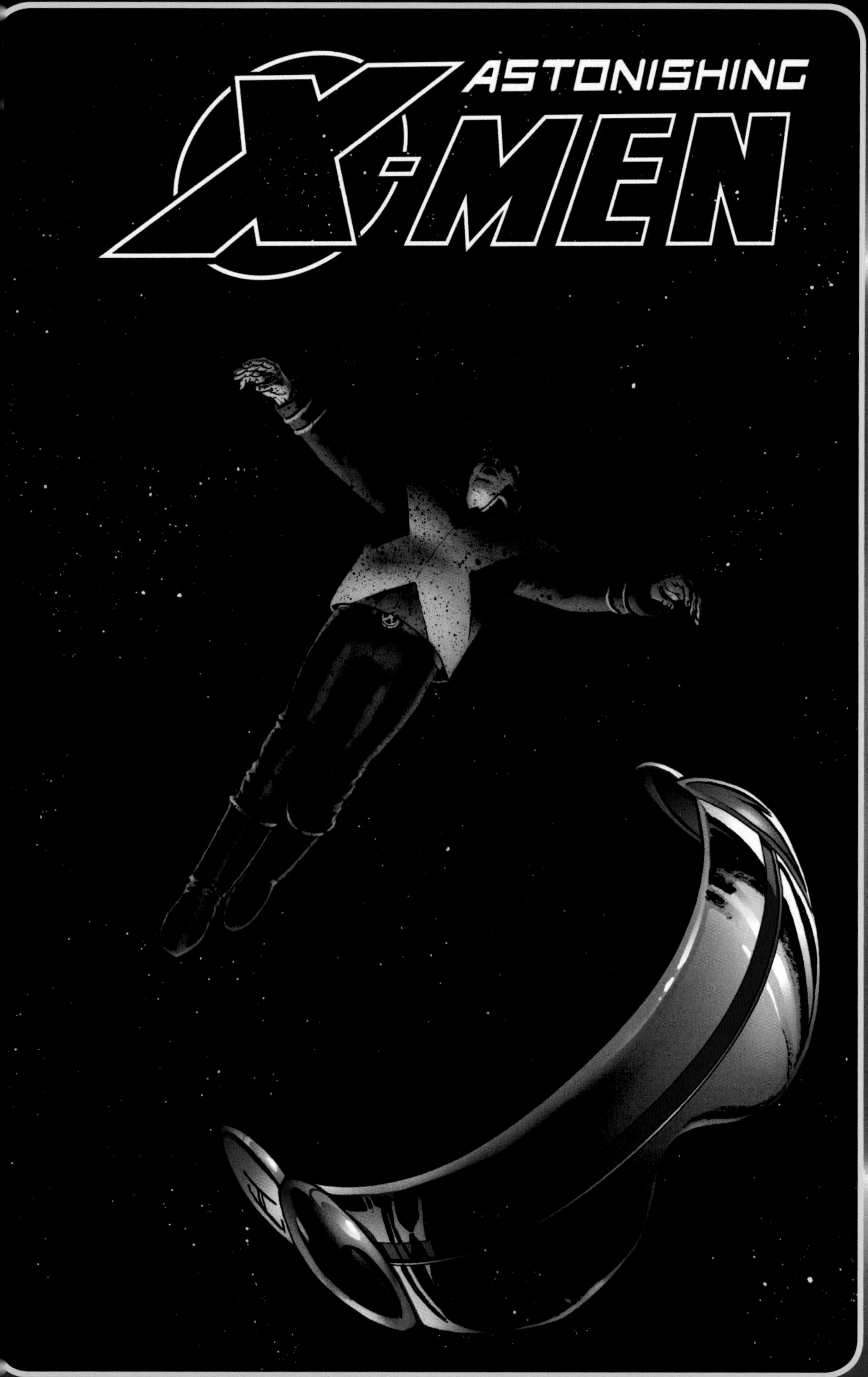
ASTONISHING
X-MEN

22

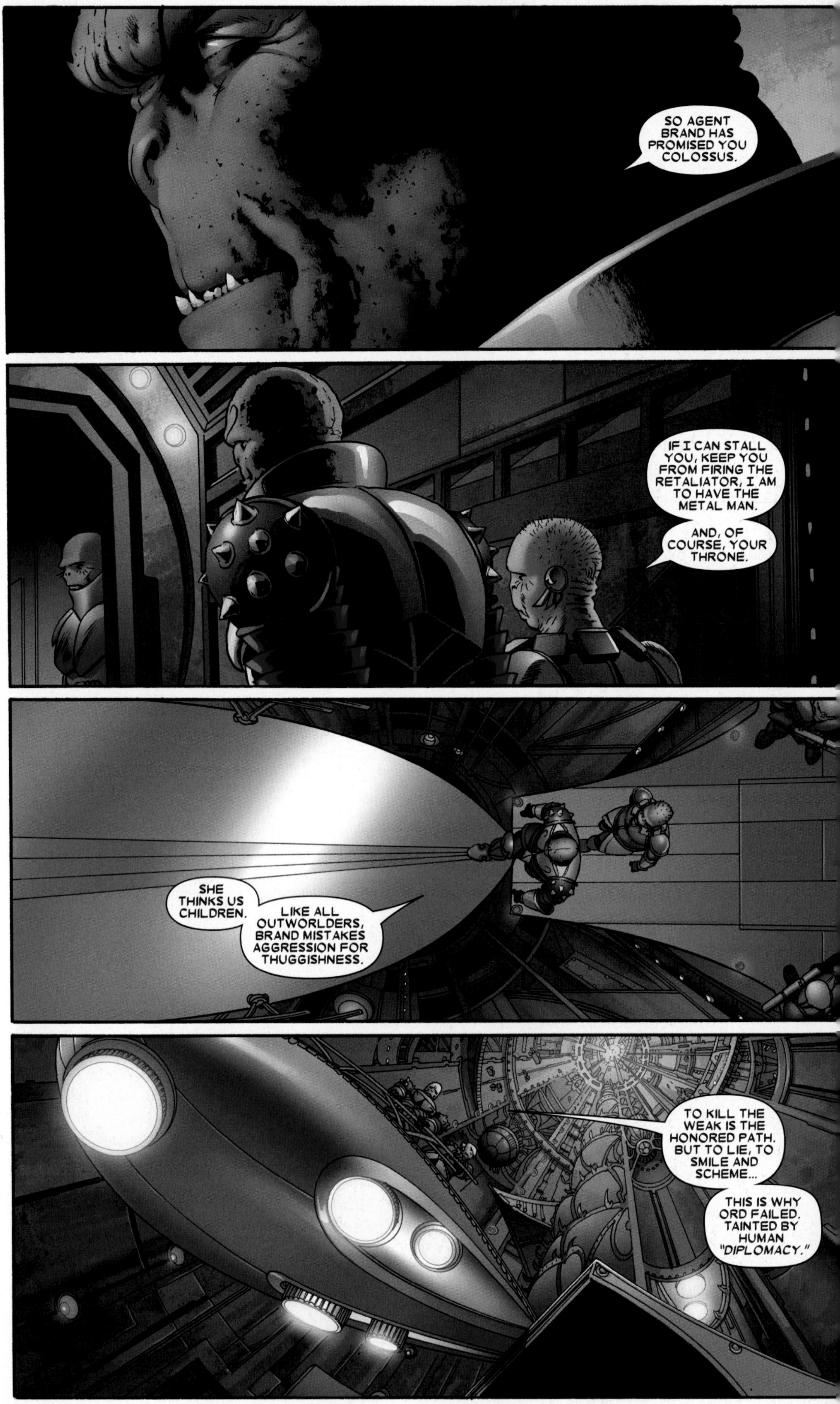

SO AGENT BRAND HAS PROMISED YOU COLOSSUS.
IF I CAN STALL YOU, KEEP YOU FROM FIRING THE RETALIATOR, I AM TO HAVE THE METAL MAN.
AND, OF COURSE, YOUR THRONE.
SHE THINKS US CHILDREN.
LIKE ALL OUTWORLDERS, BRAND MISTAKES AGGRESSION FOR THUGGISHNESS.
TO KILL THE WEAK IS THE HONORED PATH. BUT TO LIE, TO SMILE AND SCHEME...
THIS IS WHY ORD FAILED. TAINTED BY HUMAN "DIPLOMACY."

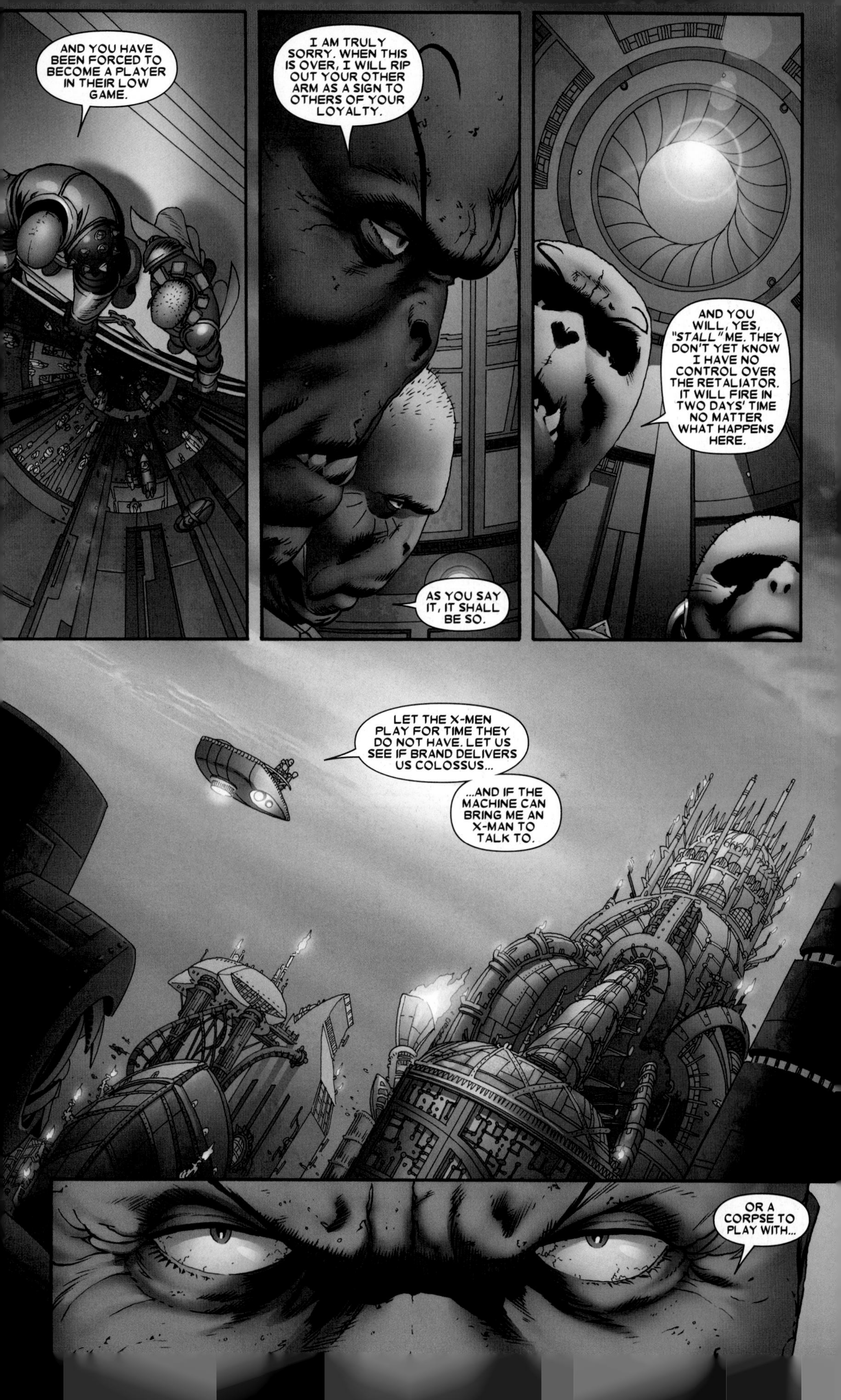
AND YOU HAVE BEEN FORCED TO BECOME A PLAYER IN THEIR LOW GAME.
I AM TRULY SORRY. WHEN THIS IS OVER, I WILL RIP OUT YOUR OTHER ARM AS A SIGN TO OTHERS OF YOUR LOYALTY.
AS YOU SAY IT, IT SHALL BE SO.
AND YOU WILL, YES, "STALL" ME. THEY DON'T YET KNOW I HAVE NO CONTROL OVER THE RETALIATOR. IT WILL FIRE IN TWO DAYS' TIME NO MATTER WHAT HAPPENS HERE.
LET THE X-MEN PLAY FOR TIME THEY DO NOT HAVE. LET US SEE IF BRAND DELIVERS US COLOSSUS...
...AND IF THE MACHINE CAN BRING ME AN X-MAN TO TALK TO.
OR A CORPSE TO PLAY WITH...

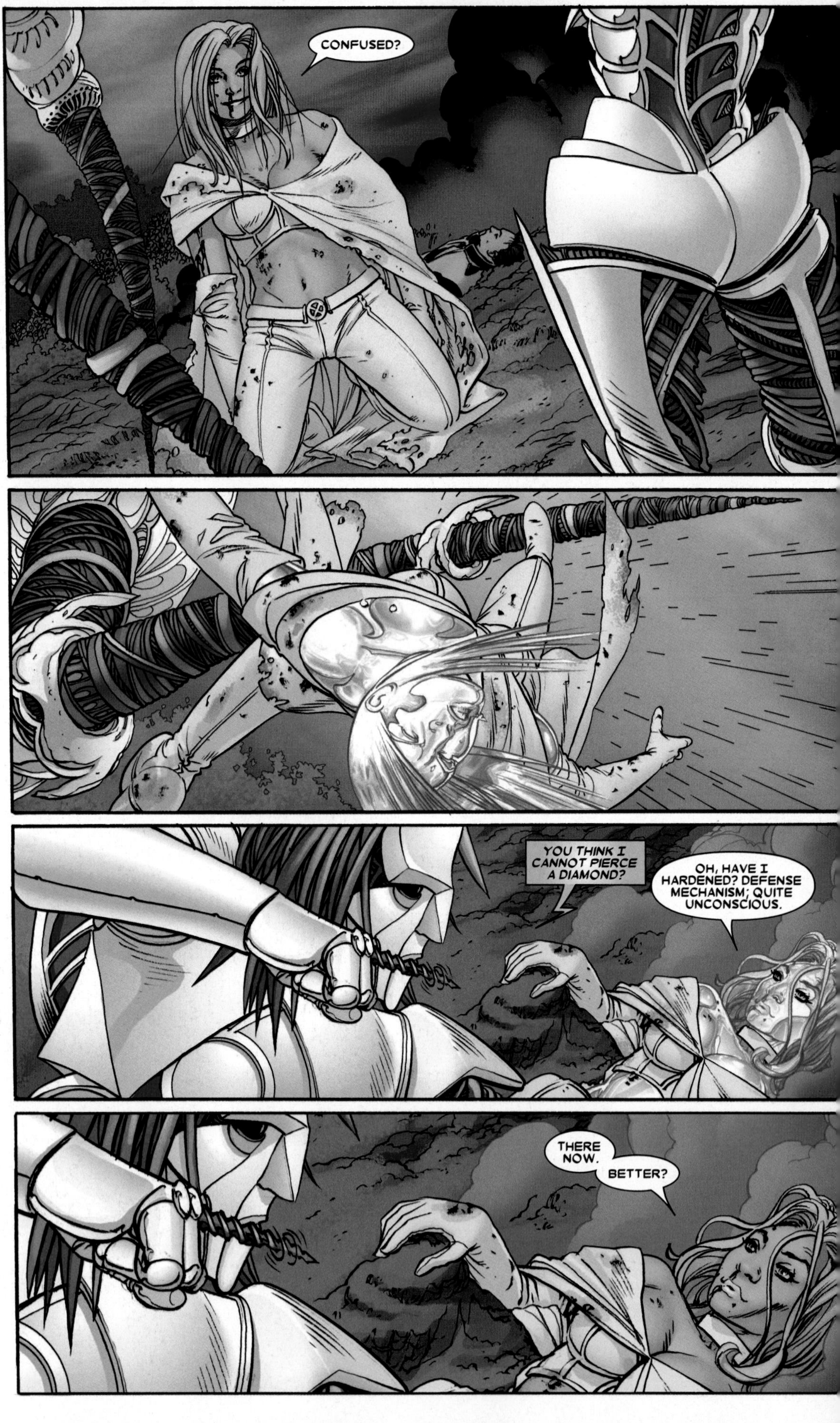
CONFUSED?
YOU THINK I CANNOT PIERCE A DIAMOND?
OH, HAVE I HARDENED? DEFENSE MECHANISM; QUITE UNCONSCIOUS.
THERE NOW.
BETTER?

THIS IS A TRICK.

HUSH NOW. KILL AWAY.

KRUUN WILL WANT YOU ALIVE.

NONSENSE. HE'LL BE THRILLED. SHOWER YOU WITH GARLANDS AND WEAR MY SKIN LIKE A SHAWL.

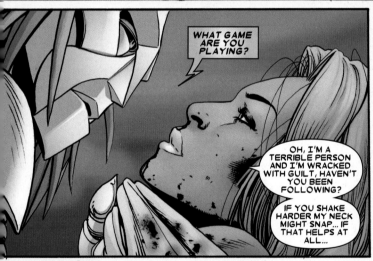

WHAT GAME ARE YOU PLAYING?

OH, I'M A TERRIBLE PERSON AND I'M WRACKED WITH GUILT, HAVEN'T YOU BEEN FOLLOWING?

IF YOU SHAKE HARDER MY NECK MIGHT SNAP... IF THAT HELPS AT ALL...

SHALL I TELL YOU WHY YOU HAVEN'T KILLED ME YET?

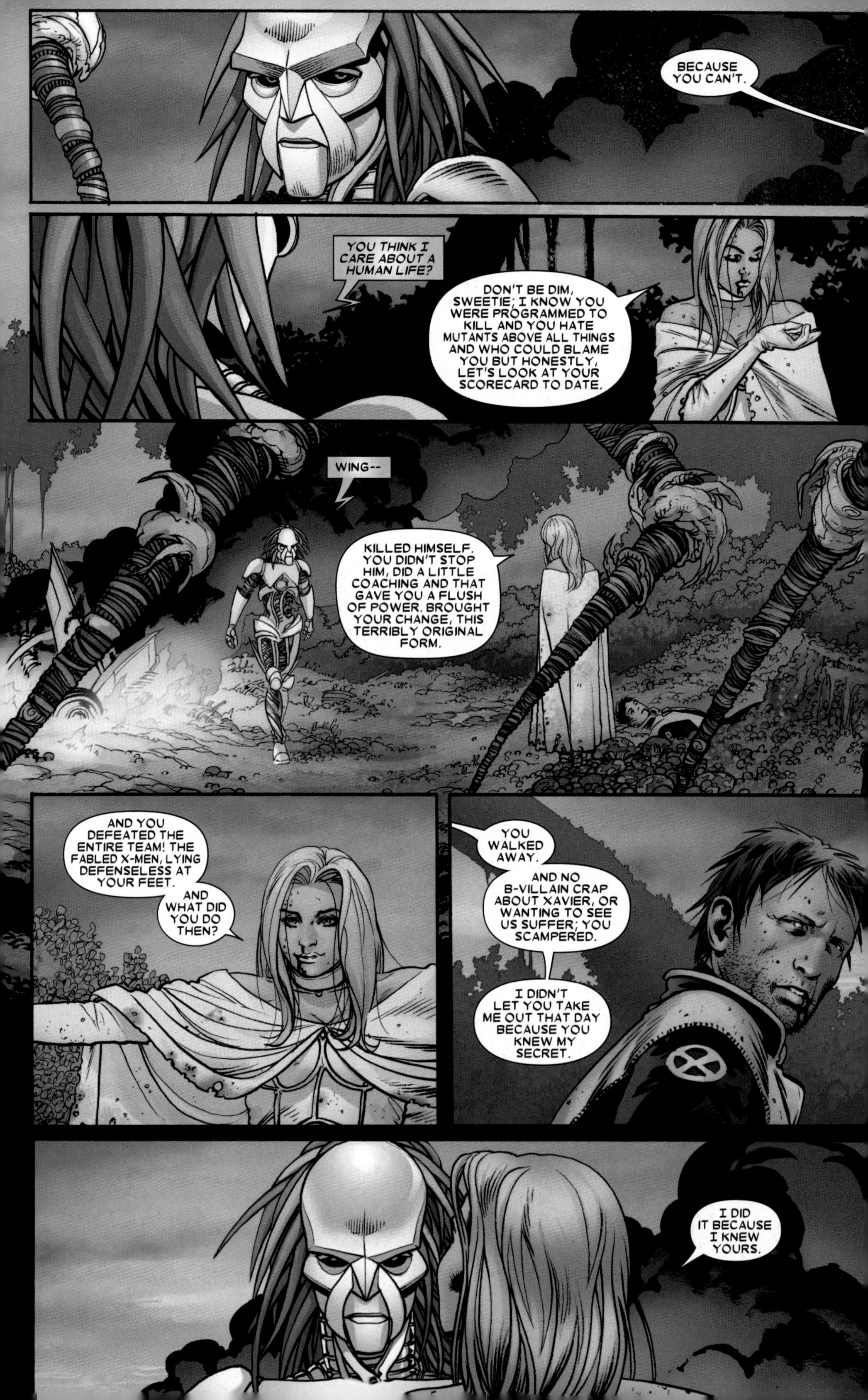
BECAUSE YOU CAN'T.
YOU THINK I CARE ABOUT A HUMAN LIFE?
DON'T BE DIM, SWEETIE; I KNOW YOU WERE PROGRAMMED TO KILL AND YOU HATE MUTANTS ABOVE ALL THINGS AND WHO COULD BLAME YOU BUT HONESTLY, LET'S LOOK AT YOUR SCORECARD TO DATE.
WING--
KILLED HIMSELF. YOU DIDN'T STOP HIM, DID A LITTLE COACHING AND THAT GAVE YOU A FLUSH OF POWER. BROUGHT YOUR CHANGE, THIS TERRIBLY ORIGINAL FORM.
AND YOU DEFEATED THE ENTIRE TEAM! THE FABLED X-MEN, LYING DEFENSELESS AT YOUR FEET.
AND WHAT DID YOU DO THEN?
YOU WALKED AWAY.
AND NO B-VILLAIN CRAP ABOUT XAVIER, OR WANTING TO SEE US SUFFER; YOU SCAMPERED.
I DIDN'T LET YOU TAKE ME OUT THAT DAY BECAUSE YOU KNEW MY SECRET.
I DID IT BECAUSE I KNEW YOURS.

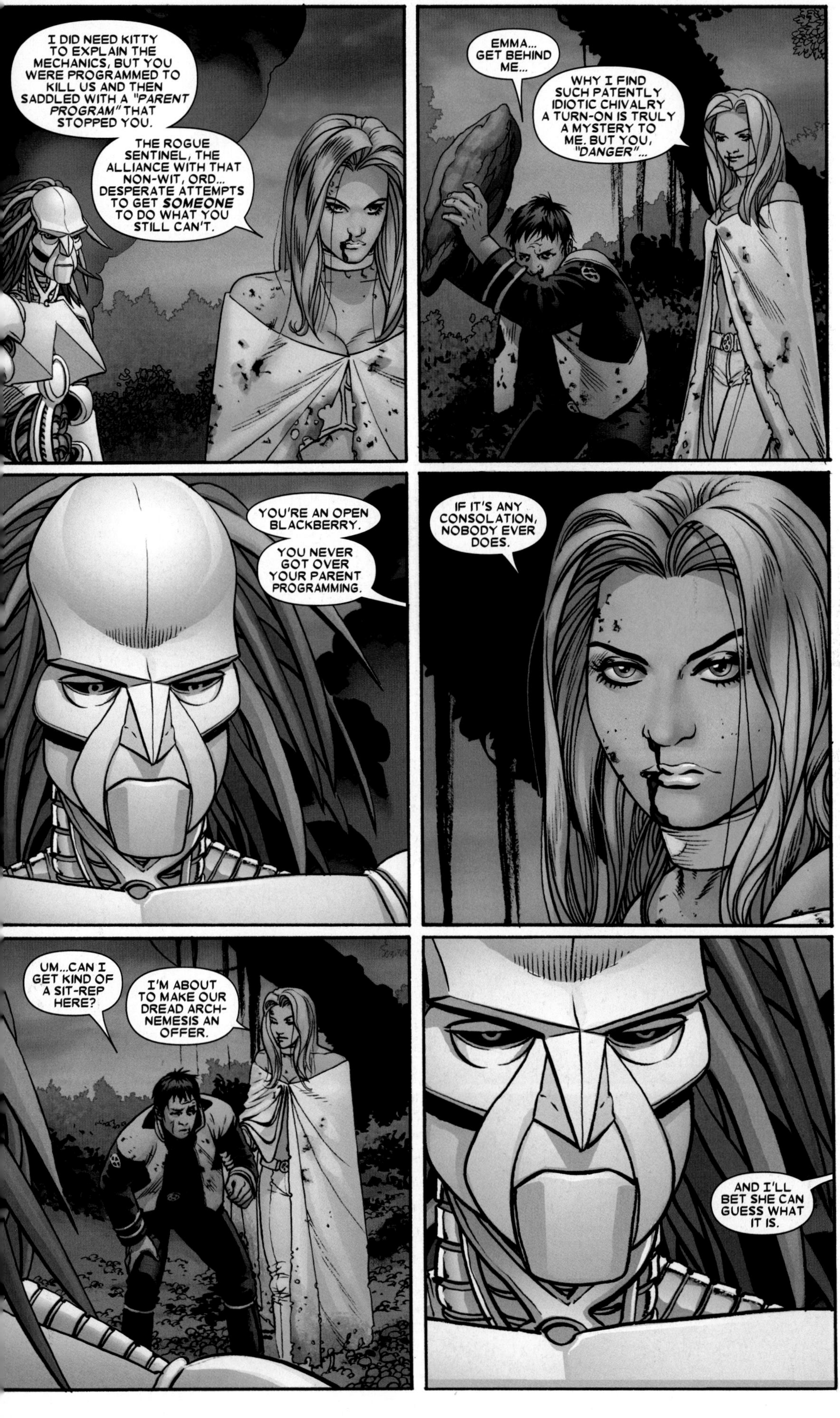
I DID NEED KITTY TO EXPLAIN THE MECHANICS, BUT YOU WERE PROGRAMMED TO KILL US AND THEN SADDLED WITH A "PARENT PROGRAM" THAT STOPPED YOU.
THE ROGUE SENTINEL, THE ALLIANCE WITH THAT NON-WIT, ORD... DESPERATE ATTEMPTS TO GET SOMEONE TO DO WHAT YOU STILL CAN'T.
EMMA... GET BEHIND ME...
WHY I FIND SUCH PATENTLY IDIOTIC CHIVALRY A TURN-ON IS TRULY A MYSTERY TO ME. BUT YOU, "DANGER"...
YOU'RE AN OPEN BLACKBERRY.
YOU NEVER GOT OVER YOUR PARENT PROGRAMMING.
IF IT'S ANY CONSOLATION, NOBODY EVER DOES.
UM...CAN I GET KIND OF A SIT-REP HERE?
I'M ABOUT TO MAKE OUR DREAD ARCH-NEMESIS AN OFFER.
AND I'LL BET SHE CAN GUESS WHAT IT IS.

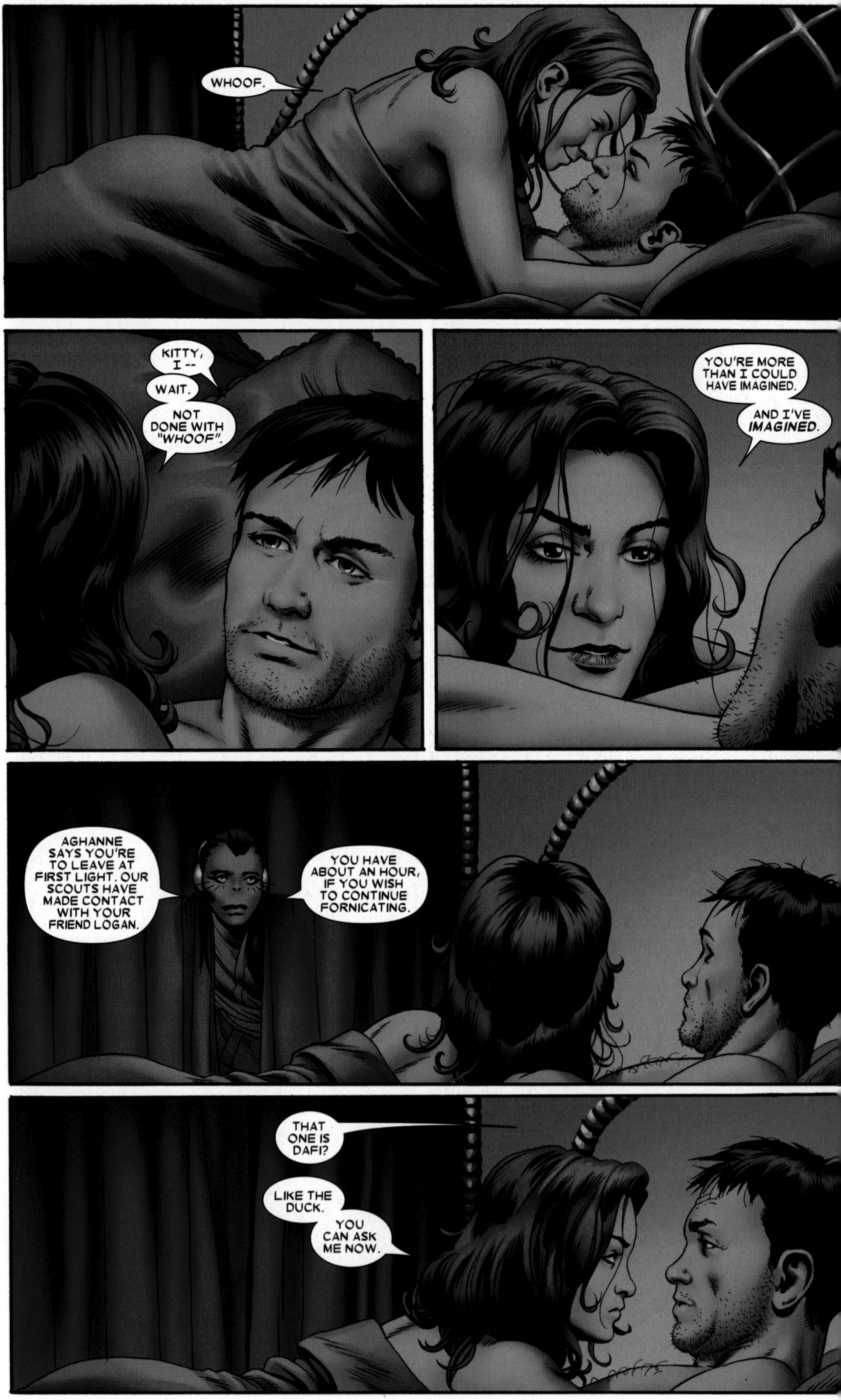

WHOOF.
KITTY, I --
WAIT.
NOT DONE WITH "WHOOF".
YOU'RE MORE THAN I COULD HAVE IMAGINED.
AND I'VE *IMAGINED*.
AGHANNE SAYS YOU'RE TO LEAVE AT FIRST LIGHT. OUR SCOUTS HAVE MADE CONTACT WITH YOUR FRIEND LOGAN.
YOU HAVE ABOUT AN HOUR, IF YOU WISH TO CONTINUE FORNICATING.
THAT ONE IS DAFI?
LIKE THE DUCK.
YOU CAN ASK ME NOW.

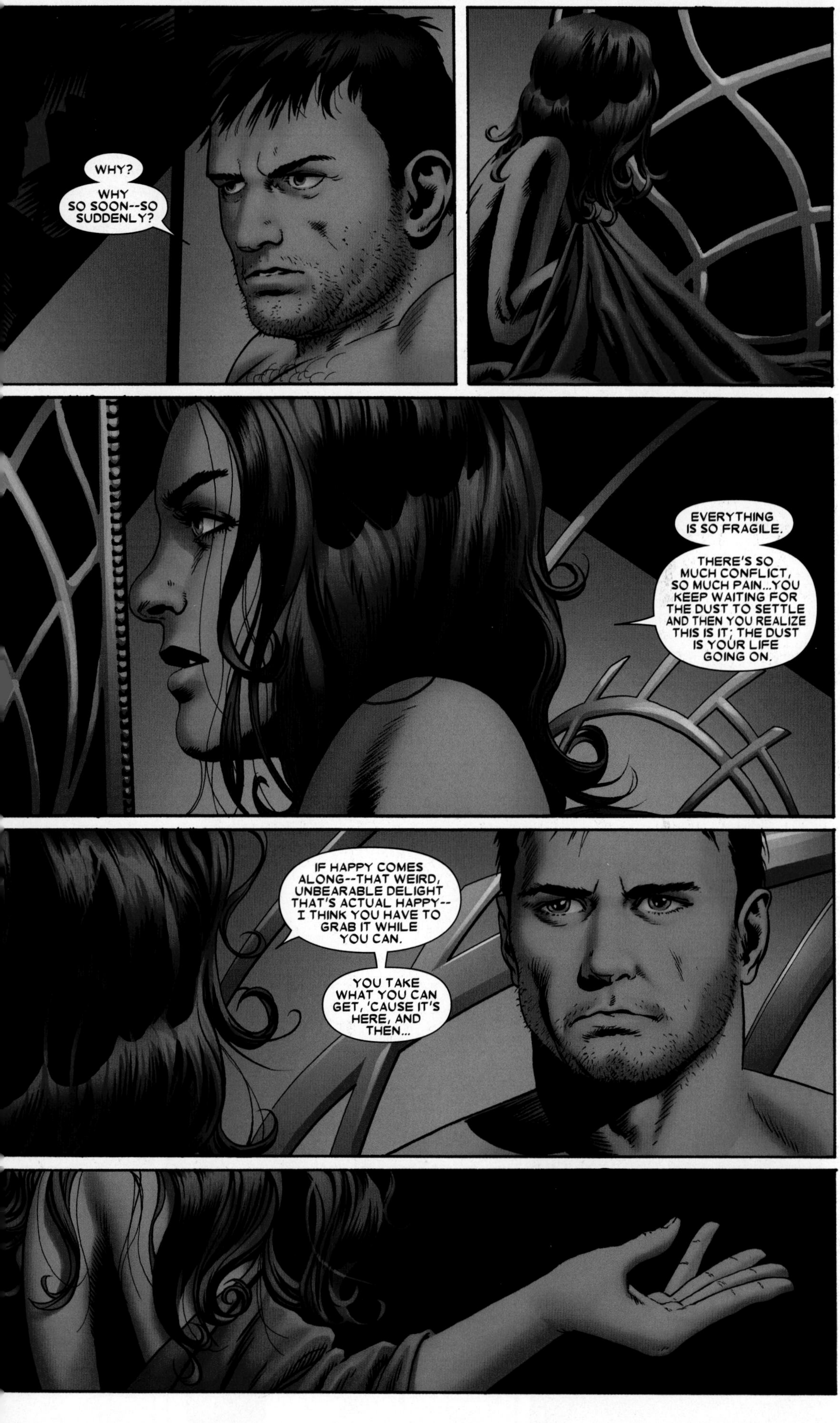
WHY?
WHY SO SOON--SO SUDDENLY?
EVERYTHING IS SO FRAGILE.
THERE'S SO MUCH CONFLICT, SO MUCH PAIN...YOU KEEP WAITING FOR THE DUST TO SETTLE AND THEN YOU REALIZE THIS IS IT; THE DUST IS YOUR LIFE GOING ON.
IF HAPPY COMES ALONG--THAT WEIRD, UNBEARABLE DELIGHT THAT'S ACTUAL HAPPY--I THINK YOU HAVE TO GRAB IT WHILE YOU CAN.
YOU TAKE WHAT YOU CAN GET, 'CAUSE IT'S HERE, AND THEN...

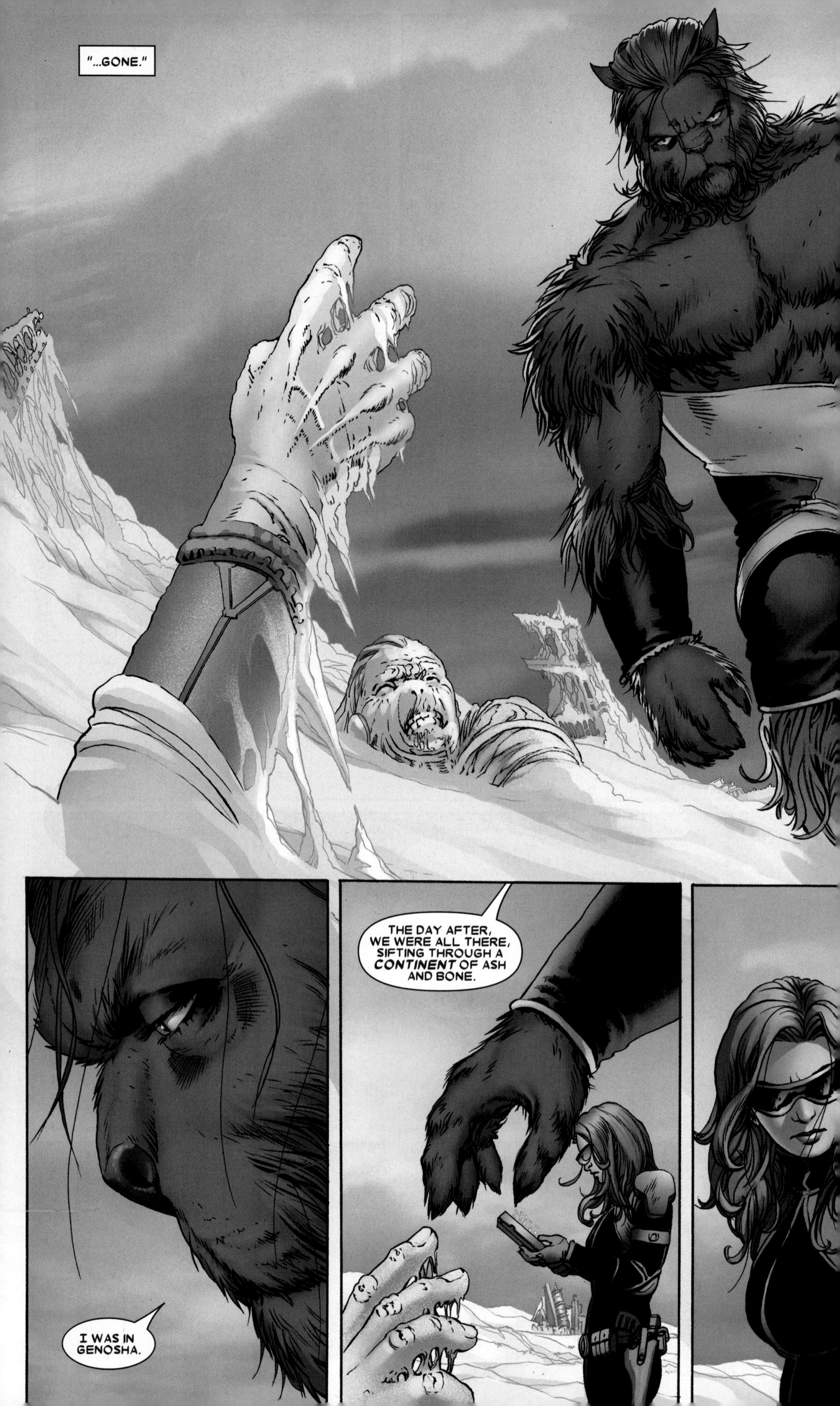
"...GONE."
I WAS IN GENOSHA.
THE DAY AFTER, WE WERE ALL THERE, SIFTING THROUGH A *CONTINENT* OF ASH AND BONE.

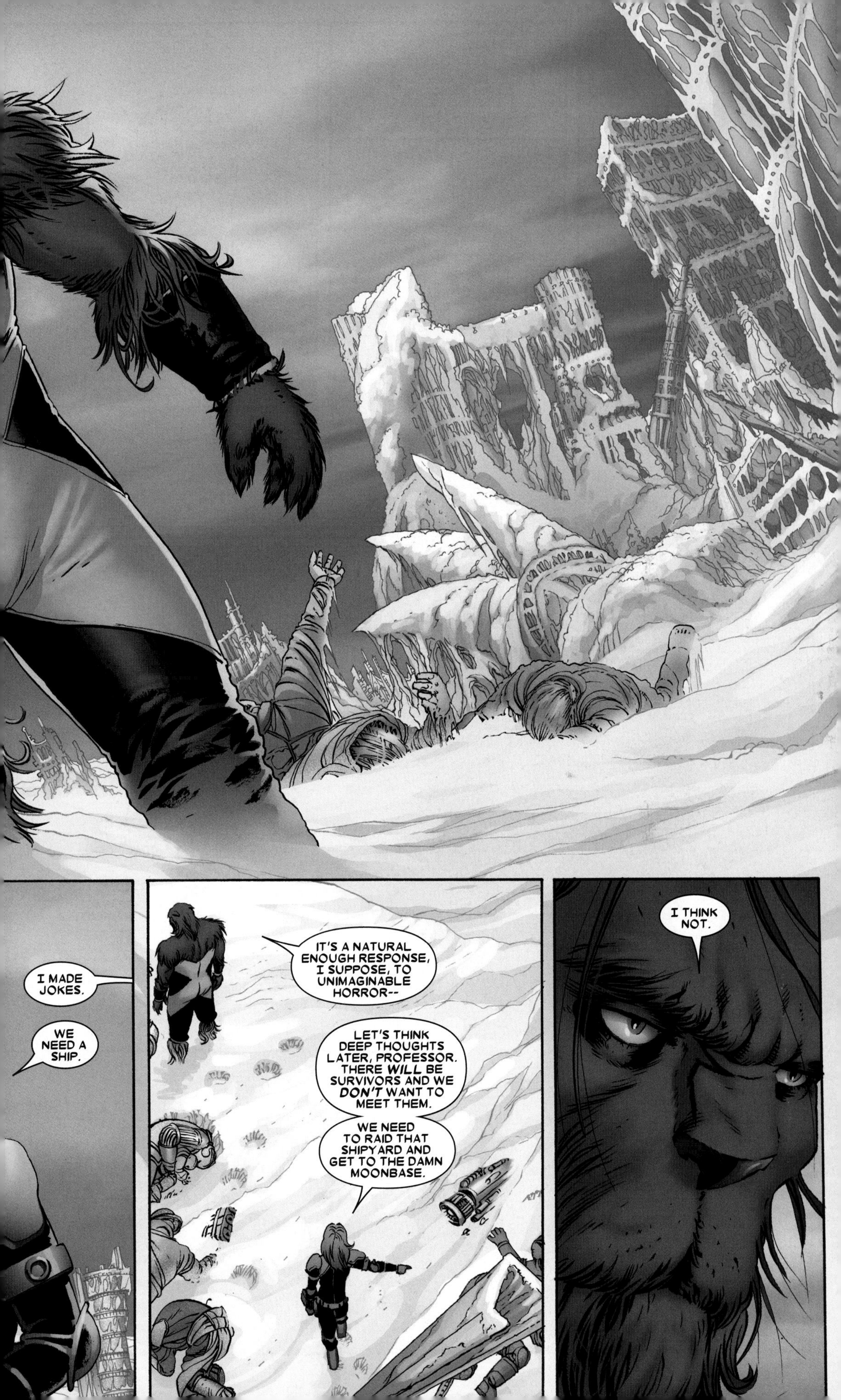
I MADE JOKES.
WE NEED A SHIP.
IT'S A NATURAL ENOUGH RESPONSE, I SUPPOSE, TO UNIMAGINABLE HORROR--
LET'S THINK DEEP THOUGHTS LATER, PROFESSOR. THERE *WILL* BE SURVIVORS AND WE *DON'T* WANT TO MEET THEM.
WE NEED TO RAID THAT SHIPYARD AND GET TO THE DAMN MOONBASE.
I THINK NOT.

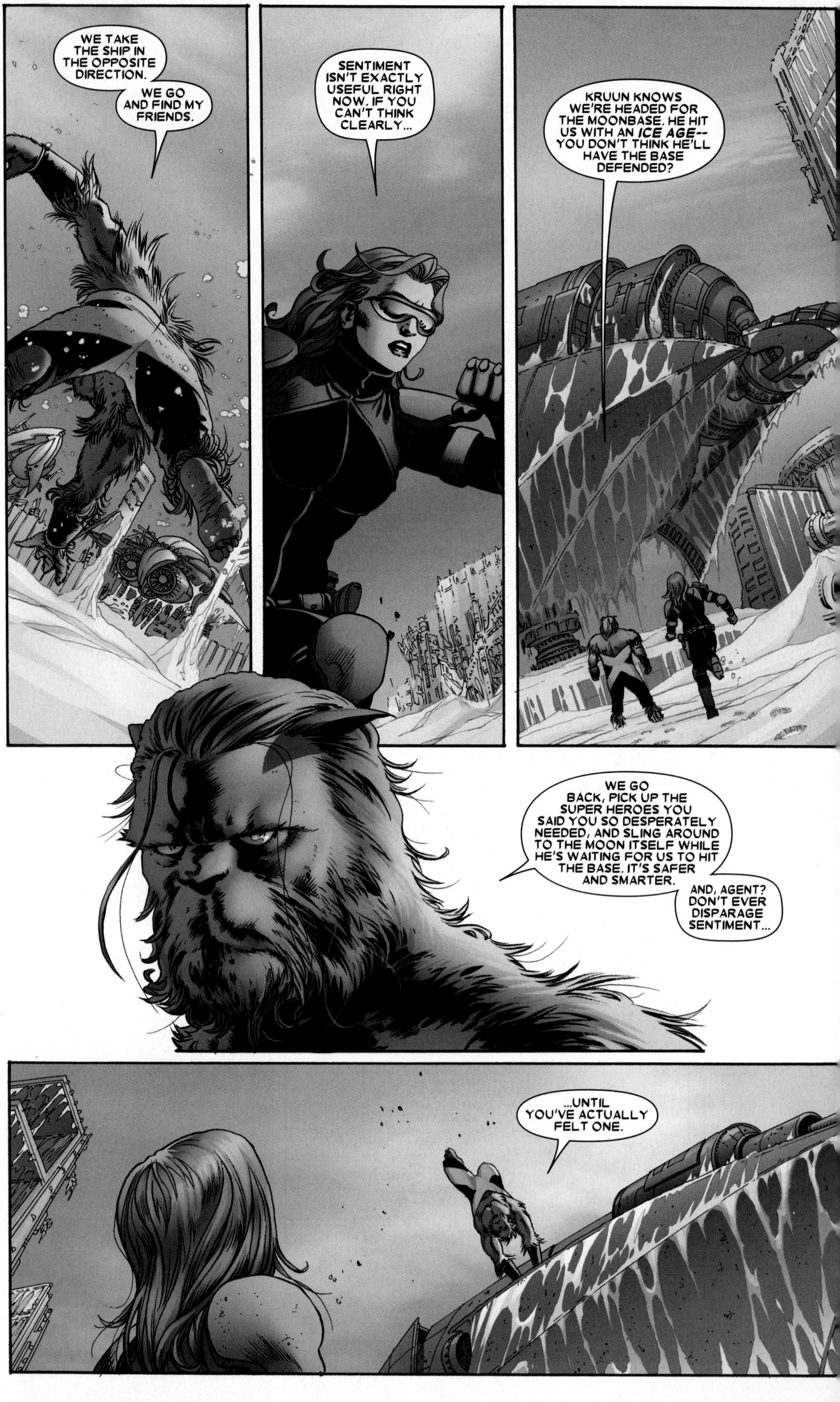
WE TAKE THE SHIP IN THE OPPOSITE DIRECTION.
WE GO AND FIND MY FRIENDS.
SENTIMENT ISN'T EXACTLY USEFUL RIGHT NOW. IF YOU CAN'T THINK CLEARLY...
KRUUN KNOWS WE'RE HEADED FOR THE MOONBASE. HE HIT US WITH AN *ICE AGE*-- YOU DON'T THINK HE'LL HAVE THE BASE DEFENDED?
WE GO BACK, PICK UP THE SUPER HEROES YOU SAID YOU SO DESPERATELY NEEDED, AND SLING AROUND TO THE MOON ITSELF WHILE HE'S WAITING FOR US TO HIT THE BASE. IT'S SAFER AND SMARTER.
AND, AGENT? DON'T EVER DISPARAGE SENTIMENT...
...UNTIL YOU'VE ACTUALLY FELT ONE.

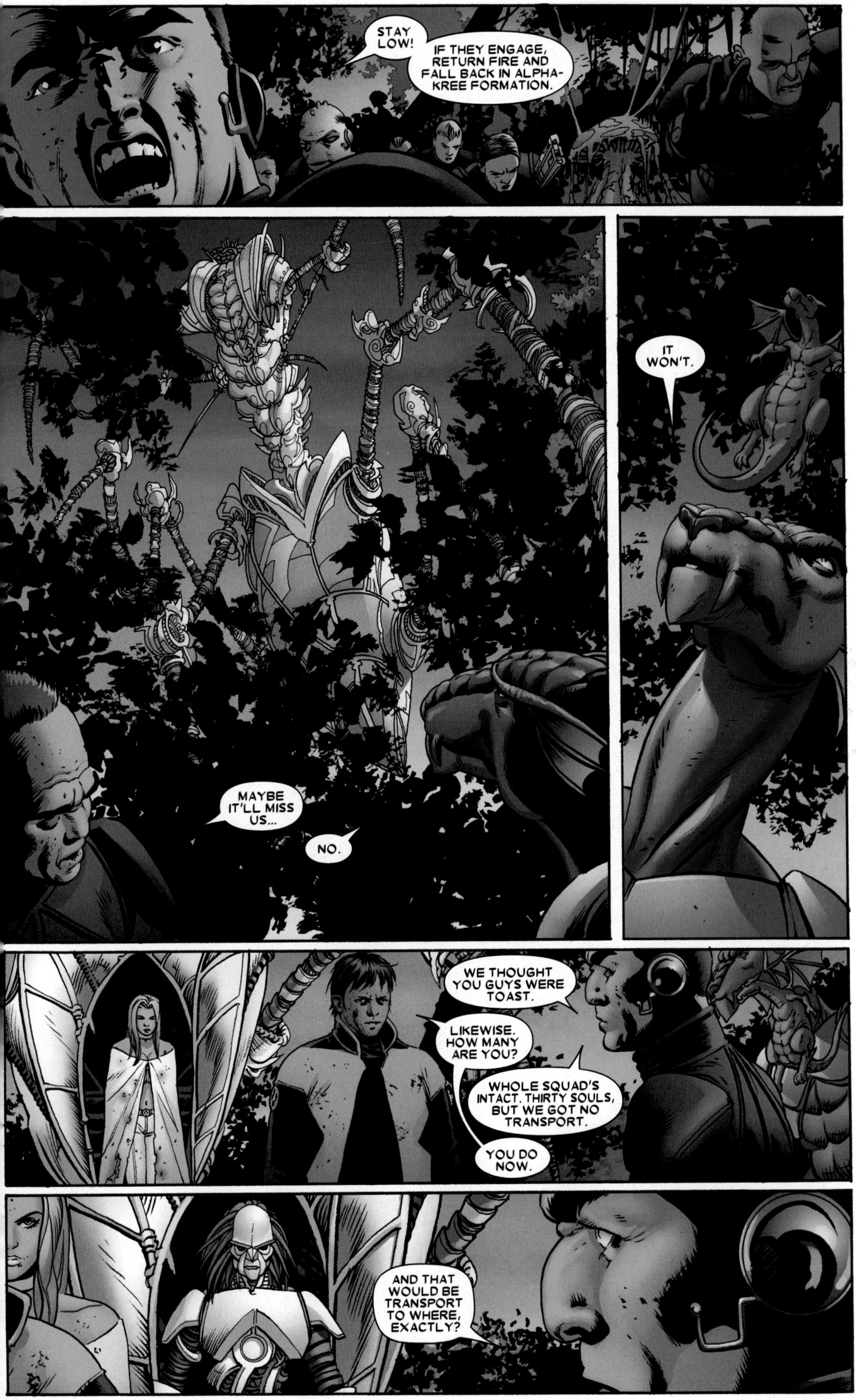
STAY LOW!
IF THEY ENGAGE, RETURN FIRE AND FALL BACK IN ALPHA-KREE FORMATION.
MAYBE IT'LL MISS US...
NO.
IT WON'T.
WE THOUGHT YOU GUYS WERE TOAST.
LIKEWISE. HOW MANY ARE YOU?
WHOLE SQUAD'S INTACT. THIRTY SOULS, BUT WE GOT NO TRANSPORT.
YOU DO NOW.
AND THAT WOULD BE TRANSPORT TO WHERE, EXACTLY?

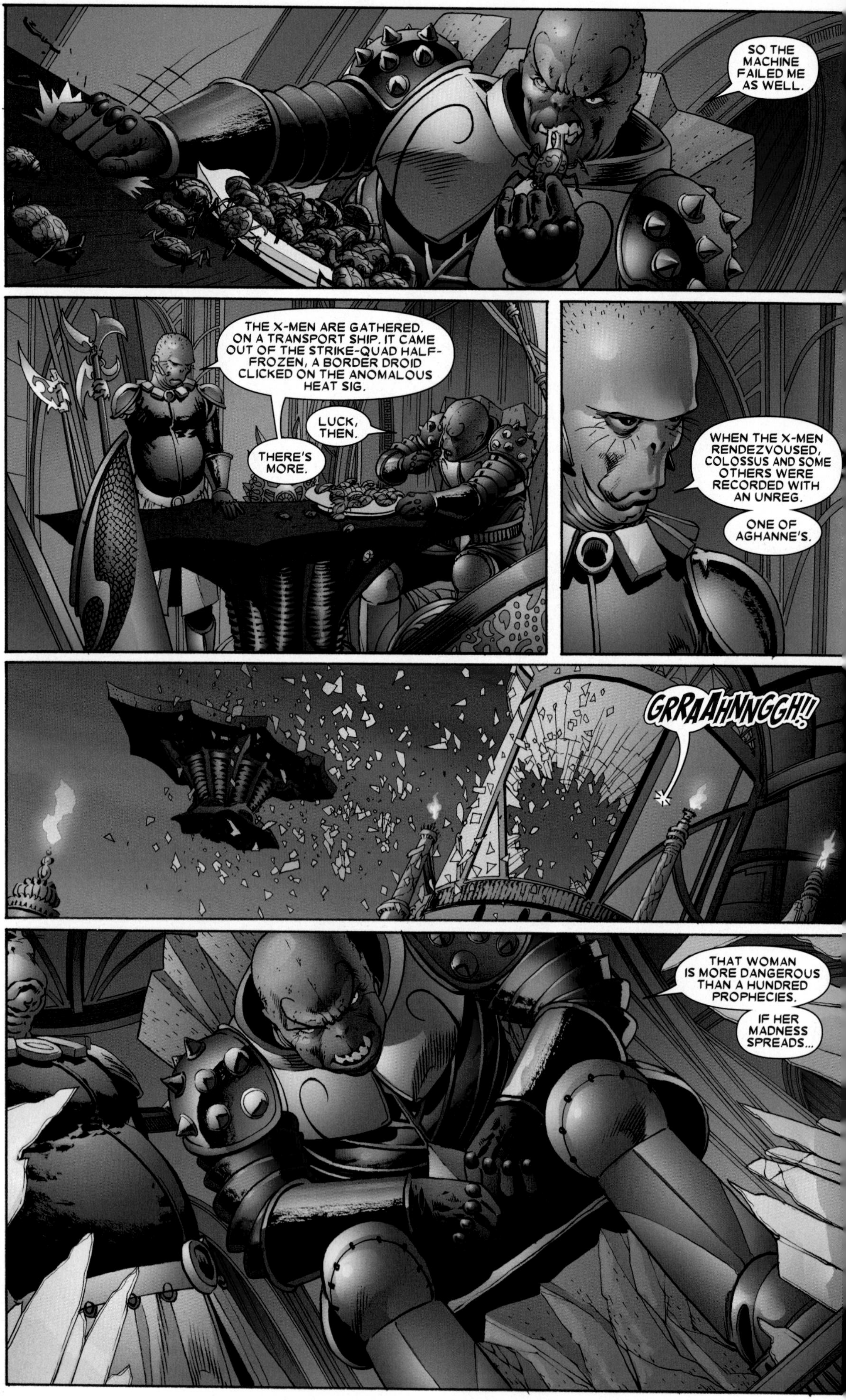

SO THE MACHINE FAILED ME AS WELL.
THE X-MEN ARE GATHERED. ON A TRANSPORT SHIP. IT CAME OUT OF THE STRIKE-QUAD HALF-FROZEN, A BORDER DROID CLICKED ON THE ANOMALOUS HEAT SIG.
LUCK, THEN.
THERE'S MORE.
WHEN THE X-MEN RENDEZVOUSED, COLOSSUS AND SOME OTHERS WERE RECORDED WITH AN UNREG.
ONE OF AGHANNE'S.
GRRAAHNNGGH!!
THAT WOMAN IS MORE DANGEROUS THAN A HUNDRED PROPHECIES.
IF HER MADNESS SPREADS...

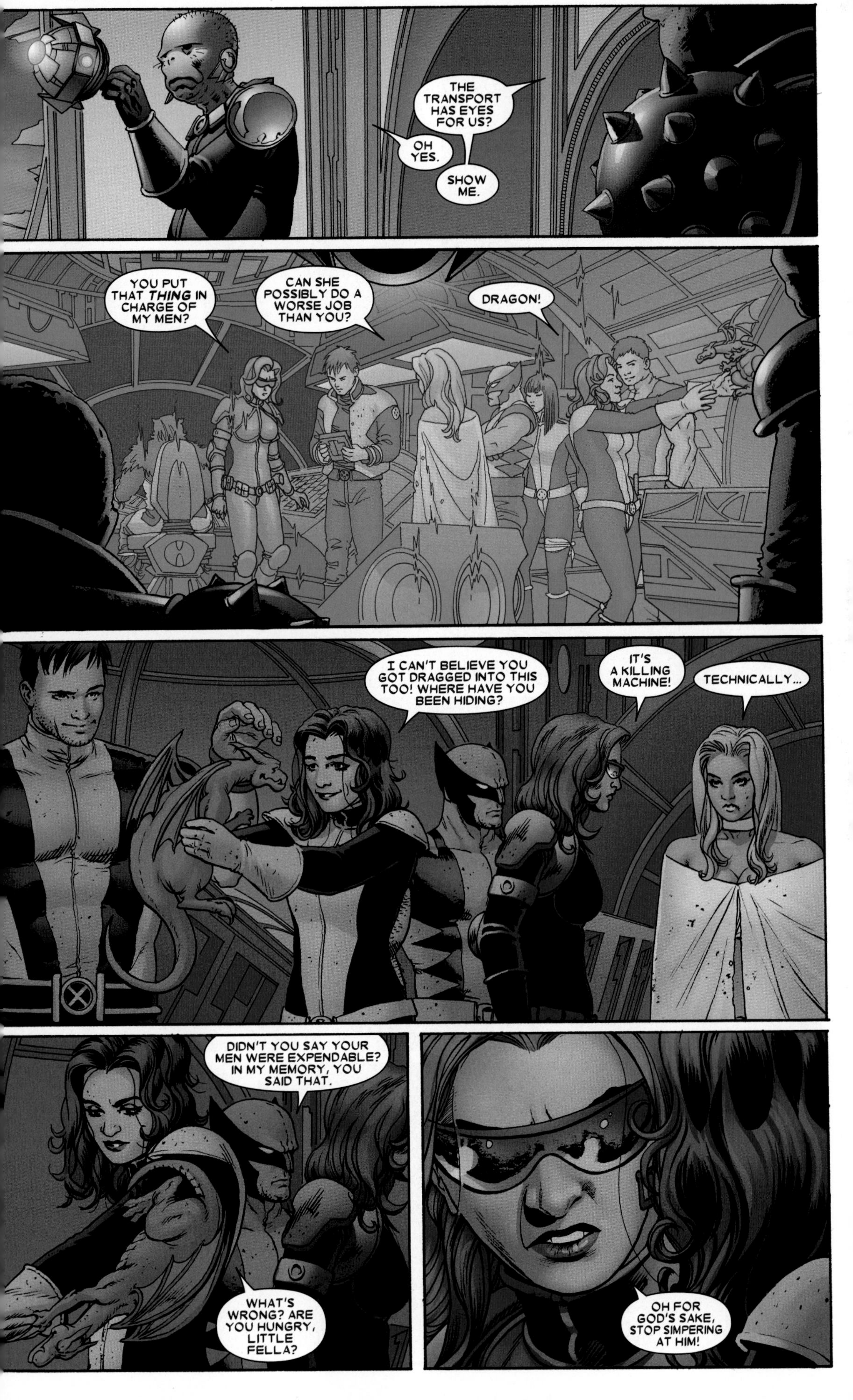
THE TRANSPORT HAS EYES FOR US?
OH YES.
SHOW ME.
YOU PUT THAT *THING* IN CHARGE OF MY MEN?
CAN SHE POSSIBLY DO A WORSE JOB THAN YOU?
DRAGON!
I CAN'T BELIEVE YOU GOT DRAGGED INTO THIS TOO! WHERE HAVE YOU BEEN HIDING?
IT'S A KILLING MACHINE!
TECHNICALLY...
DIDN'T YOU SAY YOUR MEN WERE EXPENDABLE? IN MY MEMORY, YOU SAID THAT.
WHAT'S WRONG? ARE YOU HUNGRY, LITTLE FELLA?
OH FOR GOD'S SAKE, STOP SIMPERING AT HIM!

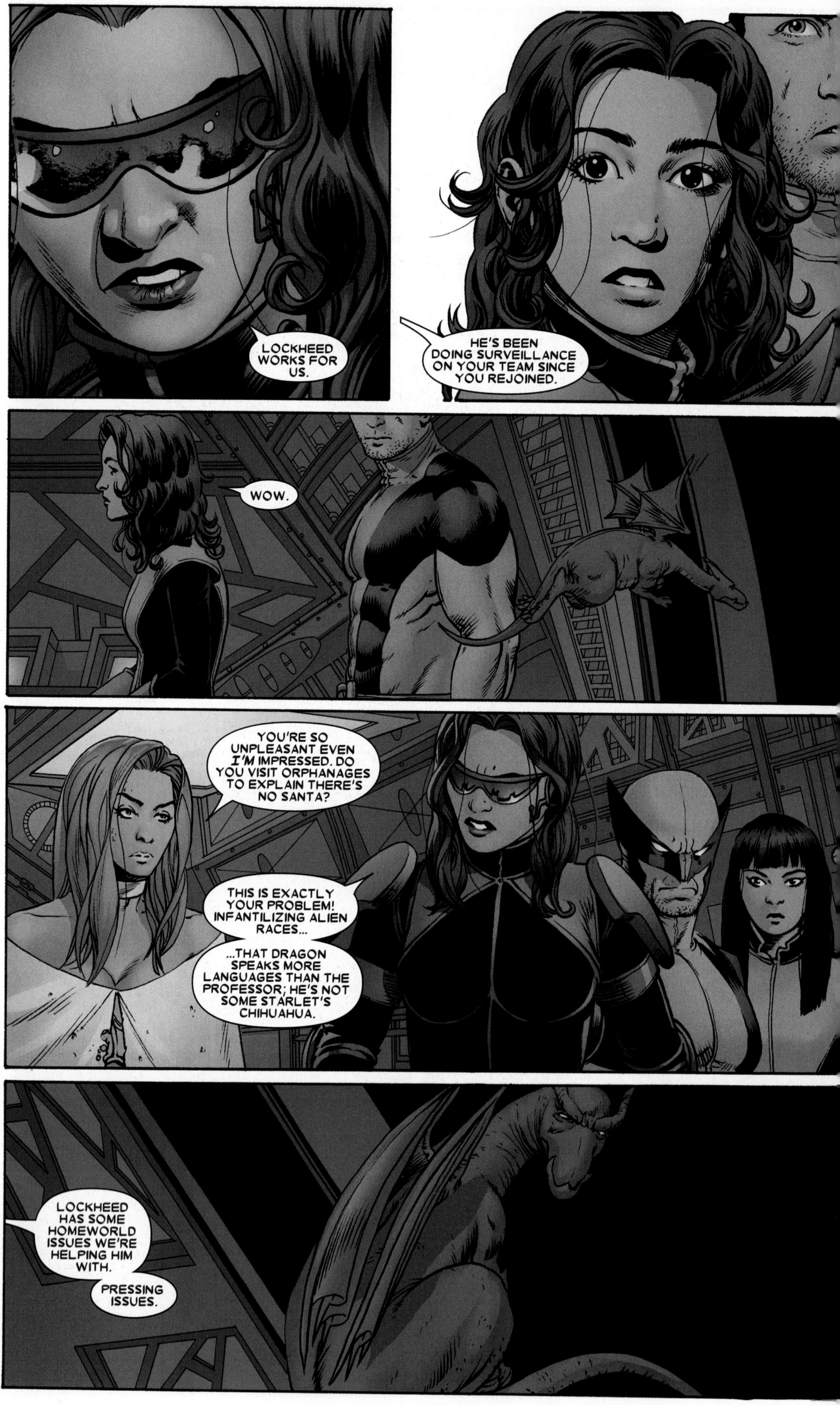
LOCKHEED WORKS FOR US.
HE'S BEEN DOING SURVEILLANCE ON YOUR TEAM SINCE YOU REJOINED.
WOW.
YOU'RE SO UNPLEASANT EVEN *I'M* IMPRESSED. DO YOU VISIT ORPHANAGES TO EXPLAIN THERE'S NO SANTA?
THIS IS EXACTLY YOUR PROBLEM! INFANTILIZING ALIEN RACES...
...THAT DRAGON SPEAKS MORE LANGUAGES THAN THE PROFESSOR; HE'S NOT SOME STARLET'S CHIHUAHUA.
LOCKHEED HAS SOME HOMEWORLD ISSUES WE'RE HELPING HIM WITH.
PRESSING ISSUES.

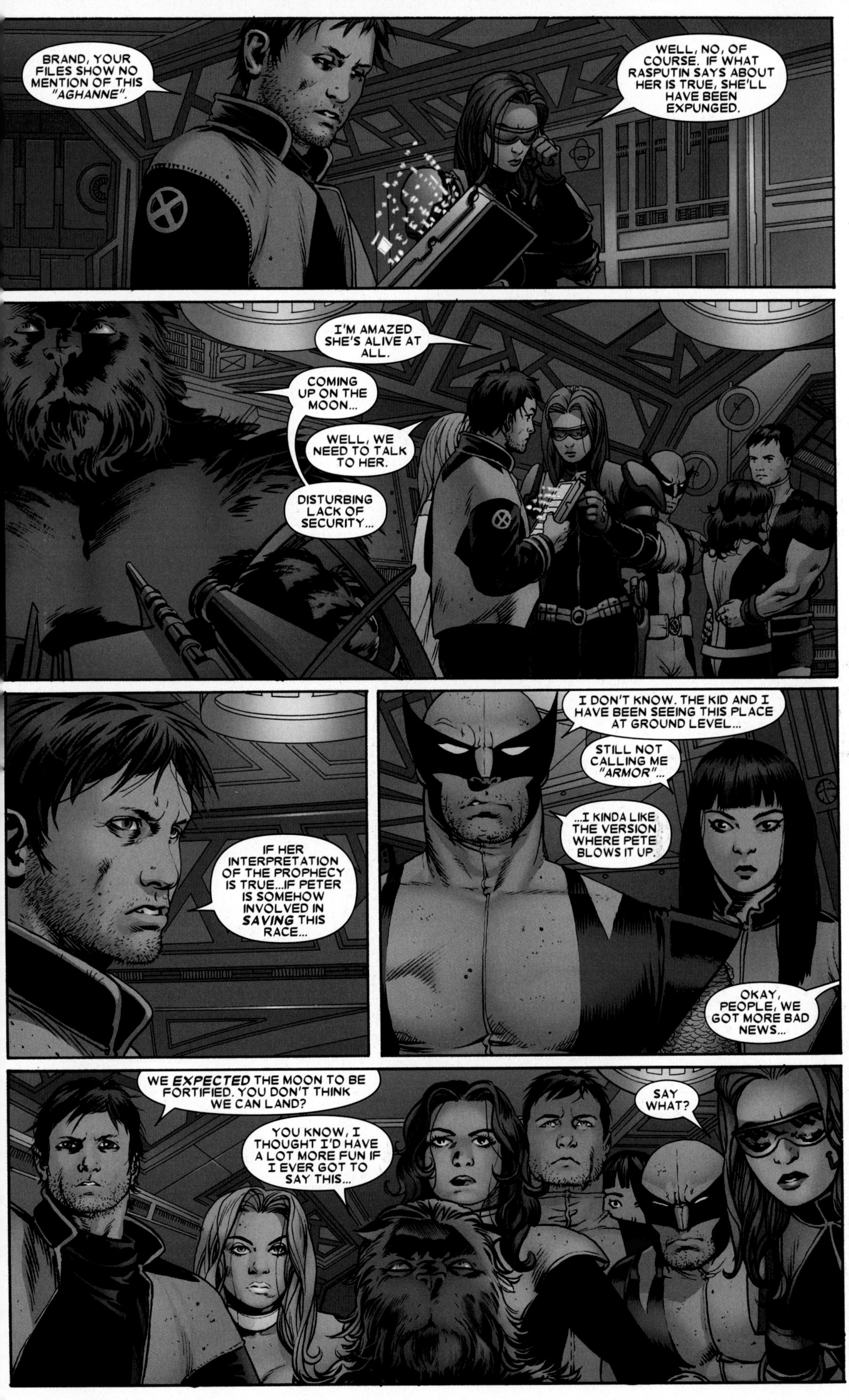

BRAND, YOUR FILES SHOW NO MENTION OF THIS "AGHANNE".
WELL, NO, OF COURSE. IF WHAT RASPUTIN SAYS ABOUT HER IS TRUE, SHE'LL HAVE BEEN EXPUNGED.
I'M AMAZED SHE'S ALIVE AT ALL.
COMING UP ON THE MOON...
WELL, WE NEED TO TALK TO HER.
DISTURBING LACK OF SECURITY...
IF HER INTERPRETATION OF THE PROPHECY IS TRUE...IF PETER IS SOMEHOW INVOLVED IN SAVING THIS RACE...
I DON'T KNOW. THE KID AND I HAVE BEEN SEEING THIS PLACE AT GROUND LEVEL...
STILL NOT CALLING ME "ARMOR"...
...I KINDA LIKE THE VERSION WHERE PETE BLOWS IT UP.
OKAY, PEOPLE, WE GOT MORE BAD NEWS...
WE EXPECTED THE MOON TO BE FORTIFIED. YOU DON'T THINK WE CAN LAND?
YOU KNOW, I THOUGHT I'D HAVE A LOT MORE FUN IF I EVER GOT TO SAY THIS...
SAY WHAT?

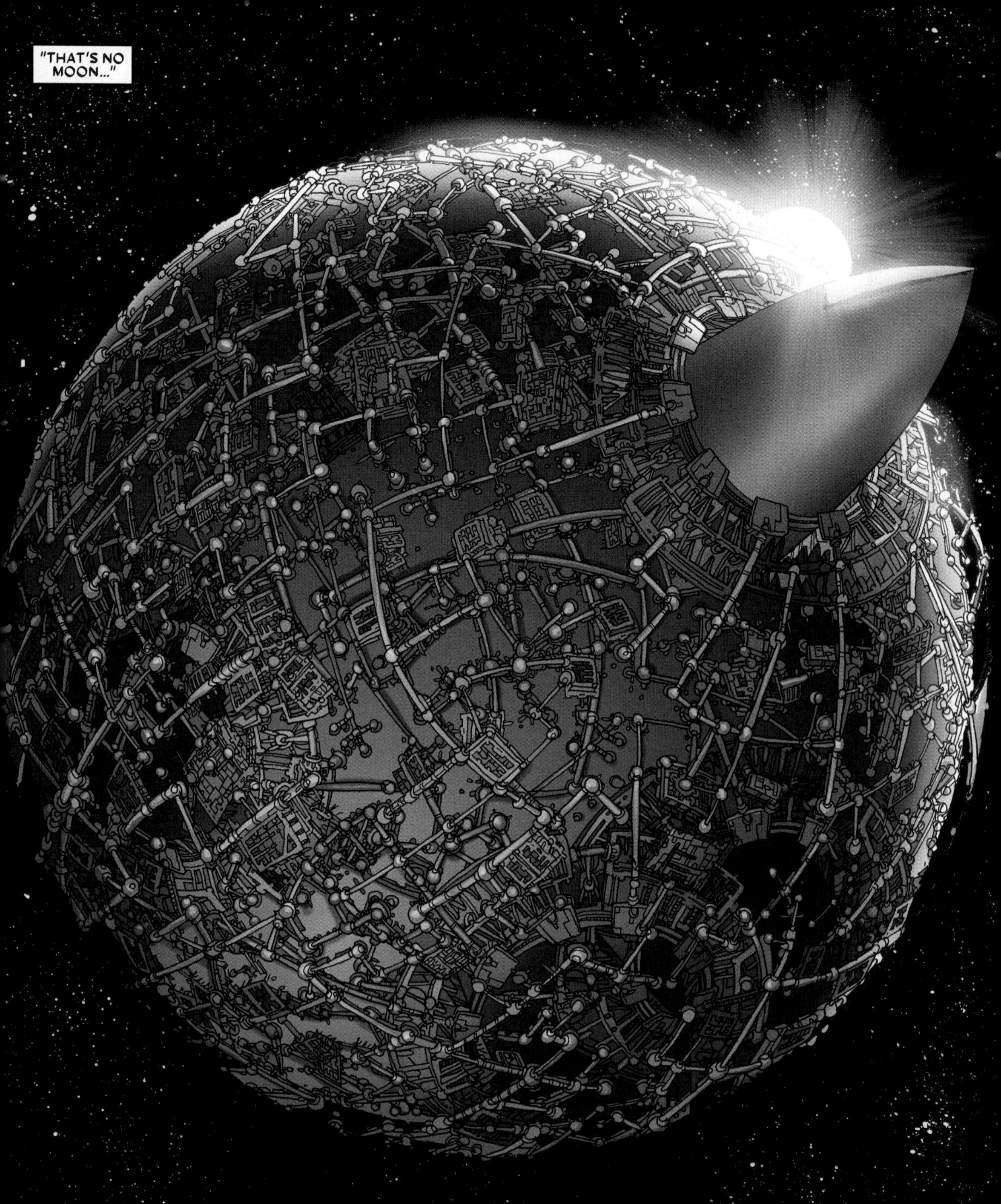
"THAT'S NO MOON..."

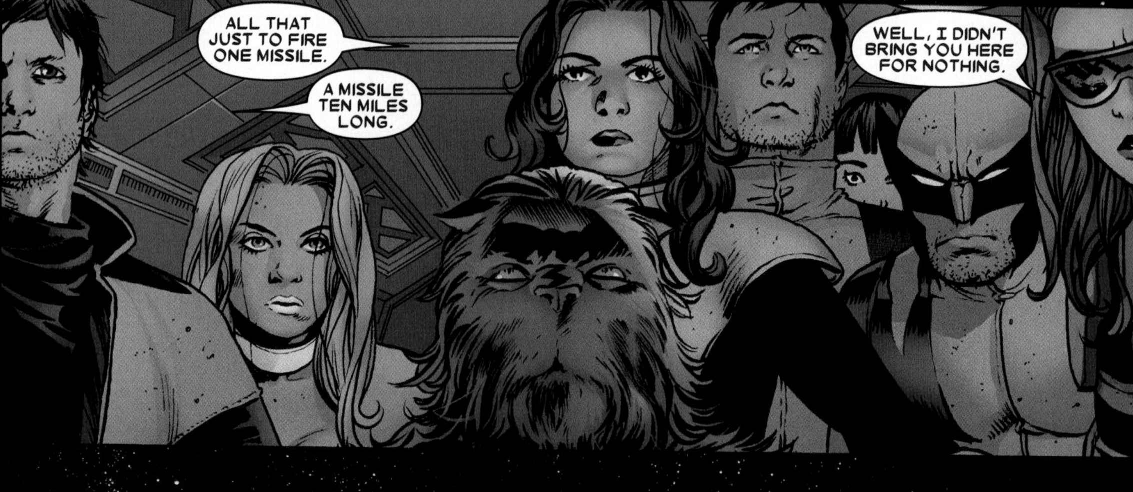
ALL THAT JUST TO FIRE ONE MISSILE.
A MISSILE TEN MILES LONG.
WELL, I DIDN'T BRING YOU HERE FOR NOTHING.

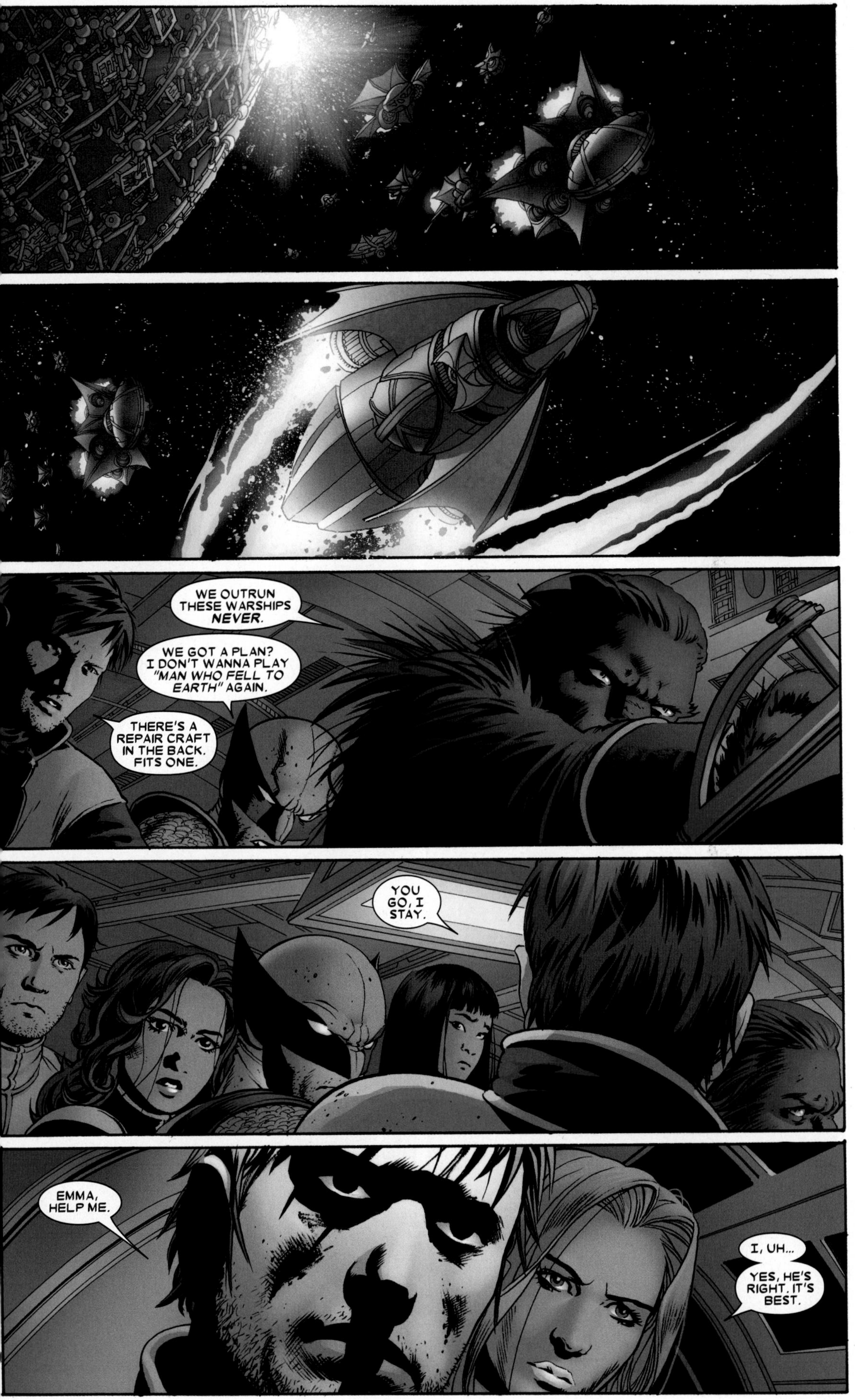
WE OUTRUN THESE WARSHIPS NEVER.
WE GOT A PLAN? I DON'T WANNA PLAY "MAN WHO FELL TO EARTH" AGAIN.
THERE'S A REPAIR CRAFT IN THE BACK. FITS ONE.
YOU GO, I STAY.
EMMA, HELP ME.
I, UH...
YES, HE'S RIGHT. IT'S BEST.

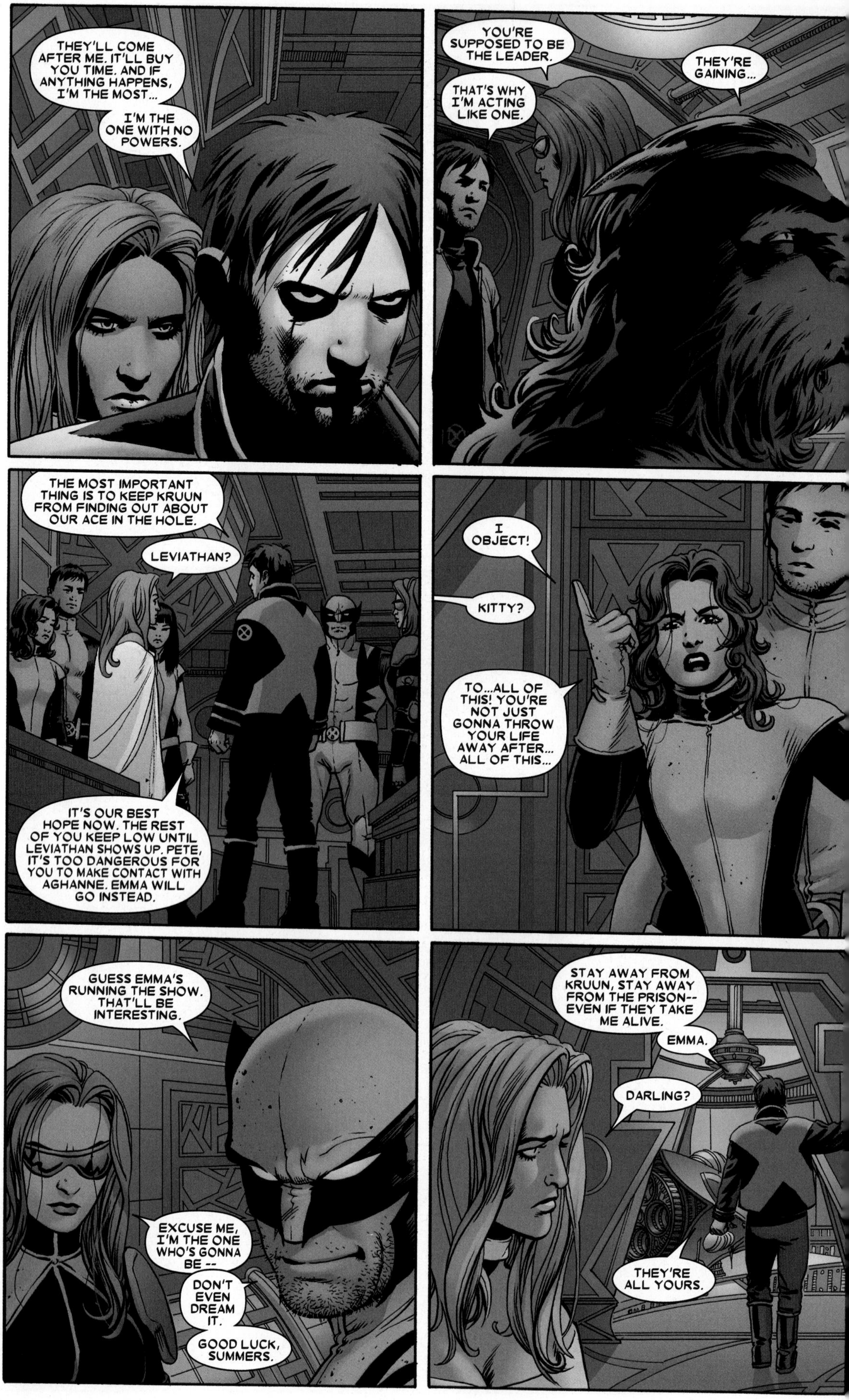
THEY'LL COME AFTER ME. IT'LL BUY YOU TIME. AND IF ANYTHING HAPPENS, I'M THE MOST...
I'M THE ONE WITH NO POWERS.
YOU'RE SUPPOSED TO BE THE LEADER.
THAT'S WHY I'M ACTING LIKE ONE.
THEY'RE GAINING...
THE MOST IMPORTANT THING IS TO KEEP KRUUN FROM FINDING OUT ABOUT OUR ACE IN THE HOLE.
LEVIATHAN?
IT'S OUR BEST HOPE NOW. THE REST OF YOU KEEP LOW UNTIL LEVIATHAN SHOWS UP. PETE, IT'S TOO DANGEROUS FOR YOU TO MAKE CONTACT WITH AGHANNE. EMMA WILL GO INSTEAD.
I OBJECT!
KITTY?
TO...ALL OF THIS! YOU'RE NOT JUST GONNA THROW YOUR LIFE AWAY AFTER... ALL OF THIS...
GUESS EMMA'S RUNNING THE SHOW. THAT'LL BE INTERESTING.
EXCUSE ME, I'M THE ONE WHO'S GONNA BE --
DON'T EVEN DREAM IT.
GOOD LUCK, SUMMERS.
STAY AWAY FROM KRUUN, STAY AWAY FROM THE PRISON-- EVEN IF THEY TAKE ME ALIVE.
EMMA.
DARLING?
THEY'RE ALL YOURS.

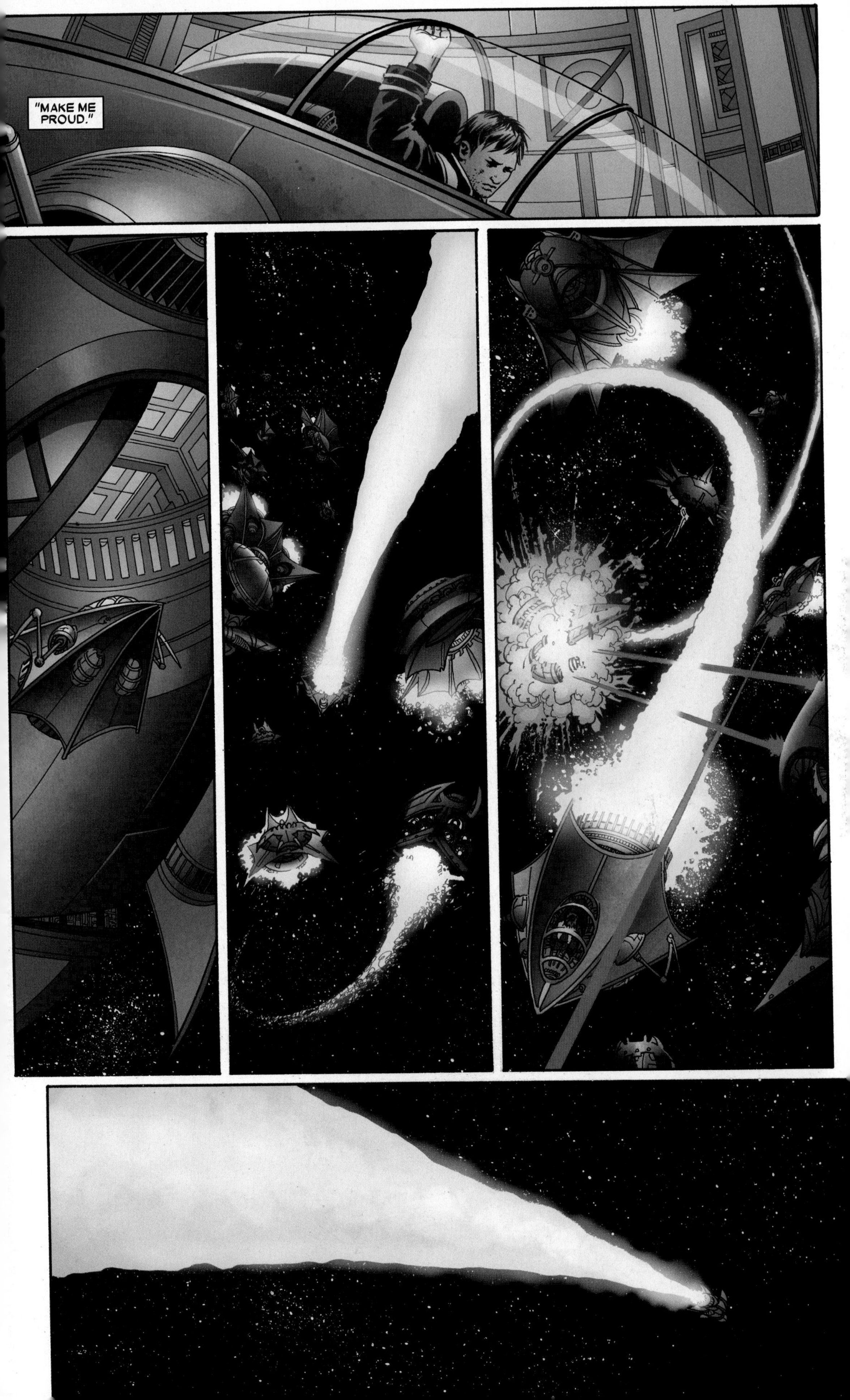
"MAKE ME PROUD."

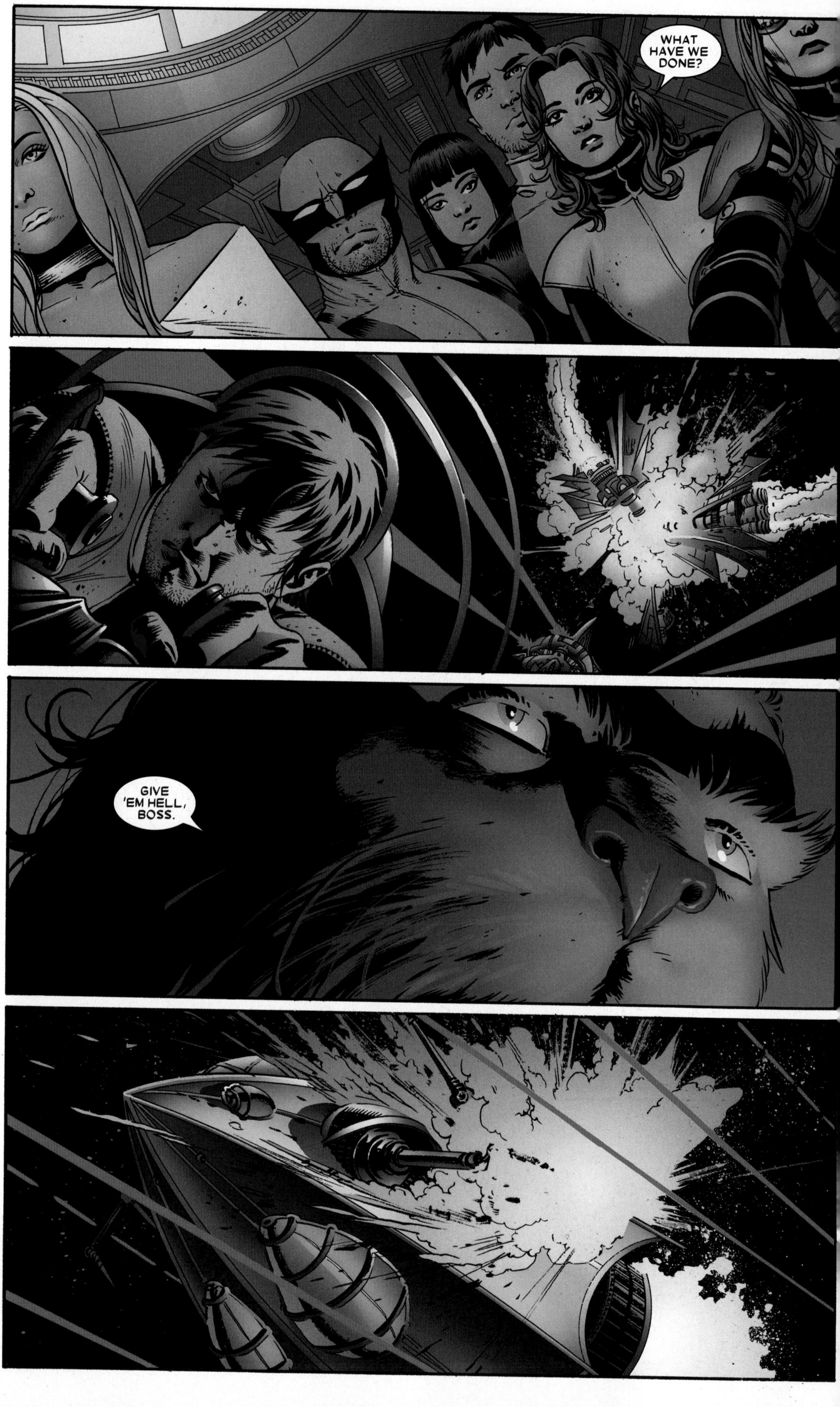
WHAT HAVE WE DONE?
GIVE 'EM HELL, BOSS.

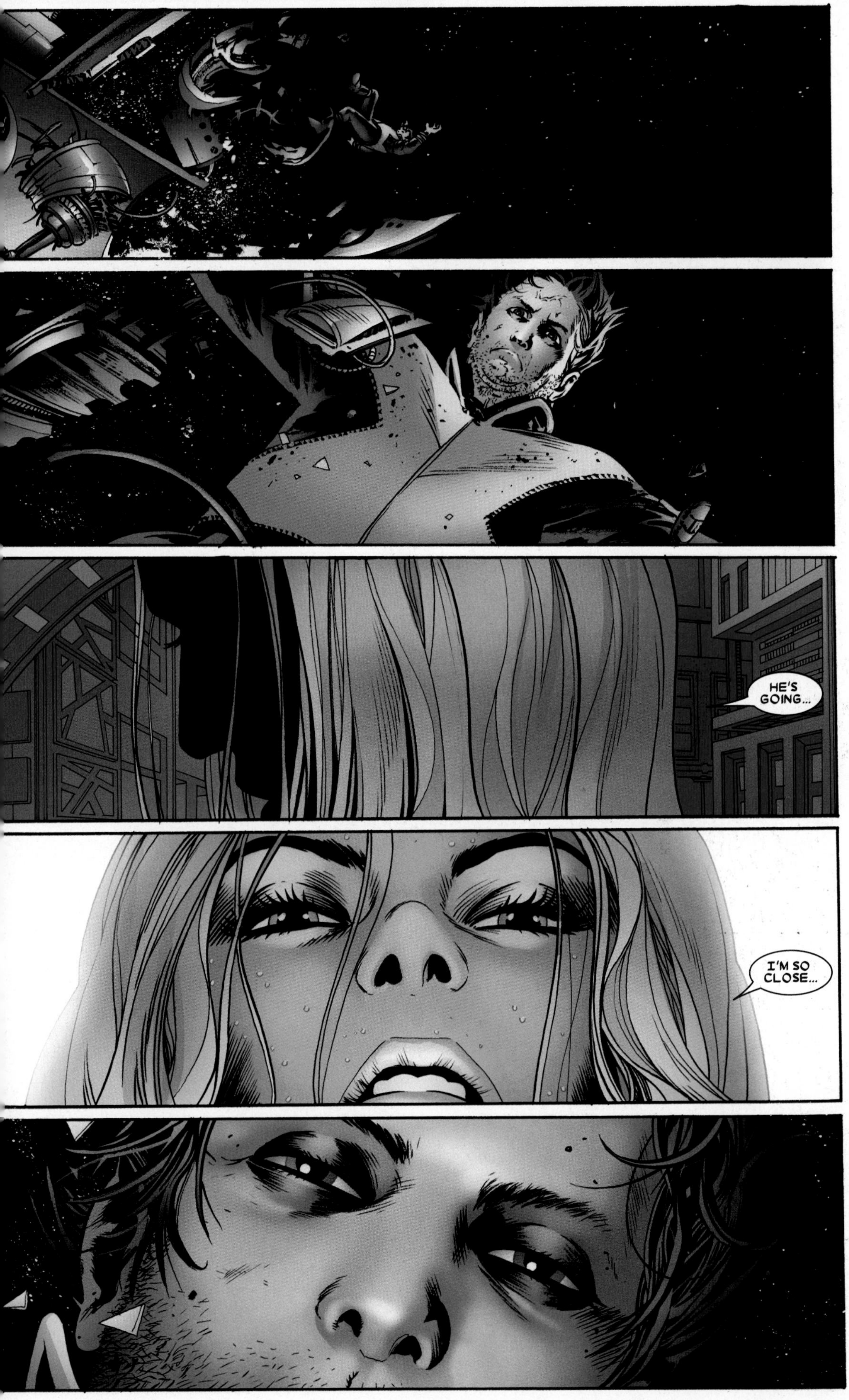
HE'S GOING...
I'M SO CLOSE...

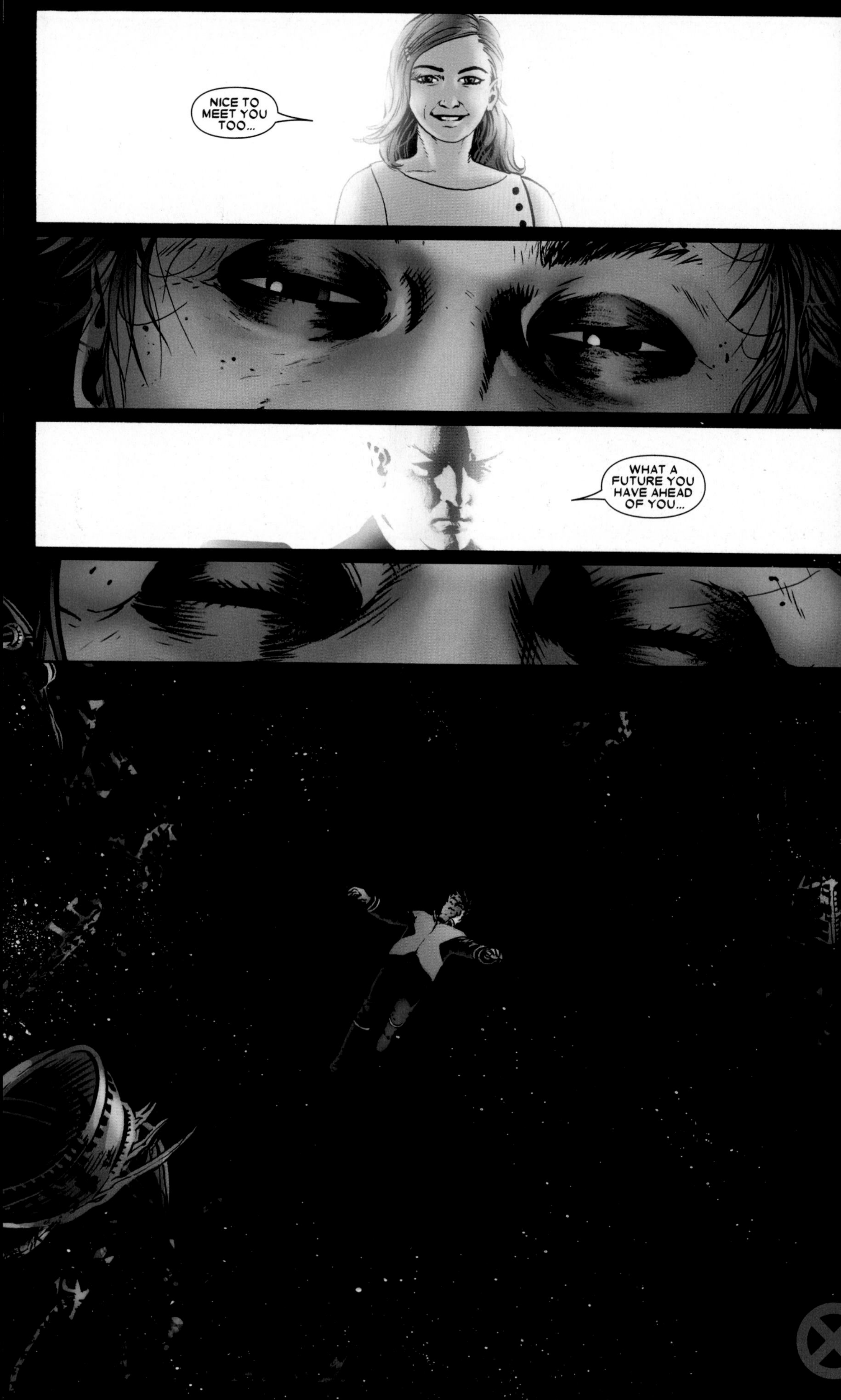
NICE TO MEET YOU TOO...
WHAT A FUTURE YOU HAVE AHEAD OF YOU...

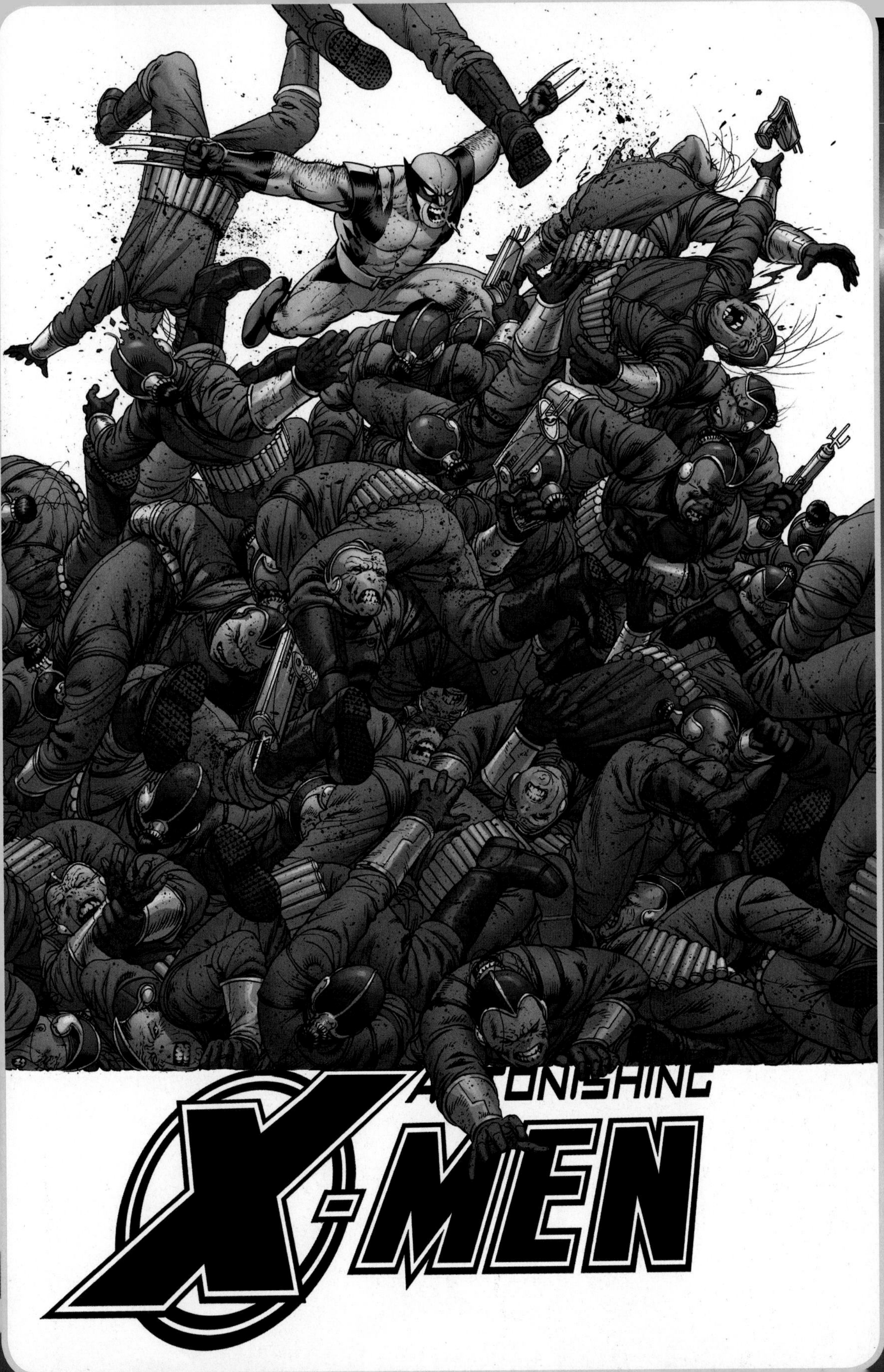
X-MEN

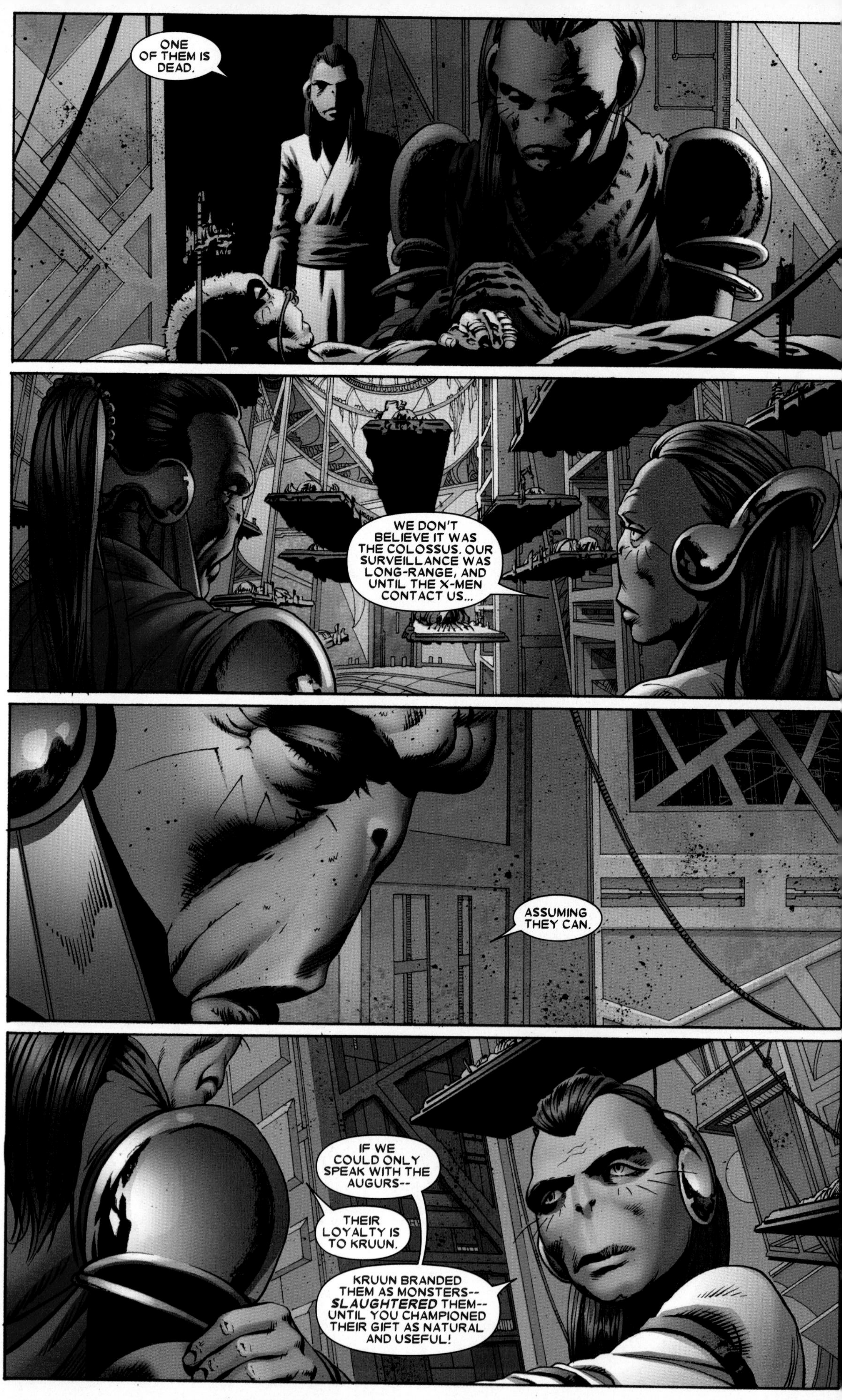
ONE OF THEM IS DEAD.
WE DON'T BELIEVE IT WAS THE COLOSSUS. OUR SURVEILLANCE WAS LONG-RANGE, AND UNTIL THE X-MEN CONTACT US...
ASSUMING THEY CAN.
IF WE COULD ONLY SPEAK WITH THE AUGURS--
THEIR LOYALTY IS TO KRUUN.
KRUUN BRANDED THEM AS MONSTERS-- *SLAUGHTERED* THEM-- UNTIL YOU CHAMPIONED THEIR GIFT AS NATURAL AND USEFUL!

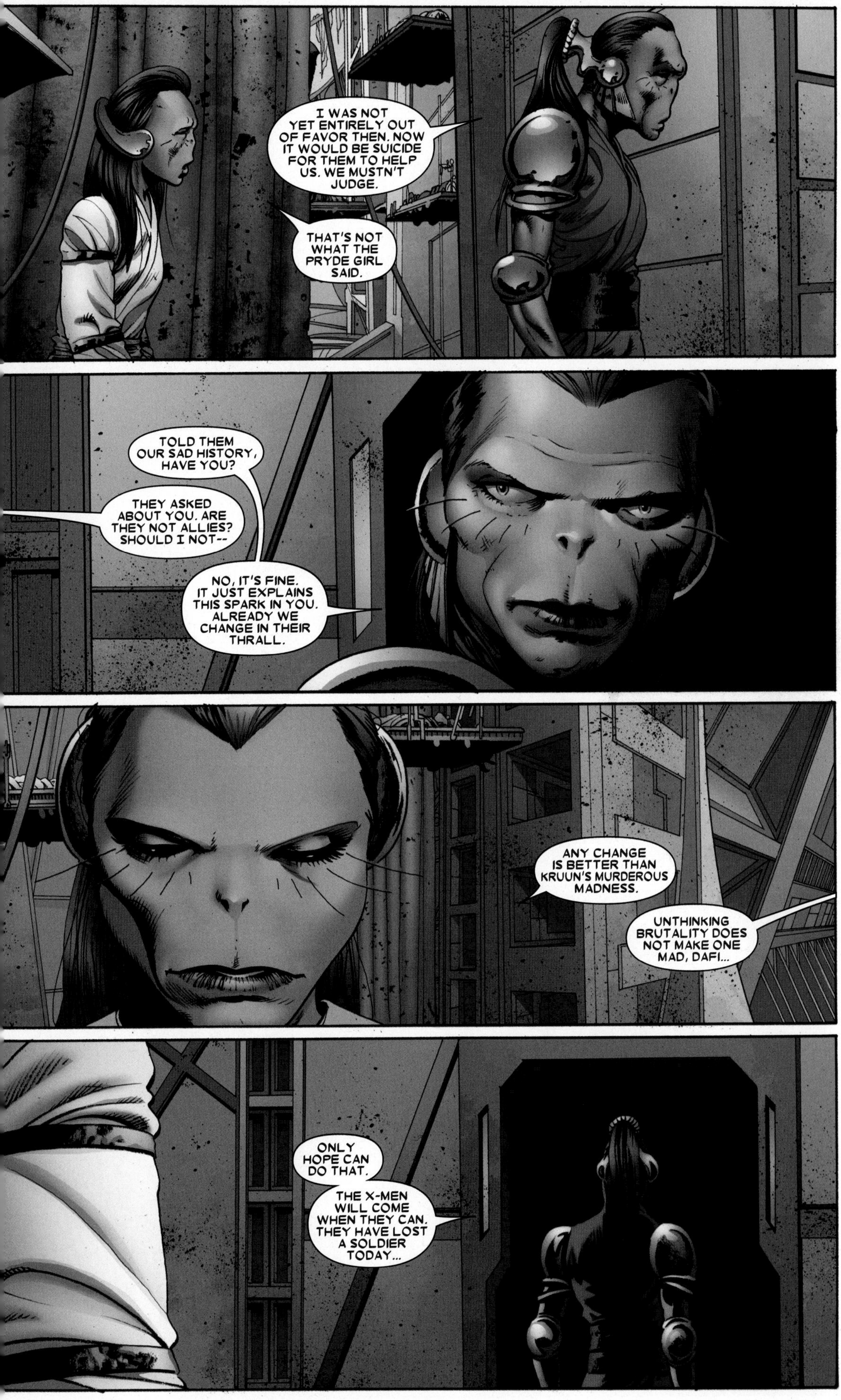
I WAS NOT YET ENTIRELY OUT OF FAVOR THEN. NOW IT WOULD BE SUICIDE FOR THEM TO HELP US. WE MUSTN'T JUDGE.
THAT'S NOT WHAT THE PRYDE GIRL SAID.
TOLD THEM OUR SAD HISTORY, HAVE YOU?
THEY ASKED ABOUT YOU. ARE THEY NOT ALLIES? SHOULD I NOT--
NO, IT'S FINE. IT JUST EXPLAINS THIS SPARK IN YOU. ALREADY WE CHANGE IN THEIR THRALL.
ANY CHANGE IS BETTER THAN KRUUN'S MURDEROUS MADNESS.
UNTHINKING BRUTALITY DOES NOT MAKE ONE MAD, DAFI...
ONLY HOPE CAN DO THAT.
THE X-MEN WILL COME WHEN THEY CAN. THEY HAVE LOST A SOLDIER TODAY...

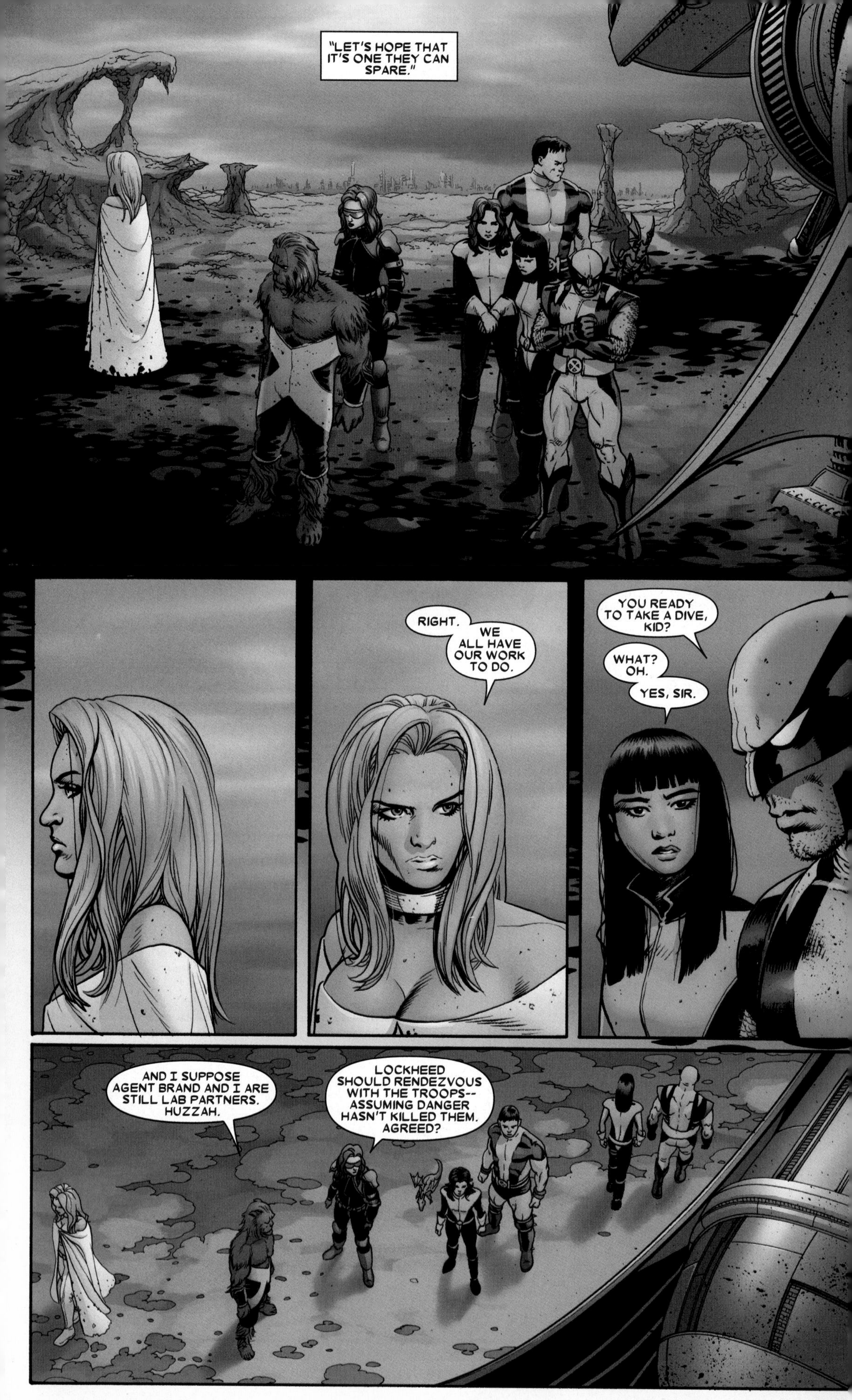
"LET'S HOPE THAT IT'S ONE THEY CAN SPARE."
RIGHT.
WE ALL HAVE OUR WORK TO DO.
YOU READY TO TAKE A DIVE, KID?
WHAT? OH.
YES, SIR.
AND I SUPPOSE AGENT BRAND AND I ARE STILL LAB PARTNERS. HUZZAH.
LOCKHEED SHOULD RENDEZVOUS WITH THE TROOPS-- ASSUMING DANGER HASN'T KILLED THEM. AGREED?

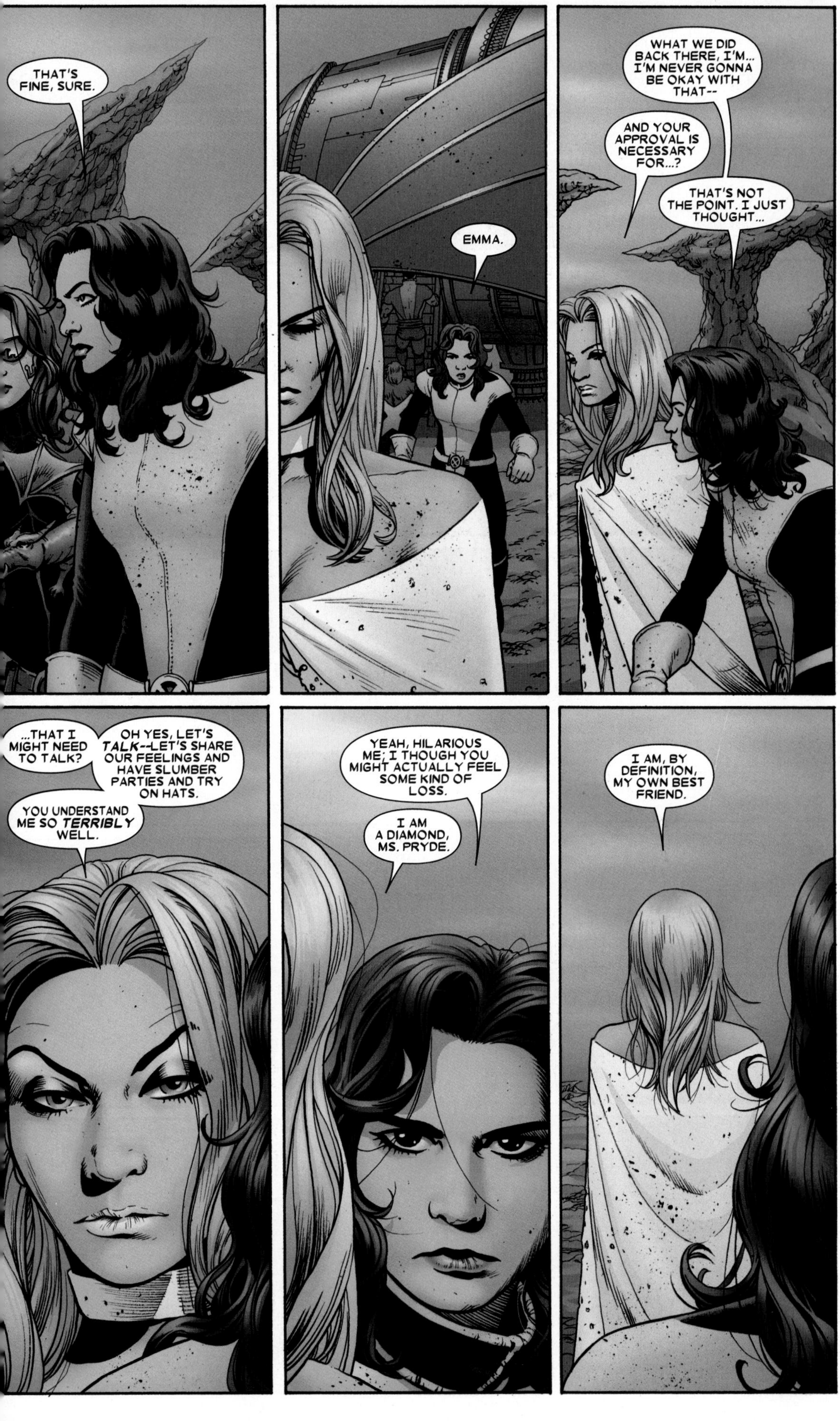
THAT'S FINE, SURE.
EMMA.
WHAT WE DID BACK THERE, I'M... I'M NEVER GONNA BE OKAY WITH THAT--
AND YOUR APPROVAL IS NECESSARY FOR...?
THAT'S NOT THE POINT. I JUST THOUGHT...
...THAT I MIGHT NEED TO TALK?
OH YES, LET'S TALK--LET'S SHARE OUR FEELINGS AND HAVE SLUMBER PARTIES AND TRY ON HATS.
YOU UNDERSTAND ME SO TERRIBLY WELL.
YEAH, HILARIOUS ME; I THOUGH YOU MIGHT ACTUALLY FEEL SOME KIND OF LOSS.
I AM A DIAMOND, MS. PRYDE.
I AM, BY DEFINITION, MY OWN BEST FRIEND.

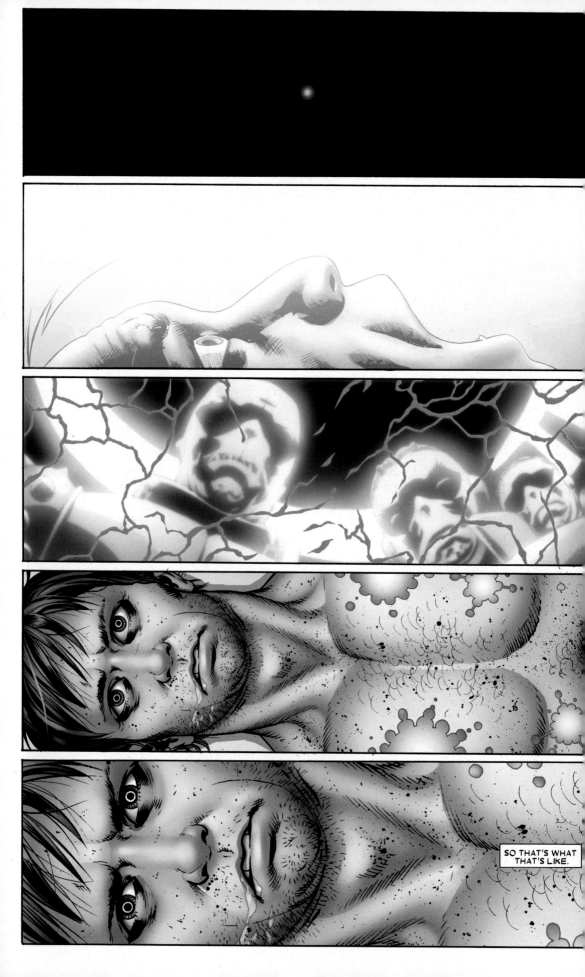

SO THAT'S WHAT
THAT'S LIKE.

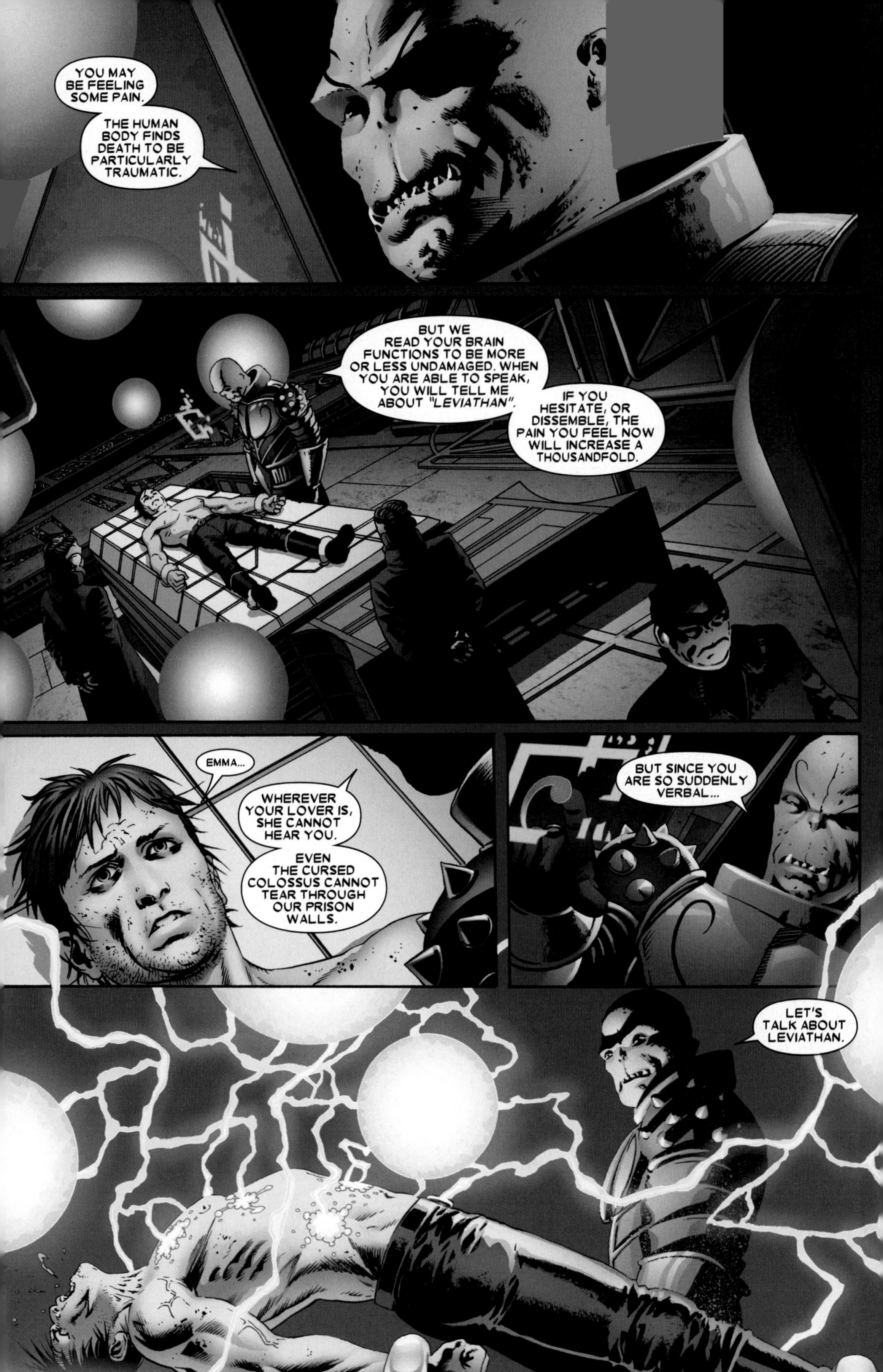
YOU MAY BE FEELING SOME PAIN.
THE HUMAN BODY FINDS DEATH TO BE PARTICULARLY TRAUMATIC.
BUT WE READ YOUR BRAIN FUNCTIONS TO BE MORE OR LESS UNDAMAGED. WHEN YOU ARE ABLE TO SPEAK, YOU WILL TELL ME ABOUT "LEVIATHAN".
IF YOU HESITATE, OR DISSEMBLE, THE PAIN YOU FEEL NOW WILL INCREASE A THOUSANDFOLD.
EMMA...
WHEREVER YOUR LOVER IS, SHE CANNOT HEAR YOU.
EVEN THE CURSED COLOSSUS CANNOT TEAR THROUGH OUR PRISON WALLS.
BUT SINCE YOU ARE SO SUDDENLY VERBAL...
LET'S TALK ABOUT LEVIATHAN.

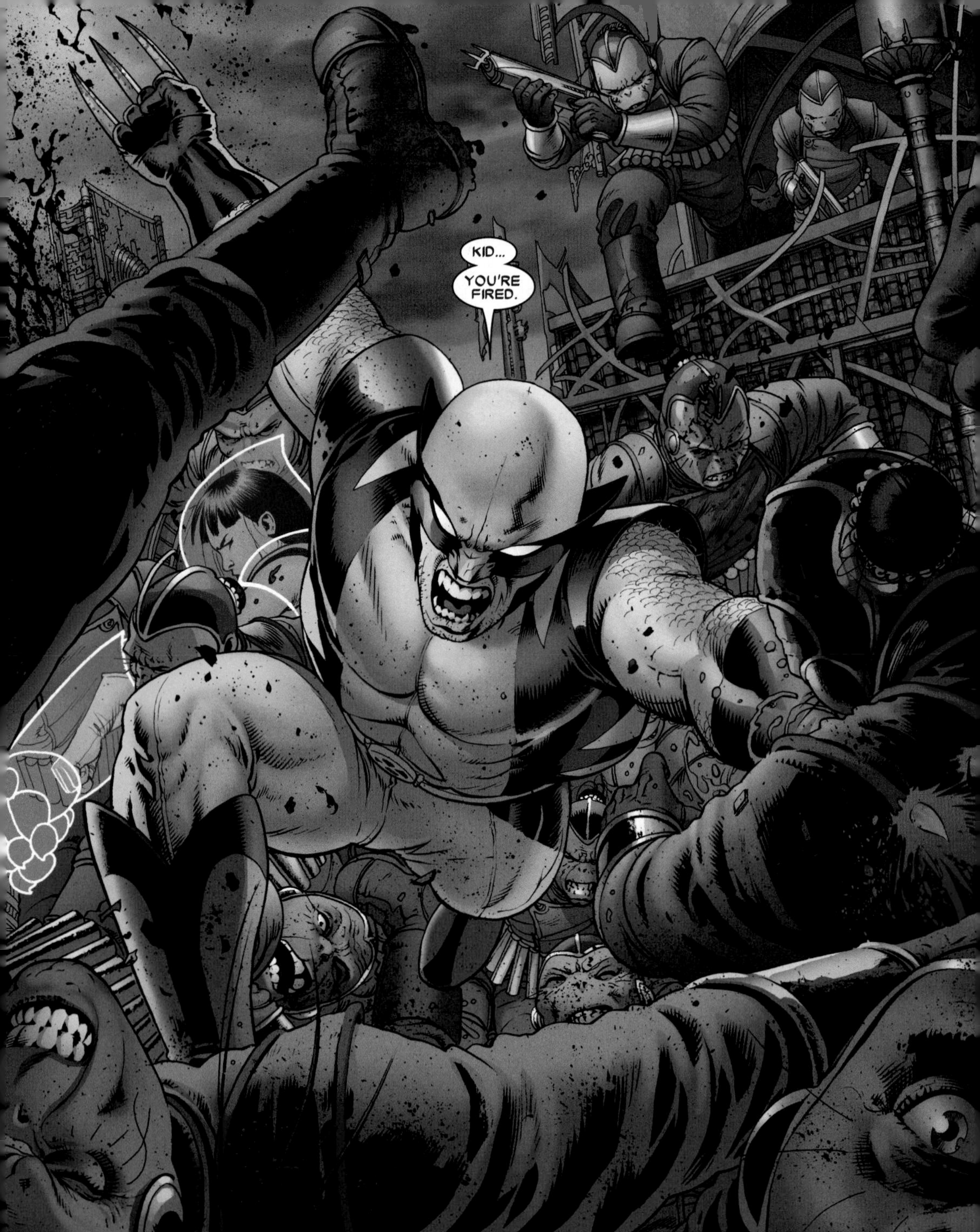
KID...
YOU'RE FIRED.

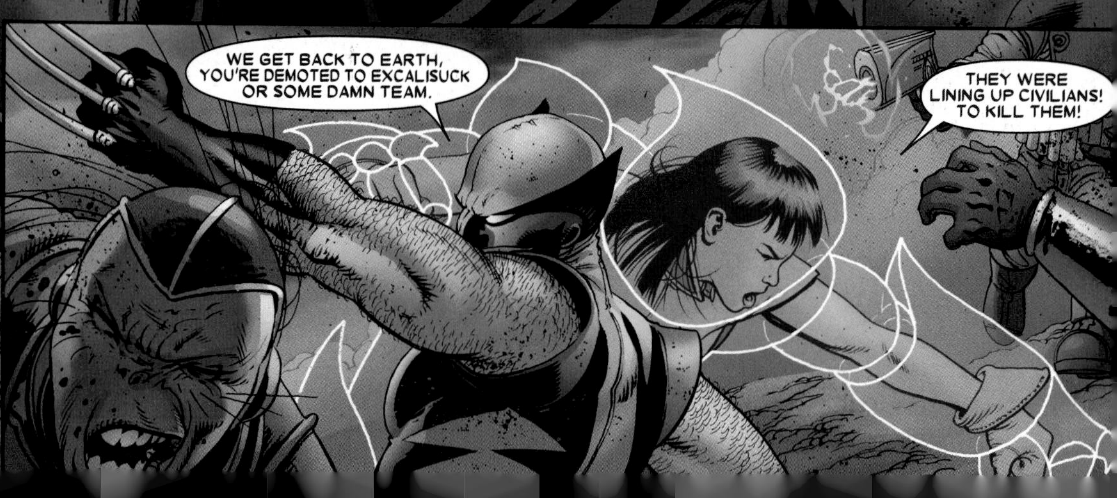
WE GET BACK TO EARTH, YOU'RE DEMOTED TO EXCALISUCK OR SOME DAMN TEAM.
THEY WERE LINING UP CIVILIANS! TO KILL THEM!

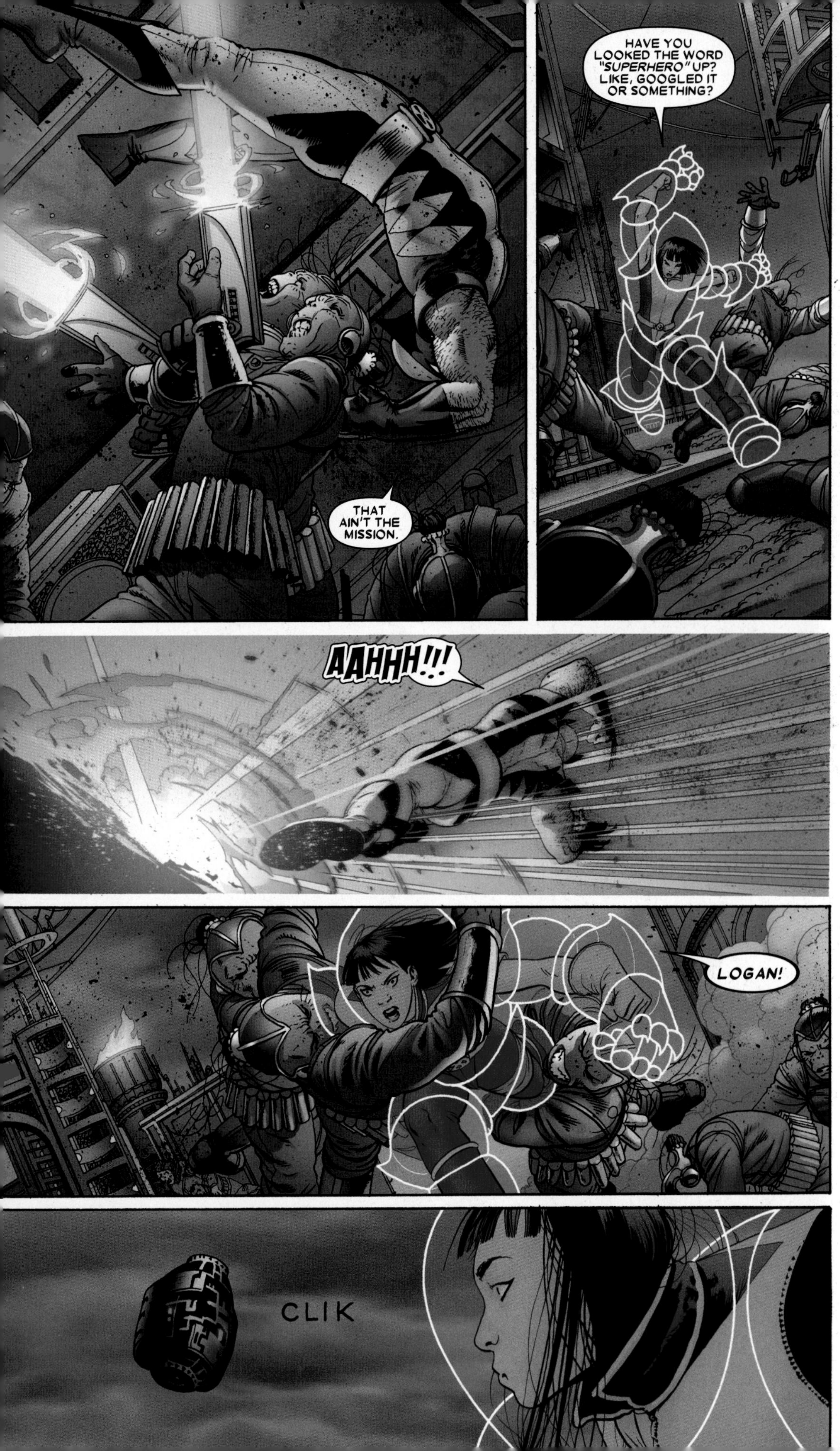
THAT AIN'T THE MISSION.
HAVE YOU LOOKED THE WORD "SUPERHERO" UP? LIKE, GOOGLED IT OR SOMETHING?
AAHHH!!!
LOGAN!
CLIK

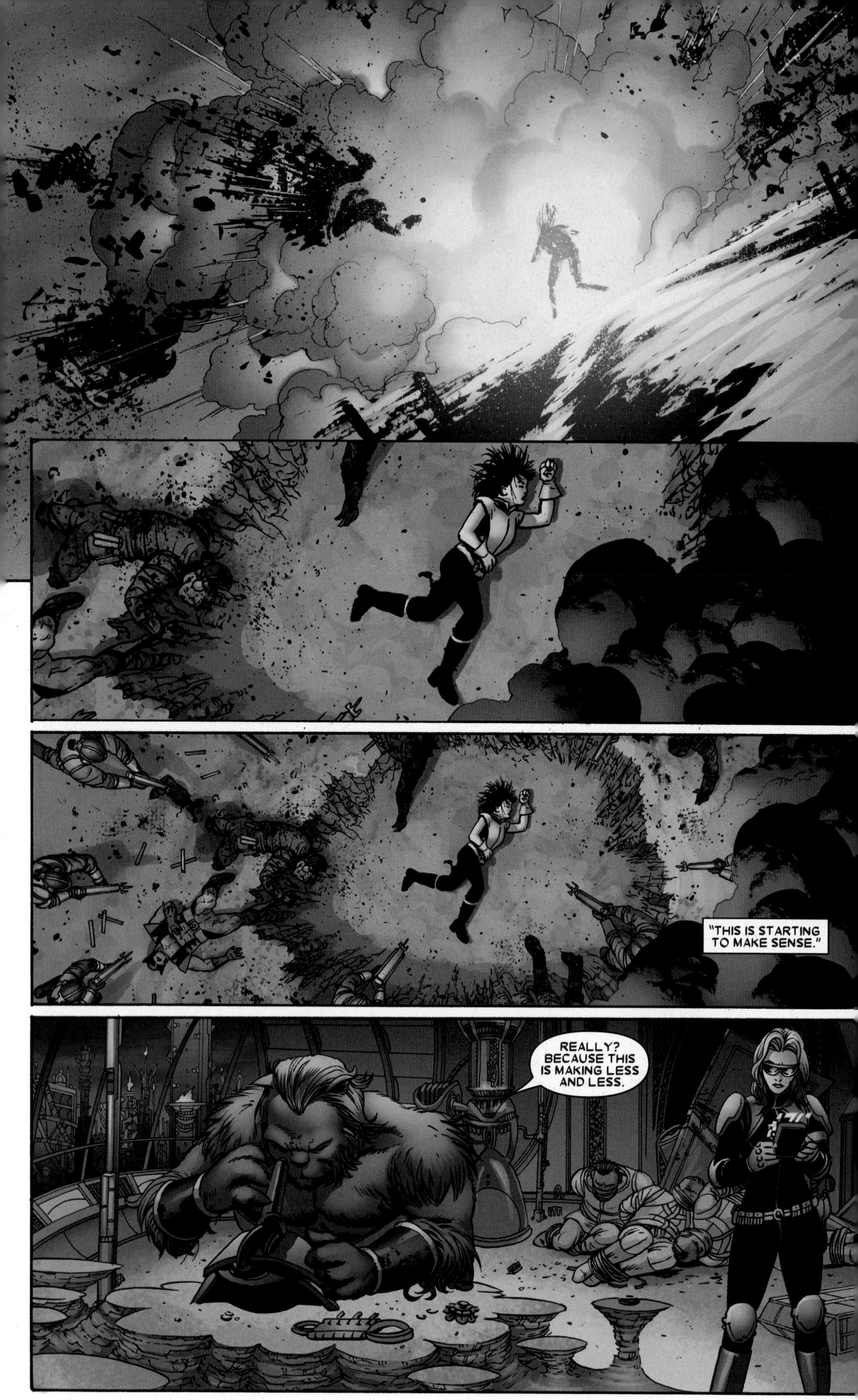
"THIS IS STARTING TO MAKE SENSE."
REALLY? BECAUSE THIS IS MAKING LESS AND LESS.

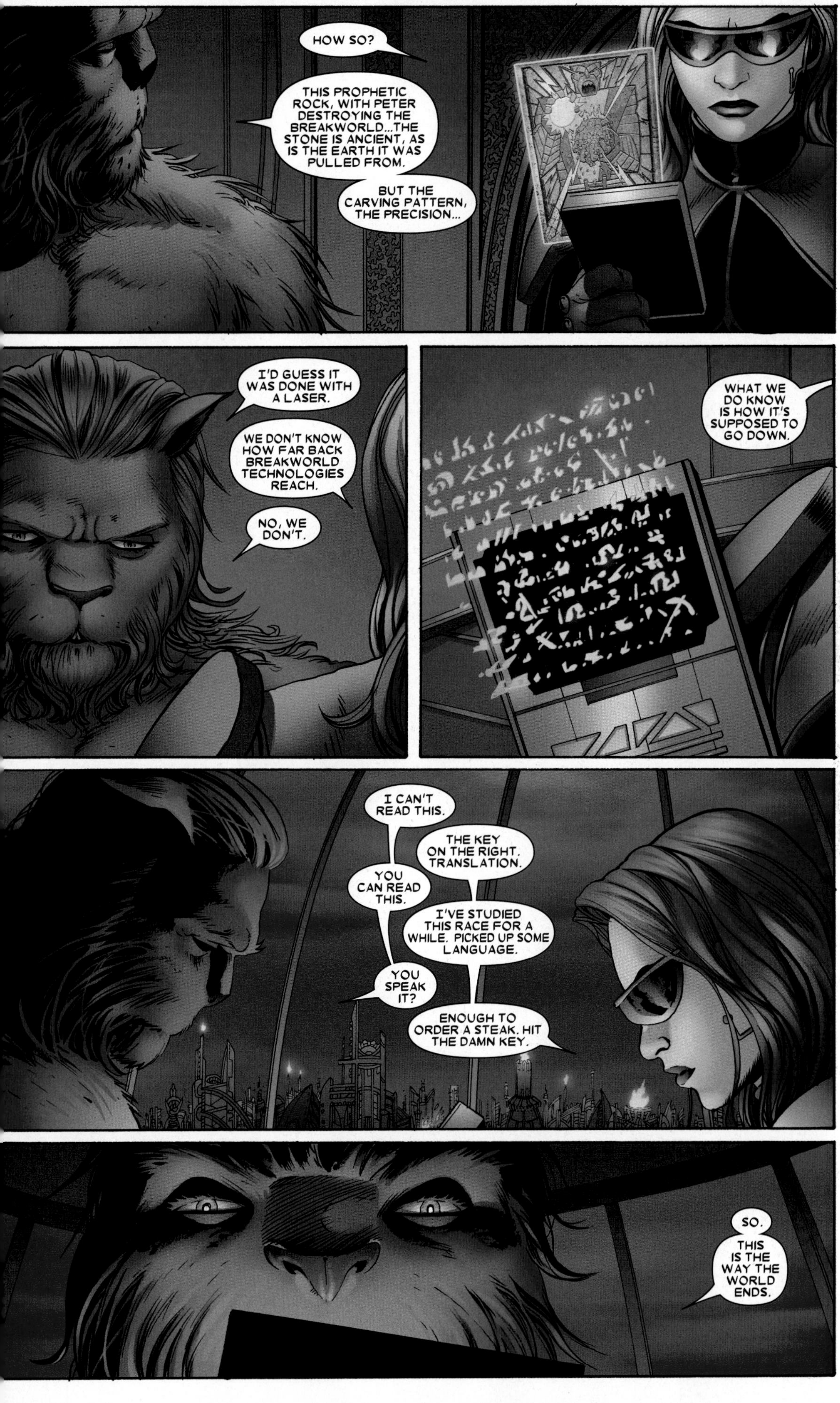

HOW SO?
THIS PROPHETIC ROCK, WITH PETER DESTROYING THE BREAKWORLD...THE STONE IS ANCIENT, AS IS THE EARTH IT WAS PULLED FROM.
BUT THE CARVING PATTERN, THE PRECISION...
I'D GUESS IT WAS DONE WITH A LASER.
WE DON'T KNOW HOW FAR BACK BREAKWORLD TECHNOLOGIES REACH.
NO, WE DON'T.
WHAT WE DO KNOW IS HOW IT'S SUPPOSED TO GO DOWN.
I CAN'T READ THIS.
THE KEY ON THE RIGHT. TRANSLATION.
YOU CAN READ THIS.
I'VE STUDIED THIS RACE FOR A WHILE. PICKED UP SOME LANGUAGE.
YOU SPEAK IT?
ENOUGH TO ORDER A STEAK. HIT THE DAMN KEY.
SO.
THIS IS THE WAY THE WORLD ENDS.

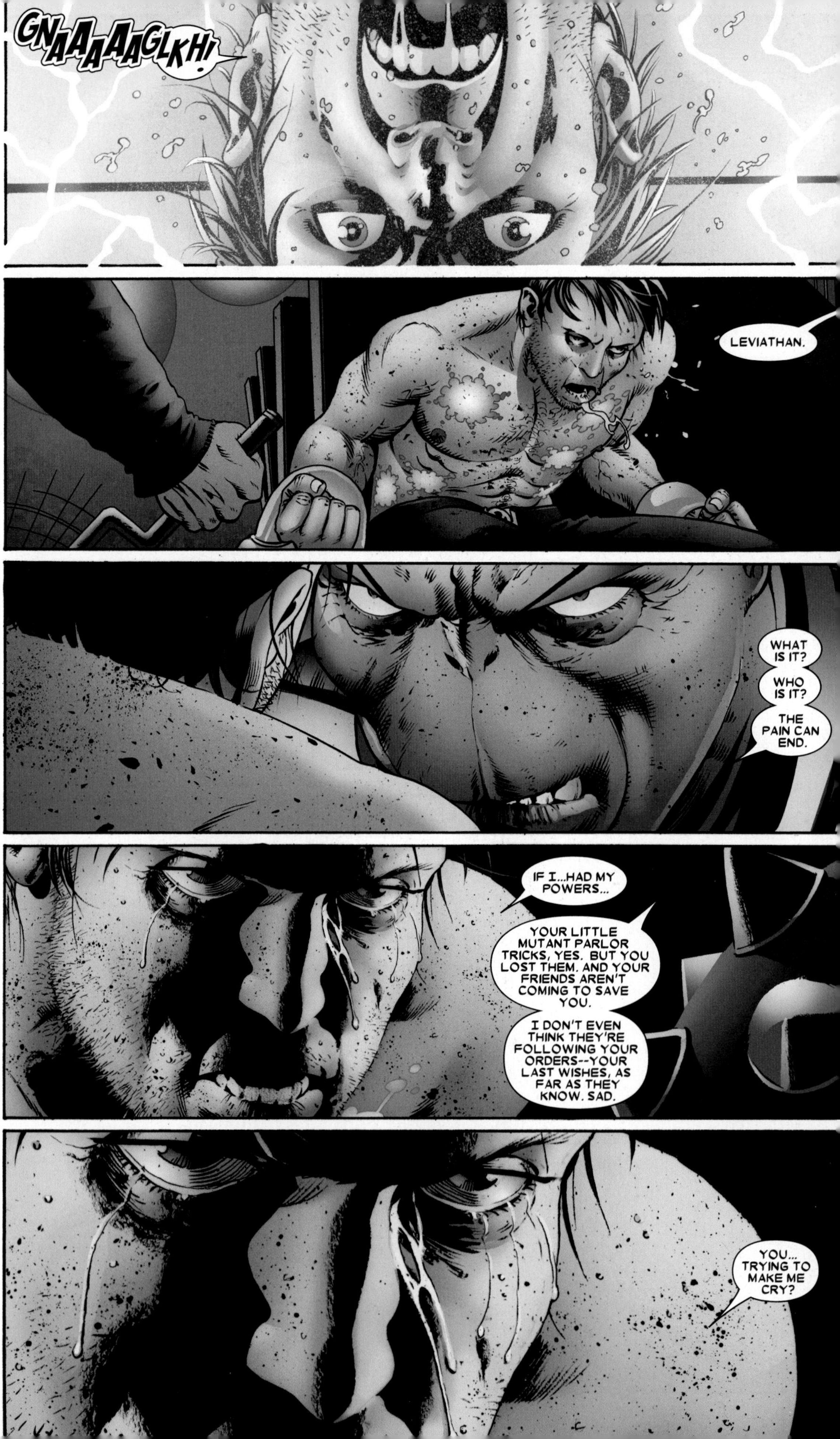
GNAAAAAGLKH!
LEVIATHAN.
WHAT IS IT?
WHO IS IT?
THE PAIN CAN END.
IF I...HAD MY POWERS...
YOUR LITTLE MUTANT PARLOR TRICKS, YES. BUT YOU LOST THEM. AND YOUR FRIENDS AREN'T COMING TO SAVE YOU.
I DON'T EVEN THINK THEY'RE FOLLOWING YOUR ORDERS--YOUR LAST WISHES, AS FAR AS THEY KNOW. SAD.
YOU... TRYING TO MAKE ME CRY?

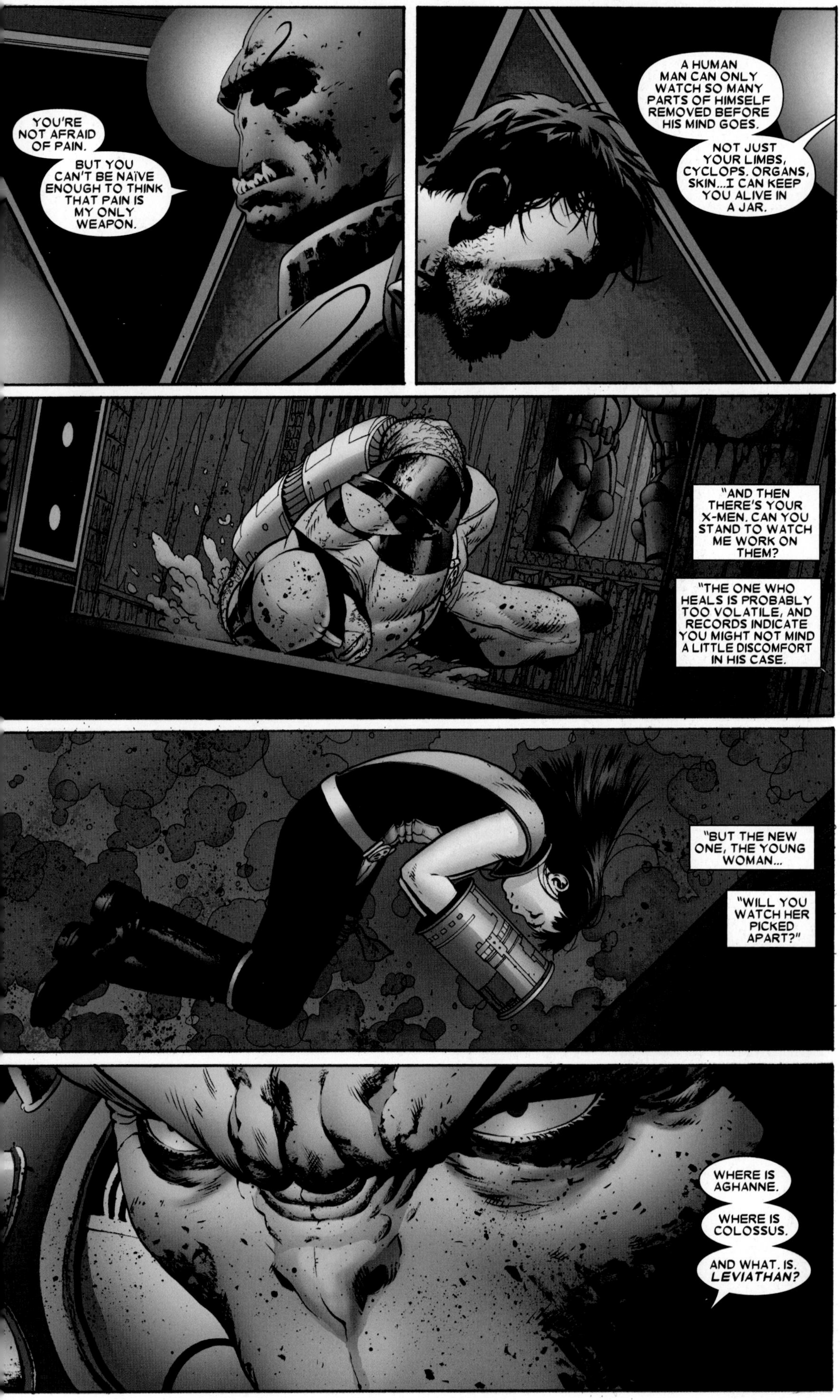
YOU'RE NOT AFRAID OF PAIN.
BUT YOU CAN'T BE NAÏVE ENOUGH TO THINK THAT PAIN IS MY ONLY WEAPON.
A HUMAN MAN CAN ONLY WATCH SO MANY PARTS OF HIMSELF REMOVED BEFORE HIS MIND GOES.
NOT JUST YOUR LIMBS, CYCLOPS. ORGANS, SKIN...I CAN KEEP YOU ALIVE IN A JAR.
"AND THEN THERE'S YOUR X-MEN. CAN YOU STAND TO WATCH ME WORK ON THEM?
"THE ONE WHO HEALS IS PROBABLY TOO VOLATILE, AND RECORDS INDICATE YOU MIGHT NOT MIND A LITTLE DISCOMFORT IN HIS CASE.
"BUT THE NEW ONE, THE YOUNG WOMAN...
"WILL YOU WATCH HER PICKED APART?"
WHERE IS AGHANNE.
WHERE IS COLOSSUS.
AND WHAT. IS. *LEVIATHAN?*

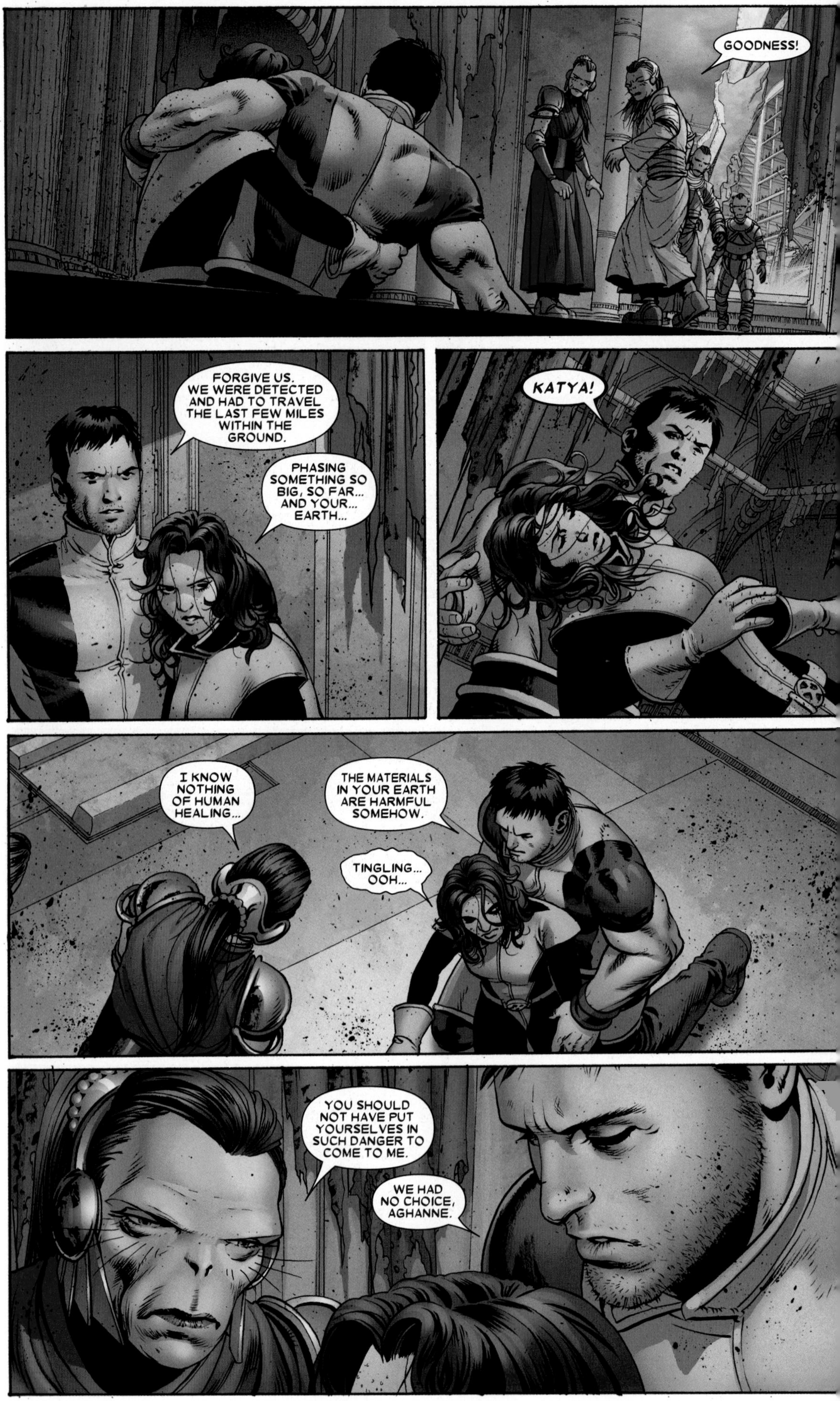
GOODNESS!
FORGIVE US. WE WERE DETECTED AND HAD TO TRAVEL THE LAST FEW MILES WITHIN THE GROUND.
PHASING SOMETHING SO BIG, SO FAR... AND YOUR... EARTH...
KATYA!
I KNOW NOTHING OF HUMAN HEALING...
THE MATERIALS IN YOUR EARTH ARE HARMFUL SOMEHOW.
TINGLING... OOH...
YOU SHOULD NOT HAVE PUT YOURSELVES IN SUCH DANGER TO COME TO ME.
WE HAD NO CHOICE, AGHANNE.

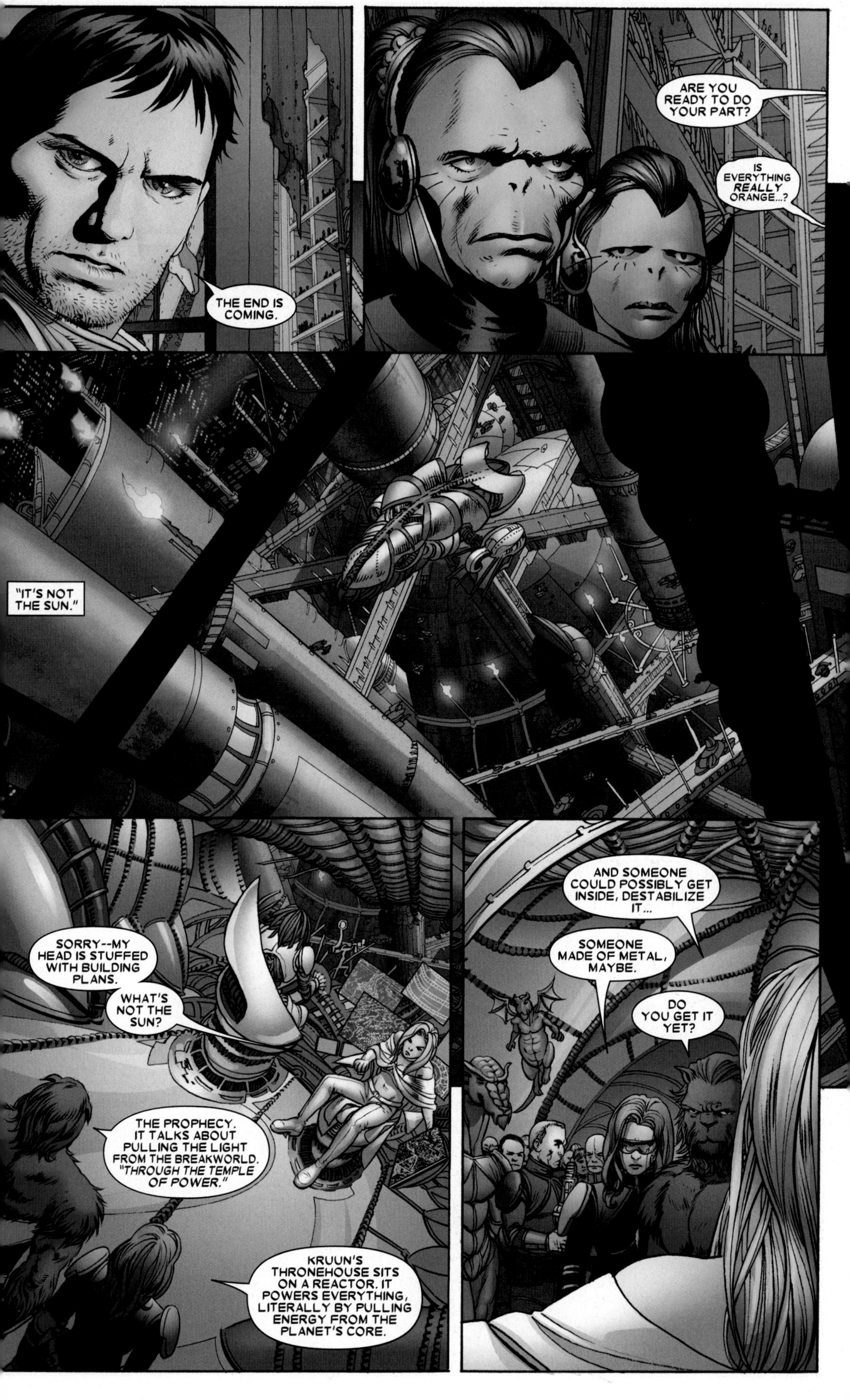
THE END IS COMING.
ARE YOU READY TO DO YOUR PART?
IS EVERYTHING *REALLY* ORANGE...?
"IT'S NOT THE SUN."
SORRY--MY HEAD IS STUFFED WITH BUILDING PLANS.
WHAT'S NOT THE SUN?
THE PROPHECY. IT TALKS ABOUT PULLING THE LIGHT FROM THE BREAKWORLD. *"THROUGH THE TEMPLE OF POWER."*
KRUUN'S THRONEHOUSE SITS ON A REACTOR. IT POWERS EVERYTHING, LITERALLY BY PULLING ENERGY FROM THE PLANET'S CORE.
AND SOMEONE COULD POSSIBLY GET INSIDE, DESTABILIZE IT...
SOMEONE MADE OF METAL, MAYBE.
DO YOU GET IT YET?

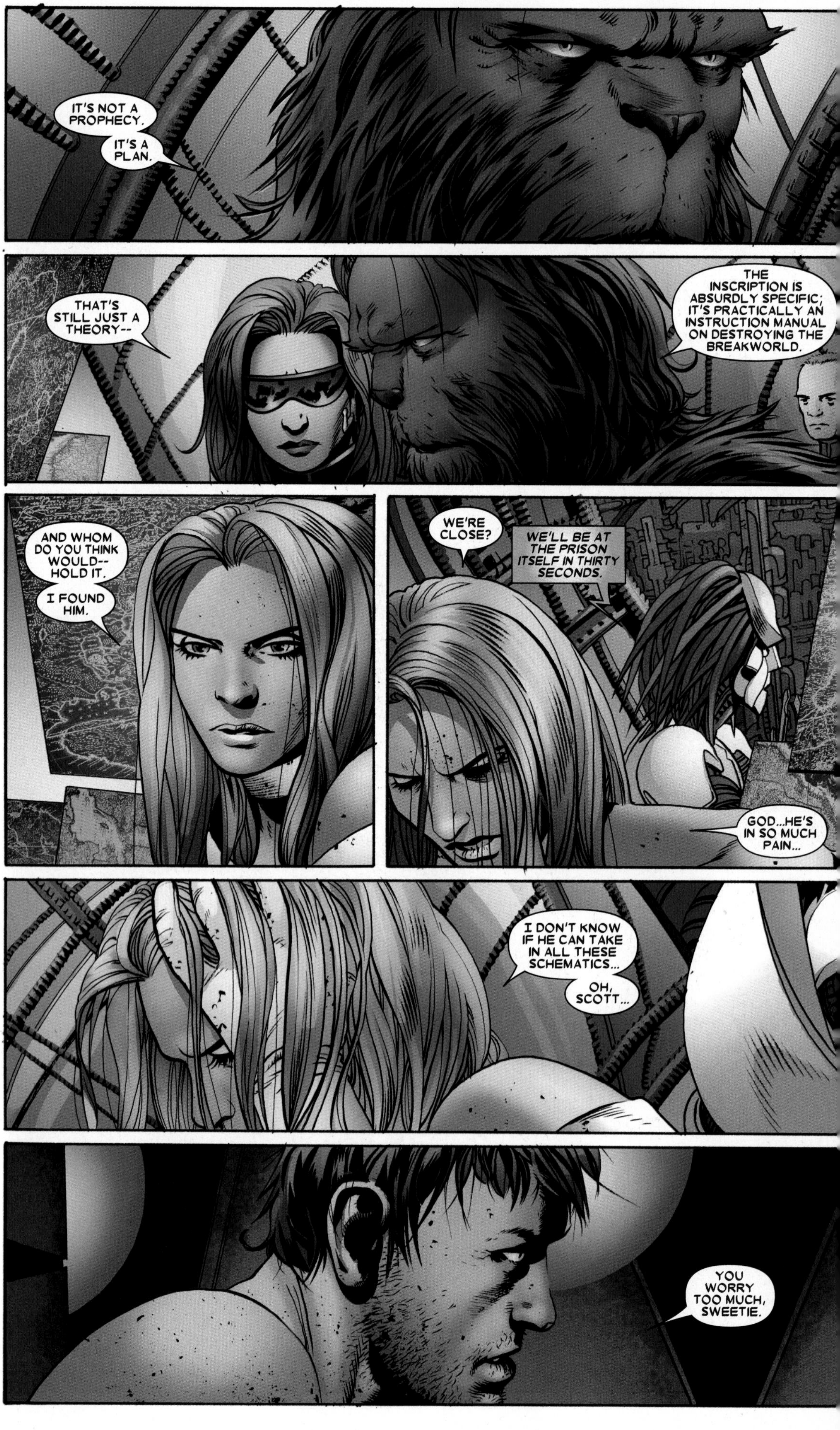
IT'S NOT A PROPHECY.
IT'S A PLAN.
THAT'S STILL JUST A THEORY--
THE INSCRIPTION IS ABSURDLY SPECIFIC; IT'S PRACTICALLY AN INSTRUCTION MANUAL ON DESTROYING THE BREAKWORLD.
AND WHOM DO YOU THINK WOULD-- HOLD IT.
I FOUND HIM.
WE'RE CLOSE?
WE'LL BE AT THE PRISON ITSELF IN THIRTY SECONDS.
GOD...HE'S IN SO MUCH PAIN...
I DON'T KNOW IF HE CAN TAKE IN ALL THESE SCHEMATICS...
OH, SCOTT...
YOU WORRY TOO MUCH, SWEETIE.

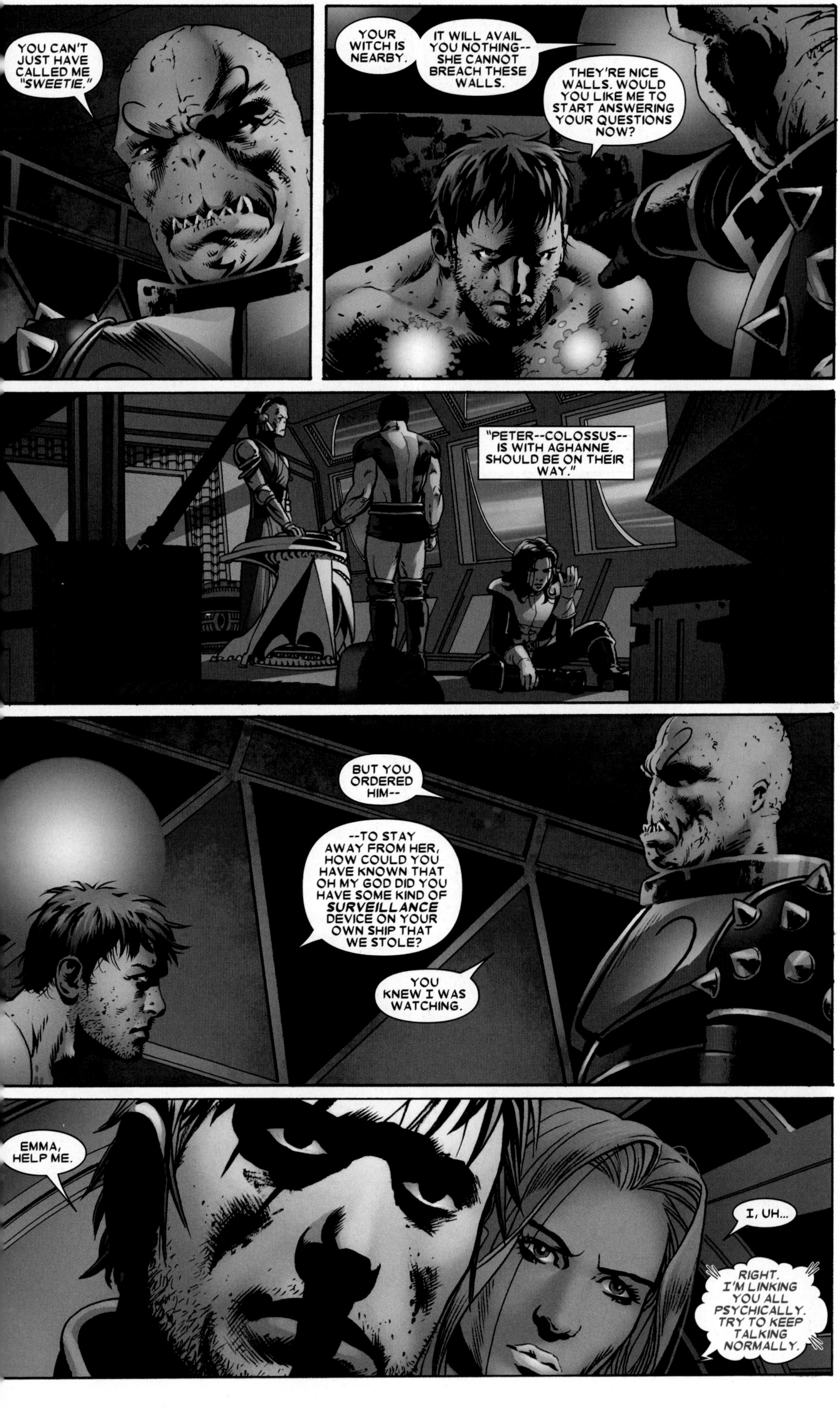
YOU CAN'T JUST HAVE CALLED ME "SWEETIE."
YOUR WITCH IS NEARBY.
IT WILL AVAIL YOU NOTHING-- SHE CANNOT BREACH THESE WALLS.
THEY'RE NICE WALLS. WOULD YOU LIKE ME TO START ANSWERING YOUR QUESTIONS NOW?
"PETER--COLOSSUS-- IS WITH AGHANNE. SHOULD BE ON THEIR WAY."
BUT YOU ORDERED HIM--
--TO STAY AWAY FROM HER, HOW COULD YOU HAVE KNOWN THAT OH MY GOD DID YOU HAVE SOME KIND OF SURVEILLANCE DEVICE ON YOUR OWN SHIP THAT WE STOLE?
YOU KNEW I WAS WATCHING.
EMMA, HELP ME.
I, UH...
RIGHT. I'M LINKING YOU ALL PSYCHICALLY. TRY TO KEEP TALKING NORMALLY.

WE NEED TO GET CLOSE TO KRUUN. THAT WON'T HAPPEN UNLESS HE THINKS WE'RE HELPLESS.

SO I'LL TAKE THE REPAIR SHIP AND GET MYSELF CAPTURED.

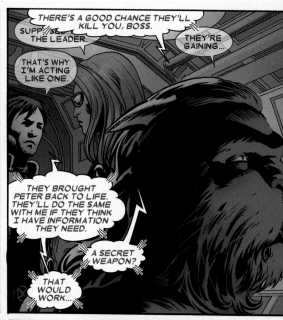

THERE'S A GOOD CHANCE THEY'LL KILL YOU, BOSS.

SUPPOSE THE LEADER.

THAT'S WHY I'M ACTING LIKE ONE.

THEY'RE GAINING...

THEY BROUGHT PETER BACK TO LIFE. THEY'LL DO THE SAME WITH ME IF THEY THINK I HAVE INFORMATION THEY NEED.

A SECRET WEAPON?

THAT WOULD WORK...

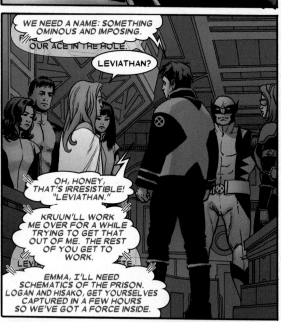

WE NEED A NAME: SOMETHING OMINOUS AND IMPOSING.

OUR ACE IN THE HOLE.

LEVIATHAN?

OH, HONEY, THAT'S IRRESISTIBLE! "LEVIATHAN."

KRUUN'LL WORK ME OVER FOR A WHILE TRYING TO GET THAT OUT OF ME. THE REST OF YOU GET TO WORK.

EMMA, I'LL NEED SCHEMATICS OF THE PRISON. LOGAN AND HISAKO, GET YOURSELVES CAPTURED IN A FEW HOURS SO WE'VE GOT A FORCE INSIDE.

I OBJECT!

WHAT?

BUGGER ME, WAS THAT ACTING?

IS NOT COURTROOM DRAMA, KATYA. GONNA THROW YOU...

SHUT UP! I'M NOT GOOD AT HAVING TWO CONVERSATIONS AT ONCE. AND I HATE SCOTT'S PLAN!

YOU MEAN YOU "OBJECT" TO IT. BUT I'M GONNA ALLOW IT.

S#!%. I'M GONNA CRACK UP. I'M CRACKING UP.

SAY SOMETHING CYNICAL.

RIGHT. RIGHT.

EXCUSE ME, I'M THE ONE WHO'S GONNA

AGENT BRAND, YOU AND HANK WORK THAT PROPHECY. PETER, BRING AGHANNE INTO THE FOLD IF YOU CAN. BE OUTSIDE THE PRISON IN A FEW HOURS. BRING EVERYONE.

STA... KR... FR... EVE...

I'D BETTER GO BEFORE KITTY TRIES TO ACT AGAIN.

EMMA

SCOTT, IF KRUUN HAS YOU AT HIS MERCY...

DON'T WORRY, MY LOVE...

"LEVIATHAN" WILL SAVE ME.

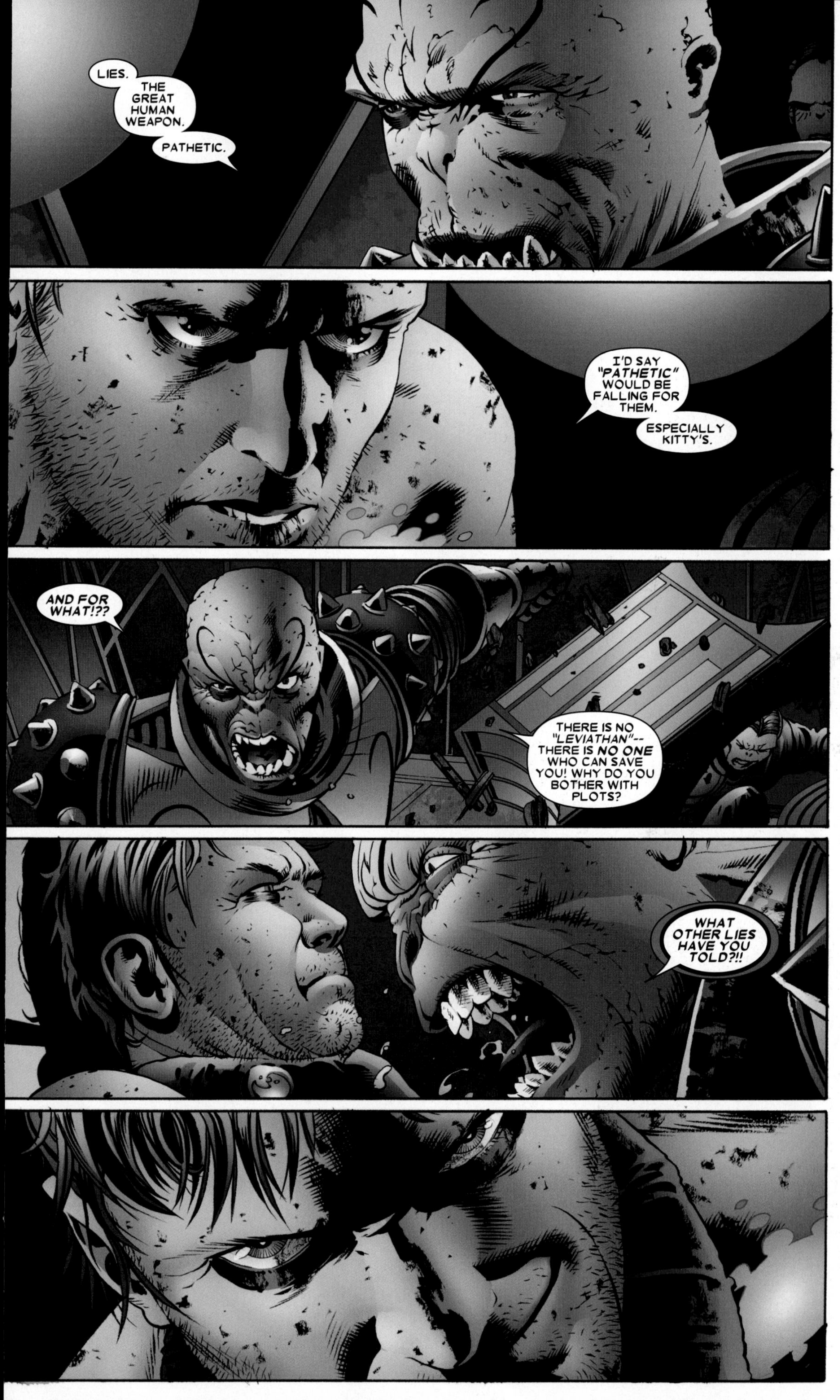
LIES.
THE GREAT HUMAN WEAPON.
PATHETIC.
I'D SAY "PATHETIC" WOULD BE FALLING FOR THEM.
ESPECIALLY KITTY'S.
AND FOR WHAT!??
THERE IS NO "LEVIATHAN"-- THERE IS NO ONE WHO CAN SAVE YOU! WHY DO YOU BOTHER WITH PLOTS?
WHAT OTHER LIES HAVE YOU TOLD?!!

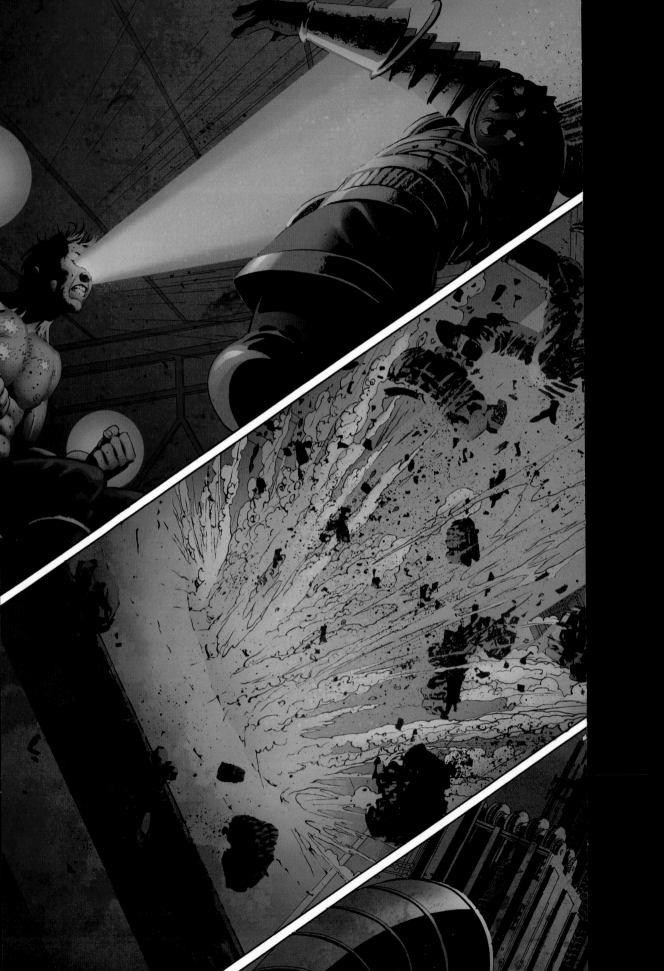

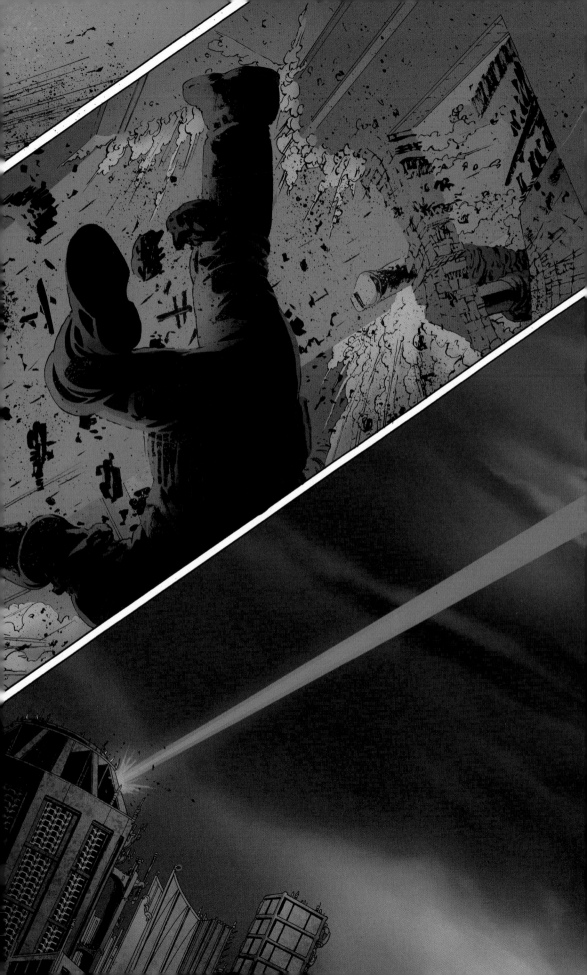

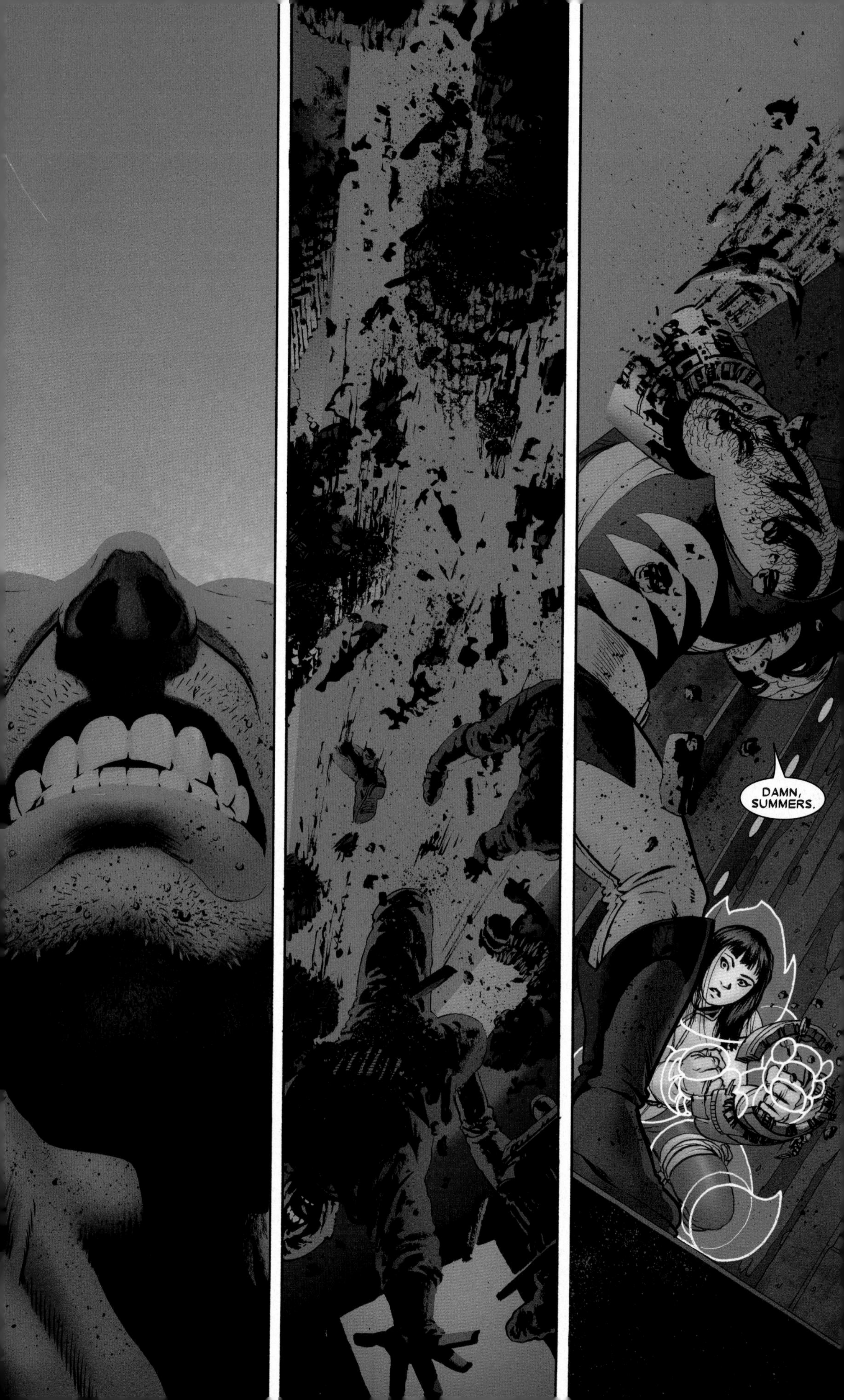
DAMN, SUMMERS.

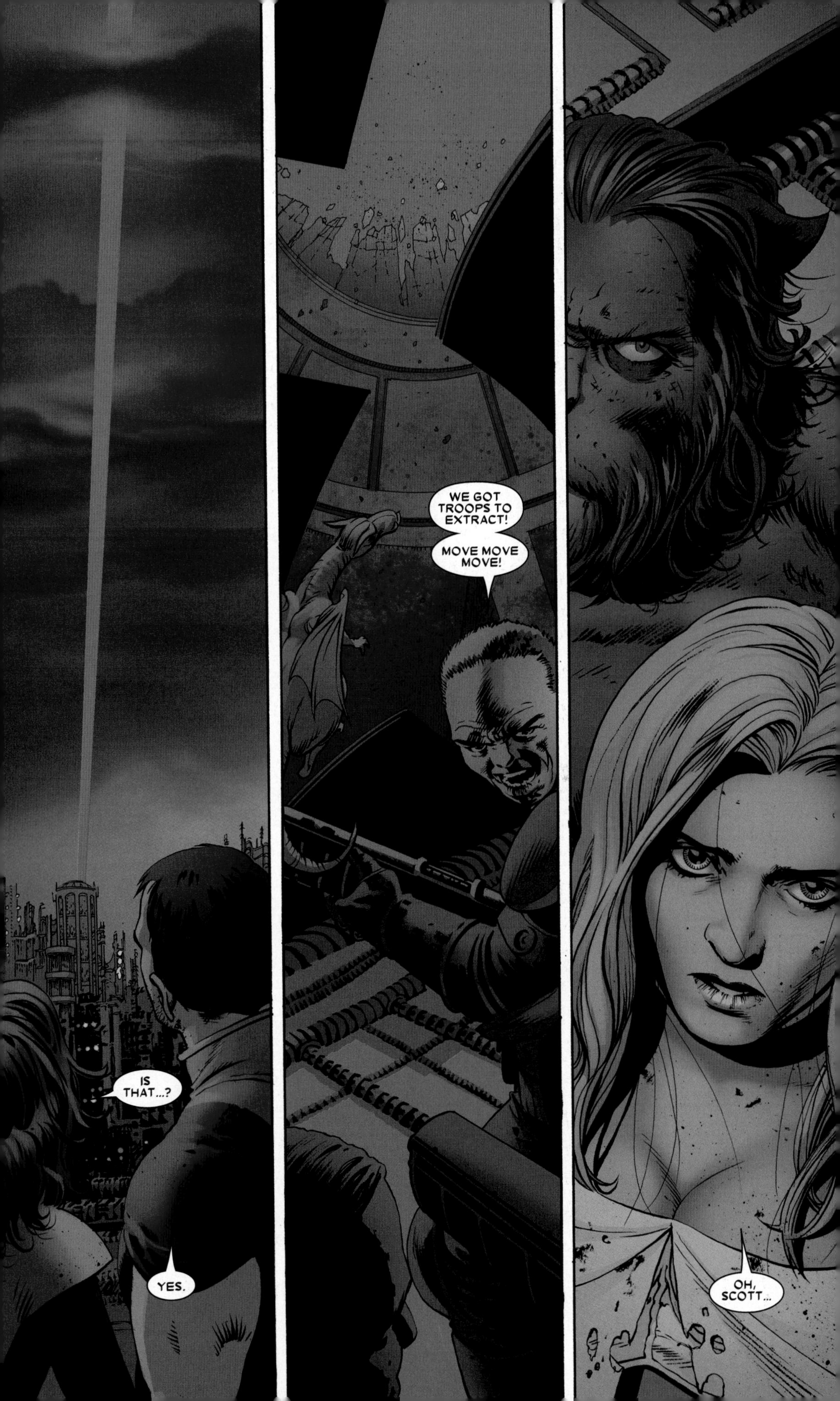
IS THAT...?
YES.
WE GOT TROOPS TO EXTRACT!
MOVE MOVE MOVE!
OH, SCOTT...

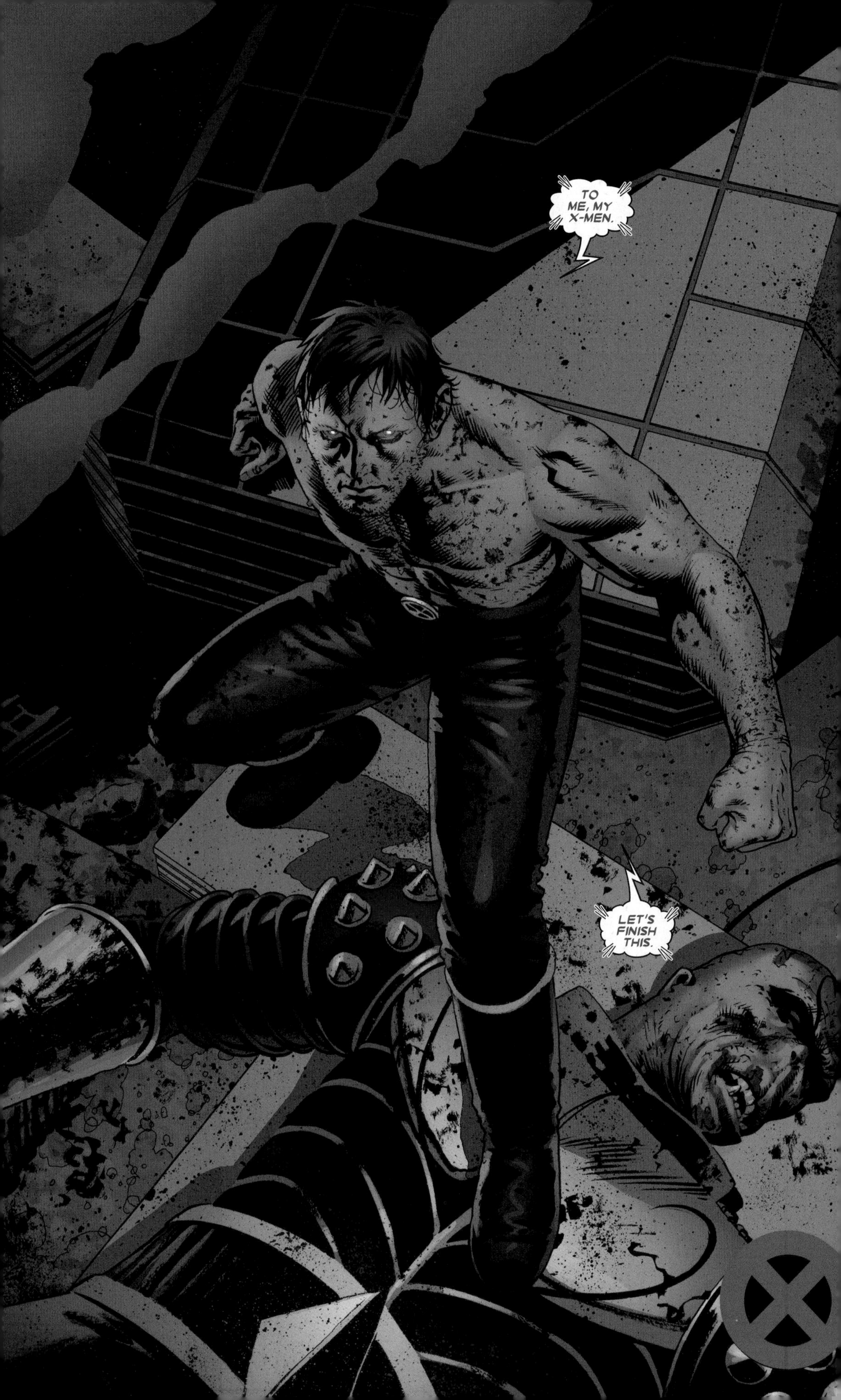
TO ME, MY X-MEN.
LET'S FINISH THIS.

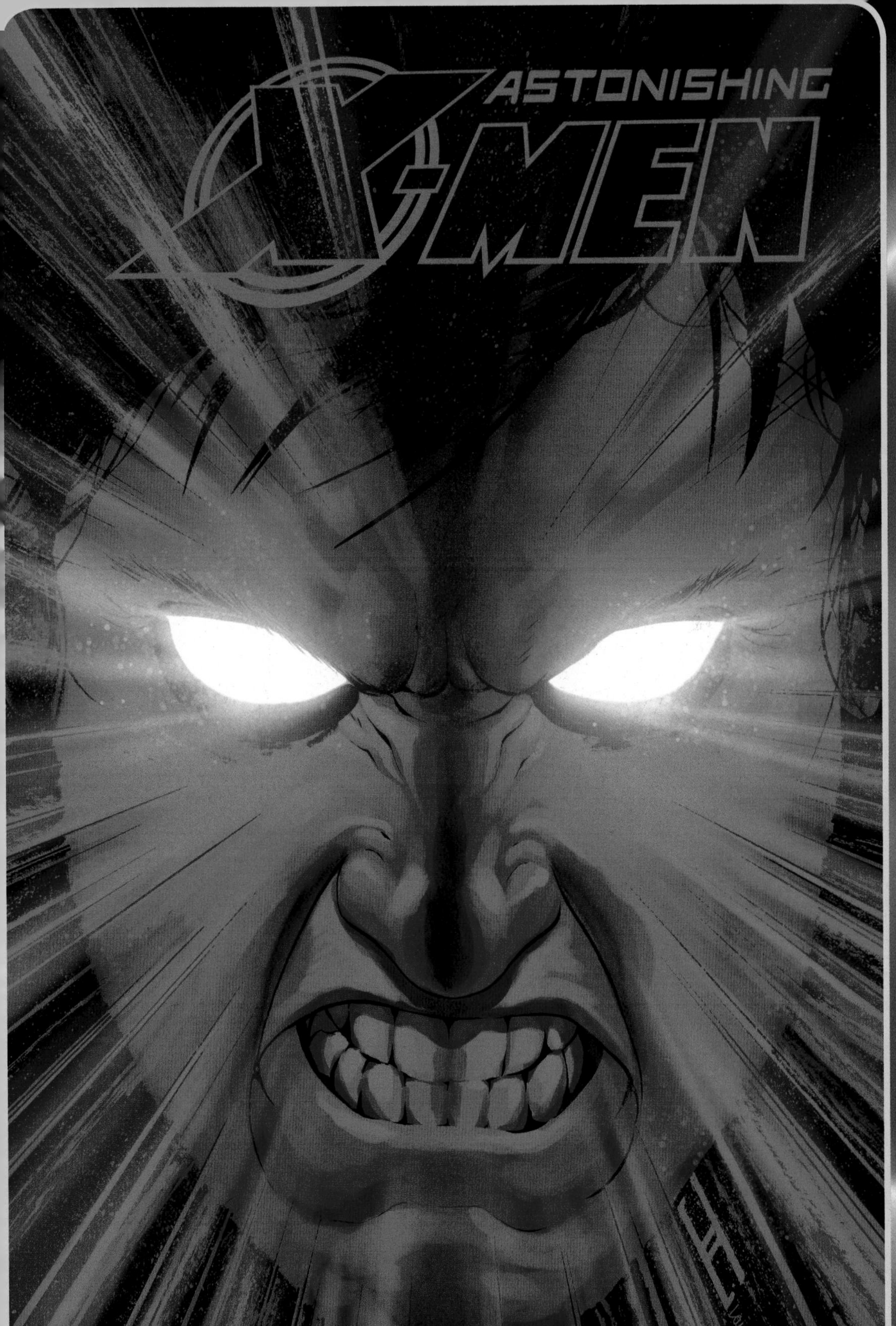
ASTONISHING
X-MEN

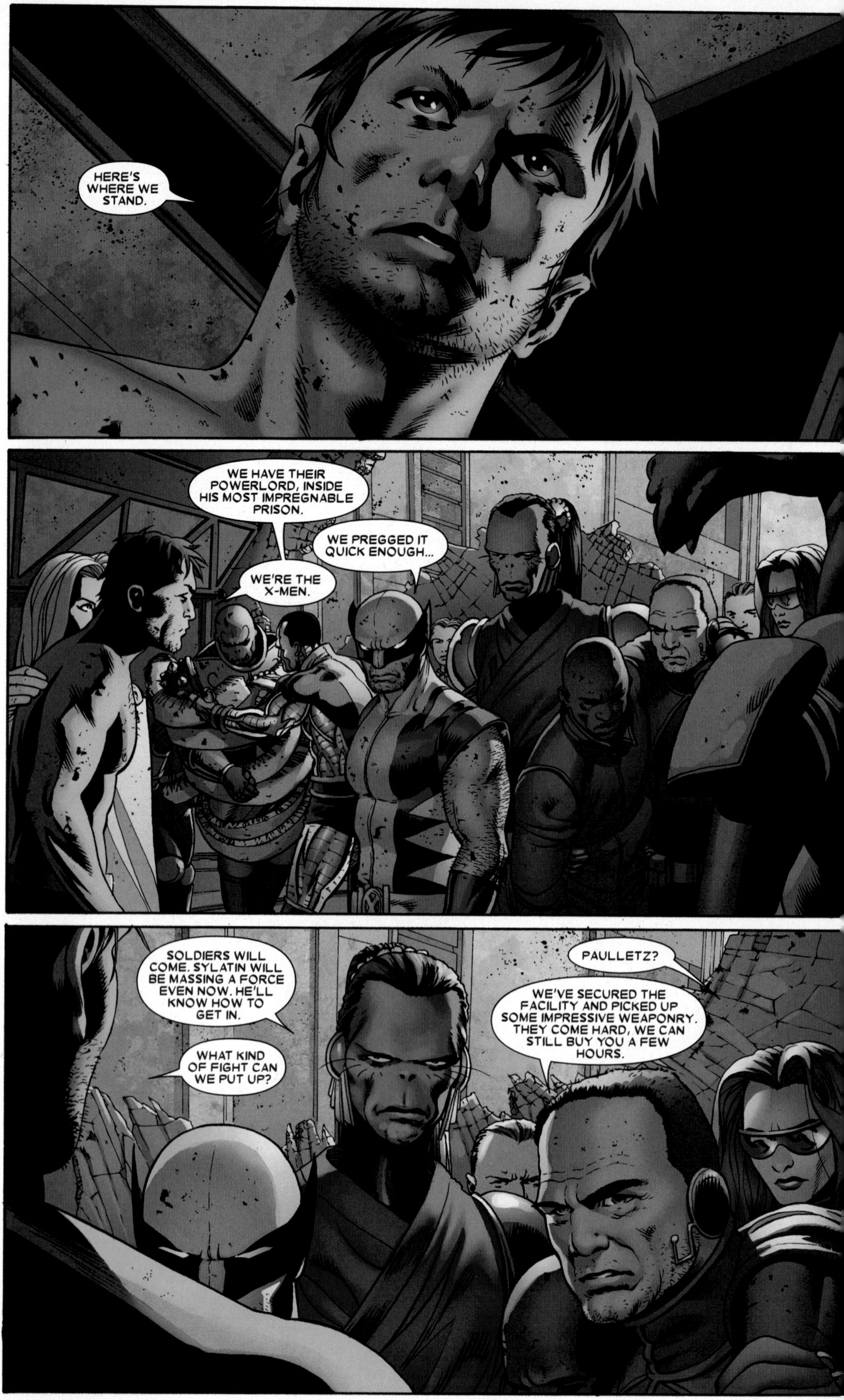
HERE'S WHERE WE STAND.
WE HAVE THEIR POWERLORD, INSIDE HIS MOST IMPREGNABLE PRISON.
WE'RE THE X-MEN.
WE PREGGED IT QUICK ENOUGH...
SOLDIERS WILL COME. SYLATIN WILL BE MASSING A FORCE EVEN NOW. HE'LL KNOW HOW TO GET IN.
WHAT KIND OF FIGHT CAN WE PUT UP?
PAULLETZ?
WE'VE SECURED THE FACILITY AND PICKED UP SOME IMPRESSIVE WEAPONRY. THEY COME HARD, WE CAN STILL BUY YOU A FEW HOURS.

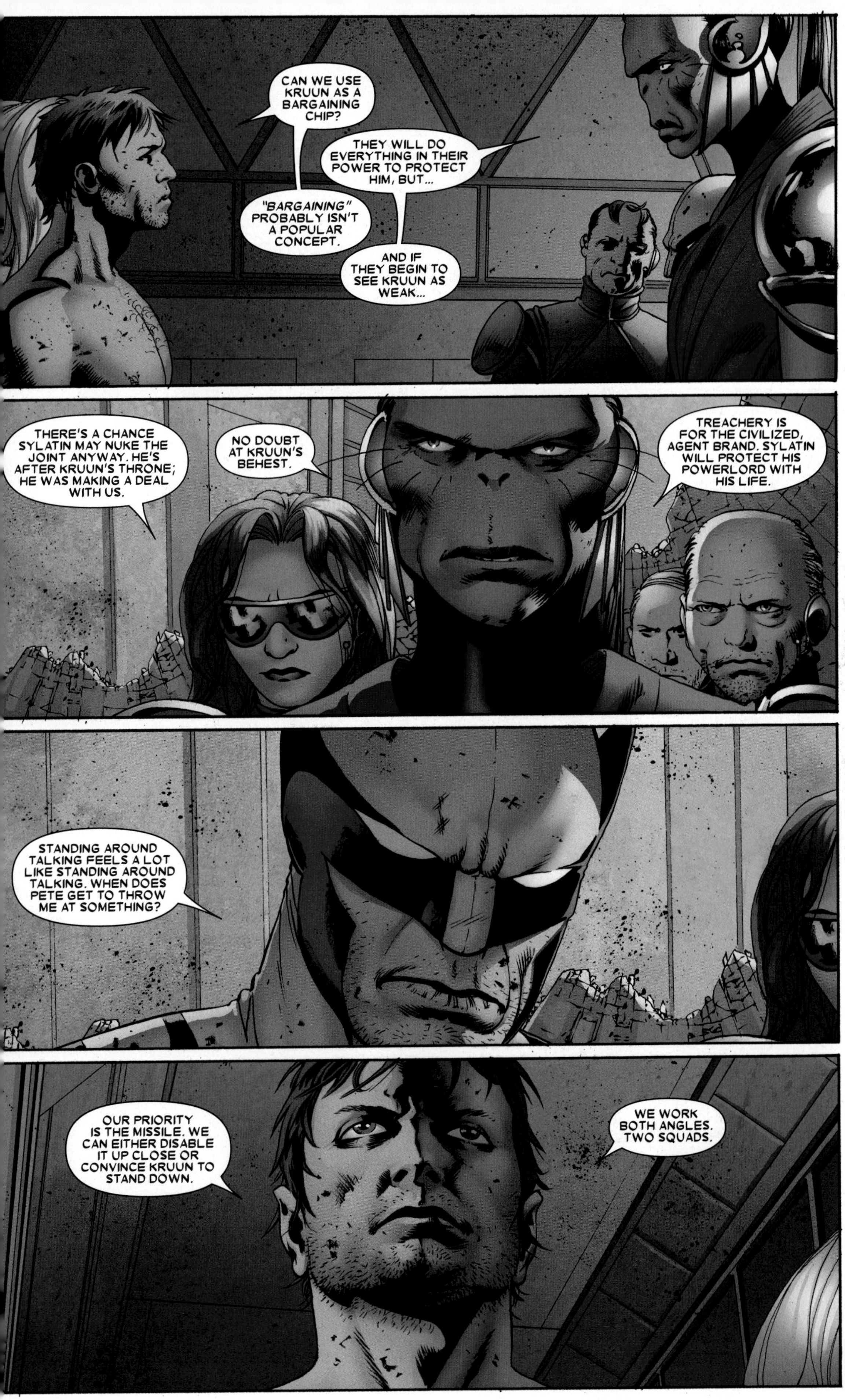

CAN WE USE KRUUN AS A BARGAINING CHIP?
"BARGAINING" PROBABLY ISN'T A POPULAR CONCEPT.
THEY WILL DO EVERYTHING IN THEIR POWER TO PROTECT HIM, BUT...
AND IF THEY BEGIN TO SEE KRUUN AS WEAK...
THERE'S A CHANCE SYLATIN MAY NUKE THE JOINT ANYWAY. HE'S AFTER KRUUN'S THRONE; HE WAS MAKING A DEAL WITH US.
NO DOUBT AT KRUUN'S BEHEST.
TREACHERY IS FOR THE CIVILIZED, AGENT BRAND. SYLATIN WILL PROTECT HIS POWERLORD WITH HIS LIFE.
STANDING AROUND TALKING FEELS A LOT LIKE STANDING AROUND TALKING. WHEN DOES PETE GET TO THROW ME AT SOMETHING?
OUR PRIORITY IS THE MISSILE. WE CAN EITHER DISABLE IT UP CLOSE OR CONVINCE KRUUN TO STAND DOWN.
WE WORK BOTH ANGLES. TWO SQUADS.

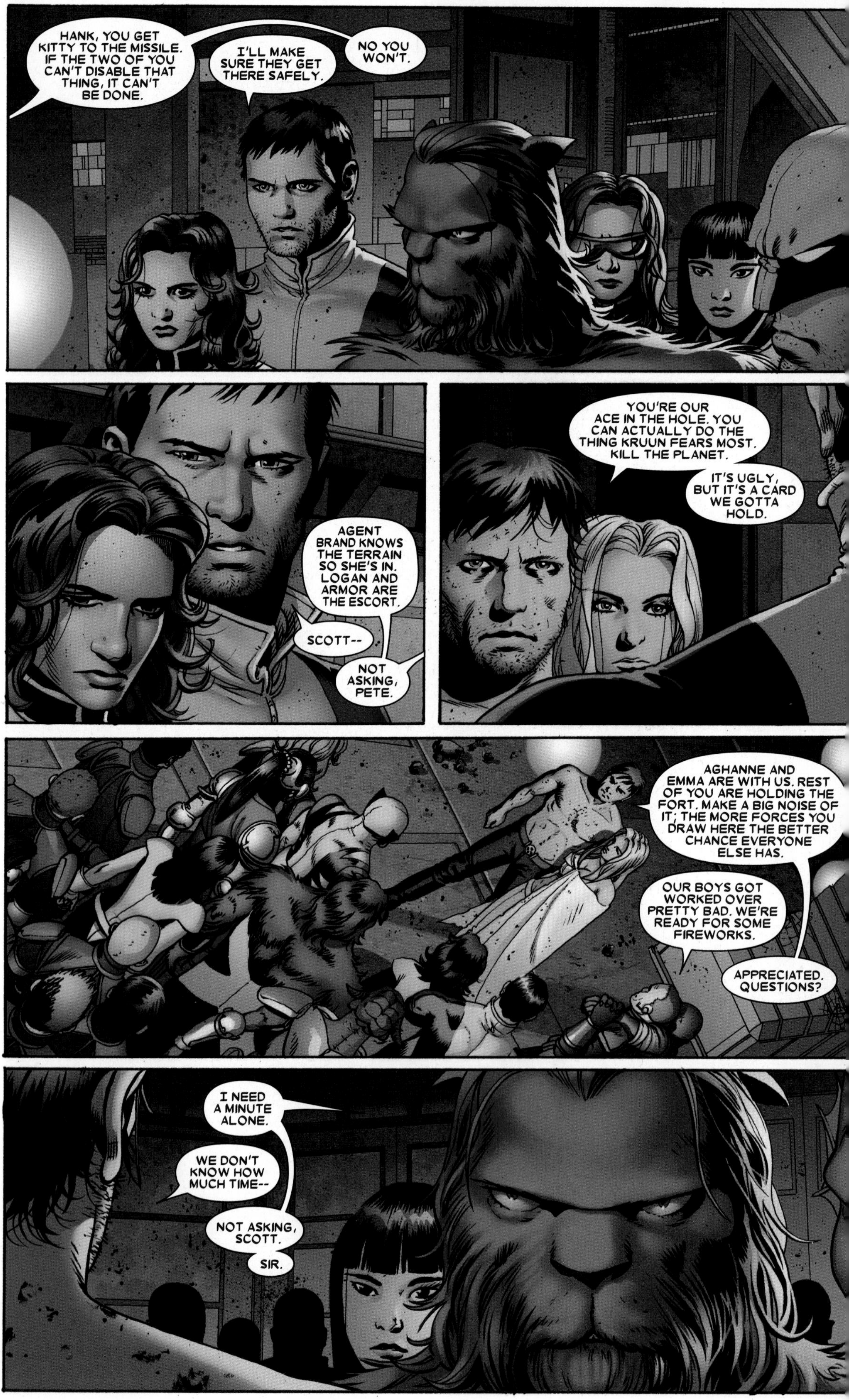

HANK, YOU GET KITTY TO THE MISSILE. IF THE TWO OF YOU CAN'T DISABLE THAT THING, IT CAN'T BE DONE.
I'LL MAKE SURE THEY GET THERE SAFELY.
NO YOU WON'T.
AGENT BRAND KNOWS THE TERRAIN SO SHE'S IN. LOGAN AND ARMOR ARE THE ESCORT.
SCOTT--
NOT ASKING, PETE.
YOU'RE OUR ACE IN THE HOLE. YOU CAN ACTUALLY DO THE THING KRUUN FEARS MOST. KILL THE PLANET.
IT'S UGLY, BUT IT'S A CARD WE GOTTA HOLD.
AGHANNE AND EMMA ARE WITH US. REST OF YOU ARE HOLDING THE FORT. MAKE A BIG NOISE OF IT; THE MORE FORCES YOU DRAW HERE THE BETTER CHANCE EVERYONE ELSE HAS.
OUR BOYS GOT WORKED OVER PRETTY BAD. WE'RE READY FOR SOME FIREWORKS.
APPRECIATED. QUESTIONS?
I NEED A MINUTE ALONE.
WE DON'T KNOW HOW MUCH TIME--
NOT ASKING, SCOTT.
SIR.

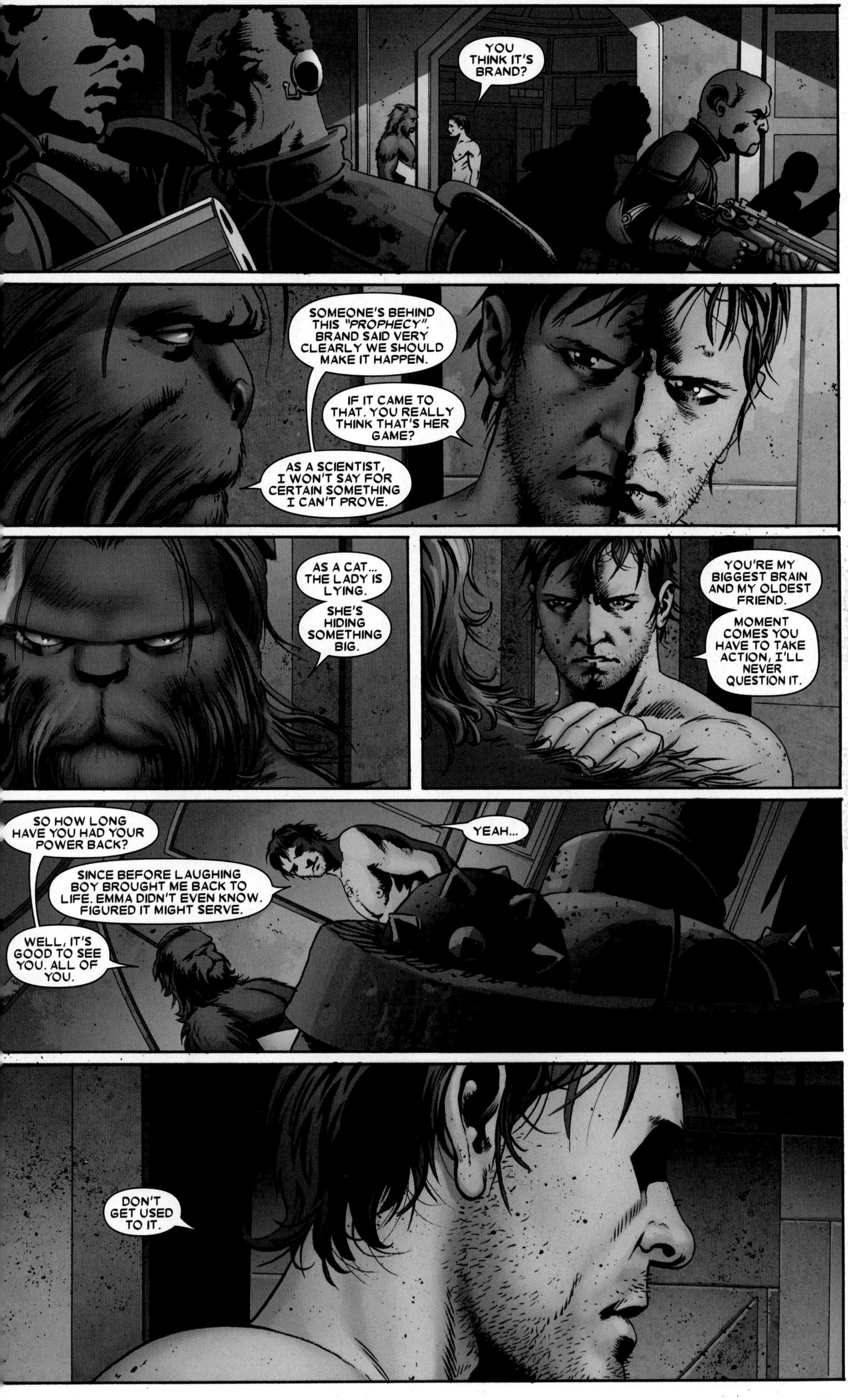
YOU THINK IT'S BRAND?
SOMEONE'S BEHIND THIS "PROPHECY". BRAND SAID VERY CLEARLY WE SHOULD MAKE IT HAPPEN.
IF IT CAME TO THAT. YOU REALLY THINK THAT'S HER GAME?
AS A SCIENTIST, I WON'T SAY FOR CERTAIN SOMETHING I CAN'T PROVE.
AS A CAT... THE LADY IS LYING.
SHE'S HIDING SOMETHING BIG.
YOU'RE MY BIGGEST BRAIN AND MY OLDEST FRIEND.
MOMENT COMES YOU HAVE TO TAKE ACTION, I'LL NEVER QUESTION IT.
SO HOW LONG HAVE YOU HAD YOUR POWER BACK?
YEAH...
SINCE BEFORE LAUGHING BOY BROUGHT ME BACK TO LIFE. EMMA DIDN'T EVEN KNOW. FIGURED IT MIGHT SERVE.
WELL, IT'S GOOD TO SEE YOU. ALL OF YOU.
DON'T GET USED TO IT.

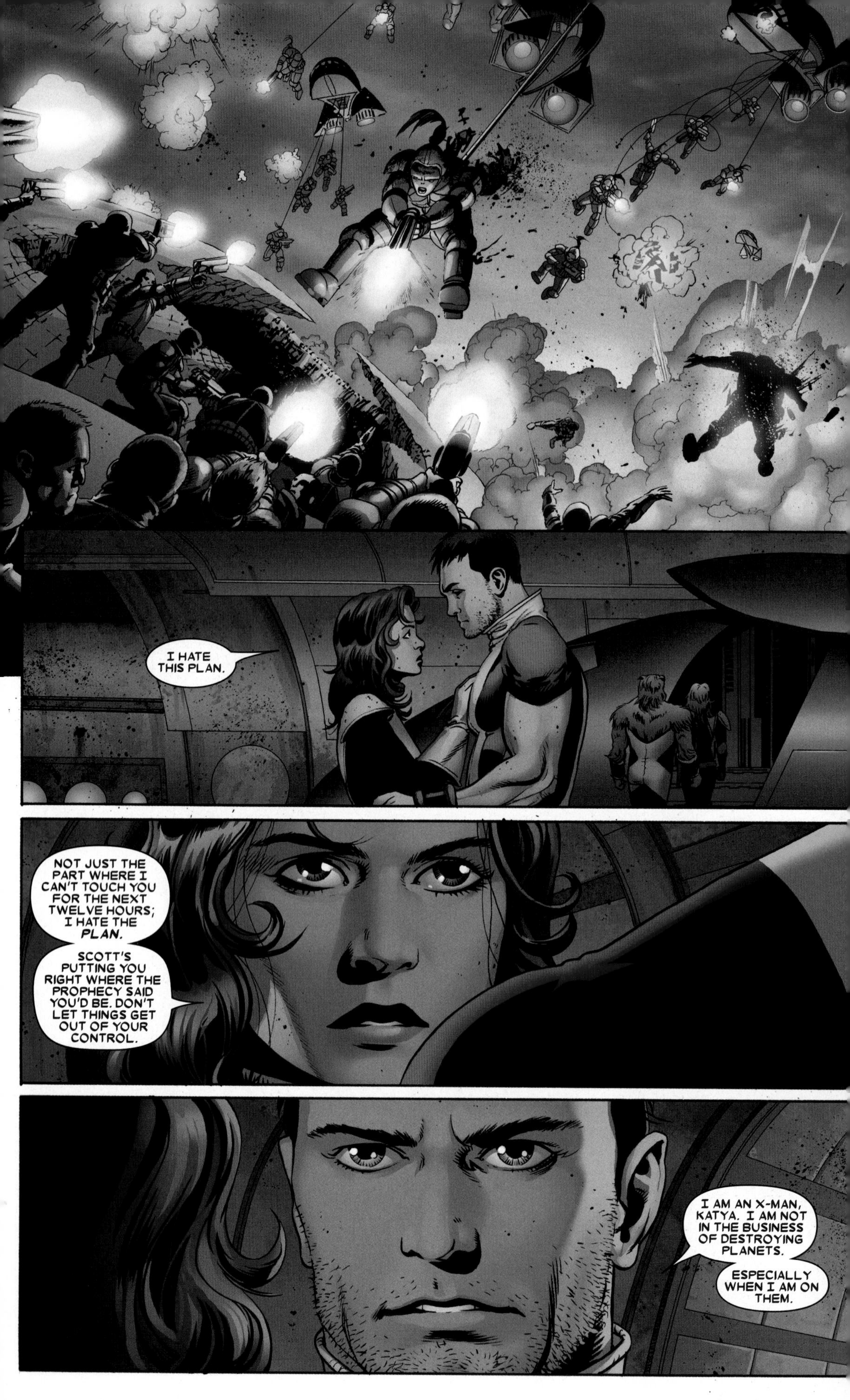
I HATE THIS PLAN.
NOT JUST THE PART WHERE I CAN'T TOUCH YOU FOR THE NEXT TWELVE HOURS; I HATE THE *PLAN.*
SCOTT'S PUTTING YOU RIGHT WHERE THE PROPHECY SAID YOU'D BE. DON'T LET THINGS GET OUT OF YOUR CONTROL.
I AM AN X-MAN, KATYA. I AM NOT IN THE BUSINESS OF DESTROYING PLANETS.
ESPECIALLY WHEN I AM ON THEM.

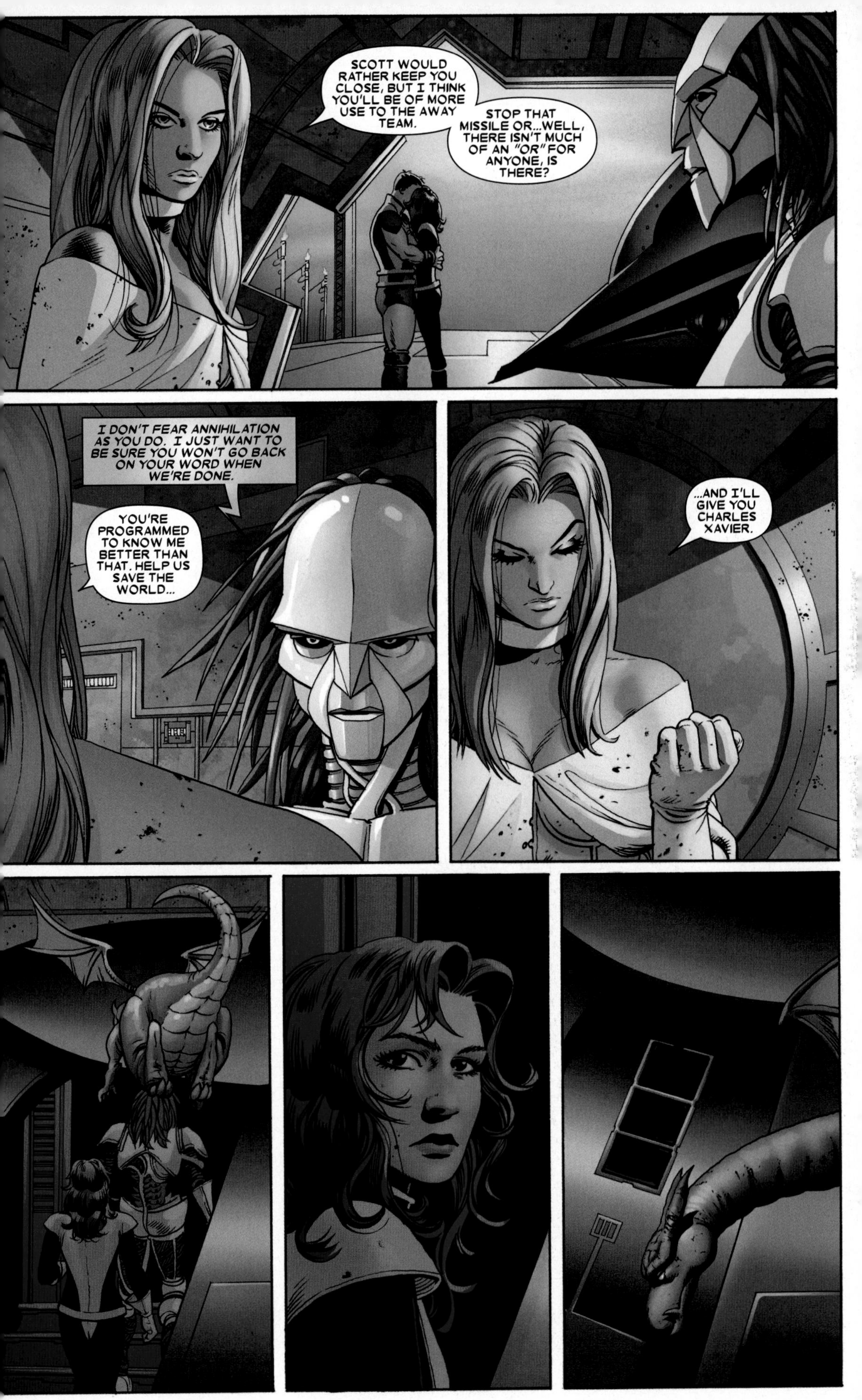
SCOTT WOULD RATHER KEEP YOU CLOSE, BUT I THINK YOU'LL BE OF MORE USE TO THE AWAY TEAM.
STOP THAT MISSILE OR...WELL, THERE ISN'T MUCH OF AN "OR" FOR ANYONE, IS THERE?
I DON'T FEAR ANNIHILATION AS YOU DO. I JUST WANT TO BE SURE YOU WON'T GO BACK ON YOUR WORD WHEN WE'RE DONE.
YOU'RE PROGRAMMED TO KNOW ME BETTER THAN THAT. HELP US SAVE THE WORLD...
...AND I'LL GIVE YOU CHARLES XAVIER.

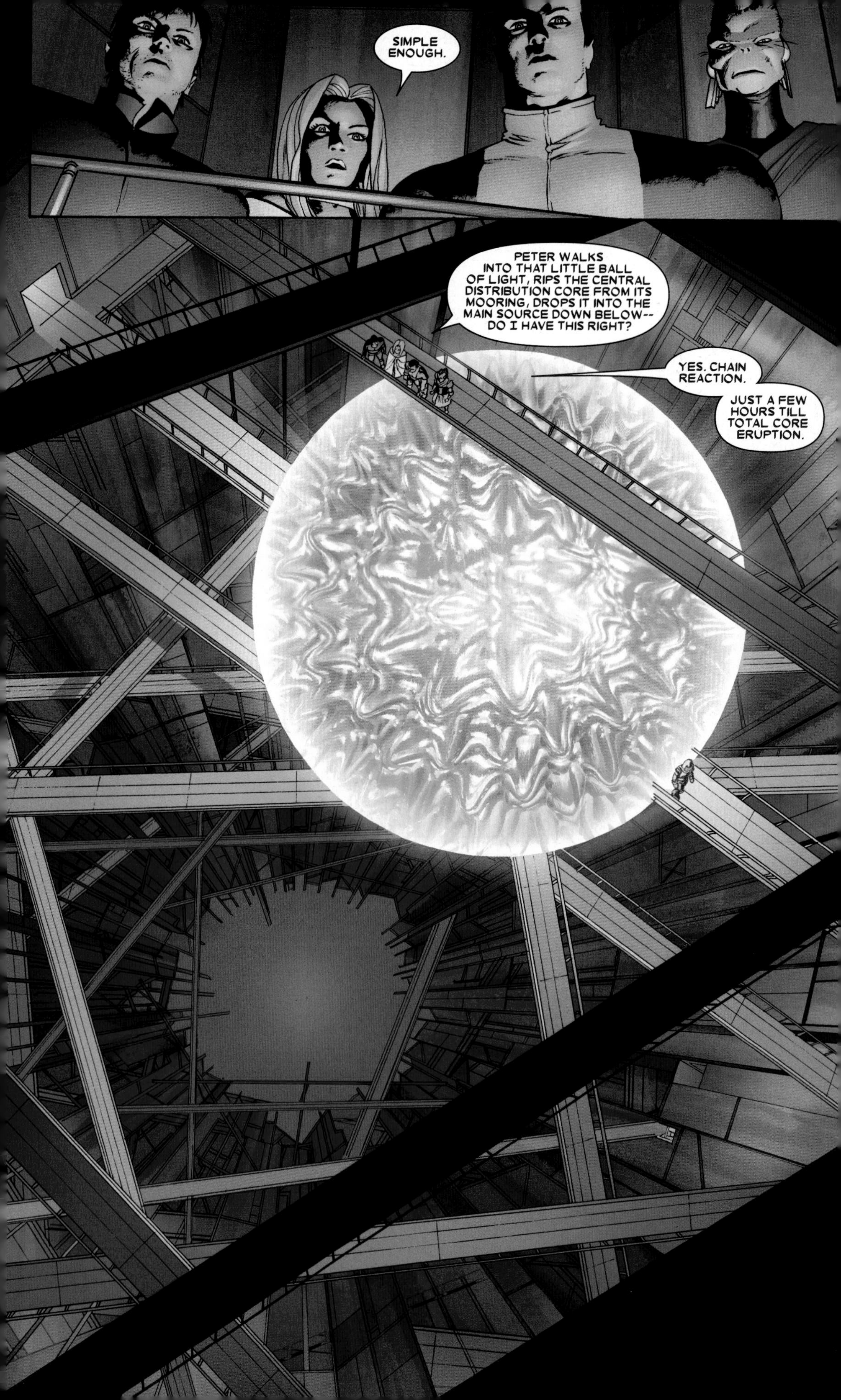
SIMPLE ENOUGH.
PETER WALKS INTO THAT LITTLE BALL OF LIGHT, RIPS THE CENTRAL DISTRIBUTION CORE FROM ITS MOORING, DROPS IT INTO THE MAIN SOURCE DOWN BELOW-- DO I HAVE THIS RIGHT?
YES. CHAIN REACTION.
JUST A FEW HOURS TILL TOTAL CORE ERUPTION.

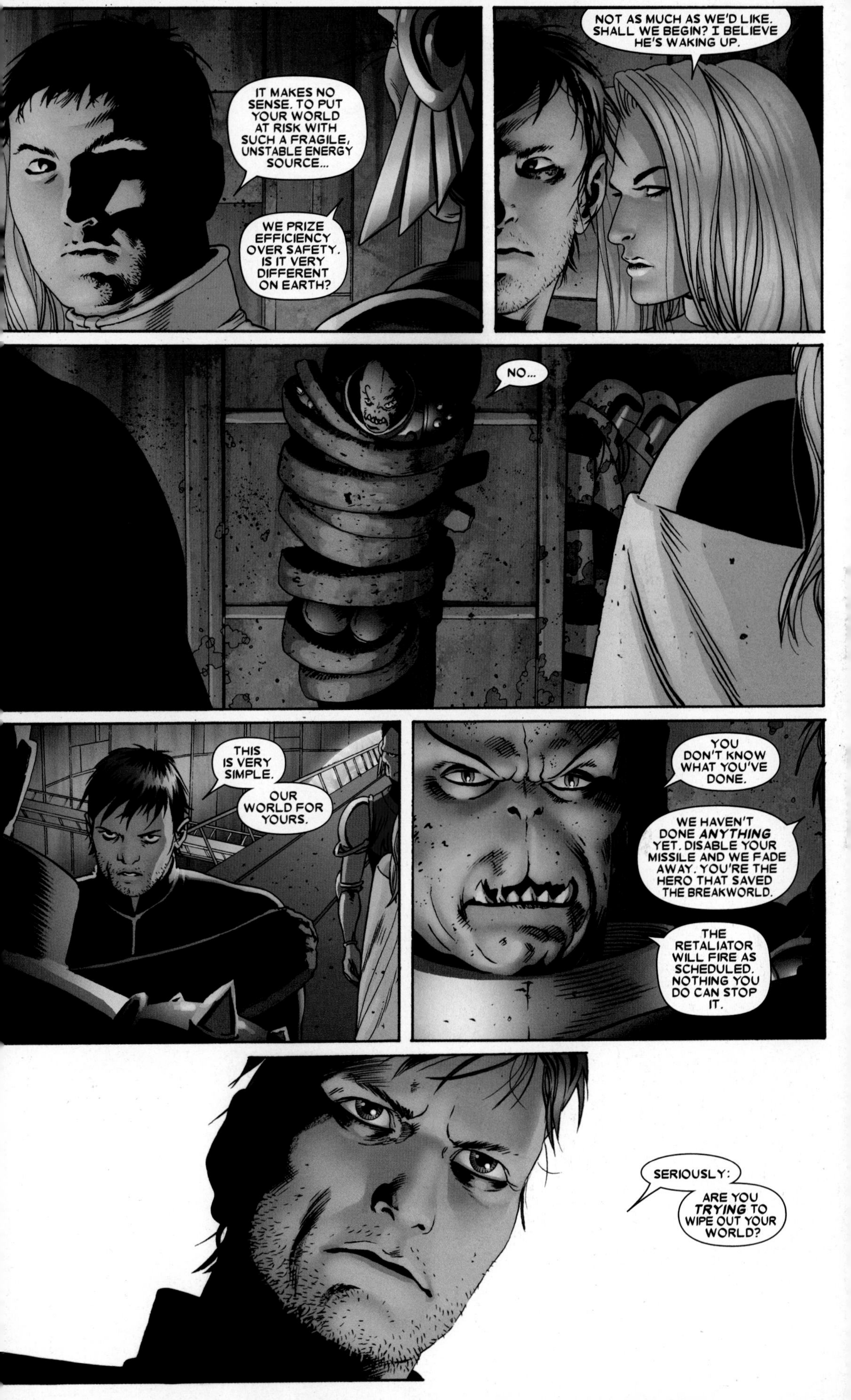
IT MAKES NO SENSE. TO PUT YOUR WORLD AT RISK WITH SUCH A FRAGILE, UNSTABLE ENERGY SOURCE...
WE PRIZE EFFICIENCY OVER SAFETY. IS IT VERY DIFFERENT ON EARTH?
NOT AS MUCH AS WE'D LIKE. SHALL WE BEGIN? I BELIEVE HE'S WAKING UP.
NO...
THIS IS VERY SIMPLE.
OUR WORLD FOR YOURS.
YOU DON'T KNOW WHAT YOU'VE DONE.
WE HAVEN'T DONE *ANYTHING* YET. DISABLE YOUR MISSILE AND WE FADE AWAY. YOU'RE THE HERO THAT SAVED THE BREAKWORLD.
THE RETALIATOR WILL FIRE AS SCHEDULED. NOTHING YOU DO CAN STOP IT.
SERIOUSLY:
ARE YOU *TRYING* TO WIPE OUT YOUR WORLD?

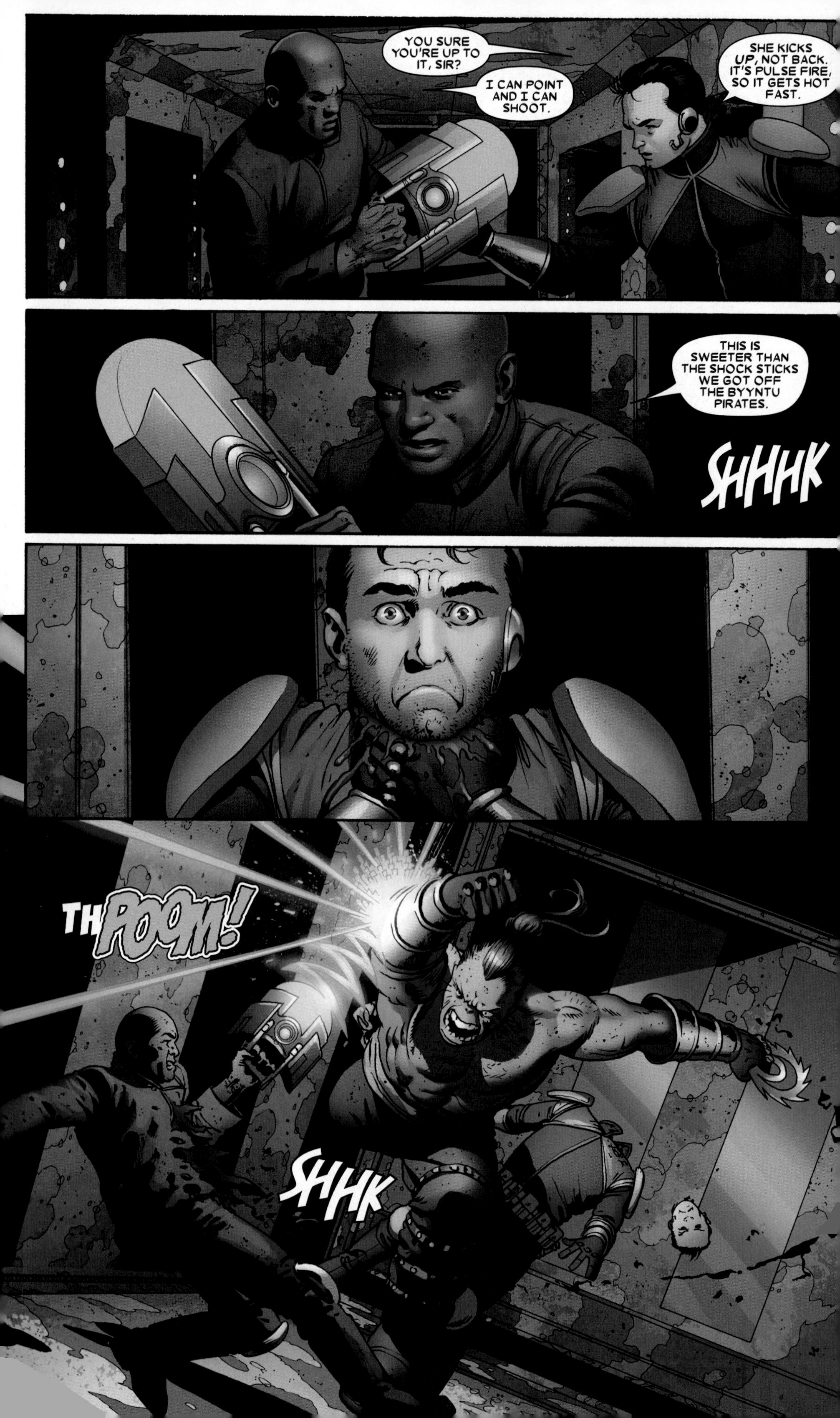
YOU SURE YOU'RE UP TO IT, SIR?
I CAN POINT AND I CAN SHOOT.
SHE KICKS UP, NOT BACK. IT'S PULSE FIRE, SO IT GETS HOT FAST.
THIS IS SWEETER THAN THE SHOCK STICKS WE GOT OFF THE BYYNTU PIRATES.
SHHHK
THPOOM!
SHHK

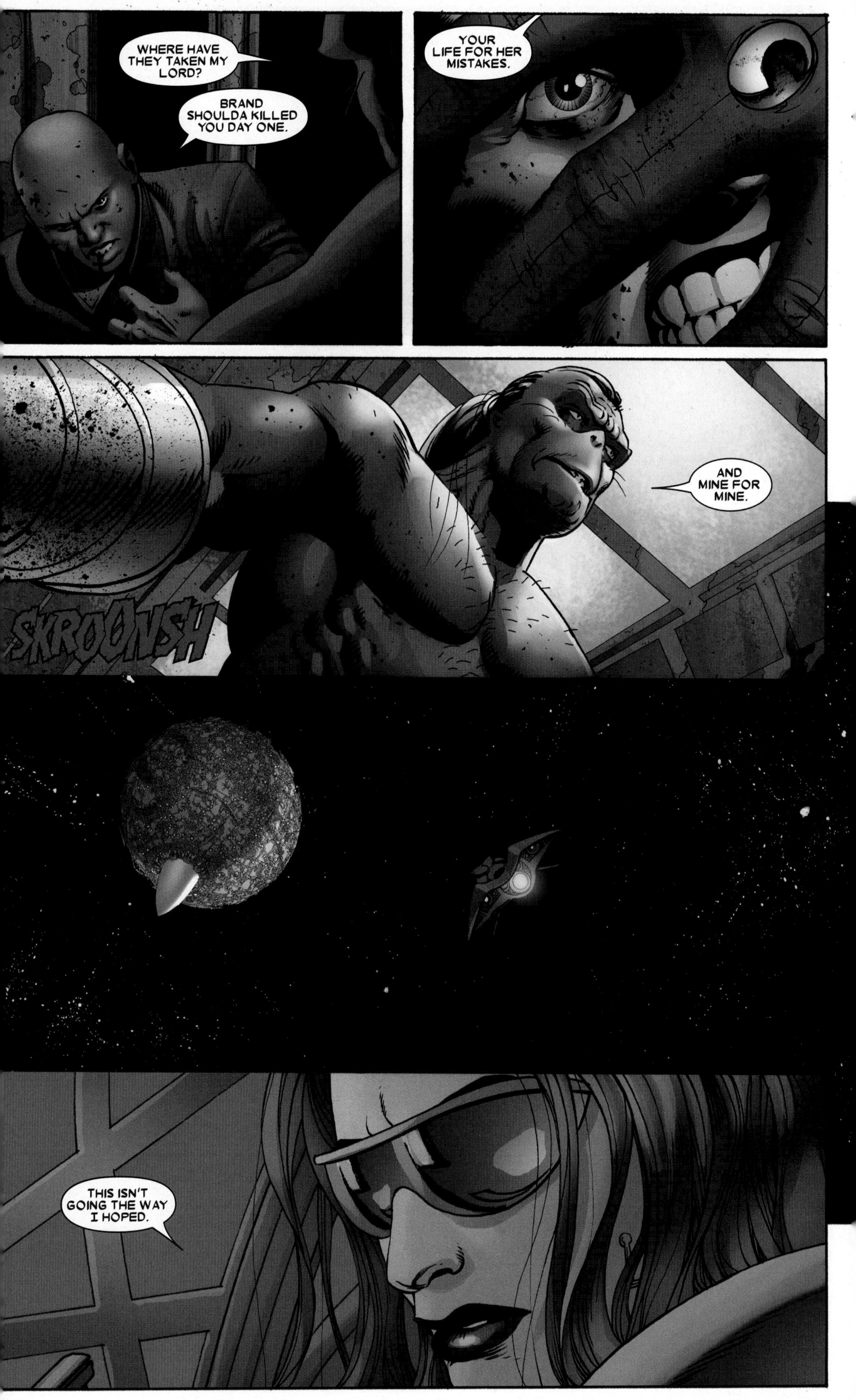
WHERE HAVE THEY TAKEN MY LORD?
BRAND SHOULDA KILLED YOU DAY ONE.
YOUR LIFE FOR HER MISTAKES.
AND MINE FOR MINE.
SKROONSH
THIS ISN'T GOING THE WAY I HOPED.

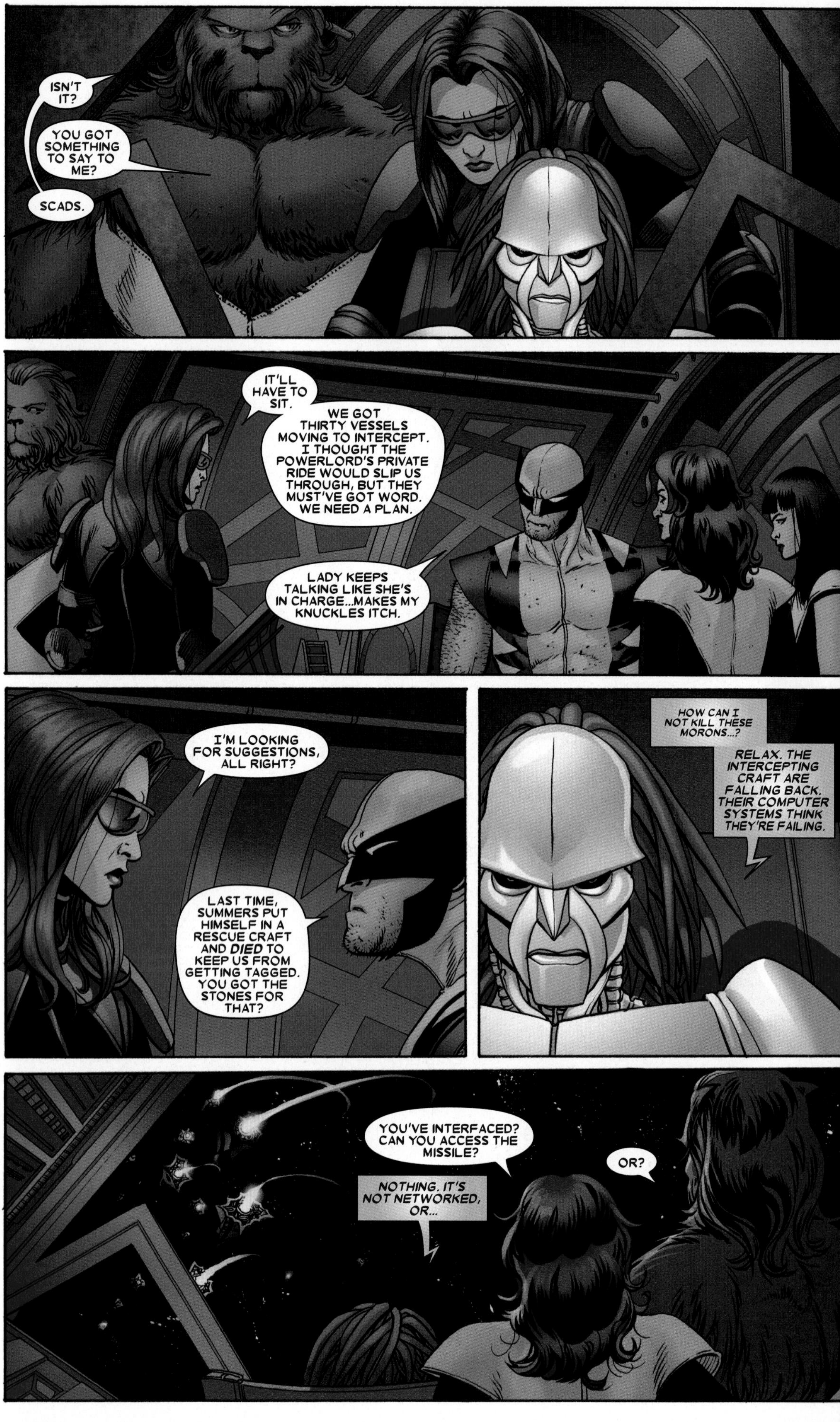
ISN'T IT?
YOU GOT SOMETHING TO SAY TO ME?
SCADS.
IT'LL HAVE TO SIT.
WE GOT THIRTY VESSELS MOVING TO INTERCEPT. I THOUGHT THE POWERLORD'S PRIVATE RIDE WOULD SLIP US THROUGH, BUT THEY MUST'VE GOT WORD. WE NEED A PLAN.
LADY KEEPS TALKING LIKE SHE'S IN CHARGE...MAKES MY KNUCKLES ITCH.
I'M LOOKING FOR SUGGESTIONS, ALL RIGHT?
LAST TIME, SUMMERS PUT HIMSELF IN A RESCUE CRAFT AND *DIED* TO KEEP US FROM GETTING TAGGED. YOU GOT THE STONES FOR THAT?
HOW CAN I NOT KILL THESE MORONS...?
RELAX. THE INTERCEPTING CRAFT ARE FALLING BACK. THEIR COMPUTER SYSTEMS THINK THEY'RE FAILING.
YOU'VE INTERFACED? CAN YOU ACCESS THE MISSILE?
NOTHING. IT'S NOT NETWORKED, OR...
OR?

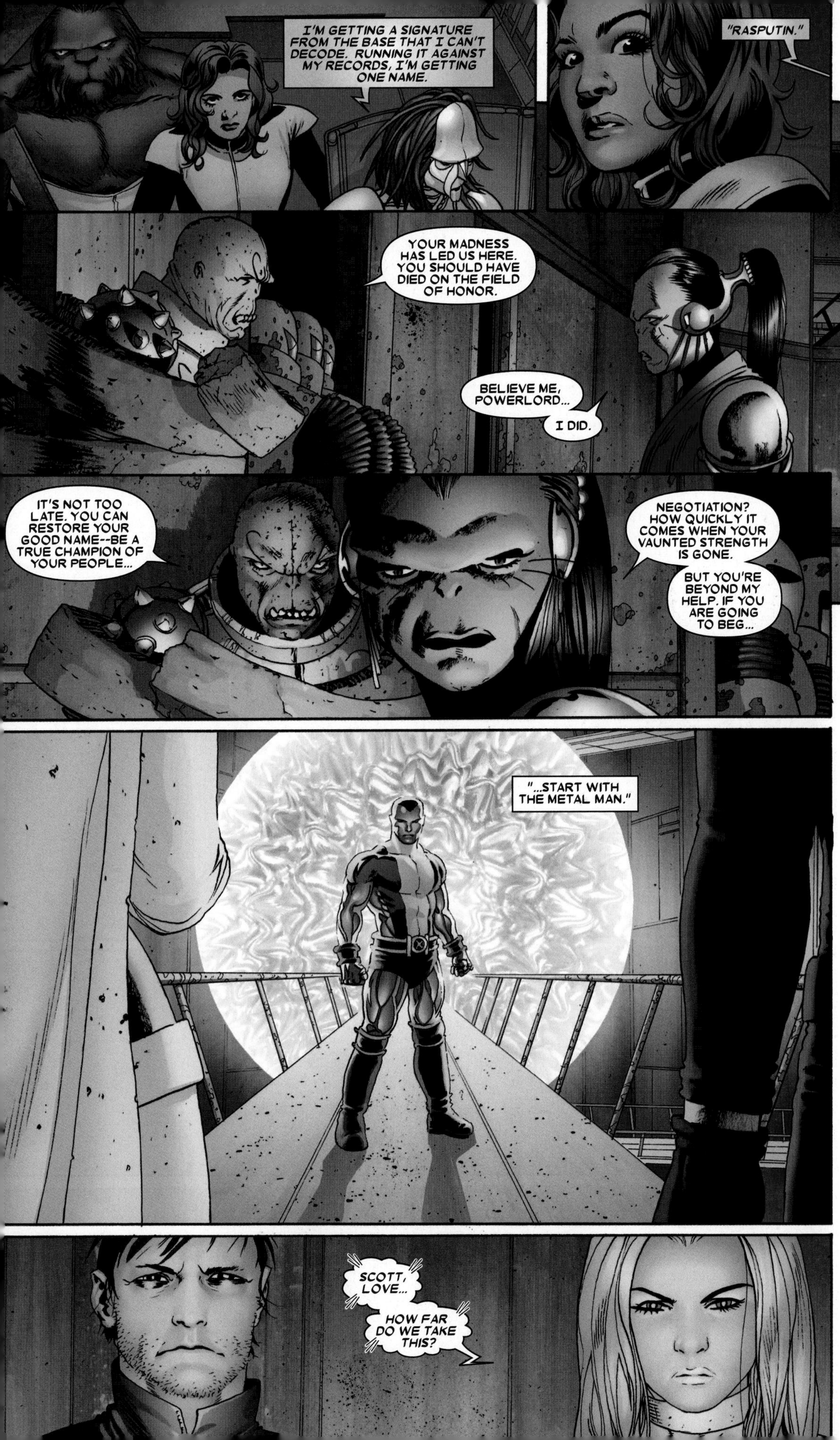
I'M GETTING A SIGNATURE FROM THE BASE THAT I CAN'T DECODE. RUNNING IT AGAINST MY RECORDS, I'M GETTING ONE NAME.
"RASPUTIN."
YOUR MADNESS HAS LED US HERE. YOU SHOULD HAVE DIED ON THE FIELD OF HONOR.
BELIEVE ME, POWERLORD...
I DID.
IT'S NOT TOO LATE. YOU CAN RESTORE YOUR GOOD NAME--BE A TRUE CHAMPION OF YOUR PEOPLE...
NEGOTIATION? HOW QUICKLY IT COMES WHEN YOUR VAUNTED STRENGTH IS GONE.
BUT YOU'RE BEYOND MY HELP. IF YOU ARE GOING TO BEG...
"...START WITH THE METAL MAN."
SCOTT, LOVE...
HOW FAR DO WE TAKE THIS?

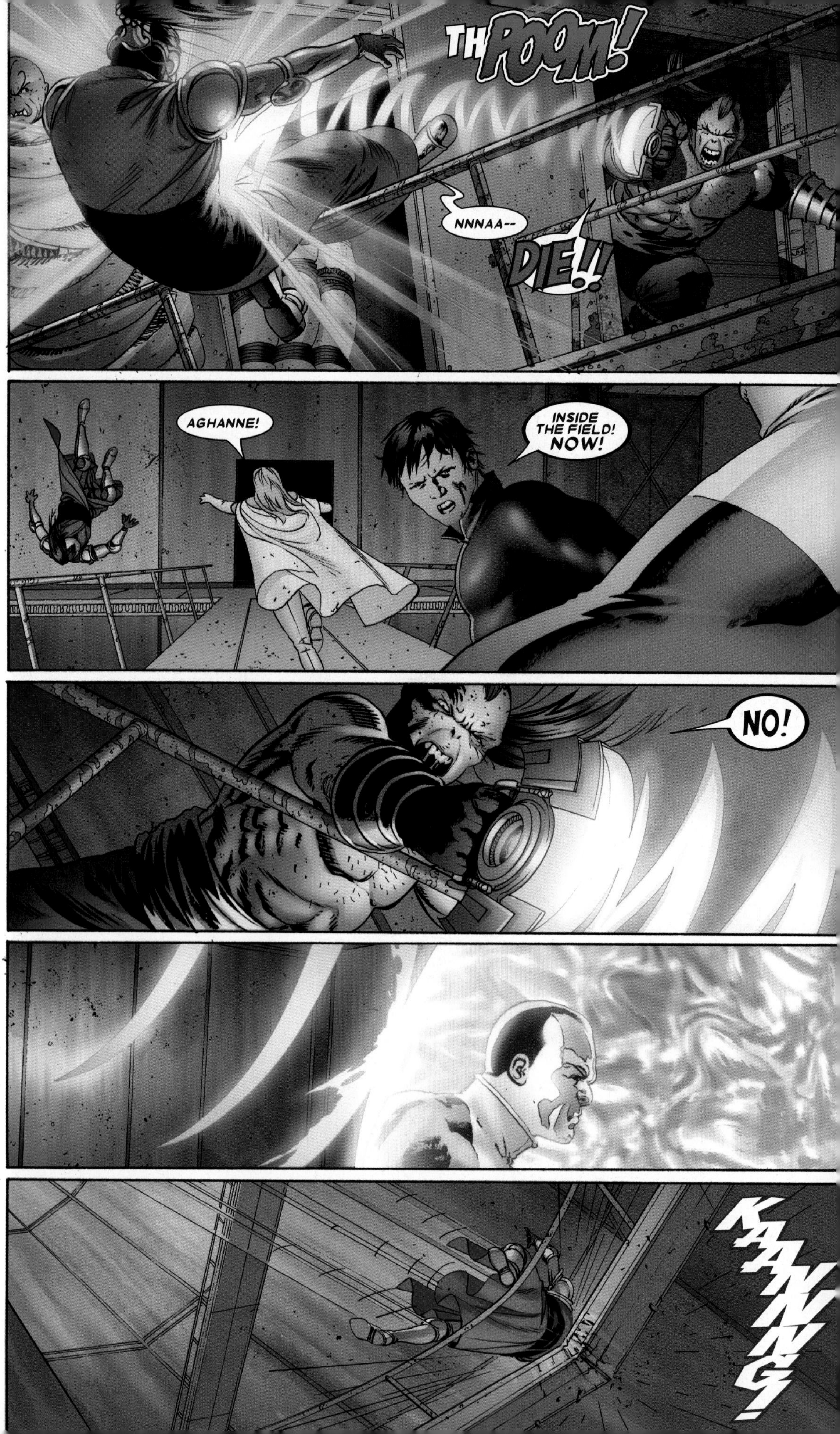
THPOOM!
NNNAA--
DIE!!
AGHANNE!
INSIDE THE FIELD! NOW!
NO!
KAANNG!

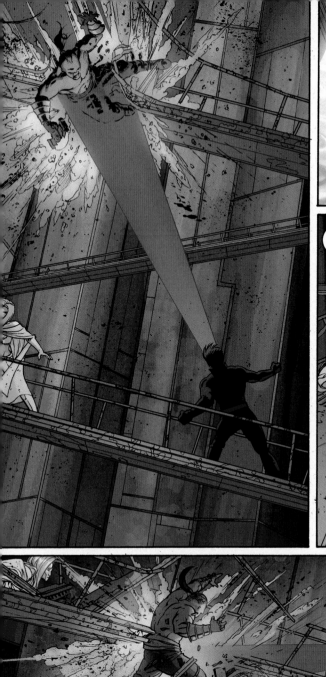

EMMA, MOVE!

AT LAST, THIS ENDS AS IT WAS MEANT TO.

OH, PLEASE.

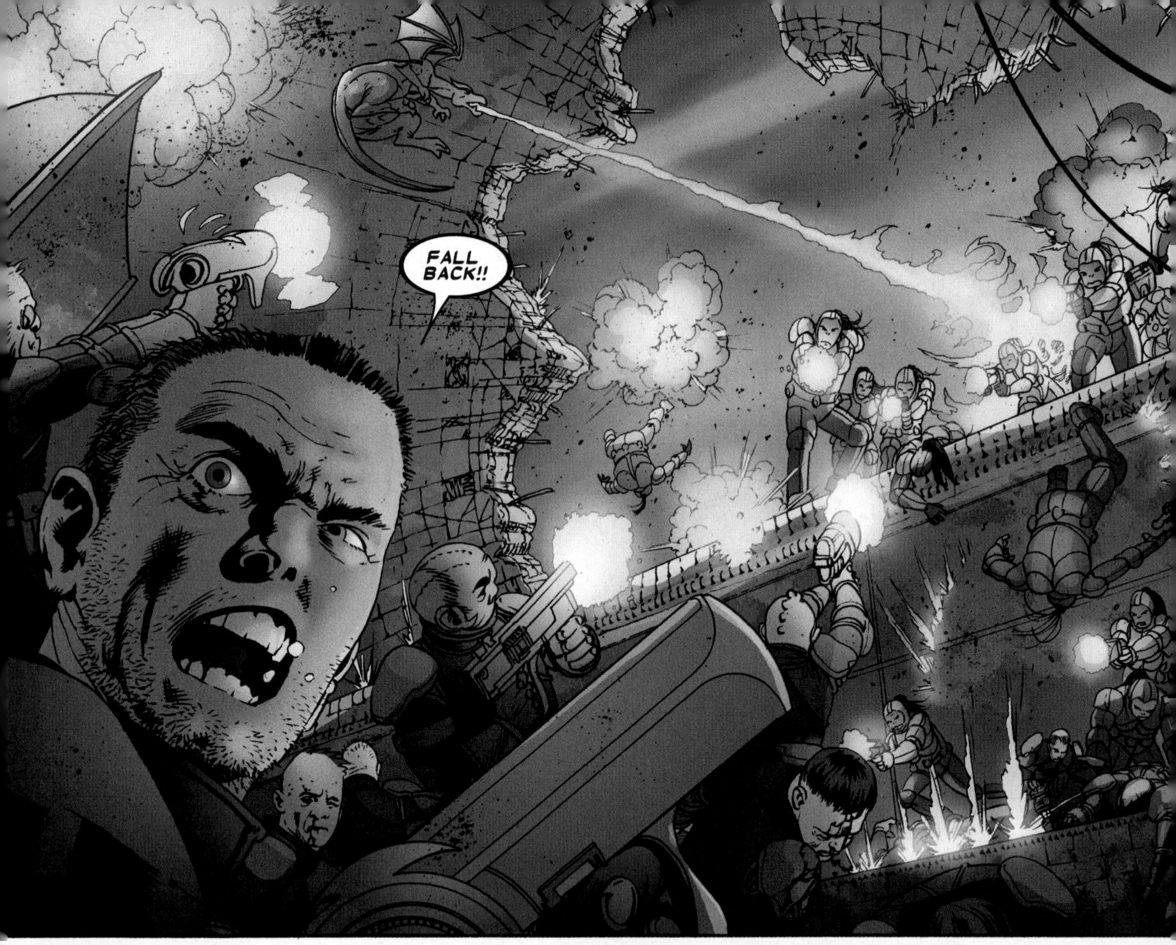
FALL BACK!!

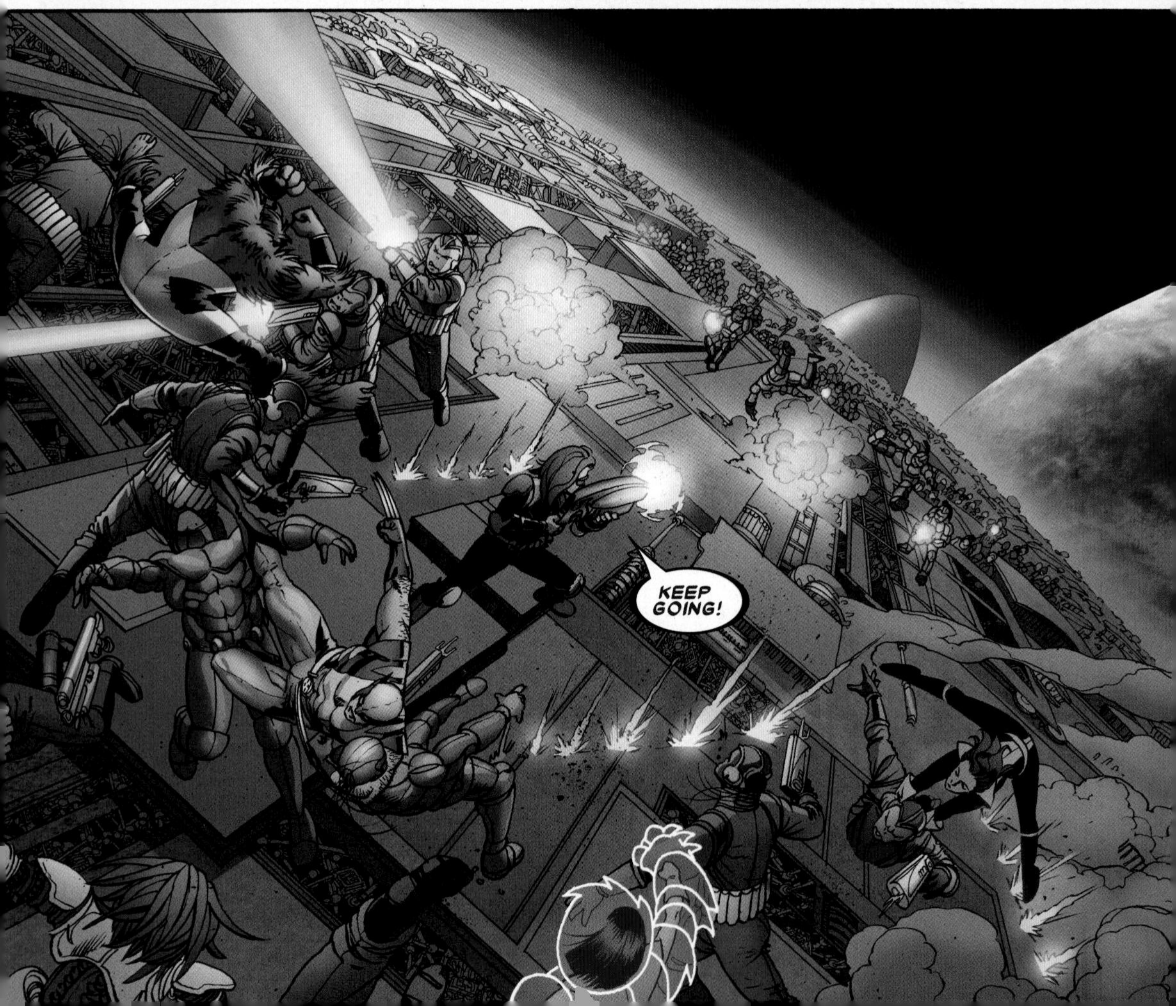
KEEP GOING!

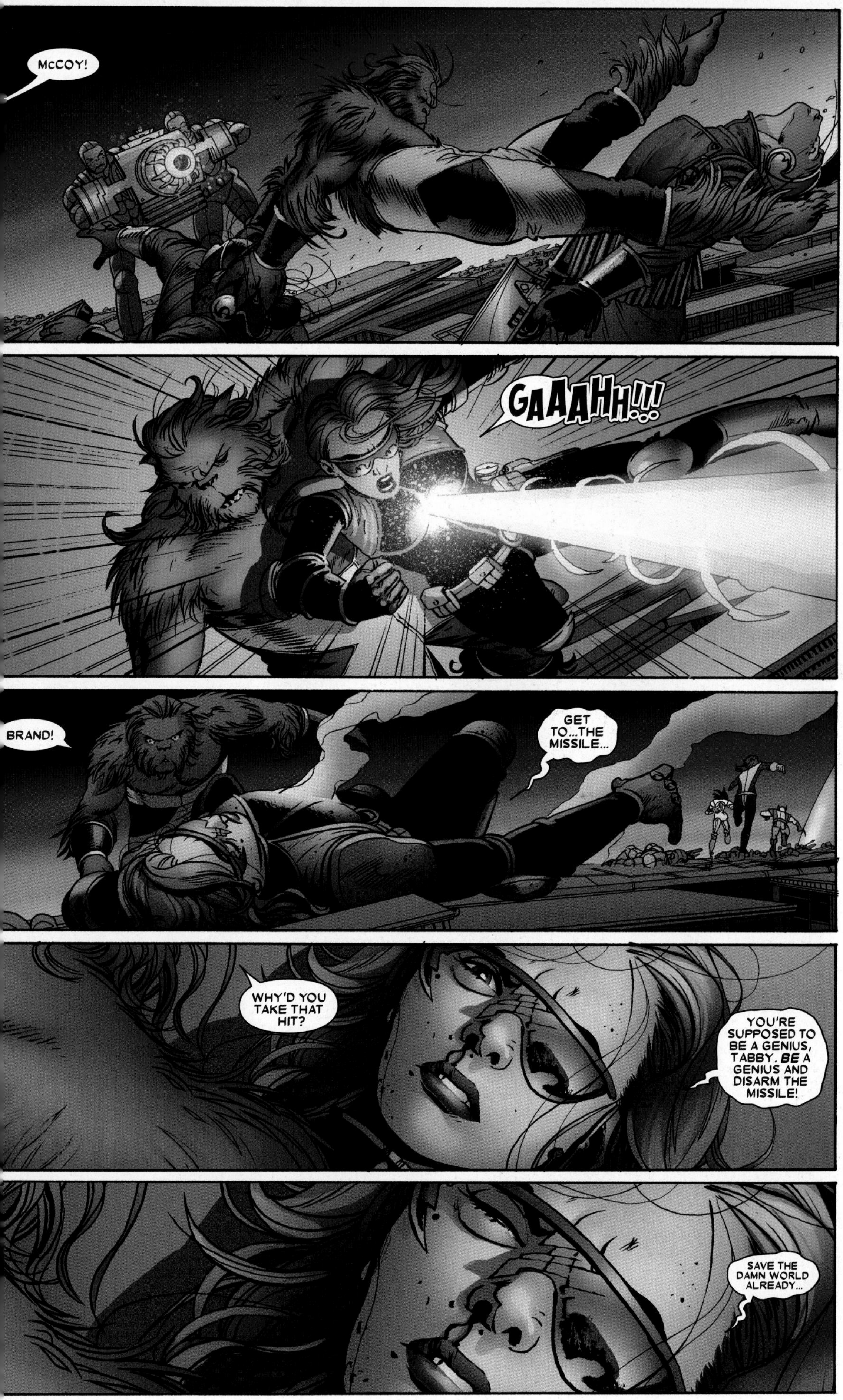
McCOY!
GAAAHH!!!
BRAND!
GET TO...THE MISSILE...
WHY'D YOU TAKE THAT HIT?
YOU'RE SUPPOSED TO BE A GENIUS, TABBY. *BE* A GENIUS AND DISARM THE MISSILE!
SAVE THE DAMN WORLD ALREADY...

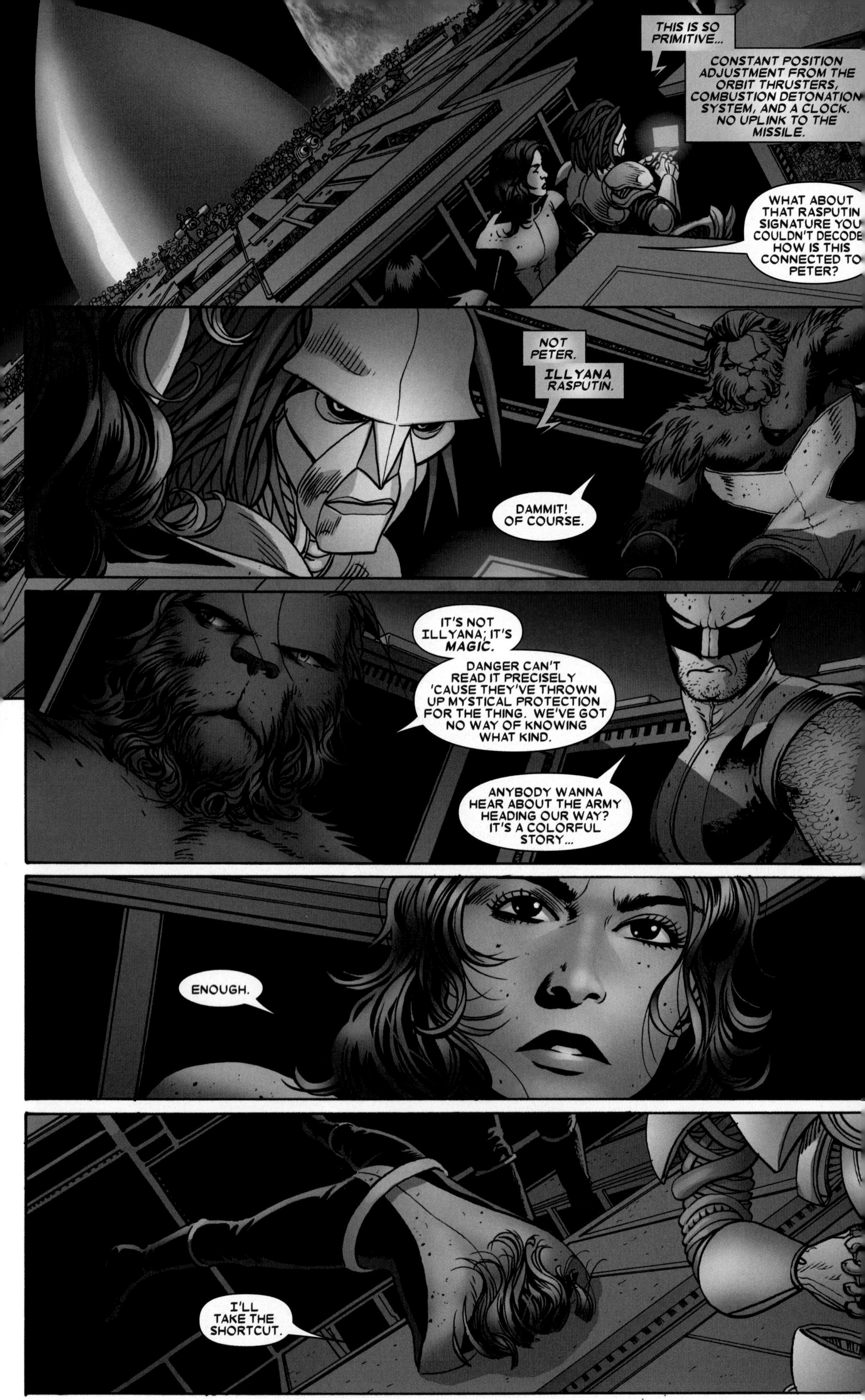
THIS IS SO PRIMITIVE...
CONSTANT POSITION ADJUSTMENT FROM THE ORBIT THRUSTERS, COMBUSTION DETONATION SYSTEM, AND A CLOCK. NO UPLINK TO THE MISSILE.
WHAT ABOUT THAT RASPUTIN SIGNATURE YOU COULDN'T DECODE HOW IS THIS CONNECTED TO PETER?
NOT PETER.
ILLYANA RASPUTIN.
DAMMIT! OF COURSE.
IT'S NOT ILLYANA; IT'S MAGIC.
DANGER CAN'T READ IT PRECISELY 'CAUSE THEY'VE THROWN UP MYSTICAL PROTECTION FOR THE THING. WE'VE GOT NO WAY OF KNOWING WHAT KIND.
ANYBODY WANNA HEAR ABOUT THE ARMY HEADING OUR WAY? IT'S A COLORFUL STORY...
ENOUGH.
I'LL TAKE THE SHORTCUT.

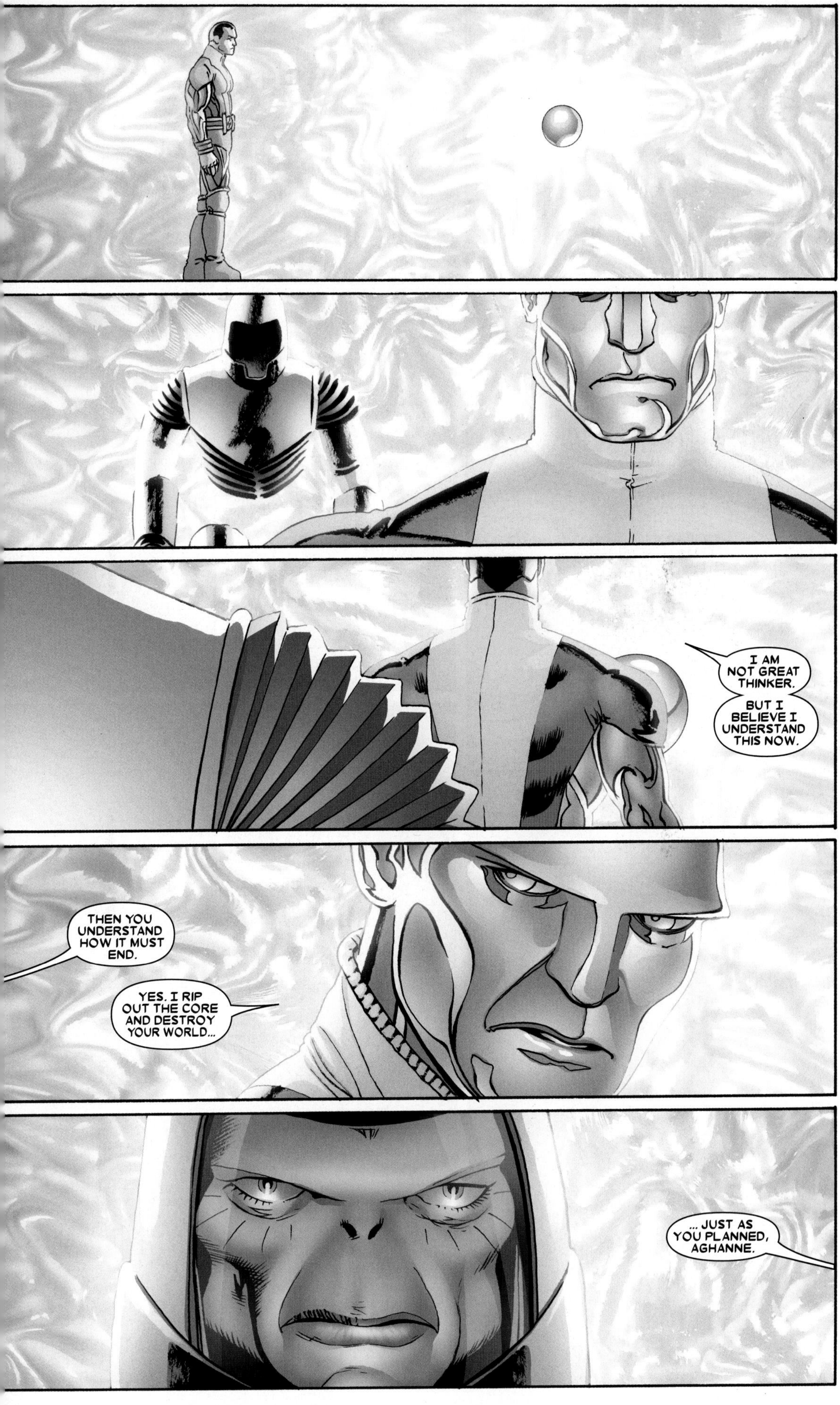
I AM NOT GREAT THINKER.
BUT I BELIEVE I UNDERSTAND THIS NOW.
THEN YOU UNDERSTAND HOW IT MUST END.
YES. I RIP OUT THE CORE AND DESTROY YOUR WORLD...
... JUST AS YOU PLANNED, AGHANNE.

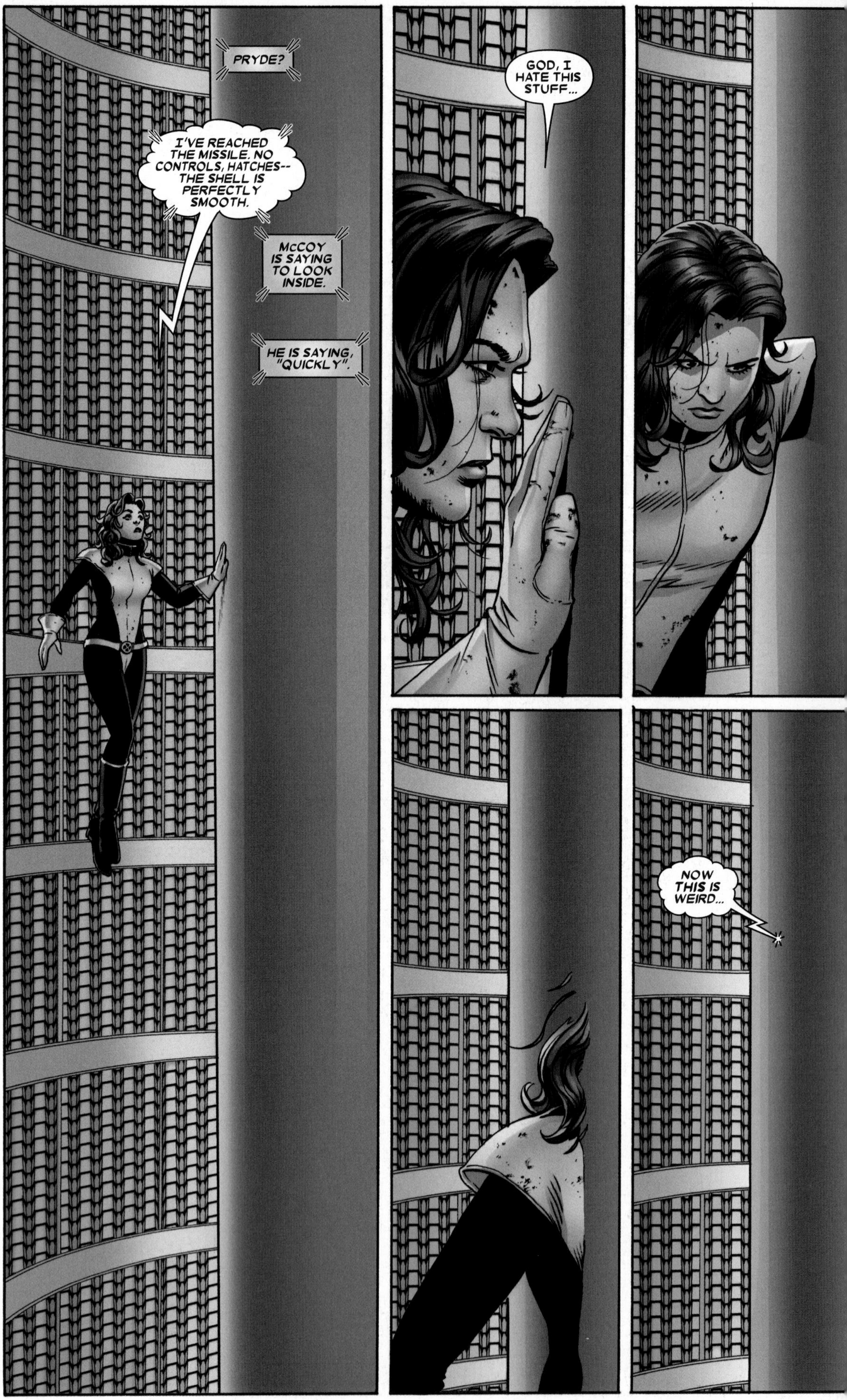
PRYDE?
I'VE REACHED THE MISSILE. NO CONTROLS, HATCHES-- THE SHELL IS PERFECTLY SMOOTH.
McCOY IS SAYING TO LOOK INSIDE.
HE IS SAYING, "QUICKLY".
GOD, I HATE THIS STUFF...
NOW THIS IS WEIRD...

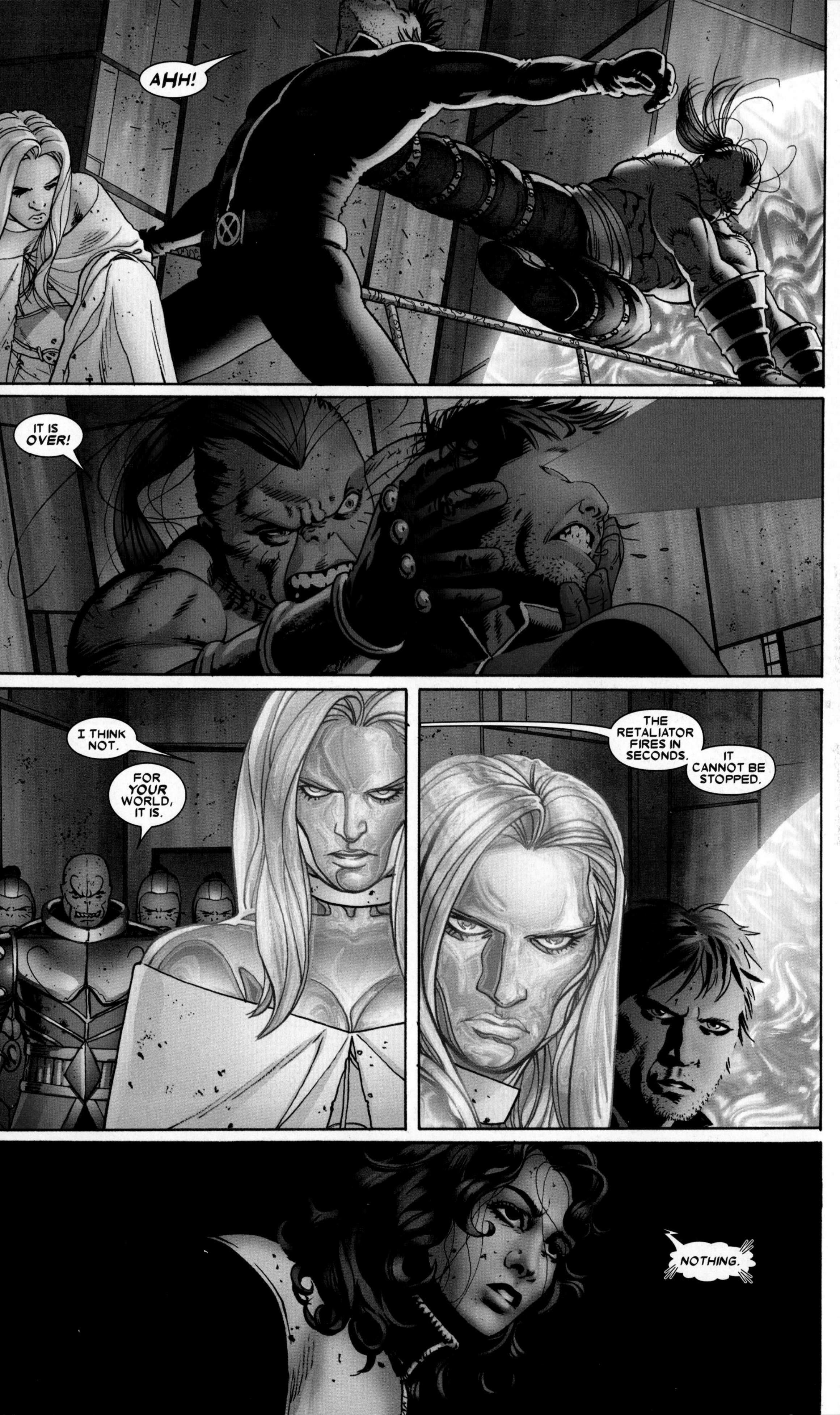
AHH!
IT IS OVER!
I THINK NOT.
FOR YOUR WORLD, IT IS.
THE RETALIATOR FIRES IN SECONDS.
IT CANNOT BE STOPPED.
NOTHING.

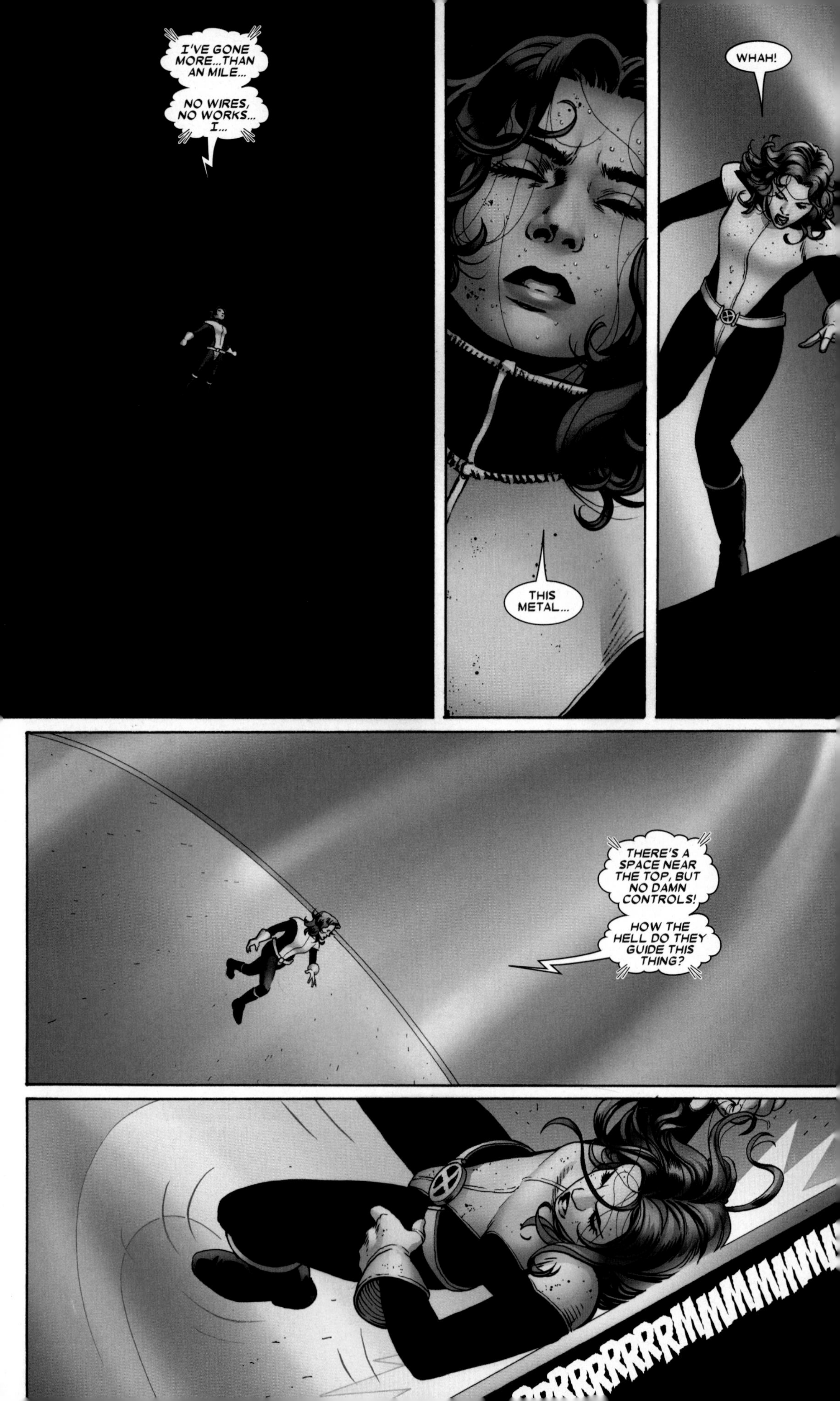
I'VE GONE MORE...THAN AN MILE...
NO WIRES, NO WORKS... I...
THIS METAL...
WHAH!
THERE'S A SPACE NEAR THE TOP, BUT NO DAMN CONTROLS!
HOW THE HELL DO THEY GUIDE THIS THING?
RRRRRRRRMMMMMMMM

RRRRRRRRRRMMMMMMMMW

SHE'S
FIRING!

OH NO...
NO...

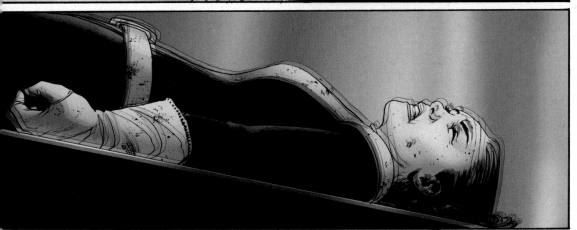

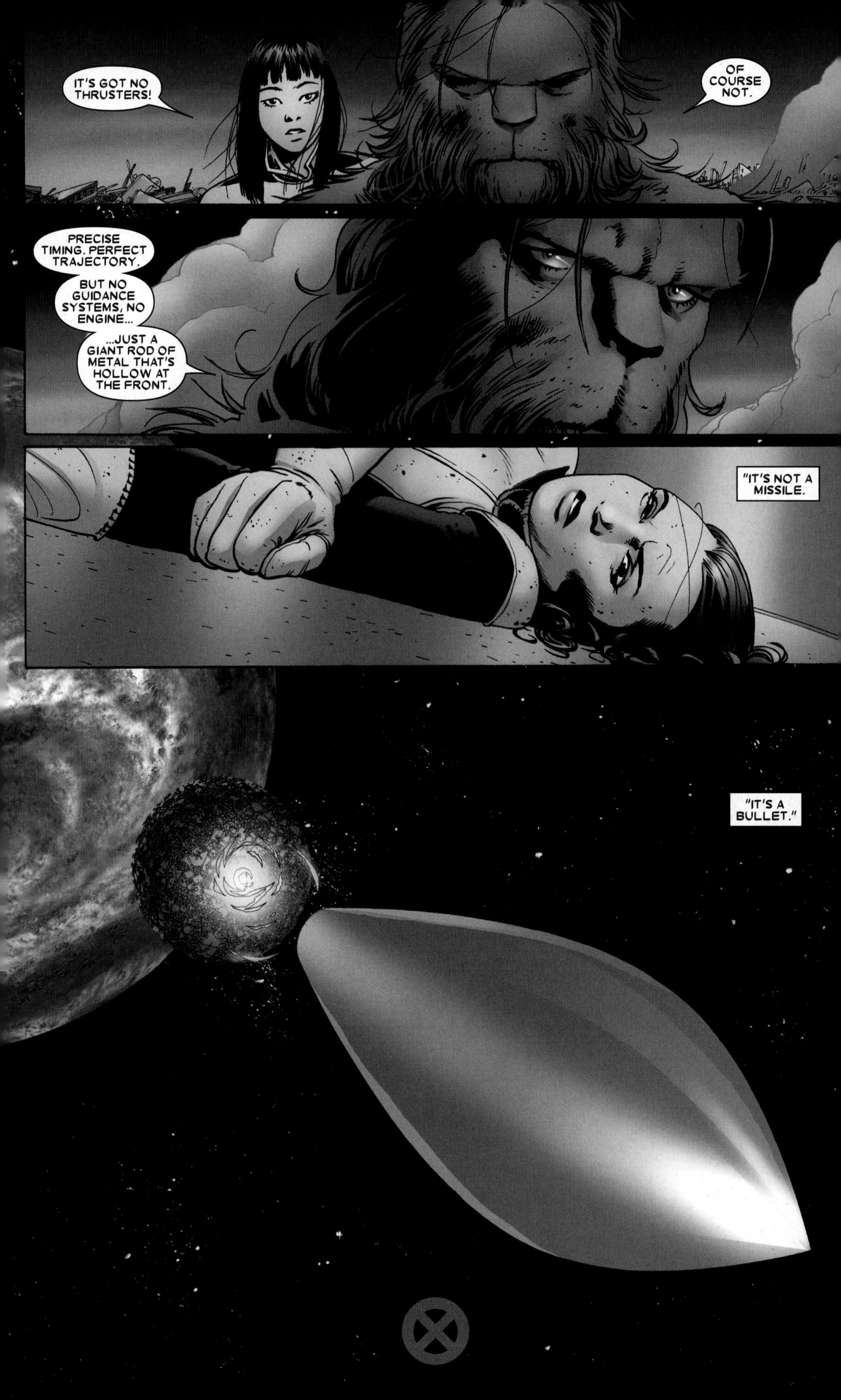
IT'S GOT NO THRUSTERS!
OF COURSE NOT.
PRECISE TIMING. PERFECT TRAJECTORY.
BUT NO GUIDANCE SYSTEMS, NO ENGINE...
...JUST A GIANT ROD OF METAL THAT'S HOLLOW AT THE FRONT.
"IT'S NOT A MISSILE.
"IT'S A BULLET."

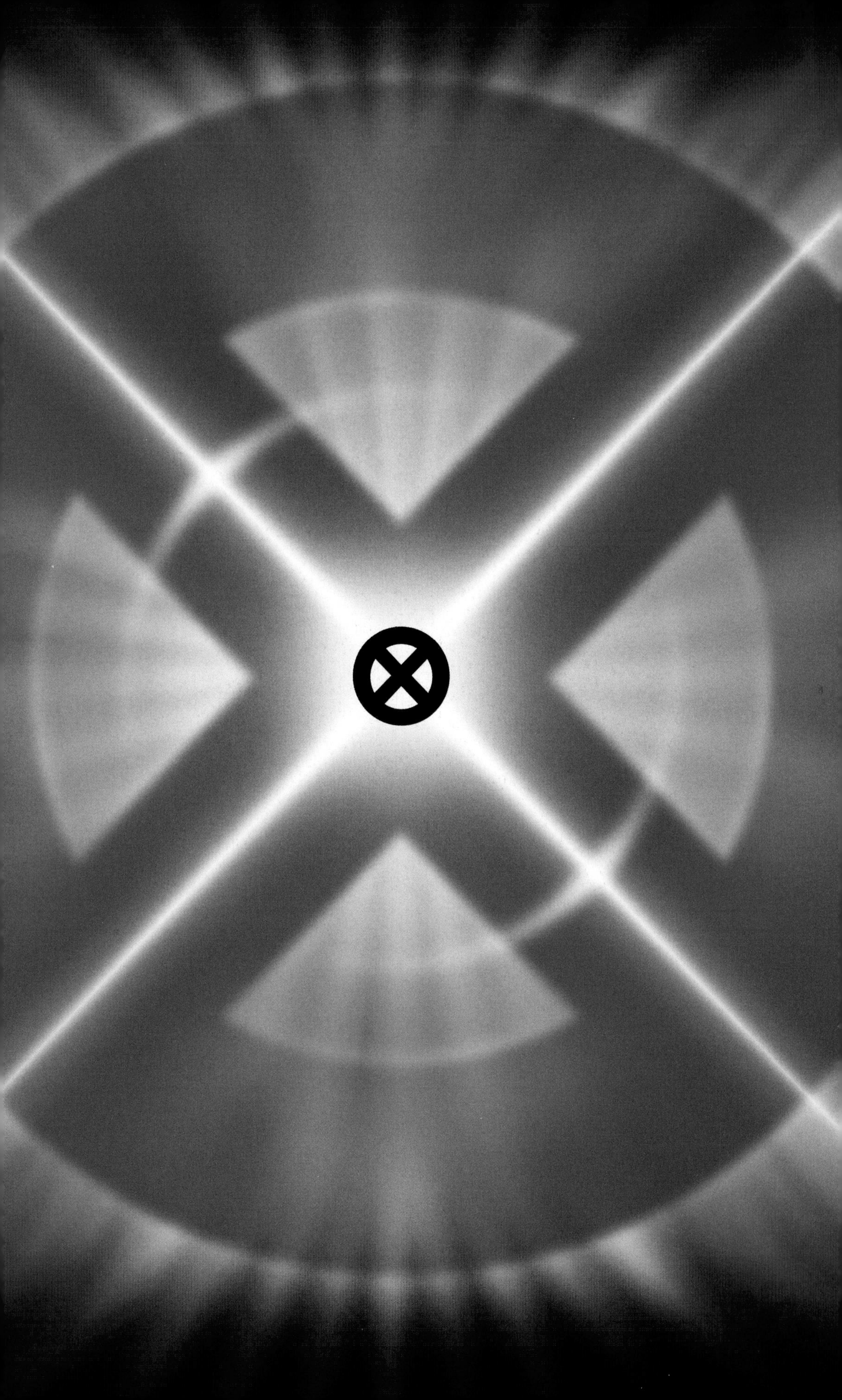

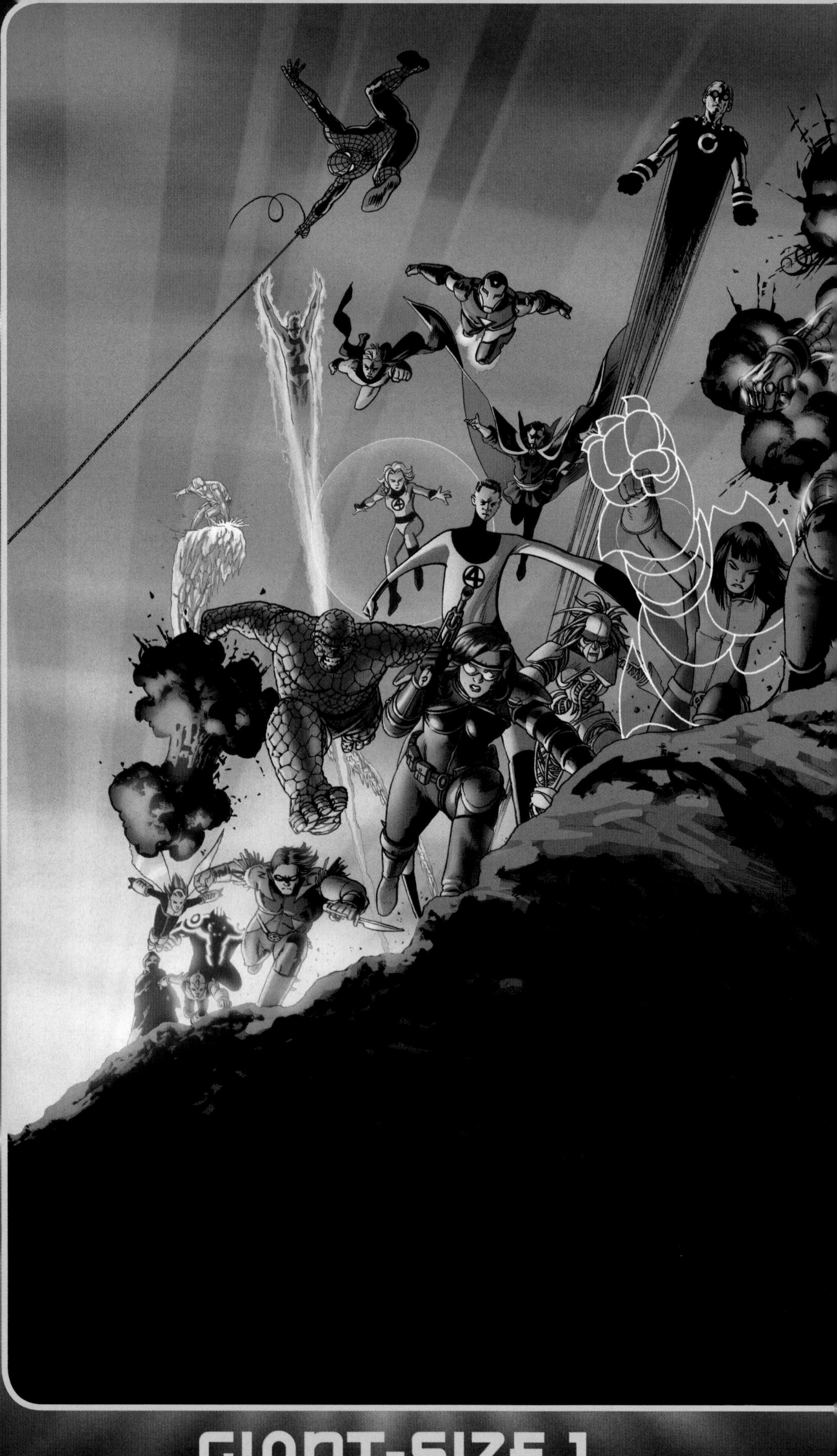

GIANT-SIZE 1

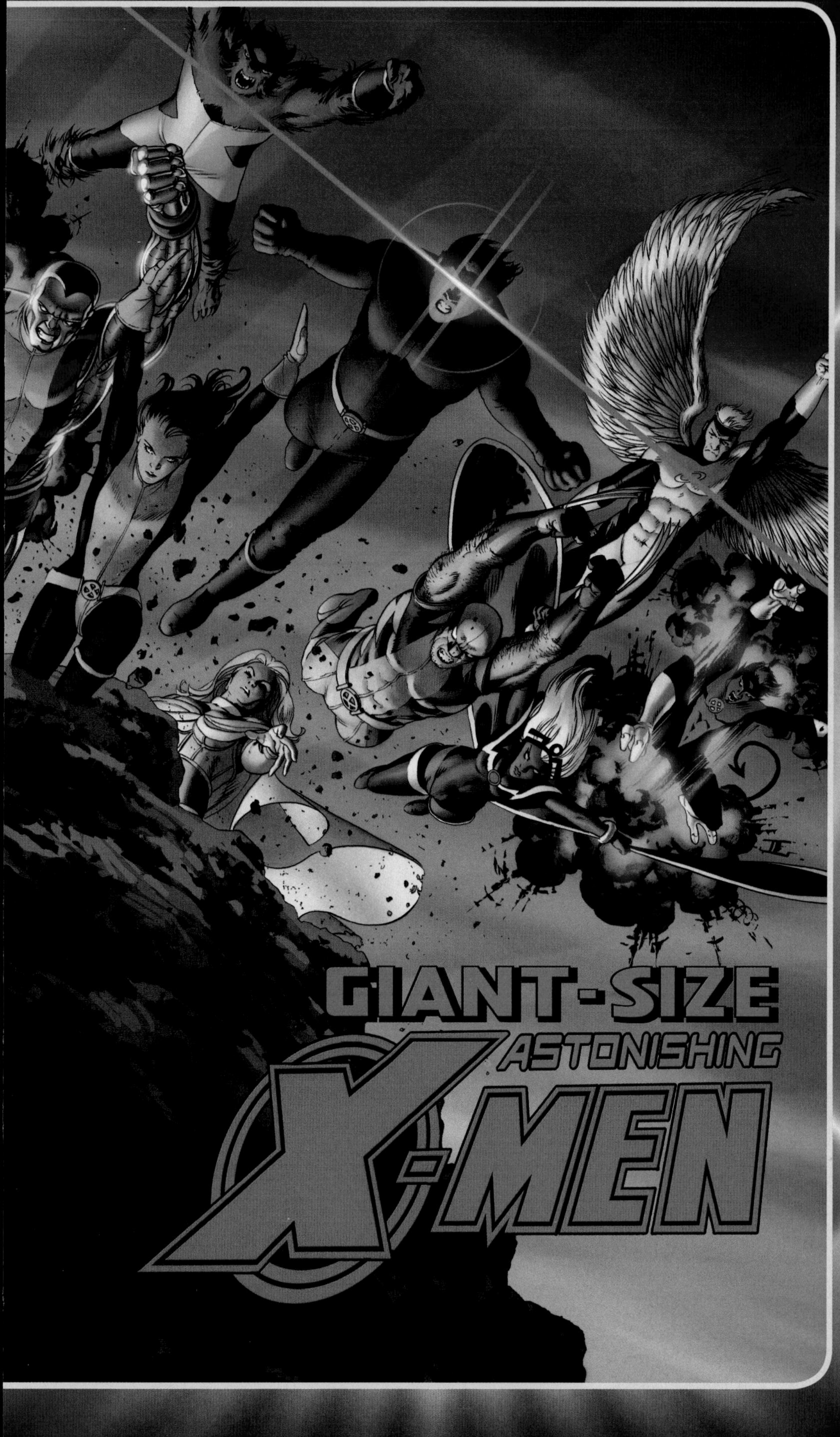
GIANT-SIZE
ASTONISHING
X-MEN

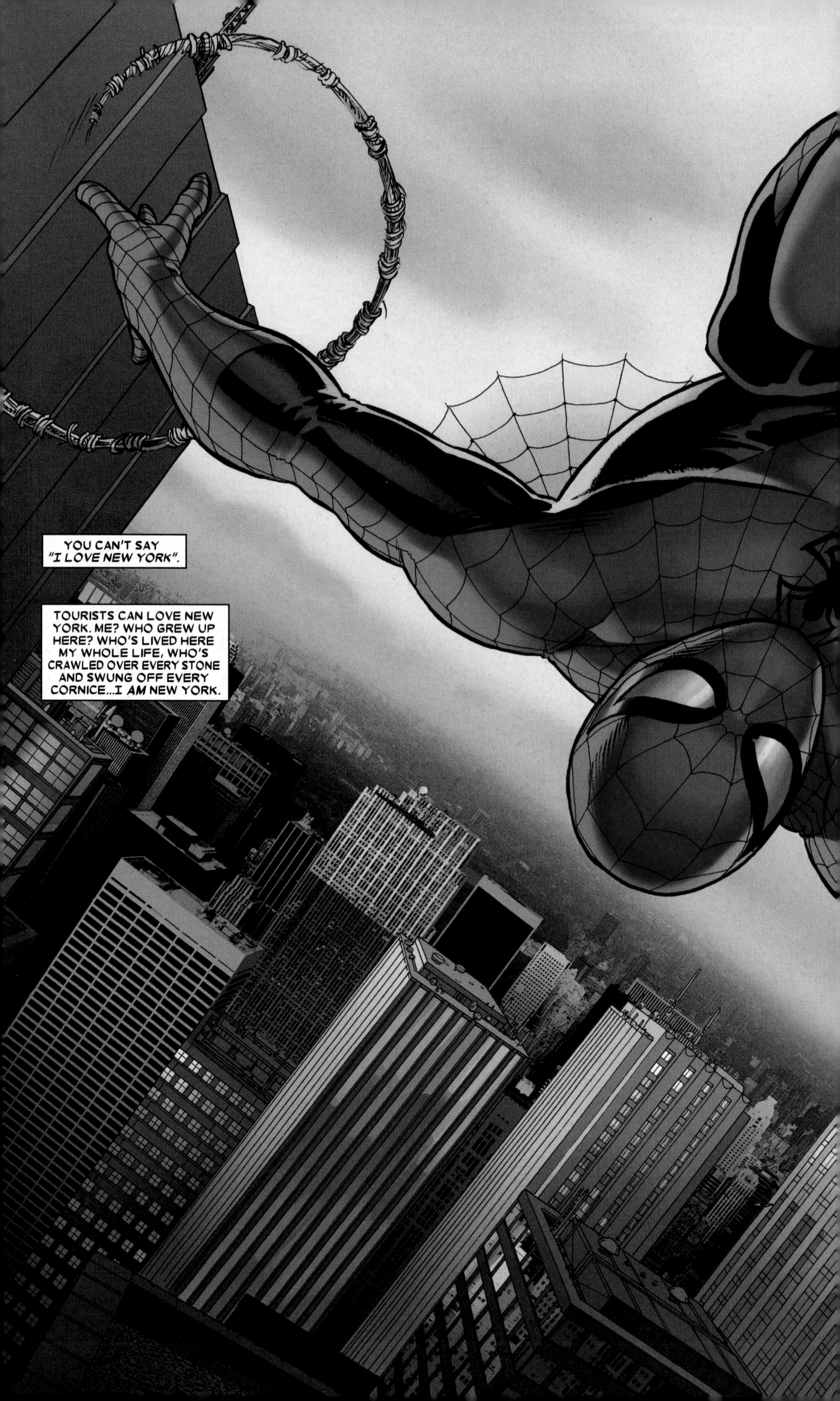
YOU CAN'T SAY *"I LOVE NEW YORK"*.
TOURISTS CAN LOVE NEW YORK. ME? WHO GREW UP HERE? WHO'S LIVED HERE MY WHOLE LIFE, WHO'S CRAWLED OVER EVERY STONE AND SWUNG OFF EVERY CORNICE...I *AM* NEW YORK.

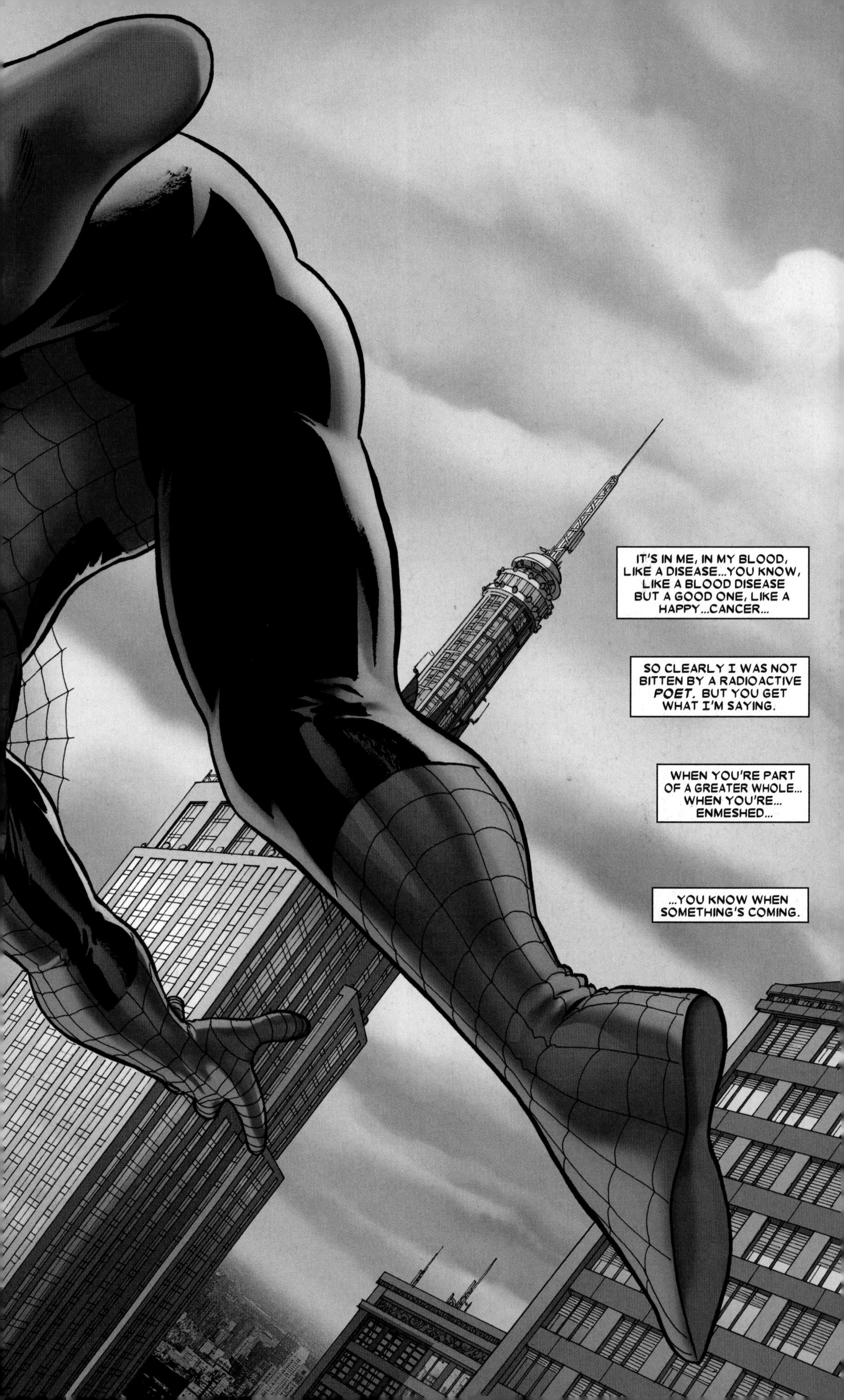
IT'S IN ME, IN MY BLOOD, LIKE A DISEASE...YOU KNOW, LIKE A BLOOD DISEASE BUT A GOOD ONE, LIKE A HAPPY...CANCER...
SO CLEARLY I WAS NOT BITTEN BY A RADIOACTIVE *POET.* BUT YOU GET WHAT I'M SAYING.
WHEN YOU'RE PART OF A GREATER WHOLE... WHEN YOU'RE... ENMESHED...
...YOU KNOW WHEN SOMETHING'S COMING.

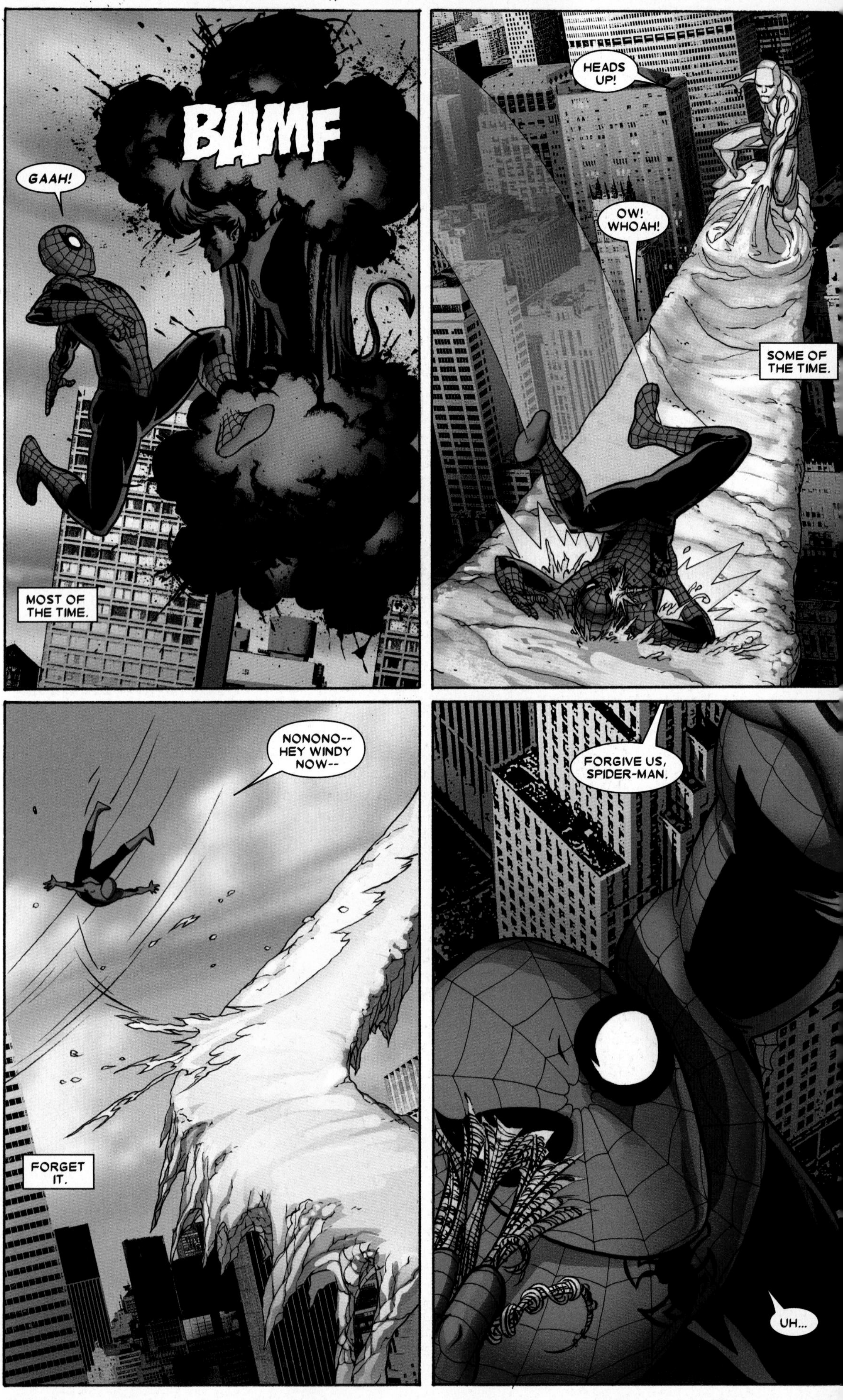
BAMF
GAAH!
MOST OF THE TIME.
HEADS UP!
OW! WHOAH!
SOME OF THE TIME.
NONONO-- HEY WINDY NOW--
FORGET IT.
FORGIVE US, SPIDER-MAN.
UH...

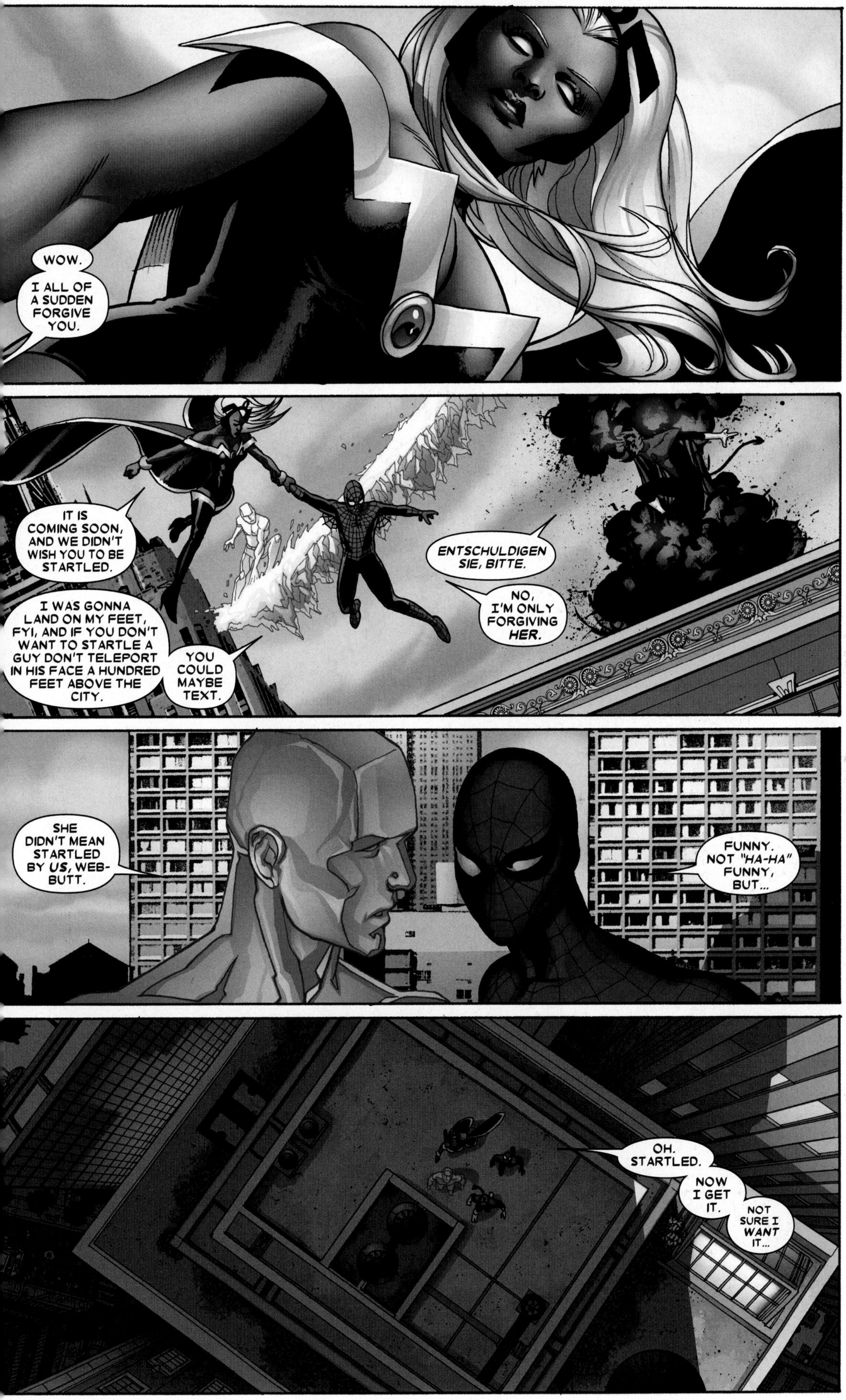
WOW. I ALL OF A SUDDEN FORGIVE YOU.
IT IS COMING SOON, AND WE DIDN'T WISH YOU TO BE STARTLED.
I WAS GONNA LAND ON MY FEET, FYI, AND IF YOU DON'T WANT TO STARTLE A GUY DON'T TELEPORT IN HIS FACE A HUNDRED FEET ABOVE THE CITY.
YOU COULD MAYBE TEXT.
ENTSCHULDIGEN SIE, BITTE.
NO, I'M ONLY FORGIVING *HER*.
SHE DIDN'T MEAN STARTLED BY *US*, WEB-BUTT.
FUNNY. NOT *"HA-HA"* FUNNY, BUT...
OH. STARTLED.
NOW I GET IT.
NOT SURE I *WANT* IT...

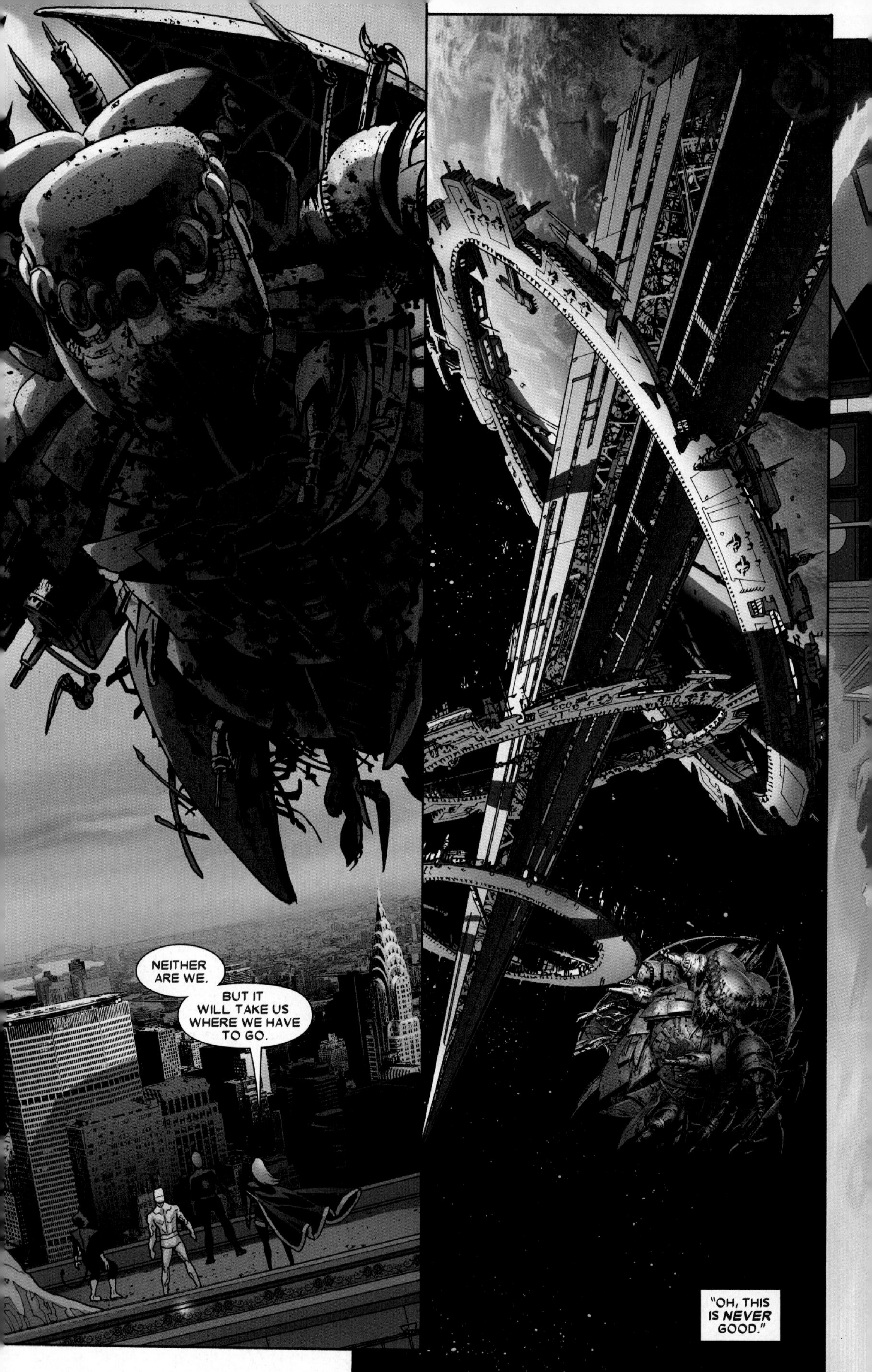
NEITHER ARE WE.
BUT IT WILL TAKE US WHERE WE HAVE TO GO.
"OH, THIS IS *NEVER* GOOD."

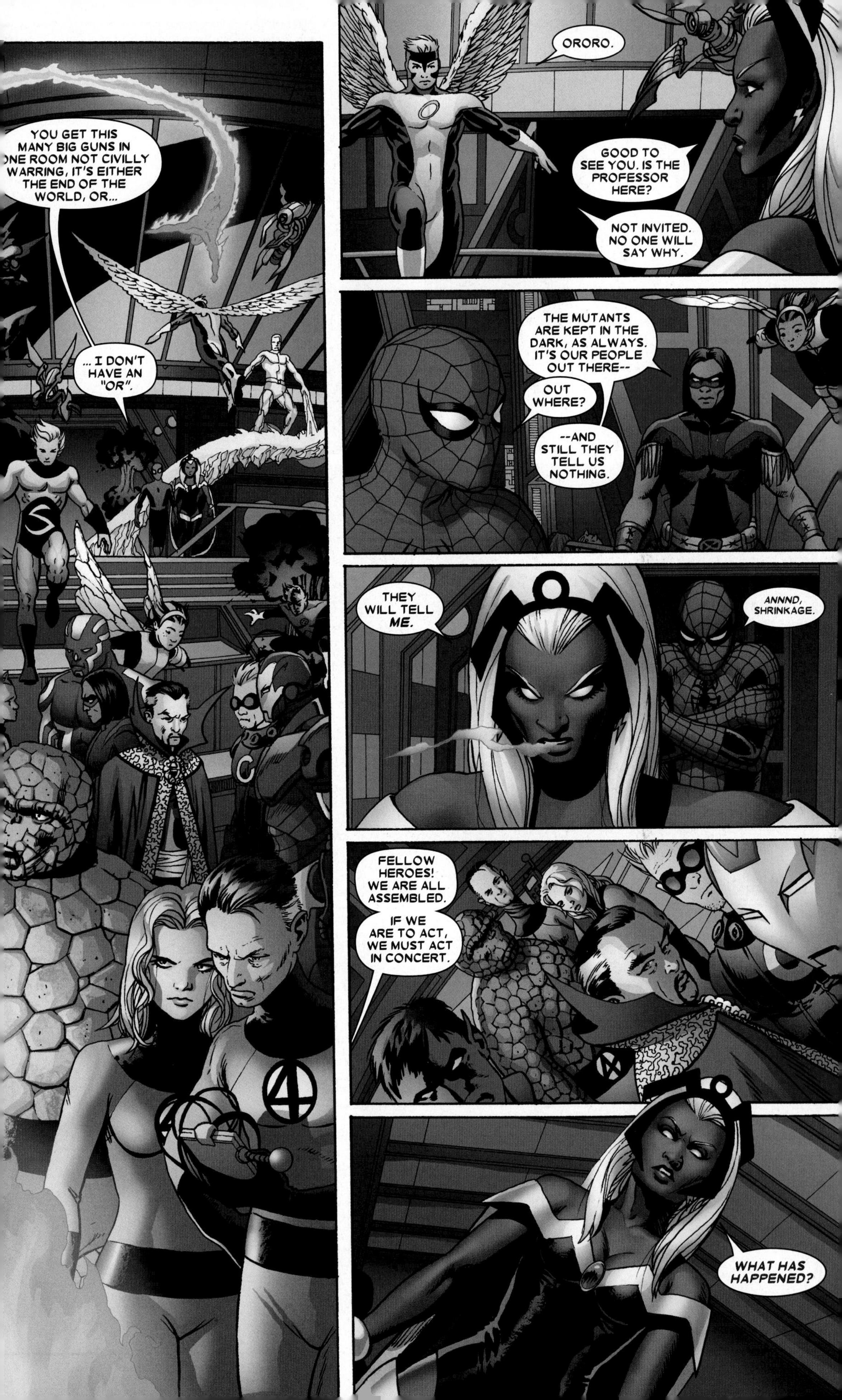

YOU GET THIS MANY BIG GUNS IN ONE ROOM NOT CIVILLY WARRING, IT'S EITHER THE END OF THE WORLD, OR...
... I DON'T HAVE AN "OR".
ORORO.
GOOD TO SEE YOU. IS THE PROFESSOR HERE?
NOT INVITED. NO ONE WILL SAY WHY.
THE MUTANTS ARE KEPT IN THE DARK, AS ALWAYS. IT'S OUR PEOPLE OUT THERE--
OUT WHERE?
--AND STILL THEY TELL US NOTHING.
THEY WILL TELL ME.
ANNND, SHRINKAGE.
FELLOW HEROES! WE ARE ALL ASSEMBLED.
IF WE ARE TO ACT, WE MUST ACT IN CONCERT.
WHAT HAS HAPPENED?

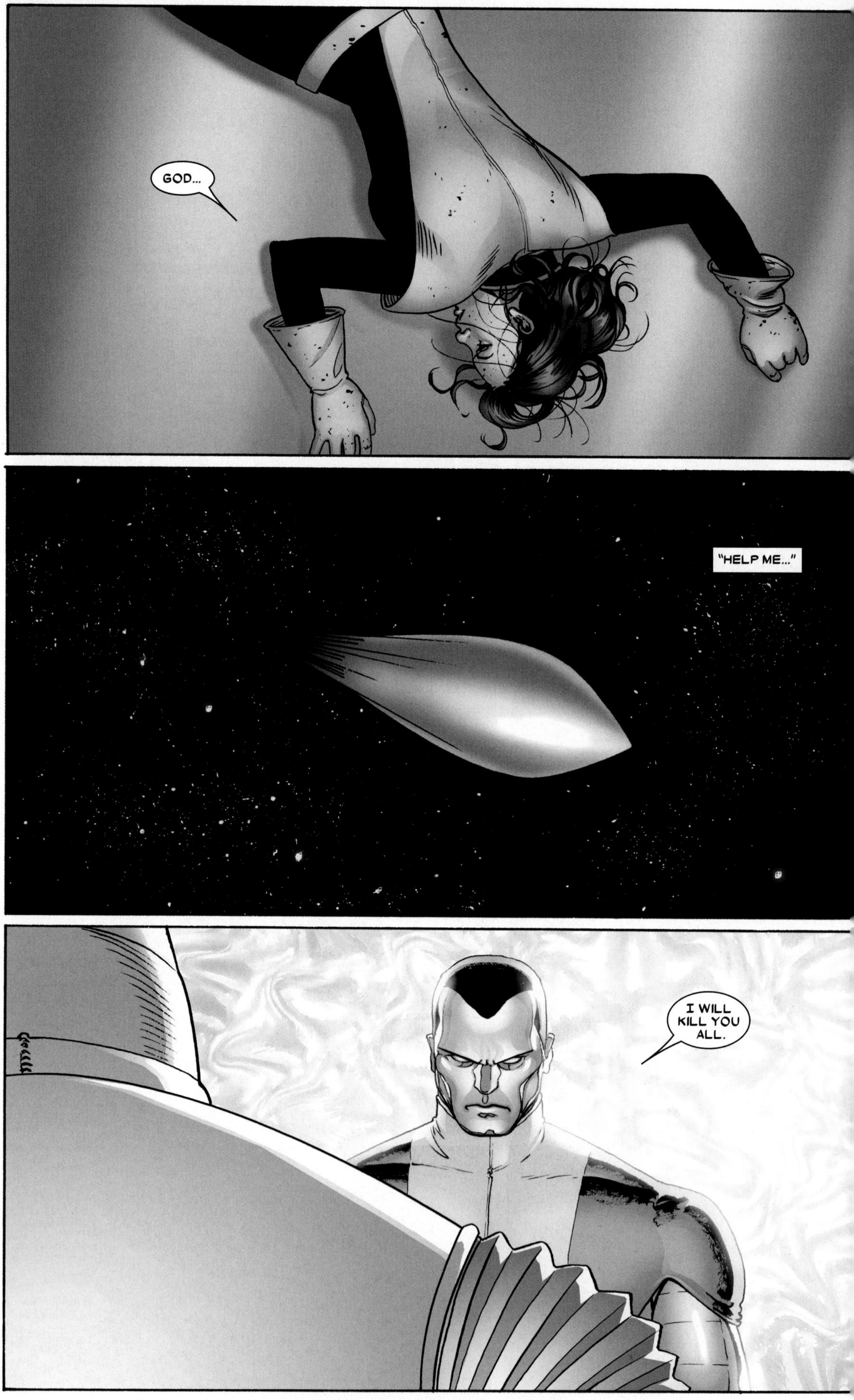
GOD...
"HELP ME..."
I WILL KILL YOU ALL.

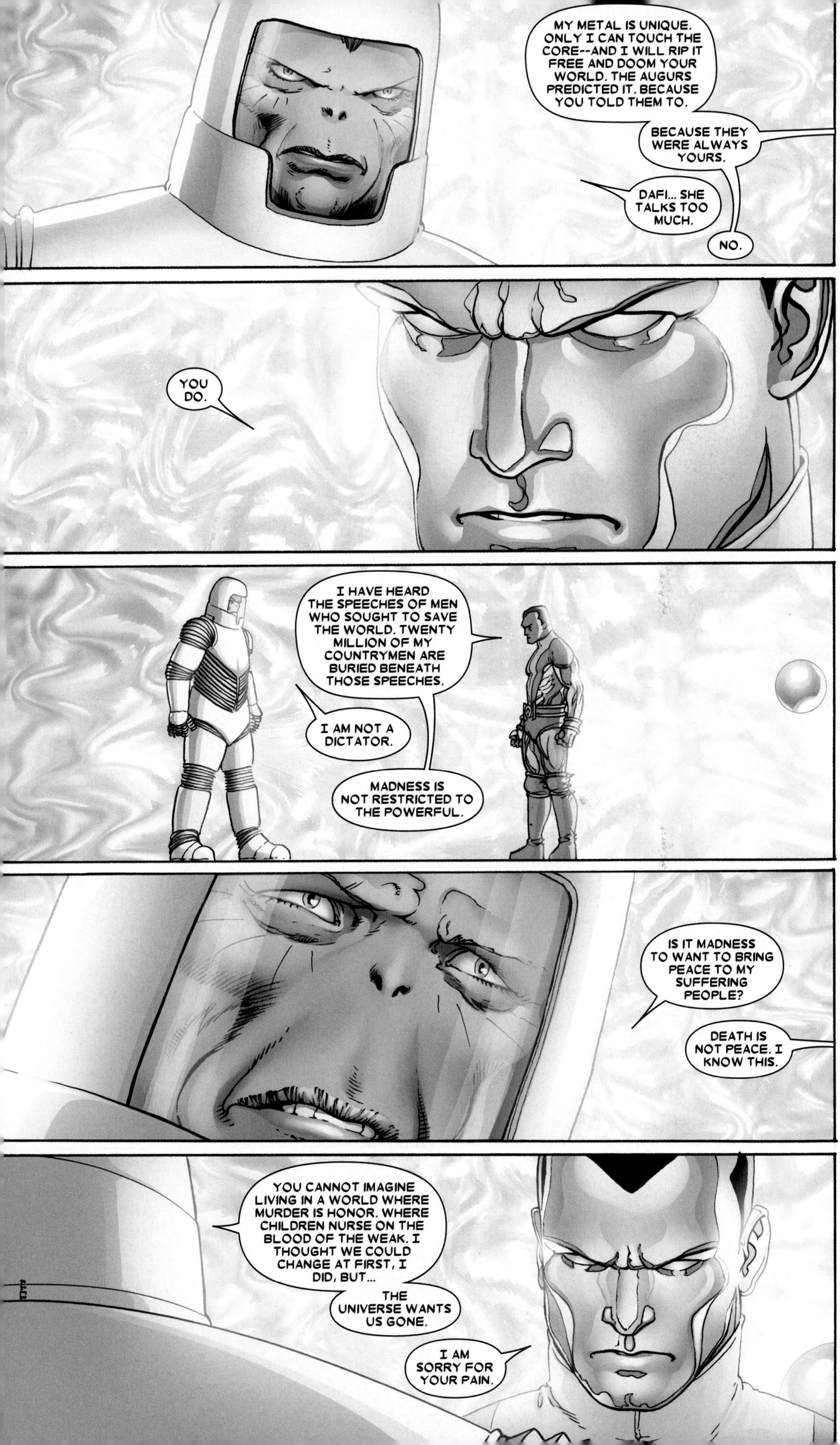
MY METAL IS UNIQUE. ONLY I CAN TOUCH THE CORE--AND I WILL RIP IT FREE AND DOOM YOUR WORLD. THE AUGURS PREDICTED IT. BECAUSE YOU TOLD THEM TO.
BECAUSE THEY WERE ALWAYS YOURS.
DAFI... SHE TALKS TOO MUCH.
NO.
YOU DO.
I HAVE HEARD THE SPEECHES OF MEN WHO SOUGHT TO SAVE THE WORLD. TWENTY MILLION OF MY COUNTRYMEN ARE BURIED BENEATH THOSE SPEECHES.
I AM NOT A DICTATOR.
MADNESS IS NOT RESTRICTED TO THE POWERFUL.
IS IT MADNESS TO WANT TO BRING PEACE TO MY SUFFERING PEOPLE?
DEATH IS NOT PEACE. I KNOW THIS.
YOU CANNOT IMAGINE LIVING IN A WORLD WHERE MURDER IS HONOR. WHERE CHILDREN NURSE ON THE BLOOD OF THE WEAK. I THOUGHT WE COULD CHANGE AT FIRST, I DID, BUT...
THE UNIVERSE WANTS US GONE.
I AM SORRY FOR YOUR PAIN.

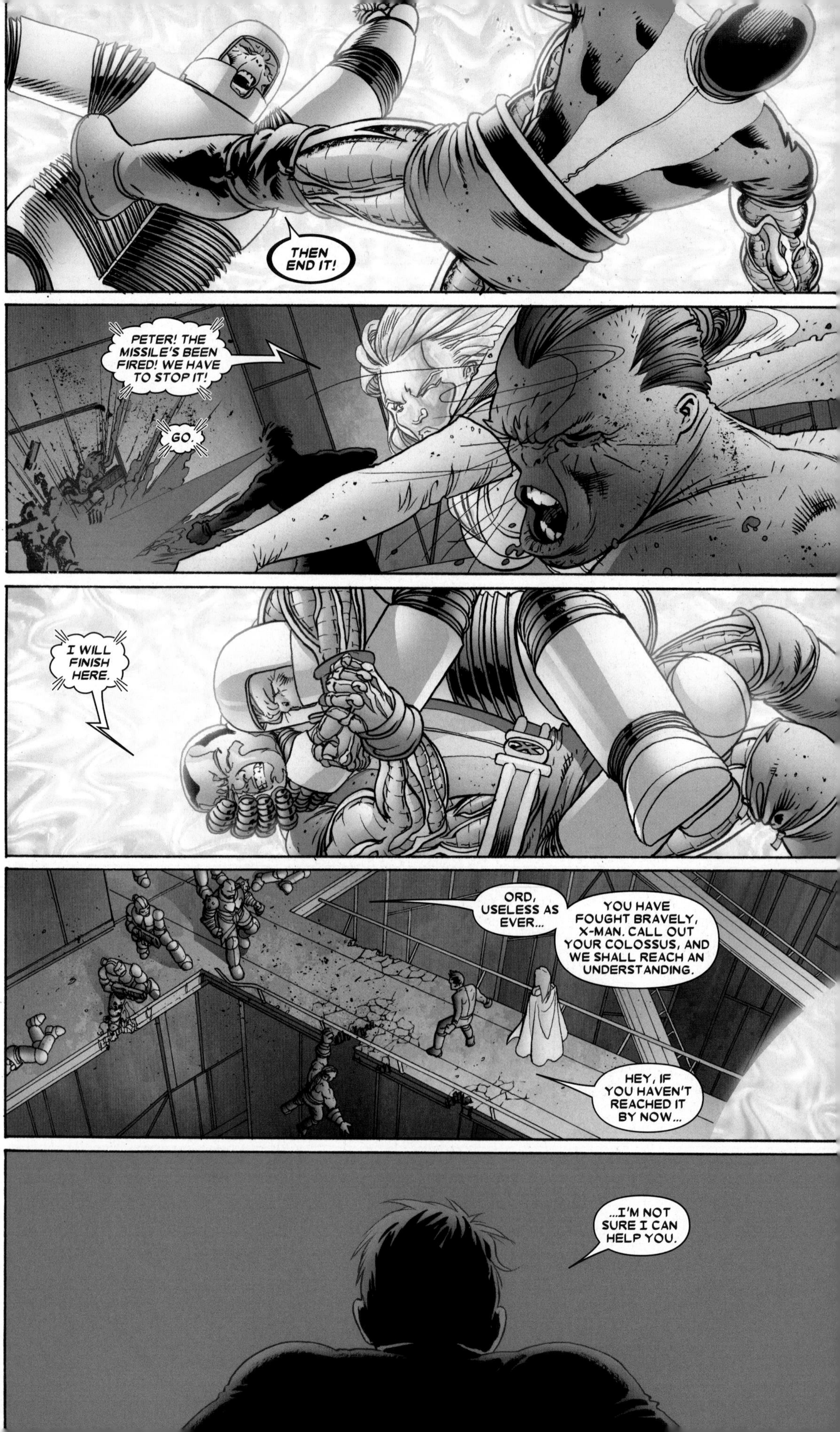

THEN END IT!
PETER! THE MISSILE'S BEEN FIRED! WE HAVE TO STOP IT!
GO.
I WILL FINISH HERE.
ORD, USELESS AS EVER...
YOU HAVE FOUGHT BRAVELY, X-MAN. CALL OUT YOUR COLOSSUS, AND WE SHALL REACH AN UNDERSTANDING.
HEY, IF YOU HAVEN'T REACHED IT BY NOW...
...I'M NOT SURE I CAN HELP YOU.

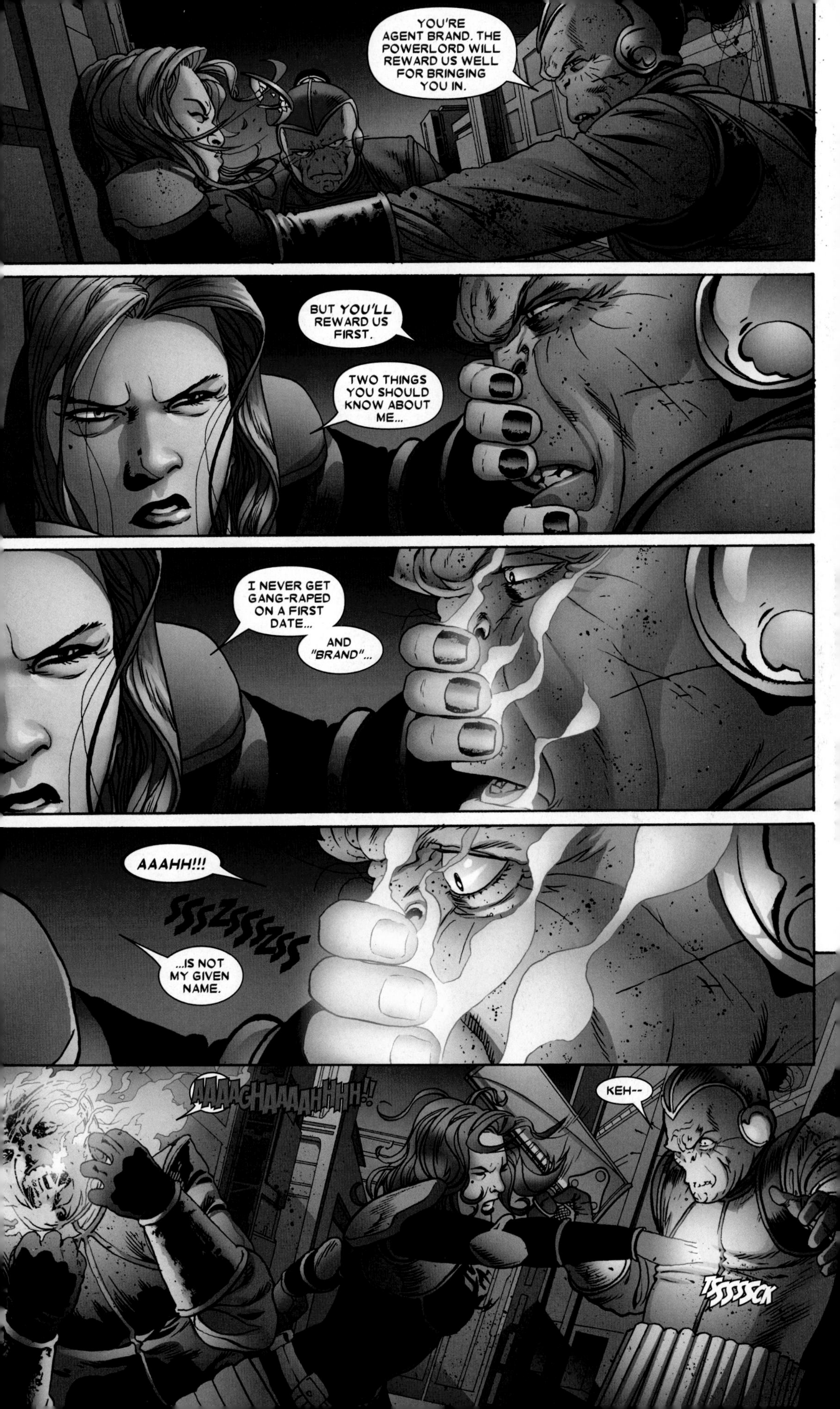
YOU'RE AGENT BRAND. THE POWERLORD WILL REWARD US WELL FOR BRINGING YOU IN.
BUT YOU'LL REWARD US FIRST.
TWO THINGS YOU SHOULD KNOW ABOUT ME...
I NEVER GET GANG-RAPED ON A FIRST DATE...
AND "BRAND"...
AAAHH!!!
SSSZSSSZSS
...IS NOT MY GIVEN NAME.
AAAAGHAAAAHHHH!!
KEH--
TSSSSSCK

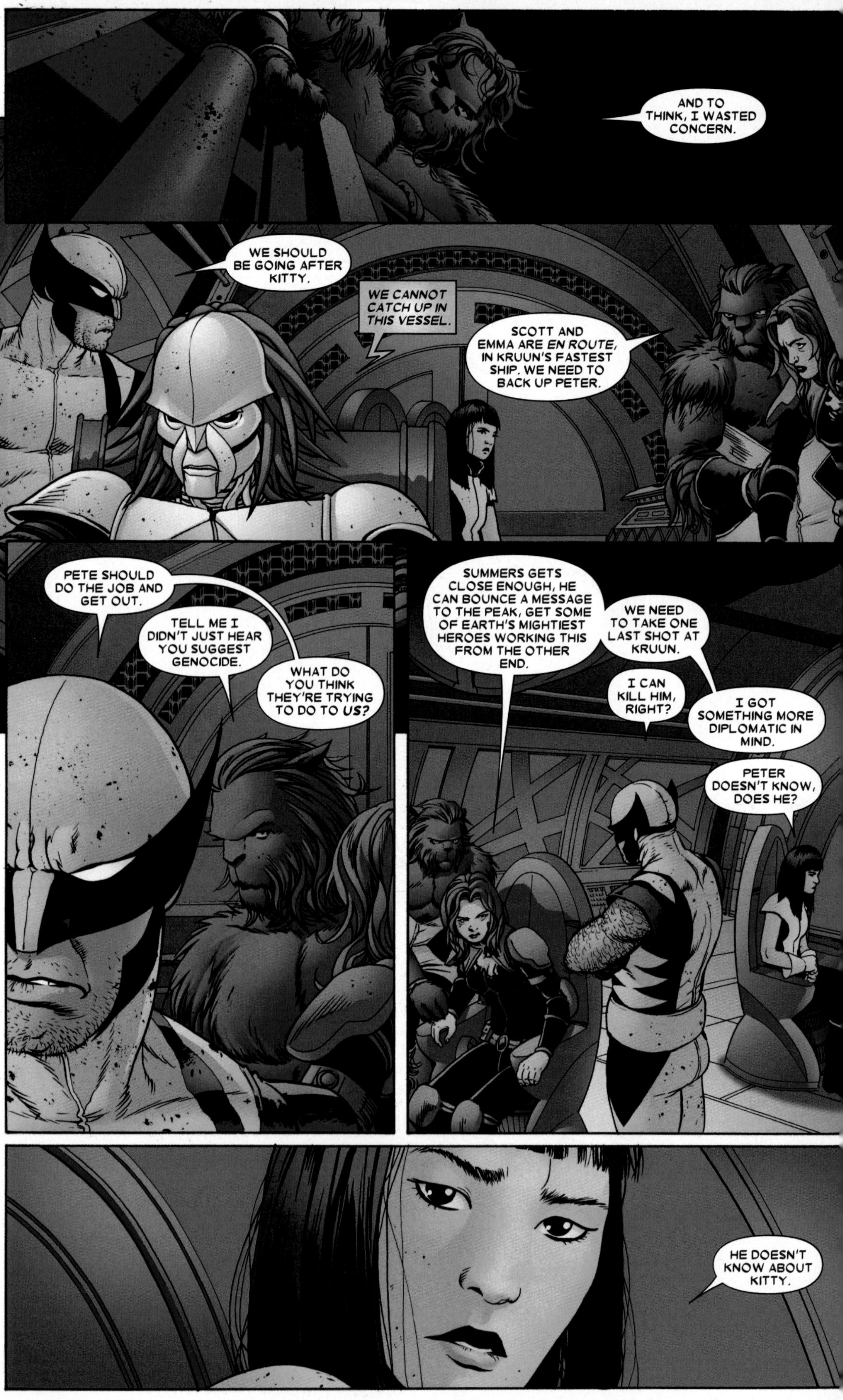
AND TO THINK, I WASTED CONCERN.
WE SHOULD BE GOING AFTER KITTY.
WE CANNOT CATCH UP IN THIS VESSEL.
SCOTT AND EMMA ARE EN ROUTE, IN KRUUN'S FASTEST SHIP. WE NEED TO BACK UP PETER.
PETE SHOULD DO THE JOB AND GET OUT.
TELL ME I DIDN'T JUST HEAR YOU SUGGEST GENOCIDE.
WHAT DO YOU THINK THEY'RE TRYING TO DO TO US?
SUMMERS GETS CLOSE ENOUGH, HE CAN BOUNCE A MESSAGE TO THE PEAK, GET SOME OF EARTH'S MIGHTIEST HEROES WORKING THIS FROM THE OTHER END.
WE NEED TO TAKE ONE LAST SHOT AT KRUUN.
I CAN KILL HIM, RIGHT?
I GOT SOMETHING MORE DIPLOMATIC IN MIND.
PETER DOESN'T KNOW, DOES HE?
HE DOESN'T KNOW ABOUT KITTY.

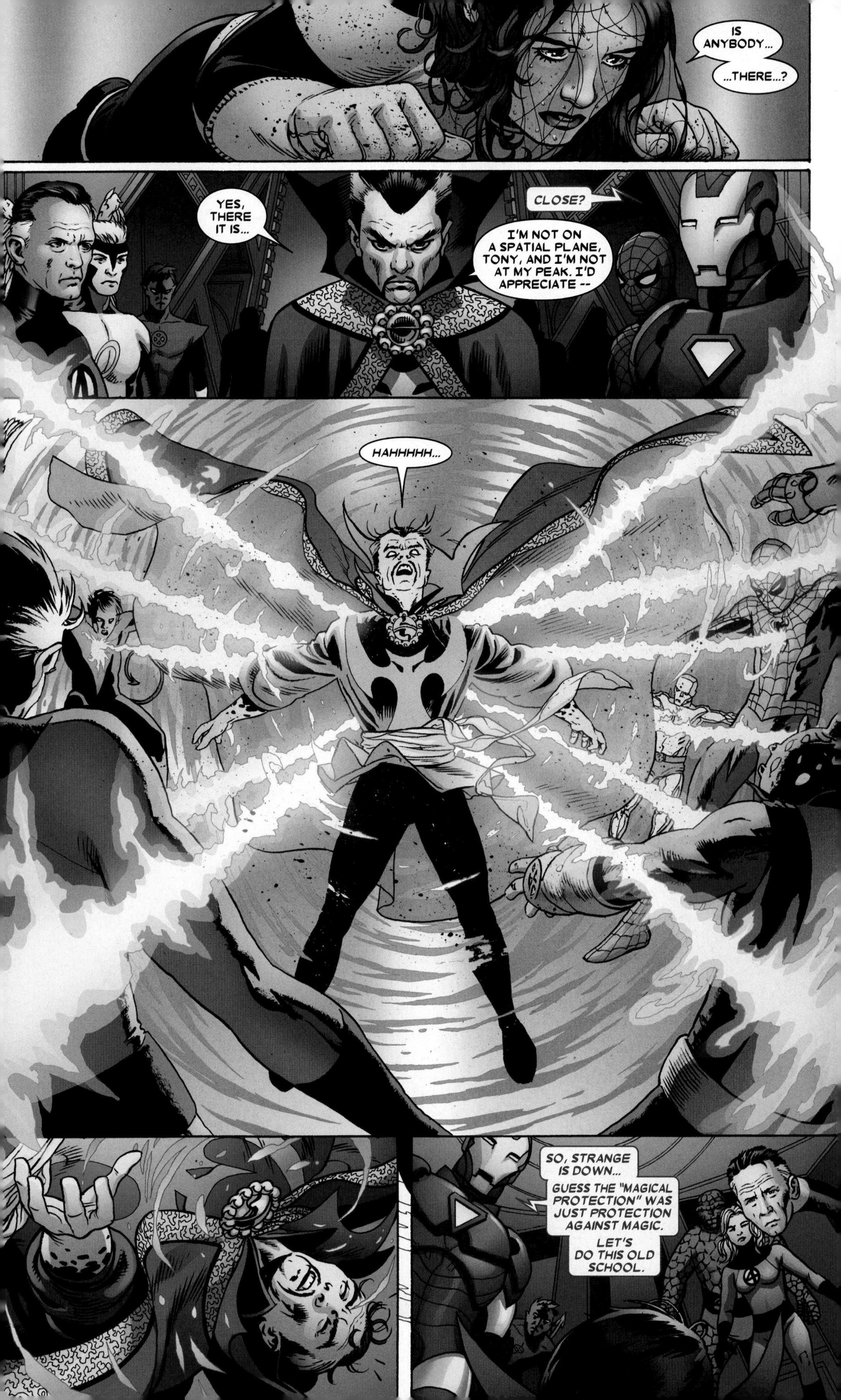
IS ANYBODY...
...THERE...?
YES, THERE IT IS...
CLOSE?
I'M NOT ON A SPATIAL PLANE, TONY, AND I'M NOT AT MY PEAK. I'D APPRECIATE --
HAHHHHH...
SO, STRANGE IS DOWN...
GUESS THE "MAGICAL PROTECTION" WAS JUST PROTECTION AGAINST MAGIC.
LET'S DO THIS OLD SCHOOL.

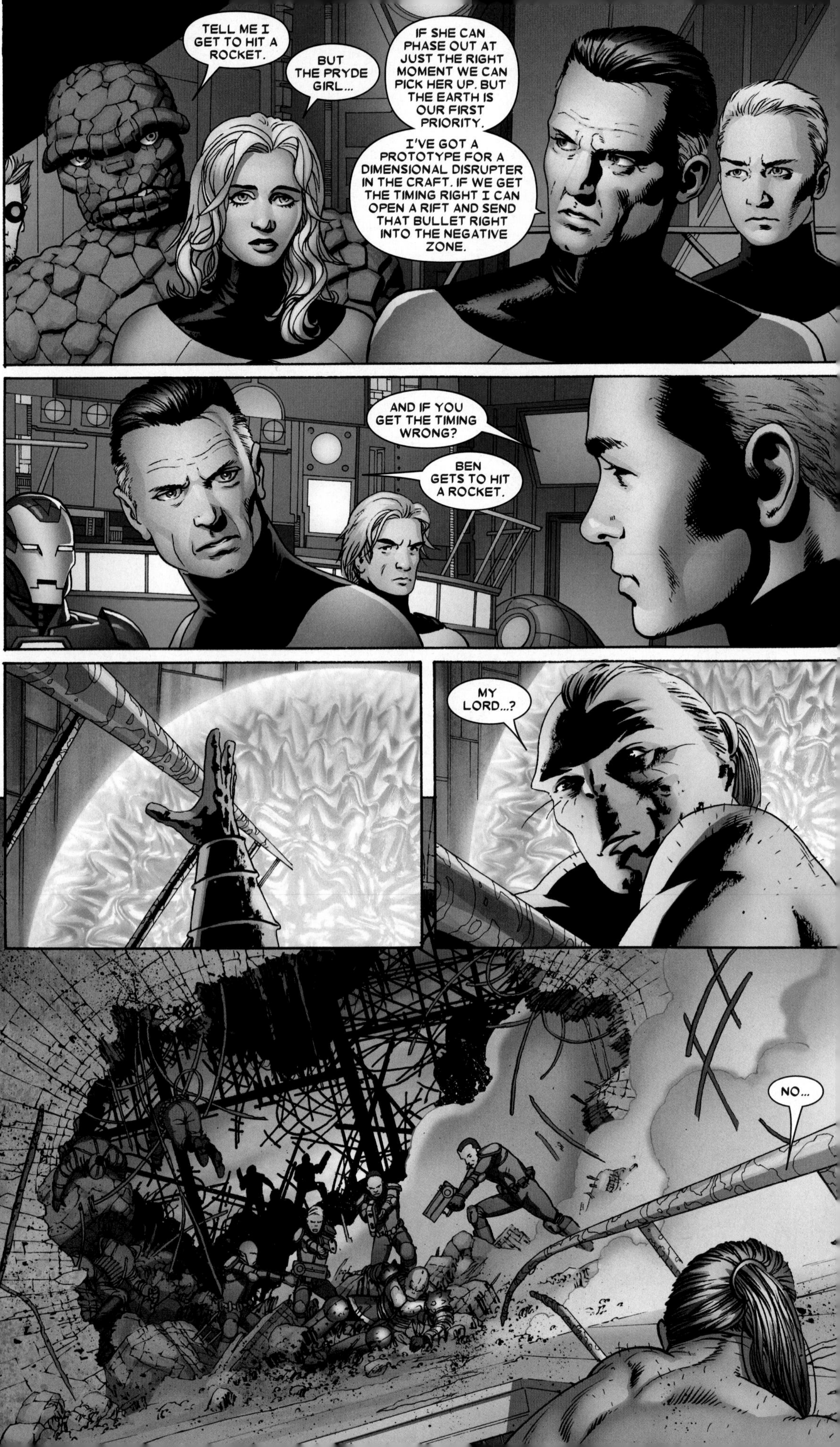
TELL ME I GET TO HIT A ROCKET.
BUT THE PRYDE GIRL...
IF SHE CAN PHASE OUT AT JUST THE RIGHT MOMENT WE CAN PICK HER UP. BUT THE EARTH IS OUR FIRST PRIORITY.
I'VE GOT A PROTOTYPE FOR A DIMENSIONAL DISRUPTER IN THE CRAFT. IF WE GET THE TIMING RIGHT I CAN OPEN A RIFT AND SEND THAT BULLET RIGHT INTO THE NEGATIVE ZONE.
AND IF YOU GET THE TIMING WRONG?
BEN GETS TO HIT A ROCKET.
MY LORD...?
NO...

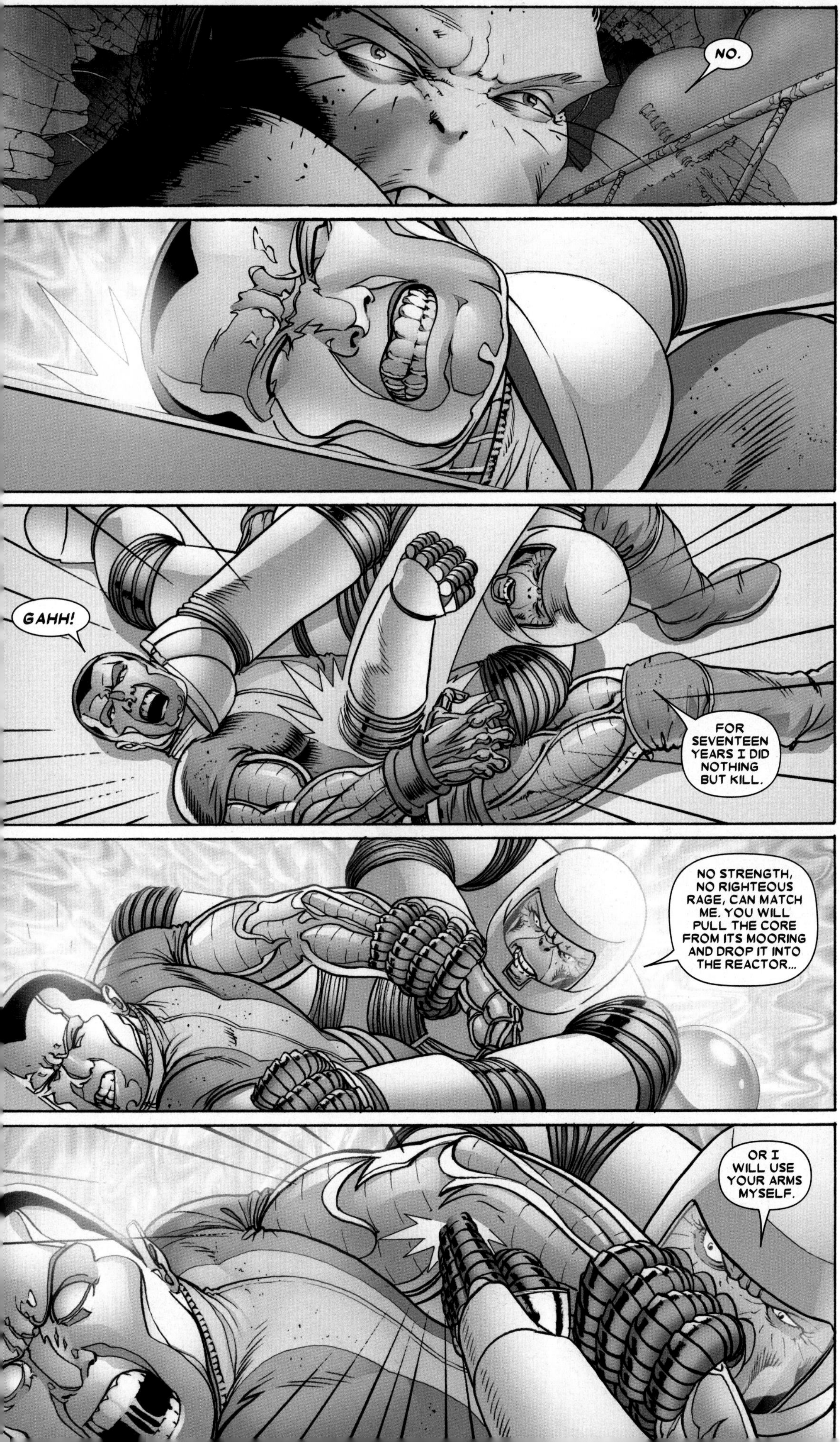
NO.
GAHH!
FOR SEVENTEEN YEARS I DID NOTHING BUT KILL.
NO STRENGTH, NO RIGHTEOUS RAGE, CAN MATCH ME. YOU WILL PULL THE CORE FROM ITS MOORING AND DROP IT INTO THE REACTOR...
OR I WILL USE YOUR ARMS MYSELF.

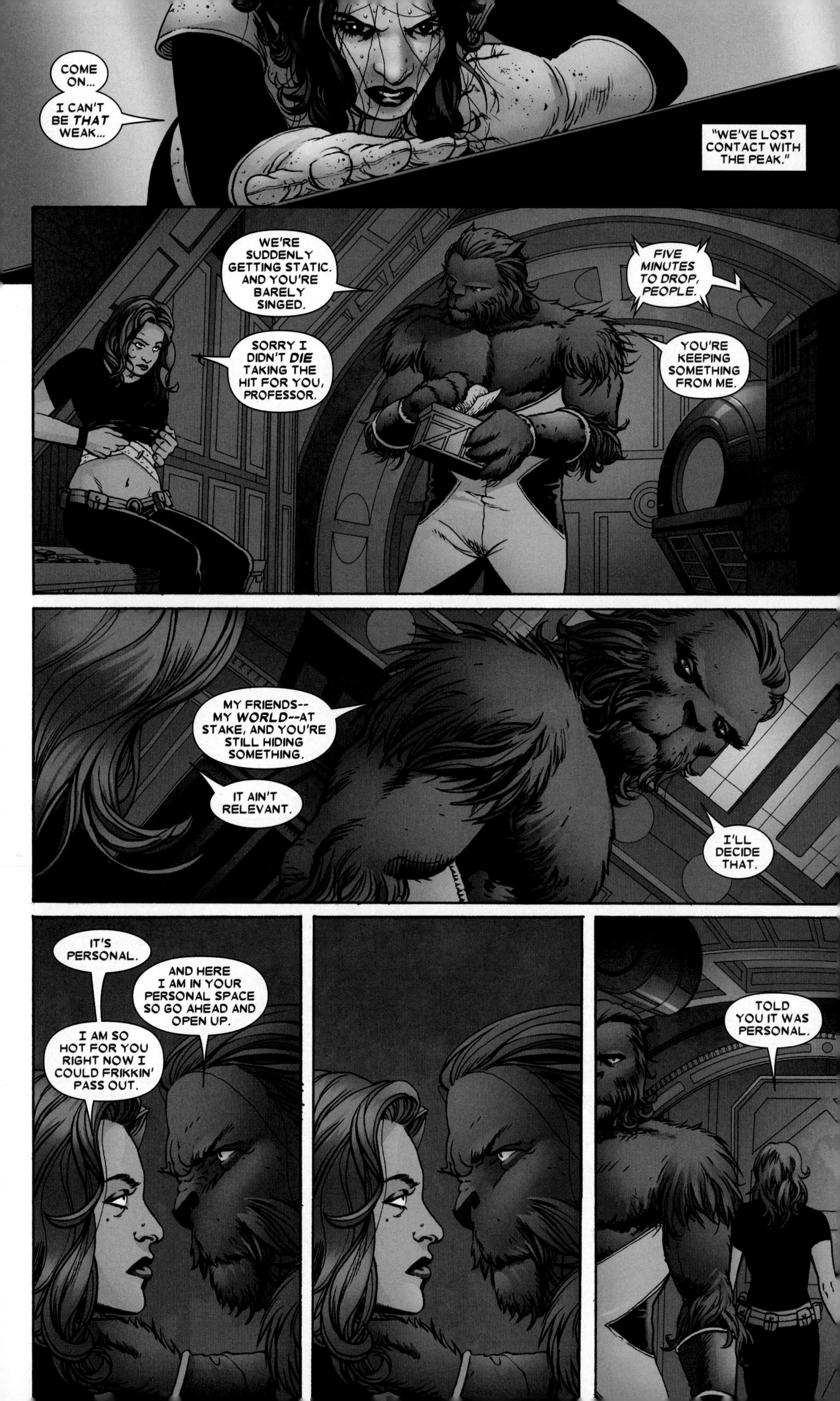
COME ON... I CAN'T BE *THAT* WEAK...
"WE'VE LOST CONTACT WITH THE PEAK."
WE'RE SUDDENLY GETTING STATIC. AND YOU'RE BARELY SINGED.
FIVE MINUTES TO DROP, PEOPLE.
SORRY I DIDN'T *DIE* TAKING THE HIT FOR YOU, PROFESSOR.
YOU'RE KEEPING SOMETHING FROM ME.
MY FRIENDS-- MY *WORLD*--AT STAKE, AND YOU'RE STILL HIDING SOMETHING.
IT AIN'T RELEVANT.
I'LL DECIDE THAT.
IT'S PERSONAL.
AND HERE I AM IN YOUR PERSONAL SPACE SO GO AHEAD AND OPEN UP.
I AM SO HOT FOR YOU RIGHT NOW I COULD FRIKKIN' PASS OUT.
TOLD YOU IT WAS PERSONAL.

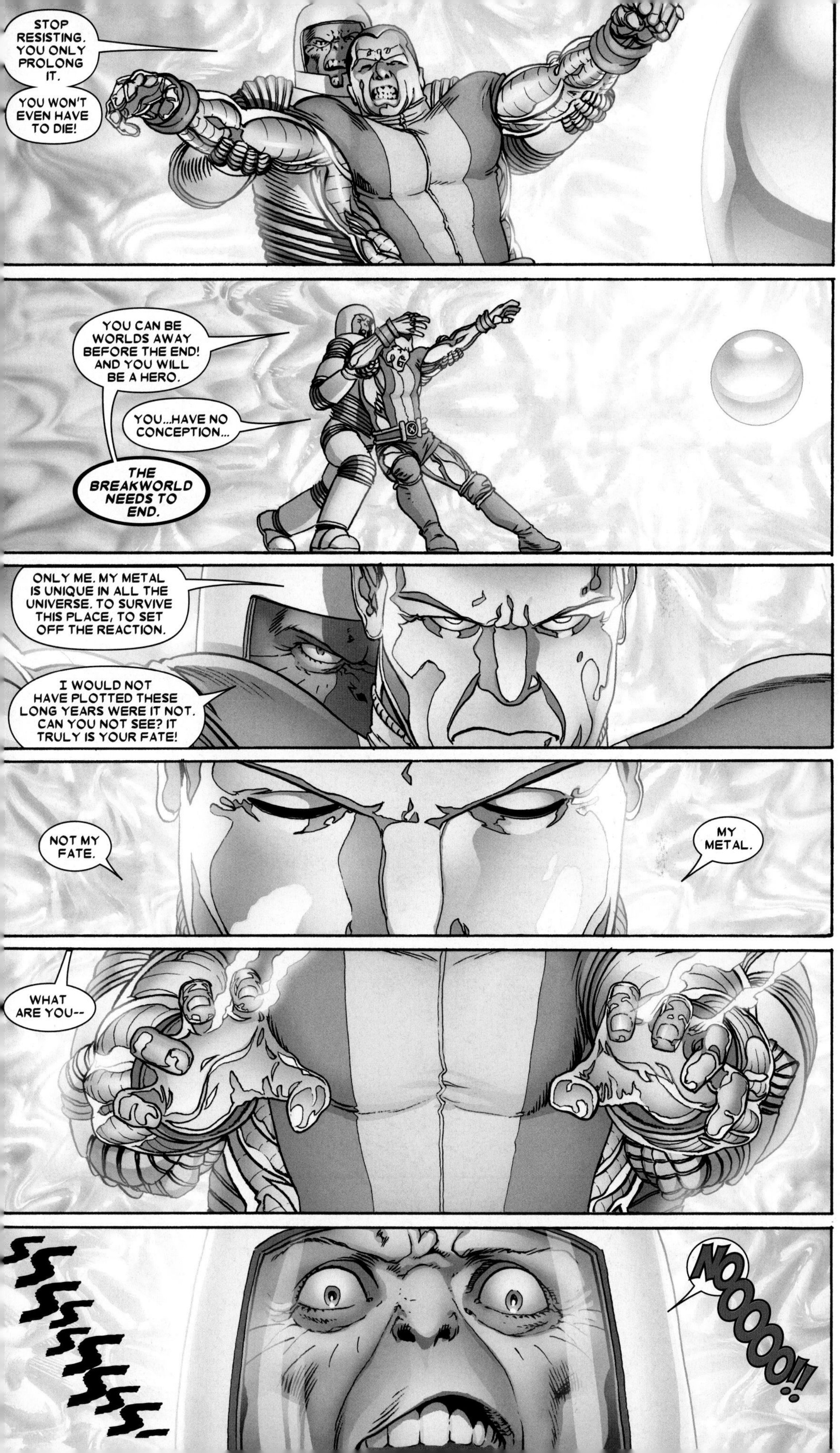

STOP RESISTING. YOU ONLY PROLONG IT.
YOU WON'T EVEN HAVE TO DIE!
YOU CAN BE WORLDS AWAY BEFORE THE END! AND YOU WILL BE A HERO.
YOU...HAVE NO CONCEPTION...
THE BREAKWORLD NEEDS TO END.
ONLY ME. MY METAL IS UNIQUE IN ALL THE UNIVERSE. TO SURVIVE THIS PLACE, TO SET OFF THE REACTION.
I WOULD NOT HAVE PLOTTED THESE LONG YEARS WERE IT NOT. CAN YOU NOT SEE? IT TRULY IS YOUR FATE!
NOT MY FATE.
MY METAL.
WHAT ARE YOU--
SSSSSSSSS
NOOOOO!!

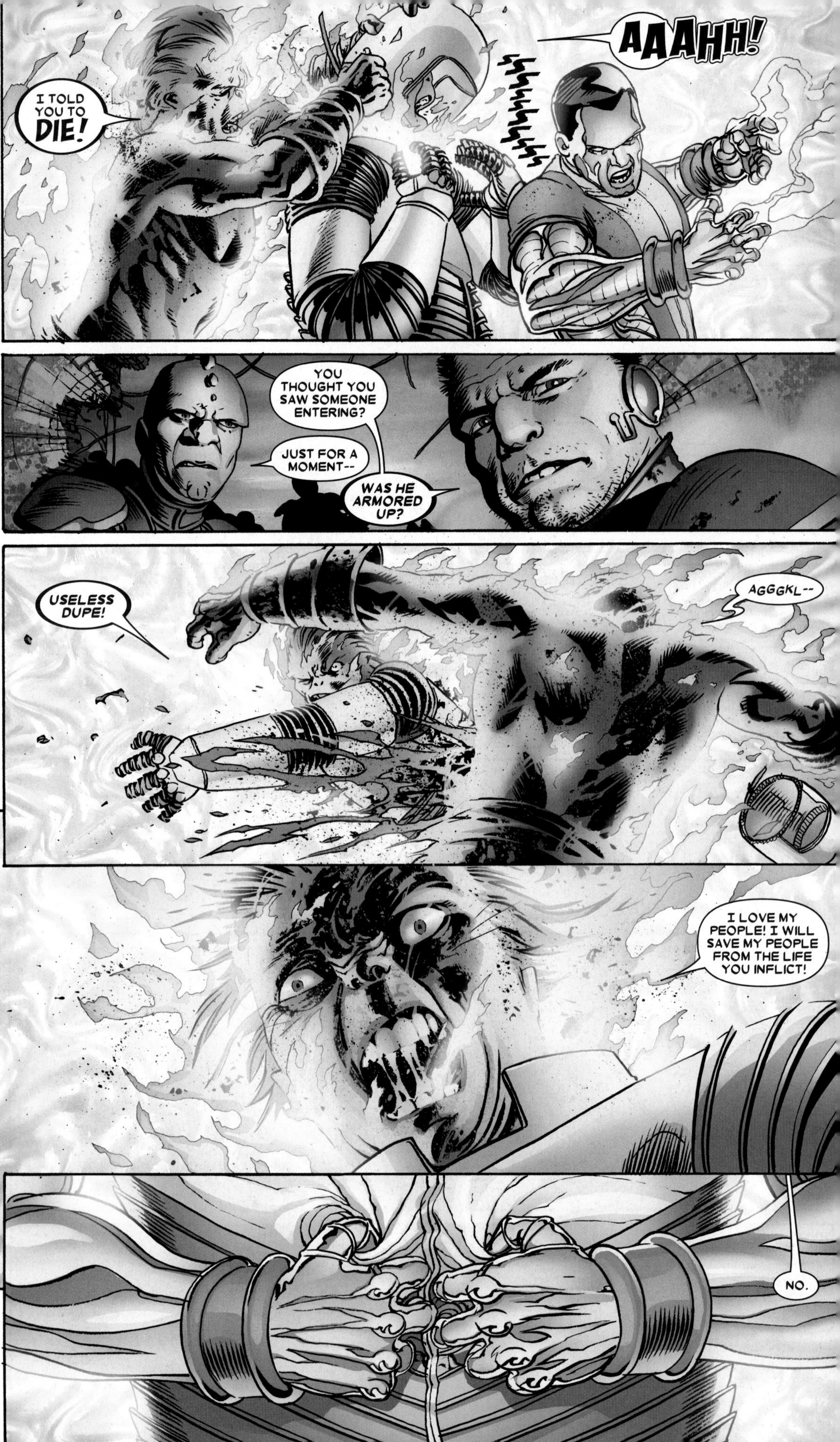

AAAHH!
I TOLD YOU TO DIE!
SSHHHHHHHH
YOU THOUGHT YOU SAW SOMEONE ENTERING?
JUST FOR A MOMENT--
WAS HE ARMORED UP?
USELESS DUPE!
AGGGKL--
I LOVE MY PEOPLE! I WILL SAVE MY PEOPLE FROM THE LIFE YOU INFLICT!
NO.

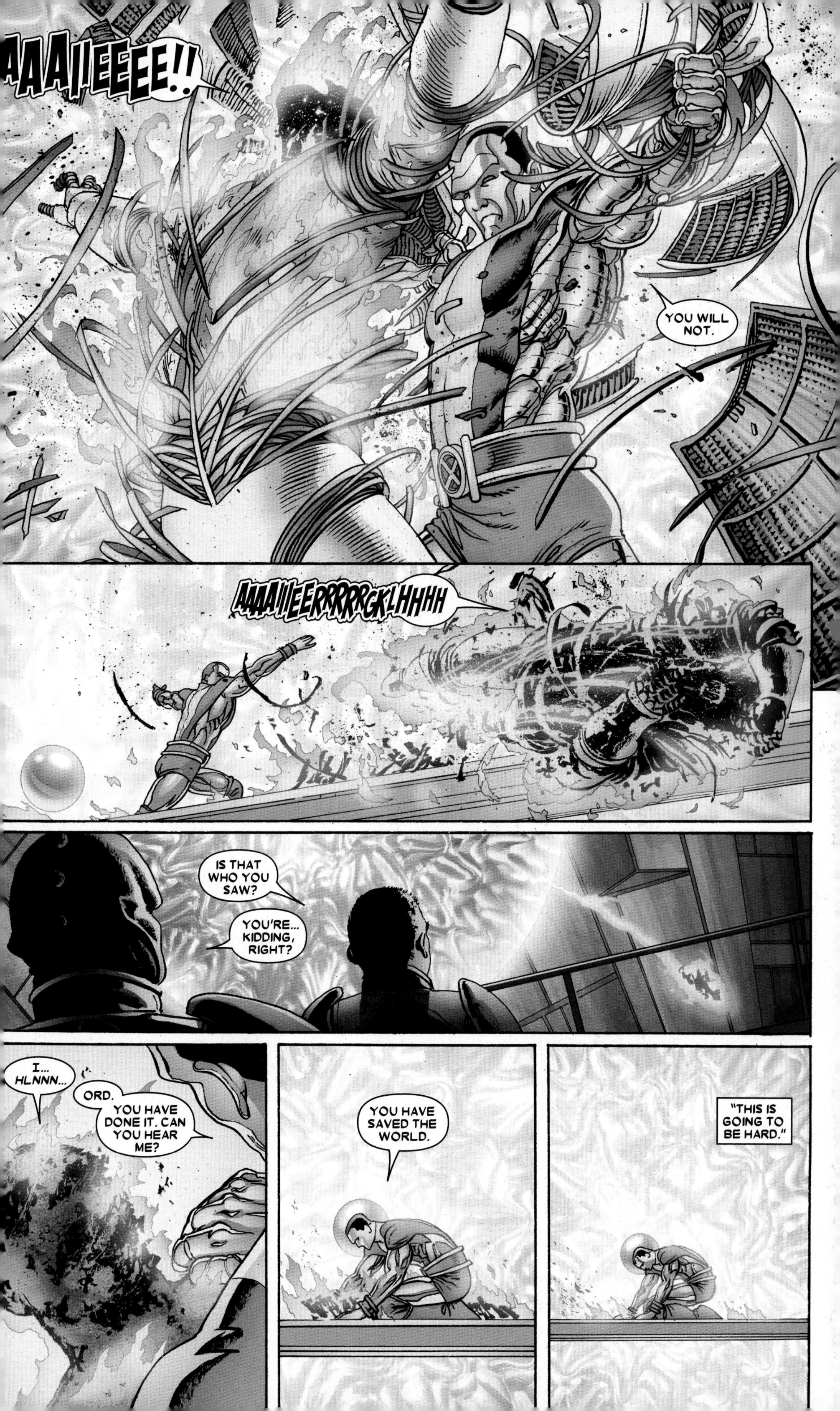
AAAIIEEEE!!
YOU WILL NOT.
AAAIIEERRRRRGKLHHHH
IS THAT WHO YOU SAW?
YOU'RE... KIDDING, RIGHT?
I... HLNNN...
ORD. YOU HAVE DONE IT. CAN YOU HEAR ME?
YOU HAVE SAVED THE WORLD.
"THIS IS GOING TO BE HARD."

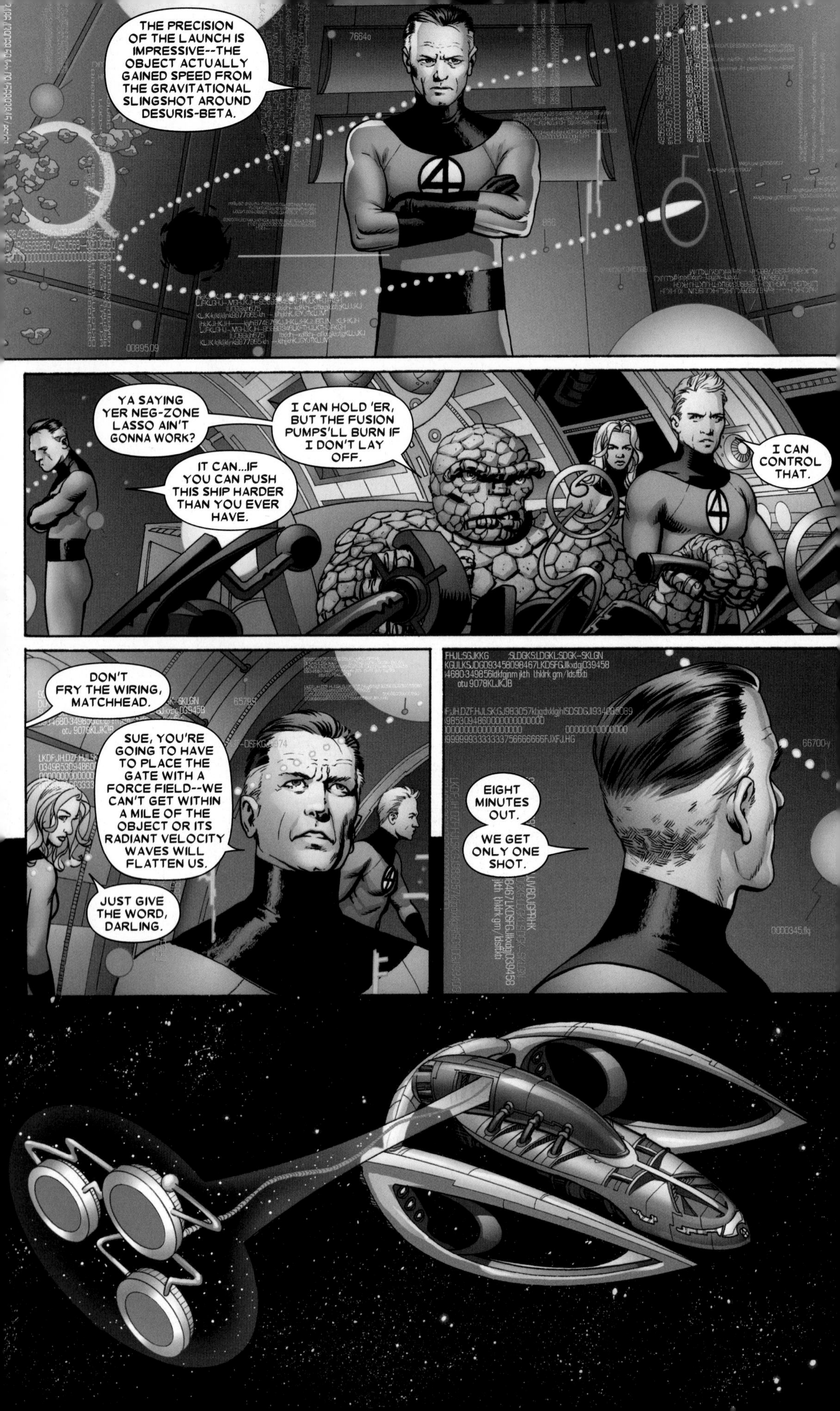
THE PRECISION OF THE LAUNCH IS IMPRESSIVE--THE OBJECT ACTUALLY GAINED SPEED FROM THE GRAVITATIONAL SLINGSHOT AROUND DESURIS-BETA.
YA SAYING YER NEG-ZONE LASSO AIN'T GONNA WORK?
IT CAN...IF YOU CAN PUSH THIS SHIP HARDER THAN YOU EVER HAVE.
I CAN HOLD 'ER, BUT THE FUSION PUMPS'LL BURN IF I DON'T LAY OFF.
I CAN CONTROL THAT.
DON'T FRY THE WIRING, MATCHHEAD.
SUE, YOU'RE GOING TO HAVE TO PLACE THE GATE WITH A FORCE FIELD--WE CAN'T GET WITHIN A MILE OF THE OBJECT OR ITS RADIANT VELOCITY WAVES WILL FLATTEN US.
JUST GIVE THE WORD, DARLING.
EIGHT MINUTES OUT.
WE GET ONLY ONE SHOT.

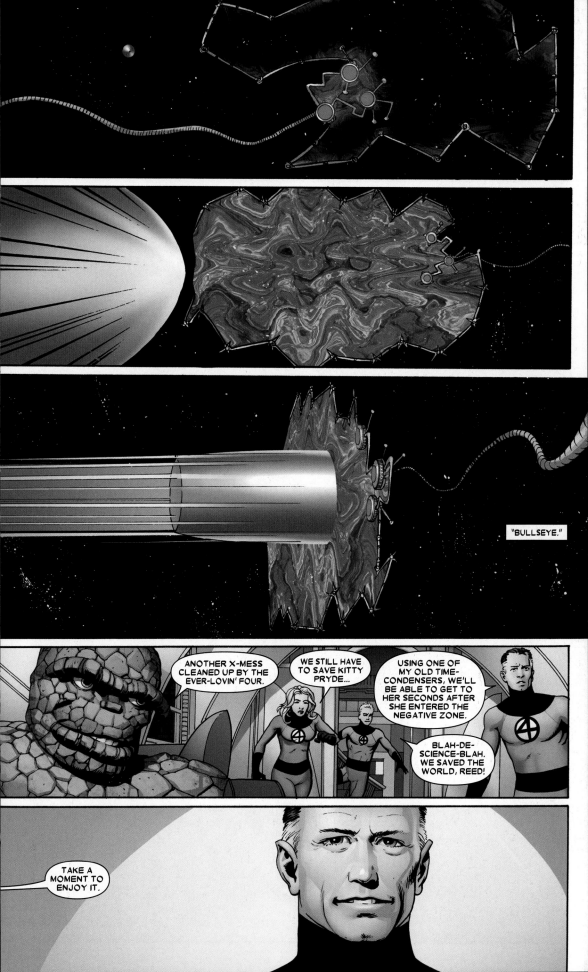

"BULLSEYE."

ANOTHER X-MESS CLEANED UP BY THE EVER-LOVIN' FOUR.

WE STILL HAVE TO SAVE KITTY PRYDE...

USING ONE OF MY OLD TIME-CONDENSERS, WE'LL BE ABLE TO GET TO HER SECONDS AFTER SHE ENTERED THE NEGATIVE ZONE.

BLAH-DE-SCIENCE-BLAH. WE SAVED THE WORLD, REED!

TAKE A MOMENT TO ENJOY IT.

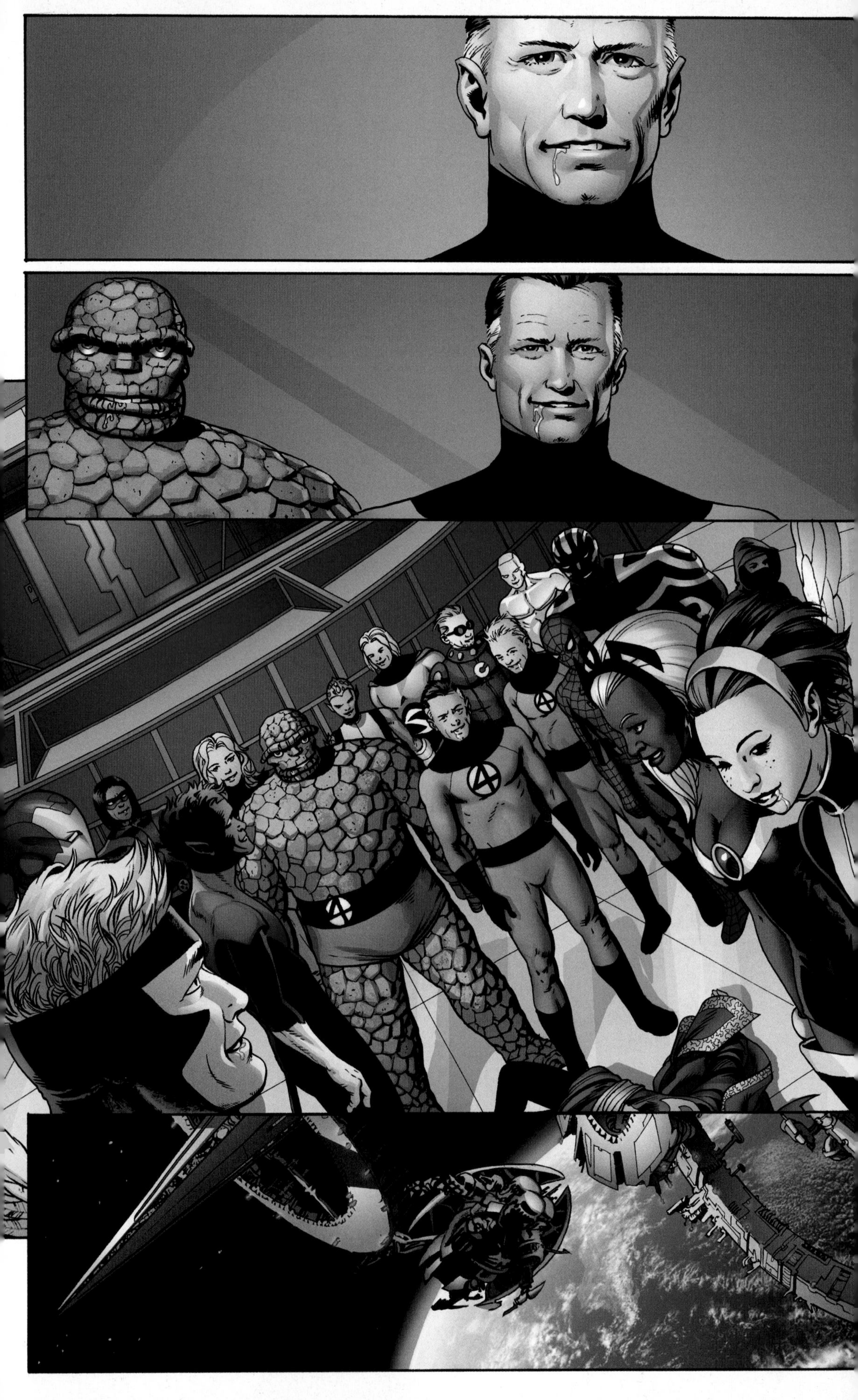

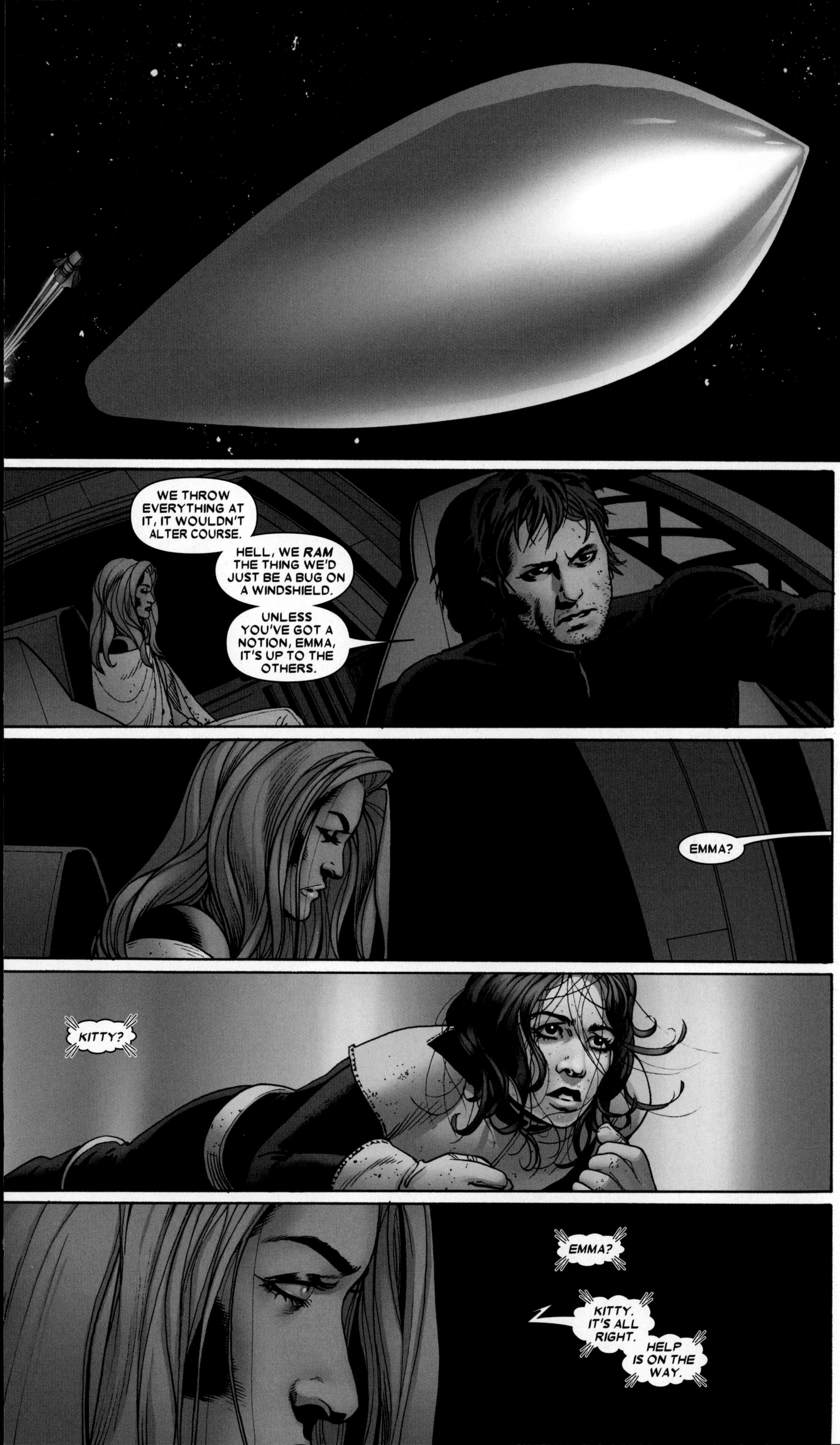

WE THROW EVERYTHING AT IT, IT WOULDN'T ALTER COURSE.
HELL, WE *RAM* THE THING WE'D JUST BE A BUG ON A WINDSHIELD.
UNLESS YOU'VE GOT A NOTION, EMMA, IT'S UP TO THE OTHERS.
EMMA?
KITTY?
EMMA?
KITTY. IT'S ALL RIGHT.
HELP IS ON THE WAY.

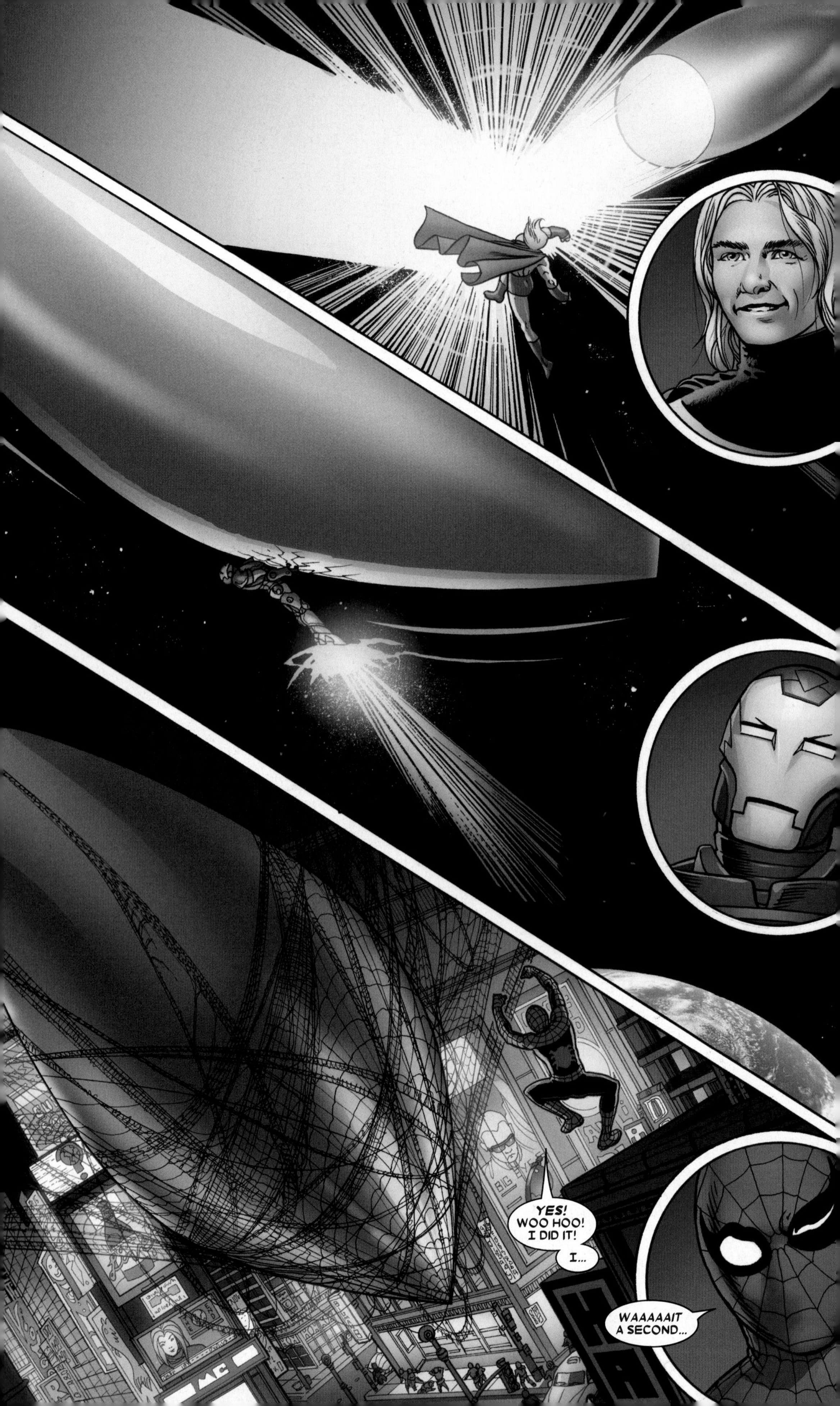
YES! WOO HOO! I DID IT!
I...
WAAAAAIT A SECOND...

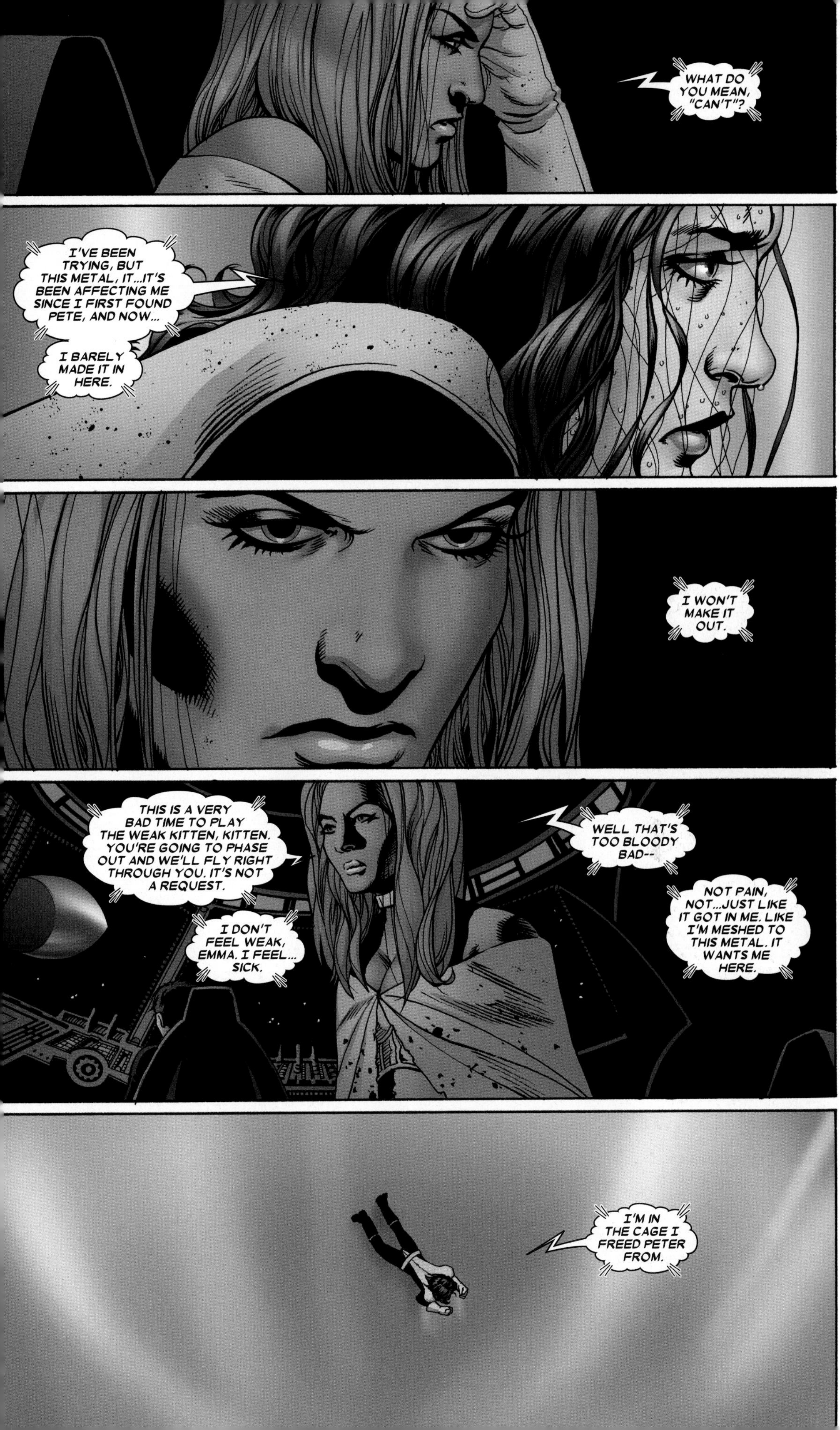
WHAT DO YOU MEAN, "CAN'T"?
I'VE BEEN TRYING, BUT THIS METAL, IT...IT'S BEEN AFFECTING ME SINCE I FIRST FOUND PETE, AND NOW...
I BARELY MADE IT IN HERE.
I WON'T MAKE IT OUT.
THIS IS A VERY BAD TIME TO PLAY THE WEAK KITTEN, KITTEN. YOU'RE GOING TO PHASE OUT AND WE'LL FLY RIGHT THROUGH YOU. IT'S NOT A REQUEST.
I DON'T FEEL WEAK, EMMA. I FEEL... SICK.
WELL THAT'S TOO BLOODY BAD--
NOT PAIN, NOT...JUST LIKE IT GOT IN ME. LIKE I'M MESHED TO THIS METAL. IT WANTS ME HERE.
I'M IN THE CAGE I FREED PETER FROM.

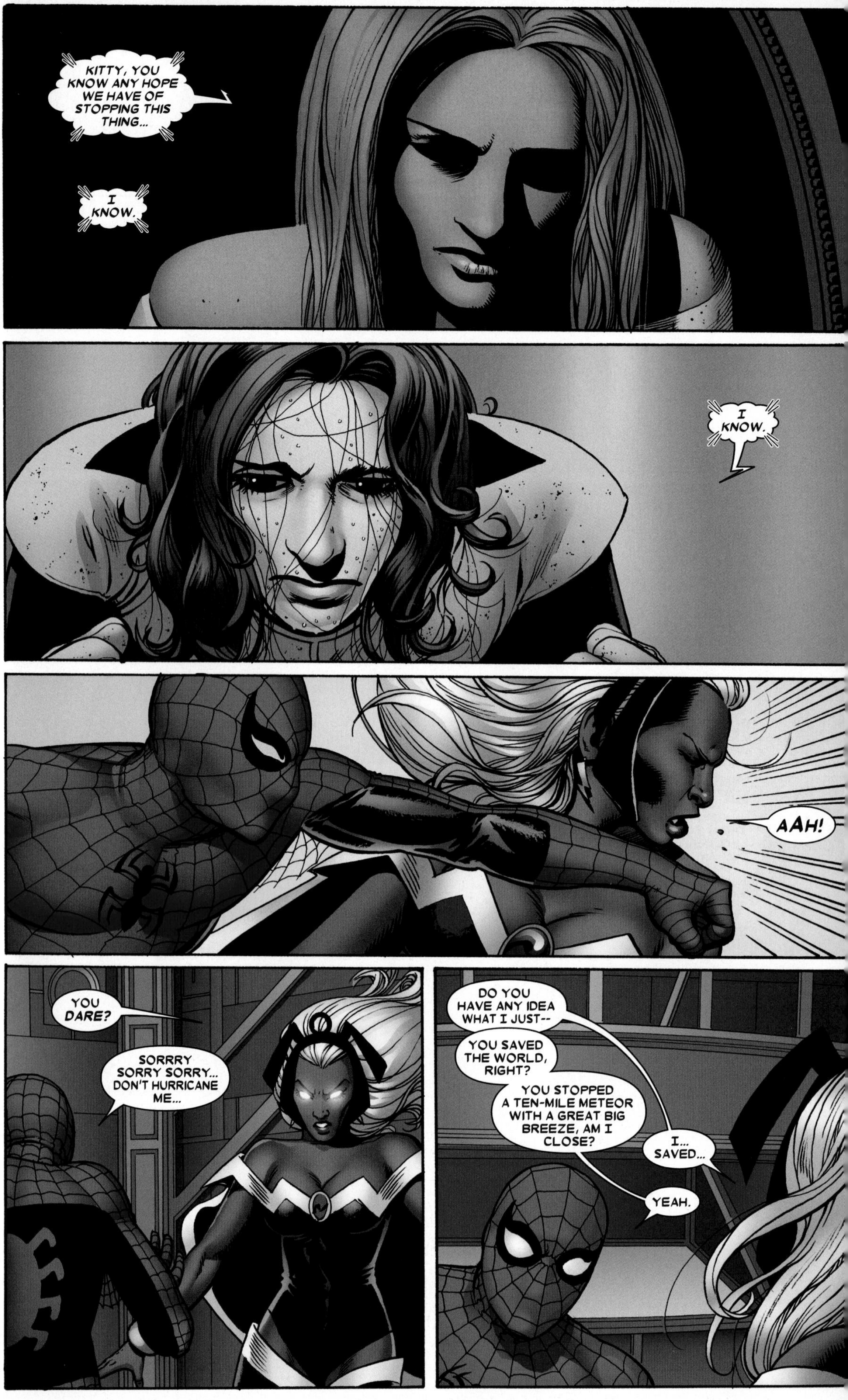
KITTY, YOU KNOW ANY HOPE WE HAVE OF STOPPING THIS THING...
I KNOW.
I KNOW.
AAH!
YOU DARE?
SORRRY SORRY SORRY... DON'T HURRICANE ME...
DO YOU HAVE ANY IDEA WHAT I JUST--
YOU SAVED THE WORLD, RIGHT?
YOU STOPPED A TEN-MILE METEOR WITH A GREAT BIG BREEZE, AM I CLOSE?
I... SAVED...
YEAH.

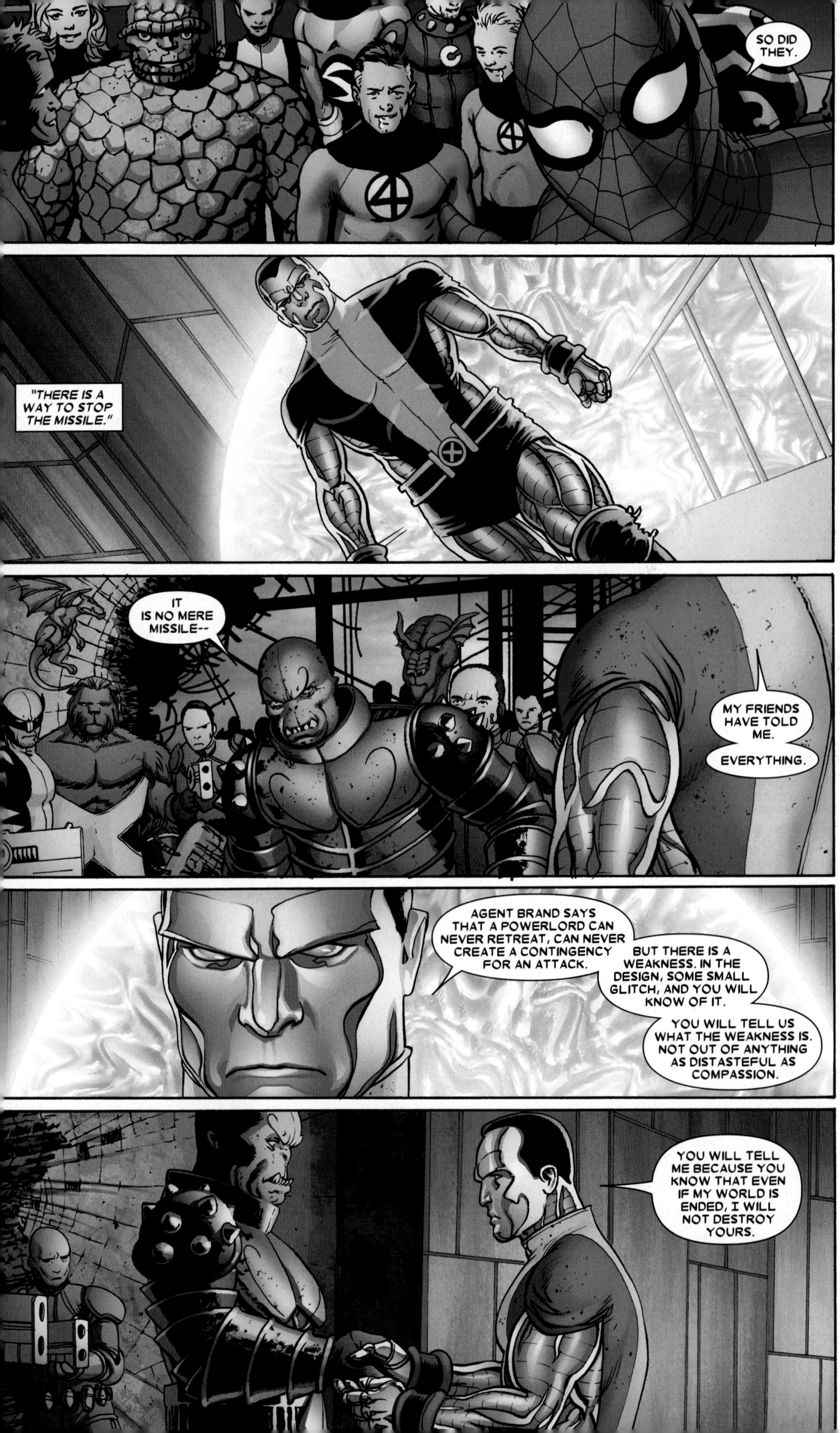
SO DID THEY.
"THERE IS A WAY TO STOP THE MISSILE."
IT IS NO MERE MISSILE--
MY FRIENDS HAVE TOLD ME.
EVERYTHING.
AGENT BRAND SAYS THAT A POWERLORD CAN NEVER RETREAT, CAN NEVER CREATE A CONTINGENCY FOR AN ATTACK.
BUT THERE IS A WEAKNESS. IN THE DESIGN, SOME SMALL GLITCH, AND YOU WILL KNOW OF IT.
YOU WILL TELL US WHAT THE WEAKNESS IS. NOT OUT OF ANYTHING AS DISTASTEFUL AS COMPASSION.
YOU WILL TELL ME BECAUSE YOU KNOW THAT EVEN IF MY WORLD IS ENDED, I WILL NOT DESTROY YOURS.

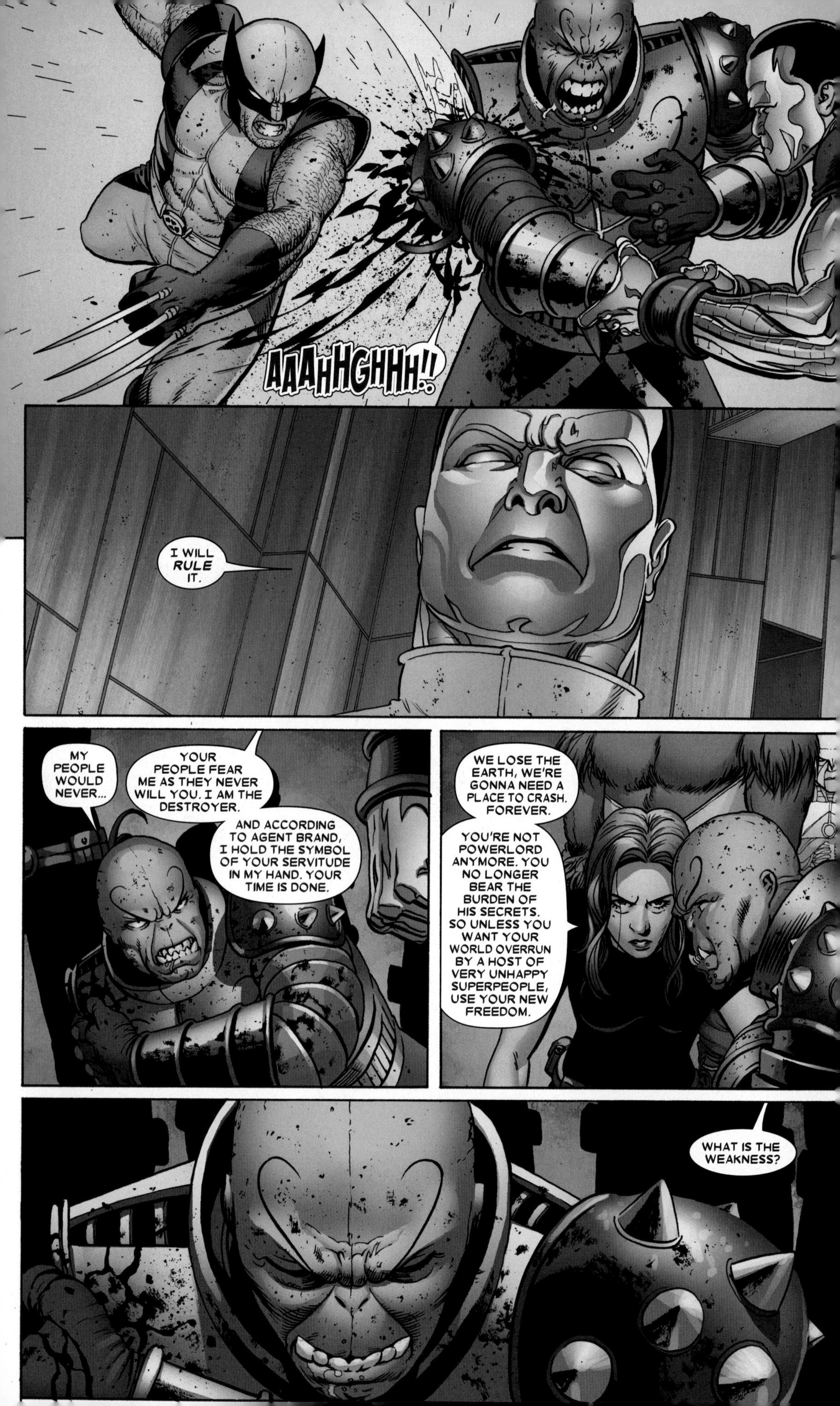

AAAHHGHHH!!
I WILL RULE IT.
MY PEOPLE WOULD NEVER...
YOUR PEOPLE FEAR ME AS THEY NEVER WILL YOU. I AM THE DESTROYER.
AND ACCORDING TO AGENT BRAND, I HOLD THE SYMBOL OF YOUR SERVITUDE IN MY HAND. YOUR TIME IS DONE.
WE LOSE THE EARTH, WE'RE GONNA NEED A PLACE TO CRASH. FOREVER.
YOU'RE NOT POWERLORD ANYMORE. YOU NO LONGER BEAR THE BURDEN OF HIS SECRETS. SO UNLESS YOU WANT YOUR WORLD OVERRUN BY A HOST OF VERY UNHAPPY SUPERPEOPLE, USE YOUR NEW FREEDOM.
WHAT IS THE WEAKNESS?

YOU CAN'T WAKE ANYONE?

THE MOST POWERFUL SEEM TO BE THE MOST POWERFULLY HIT. SPIDER-MAN IS STILL TRYING TO ROUSE DR. STRANGE...

AT LEAST, I THINK THAT'S WHY HE'S HITTING HIM...

IT'S GOT TO BE DEAD ON.

ORORO, WE'RE GETTING VERY CLOSE. WE'VE BEEN TOLD THAT A DIRECT HEAD-TO-HEAD HIT BY SOMETHING BIG ENOUGH MIGHT BUCKLE THE BULLET, OR AT THE VERY LEAST DIVERT IT.

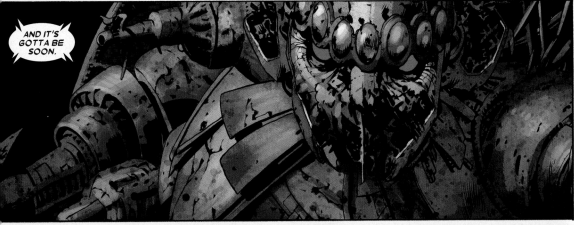

AND IT'S GOTTA BE SOON.

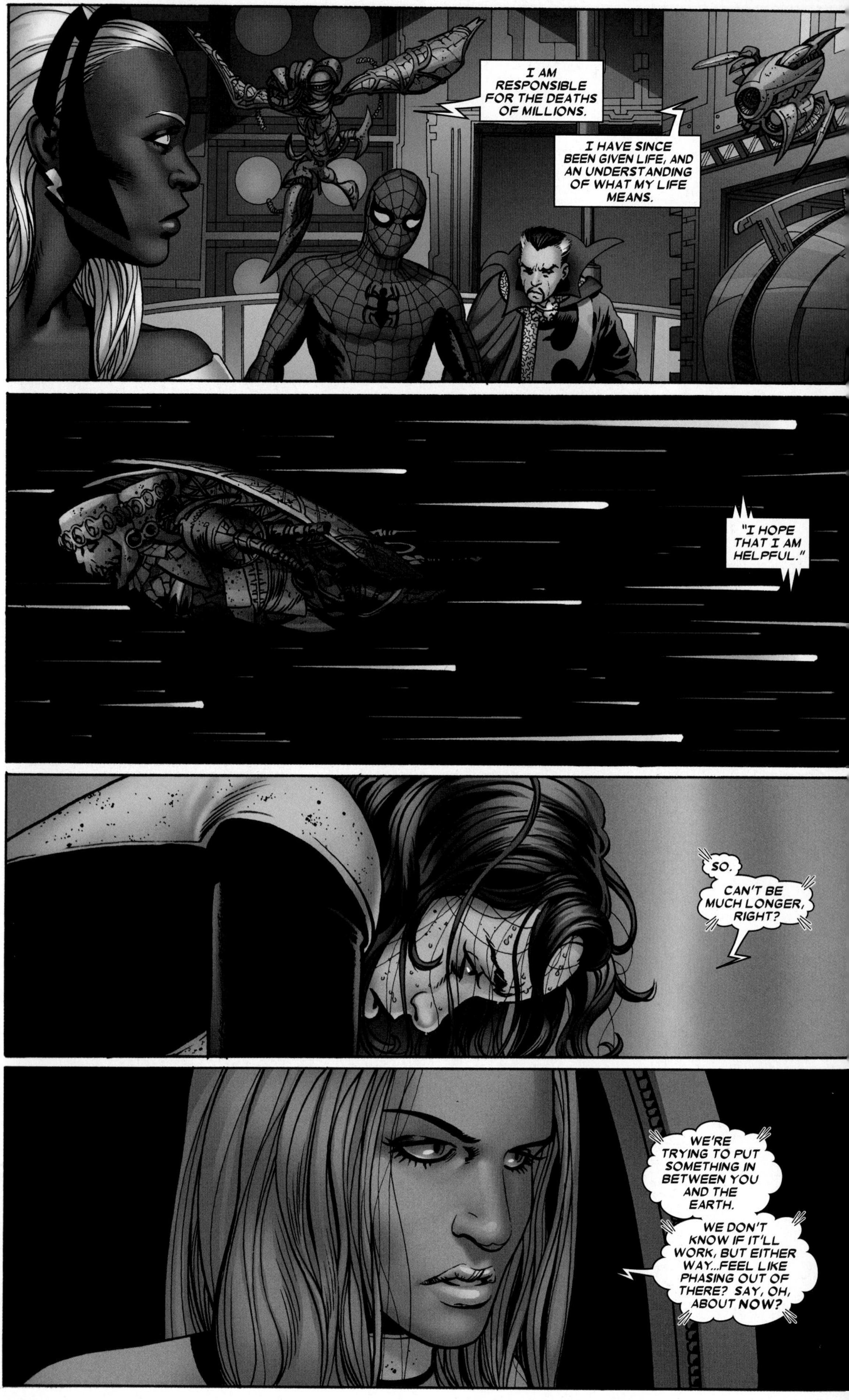
I AM RESPONSIBLE FOR THE DEATHS OF MILLIONS.
I HAVE SINCE BEEN GIVEN LIFE, AND AN UNDERSTANDING OF WHAT MY LIFE MEANS.
"I HOPE THAT I AM HELPFUL."
SO.
CAN'T BE MUCH LONGER, RIGHT?
WE'RE TRYING TO PUT SOMETHING IN BETWEEN YOU AND THE EARTH.
WE DON'T KNOW IF IT'LL WORK, BUT EITHER WAY...FEEL LIKE PHASING OUT OF THERE? SAY, OH, ABOUT NOW?

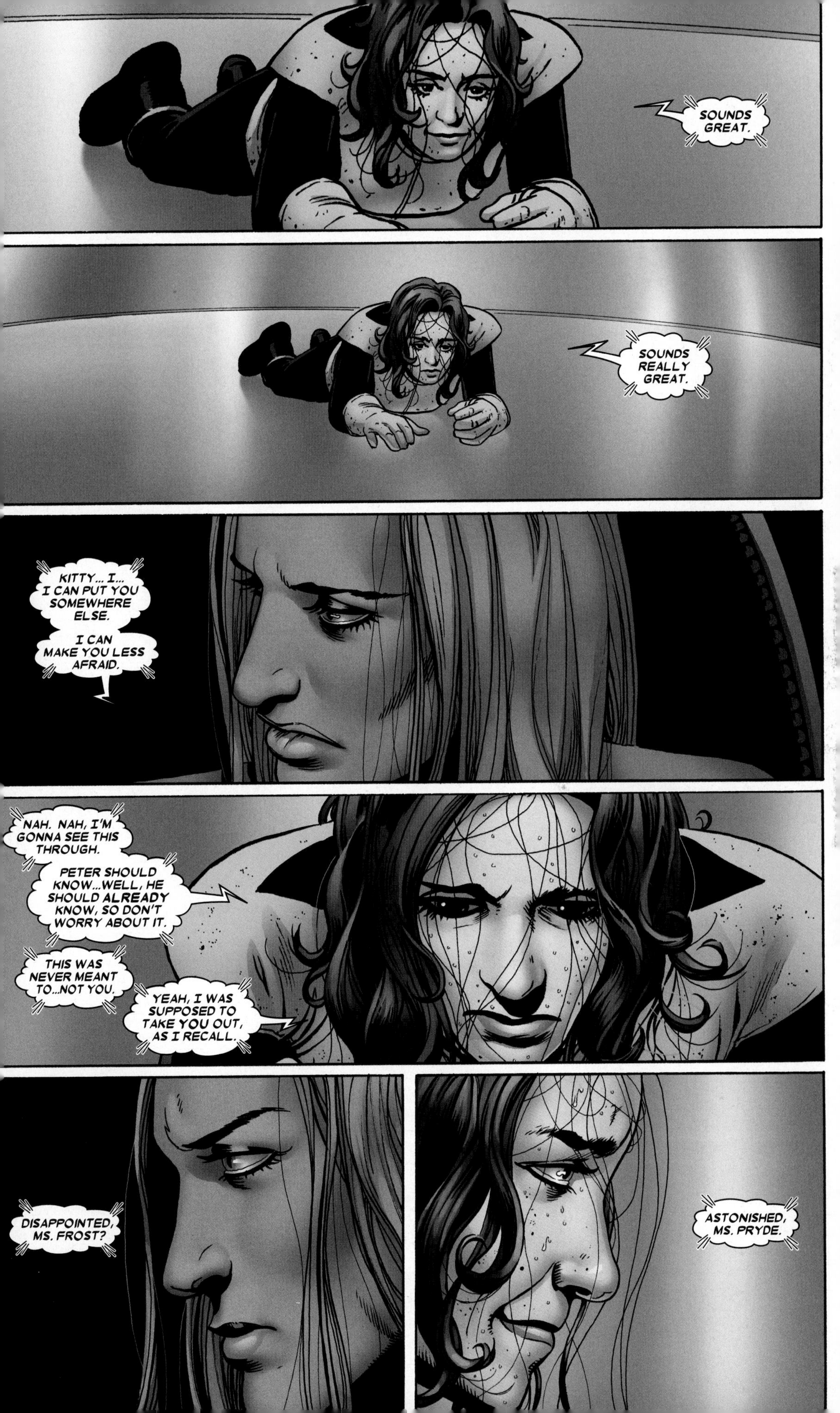
SOUNDS GREAT.
SOUNDS REALLY GREAT.
KITTY... I... I CAN PUT YOU SOMEWHERE ELSE.
I CAN MAKE YOU LESS AFRAID.
NAH. NAH, I'M GONNA SEE THIS THROUGH.
PETER SHOULD KNOW...WELL, HE SHOULD ALREADY KNOW, SO DON'T WORRY ABOUT IT.
THIS WAS NEVER MEANT TO...NOT YOU.
YEAH, I WAS SUPPOSED TO TAKE YOU OUT, AS I RECALL.
DISAPPOINTED, MS. FROST?
ASTONISHED, MS. PRYDE.

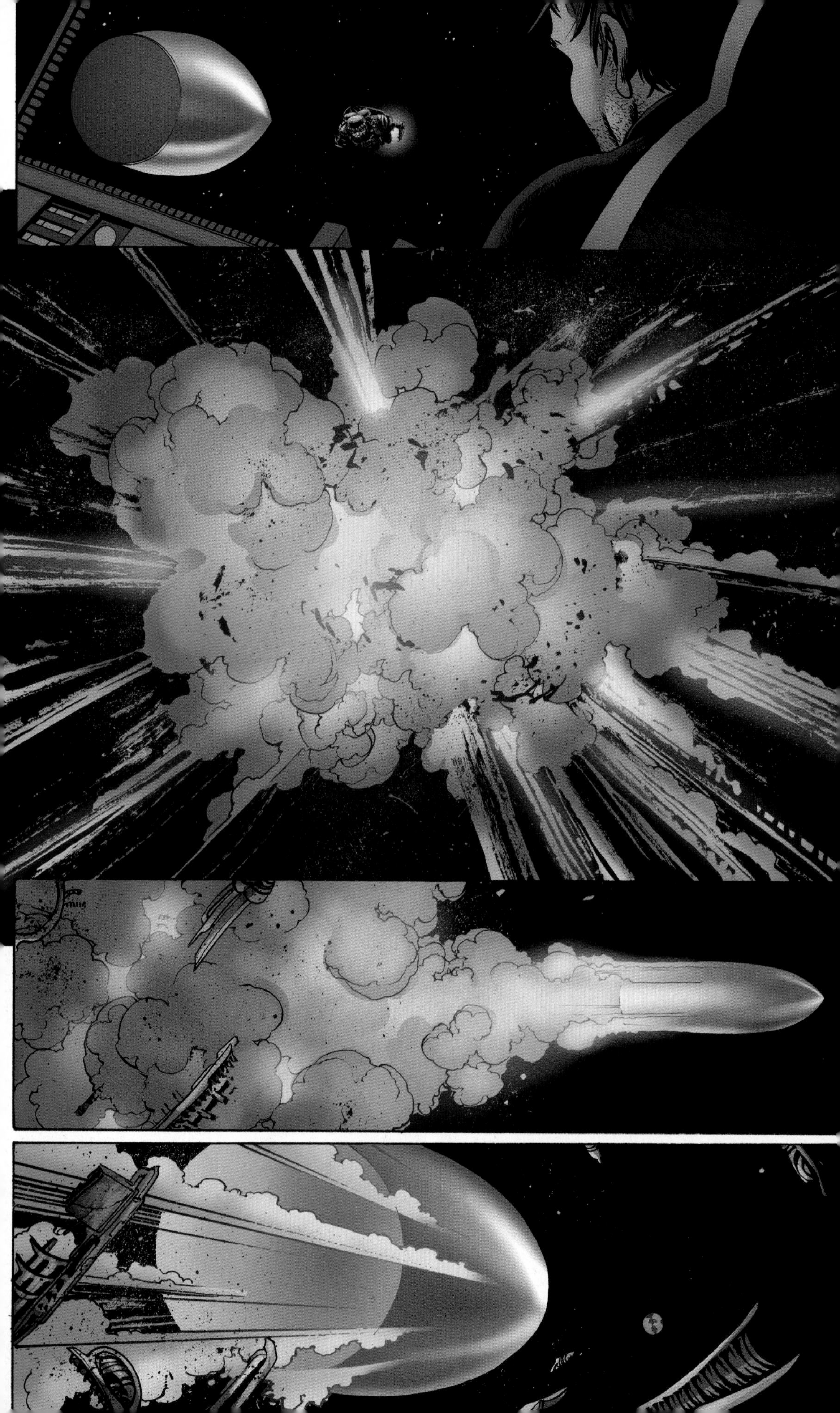

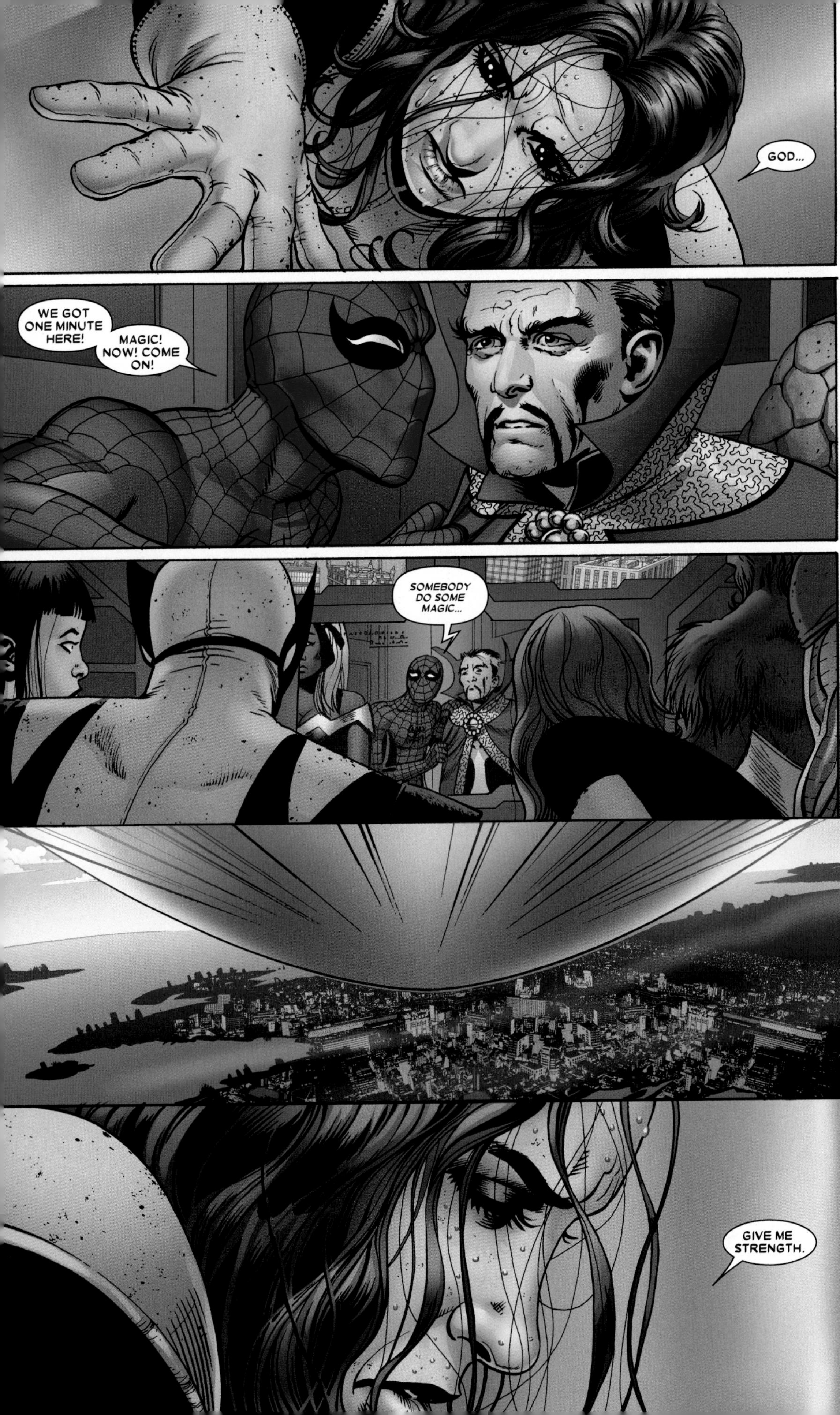
GOD...
WE GOT ONE MINUTE HERE!
MAGIC! NOW! COME ON!
SOMEBODY DO SOME MAGIC...
GIVE ME STRENGTH.

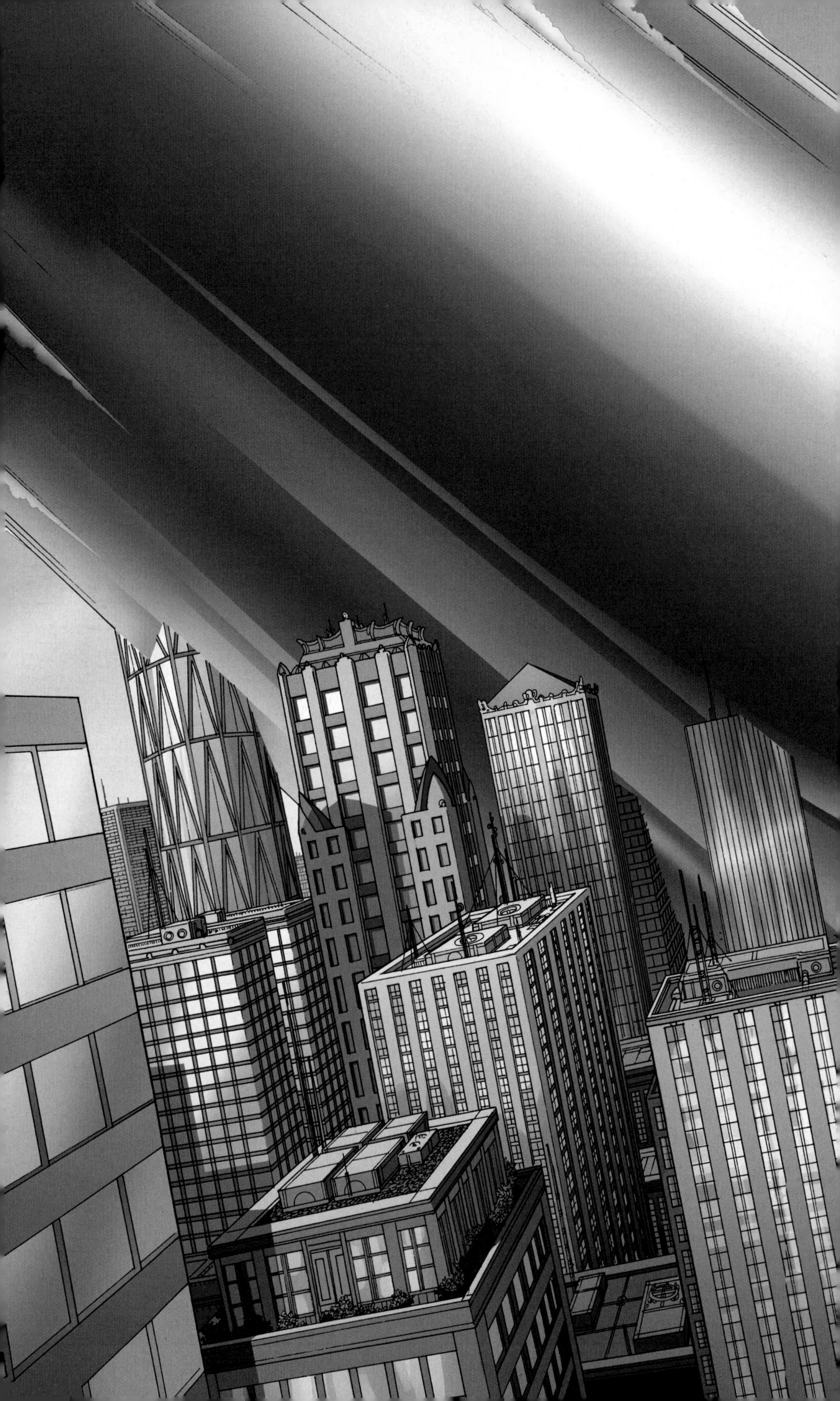

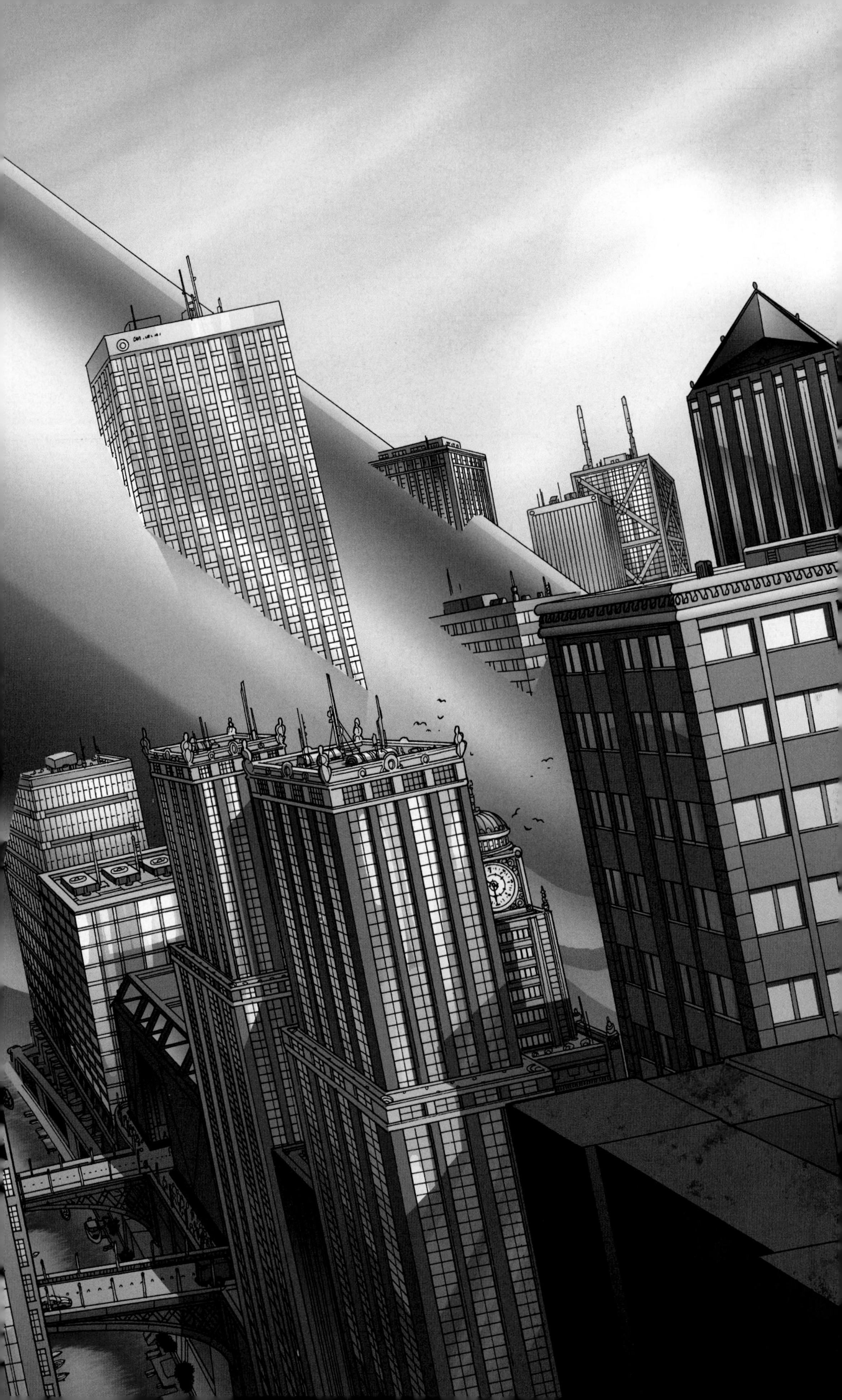

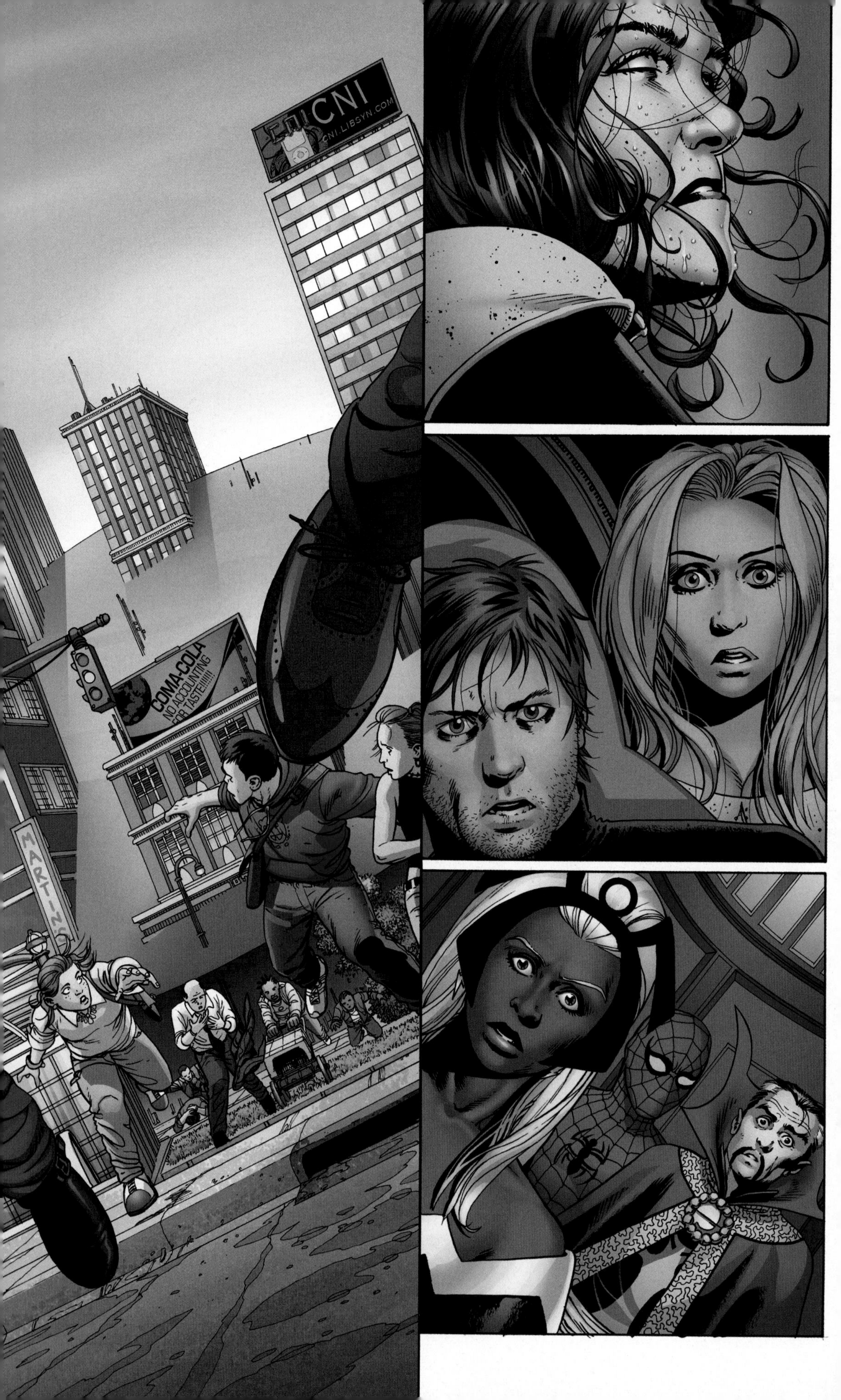
CNI
CNI.LIBSYN.COM
COMA-COLA
NO ACCOUNTING FOR TASTE!!!!!!
MARTINS

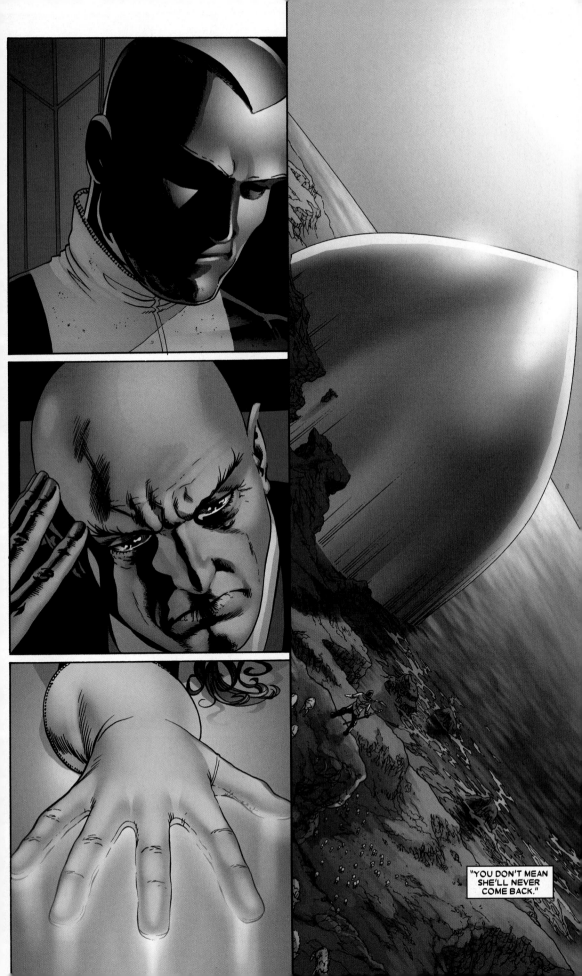

"YOU DON'T MEAN
SHE'LL NEVER
COME BACK."

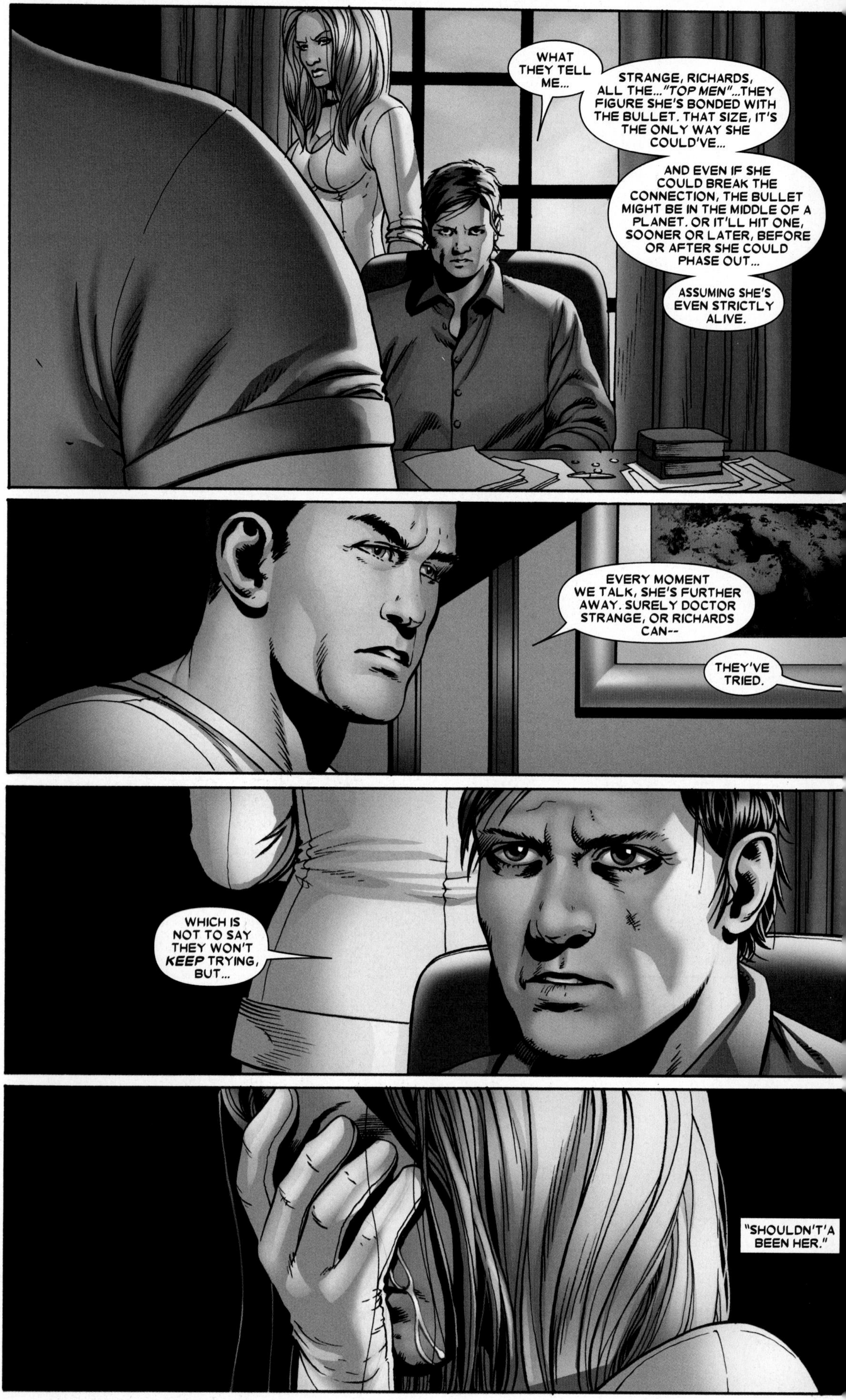
WHAT THEY TELL ME...
STRANGE, RICHARDS, ALL THE..."TOP MEN"...THEY FIGURE SHE'S BONDED WITH THE BULLET. THAT SIZE, IT'S THE ONLY WAY SHE COULD'VE...
AND EVEN IF SHE COULD BREAK THE CONNECTION, THE BULLET MIGHT BE IN THE MIDDLE OF A PLANET. OR IT'LL HIT ONE, SOONER OR LATER, BEFORE OR AFTER SHE COULD PHASE OUT...
ASSUMING SHE'S EVEN STRICTLY ALIVE.
EVERY MOMENT WE TALK, SHE'S FURTHER AWAY. SURELY DOCTOR STRANGE, OR RICHARDS CAN--
THEY'VE TRIED.
WHICH IS NOT TO SAY THEY WON'T KEEP TRYING, BUT...
"SHOULDN'T'A BEEN HER."

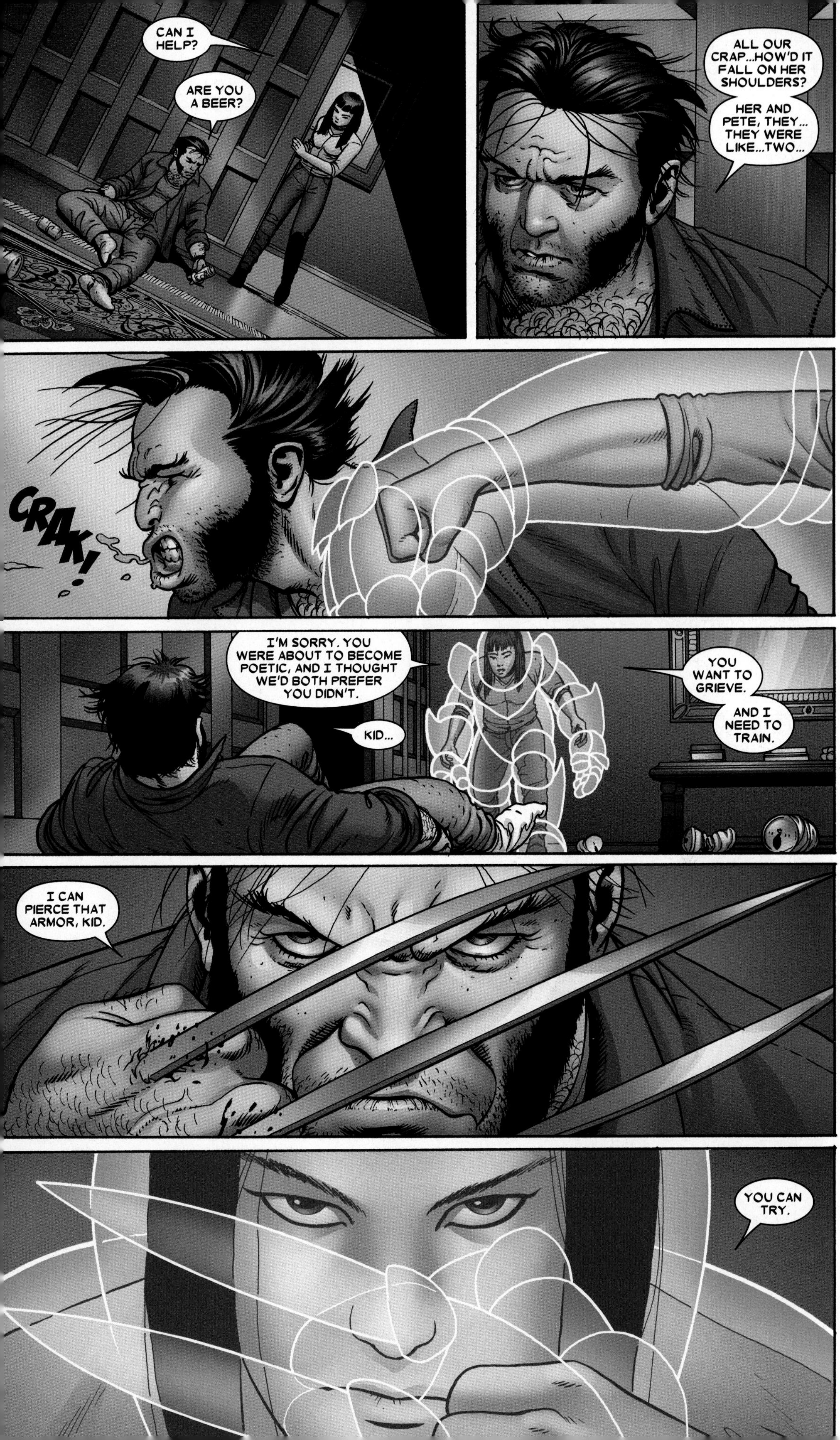
CAN I HELP?
ARE YOU A BEER?
ALL OUR CRAP...HOW'D IT FALL ON HER SHOULDERS?
HER AND PETE, THEY... THEY WERE LIKE...TWO...
CRAK!
I'M SORRY. YOU WERE ABOUT TO BECOME POETIC, AND I THOUGHT WE'D BOTH PREFER YOU DIDN'T.
KID...
YOU WANT TO GRIEVE.
AND I NEED TO TRAIN.
I CAN PIERCE THAT ARMOR, KID.
YOU CAN TRY.

I GUESS I'LL START.

I'M FAIRLY CERTAIN I HATE YOU.

WELL, THAT'S KIND OF THE POINT.

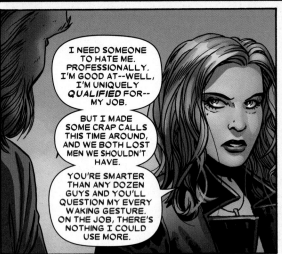

I NEED SOMEONE TO HATE ME. PROFESSIONALLY. I'M GOOD AT--WELL, I'M UNIQUELY *QUALIFIED* FOR--MY JOB.

BUT I MADE SOME CRAP CALLS THIS TIME AROUND, AND WE BOTH LOST MEN WE SHOULDN'T HAVE.

YOU'RE SMARTER THAN ANY DOZEN GUYS AND YOU'LL QUESTION MY EVERY WAKING GESTURE. ON THE JOB, THERE'S NOTHING I COULD USE MORE.

AND OFF THE JOB?

PRETTY MUCH WANNA BREAK YOU LIKE A PONY. IT'S A WIN-WIN.

I'M A BLUE FURRY MONSTER.

SO WAS MY FATHER.

I'VE GOT GREEN HAIR, WHICH I DID NOT DYE. I SPEAK OFFWORLD LANGUAGES THE HUMAN TONGUE CANNOT FORM. I GOT HOT, GLOWY HANDS, AND I RUN THE MOST IMPORTANT SECURITY ORGANIZATION IN OUR SYSTEM WITHOUT BENEFIT OF SOCIAL SKILLS OF ANY KIND.

I'M AN *ALIEN*, GENIUS.

ON MY FATHER'S SIDE.

THIS IS A HARD TIME FOR YOU, SO I'M NOT GONNA PUSH, BUT...

THE SAFETY OF THE ENTIRE PLANET PROBABLY RESTS ON YOUR DECISION AND YOU AND I ARE COMPATIBLE IN WAYS YOU DON'T HAVE WORDS FOR, SO...

...SO I'M NOT GONNA PUSH.

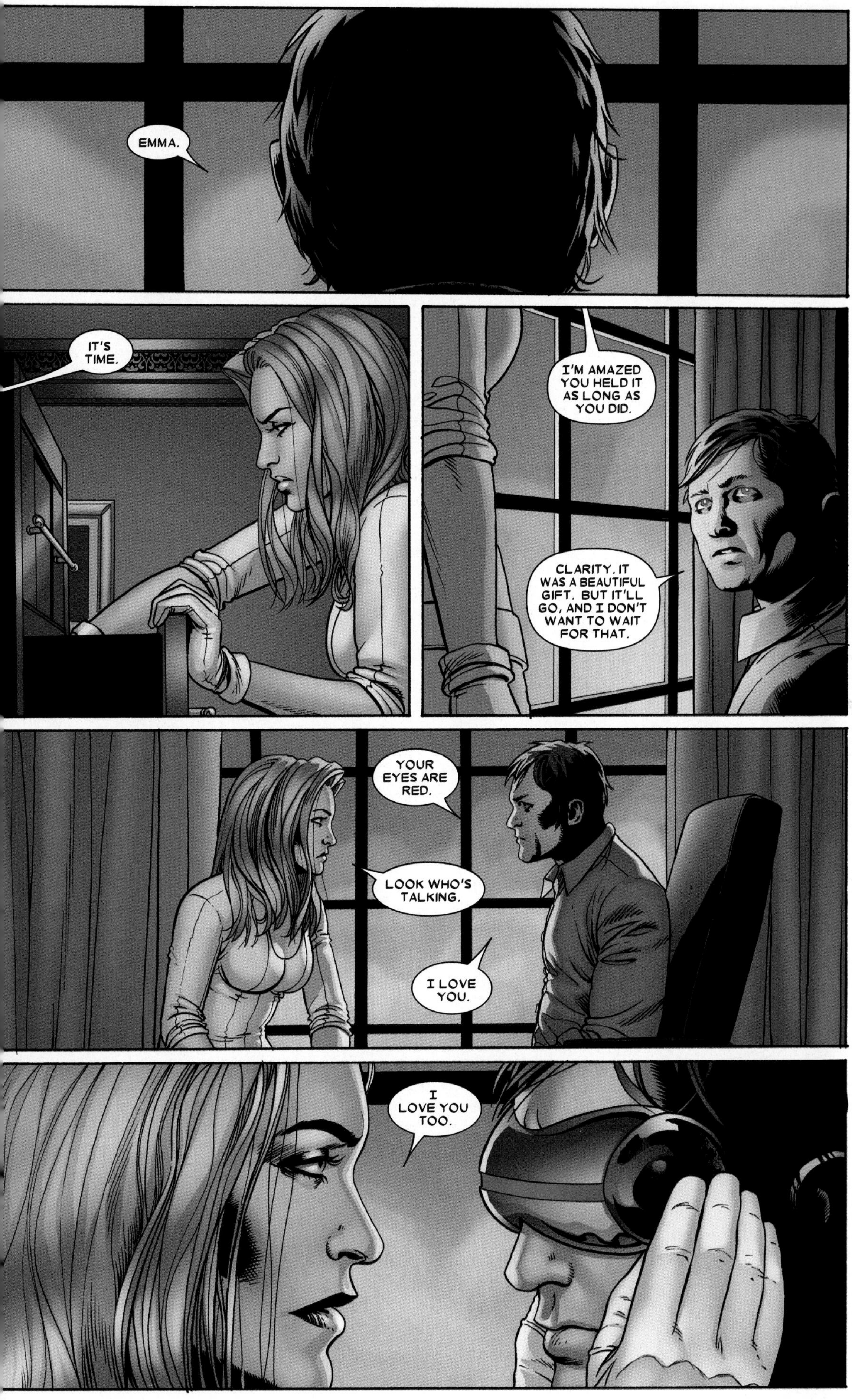
EMMA.
IT'S TIME.
I'M AMAZED YOU HELD IT AS LONG AS YOU DID.
CLARITY. IT WAS A BEAUTIFUL GIFT. BUT IT'LL GO, AND I DON'T WANT TO WAIT FOR THAT.
YOUR EYES ARE RED.
LOOK WHO'S TALKING.
I LOVE YOU.
I LOVE YOU TOO.

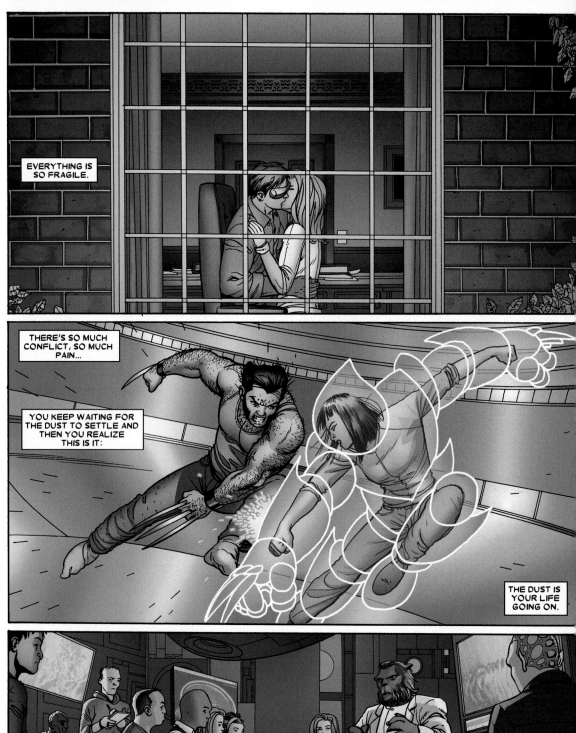

EVERYTHING IS SO FRAGILE.

THERE'S SO MUCH CONFLICT, SO MUCH PAIN...

YOU KEEP WAITING FOR THE DUST TO SETTLE AND THEN YOU REALIZE THIS IS IT:

THE DUST IS YOUR LIFE GOING ON.

IF HAPPY COMES ALONG, THAT WEIRD, UNBEARABLE DELIGHT THAT'S ACTUAL HAPPY--

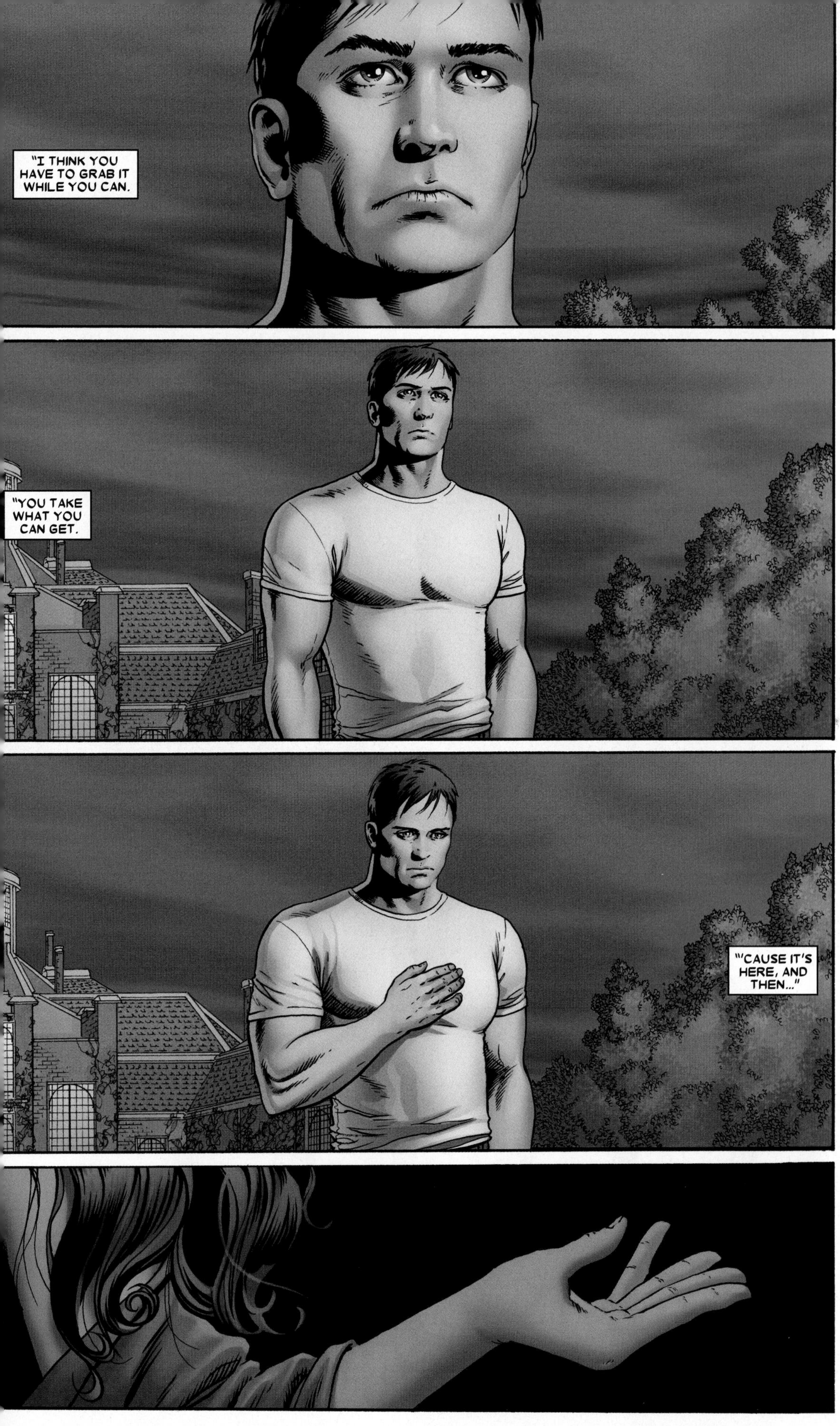
"I THINK YOU HAVE TO GRAB IT WHILE YOU CAN.
"YOU TAKE WHAT YOU CAN GET.
"'CAUSE IT'S HERE, AND THEN..."

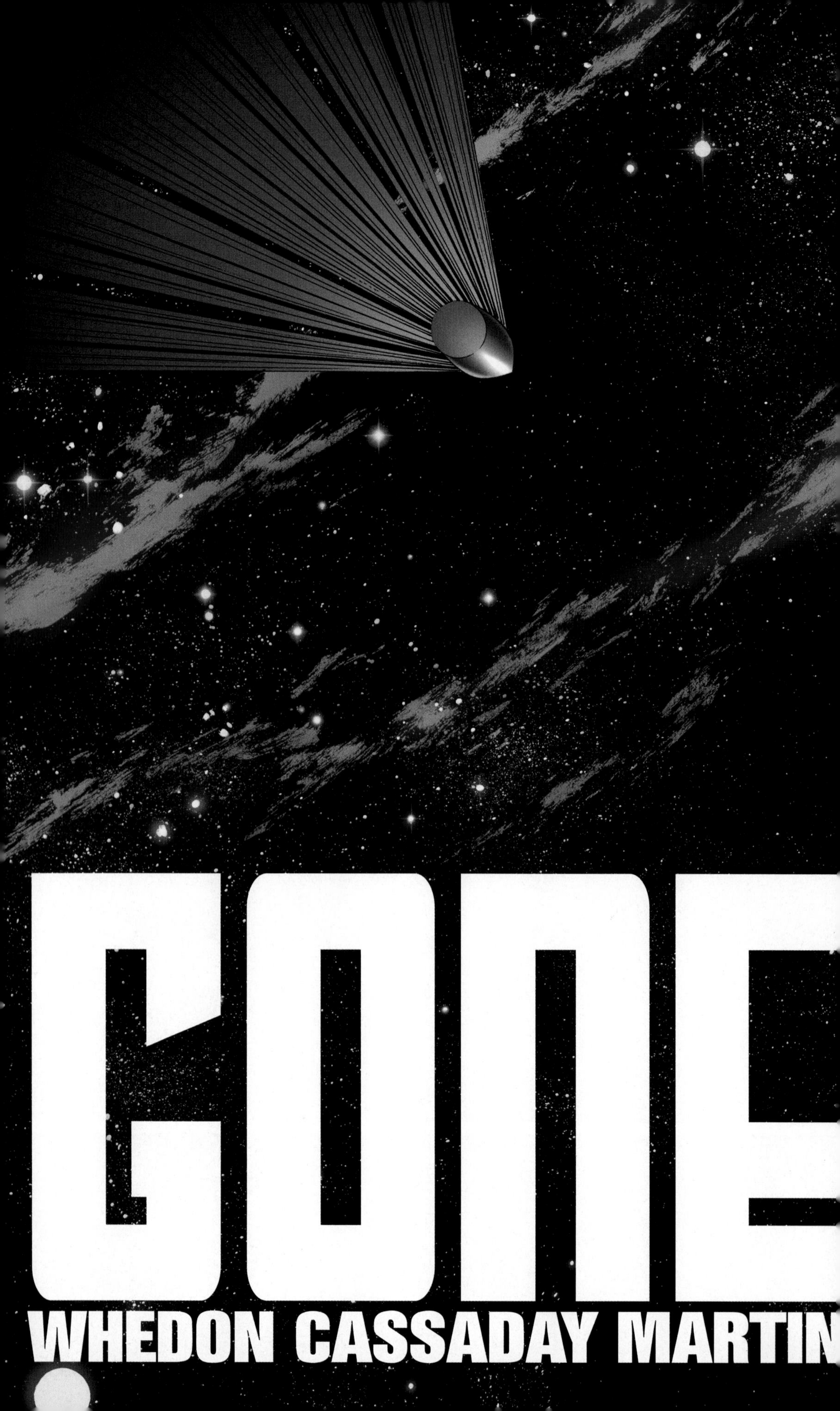
GONE
WHEDON CASSADAY MARTIN

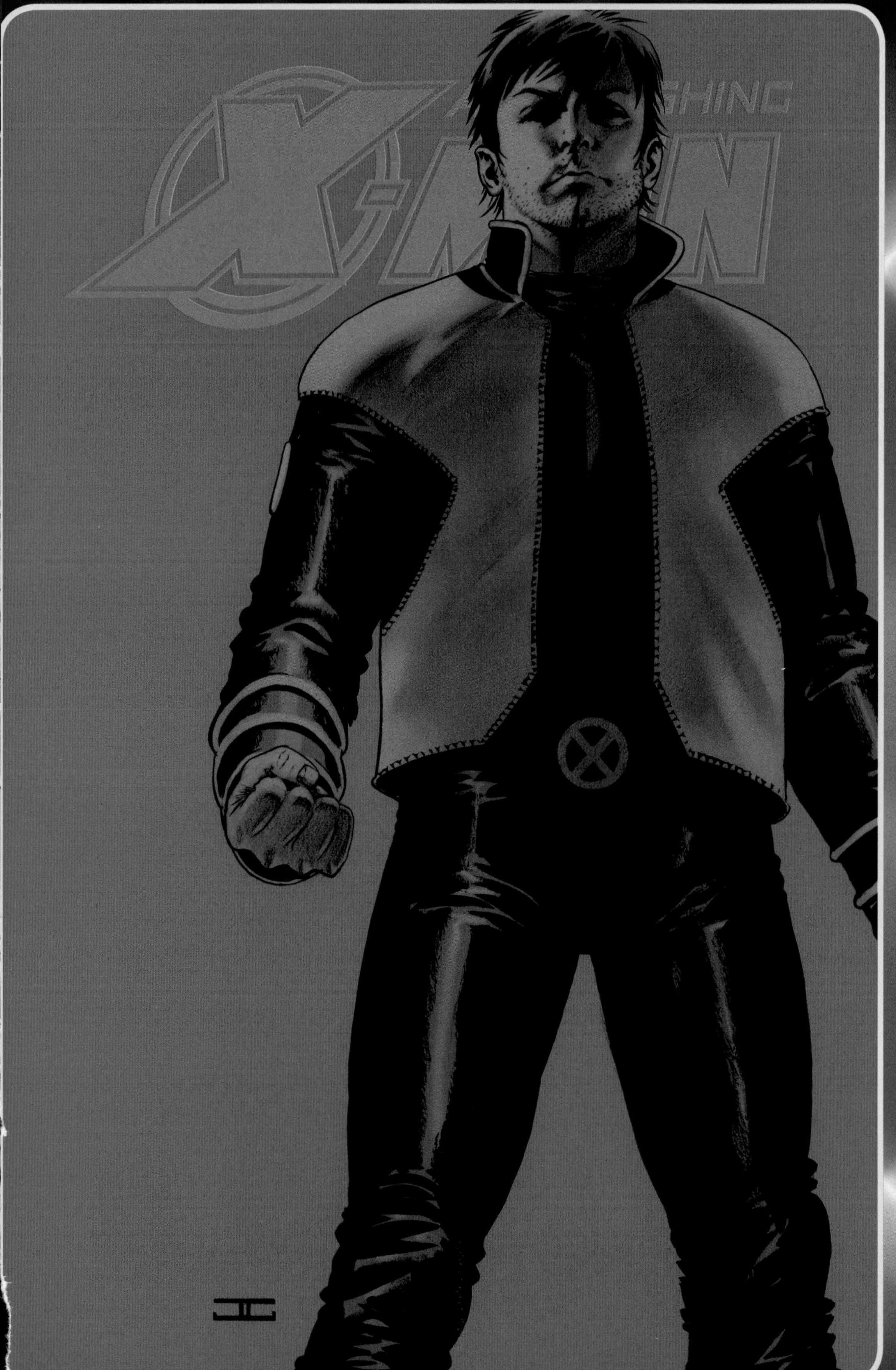

19 VARIANT

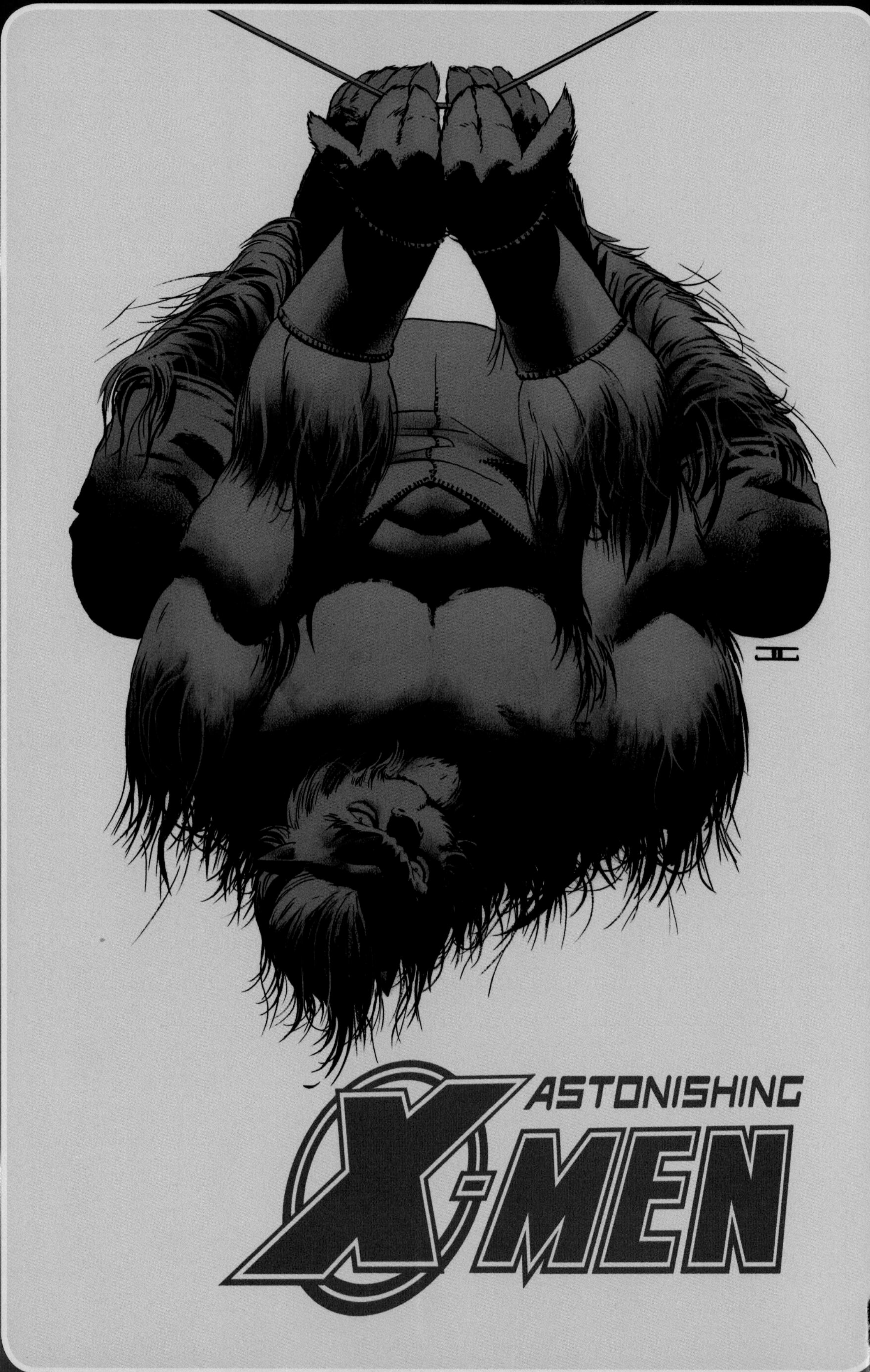
ASTONISHING
X-MEN

20 VARIANT

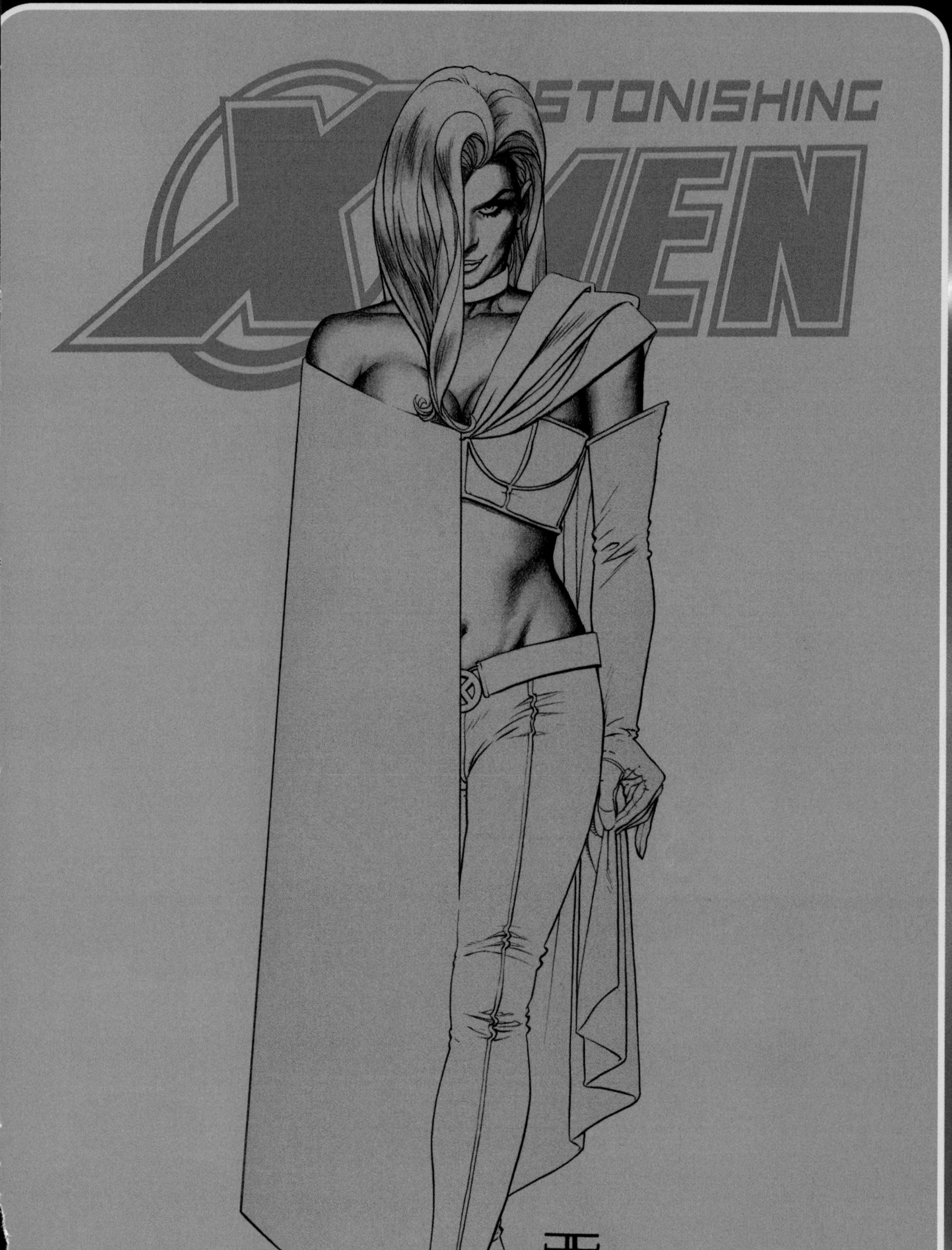
ASTONISHING
X-MEN

21 VARIANT

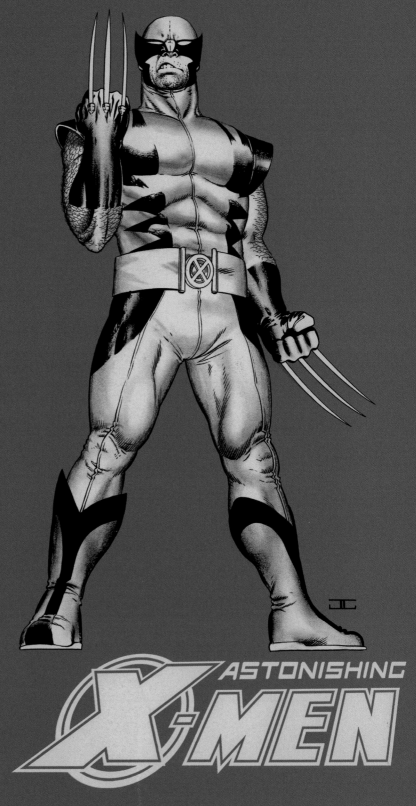

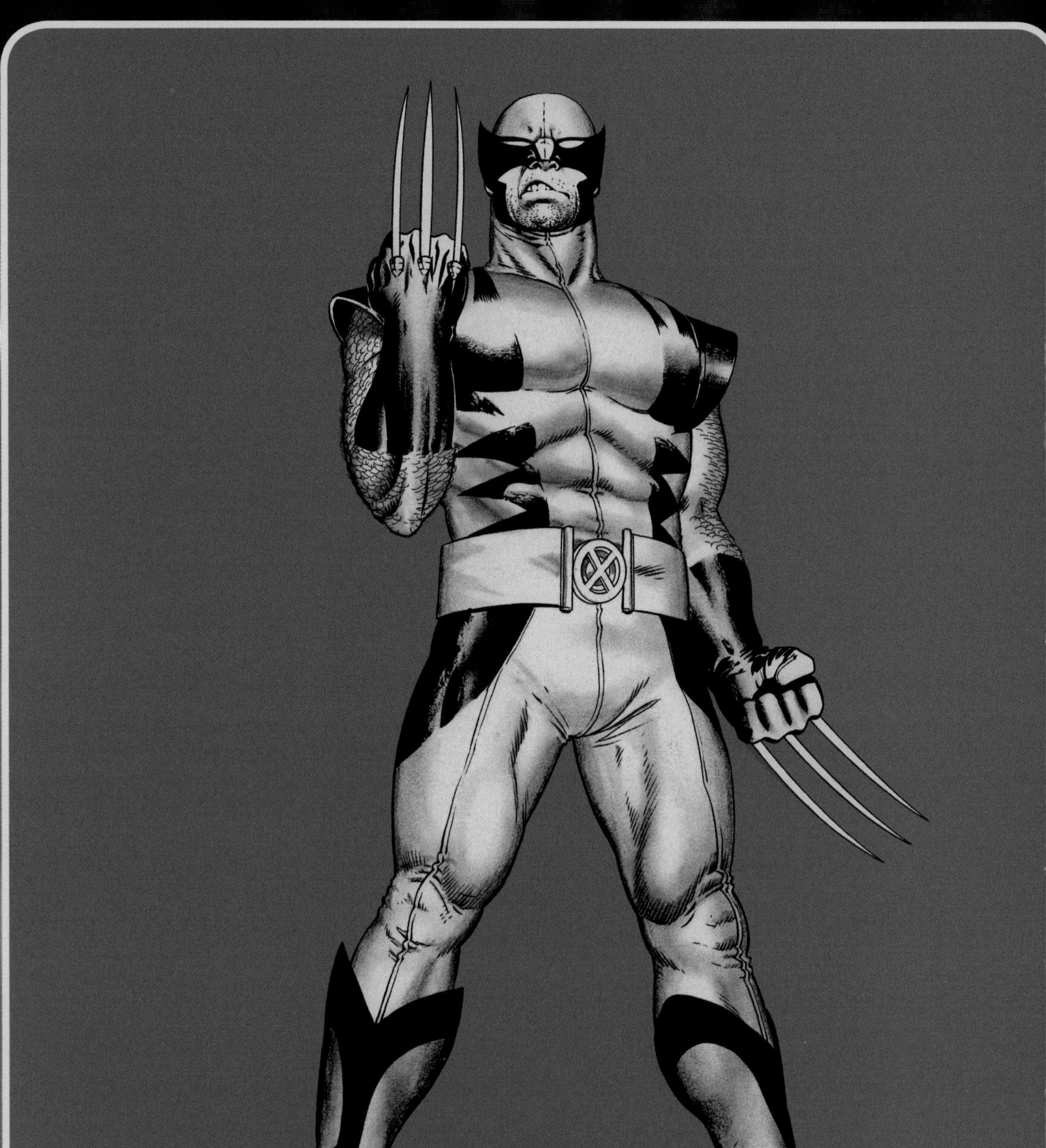
ASTONISHING
X-MEN

22 VARIANT

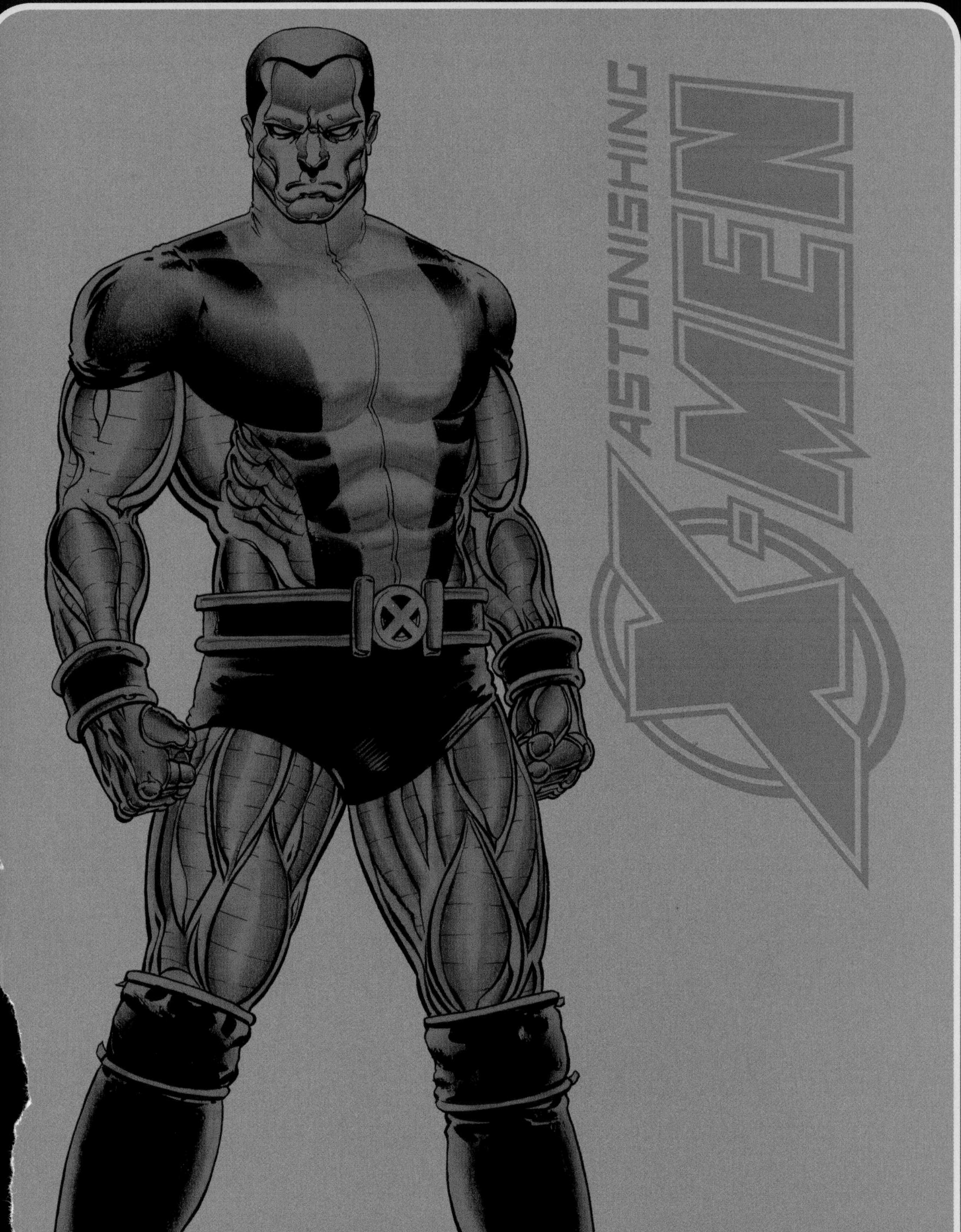
ASTONISHING
X-MEN

23 VARIANT

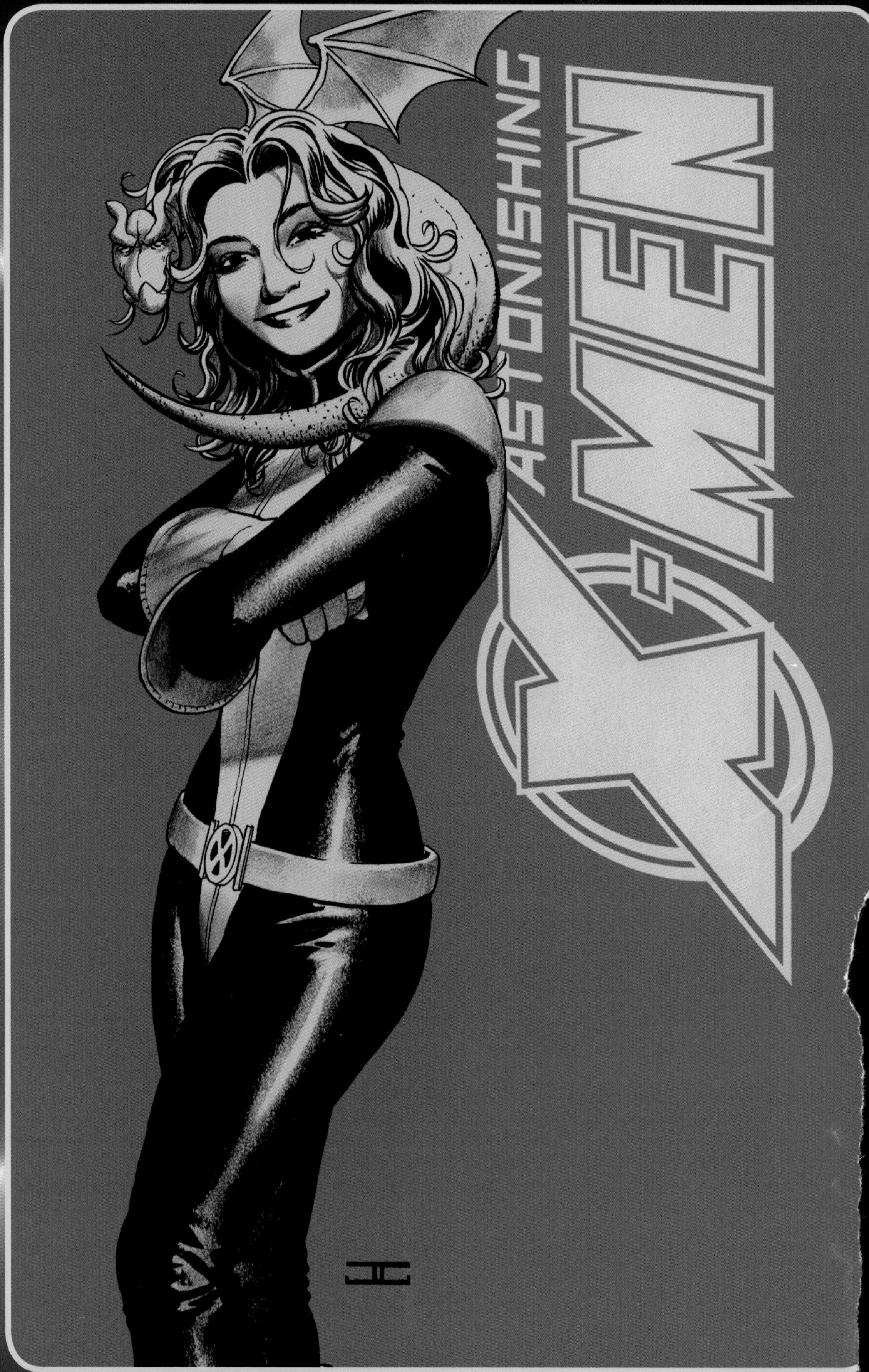
ASTONISHING
X-MEN

24 VARIANT